Plant Hardiness Zones

This plant hardiness map, which was developed by the Agricultural Research Service of the U.S. Department of Agriculture, will help you find the most suitable plants for your garden. Every plant in the 'A–Z Directory' (see pp. 106– 336) is given a zone range. The zones 1-11 are based on the average annual minimum temperature. In the zone range, the smaller number indicates the northern-most zone in which a plant can survive the winter and the higher number gives the most southerly area in which it will perform consistently. It is important to bear in mind that factors such as altitude, wind exposure, proximity to water, soil type, snow, night temperature, shade, and the level of water received by a plant may alter a plant's hardiness by as much as two zones.

The Perfect
Plant

The Perfect
Plant

for Every Site, Habitat, and Garden Style

DAVID JOYCE
U.S. CONSULTANT JOHN ELSLEY

photography by JERRY HARPUR
additional photography by MARCUS HARPUR

STEWART, TABORI & CHANG
NEW YORK

First published in 1998 by
Ryland Peters & Small
Cavendish House
51-55 Mortimer Street
London W1N 7TD

Text ©1998 David Joyce
Design and illustration © Ryland Peters & Small

Published in 1998 and distributed in the U.S. by
Stewart, Tabori & Chang,
a division of U.S. Media Holdings, Inc.
115 West 18th Street, New York, NY 10011

Distributed in Canada by
General Publishing Company Ltd.
30 Lesmill Road
Don Mills, Ontario, Canada, M3B 2T6

Library of Congress Cataloging-in-Publication
Data

Joyce, David
    The perfect plant : for every site, habitat, and, garden style / by David Joyce ; photography by Jerry Harpur.
        p.   cm.
    Includes index.
    ISBN 1-55670-607-3 (hardcover)
1. Plants, Ornamental—Selection. 2. Plants, Ornamental—Pictorial works. 3. Plant selection. 4. Landscape gardening. I. Title.
SB407.J69   1998
635.9'52—DC21   97-41165
                                     CIP

Printed in China

10 9 8 7 6 5 4 3 2 1

Project Editor Caroline Davison

Editors Polly Boyd, Jane Chapman,
    Mary Lambert, Annabel Morgan, Helen Ridge,
    Sian Parkhouse, Lesley Riley, Stella Vayne

Copy Editors Mary Green, Ann Snyder

Editorial Assistant Maddalena Bastianelli

Art Editor Paul Tilby

Designers Michael Whitehead, John Grain,
    Richard Scott, Alison Shackleton

Art Assistant Sailesh Patel

Picture Research Emily Hedges

Production Manager Kate Mackillop

Production Consultant Norman de Brackinghe

Art Director Jacqui Small

Publishing Director Anne Ryland

Jacket photography by Jerry Harpur
Front jacket:
Inset: RHS Rosemoor in Great Torrington, Devon. In the foreground are red *Crocosmia* 'Lucifer', yellow *Achillea filipendulina* 'Gold Plate', yellow day lilies (*Hemerocallis*), golden rod (*Solidago*) and rudbeckias. In the background are *Buddleja globosa* and *Robinia pseudoacacia* 'Frisia'.

Back jacket:
Top left Lobelia 'Bees' Flame' and
    Crocosmia masoniorum
Top right Taxus baccata 'Standishii'
Bottom left Tulipa kaiserkroon
Bottom right Ribes speciosum
Page 1 Bletilla striata
Page 2 Lobelia 'Bees' Flame' and
    Crocosmia masoniorum
Page 3 Iris 'Cantab'
Page 4-5 Molinia caerulea subsp.
    arundinacea 'Windspiel', *Sedum*
    'Herbstfreude' and *Rudbeckia fulgida* var.
    sullivantii 'Goldsturm'

CONTENTS

Introduction

Without an agricultural prelude, beginning with the early cultivation of grain crops in about 7000 BC, the making of gardens would have been inconceivable. However, the history of gardens has its own long course, with ample evidence of sophisticated gardens even in ancient civilizations such as those of Assyria, China, and Egypt. Along the way, large numbers of plants have been brought into cultivation, culminating in an orgy of introductions in the 19th and early 20th centuries. Miraculously, even now, when it seems as though the remotest and wildest regions of the world have been scoured for plants of potential value, a small stream of introductions, in some cases reintroductions, continues to increase the encyclopedic plant collections in great gardens of the world.

As with agricultural crops, ornamentals have their origins in plants found in the wild. It comes as a surprise to many gardeners to recognize some of the plants that they value, particularly trees and shrubs, in natural habitats in various parts of the world. In addition to the species and their localized variants and forms, there are numerous selections, distinguished by such features as unusual leaf shape or flower color, that would appear to be the result of genetic playfulness. There are also innumerable hybrids that are the result of interbreeding between species. Hybrids occasionally occur naturally, but it is not often that the compatible plants necessary to create a new hybrid grow beside one another in the wild. On the other hand, the promiscuous gathering of plants in gardens provides ideal opportunities for new crosses, which sharp-eyed gardeners can spot and propagate if they look promising. Far more hybrids, however, are the result of deliberate breeding. Amateurs can play an important role in this process, although their contribution to the range of popular plants such as annuals, lilies, roses, and orchids (a group of plants in which dizzyingly complex crosses occur between genera) is dwarfed by the output of commercial nurseries for which plant breeding is big business.

Opposite **This well-drained garden contains ornamental grasses mixed with flowering perennials. Orange-flowered red-hot pokers (*Kniphofia*) contrast with small purple-flowered *Verbena bonariensis*, steely blue sea hollies (*Eryngium*), alliums, and globe thistles (*Echinops*).**

When choosing plants for a garden, it is exhilarating to scan the vast armies of plants from the wild that are worth a place in gardens and the countless auxiliaries ranked behind them that are the result of selection and breeding.

7

Above A sunny border with a moist soil will improve the growth and flowering displays of many perennials. Here, pure white *Phlox* grows alongside knotweed (*Persicaria*) and the yellow daisy-like flowers of *Ligularia dentata.*

Opposite This sunny border is home to hollyhocks (*Alcea rosea*) which have been planted behind the distinctive dark orange *Lilium* 'Fire King'. At the front, *Lychnis coronaria* Alba Group and lavender (*Lavandula*) grow happily with perennial lady's mantle (*Alchemilla mollis*). This provides a frilly edge along the length of the whole border, which is backed by sun-loving rambling and climbing roses.

Right Cool attractive planting can be created by using plants with striking foliage. Here, the straplike leaves of *Iris sibirica* contrast with the rounded leaves of *Ligularia dentata* and the graceful stems of Solomon's seal (*Polygonatum hybridum*). These plants will all thrive in a sunny, sheltered position with a moist, well-drained soil.

Choosing plants that are suitable for a particular garden from this vast array can be a daunting process. A major purpose of this book is to provide gardeners with a manageable selection in the "A–Z Directory" (pp. 105–336), which focuses mainly on plants that are suitable for growing in temperate regions. The selection is inevitably a personal one, but prejudices have been held sufficiently in check so that the book covers a comprehensive range of plants. Unashamed favoritism is also frankly expressed in a selection of 250 plants which are highlighted in the Plant Index (pp. 344–351). These would provide the material for a truly delectable paradise garden, though admittedly it would be one that offers an astonishing range of growing conditions.

To make best use of the selection, gardeners need to embrace the theme running through "Plant Communities in Nature" (pp. 16–47) and "Plant Associations in the Garden" (pp. 50–101). Stated simply, this is that plants differ in their requirements, and the conditions in which they thrive in the wild give the best indication of the conditions in which they are most likely to succeed in gardens. In these sections, plants from largely temperate regions are set in a worldwide context of natural environments and gardens.

A happy consequence of relatively cheap travel is that many of us are now acquainted with regions of the world with markedly different land forms, climates, and vegetation. Even if we do not express our experiences in a very scientific way, most of us register these differences and recognize the broad connections between our own environments and those we have seen elsewhere. This is even true when we do not see the original vegetation of a country or region, but only what has been modified by farming and other kinds of human exploitation. In discerning these patterns in the environment, we can recognize the features, even if only the most obvious, of habitats and plant communities which are more specifically defined by ecologists.

One of the most enjoyable features of preparing this book has been to review the relationship between natural conditions and the wild plants that are found in them (see "Plant Communities in Nature," pp. 16–47). The brush strokes are necessarily broad, and readers will be disappointed if they expect an analysis of different habitats and their plant communities. However, what emerges is that a broad range of factors, such as climate, drainage, exposure to sun and shade, and soil chemistry, is critical in determining what grows where. This not only has its own intrinsic interest, it teaches us a fundamental truth: a successful garden matches the plants to the available conditions.

By definition, a garden is an environment that has been meddled with, more or less artfully, even when it it looks like natural woodland

Above Ornamental grasses such as *Miscanthus sinensis* and *Stipa tenuissima*—both of which prefer well-drained soil in full sun—give the impression of a natural habitat in the garden, providing a "misty" look when the sun shines through their foliage.

Opposite A variety of perennials have been naturalized in grass to create a meadowlike garden. They include thick swathes of purple-flowered *Verbena bonariensis*, which thrives in moist but well-drained soil in full sun.

Below Many spring-flowering bulbs adapt to the conditions under deciduous trees. Here, the American trout lily (*Erythronium revolutum*) has successfully naturalized in the dappled shade provided by a tree.

or a boggy streamside. It has, however, an underlying character, more frequently a mixture of characters, which is defined by the climate of the region and by physical factors such as orientation, soil chemistry, and drainage. Cultivation can undoubtedly modify this character to some extent: for example, improved drainage and the addition of organic matter, such as well-rotted humus, will broaden the range of plants that can be grown. Nonetheless, the principle remains that plants have optimum growing conditions, and gardening is made easier when these are taken into account. Discovering the conditions that prevail in a garden is the first step to choosing the right plants, and these are discussed in "Plant Associations in the Garden" (pp. 50-101).

The simplest way of finding the right plants for a particular area of the garden is to look up the conditions—whether these are full sun with dry soil or partial shade with moist soil—in the "Special Plant Lists" (pp. 337-40). These give a selection of plants for different growing conditions that are then described in much more detail in an "A-Z Directory" (pp.105-336). This is organized by major plant categories (Trees; Shrubs; Conifers; Climbers; Roses; Perennials; Bulbs, Corms, and Tubers;Annuals and Biennials; Bamboos, Grasses, and Grasslike Plants; and Ferns). The plants in each category are arranged alphabetically by the internationally accepted botanical name. Common names with wide currency are given with the entries, and these, as well as any botanical synonyms, are listed in the Plant Index (pp. 344-51).

Above These Mediterranean or Italian cypresses (*Cupressus sempervirens*), underplanted with a mass of lavender (*Lavandula*), revel in the full sun and well-drained soil in this garden on the Scilly Isles off the southwestern coast of England.

Right Ornamental onions (*Allium aflatunense*), with spherical purple flowerheads, and perennial wallflowers (*Erysimum* 'Bowles' Mauve') prefer hot, dry growing conditions. They survive because their roots can penetrate deep into the ground in search of water.

Far left These yellow spires of mullein (*Verbascum*) and the white frothy flowers of kale (*Crambe cordifolia*) produce their best displays when they are grown on poor alkaline soils in full sun.

PLANT COMMUNITIES
IN NATURE

The Making of Plant Communities

The way we respond to the natural world has influenced the aesthetic notions that we bring to gardens. At present, we are generally taking much of our inspiration from nature. In part, this reflects the influence of the 19th-century garden writer William Robinson, advocate of what he called the "wild garden." It has not always been so. Dutch gardens of the 17th century were like an outdoor cabinet of horticultural curiosities. Superficially the formal Dutch garden and the Robinsonian wild garden seem miles apart. But they have something fundamental in common that separates gardens from natural landscapes. In the garden, gardeners choose plants eclectically and arrange them with a strong element of fantasy according to the fashionable ideas of the day.

We miss the point if we look at forest, steppe, or marsh simply as landscapes with plants that please the eye. The plant component is conspicuous but represents only a part of a complex, self-perpetuating community of living things in a distinctive landscape. At a simple level different life forms are interconnected in deciduous woodland, where animals, birds, and insects find shelter and food, pollinating flowers and distributing seed. In comparison, tropical rainforest fizzes with the complex interrelationships of countless life forms: giant trees loaded with lianas and epiphytes, pollinating birds and bats, fruit-eating monkeys, fungi, and microscopic bacteria. The forces giving these communities their essential character and marking their boundaries are environmental. It is here that our interest as gardeners quickens, because the broad factors, particularly climatic, that influence natural plant communities also affect the conditions in our gardens.

TEMPERATURE

We respond to temperature ourselves, so it is one of the most easily appreciated of climatic factors. In 1802, when the Prussian naturalist Alexander von Humboldt ascended Mount Chimborazo in Ecuador, rising from tropical lowlands to a height of 20,000ft (6096m), he found that zonation of vegetation on mountains paralleled latitudinal zonation from the equator to the poles. The exactitude of these vegetation zones was oversimplified but the connection is not surprising. In fact, many other factors make it difficult to relate precisely the distribution of plants to isotherms, the lines on a map linking the same temperature readings (calculated, say, as averages). Nonetheless, for all plants there is a range of tolerance and an optimum temperature at which, all other factors being equal, they grow best.

The hardiness of garden plants is reflected in the distribution of wild plants. Very high temperatures, 104°F (40°C) or more, cause an increase in transpiration and affect the proper function of the enzymes that play a key role in biochemical reactions. Even so, there are plants that survive scorching temperatures, among them date palms (*Phoenix*

Top **The vegetation of Japan reflects varying climatic influences over its four main mountainous islands. The rainfall is generally high, the southeast monsoon bringing heavy summer rains but, due to the northwest monsoon, the center has cold winters. Much of the original vegetation was deciduous forest with a rich layer of herbaceous plants.**

Above **The coastal plain on the Caribbean side of Costa Rica has a hot, humid climate and a tropical vegetation to match. The flowering plant is a species of *Heliconia*, many species of which are found in tropical forests in Central and South America. Some, however, live in drier and more open scrub.**

dactylifera) in Saharan oases. Cold that limits plant growth is more familiar to most gardeners. In temperate regions, where the climate is markedly seasonal, many plants lose their leaves in fall and shut down until the favorable growing conditions of spring. Frost, which is a killer because we try to grow plants outside their natural range, requires a special adaptation of the cells to prevent them being ruptured by the formation of ice. The plantless polar regions of today are a reminder that the present world distribution of plants has been profoundly influenced by climatic changes of the distant past, the ice ages accounting for many characteristic features of the vegetation in Europe and North America.

The temperature at which the seed of a particular plant germinates best has much to do with the climatic conditions in which it is found growing naturally. The seed of most plants from cold regions only germinates if subjected to a cold period. Many Mediterranean plants germinate at relatively low temperatures, about 50°F (10°C), the Mediterranean climate being one where winter is the wet season, providing young plants with a much better chance of survival than the long hot summers. In habitats where the rainfall is irregular, as in the grassland of steppes, plants will often germinate over a much broader range of temperatures, the key to successful establishment being an adequate but unpredictable water supply.

RAINFALL, HUMIDITY, AND MOISTURE IN THE SOIL

Water is essential for plants, as it is for all living creatures. It provides hydrogen for photosynthesis, the key process by which green plants convert solar energy into food. It is also important because nutrients are only available to plants when dissolved in it. For nonwoody plants it plays yet another role, acting as a filling that gives rigidity to the structure. Plants take up water through fine root hairs, situated near the root tip, but lose it through their pores (stomata), the openings on the leaves through which gases pass in and out. To survive, they must strike a balance between intake and loss. In a stable environment where there is a regular and generous supply of moisture, plants maintain this balance without special adaptations, although they have guard cells which can close the pores to reduce transpiration.

Top Alaska is a region of mountainous topography and harsh climate, a large part of it lying inside the Arctic Circle. The main vegetation is coniferous forest and, in the north, vast expanses of tundra.

Above center (left) The saguaro cactus (*Carnegia gigantea*) epitomizes desert Arizona where, despite low rainfall, it may live for more than 200 years, reaching a height of up to 60ft (18m).

Above center (right) In gardens, it is impossible to recreate the rather sensational display of flowers that rain brings to life in desert or semi-desert regions, as is the case here in South Africa.

Above High humidity, as in this temperate Japanese forest, encourages the rich growth of mosses. Bacteria, fungi, lichens, mosses, and ferns may not have the glamour of flowering plants but are no less important ecologically.

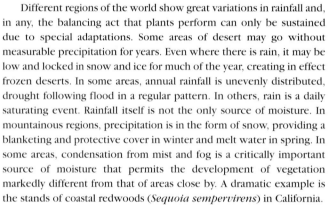

Different regions of the world show great variations in rainfall and, in any, the balancing act that plants perform can only be sustained due to special adaptations. Some areas of desert may go without measurable precipitation for years. Even where there is rain, it may be low and locked in snow and ice for much of the year, creating in effect frozen deserts. In some areas, annual rainfall is unevenly distributed, drought following flood in a regular pattern. In others, rain is a daily saturating event. Rainfall itself is not the only source of moisture. In mountainous regions, precipitation is in the form of snow, providing a blanketing and protective cover in winter and melt water in spring. In some areas, condensation from mist and fog is a critically important source of moisture that permits the development of vegetation markedly different from that of areas close by. A dramatic example is the stands of coastal redwoods (*Sequoia sempervirens*) in California.

In general, there is a correlation between distribution of rainfall and types of vegetation, the gradation from forest to grassland and desert reflecting a general reduction in the amount of moisture. Among the most remarkable of all plant adaptations are those to drought. In seasonally dry areas of the tropics, many plants are deciduous, but more radical adaptations are found in almost waterless deserts, where the harshness of the environment is made worse by an alternation of searing heat and icy cold. At the other extreme are the plants occupying the zone where land and water meet; these, too, require special adaptations for a life in poorly aerated soils.

SUN AND SHADE

The prime biological process, photosynthesis, relies on light as its energy source. All green plants need light, but they have different requirements. Differences in light demand and shade tolerance, part of the genetic constitution of plants, are major factors in the composition and ordering of plant communities. Among the plants most hungry for light are quick-growing annuals that produce many seeds in their short lives. The germination of their seed is often triggered by light of a certain intensity. Slower growing are "pioneer" trees, such as the pines (*Pinus*), which nevertheless quickly colonize disturbed open ground. Plants adapted to shade are often slow growing and often do not rely solely on flowering and seed production to maintain their populations. Yet shade tolerance is not always fixed for life. Tree seedlings, for example, can show greater shade tolerance than adults of the same species.

The light regime created by the canopy of a forest has a marked effect on the growth of plants below. It is also true that even much lower vegetation has a shady understory. Dense coniferous forest usually has very little undergrowth; this is also true under the light-trapping canopy of beech (*Fagus sylvatica*). The vegetation on the

Top left Heath and moorland, which is dominated by heather or ling (*Calluna vulgaris*) and species of *Erica*, are found on acid soils in many parts of Europe, often merging with bog and tundra.

Top right The European beech (*Fagus sylvatica*) does well on alkaline and limestone soils, beech "hangers" being a feature of the chalk downs in southern Britain.

Above Ericaceous plants—that is, members of the *Erica* family—are generally intolerant of alkaline soils. Attractive representatives from California include the pink-flowered *Phyllodoce breweri* and *Cassiope mertensiana*.

floor of temperate deciduous forests is either capable of living under low light intensities, or else plants get around the problem by growing, flowering, and setting seed before the foliage of the canopy develops. The mixture of herbaceous plants and bulbs in regularly thinned woodland benefits from periodic exposure to relatively high light levels. The floor of a tropical rainforest is usually heavily shaded, a fact that largely accounts for the relatively poor herbaceous layer. In these forests, plants below the canopy have to use sunflecks, spots of light that get through gaps. There is strong evidence that a large part of the photosynthesis carried out by plants of the understory occurs during the very brief periods when light is intense.

SOIL

The detailed processes of soil formation should be set against the large-scale geological processes that have played a defining role in the distribution of plants comparable to ice ages and other major climatic changes. Among the most intriguing relationships in the plant world are those that suggest how the continents have drifted into their present positions after the breakup of a single large land mass.

The raw material of soil is bare rock, broken down by weathering processes such as frost. Soils provide an anchor for plants and hold the water, inorganic nutrients, and air that plants need for satisfactory growth. However, they vary enormously in composition, chemistry, structure, and nutrient and organic content. Several broad soil types are strongly associated with particular types of climate and vegetation. Among the poorest soils are those of the tundra, partially decomposed peat and a sticky clay (gley) sitting over permafrost. Coniferous forest and heath in the cold north have gray podzols, the Russian name for the gray color of the soil. The brown earths are typical of temperate

Below Shade from the forest canopy inhibits the growth of many tree seedlings. Their chance of getting established may come when the canopy is removed by fire or the timely collapse of a forest giant. Other trees show a tolerance of shade when they are seedlings but not as adults.

Bottom In this Californian landscape, which is momentarily brilliant with flowers, low rainfall limits the growth of trees and shrubs, while openness allows light-demanding plants to flourish when the conditions are favorable.

deciduous forest and the black chernozems, valuable as agricultural land, of humid grasslands. Heavy rains leach the soils of tropical forests. These lateritic soils (red clay containing iron) have few nutrients, and silt is washed out to leave clay colored by iron and aluminium oxides. This is most marked where there are alternating wet and dry seasons.

In addition to these broad soil types, there are local soils, usually reflecting topography or the character of the underlying rock, which may pose problems for plants that are not especially adapted to them. In poorly drained soils, for example, the pores in the soil are filled with water, so there is little oxygen for respiration. Saline conditions near the sea complicate water uptake and comparable problems are found, in addition to the lack of water, in desert areas where salts accumulate. Deficiencies in or toxic levels of certain minerals can also pose limits to plant growth. Even when the minerals for growth and reproduction are present, marked acidity or alkalinity may hinder their uptake. The degree of acidity or alkalinity is measured on a pH scale from 0 to 14. Plants have the best chance of taking up the available nutrients when the soil has a pH of 6.5. Marked acidity or alkalinity also affects the bacterial and fungal activity that breaks down organic matter.

WIND

Large-scale wind movements cause the circulation of water vapor and form an integral part of worldwide weather patterns that result from the interaction of atmosphere and oceans powered by the heat of the sun. In areas of the world where there is a reasonably uniform distribution of rainfall, the scale of global circulatory systems is usually only evident when there is an aberration in the pattern, as happens periodically with the El Nino effect, originating in the eastern Pacific. The case is different in Southeast Asia, where the monsoon, a seasonal wind that blows from the northeast in winter and from the southeast from about April to October, sweeps in from the Indian Ocean with heavy rains that are life-giving but potentially destructive. Elsewhere, wind can be an important factor in making and molding landscapes, as in the formation of the loess plateau of northwest China, composed of wind-blown particles from the desert interior. Drought, overgrazing, the cultivation of marginal lands, and combinations of these give wind the upper hand, with consequences on the scale of the sheet erosion of America's Great Plains in the 1930s.

Apart from its role in pollination and the distribution of seeds, the main influence of wind on plants is to increase the rate at which leaves lose water. In addition, wind can cause a sand-blasting effect or more moderate abrasion from the particles it carries, while violent gusts can break branches and wrench off leaves. In coastal areas, salt carried by fierce winds can affect plants well beyond the normal spray zone. Few plants seem to be adapted to irregular violent winds, but some palms are remarkable survivors of typhoons and other tropical storms, probably

Above At high altitudes the force of prevailing winds, as in the Selkirk Mountains of British Columbia, which are shown here, can strongly modify the growth of plants. Above the tree line—the limit at which trees grow to approximately their normal size—trees are dwarfed and shaped by the wind so that the branches only develop on the side away from the wind.

because their head of pinnate leaves is not held rigidly and the division of the leaves means they offer little resistance. The very large undivided leaves of bananas (*Musa*) have regular strips of weak tissue running at right angles to the rib. Strong winds may tear these but leave the shredded leaf still able to function. The most marked adaptations to winds, however, are found near the sea and in deserts, where the leaves are often leathery or greatly reduced in size and the pores protected. In alpine and tundra regions, plants are compact and often huddled in close mats and cushions for mutual protection.

HUMAN INFLUENCE

In the wild, plants are part of communities in which the various living components interrelate in a complex way. The human race may once have been inconspicuous in these relationships although already long ago it began to have a decisive influence on plants and animals. Human exploitation has fundamentally modified much of the earth's natural vegetation. Forests have been felled, grasslands ploughed, hillsides grazed, minerals extracted, vast areas built over with factories, roads and housing, or contaminated with waste. Humans have intentionally and accidentally introduced plants and other life forms, often weeds, pests, and diseases that then need to be controlled or eradicated.

We have huge confidence in the resilience of the natural world, but alarm bells are now ringing. Gardens may be a refuge for endangered plants, but this should be a last-ditch solution and not a substitute for serious attempts to protect self-sustaining communities in the wild.

Far left The combination of wind, salt spray, and negligible soil limits the range of plants that can grow on rocky coastlines. Sea thrift (*Armeria maritima*) is widely distributed as a coastal plant in the Northern Hemisphere and is also found in mountainous regions.

Below left Cultivation has extended the range of many plants. The olive (*Olea europaea*), one of the classic plants of the Mediterranean, is now widely cultivated in regions with hot dry summers and mild moist winters. The field poppy (*Papaver rhoeas*), an annual that almost certainly originated in the eastern Mediterranean, has been widely distributed in the world along with the seed of the cereals among which it grows as a weed.

Below Tropical rainforest is the most seriously threatened of all natural ecosystems. Burning and clearing, as here in Brazil, produces land with very short-lived fertility.

Major Plant Communities

FOREST AND WOODLAND

The dedication of sacred groves and the veneration of individual trees are an indication of the reverence and awe that since ancient times humankind has felt towards the largest members of the plant world. The survival in China of the maidenhair tree (*Ginkgo biloba*), a unique living representative of an order of seed-bearing trees stretching back beyond the conifers in the geological record and unknown in the wild, can almost certainly be attributed to its cultivation in the grounds of palaces and temples.

The fate of the forests of the classical world is a reminder, if one is needed, that reverence has been shown to forests and trees very selectively. Only fragments are left of the preclassical vegetation that covered the Mediterranean region with an evergreen forest capable of withstanding long hot summers. Centuries ago, land clearance, felling for timber and firewood, heavy grazing (especially by goats), and soil erosion had reduced most of the plant communities to a form of scrub (see "Scrubland," pp. 30-31). Elsewhere in the world, what seem like vast areas of untouched forest are in most cases greatly reduced from their original extent and very often modified by human activity. In some parts of the world the level of human influence has been stabilized, and modern "sacred groves," in the form of special reserves and national parks, provide some protection for what survives. Elsewhere, particularly in the tropics (see "Tropical Forests," pp. 26-29), there is reckless exploitation that has implications for us all.

In temperate regions with moderate annual rainfall—about 30-60in (750-1,500mm)—the natural plant cover is deciduous woodland. In the cold winters that are a feature of much of the temperate zone, the movement of sap slows down and eventually stops as the temperature falls. Dropping leaves at a time of year when photosynthesis is at its most inefficient because of low light levels is a way of minimizing water loss that cannot be replaced from the ground. Deciduous woodland is uncommon in the Southern Hemisphere: in Tierra del Fuego in Argentina, forests of Antarctic beech (*Nothofagus antarctica*) drop their leaves in fall, but members of the same genus in other parts of the hemisphere are evergreen. In the Northern Hemisphere, however, deciduous forest once covered much of western Europe, eastern North America, and parts of Asia, including Japan. The onslaught of the ice ages has resulted in a relatively small range of deciduous trees in western Europe, while the forests that survive have been profoundly

Below The woodland of Britain has been greatly modified by human interference over many centuries. Oaks (*Quercus robur* and *Q. petraea*) are favored at the expense of other trees. Here, oak is the major constituent of Padley Wood, which runs along a gorge in the Derbyshire Peak District.

Bottom left Ferns and mosses provide a lush floor to a moist mixed woodland of deciduous trees and conifers in New York State.

Bottom center Even the grandest forest trees succumb to death and decay, bacteria and fungi eventually breaking down the woody carcass. This process can be slow here in cool northern woods in Sweden.

influenced by human activity. There are traditional methods of woodland management, however, which have helped to maintain some plant communities. Thinning and pollarding of trees such as oak (*Quercus robur*) and hornbeam (*Carpinus betulus*) let light onto the woodland floor, this periodic exposure favoring a number of bulbs and herbaceous perennials, including bluebells (*Hyacinthoides non-scripta*) and primulas (*Primula vulgaris*). The deciduous forest of northeast North America and Asia is much richer in tree species and also in the plants of the shrub and herbaceous layers. In Japan, as well as in New England, numerous maples (*Acer*) give the forest its fall brilliance.

The deciduous forest contains relatively few climbers, and the main epiphytic plants are ferns. The shrubs and herbaceous plants of the forest floor vary greatly according to soil moisture and chemistry, root competition from trees, and the density of the canopy. For example, the well-spread foliage of common beech (*Fagus sylvatica*) is very efficient at trapping light, but little moisture reaches the floor of the wood, the shade cast is very dense and, as a consequence, there is little undergrowth. Even under trees with a lighter canopy, most plants of the woodland floor grow and flower before the tree foliage is fully developed. Where the shade is heavy, the main plants of the woodland floor tend to be ferns.

Below and bottom right Sugar maple (*Acer saccharum*) and silver maple (*Acer saccharinum*) are among the trees that give the deciduous forest of northeast USA, shown here in Vermont, its exceptionally rich coloring in the autumn. Other species found growing with them in these forests include American beech (*Fagus grandifolia*), white ash (*Fraxinus americana*), and red oak (*Quercus rubra*).

In evolutionary terms, it is approximately 80 to 90 million years since conifers were overtaken by flowering plants. The key advance of the flowering plants was the enclosure of the ovules which develop into seeds when fertilized. Despite the apparently evolutionary handicap of having naked seeds, which are in fact protected in woody cones, conifers remain highly successful plants in many parts of the world. Although low in the number of species represented, some of the vast coniferous stands in the Northern Hemisphere are among the largest forests in the world. The conifers also include the most massive of all living things, big tree (*Sequoiadendron giganteum*). The big tree groves, found mainly at altitudes of between 5,000 and 8,000ft (1524–2438m) in a belt about 250 miles (402km) long on the western slopes of the Californian Sierra Nevada, hold trees that are more than 265ft (80m) tall, with diameters at their base of 33ft (10m). It is estimated that some have lived to more than 4000 years. Even longer lived by several hundred years are specimens of another conifer, the bristlecone pine (*Pinus aristata*), found at over 10,000ft (3000m) in eastern California and Nevada.

A key to the usefulness of many conifers is that they are fast-growing "pioneer" plants, producing valuable timber and pulpwood. Pioneer plants, usually at a disadvantage because their seedlings are intolerant of shade, are quick off the mark when, in natural conditions, trees fall or fire clears the ground (some of the pines require fire for the cones to release their seeds). It is not surprising, therefore, that they can be successfully planted on exposed sites, stabilizing sandy soils, forming shelter belts, and protecting slower growing and more vulnerable trees. The success of *Pinus radiata* as a timber tree is astonishing when the scale of its plantations on poor soils in many parts of the world is set against its highly restricted distribution in the wild, where it is confined almost entirely to a few small areas on the Monterey Peninsula of California.

The boreal forest forms a broad belt, as much as 500 miles wide, across North America, Europe, and Siberia. At its northern extreme, before it peters out in the bleak expanses of the tundra, the forest becomes more open. In the taiga, as this chilly parkland is called, stunted specimens of conifers such as black spruce (*Picea mariana*) tip drunkenly as they hold their footing in shallow soils above permafrost. Even south of these extreme conditions the climate is harsh, with long, cold, snowy winters. Larches (*Larix*), among the few deciduous conifers, are among the hardiest survivors, the northernmost forest in the world, in eastern Siberia, being dominated by *L. gmelinii*. The small needles of other conifers, such as the spruces (*Picea*), are well adapted to conserving moisture and, because they are evergreen, photosynthesis can take place whenever conditions are

favorable. The form of the trees, narrow and conical with drooping branches furnished with needles, helps shed snow, minimizing the risk of injury. Among the few plants on the floor of these dark forests is dwarf cornel (*Cornus canadensis*).

To the south of this belt, coniferous forests commonly form a conspicuous zone on mountain slopes between broad-leaved forest and alpine tundra. In an area of North America known as the cordillera, coniferous forests of trees such as Douglas fir (*Pseudotsuga menziesii*) sweep up from the lowlands to a sharply marked tree line and form some of the most magnificent stands of trees in the world, the species varying with altitude and latitude. Where the summers are not too dry, as on the west side of the Olympic Mountains in Washington, the dominant trees are sitka spruce (*Picea sitchensis*) and western hemlock (*Tsuga heterophylla*). The mossy floors of these forests are thick with ferns. Along a narrow strip at the southwest margin of the cordillera, frequent fog modifies what would otherwise be a dry Mediterranean climate. Thanks to this quirk, the world's tallest tree,

the coastal redwood (*Sequoia sempervirens*), here forms dense stands in which specimens can regularly reach 330ft (100m).

The distinctive conifers from the Southern Hemisphere include the spiny-leaved monkey puzzle (*Araucaria araucana*) and its relatives. They are often plants of mixed forest, the New Zealand kauri (*Agathis australis*) usually towering massively among evergreen broad-leaved trees. The evergreen rainforests of warm temperate regions have a distinct annual rhythm, but the high rainfall, about 60–120in (1,500–3,000mm), is distributed quite evenly throughout the year. These forests are similar to tropical and subtropical rainforest, especially that at higher altitudes. Climbers and epiphytes are common and the numerous ferns include tree-like species of *Dicksonia*.

Top left This Pacific dogwood (*Cornus nuttallii*) here frames a stand of the giant redwood (*Sequoiadendron giganteum*) in the Sequoia National Forest, California. No other tree can match the giant redwood for bulk. It is remarkably resistant to fire and there is a healthy population of young trees in the groves, but these are, nonetheless, limited to a small area of the Sierra Nevada.

Left Although conifers can be found in many regions of the world, their key territory is the cold north and the mountain ranges of the Northern Hemisphere. Their evergreen foliage, adapted to conserve moisture, allows them to grow when conditions are favorable, without having to put energy into the formation of leaves.

Below The warm temperate rainforests of Tasmania have many similarities with tropical and subtropical rainforest. A striking feature is the wealth of tree ferns.

TROPICAL FORESTS

To those whose view of the plant kingdom has been formed by the prairies, fields, and meadows of temperate regions, a first encounter with the luxuriance of a tropical rain forest is startling and even disorienting. The prodigious, space-grabbing energy of tropical plants makes their temperate relatives seem prissily decorous. Their flamboyant and curious flowers imply ingenious sexual habits. The profusion and variety is so overwhelming that by comparison the temperate flora seems impoverished. Perhaps most bewildering of all is the apparent abandonment of seasonal rhythms. Instead of a synchronized burst in spring, heralding a season of growth followed by autumnal decline and winter dormancy, there seems to be random flowering, fruiting, and leaf fall throughout the year. If the impression left by the luxuriance of tropical forests is of biological chaos, this is

Below Palms can be found in a wide range of habitats. Although these trees are mainly native to tropical areas, the European *Chamaerops europaeus* is also included in this family. In fact, *Chamaerops* grow on sandy or rocky slopes as well as in shrub in the western Mediterranean. In tropical rainforest, palms, with their large, pinnate leaves, often make a conspicuous and rather dramatic contribution to the vegetation beneath the canopy. An Australian species of *Licuala*, which is a large genus strongly represented in Southeast Asia, is seen here in Queensland rainforest.

Bottom The canopy of tropical rainforest, such as the one here in Belize in Central America, is composed of a large number of species, through which isolated taller trees emerge.

Below Even where water courses run though tropical rainforest, light reaches the floor only as fleeting patches and flecks.

Bottom left and right Many of the tropical trees most familiar as ornamentals come from areas with a marked wet and dry season. This is so for jacaranda (*Jacaranda mimosifolia*) from savanna country in Brazil, deciduous in the dry season and with violet-blue flowers before the leaves open. The pink poui or rosy trumpet tree (*Tabebuia rosea*), the national plant of El Salvador, is seasonally deciduous and usually flowers when leafless.

misleading. Their amazing fecundity, geared to a wildly accelerated growth rate, operates according to its own complex rhythms.

Tropical rainforest is found in a number of areas near the equator: on a large scale in the Amazon basin of South America, in western Africa, and in southeast Asia. These are regions with very high annual rainfall: over 78in (200cm) is quite normal, and in some areas rainfall can even exceed 394in (1000cm). In the tropical heartlands, the sluicing of torrential rains can be expected throughout the year, the temperature remains fairly constant, with the yearly mean about 79–81°F (26–27°C), and the humidity (near saturation most of the time) is exhausting for those who are unaccustomed to it. The phenomenal growth creates a misleading impression of soil fertility. As rain water leaches through the soil, it removes nutrients, and what is returned through decomposition is not retained. The forest is its own powerhouse, and once the land is cleared, as is happening at a staggering rate, its future is very bleak.

After the first few crops, the nutrients are exhausted and the land is permanently degraded, with the likelihood of heavy erosion.

The distinctive hierarchical structure of the trees in a tropical forest has no parallel in the deciduous broadleaf and coniferous forests. Very tall trees, 150–200ft (45–60m) high and only branching near the crown, stand above the general level of the forest. Like most of the vegetation in the rainforest, the "emergents," as they are called, are shallow-rooted, but buttress roots help to stabilize these exposed trees. The layer of trees below them, usually without buttress roots, forms a canopy at a height of about 100–130ft (30–39m). Beneath this, there is usually a third layer of narrow-crowned trees and what might be thought of as a shrub layer, in which palms are often a conspicuous feature. As well as being very rich in species, the composition of the rainforest is extraordinarily diverse even in quite small areas, and it is rare for a single species to dominate.

From ground level, it is very difficult to get an idea of what is going on in the tropical forest. The place to be is in the canopy, where

Far left The rainforests of Southeast Asia are the most complex in the tropics. In Sumatra, where this photograph was taken, there is high rainfall throughout the year, which is brought by both the southeast and northeast monsoons. Forests that are rich in trees of commercial value have, however, suffered from heavy exploitation.

Top left The emerald creeper or jade vine (*Strongylodon macrobotrys*) gets its name from the spectacular trail of blue-green flowers that hang from the twining stems. In its vigor this native of the Philippines is like many tropical climbers, growing from the shady floor of the forest to a height of 70ft (22m) or more.

Center left (top) Orchids are found in almost every region of the world and in a wide range of habitats. It is in the tropics, however, that they achieve their fullest development. Many tropical species, such as this *Cymbidium*, are epiphytic, with gray or white tangled aerial roots. The green tip of these roots absorbs moisture and nutrients.

Center left (bottom) A large number of tropical ferns are epiphytic, including the widely distributed bird's-nest fern (*Asplenium nidus*).

Bottom left A large number of the bromeliads, such as this species of Nidularium, are plants of tropical rainforest, and many of them are epiphytic.

Below In comparison with the canopy or even the various levels of vegetation beneath it where there are perching plants, the floor of a tropical rainforest often seems uncrowded. In this Costa Rican forest, ferns compete with various shade-tolerant herbaceous plants, including a species of *Aphelandra* that is in flower.

insects, birds, mammals (including pollinating bats), reptiles, and amphibians are busy in a way that can scarcely be guessed at from below. Some fresh insights into the complex life of the tropical forest have been made possible by specialized climbing techniques that have given scientists access to the canopy. It is possible, as a poor second best, to get an idea from the channel of a river that activity is taking place high up. When the forest is looked at from such a vantage point, two other categories of plants stand out: lianas and epiphytes. The criss-crossing stems of lianas occur almost everywhere but are very thick along watercourses. These nimble vines, rooted in the floor of the forest but desperate for the light of the canopy, make up the tangle that is the principal obstacle to those penetrating the forest.

Light is also important for a large number of epiphytes. These are perching plants that shun the dark forest floor in favor of a better position higher up in the trees. The great variety and abundance of these flowering plants and ferns, staged at various levels, give the upper levels of the forest the appearance of hanging gardens. Many epiphytes have specialized roots which help secure the plant and also absorb moisture directly from the air. This is so for the large numbers of epiphytic tropical orchids (see pp. 100–101). The epiphytic bromeliads, mainly from Central and South America, include a number that have become popular ornamentally for their curious flowers. These are cupped in a colorful "leaf-vase" at the center of the leaf rosette, forming a reservoir for the plant. Not all the plants lodged in the canopy are as innocent as they seem. Some of the figs, including the weeping fig (*Ficus benjamina*), widely grown as a houseplant, turn stranglers if their seed germinates in the crook of a branch. For a while the fig seems like a simple epiphyte but with a criss-cross of roots around its host. Eventually, it sends down vertical roots; once it gets its feet in the ground, it forms a strangling network of roots, although shade cast by its top growth is probably the real killer. When the host dies and decays, the fig is left as a self-supporting cylinder.

Far from all tropical areas have the rainfall to support true rainforest. Where there is a distinct dry season, as in areas affected by the monsoon, the forest is much less varied and many of the trees are semideciduous or deciduous, losing their leaves during the dry season and most coming into flower with the onset of the rains. Some widely planted ornamentals in tropical and subtropical regions, among them the flamboyant tree (*Delonix regia*) of Madagascar, come from regions in the tropics with a marked seasonal rhythm. In areas with a long dry season the forest no longer forms a continuous cover, and it is reduced to trees such as thorny acacias scattered in grassland.

The cycles and rhythms of plants in the tropical rainforests, which are richest in Southeast Asia, cannot be isolated from those of the many other life forms in the forest. Something of the interdependence of these life forms is understood. Much will never be known, so great and accelerating is the scale of devastation.

Left Throughout much of the Mediterranean, hot dry slopes are covered with low scrub or garrigue, (known as phrygana in Greece). It is surprisingly rich in species. There are many aromatic shrubs such as rosemary (*Rosmarinus*). Numerous bulbs make the hillsides colorful in spring. Species of rock or sun rose (*Cistus*), some of which are flowering here, are also common in taller scrub known as maquis.

Below The Cape Peninsula of South Africa has a unique and very rich flora. Most of the region has evergreen scrub, Mediterranean in character but with a different range of shrubs. In spring and summer, annuals, bulbs, and herbaceous perennials flower in profusion.

SCRUBLAND

Of all the words describing scrub, none is more evocative than maquis (or its Corsican equivalent, macchia) with its romantic associations of banditry and its sense of wildness. For such an apparently undistinguished kind of vegetation, it is surprising how many terms are applied to its various forms: chaparral in California, fynbos in South Africa, mallee scrub in Australia, matorral in Chile, phrygana in Greece, and tomillares in Spain. These represent variants of a type of vegetation found in the Mediterranean or in regions with a similar climate, characterized by hot, dry summers and relatively mild winters. The moderate annual rainfall, in the range of 12–36in (300–900mm), is concentrated in the winter months.

In addition to the vegetation of these regions, there are large tracts of continental interiors with semidesert scrub. South of the Sahara, for example, in areas where the rainfall may be as little as 5in (120mm) a year, acacias and other thorny plants, sometimes mixed with succulents such as the shrubby euphorbias, form open scrub that reaches a height of about 6ft (1.8m) with a rough understory of thorny herbs. Scrub also occupies various marginal zones where climatic and environmental factors limit the growth of trees. For instance, in mountains there is often a shrub zone above the tree line.

The influence of the classical world on western culture permeates even our attitude toward plants, many from the Mediterranean region holding a privileged place in gardens. The maquis itself, of which many are a constituent, is composed largely of hard-leaved evergreen shrubs or small trees making more or less dense cover to a height of about 10ft (3m). The maquis may be the natural plant community in some parts of the Mediterranean, but elsewhere it is certainly the result of modifications to evergreen forest, including the holm oak (*Quercus ilex*), which once covered large areas. Characteristic plants of the maquis include: strawberry trees (*Arbutus*), rock or sun roses (*Cistus*), myrtle (*Myrtus communis*), olive (*Olea europaea*), Jerusalem sage (*Phlomis fruticosa*), lentisc (*Pistacia lentiscus*) and Spanish broom (*Spartium junceum*).

Right In the vast, ancient island of Australia, the genus *Eucalyptus* holds a dominant position. Among the 500 or so species, some are forest trees but many are found in scrub and semidesert. Like the eucalyptus of scrubland, the curious grass trees (*Xanthorrhoea*), known as blackboys, are fire-resistant.

Bottom There is rarely a sharp divide between scrubland and desert. Here, the merging of scrub and desert vegetation can be seen in the Saguaro National Monument, in Arizona. Cacti, including the columnar saguaro (*Carnegia gigantea*), grow with various other drought-resistant shrubs, including the yellow-flowered brittle bush or incienso (*Encelia farinosa*).

Heavy grazing, fires, and cutting are responsible for the relatively stable low-scrub communities described as garrigue, phrygana, and tomillares. However, the vegetation can be so degraded that it only consists of a few spiny shrubs thinly scattered over stony ground where there is barely a vestige of soil. Many maquis plants, including the rock or sun roses and Spanish broom, are also found in garrigue and comparable communities. Many of the shrubs, such as lavenders (*Lavandula*), rosemary (*Rosmarinus officinalis*), members of the savory family (*Satureja*), and thymes (*Thymus*), are aromatic. As with the shrubs of the maquis, growth occurs in late winter, and the main flowering season is spring, before the long, parching and bleaching summer. In late winter and spring, and to a lesser degree in fall, the shrubs are overshadowed by bulbous plants such as various onions (*Allium*), anemones, autumn crocus (*Colchicum*), true crocuses, and sternbergias. In addition, there are a large number of terrestrial orchids.

Many parallels can be drawn between Mediterranean communities and the chaparral of southern California, in which the dominant plants are also hard-leaved evergreen shrubs growing to a height of about 10ft (3m). On some of the driest slopes, chamise (*Adenostoma fasciculatum*) forms almost pure stands. More mixed scrub includes manzanitas (*Arctostaphylos*), Californian lilac (*Ceanothus*), and scrub oak (*Quercus dumosa*). The word chaparral is, in fact, derived from *chaparra*, a Spanish word for evergreen oak. An aspect of the chaparral and of scrubland in general that is difficult to reconcile with building development is the part fire plays in its renewal. In the natural cycle, chaparral produces shrub litter that builds up to form a flammable accumulation. This is cleared, as is most of the top growth, by fire caused by lightning every 20 to 35 years. During this temporary phase, grasses, annuals, and perennials, such as lobelias, phacelias, and Californian poppies (*Romneya*), flourish. Many shrubs shoot from ground level after a few months, while fire triggers others to germinate. Within a few years, the shrubs dominate once more, some chemically inhibiting the germination and growth of herbs.

Clearly, the plant communities of the Mediterranean and regions with similar climates are of intrinsic interest and a vital source of ideas for gardeners facing long hot summers and reduced water supplies.

Grasslands

In hunter-gatherer communities, 10,000 to 20,000 years ago, humans were already dipping in to the cereal bowl. They fed omniverously, opportunistically gathering ripening grain on the stem before the heads shattered, or feasting on meat after the lucky kill of a grazing animal. From this, a world economy has developed that is based on grasses (Poaceae), to remarkable degree. A major advance made in southwest Asia and the Middle East was the development, from wild *Triticum* and *Hordeum* species, of wheat and rye that did not shatter before the grain could be harvested. In tropical Asia the principal cereal was rice (*Oryza sativa*). In America it was maize (*Zea mays*). Africa has several indigenous cereals, of which sorghum (*Sorghum*

bicolor) and pearl millet (*Pennisetum glaucum*) were brought into cultivation early. Vast areas of the earth's surface are now cultivated to raise annual grasses that provide grain crops, and a few perennial grasses, the most important of which is sugar cane (*Saccharum officinarum*), originally from Southeast Asia. Large areas are also maintained with a perennial grass cover to feed flocks and herds of domesticated grazing animals. All of this is on such a scale that it can give a misleading impression of the earth's natural grass cover.

It seems that grasses, late developers among the flowering plants, started off in forests. Some grasses, such as the European wood millet (*Milium effusum*), are still found under a tree canopy. The best move that grasses made, however, was to get out into the open. Many grasses can grow well enough in a forest climate; the farmlands of western Europe, once wooded, are testimony to this. It is shade that puts them at a disadvantage. Grasses have succeeded where climate does not favor trees or where other factors, including human intervention, prevent the development of forest. Rainfall rather than temperature is the key factor. As a broad generalization, it can be said that the great natural grasslands of the world are found in a climatic zone that is too dry for forest but not as dry as desert. The majority of grasses show some degree of adaption to or tolerance of drought. The annuals avoid the problem by moving quickly through their life cycle in what may be a very short rainy season. Perennial grasses have adapted

Top left The bond that has always existed between nomadic tribes and their horses was originally forged in the grasslands of central Asia. Although nomadism as a way of life has declined, horse raising continues to this day, even here at the western edge of the Tibetan plateau.

Above The pressure of growing populations threatens even the vast grasslands of Africa. Here, in Tanzania's plateau, the rainy season that takes place in the summer brings new growth to the savanna and more open expanses on which herds of wildebeest and buffalo depend.

to drought, the breathing pores (stomata) of some being protected inside furled leaves. They have dormant winter buds, often below the surface of the soil, while the collapsed litter of the previous season's leaves helps reduce the loss of moisture.

The tall grasslands that still cover large areas of Africa, providing pasture for the last remaining large herds of wild grazing animals, represent a type found throughout tropical regions where there are marked wet and dry seasons. The term "savanna" that is applied to these grasslands is a broad category covering almost pure grassland, a more parklike landscape in which open areas of grassland are more or less sparsely dotted with thorny trees and bushes, and country where trees grow more closely but where the canopy is still well broken up. These variations reflect differences in the length of the dry season,

Top right There are three broad zones of North American prairie, broadly related to the height of the grass: tall in the east, short in the west, and mixed in between. Short-grass prairie formerly supported large bison herds. In areas like Montana and South Dakota, as here, ponderosa pine (*Pinus ponderosa*) grows in short-grass prairie.

Above right Tussock grasses are the dominant plants among the treeless vegetation of the islands in the southern oceans. On Campbell Island, which lies south of New Zealand, the herbaceous perennial *Bulbinella rossii* shelters among the tussocks.

usually 3 to 5 months, and in an annual rainfall range of 8–39in (200–1000mm). The greater the rainfall, the denser the tree cover. Nutrients tend to be washed out of the soil when heavy rains fall in a relatively short season, and these soils often drain poorly because of the formation of a hardpan. Where they are used for ranching, as in the llanos of northern Columbia, Argentina, and Venezuela, the original grasses have been largely replaced by introduced species, and fire is used to lift nutrient levels and prevent the growth of scrub or trees.

Since pioneer days, the boundaries of the vast grasslands of central North America have been obscured and their character altered by agriculture, forest clearing, and urban development. But the broad outlines are still clear. The prairies, bordered by the coniferous forests of Canada in the north and the deserts of Mexico in the south, are brought to a halt in the west by the Rocky Mountains. In the east, the prairie meets forest. The divide was never sharp, accidents of topography and microclimates ensuring a complex mixture of grassland and forest. The broad frontier has moved backwards and forwards. For example, the use of fire by Indians in hunting checked the growth of trees and the prairie moved east.

The variation in the composition of the prairie grasslands from east to west is also an indication of the effect of climate. In the east, in a zone now mainly devoted to the cultivation of corn and soybean, there was tall-grass prairie, in which grasses such as big bluestem

Below Texas bluebonnet (*Lupinus texensis*) grows with other annuals and perennials in grasssland.

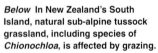

Below In New Zealand's South Island, natural sub-alpine tussock grassland, including species of *Chionochloa*, is affected by grazing.

Bottom The poet's narcissus (*Narcissus poeticus*) is widely distributed in the moist alpine meadows of southern Europe.

(*Andropogon gerardii*) formed a dense sward that reached a height of 6–10ft (1.8–3m) in summer. Numerous herbaceous plants, including species of *Aster, Baptisia, Lupinus, Monarda,* and *Solidago*, are native to this zone. Reflecting their much lower rainfall, 10–15in (25–33mm) a year, the Great Plains east of the Rocky Mountains had a short-grass prairie, usually under 10in (25cm) high, which included buffalo grass (*Buchloe dactyloides*) and blue grama or mosquito grass (*Bouteloua gracilis*). This prairie once supported great herds of bison but they have now gone, and heavy grazing, managed by humans, has taken its toll on the natural vegetation. In the Great Drought of the 1930s, the blowing of topsoil was worst where cropping, especially of wheat, had been pushed into short-grass prairie. The transitional character of the zone between these two prairies, now more or less occupied by the wheat belt, was reflected in a mixture of grasses.

Rainfall too low or sporadic for trees has favored the development of grasslands in the pampas of Argentina and the steppes that extend from central Hungary eastwards through the former USSR and on to northern Mongolia and northeast China. From the Russian *chernaya zemlya*, which means black earth, has come the word chernozem, used to describe the characteristically rich black soil that in cool or temperate regions develops in grassland. There are enormous variations in this region of cold steppe, where for at least 4 months of the year temperatures are often well below freezing and where the fierce heat of summer leads to drought. Where the rainfall is low, grassland becomes desert. Many other areas that are less bleak in winter, including the South African veld, have a dense grass cover, but where winter rains are uncertain, as in the Sahel steppe south of the Sahara, semidesert scrub develops. A tundra-like vegetation dominated by tussock grasses is found in the islands of the southern ocean and also in subalpine zones in the Southern Hemisphere.

Many grasses are native to temperate regions such as western Europe and the eastern United States, where rainfall favors the growth of trees but natural expanses of grassland are limited. The pastures and meadows of Europe owe much of their character to human interference over the centuries. The Romans are said to have been the first to use hay as winter fodder for livestock on a large scale. In subalpine

Below These subalpine meadows in the Alps fill with flowers in late spring and early summer.

Above left Subalpine meadows in the Pyrenees are full of perennials including clover (*Trifolium*), hawkweeds (*Hieraceum*), and yellow rattle (*Rhinanthus minor*).

Bottom Cotton grasses (*Eriophorum*) are sedges, found in bog and tundra in the Northern Hemisphere.

regions of Europe, the combination of mowing and grazing regimes has favored the development of meadows rich in bulbs and herbaceous perennials. The timing of the mowing is critical; if it is too early, plants do not have a chance to flower and set seed. Ancient management of grassland in Britain has resulted in one of the floral highlights of a country where the devastation of the ice ages left the natural flora impoverished. Sheep and rabbit grazing on chalk downs has enabled several attractive flowers to compete with the grasses. Small scabious (*Scabiosa columbaria*), rampion (*Phyteuma orbiculare*), horseshoe vetch (*Hippocrepis comosa*), and a number of terrestrial orchids are found on the thin soils. Species of *Ophrys* take pollination to bizarre extremes by relying on the copulatory motions of bees and wasps that they resemble. Grazing also prevents the establishment of shrub and tree seedlings that might lead to the reclothing of chalk downland with woods of beech (*Fagus sylvaticus*). A fall in the rabbit population, dramatic when the disease myxomatosis was first prevalent, combined with a reduction in sheep grazing, has shown what a fragile hold these small flowers have on downland. For those who find lawn rather dull, chalk downland, old meadows, and ancient churchyards sometimes serve as models for ornamental mixtures of grasses and flowers. The recovery of downland after plowing is painfully slow, leaving discernible effects for hundreds of years. This serves as a reminder that rich and stable plant communities cannot be created overnight.

Due to a superficial resemblance to grasses, several other groups of plants are often lumped with them. These include reeds and sedges (Cyperaceae) which are major components of wetland and marshy vegetation. One of the largest of the sedges is papyrus (*Cyperus papyrus*), the stalks of which were used by the ancient Egyptians to make a writing material. Extensive papyrus swamps on the Nile Delta, depicted in reliefs and murals of the pharaonic period as the haunt of wildfowl, have more or less been eliminated as a result of drainage and irrigation schemes. In the Northern Hemisphere the cotton grasses (*Eriophorum*) animate vast areas of bog and tundra with the rabbit-tail bobbing of their tufts. The species of two other families, the rushes (Juncaceae) and reedmaces (Typhaceae), are also mainly plants of swampland and often form very large colonies.

Heath, Moorland, and Tundra

The empty landscapes of western Europe that are stained purple with heather in late summer are exhilarating and monotonous in equal measure. The meeting of land and sky is dramatically uncluttered, but the low vegetation stretching in all directions lacks incident. Heather or ling (*Calluna vulgaris*) is one of the most widespread members of the heath family, many of which are dwarf evergreen shrubs, with a few exceptions intolerant of alkaline soils. They show a strong family resemblance: their tough leaves are scale- or needle-like and their numerous small flowers are bell- or urn-shaped. Like heather, various heaths (*Erica*) and species of *Daboecia* are major constituents of the low shrub cover that is often found on the poor soils of sandy heathland or on moorland over peat. They frequently form a low canopy 3–4ft (90-120cm) high, beneath which there is a layer of a few herbs and grasses in a mosaic of mosses and lichens. Other dwarf shrubs of the heath family that accompany them include berrying species such as the bilberry (*Vaccinium myrtillus*) and shrubs that resemble heaths, such as crowberries (*Empetrum*). In peat bog, the main plants of the wet hollows are sphagnum mosses and sedges, but typical heathland plants are conspicuous in the drier parts.

In North America, very similar communities of plants but with slightly different species are found on acidic soils where there is a moist maritime climate. The concentration of *Erica* species in South Africa give a different complexion to the heaths found in the area known as "mountain fynbos" in the southern part of Cape Province. Here the "Cape heaths" make a low scrub with related plants such as species of Cape myrtle (*Phylica*). Australia has virtually no members of the heath family, but heathlike communities exist in which the dominant plants are members of a mainly Australian family, Epacridaceae. In South America, even on the remote island of Tristan da Cunha, crowberries make a surprising reappearance in plant communities that have similarities to the heaths of Northern Europe.

There is much debate about the role humans have played in the formation of the heathland and moorland of western Europe, but there is no doubt that human interference maintains many of these landscapes. In Britain, much heath on poor sandy soils is degraded woodland, the exercise of commoners' rights to grazing and gathering of fuel helping to keep the vegetation of the heathland to a low cover of heather, gorse (*Ulex europaea*), bracken (*Pteridium aquilinum*) and grasses. In the medieval period and later, heathland was often used for the managed grazing of rabbits. It is clear from old legislation against burning that heathland fires were often intentionally lit. Burning is still the major method of managing grazed moorland and grouse moor. Left to itself, heather (*Calluna vulgaris*) degenerates after 30 or 40 years, the plant eventually dying. Firing heather every 10 to 12 years keeps the plants dense and encourages the growth of numerous soft young shoots that feed animals and grouse. When burning and grazing stop, "pioneer" trees are often quick to establish. In the Scottish Highlands, much of the browsing pressure comes from red deer, and the case is often made for controlling their numbers to allow the regeneration of pine forests.

At their northernmost limits, heath communities merge imperceptibly with the vegetation of the tundra, a vast circumpolar region beyond the tree line. Although low in rainfall, usually less than 8in (200mm) a year, this area is poorly drained in its brief summer, when only a shallow layer of soil is thawed above the permafrost, which remains frozen year in and year out. There are parallels between the vegetation of this harsh environment and that above the tree line in mountains (see pp.40-43), but the most striking feature is the small number of species: sedges, mosses, and lichens, including the reindeer moss (*Claydonia rangiferina*), a lichen not a moss, are the most characteristic. The shrubby component, less conspicuous as the tundra extends

Top left Even where members of the heath family dominate, other plants such as grasses, bracken (*Pteridium aquilinum*), and brambles (*Rubus*) form part of the vegetation.

Center left Moorland, coniferous forest, and tundra meet in the harsh climatic conditions of the far north.

Below left When grazing pressure on the open sandy heathlands of Britain is reduced, trees such as birch (*Betula pendula*) and pine (*Pinus sylvestris*) invade.

Right It is widely believed that a vast pine forest stretched across the central Highlands of Scotland even in historical times. The evidence is not persuasive, but pine (*Pinus sylvestris*) certainly occurs widely in the moorland of the Highlands, which is dominated by heather (*Calluna vulgaris*).

Below The tundralike vegetation of mountainous regions in the subarctic, as in Norway, includes mosses and lichens, members of the heath family such as species of *Vaccinium*, low-growing conifers, and stunted birches (*Betula*).

north, includes heath plants, dwarf willows (*Salix*), and birches (*Betula*). Many of these plants, such as the heath relative *Cassiope tetragona*, are distributed throughout the tundra. The ice and snow cover of Antarctica is nearly complete, so there is no vegetation to compare even with the reduced plant communities of the tundra. Other than limited patches of painfully slow-growing mosses, the vegetation is limited to a grass, *Deschampsia antarctica*, and a cushionlike herb very similar to that of the Arctic moss campion (*Silene acaulis*).

WATER AND WET PLACES

The fate of many houseplants is to be killed with kindness as over-zealous owners unwittingly execute a kind of water torture. The idea that plants can have too much water is difficult to grasp, but there is no doubt that the plants that live in water or in waterlogged soils are specially adapted to these conditions. The most common structural solution that allows the free movement of oxygen, the great problem facing these plants, is a system of air channels that run from the roots to the shoots. In watery and boggy places, plants that are adequately adapted to these conditions are easy to recognize because they produce some of the lushest growth found in the plant world.

The term "bog garden" is misleading. It defines a permanently wet area that is normally richly planted with giant-leaved perennials, such as gunneras, and brightly colored flowers like astilbes and primulas. Natural bog is, in fact, wet peatland. In temperate regions, the main plants are sphagnum mosses (several species, interestingly, having their own zonation according to preferences for wet or dry conditions) and sedges such as cotton grass (*Eriophorum angustifolium*). Heath-like vegetation only occurs in drier parts of bog, and even this does not provide a model for exuberant planting. A broader range of plants is found on fens, where the plants are also growing on peat but the water supply is rich in minerals. Familiar fen plants include the common reed (*Phragmites australis*), a plant of exceptionally wide distribution throughout the world, and bulrushes or reedmaces (*Typha*). Fen sometimes develops into a kind of damp woodland, known as carr. In Europe, the most common trees of carr are alders (*Alnus*).

For the gardener considering the range of plants that can be grown in water or watery places, a more useful model than bog, fen, or carr is provided by natural ponds or lakes and their margins. Open bodies of water tend to be converted to land, with a sequence of plant communities succeeding one another in textbook order as the water becomes more shallow. Reduction of the water depth, perhaps with the build up of planktonic debris, allows enough light to reach the bottom of the pond or lake for submerged weeds such as the pondweeds (*Elodia*) to become established. These are followed by water lilies (*Nymphaea*) and similar floating plants rooted in the mud. It is not until the water is about 3ft (90cm) deep or less that plants with

Above Yellow skunk cabbage (*Lysichiton americanus*), a member of the *Arum* family, is widespread in western North America, where the water margins and streams, as well as the bogs, are kept permanently moist. The large paddle-shaped leaves develop as the yellow spathes wither.

Below The bog arum (*Calla palustris*) is found throughout the cool Northern Hemisphere, growing in shallow water where the soils are peaty and acidic, and even thriving in the shade cast by trees at the water's edge. The small flowers with a white spathe are followed by red berries.

Above left Carnivorous plants tend to live in nitrogen-deficient soils. *Sarracenia flava* and other pitcher plants of eastern North America are found in acidic bogs that are low in nutrients.

Above right In their adaptation to a watery environment, the water lilies (*Nymphaea*) seem highly developed, but it is clear from the fossil record that they are among the most primitive of flowering plants. Water lily stems have conduits for the movement of air; these may help to give the leaves buoyancy.

Below left Fen covered with stable woodland composed of trees such as these alders (*Alnus*) is known as carr.

Below right The regal fern (*Osmunda regalis*), one of the most successful ferns in bog, is widely distributed in temperate and subtropical regions.

leaves standing above the water, the emergents, become rooted. The effect of these marginals, which are similar to those of fen, is to accelerate the reduction of the water surface. But as their marshy fringe builds up, they help create an area of moist ground in which herbaceous plants, such as kingcup (*Caltha palustris*), can grow. Shrubby alders and willows (*Salix*) may eventually be followed by a woodland of birch (*Betula*), oak (*Quercus*), and other trees. In the controlled environment of a garden these stages can be maintained, although a rapid transformation sometimes requires a brutal response.

Trees that tolerate wet ground are particularly interesting. In eastern North America, the eastern cottonwood (*Populus deltoides*) and silver maple (*Acer saccharinum*) are typical streamside trees, both of which will tolerate prolonged flooding. In the numerous peat bogs of northern North America, black spruce (*Picea mariana*) and tamarck (*Larix laricina*) are consistently found together. One of the most impressive of all the swamp trees is the swamp cypress (*Taxodium distichum*), which is, like tamarck, a deciduous conifer. Although in cultivation this conifer does not require wet soil, in the wild it is found in alluvial swamps in the southeastern states of North America. The curious kneelike protuberances that surround the trunks of old plants are called breathing roots or pneumatophores, but there is debate about their function. One of the greatest of all dendrological sensations when it was recognized as a living fossil in the 1940s, is the dawn redwood (*Metasequoia glyptostroboides*). This shows many parallels with the swamp cypress. In its tiny area of natural distribution, in China's northwest Hubei province, it is found by the edges of streams and rivers, although not in swamplike conditions.

MOUNTAINOUS AND ROCKY LANDSCAPES

Pleasure in the grandeur of alpine scenery is relatively recent. Partly as a consequence, the horticultural infatuation with alpine plants did not reach its peak until the late 19th and early 20th centuries. The appeal of these naturally trimmed and poised plants remains enormous, and they continue to inspire expeditions of athletic botanists and provide devotees with the material for a challenging kind of gardening.

On the highest mountain peaks, as in the polar regions, there are no plants, but below this alpinist's heaven of rock, snow, and ice, there are various zones of vegetation caused by changes in altitude. These altitudinal zones bear some resemblance to the latitudinal zones between the tropics and the North Pole, but the parallels can easily be pushed too far. In the classic mountain zonation, a more or less continuous forest cover, known as montane forest, is succeeded higher up by a more open zone, with trees, often stunted and deformed, growing among grasses and herbaceous plants. The upper limit of this subalpine zone is the tree line which, unlike the forest edge of the tundra, is clearly marked. Above the tree line is the alpine zone proper, sometimes known as alpine tundra, which looks surprisingly garden-like despite the generous spacing between plants.

The general pattern of zonation, and in particular the altitude of the tree line, shows considerable variations from one part of the world to another. Temperature is the key factor: the absolute minimum temperature is not crucial (this occurs anyway when trees are dormant), but the length of the growing season is. In Europe, the tree line is usually at about 6,550ft (2000m), but moisture, snowfall, and orientation all affect it. In some of the drier areas of North America, the tree line can be at more than 10,000ft (3048m). In the tropics, where the average daily temperature is about the same throughout the year, other factors come into play, especially the sharp differences between day and night temperatures, more marked with increasing altitude.

Many compact plants are found in subalpine meadows or on rocky outcrops below the true alpine zone, but it is necessary to go higher for the purist's alpines. The harshness of the conditions is in some ways comparable to the Arctic tundra, but there is no underlying layer of permafrost. There may be boggy dips, but here much of the terrain is rough and steep so that water drains quickly. Rainfall is often low but, during the growing season, melting snow maintains a good supply of moisture. Buffeting winds often rise to a shrieking nightmare, and there is neglible soil in which to gain a hold and from which to get

nourishment. During the short growing season plants are exposed to intense light. Within this broad and daunting pattern of conditions, there is often a complex pattern of microclimates and soils. Temperature, duration, and intensity of sunshine, wind speed, loss of moisture through evaporation and drainage, thickness of snow cover and its persistence are all to some extent affected by the steepness of the slope, the direction it faces, and the character of the rock.

The plants that succeed in this inhospitable environment are remarkably consistent in their refinement, even though their flowers sometimes seem a size too large. Some are prostrate shrubs, such as dwarf willows (*Salix*). There are also dwarf bulbs, including crocuses, although many other bulbous plants belong to alpine meadows at a lower altitude. A larger number are herbaceous perennials, crouching against the wind as low mats, cushions, or packed leaf rosettes. They include mealy leaved alpine primulas, saxifrages with lime-encrusted rosettes, and blue gentians. Most of these plants rely on root systems that extend deep into rocky crevices for anchorage, moisture, and nourishment. They are all equipped to some extent to withstand dessication and primed to burgeon, flower, and set seed when conditions are favorable. The heat generated by the growth of some of the first to flower is even sufficient to melt the last of the snow that covers them.

Their position in vertical crevices or the stony fragments around them ensure that they never have a soggy collar. Some of these plants, remarkably, manage to keep their balance in the unstable environment of screes, the streams and rivers made of shattered rock fragments that are constantly being replenished by frost action on parent rock. The stone chips of the topmost layer are forever slipping lower, but beneath them there is usually a more stable base through which water moves freely. The plants that live in these harsh conditions have developed specializations. Some have fleshy roots deeply bedded in relatively stable soil beneath the moving surface. Many have leaves that snap off easily damaging the stem. The underground parts characteristically trail up the slope, which is an indication of the gravitational pull on the surface of the scree.

It is the exceptions in nature that are always intriguing. In the equatorial mountains of Central Africa and the Andes, giant alpines, including lobelias and members of the sunflower family (Compositae), provide a curious contrast to more familiar small-scale alpines. In these mountains, the average temperature varies little throughout the year, but the swing between day and night temperatures can

Above The Pyrenean *Saxifraga longifolia*, found on both the French and Spanish sides but with a restricted distribution, is most commonly seen with splendid sprays spilling from a rocky crevice. The symmetrical rosettes, composed of lime-encrusted narrow leaves, build up over several years before the spectacular flowering, and then die.

Opposite top The lushness of plants in subalpine meadow makes a sharp contrast to the compact and ground-hugging growth of the true alpines. Typical plants of meadows in the European Alps include species of cranesbill (*Geranium*), *Pulsatilla* (their flowers of silky hairiness followed by heads of feathery seeds), *Ranunculus* and globe flower (*Trollius*).

Opposite center The colorful bracts of various species of Indian paintbrush (*Castilleja*) make these among the showiest perennials below and above the tree line in the Rocky Mountains of western North America. Most species are parasitic on the roots of other plants.

Above left Stunted specimens of *Abies lasiocarpa*, sometimes known as the alpine fir, are found in the upper limits of forest in the Rocky Mountains.

Left The stony hillsides of Crete, like much of the Mediterranean region, are rich in plants. The great clefts and cliffs of the island, such as the Samaria Gorge, which is shown here, have provided a refuge for a high proportion of endemic plants. The pink-flowered oleander (*Nerium oleander*), seen in the foreground, is particularly common in dry river beds.

be dramatic. Day temperatures rise quickly to as much as 104°F (40°C) but fall below freezing at night. These giants survive by using various methods of insulation, such as developing wooly leaf surfaces or retaining old leaves as overcoats.

Far from all the plants that are grown in rockeries or raised beds originate from the high alpine zone. Although they may not be as refined as the true alpine, there are many compact plants from lower altitudes found in rocky or stony ground. Some of them are pioneers seizing a new opportunity, some are refugees that have found in a harsh environment a kind of peace not to be had in a more competitive one. Among the pioneers are those that make their homes in the stony beds of dry rivers and in moraines, the almost soilless piles of rocky debris left by retreating glaciers. At Glacier Bay in Alaska, where retreat in the last 200 years has been calculated at over 40 miles (64km), species of *Dryas* and *Epilobium* have become established in a succession that leads to dominance by spruce (*Picea*) and hemlock (*Tsuga*). In the Mediterranean region, where the natural vegetation has been modified by centuries of felling, burning, and heavy grazing, steep rock faces and gorges, like the Samaria Gorge in Crete, have served as refuges for plants that are not to be found elsewhere. Plants from the gorges of Crete include several bellflowers, such as *Campanula saxatilis*, a yellow-flowered flax (*Linum arboreum*), and the Cretan dittany (*Origanum dictamnus*). The Burren in Ireland's County Clare is another example of a rocky refuge, in this case near the sea. Slabs of porous limestone form a broken pavement that has been cracked by enormous pressure during the ice ages and riddled with cavities as a result of erosion. Its clefts and niches shelter a puzzling mix of small plants, such as the dazzling spring gentian (*Gentiana verna*), which is most often seen in alpine habitats, and more than 20 species of terrestrial orchid. Although the rock is calcareous, the soil is sufficiently acidic in some hollows to allow heaths (*Erica*), heather (*Calluna vulgaris*), and other acid-loving plants to thrive.

In many rocky and stony habitats where there is a marked dry season, especially in the Mediterranean region, bulbs eclipse most other flowers in spring and sometimes in autumn. This is true in lowlands and subalpine zones as well as in true alpine regions. One of the richest areas of the world for bulbs is the Anatolian plateau of Turkey. From it have come some of the most popular dwarf bulbs, such as species of crocus, fritillary (*Fritillaria*), snowdrop (*Galanthus*), iris, and scilla. Most of these are found in free-draining stony ground that is moist in the growing season, sometimes from snow melt, but later dry. Fortunately, dwarf bulbs, low shrubs, and compact perennials from a wide range of rocky habitats work very well together in the garden.

Above left Although rock- and boulder-strewn areas are often very exposed, their shaded chinks and crevices may provide a moist environment in which ferns, such as this species of *Dryopteris*, can become established.

Center left Species of houseleeks (*Sempervivum*), a high proportion of which are alpine plants, have succulent leaves arranged in neat rosettes. Further adaptations to conserve moisture are waxy or hairy surfaces on the leaves and, in extreme conditions, an ability to curl up and reduce transpiration.

Center right The purple saxifrage (*Saxifraga oppositifolia*), one of the most widely distributed alpine and tundra plants of the Northern Hemisphere, is shown here on Canada's Somerset Island within the Arctic Circle. The flowers overwinter after being formed in the previous growing season and are ready to open within a few days of the snow cover clearing.

Above right In late spring and early summer, the Burren, an area of limestone pavement near the sea in County Clare, Ireland, brims with small flowers such as thrift (*Armeria maritima*). The rocky crevices shelter a much wider range of plants than can be found in the surrounding area, some of them lime-lovers, others lime-hating, and a few survivors of a flora that existed before the ice ages.

Right Some of the world's most majestic rocky landscapes are found in the Colorado Plateau in the southwest. The vegetation shows considerable altitudinal zonation on 2,000–3,000ft (610–914m) cliffs that are carved in the desert and semi-desert landscape of Zion National Park, Utah, by the Virgin River.

Desert

"Making the desert bloom" is a slogan that has been much used to promote and justify irrigation schemes for arid regions. At heavy financial and often environmental cost, irrigated deserts produce remarkable crops from nondesert plants. More remarkable, however, are the true desert plants that perpetuate themselves against the odds.

Harsh desert landscapes on a heroic scale are a major feature of the interior of continents, regions where mountain ranges create areas of rain shadow, and coastal regions with cold currents. Low, irregular rainfall, often less than 10in (25cm) a year, and a high evaporation rate limit plant growth. High day temperatures, often well above 100°F (20°C) in the Sahara, often fall to near freezing at night. Dessicating winds and their load of abrasive debris are a constant feature. Deserts, however, show considerable variations of land forms and soils: these include include shifting sand dunes, rock surfaces, areas of boulders and stones. The soils are often saline (see 'Coastal Areas' pp. 46-47).

A desert is a primed landscape: just after rainfall, plants burgeon, flower, and set seed within weeks. Ephemerals are most tolerant of environmental extremes as seeds, with success depending on finely tuned mechanisms to trigger germination when conditions are right.

The desert's brief exuberance after rain is a rare event but, except in the harshest environments, a community of dogged plants survives. To tap available water, roots are well developed for the size of the plants. Cactus root systems are extensive and near the surface; new root hairs develop within hours of the ground getting wet. Many shrubs, such as the creosote bush (*Larrea tridendata*) from the Mohave Desert in the southwest, have deep, far-reaching roots, while the New World mesquites (*Prosopis*) have dense, shallow roots and deep tap roots. Wide spacing between plants indicates intense competition for water—15-30ft (4.5-9m) in the creosote bush.

Adaptations to minimize water loss include small leaves, usually thick-skinned and often with a waxy bloom, or felting to reduce transpiration. Plants can shed their leaves in extreme droughts. Shrubs like

Above Death Valley, in eastern California and southern Nevada, drops to 282ft (86m) below sea level. Its most austere sand dunes and salt flats are plantless.

Bottom left and right Succulent species of *Euphorbia* in arid regions of Africa, such as the Namib Desert (left), seem to mimic the adaptions to extreme drought of cacti in Arizona (right) and other desert areas of the New World.

Below Conspicuous plants of the Sonoran Desert, extending north from western Mexico into the southwest US, include cacti and ocotillo (*Fouquieria splendens*), with flame-red flowers after light winter rains.

the mesa palo verde (*Cercidium microphyllum*), from the Sonoran Desert that straddles Mexico and the southwest US, can photosynthesize through their bark. Plants are also vulnerable to water loss through their leaf pores (stomata). In desert plants, these are often reduced in number and recessed or protected by hairs. Closing pores as day temperatures rise reduces water loss but calls for metabolic adjustments. Succulents that take in carbon dioxide through open pores at night, fix the carbon as an organic acid until photosynthesis can begin again.

Fleshy leaved and stemmed succulents are some of the most successful desert plants. In general, cacti, a feature of New Worl deserts, have no leaves and photosynthesize through green stems. Like succulent euphorbias in Africa, they have relatively few pores and often have ridged stems with the pores sheltered in the valleys. This allows for expansion and contraction according to the supply of water.

The miracle of deserts and gardens inspired directly by them is not that they respond to irrigation, but that they can support plant communities without it and that these bloom in their own time.

Top left and right In arid regions, even small amounts of water allow increases in plant densities. Prickly pear (*Opuntia*) grows thickly along the bed of a dry creek in the Grand Canyon (left), while in the Namib Desert of southwest Africa, a succulent *Aloe* is the dominant plant where moisture gathers at the base of this rocky hillock (right).

Below Sparse vegetation, including *Yucca*, grows in the wind-shaped waves of gypsum sand and alkali flats in White Sands National Monument, New Mexico.

Bottom Many drought-tolerant plants survive in this National Monument in the Mojave Desert.

Above left As described by John Gerard, author of the celebrated *Herball* (1597), the yellow horned poppy (*Glaucium flavum*) is a plant of "sandes and bankes of the sea." In fact, it is widely distributed on the coasts of Europe and adjacent regions, even as far as the Canary Islands. Gerard added the name sea poppy, but horned has stuck, the seedheads being so conspicuous. The ruffled leaves are glaucous.

Above right Extensive root systems, foliage adapted to minimize water loss, an ability to survive burial by shifting sands, and tolerance of salt are features of many plants that colonize coastal sands, including this species of *Senecio* from the Falkland Islands.

Below left Several species of grasses make highly successful colonizers of fresh sand dunes. As the dunes move inland, they are stabilized by the grasses and a much wider range of plants can become established.

Center right On rugged and rocky promontories in the Mediterranean, where there is little tidal movement and the splash zone is limited, a hillside mixture of scrub and Aleppo pines (*Pinus halepensis*) often extends almost to the water's edge, as is the case here in Puglia, southeastern Italy.

COASTAL AREAS

The meeting place of land and sea is a taxing environment for higher plants. Many just cannot cope with high levels of salinity. Despite an abundance of water, osmotic pressure prevents its absorption. The soil structure also poses problems: it is often nearly pure sand, draining almost instantaneously and burying plants as dunes move. Pure rock, the firmest defense of land against sea, is not receptive to higher plants. Sea breezes, which shape communities of plants, can turn to violent gales, dessicating, maiming, and searing with their salt content.

Some of the most successful plants of coastal regions are those that do not stand up well in competition with terrestrial plants or even those from fresh-water swamp. Mangroves are among them, and this group of about 100 species of evergreen trees and shrubs from various families provides an interesting example of converging evolutionary processes. Mangrove forest and scrub covers more than 50 per cent of tropical shoreline, reaching its fullest development on intertidal mud-flats, where often only the crowns of plants stand above water at high tide. Low tide exposes a clutter of air roots (pneumatophores) and stilt roots. Like other plants that extract water in saline conditions, they tolerate high salt concentrations in their sap, allowing osmosis to occur. They can also excrete excess salt on the surface of their leaves.

The vegetation of salt marshes in temperate regions includes grasses, sedges, and other specialized plants such as the leafless, fleshy stemmed glasswort (*Salicornia europeae*). This belongs to the beet family (Chenopodiaceae) whose members show remarkable salt tolerance and are widely distributed in saline conditions near coasts and in deserts. In British salt-marshes, the aggressive cord grass (*Spartina anglica*) is an example of accelerated evolution, starting as a sterile hybrid between European *S. maritima* and American *S. alterniflora*, and taking off in the late 19th century.

Above Silver sea holly (*Eryngium maritimum*) is often found on European beaches in much less stable sand and shingle than here. The waxy surface of the leaves helps reduce the loss of moisture, while fleshy roots, as much as 6ft (1.8m) long, tap and store any moisture and give the plants a secure anchor. The roots of eryngo, as the plant is also known, are thick enough to have been cooked as a delicacy and candied.

Below right The original home of the coconut may have been in Polynesia or South America, but the buoyancy of its fruit, allowing it to be carried on vast oceanic voyages, and its tolerance of salt makes it the characteristic tree of sandy tropical shorelines.

Mangroves are an example of seed that is transported by sea currents, in their case often germinating on the plant. The remarkably uniform shoreline vegetation of tropical islands is partly the result of viable fruits and seeds, such as the coconut (*Cocos nucifera*), being transported by sea from one island to another by shore birds. The uniformity of the shoreline vegetation is often in sharp contrast to that of the interior, which is not penetrated by oceanic birds. This frequently results in plants unique to individual islands.

As interesting ecologically as the tropical atoll is the more commonplace beach backed by sand dunes. Classic studies of it have identified successive stages that finally result in a community of plants in a state of equilibrium. The species mentioned here are European, but the stages are roughly the same in many parts of the world. The succession begins with salt-tolerant plants such as sea rocket (*Cakile maritima*) and sand couch grass (*Agropyrone junceiforme*) that germinate at the limit of the highest tide. The vegetation checks wind speed, with the result that more sand accumulates. Less frequent inundations from the sea and leaching by rain allow less salt-tolerant species to become established as the dune grows and moves inland. The most successful are those like marram grass (*Amophila arenaria*) and blue lyme grass (*Leymus arenarius*) that grow up through sand if buried. Stabilizing of the dune, further leaching, and the accumulation of organic matter allow more plants to establish, including shrubs such as sea buckthorn (*Hippophae rhamnoides*) or, on acidic dunes, ling (*Calluna vulgaris*), heaths (*Erica* species) and gorse (*Ulex europaeus*). A final but uncommon stage is stable woodland.

Building near the sea is not new. Well before Vesuvius erupted in AD 79, the Bay of Naples was the playground of rich Roman society. However, mass tourism and the development that goes with it pose a vastly increased threat to the often fragile plant communities of even remote shorelines, which till now have escaped development for farming, forestry, and industry.

PLANT ASSOCIATIONS
IN THE GARDEN

Full Sun to Deep Shade

One of the main difficulties about gardening is that we always want to try to manipulate nature, or at least influence it, as much as we possibly can. As a general rule, the most successful gardeners have always been those who are the most observant and have an eye for detail. They have an almost supernatural skill for observing how plants grow in their natural habitat and applying this to a garden situation, working with nature wherever possible. The greater the understanding we have of where plants grow best, and the more we understand their needs, the easier it becomes for us to grow them.

Plants need light in order to manufacture food and grow successfully. The leaf of a green plant is a highly efficient solar panel, and each plant has a different requirement for the amount of light needed to grow well. Some thrive in very bright sunlight, while others prefer to grow in conditions of partial or dense shade.

Any gardener who has traveled widely, to areas such as Australia, California, South Africa, and the Mediterranean, especially in the summer and early autumn, will have seen some of the many plants which thrive naturally in these bright, hot and dry parts of the world. *Eryngium, Helichrysum, Rosmarinus,* and *Brachyglottis* are all examples of plants that prefer this type of environment. In a garden with a hot, dry area that gets full midday sun in summer, these are the ideal plants to encourage, as they will flourish in these seemingly inhospitable conditions (see "Dry and Desert Gardens," pp. 88–91.)

Plants that prefer bright sunny conditions tend to have leaves that are small (and often thick), or narrow and straplike. This is a result of the good quality of light, which makes the manufacture of food relatively easy. The leaves are often arranged at an upright angle, to reduce the amount of leaf surface directly exposed to the sun. This is common in plants that originate in areas where the light intensity is so high that their needs are easily met.

Some plants can even adapt the size of their leaves in order to make the maximum use of all the available light. Lime trees (*Tilia*) have larger leaves in the lower shaded parts of the tree and smaller, thicker leaves at the top, where most of the sunlight is received. Whatever the preference of the plant for full sun or deep shade, most have evolved so there is very little overlap between their leaves, so that each one is exposed to as much sunlight as possible.

The leaves of plants that prefer to grow in bright sunlight are often paler in color than those growing in shade. They may have a gray or silvery sheen to them—an adaptation that allows the leaf to reflect sunlight and prevent heat damage. An additional feature of these plants is that in very hot conditions, especially during the middle of the day, the leaves may appear to wilt, but they quickly recover when the temperature drops in the evening.

Left The floor of a deciduous woodland is shaded in summer, but enough light filters down in spring, when the tree canopy is not fully formed, to support a variety of shade-tolerant plants such as these daffodils (*Narcissus*) and blue-flowered *Brunnera macrophylla.*

Far right (top) The perennial *Trillium grandiforum* is perfectly suited to the conditions in this shady corner of a garden, making a pleasing composition when backed by some feathery shuttlecock ferns (*Matteuccia struthiopteris*). The pure white of the flowers stands out startlingly against the green fronds.

Far right (bottom) Roses prefer an open site in full sun, although they can adapt to a range of conditions. Here, a rose trained over an elegant arch is intermingled with two *Clematis*. Climbing clematis flourish in full sun but are also happy if they have their bases in partial shade.

Opposite Tulips (*Tulipa*) revel in fertile, well-drained soil in full sun, but need shelter from the wind. Here, these spring tulips create a bold splash of color and are strikingly underplanted with vivid blue forget-me-nots (*Myosotis*).

Below *Verbena rigida*, a perennial that is usually grown as an annual, has fragrant purple flowers and produces a striking contrast when planted with a host of brightly colored annual marigolds (*Tagetes*). Both these plants thrive well in the full sun and fertile, well-drained soil of this site.

Shade-loving plants tend to have a rather different appearance from those preferring full sun. They often have large deep-green leaves, which provide a broad, flat surface to catch any light filtering through the canopy of plants overhead. *Aucuba, Hedera, Mahonia,* and *Pachysandra* all have glossy dark-green leaves, and even green stems (in plants such as *Sarcococca*) to catch the maximum amount of available light as it filters through from above. Many shade-loving plants have smaller, paler-colored flowers than their brightly colored sun-loving counterparts, but this is often compensated for by the number of flowers produced and their heavy scent.

It is unusual to find shade-loving plants with variegated leaves, as the plants, need as much green surface as possible for manufacturing food. In a garden situation, variegated plants that are planted in a shady position will often "revert" to plain green, as the yellow or white colors within the leaf (which contain no chlorophyll) are gradually replaced by cells containing the green pigment. However, there is one exception of a variegated plant that does prefer at least partial shade. Members of the dead nettle family, such as *Lamium galeobdolon,* have a metallic-gray coloration in their leaves, which fades considerably when the plants are grown in brighter light.

There are different levels of shade as far as plants are concerned. Dappled or partial shade occurs where sunlight is filtered through the branches and foliage of trees and shrubs, and many plants are able to grow in these conditions. Dense shade occurs where very low levels of light penetrate the higher levels of vegetation, or most of the available light is blocked by a tall building. In some instances, such as in a coniferous forest, it can be so dark that nothing will grow beneath the trees, and this is often referred to as permanent shade.

Below In a classic arrangement, a pair of herbaceous borders backed by shrubs flanks a narrow path. Apparently casual repetition in the planting creates a subtle rhythm.

Bottom Compact annuals and biennials—daisies (Bellis perennis, for instance) or *Dianthus* hybrids—are useful low plants for front positions in borders.

SUNNY FLOWER BORDERS AND BEDS

Flower borders of a kind existed long before the 19th century. On the whole, however, they were clearly defined areas in which floral treasures, including choice tulips and carnations (*Dianthus*), were sparingly planted, with a considerable amount of bare soil showing between them. Fashionable and intelligent interest in the large number of herbaceous plants introduced in the 19th and early 20th centuries, the availability of cheap labor, and the influence of persuasive and eminent gardening writers such as Gertrude Jekyll, saw the border transformed. What had been a collection of individual plants became a coordinated assembly, the beauty of the whole exceeding that of the individual plants of which it was composed.

The herbaceous border of the kind described by Gertrude Jekyll, its most influential exponent, is not well suited to small gardens and requires considerable maintenance. Nonetheless, it continues to exercise a tremendous hold on the imagination of gardeners. Fortunately, there is still much that can be learned from imaginatively planned and well-managed borders and applied to gardening on a smaller scale. It is, however, the new developments in gardening with perennials that are much closer to the spirit of this book.

HERBACEOUS BORDERS

The classic herbaceous border consists of a rectangular plot, rarely less than 20ft (6m) long and 6–12ft (1.8–3.7m) deep, in an open sunny position, backed along its length by a hedge or wall and flanked on its other side by a grassy walk. In the grandest arrangements, a pair of borders flanks a broad grassed walk. Sometimes a paved path runs along the edge of a border. Where this is not the case, mowing is made easier if a narrow run of paving stones or bricks is set just below the level of the grass. Plants that flop forward are not then damaged. If the border is particularly wide, a narrow gap along the base of the wall or hedge provides useful access and simplifies trimming.

The border's dramatic impact is partly achieved by staged variations in the height of component plants. While avoiding a rigid ranking, the aim is to encourage the eye to work easily backward and forward, with the shortest plants at the front and the tallest at the back. Borders composed of dwarf plants (disproportionately numerous in nursery

lists) give an idea of the dulling effect of uniform height. Gertrude Jekyll recommended planting in drifts, with plants of a kind grouped in irregular bands that interweave as they run at an angle across the border. In addition to resulting in complex juxtapositions of form and color, this method of planting helps to introduce a pleasing irregularity in heights, but it is not effective in a narrow border. In many interesting borders, the occasional straying of a tall, airy plant such as *Salvia uliginosa* toward the front makes a slightly eccentric but welcome variation. If there is a backing wall, its planting should make a vertical extension of the border. At Sissinghurst, the garden created by Vita Sackville-West and her husband Sir Harold Nicolson, and now one of the best-known National Trust properties in England, the purple border provides a superb example, with clematis and other climbers providing a remarkable interplay of rich and light tones.

Contrasts of scale, shape, and form add to the dynamic aesthetics of the border, but nothing counts for quite as much as color. Among the successes of plant breeders is a remarkable extension in the color range available in perennials. The choices make it possible to build up monochromatic schemes, lifted by touches of color; quiet harmonies such as silver-grays and pastels; vibrant contrasts—orange, say, intensified by blue; flaunted clashes of reds; and apparently random mixtures, given sense, perhaps, by the repetition of key colors.

The herbaceous border is in its prime in mid- to late summer, and there is a long period between autumn and spring when there is very little vegetation and a lot of bare soil showing. In small to medium-sized gardens, this is a strong case for a border to be mixed, in which a framework of branches and evergreen leaves gives body and interest even in the winter months. To turn-of-the-century owners of large gardens, the border's short season hardly mattered. They might be away when it was out of season or the spotlight might be turned on other horticultural splendors so that the blankness of the border could be forgotten.

Top left Beds crowded with plants that flower in early summer—among them alliums, bearded irises, and peonies—risk becoming dull later in the season.

Top The highly bred phloxes derived from *Phlox paniculata* reach their peak in late summer.

Above The genus *Campanula* includes many species that excel in temperate gardens. Many, like *C. latiloba*, are suitable for borders, but other bellflowers are choice alpines.

53

However, it is worth making the effort to extend the border's season. Spring bulbs can be added, tulips being more suitable than daffodils, for their foliage dies down more neatly. The customary practice is to lift tulips annually, but left in the ground, a surprising number persist from year to year, although they may need to be topped up. Bulbs are often considered a nuisance in the border but, provided their location is well noted, there is no need to disturb them when the ground is being cultivated. Biennial wallflowers planted in autumn provide clumps of green through the winter and become deliciously scented warm-colored distractions in spring. They have to be positioned where their replacements—argyranthemums or dahlias are possibilities—will fit in. Other early-flowering plants that can help to set the border season going are more often associated with rock gardens, but their compact growth makes them very suitable for front positions. Sea thrift (*Armeria maritima*) or even aubrietas can be used, but aubrietas need to be trimmed after flowering.

Early summer is exaggeratedly lamented in many temperate places as the June gap. There is no *embarras de richesses*, but there are plants of superb quality, especially geraniums, bearded irises, peonies, and oriental poppies, as well as old favorites, such as lupines and columbines. One pays for the magnificence of oriental poppies, which are messy as they die back, and they need to be carefully positioned so the gap left by the collapsing foliage is obscured as the season advances.

The great wealth of material to chose from for the high season can be a source of frustration. A lifetime is too short for many major rework-ings of a border. It is not surprising that some long-established borders in historic gardens have retained their initial color scheme and a core of good plants, although often enriched by exciting new introductions. The professionally designed border, laid out all of a piece, frequently requires modification, even radical alterations. The amateur can allow a border to evolve more gradually, perhaps in the early stages using annuals and tender plants to try out color schemes and to experiment with heights and shapes. These same plants—including argyranthe-mums, dahlias, penstemons, and salvias—are of great value, too, for extending the border season into late summer and even into autumn. But for really effective autumn displays, few plants can match the chrysanthemums (*Dendranthema*).

Cutting back dead growth and clearing up the border in autumn and applying a mulch in spring are basic to the maintenance of a border. There must also be a regular program of renovation. Some perennials, including peonies, are very long-lived and better left undisturbed. Others, among them delphiniums, are short-lived, and the performance of many perennials declines after two or three years if they are not lifted and divided. This is best done selectively on an annual basis

Above For the military at heart, the only solution for tulips is to arrange them in platoons, even companies, but informal arrangements with other bulbs are more suitable for small gardens.

Below Mulleins (*Verbascum*), which are biennials or short-lived perennials, and the annual opium poppy (*Papaver somniferum*) are tall, sun-loving plants that make useful fillers in new gardens.

Below right Corn cockle (*Agrostemma githago*), formerly a troublesome weed of grain crops, makes an airy clump in a small bed that includes the rose 'Gruss an Aachen', deep pink Peruvian lilies (*Alstroemeria*), and yellow day lilies (*Hemerocallis*).

during the dormant season, between autumn and spring. Diseased plants should be burned, and the old woody centers that no longer produce vigorous growth can be discarded.

Staking is the border job that gives cause for most complaints. In well-manured soil, close planting and the proximity of a backing wall or hedge tend to encourage lanky growth. The solid background also helps to create turbulent conditions. To prevent the tallest plants, particularly delphiniums, from being knocked about and toppling, some staking is necessary. In a large border this can be laborious work, and it must be well timed so that plants are not damaged before or while supports are being put in. It comes at a busy time, between mid- and late spring. Bamboo stakes that stand above plants that have reached their ultimate height are unsightly. To be inconspicuous, stakes should be kept within the upper limit of the foliage. Soft string looped around stems, and two or more stakes to a plant should allow a certain amount of free movement. Large areas of a border and smaller groups of plants can be stiffened with brushwood that has had the tops bent over to form an interlocking mesh. Sloping panels of wide-mesh plastic netting can also be used to give support. They need to be about 1ft (30cm) high where they start, set back from the front of the border, and about 3ft (90cm) high at the back. If only a few plants need support, purpose-made frames are an alternative to stakes or brushwood.

Island beds, championed by the British nurseryman Alan Bloom, free the border from its backing wall or hedge and reduce the need for staking. Without a wall or hedge, there is better air circulation, plants are stronger and more erect, and the tallest, grouped toward the center, do not lean out and shade lower plants at the edges. Island beds work well in large gardens, but are less satisfactory within the rectilinear framework of small to medium-sized ones.

Above Tall delphinium hybrids demand staking, but lupines can usually be left to their own devices.

Below Astilbes, Siberian irises, and the royal fern (*Osmunda regalis*) thrive in moist or even boggy ground in sun or partial shade. The feathery plumes of astilbes come in shades of pink, red, mauve, or white.

Left Perennials such as columbines, tall campanulas, and thalictrums are the dominant components of this freely planted, sunny hillside garden backed by shrubs and trees.

Below left A deep pink rock rose (Cistus), the ornamental onion (*Allium cristophii*), and euphorbias suggest the Mediterranean, but this collection of plants is eclectic, the brightest component being hybrid penstemons.

Below In a dry garden, where texture counts for just as much as color, the purple-flowered *Verbena bonariensis*, which is usually short-lived, and the prickly biennial *Eryngium giganteum* self-seed among perennials. These include the feather grass (*Stipa tenuissima*) and the lemon-yellow *Anthemis tinctoria* 'E. C. Buxton'.

A FRESH APPROACH TO PERENNIALS

A reaction to the sophistication of herbaceous borders and the labor involved in maintaining them has coincided with a growing interest in plant ecology. A much freer approach to gardening with perennials, strongly influenced by the ideas of the German nurseryman Karl Foerster, exploits the large number of species and less highly-bred perennials, of which there are enough to provide planting material for almost any garden situation. In this style of gardening, which is not constrained by a need to create massed effects, the first principle of planting is to choose perennials that suit the growing conditions. It does not rely on a conventional layout of borders and lawns, although these are not necessarily excluded. More commonly it is created in an area defined by trees and shrubs and crossed by paths, with well-placed groups of plants combined in a variety of sizes to provide a subtle rhythm.

A different frame of mind is needed to fully enjoy this kind of gardening. Flower size is smaller and flower color less vivid and varied than in the border. Texture and form become more important, with greater weight being given to ferns and grasses, plants often poorly represented in traditional borders. The whole plant matters: the poise of its stem and foliage is just as important as its flowers, and also its full seasonal progression from first shoots to winter russet foliage and dry seeds and fruits. And the plants need to be seen as only one part of an environment sympathetic to wildlife of all kinds.

For the gardener, one of the main attractions of this approach is that it involves relatively low maintenance. There is initial work clearing ground of perennial weeds and lightly working the soil, partly to find out about its character so that a workable planting scheme can be devised. Weeding in the initial stages is necessary, but the aim should be to allow plants to develop a reasonably close ground-cover—although not monoculture groundcovers exclusively for weed control. Initial close planting to limit weed competition can be thinned as groups spread. Expansion and self-seeding are taken for granted, but the gardener may sometimes have to intervene, controlling plants that threaten to overwhelm less-vigorous neighbors. The selection of plants means that watering and protection from cold are only necessary in exceptional circumstances, and many of the pest and disease problems resulting from lush growth are eliminated by not feeding. As the following pages show, gardening with a light rein can be applied to many situations, as long as the right plants are chosen.

Above In this meadowlike garden, low perennials, such as violas, are combined with taller plants, including columbines, bearded irises, and poppies (*Meconopsis* and *Papaver*). Old walls have been colonized by dwarf campanulas, sedums, and other rock plants.

Sunny Mixed Borders

The commonsense solution of combining shrubs, perennials, bulbs, and a few annuals to form integrated plantings is far from new. All of these components could sometimes be found in turn-of-the-century herbaceous borders and certainly jostled together in the cottage garden. Mixed borders, as these plantings are usually described (the term does not imply that the plantings occupy a geometrically regular space) make sense in small and medium-sized gardens, where they provide the best chance of creating a well-furnished look for all 12 months of the year. They make sense, too, because their own layered structure reflects that of plant communities in the wild. The aesthetic and horticultural interest of a mixed border is much greater than that

of a shrubbery, an area devoted to a close planting of shrubs, usually with an underplanting of vigorous groundcover. Tired remnants of old-fashioned planting have been partly responsible for the bad press shrubberies get. There is a place for them at the outer reaches of large gardens, but as self-evidently dull solutions, they make a garden seem a horticultural problem, not the delight it might be with the leavening power of bulbs and perennials.

SHRUBS FOR FOLIAGE

The spine of a mixed border is usually composed of interlocking shrubs. Evergreen broad-leaved shrubs, including hollies (*Ilex*), laurels (*Prunus*), mahonias, and *Osmanthus* are rated for the way they provide bulk throughout the year. The varied forms and foliage color of the dwarf and slow-growing conifers seem to offer much but often disappoint. When used in large numbers, these plants, with their crowded twigs and leaves, can make the border congested; the deadening effect of their appalling stillness often leaves one craving bare earth.

Foliage is given much more weight in the mixed than the herbaceous border. In addition to giving body to the border, the foliage of evergreens provides a background that shows off a succession of incidents. In intensity these may fall short of high moments in the herbaceous borders, but any loss of drama is compensated for by the integration of components that keeps interest alive all year. It is the variation of scale, shape, texture, and color that makes the mixed border such a rich tapestry. The seasonal changes, marked enough even in some evergreens, take a dramatic turn with deciduous shrubs such as the smoke bushes (*Cotinus*) and *Euonymus alatus*.

Below left The jagged leaves and pale green flowers of *Helleborus argutifolius*, a shrubby evergreen perennial, complement a planting of bulbs, from early dwarf irises to late tulips, over a long spring period.

Below right The sumptuous flowers of the perennial *Paeonia lactiflora* 'Sarah Bernhardt' are bedded here with shrubs such as *Rosa glauca* and *Pittosporum tenuifolium*. The cool *Iris pallida* 'Variegata' skirts the front of the border.

Bottom A wave of brightly colored perennials, including the fiery *Crocosmia* 'Lucifer', the yellow-flowered *Achillea filipendulina* 'Gold Plate', day lilies (*Hemerocallis*), goldenrod (*Solidago*), and rudbeckias, seem poised to overwhelm the shrubs and trees. These include *Buddleja globosa*, *Hypericum* 'Hidcote', and *Robinia pseudoacacia* 'Frisia'.

Top There is a place for *Buddleja alternifolia* in mixed borders. Here it dominates a mixture containing the rose 'Fritz Nobis', a white peony (*Paeonia lactiflora*), and *campanula persicifolia.*

Above The vivid bracts of *Euphorbia griffithii* 'Dixter' are dramatic, but it can be too much of a good thing on sandy soils.

FLOWERING SHRUBS

Although very satisfying borders that rely almost exclusively on foliage effects can be planted, flowers usually play an important role. Shrubs that flower over a long season—examples include *Abelia × grandiflora*, hardy fuchsias, the mophead hydrangeas, several hypericums, and shrubby mallows such as *Lavatera* 'Barnsley'—are understandably popular, but a border packed with them can become monotonous. Shrubs that offer a welcome pause after their first flush before flowering again include the Mexican orange (*Choisya ternata*) and *Syringa microphylla* 'Superba', a lightly built deciduous lilac.

Shrubs that flower either side of the main season and contribute to the border's interest year-round have a special value. A surprising number of the best-scented plants are shrubs that flower in winter and early spring, competing for the attentions of the relatively few pollinating insects that are around. Among the pick are several viburnums, the deciduous *Viburnum × bodnantense* bearing fragrant flowers on naked wood over a long period between autumn and spring. Several daphnes are also winter flowering, among them the deciduous mezereon (*Daphne mezereum*) and the evergreen *D. odora*.

All of these are reasonably ornamental, at least while in flower. By comparison the shrubby winter-flowering honeysuckles, of which *Lonicera × purpusii* is the best, are nondescript. Dullness when out of flower is a problem with many fragrant shrubs of spring and summer, among them the richly scented viburnums, for example *Viburnum carlesii*, the lilacs (cultivars of *Syringa vulgaris*), and the mock oranges (*Philadelphus*). At least with mock oranges, the scent is so far-reaching that they do not need a prominent position, and the choice of cultivars includes several that are compact. One way to give drab shrubs a new lease on life is to use them as supports for climbers of moderate vigor, the small-flowered clematis that flower in late summer and autumn being well suited to this purpose (see pp. 179–80). The ornamental shortcomings of important fragrant shrubs makes one reappraise several that stand up well throughout the year. The winter-flowering and evergreen *Mahonia japonica*, more richly scented than the hybrid mahonias, is a conspicuously jagged plant throughout the year. And *Choisya ternata*, which continues to flower intermittently after its main spring flush, is furnished year-round with glossy aromatic leaves.

Just as valuable as the shrubs of winter and early spring are those that add a sequel to the main summer season. Many of these flower on the current season's wood and need cutting back in spring. Several in the blue range are very effective at freshening the border in late summer and autumn. Russian sage (*Perovskia atriplicifolia*), a subshrub that can be cut back to near ground level in spring, has small violet-blue flowers carried on downy white stems above aromatic gray-green leaves. A blue of great intensity is that of *Caryopteris* × *clandonensis*, a shrub that also has aromatic foliage. *Ceratostigma willmottianum* has flowers of clear blue, and the foliage colors well in autumn.

ROSES

The large-flowered and cluster-flowered bush roses (Hybrid Teas and Floribundas) are remarkable for their long season and the quantity of flower they produce, but their gawky stiffness and their cultivation requirements make them far less satisfactory for mixed borders than the old and modern shrub roses. Some of the modern shrubs such as *Rosa* 'Golden Wings', and many of the English Roses bred and introduced by David Austin, repeat well, but others, and nearly all the old shrub roses, have a single glorious flush lasting a few weeks.

Many of these roses look perfectly at home in mixed borders, but there comes a point when there are enough of them to demand their own territory. If you have admitted defeat on this front, the best solution is to combine them with an underplanting and edging of sympathetic perennials and low shrubs. Lady's mantle (*Alchemilla mollis*), aquilegias, old-fashioned pinks (*Dianthus*), diascias, low geraniums, compact lavenders, lambs' ears (*Stachys byzantina*), *Viola cornuta*, and the biennial foxglove (*Digitalis purpurea*) are among plants that will help to sustain a border largely devoted to shrub roses.

BERRIES AND STEMS

Although not a substitute for flowers, berries and stems enrich mixed borders with their colors and textures. Rose hips and many berries are often well colored by late summer, but it is those that persist into autumn and even winter that warrant special plantings. Disappointments are sometimes the result of unfavorable weather or early losses to birds, which seem oddly inconsistent in the interest they show in berry crops. However, the most common causes of failure are to do with pollination. Several berrying shrubs, among them hollies, have male and female flowers on separate plants. Female plants of these kinds must have a male in the vicinity if they are to bear crops. Some other shrubs, among them viburnums, only crop freely when there are two or more specimens in close proximity to insure cross-pollination. Cotoneasters, somewhat lacking in other respects, are in the first rank of berrying shrubs, with a color range that includes black, yellow, and coral, as well as reds and oranges. Among the most surprising berry colors are the blues of *Clerodendrum trichotomum* var. *fargesii* and *Viburnum davidii* and the violet of *Callicarpa bodinieri* var. *giraldii*.

Above left Roses do not have to be grown in isolation in a rose garden. Grow them in mixed borders with carpets of low-growing perennials for added interest.

Above right 'Iceberg' and other roses are important in this garden, but so, too, are the numerous perennials and shrubs that anchor the planting.

Main picture opposite The bold plumes of pampas grass (*Cortaderia selloana* 'Sunningdale Silver') and a yellow-leaved Indian bean tree (*Catalpa bignonioides* 'Aurea') are bracketed with *Dahlia* 'Bishop of Llandaff' and *Sedum spectabile* 'Brilliant' for a dramatic autumn display.

Below Its flowers do not count for much, but the vigorous *Rosa glauca* is a strong candidate for mixed borders. The foliage is blue-green in summer and the hips vivid red in autumn.

The rich color or grayish bloom on the young stems of several deciduous shrubs and trees, including several dogwoods (*Cornus*) and willows (*Salix*), can be an important winter feature. Plants grown for this need to be pollarded regularly to insure a supply of young stems, which are more colorful than old wood.

ANNUALS AND BIENNIALS

While a border is still young and shrubs and perennials have yet to reach their mature size, annuals and biennials are the ideal fillers. The more expensive alternative is to plant closely, thinning as the shrubs and perennials begin to fill out, a necessary operation but calling for resolution that the faint-hearted may find it difficult to muster. Some annuals and biennials choose to stay on, self-seeding with differing degrees of success. The poached egg flower (*Limnanthes douglasii*), the money plant (*Lunaria annua*), and forget-me-not (*Myosotis*) will come up year after year, as will several short-lived perennials, among them *Campanula persicifolia*, *Salvia sclarea* var. *turkestanica,* and the tall *Verbena bonariensis*. Some annuals wheedle their way into one's affections and are difficult to dispense with even though they must be sown annually. Leaving areas free for annual planting means more work, but it is easy to be convinced that clumps of cosmos or the annual mallow *Lavatera trimestris* 'Mont Blanc' will give the border a timely lift.

BULBS

Bulbs that are positioned among other plants tend to get dug up during cultivation. This is a disadvantage, especially when perennials are being lifted and divided, but set against the effect bulbs make in a mixed border it is trivial. Many of the smaller bulbs—among them crocuses, chionodoxas, grape hyacinths (*Muscari*), puschkinias, and scillas—can be planted under the canopy of deciduous shrubs. A position under shrubs also suits daffodils (*Narcissus*), the growth of perennials helping to mask the untidiness of their dying leaves. In a more open position, spring foliage will grow over the less conspicuous leaves of tulips. By the time the ornamental onions (*Allium*), most with splendid spherical heads, come into flower, their foliage is already looking messy and they need to be planted behind perennials, such as geraniums, that make early growth. The key bulbs later in the season are lilies; there are few bulbs that can give borders such a shot in the arm. They are well suited to planting in bays among shrubs, so that the base of the plant is lightly shaded and the top exposed to full sun.

Far left Bulbs add much to borders but they undoubtedly complicate cultivation. The messy foliage of alliums, often dying while the plants are still in flower, needs to be masked by *Stachys byzantina* or similar foreground plants.

Left Planting tulips to grow through forget-me-nots (*Myosotis*) is a gardening cliché, but it does bear repetition. The yellow lily-flowered tulip here is 'West Point'.

Below The yellow-green foliage of the trees and shrubs enhances the warm colors of late-summer flowers. Day lilies (*Hemerocallis*), red hot pokers (*Kniphofia*), and the yellow-flowered *Coreopsis verticillata* will all stand up to some degree of frost, but where frosts are usual in winter the tubers of dahlias need to be lifted annually.

PERENNIALS

In a mixed border there is room for great variation in the proportion of perennials to shrubs. At one extreme the border can be largely dominated by perennials with a light stiffening of shrubs. At the other, perennials may be used as little more than fillers and edging. In a balanced border on an open site where there are inlets between the shrubby plants, it is possible to have a wide seasonal variation and various heights, representing preferences for full sun and part shade. Staking for the tallest may be necessary. Front open positions can be filled with low-growing plants such as *Campanula carpatica* and *Geranium renardii* mixed with low shrubs such as the rock roses (*Helianthemum*). Taller-growing perennials, such as the catnip *Nepeta* 'Six Hills Giant', can be used to hide the dying leaves of bulbs. For the middle ground some of the most suitable will tolerate partial shade. Particularly attractive are those perennials that work their way up through other plants, such as *Viola cornuta*. To some extent the scale of the border will dictate the height of the tallest, but even very large perennials such as *Crambe cordifolium*, cardoon (*Cynara cardunculus*), and plume poppies (*Macleaya*) do not look out of place overtopping the backbone of shrubs.

ORNAMENTALS COMPETING WITH GRASS

A flowery meadow scattered with splendid trees was a medieval ideal of a paradise garden. The appeal of flowers in grass is easily appreciated, but its first great advocate as a style of gardening was the influential 19th-century garden writer William Robinson, who was reacting against the formal beds that dominated gardens of his day. In our own time, the loss of wildflower meadows in agricultural land has encouraged many to create meadows of their own.

The open grasslands that provide the model for flowered lawns and wildflower meadows are far from being truly natural. Human intervention has controlled the growth of trees and shrubs, and in the most flower-rich meadows, annual removal of hay without the application of fertilizers has kept the soil poor, so that grasses, which are usually strongly dominant, do not overwhelm the other plants. This delicate balance depends on the grasses being relatively uncompetitive species, not bullies like agricultural rye grass (*Lolium* species).

Encouraging flowers to grow in grass holds out the prospect of relaxed gardening. There is, however, considerable work involved in the early stages of creating a wildflower meadow, and it may take several years for a stable community of desirable plants that can be maintained by a few cuts a year to become established. In the short term, prospects are brighter for nonpurists who are happy to include exotic species in grass that can be cut less often than a conventional lawn.

THE GRASS AND FLOWER COMPONENTS

Commercially available mixtures for sowing wildflower meadows are usually three parts grass, in which several species are represented, and one part wildflowers. Most of the flower seed is of perennials. In addition to being appropriate to the acid or alkaline chemistry of the soil and its moisture content, the mixture should contain seed of plants that grow locally. The ideal is to have seed gathered locally, so you do not bring in different genetic material. Conservation-minded gardeners are sometimes surprisingly comfortable with the degree to which mixtures are manipulated. Yarrow (*Achillea millefolium*) and oxeye daisy (*Leucanthemum vulgare*) may be common locally, but mixtures containing them are sometimes rejected because they are quick developers and do not give other plants a chance to get started.

Top Daffodils are the easiest of bulbs to grow in grass. They will multiply steadily if the mowing regimen does not begin until leaves die down in summer. 'February Gold' and other Cyclamineus hybrids are better suited in scale than some of the heavily built daffodils often favored for naturalizing.

Above Lupines growing wild on roadsides and railway embankments demonstrate their ability to form self-sustaining colonies.

Many gardeners will be happy to add non-native perennials to a wildflower meadow, or even allow them to dominate. Plants suitable for meadows on alkaline soil include *Aster amellus*, the bellflower *Campanula persicifolia*, several pinks (*Dianthus*), the blue flax *Linum perenne*, and the silky Pasque flower (*Pulsatilla vulgaris*). Among the most lovely for growing on moist soils are the meadow cranesbill (*Geranium pratense*), Jacob's ladder (*Polemonium caeruleum*), and several primulas.

Annuals are opportunists that flourish in disturbed ground, not true grassland plants. But corn cockle (*Agrostemma githago*), bachelor's buttons (*Centaurea cyanus*), and field poppies (*Papaver rhoeas*) are showy plants often included in seed mixtures as a nurse crop. Eventually they are crowded out unless the ground is disturbed again.

Above Damp meadows suit a European species of fritillary, (*Fritillaria meleagris*), which holds on as a wild plant or naturalized introduction in parts of Britain. The snake's head fritillary, as it is known, is more commonly a checkered purple, but there are many gradations between this and the white form (f. *alba*) on which the tessellation is no more than a greenish shadow.

Below In the wild, quamash (*Camassia quamash)* is found in very varied habitats, not merely marshy ground, and readily naturalizes in damp grass.

Bulbs are among the easiest and most satisfying plants to establish in grass, and if gardeners are prepared to draw on the plants that are not native to their area, the available choices are considerable. Many bulbs that are suitable for naturalizing in woodland thrive in sunny open positions. Dwarf bulbs include spring- and autumn-flowering crocuses and winter aconites (*Eranthis*). The most widely planted of the taller bulbs are daffodils such as the Lent lily (*Narcissus pseudonarcissus*) and the Cyclamineus hybrids, but the dwarf *N. cyclamineus* itself and *N. bulbocodium* are of incomparable beauty when planted in large drifts. The snake's head fritillary (*Fritillaria meleagris*), with nodding checkered flowers, and the camassias are suitable for moist soils.

CREATING AND MAINTAINING FLOWERED LAWNS AND MEADOWS

If the prime aim is to create a pleasing ornamental effect rather than to conserve wildflowers, changing the mowing regimen of an existing lawn is a simple and reasonably satisfactory option. Unlike a wildflower meadow, this can be effective even on a small scale. Some wildflowers may establish themselves, daisies (*Bellis perennis*), bird's-foot trefoil (*Lotus corniculatus*), and germander speedwell (*Veronica chamaedrys*) competing with fine lawn grasses. These grasses should be used if sowing a lawn, perhaps with some wildflower seed added. If you buy sod, make sure it is of good quality and contains no rye grass. Bulbs supplemented by plants such as primroses (*Primula vulgaris*) are the obvious plants to enrich this kind of lawn.

The best chance of establishing a wildflower meadow is on very poor soil, especially on alkaline soil. The removal of topsoil is a drastic measure that is sometimes advocated. Repeated mowing and removal of cut grass is a slower and less radical way of reducing fertility. Sowing cleared ground with an appropriate mixture of grass and wildflower seed is the most economic and effective method of establishing plants. Sowing in small patches of ground that have been cleared in existing areas of grass is usually less effective. Other options include planting out growing mixtures of grass and wildflowers, either as wildflower sods or, more economically, in the form of small plugs spaced evenly on prepared ground. Large-scale planting into existing sod is generally ruled out on grounds of expense, but on a small scale can be a successful way of establishing perennials. To be effective, however, competition from surrounding grasses must be reduced, which usually means applying a weedkiller before planting. Mowing at an early stage helps to control weeds while desirable plants become established. Thereafter, the mowing regimen must be geared to the cycle of the plants growing in the grass. The first cut of the year can be made in early summer if crocuses and other dwarf and early-flowering bulbs have been used. Where there are daffodils, the first cut must be delayed until mid-summer. If there are autumn-flowering bulbs, cutting must stop in late summer or early autumn. The cut grass needs to be raked off, but if it is left to dry first, there is a chance of valuable seeds being left behind. Closely mown paths through flowery lawns and meadows are practical and attractive, and they provide opportunities for imaginative contrasts of short and long grass.

Above A backdrop of small trees creates the impression that a garden is emerging from the fringes of woodland.

Below Japanese maples (*Acer japonicum*), delicate in spring and summer and smoldering or incandescent in autumn, thrive on moist soils in the protection of a gladelike setting.

TREES

Trees are the ultimate plant sculptures, wonderfully varied in the structure of their woody frames and in the canopies that these support. By the measure of most other plants, they are slow to reach maturity, but once mature they seem, at least when set against a human's life span, permanent features of the garden. Their stature and presence in woods and forests, or even in carefully assembled clumps in parks, can be on an awesome scale. The planting of some trees is the gift of a giant to future generations, but there are a surprising number of trees for medium-sized gardens that will even give pleasure to impatient gardeners. Others are planted principally because they grow rapidly, providing shelter at the boundaries of gardens.

WOODLAND GARDENS

Lucky are the gardeners who start with established woodland. The shaded and sheltered environment under trees provides conditions in which a wide variety of shrubs, perennials, and bulbs will thrive. The broadest range of plants can be grown where the shade is dappled and where there are glades resulting from occasional breaks in the canopy.

A woodland effect of sorts can be created on a surprisingly small scale, perhaps using an existing tree or clump as the nucleus. The remnants of an old orchard could be the starting point, although the ordered planting of an orchard goes against the free spirit of woodland, where the art is to seem artless. This is a point to bear in mind when choosing trees to supplement the nucleus or when starting from scratch. A large variety of trees grouped in contrasting shapes, colors, and textures is too self-conscious for woodland.

SPECIMEN TREES AND FORMAL PLANTING

The ornamental qualities of individual trees are particularly important when there is room for only one or two trees and where specimens are to be isolated, for example as focal points in lawns. The shape and stance of a tree can be its principal recommendation. Most trees growing naturally have a strong central leader supporting a balanced

arrangement of branches, as in *Liquidambar*, or develop a more rounded branched head, as in ornamental cherries (*Prunus*) and crab apples (*Malus*). Gardeners show an interest in shapes that are less common in nature, often preferring weeping trees, those with tiered horizontal branches or contorted stems, and others with growth that is narrowly upright (fastigiate) or densely columnar.

Flowers are a principal feature of many trees, among them the thorns (*Crataegus*), the magnolias, and the crab apples. In their flowering season, some of these trees can make a sensational impact, and it is asking a lot to expect their ornamental qualities to be sustained throughout the whole year. Fortunately, among the small trees there are a good number that are beautiful in flower and produce impressive crops of fruits. The crab apples and the thorns are outstanding, while some of the ornamental cherries follow their high point in spring with richly colored foliage in autumn. The flowers of *Sorbus* are less impressive, but the genus includes trees suitable for small gardens that have good autumn color and plentiful crops of attractive fruits.

Colorful foliage year-round or, in the case of deciduous trees, from spring to autumn, has merits and drawbacks. Distinctive bark, on the other hand, is almost invariably a feature worth noting. The rich patterning of *Parrotia persica*, the cinnamon-red of *Arbutus × andrachnoides*, the burnished red-brown of *Prunus serrula,* and the ghostly whiteness of *Betula utilis* var. *jacquemontii* are enough to make these plants stand out in any garden.

The shade that trees create can be a vice or a virtue. Too near the house and it takes light from rooms—and the roots of trees may cause damage to foundations and to drains. Too dense and over too large an area, and the garden becomes dank and sunless. There is no denying that the choice of trees for small gardens is limited. The most suitable, like the Mount Etna broom (*Genista aetnensis*), have an airy canopy that lets plenty of light through. Thinning the canopy of denser trees can help to let more light in, but this is work for a qualified arboriculturist. An easier operation is the removal of lower branches, allowing light to reach under the canopy at an angle. Trees of fastigiate growth are widely recommended, but they often make awkward and graceless substitutes for close relatives that are well balanced. In a small garden it may be better to create height and manageable shade with climbers growing on a well-proportioned pergola or arch (see pp.68–69).

Except in orchards, the formal planting of trees is now largely confined to ordered rows. To achieve the even and regular appearance of an "avenue," the plants should be of the same clone or grafted onto the same reliable stock.

Above Topiary, or even very gentle shaping of trees, in this case the silver-leaved *Pyrus salicifolia* 'Pendula', arouses strong feelings. There is, however, a place for it in more formal areas of the garden.

Below Some botanists believe that the magnolias belong to one of the most primitive families of flowering plants. It is universally acknowledged that they are in the first rank of ornamental trees.

Bottom Gardeners who plant *Prunus* 'Shirotae' and other flowering cherries must be reconciled to the brief duration of their blossom.

CLIMBERS

Climbers are the athletic opportunists of the vegetable world, relying on more plodding growers to provide support as they rush skyward. Their questing nimbleness, which makes them so successful in the wild, is also their great asset in the garden. They provide a link between garden floor and canopy, and where no canopy exists they make their own. With supple grace they create an impression of profusion and yet are not space-consuming. Climbers are malleable, readily responding to the hand of the gardener, who can train them around architectural features, up screens to block out unsightly views, and over arbors and arches to create shade. And they do not necessarily have to climb. Wisterias trained as standards, roses trailing down banks, ivies sprawling along a woodland floor, and clematis spilling out of a tall jar are reminders of the versatility of this group of plants.

CLIMBERS ON LIVING SUPPORTS

The most natural way of growing climbers, training them through other plants, is curiously neglected by many gardeners, despite its many advantages. The tapestry interweaving of climber with shrubs or trees, climber with climber, even climber with herbaceous perennials, is one of the most effective ways of creating an integrated planting. At its simplest, it mimics the airy nonchalance of plants growing in the wild. The effect is particularly telling when the climber adds another season of beauty to its support. In the classic combination, rambler roses climb into old fruit trees that are no longer yielding useful crops but produce a good display of blossom and a few colorful fruits in autumn. A vigorous rambler such as *Rosa* 'Bobbie James' needs little encouragement to race high into the canopy, from where in mid-summer it spills showers of fragrant flowers, like a magically improved second crop of blossom. It has to be said that the rose's embrace can eventually be too much for an old fruit tree and that pruning of the rose (ramblers flower most freely if stems are cut out after they have flowered) is problematic.

The success of these marriages depends on matching the vigor of climber and support. Climbers also need help to start. Where trees have made a close network of roots near the surface, the climber may need to be planted outside the area of the canopy and then trained in. Large forest trees are needed for giant climbers such as *Hydrangea anomala* subsp. *petiolaris*, *Vitis coignetiae,* and wisterias. For shrubs and trees with light frames, clematis are often the climbers of first choice. They are particularly useful for shrubs that flower in spring or early summer, some of which, like the cultivars of the common lilac (*Syringa vulgaris*), are ponderously boring when not in flower. A slender climber of great appeal in late summer is the flame creeper (*Tropaeolum speciosum*). It is, however, in danger of becoming something of a cliché as a wandering decoration on dark hedges of yew that show off the vivid scarlet of its flowers to perfection.

CLIMBERS ON WALLS

The most common way of training climbers in the garden, in two planes on walls, is highly effective at integrating house and garden and producing dramatic effects in small enclosures where there is barely

Top left In the wild, clematis climb from shade to light, clinging to supports with hitches of their leaf stalks. In the garden, the moderately vigorous Viticella hybrids, such as 'Etoile Violette' and 'Abundance', can be planted to scramble over and through vigorous shrubs.

Top The ornamental gourds (*Cucurbita pepo*) are hardskinned and inedible versions of squashes and pumpkins. Their romping growth and quaintly shaped and colored fruits make them amusing annual climbers.

Above The rambling rose 'Albertine', often cursed by mildew but glorious in mid-summer, is backed by the sweetly scented *Lonicera periclymenum* 'Graham Thomas', a yellow-flowered form of the European woodbine.

room for narrow borders. By combining climbers and wall-trained shrubs, there is plenty of opportunity for well-timed coincidences of flowering and long successions of bloom. In fully paved yards, climbers and shrubs can be planted in containers, but when grown in this way they need more attention than those in the open ground, and regular watering is essential. Walls that are in good condition are not likely to be damaged by self-clinging climbers such as ivy (*Hedera*) and Virginia creeper (*Parthenocissus*). Climbers that pull themselves up by other means need wires or trellis to get a purchase. Whatever the support, it should stand out from the wall by about 4in (10cm); climbers growing tightly against a wall tend to be more prone to disease than those that have air moving more freely about their leaves and stems.

Preference for sun or shade, less critical when climbers are growing in three dimensions, becomes an issue when the orientation is dictated by a wall. One that gets full sun (in the Northern Hemisphere a a south-facing wall) seems on the face of it a choice position. It does provide conditions in which growth ripens well, encouraging frost resistance and generous flowering. When grown on a shady wall, wisterias and other sun-lovers are likely to produce lush foliage but poor crops of flowers. However, the growing conditions at the wall's base often pose problems. Most climbers like well-drained but moist rather than dry soil, and the base of a wall, particularly a sunny wall, is often the driest area of a garden, partly because a wall creates its own rain shadow, and it is sometimes stony. Measures that help get around these problems include the addition of generous quantities of well-rotted compost or similar organic material that boosts the humus content; planting about 18in (45cm) from the wall with the roots trained away from it; and additional planting—but not so that there is strong competition for moisture and nutrients—to shade the roots of climbers. (See also p.75 for shade-tolerant climbers.)

Top right *Solanum crispum* 'Glasnevin', usually grown as a wall shrub, is here trained on a metal arch, with *Clematis* 'Venosa Violacea' providing a bright accent at the base.

Above The ivies, including large-leaved kinds such as *Hedera canariensis* 'Gloire de Marengo', are as useful covering ground as they are on walls.

CLIMBERS ON FREESTANDING SUPPORTS

Architectural features in a garden are prime sites for climbers. Arbors and arches that are not clothed with climbers barely make sense; an ornamental bridge festooned with blossom is a delicious and romantic surprise. It has already been suggested that a simple structure such as an arch supporting climbers can be a more manageable way of introducing height in a small garden than the planting of a tree (see p.67). The same principle can equally be applied when a larger garden is being established; an arbor can be smothered by rampant vines long before trees are making an impression. Screens made of trellis and planted with climbers are an alternative to hedges. Sprinters for quick cover include annuals such as morning glory (*Ipomoea*), the canary creeper (*Tropaeolum peregrinum*), and several perennials that can be grown as annuals, among them the cup and saucer plant (*Cobaea scandens*) and the Chilean glory flower (*Eccremocarpus scaber*). Matching the sturdiness of the support and the vigor of the climber is, of course, very important. Tall focal points can be created in borders with pyramids of trellis and metal frames around and through which plants are trained. Less pretentious and just as pleasing are tripods and wigwams of bamboo.

Top The contrast between formal and informal components, full sun and shade, and areas of dense and spare planting can create dramatic tensions in a garden. A yew hedge (*Taxus baccata*), one of the best hedging plants in shade, marks the divide between an area under trees, planted informally with shrubs such as *Viburnum* x *burkwoodii*, and a broad expanse of grass.

Above The brilliant, even shrieking, colors of some azaleas and rhododendrons, such as *Rhododendron augustinii*, can strike a harsh note in a woodland setting. The company of other shade-tolerant shrubs that thrive in acidic conditions helps establish a balance. *Corylopsis*, a small Asiatic genus of deciduous shrubs with dangling clusters of pale yellow flowers, is ideal.

Above right Since the late 19th century, a large number of rhododendron species have been introduced from Asia, and their hybrids are legion. In scale, flower color, leaf size and shape, they show great diversity but all need acidic growing conditions and most, especially those that flower early, benefit from light overhead protection.

SHRUBS IN WOODLAND

Woodland gardening as a style is surprisingly modern. It represents an important shift in taste in the latter half of the 19th century, but it was also a response to the dramatic increase in plant introductions from temperate regions of the world, especially the Himalayas, western China, and Japan. In woodland gardening at its best, there is an effortless combination of exotic and native plants creating an impression of perfected nature.

Many of the shrubs best suited to the woodland garden are to some extent shade tolerant, but few thrive in dense shade. In the wild, they are often plants of glades and woodland margins, where they get filtered sunlight and often direct sunlight during part of the day. A large number thrive only on soils that are neutral to acidic, well-drained but moist, and rich in organic matter. Non-native shrubs are usually vigorous enough to compete with many existing plants, but aggressive spreaders should be cleared before shrubs are planted.

The tree canopy of a woodland garden is the protector of the plants layered beneath it. The microclimate it creates reduces the risk of frost damage, cuts water loss, and gives shelter from wind. The ideal canopy is that of deep-rooting trees that cast dappled shade, such as oak (*Quercus*). Woodland gardens in exposed areas need the additional defense of well-maintained shelter belts composed of tough plants such as Leyland cypress (× *Cupressocyparis leylandii*).

RHODODENDRONS

The great woodland gardens of the 19th and early 20th centuries were repositories for the hundreds of rhododendron species introduced from the Himalayas and western China and were also nurseries for the breeding of hybrids. The rhododendron in its many forms remains the

woodland shrub par excellence. This is especially so on acidic soils in northwestern North America, New Zealand, and areas of western Europe where the climate is mild and moist. The many enthusiasts of the genus point to its variety: in size, plants range from midgets to large trees, with considerable variation in plant growth; there is an impressive choice of flower color, size, and shape; and a judicious selection can give a very long flowering season. The foliage itself can be a feature, some of the evergreens being interesting for the color, texture, and size of their leaves, while numerous deciduous azaleas color well in autumn. Detractors, however, point to the conflict between the character of the rhododendron hybrids and their use in naturalistic planting. The colors of some have a synthetic stridency, the dense massing of the flowers is like that of bedding plants writ large, and out of flower many turn sullen. By a discriminating choice of species and hybrids, and a willingness to use them with other shrubs, however, the pitfalls of woodland gardening with rhododendrons and azaleas can be avoided. Their fibrous root system allows them to be moved with relative ease, so there should be no hesitation about rectifying mistakes in initial planting.

BEYOND RHODODENDRONS

Other plants for dappled shade on neutral to acidic soils include the calico bush (*Kalmia latifolia*) and the Japanese *Enkianthus campanulatus*. Quite outside the ericaceous camp are the hydrangeas. By far the most widely grown are the mophead and lacecap forms of *Hydrangea macrophylla*. On acidic soils, where they do best, there are strong blues; on alkaline soils they are pink. The mopheads can look very "towny," and it is easy to feel that they strike a false note in a woodland setting. More suitable choices can be found among the lacecaps and other species, including the oak-leaved hydrangea (*H. quercifolia*).

Some shrubs, including species of *Corylopsis* and *Fothergilla*, that are valued for their spring flowers are also impressive for their autumn color. A continental climate is needed to bring a woodland garden to its full autumn climax, but even where contrasts between summer and winter are less marked, it is worth planting for a blaze of color at leaf fall. Maples (*Acer*) are the supreme genus for autumn color. The Asiatic species *A. japonicum* and *A. palmatum* tolerate lime, but need moist soils rich in organic matter. A sheltered position in woodland protects their delicate foliage from cold winds and rapid thaw following frost. The pleasing outlines of these trees and shrubs and the rich colors of their autumn leaves are seen to best effect against broad-leaved and coniferous evergreens such as holly (*Ilex*) and yew (*Taxus*).

Those who garden on a grand scale can include shrubs and small trees that thrive in the sheltering embrace of woodland but do not need shade. These include dogwoods such as *Cornus kousa*, winter-flowering witch hazels (*Hamamelis*), and spring-flowering magnolias.

Below Shrub planting in gardens is more often inspired by woodland edge than by woodland depths, where only very shade-tolerant species thrive under a full deciduous or even denser evergreen canopy. Here, autumn sunshine lights the bright foliage of deciduous shrubs such as maples (*Acer*).

Bottom The tiered branches of *Viburnum plicatum* 'Mariesii', laden with a greenish show of sterile florets, stand out in a gladelike setting or backed by larger shrubs and trees.

THE WOODLAND FLOOR

Shade-tolerant bulbs and perennials make the tapestried beauty of the woodland floor. The mix is usually international, including daffodils (*Narcissus*) and primroses (*Primula vulgaris*) from Europe, trilliums and trout lilies (*Erythronium*) from North America, hostas from Japan, and blue poppies (*Meconopsis*) from the Himalayas and China. Few of these plants will grow in deep shade, and even ferns, more tolerant of shade than most flowering plants, do best in reasonably bright conditions. Many of the bulbs burgeon, flower, and start to die down before deciduous trees overhead are in full leaf. Most of the perennials do best beneath the edges of the tree canopy, where they get some angled light for at least part of the day as well as filtered light from overhead. In comparison, the dark shade under conifers or the secondary canopy of evergreen rhododendrons is a hostile environment. Most of the bulbs, as well as the perennials, flourish in soils that are moist and rich in organic matter, and some require neutral to acidic conditions. Few will grow in dry shade under beech trees (*Fagus sylvatica*), and even trees that cast light shade but are surface rooting, such as birches (*Betula*), leave little moisture for bulbs and perennials.

Below left In the wild, many lilies are plants of forest glades. This kind of setting suits even such spectacular hybrids as 'Casa Blanca'.

Below The hellebores (*Helleborus*) are a major group of winter- and spring-flowering perennials that are particularly suitable for woodland conditions. Here, purple-flowered *Hepatica nobilis* 'Rubra Plena' has been planted with a long-flowering Lenten rose (*Helleborus orientalis*). The prettily silvered leaves of the autumn-flowering *Cyclamen hederifolium* will last until early summer.

Once established, many native and non-native plants are capable of looking after themselves with a very low level of maintenance. Some are altogether too successful. In a large piece of woodland there is a place for coarse and vigorous plants such as comfrey (*Symphytum*), yellow archangel (*Lamium galeobdolon*), and the greater periwinkle (*Vinca major*); but they are bullies that will overwhelm choicer plants, and a decision to plant them should not be taken lightly.

For the choicest of the woodland plants, including the blue poppies (*Meconopsis*) and trilliums, the garden needs stronger management. Although the charm of wildness is to some extent sacrificed, the ground needs to be cleared, dug over, and improved with the addition of well-rotted organic matter. A mulch, ideally of leaf mold, helps to keep down weeds and conserve moisture. This level of management is less a problem where a limited area under the canopy of a small cluster of trees is gardened to create a woodland effect. For the area covered, the proportion of bulbs and perennials used will be higher than in true woodland, but the aim must still be to convey in the casual grouping of clumps and the placing of individual specimens an impression that plants have found their own way into the garden.

Above Bulbs that flower early and are dormant by mid-summer are an important feature of natural woodland in the temperate Northern Hemisphere. Among the easiest plants to naturalize under deciduous trees are the yellow-flowered winter aconite (*Eranthis hyemalis*) and snowdrops (*Galanthus* species).

Below When allowed to spread freely in semiwild conditions, either under trees or in more open conditions, the English bluebell (*Hyacinthoides non-scripta*) produces a unique massed spring display of blue flowers. In the more ordered parts of the garden, it can quickly become a nuisance.

BULBS

The woodland garden bright with bulbs before the leaves of deciduous trees unfurl is the epitome of spring. A relatively narrow range of plants is enough and should not include large-flowered hybrids. The vigorous hybrid daffodils may seem to offer more than small-flowered hybrids and species such as *Narcissus pseudonarcissus,* but in a woodland garden they look showy and overdressed. For a large area, expense will probably dictate the choice, for example, of the common snowdrop (*Galanthus nivalis*) and the dog's-tooth violet (*Erythronium dens-canis*) rather than their less commonly cultivated relatives, but these could be made a special feature of a small-scale woodland garden.

Bulbs should be planted, not too densely, in small irregular groups with a few outliers. Winter aconite (*Eranthis hyemalis*) and snowdrops (*Galanthus*) settle down more quickly if planted immediately after flowering, rather than as dry bulbs. In time, some bulbs, including wood anemone (*Anemone nemorosa*), winter aconite, and dwarf daffodils such as *Narcissus cyclamineus*, will form very large colonies if grown in conditions that suit them. *Crocus tommasinianus*, best in a glade-like opening, also spreads freely, and *Cyclamen hederifolium* will even self-seed in quite dry shade. The blue tides of English bluebells (*Hyacinthoides non-scripta*), it must be admitted, are at the expense of other plants, squeezed out as the bulbs become congested.

Lilies, the principal bulbs of summer, include many that are well suited to woodland conditions. Turk's-cap lilies such as *Lilium martagon* are easy to naturalize in dappled shade. However, they cannot match the giant lily (*Cardiocrinum giganteum*), which has a massive stem up to 12ft (3.7ft) high and steeply angled, richly scented, white trumpets. A colony should consist of several generations.

PERENNIALS

Cool refinement marks the best of the woodland perennials. Their character is typified by plants such as the Lenten roses (*Helleborus orientalis*) and Solomon's seal (*Polygonatum × hybridum*) of spring, early summer geraniums such as the mourning widow (*Geranium phaeum*), and the autumn-flowering *Kirengeshoma palmata*. Even the most eye-catching plants have an aristocratic reserve. The pristine radiance of the wake robin (*Trillium grandiflorum*) gives it high rank in a family that is distinctive for the arrangement of its leaves and flower parts in threes. And with their improbable azure, the Himalayan blue poppies seem like envoys from a remote and magical region.

73

Left The frothy yellow-green flowers of lady's mantle *(Alchemilla mollis)* intermingle freely with the cream pincushion flowers of masterwort *(Astrantia major)*. Both these perennials perform well in either sun or partial shade in a moist soil that is rich in organic matter.

BORDERS IN SHADE (ARCHITECTURAL SHADE)

Trees and shrubs in the garden create shady conditions that relate closely to those of forest and woodland. In small gardens, additional shade is cast by buildings, walls, or fences. In southern heat, architectural shade may have a special value as a place of retreat, but in cooler climates we want to sit on sunny lawns or patios, surveying an idyll of foliage and flowers that is often relegated to shady areas.

Some of the problems attributed to shade have to do with other aspects of the growing conditions. The soil at the base of walls is commonly the poorest in the garden, choked with limy stones and dry, the walls themselves causing areas of rain shadow. In addition, walls cause turbulence, which can wreck long-stemmed and fragile plants. Removing stones and replacing them with organic-rich soil is worth it where practicable. The minimum aim should be to work in plenty of organic material every year. The perennial problem of rain shadow can only be overcome by regular watering, even in spring and fall, combined with the use of a mulch. The answer to turbulence is to use sturdy plants closely planted.

The problems that are specific to shade are largely the consequence of inappropriate planting. Plants with a low tolerance of shade become drawn, and their weak growth is prone to disease. Some plants that are reasonably tolerant of shade although essentially sun loving produce foliage at the expense of flowers when grown in shade. There is, however, compensation in that flowers in shade usually last longer than those in full sun. Tall and upright plants tend to lean out when planted close to walls. Staking is time-consuming, difficult to conceal, and plants, when fettered, lose much of their grace. A better solution is to rely more heavily on plants of rounded growth set 2–3ft (60–90cm) from walls and backed by climbers or wall-trained shrubs.

Most of the shrubs, perennials, and bulbs suitable for woodland can be grown in the shade of walls and buildings, provided the soil is organic-rich and kept reasonably moist. To these can be added a very large number of plants that grow well with little or no direct sunshine, provided they get plenty of light and there is no overhead shade.

Above left Both hellebores and epimediums are tolerant of a wide range of conditions, but perform best in bright shade where the soil is relatively moist and contains plenty of organic matter. The lenten rose *(Helleborus niger)* remains attractive in flower over many weeks, and many epimediums are evergreen.

Above Several bulbs do reasonably well in the shade of walls provided the position is well lit. Here *Scilla siberica* grows with polyanthus, almost obscuring the leaves of *Cyclamen hederifolium.*

USEFUL QUALITIES IN SHADE

Given our insatiable appetite for color in the garden, plants that flower with unstinting generosity despite the conditions have a special value. In some important categories there are relatively few plants that flower freely in shade. Roses, for example, disappoint, although among old roses, Albas such as 'Königin von Dänemark' perform reasonably well, and a few climbers, famously the white 'Madame Alfred Carrière', flower even on a wall that gets little direct sun. The selection is thin among annuals, biennials, and bedding plants, but among those suitable several provide a broad color range, notably *Impatiens*, polyanthus (*Primula* Polyanthus Group), and the numerous pansy and viola hybrids (*Viola*). The color range of tobacco plants (*Nicotiana*) is limited, but their height, especially of *N. sylvestris*, is an advantage.

There is, however, ample compensation for these deficiencies. Most honeysuckles (*Lonicera*) are best in shade, and many clematis flower just as freely as in sun, without the flowers being bleached of color. Major groups of shrubs that flower prolifically include camellias, fuchsias, hydrangeas, and mock oranges (*Philadelphus*). The camellias need shade where the flowers are not caught by early sun (rapid thawing of frost on flowers causes browning of the petals). Some shrubs, notably skimmias and pyracanthas, are more colorful in berry than they are in flower. Among bulbs and perennials there are plants for the whole year, strongly represented from winter to early spring and from late summer to autumn, as well as in the main flowering season. In all this floral richness, it is flowers that are white or pale that give the shady border a special lift. This is not an argument for all-white borders, but a plea for judicious lighting with touches of cool bright radiance. The sort of plants that do the trick are *Narcissus* 'Jenny', *Camellia japonica* 'Alba Simplex', *Philadelphus* 'Sybille', *Hydrangea macrophylla* 'Madame Emile Mouillère', and *Anemone* × *hybrida* 'Honorine Jobert'.

Foliage with light-enhancing qualities also has a special value. Matt dark leaves, especially heavy purples, weigh down the shady border, but leaves with polished surfaces reflect light. Evergreen shrubs with glossy leaves include the Mexican orange (*Choisya ternata*), *Fatsia japonica*, and the camellias. Several of the hostas, such as *H. plantaginea*, have leaves with sheeny surfaces, but for an effect of lustrous nobility in perennials, nothing can quite match bear's breeches (*Acanthus mollis* Latifolius Group). Variegation is a more startling and light-enhancing effect with which to freshen shady borders, but overuse can tend to create a hectic consumptive look. The contrast of white and near whites with green is generally crisp in partial shade and particularly bright in several hostas, including *H.* 'Ginko Craig'. One of the most effective of the white-variegated shrubs is *Cornus alba* 'Elegantissima', a |silvery shimmer in summer with stems that glow red for months in winter. In theory, plants with yellow leaves or yellow variegation should seem like patches of sunshine in the shady border. In practice, yellow foliage, which often burns in full sun, tends to become a jaundiced green in full shade. Relatively die-fast yellows are found in cultivars of *Euonymus fortunei*, several ivies (notably *Hedera helix* 'Oro di Bogliasco'), and the hollies (*Ilex*).

Below A position in the shade of a wall often provides the shelter from cold winds and late frosts that camellias require. But they also demand lime-free soil and an abundance of moisture. *Camellia japonica* 'Gloire de Nantes' starts flowering in winter.

Left Many species of columbine, including granny's bonnet (*Aquilegia vulgaris*), are woodland plants that adapt well to the walled and confined conditions of city gardens, provided the ground is reasonably moist. Plants are short-lived but they self-seed freely.

75

Special Conditions and Solutions

Plants are extremely adaptable and can cope with most environments, except for the frozen polar ice caps and certain desert areas. Interest in plants is inherent in most of us, and gardening is now increasingly popular. However, selecting the right plants is the most important ingredient for success in any type of gardening. Trying new plants in new places is not wrong, but every plant, regardless of how common or how rare it is, has its limitations. Gardeners quickly learn that each plant has its own preferred growing conditions, and is best positioned with other plants that have the same requirements. This is very true of plants that have very specific growing needs.

One important factor to consider is the type of soil the plant prefers. This has more to do with the size of the soil particles and how freely the soil drains than with chemical content. Clay particles are very small, enabling soils that contain a high proportion of clay to retain plenty of moisture and nutrients. On the other hand, sand has large particles, allowing soil to drain freely but retaining little nutrition.

A common preference in plants is for soil with a particular pH—how acidic or alkaline the soil is (see "The Making of Plant Communities," p. 20). This influences the solubility of minerals and how easily these are taken up by plants. Although many plants tolerate a range of pH levels, others do not. For example, *Clematis* need lime in the soil, whereas most heaths (*Erica*) and many of their relatives do not tolerate lime at all. These are called calcifuges or "lime-haters." Plants with a marked pH preference are best grown in containers.

Some plants prefer very wet growing conditions and actually need to have their "feet" in water so that the roots are submerged for at least a part of the year and, in many cases, permanently. Such plants have adapted to their preferred surroundings. For instance, water lilies (*Nymphaea*) have a system of air cavities in the stems, which means that the air can get down to parts of the plant that are under water. Another good example is the swamp cypress (*Taxodium distichum*) which has special "breathing" roots that grow above the water line.

Above A mixture of *Tulipa sprengeri*, peonies (*Paeonia*), and *Geranium* softens the outline of these paving stones. The openness of this site is perfect for sun-loving tulips, although both geraniums and peonies tolerate partial shade.

Below right A wide range of plants can be grown in dry soil. Here, the cylindrical lime-green bracts of *Euphorbia characias* and the purple spires of *Salvia nemorosa* bring shapely interest to a planting.

Below Deciduous rhododendrons *Meconopsis* and *Primula* thrive in the cool, damp, lime-free soils of a woodland edge.

At the very other extreme are plants that grow naturally in dry, impoverished soil. The soil may be almost pure sand or gravel, with little or no organic matter because any fallen leaves tend to shrivel away quickly. Such soils are often very quick to drain and, in summer, natural moisture is scarce. However, once the plants are established, they cope with bright sunlight, high temperatures, and low rainfall by using various adaptations for conserving moisture—features that are often what makes them look attractive in the garden. For example, *Convolvulus cneorum* has developed a coating of fine hairs on the surface of the leaves that reduces moisture loss and reflects sunlight. This creates the silvery-gray color of the foliage. Brooms such as *Genista aetensis* reduce moisture loss by having hardly any leaves. Instead, they have tough, thin, green stems that take on the function of leaves for the manufacture of food.

Dry soils and high altitudes, a combination of conditions that is found in mountainous regions, has given rise to a very popular form of gardening involving alpines. Alpines are very hardy, slow-growing plants that have adapted to the conditions in such regions. Their size and hardiness means that they are ideal for small modern gardens, but they only thrive well in dry, well-drained soil in a sheltered site.

Just as inhospitable as an environment for plants is the coastline. The salt-laden air (and there are also often salt residues in the soil), bright light, and high winds make coastal gardening very difficult. Plants such as *Hebe* have extra-thick coatings on their leaves, and sea holly (*Eryngium*) has tough leathery leaves as a protection against salt. Other plants have modified leaves for reducing the amount of moisture lost during windy and dry periods. These preserve any fresh water they receive, which can then be used during the growing process.

Gardeners in temperate regions, however, must accept that, in spite of their very best efforts, some plants—namely tender plants— are difficult, if not impossible, to grow outdoors year-round. Many of these plants come from tropical and subtropical regions and, although they may be grown outside in the warmest summer months, they must be taken indoors or kept in a greenhouse or conservatory during the winter for protection. Alternatively, after they have been planted outdoors for summer bedding, they can simply be discarded.

Top Here, perennial *Iris sibirica* and a swath of *Primula bulleyana* are naturalized at the base of a slope in moist soil that is also rich in organic matter.

Above The damp ground by the side of a stream, which is decorated with the floating leaves of a water lily (*Nymphaea*), provides the perfect growing conditions for a wide variety of lush architectural foliage plants, including perennial *Hosta* and ferns.

Above The mock oranges
(*Philadelphus*), heavily scented
shrubs of mid-summer, do well
even on poor, thin, alkaline soils.
Crambe cordifolia, a perennial
that makes a large cloud of small
white flowers, will also grow in
similar conditions.

Above right Highdown, near Wor-
thing, Sussex, is an inspiration to
British gardeners on alkaline soil,
having been created in the mid-20th
century on pure chalk. A remarkable range of plants was grown
there by its creators Sir Frederick
Stern and Lady Stern.

Below Red valerian (*Centranthus
ruber*), to some gardeners a
bothersome weed, especially when
its roots become established in
walls, is a splendid perennial on
dry, alkaline slopes.

THE ACID-ALKALINE DIVIDE

The terms calcifuge and calcicole express one of the great divides in the plant world. Lime-hating plants (calcifuges), which take their stand on acidic soils, and plants that flourish in lime-rich conditions (calcicoles) seem like the adherents of a major religion aligned on opposite sides of a fundamental dogma. By far the most rigid are the calcifuges, yellowing with disapproval when a trace of lime pushes the pH over 7, the point of neutrality. Most of the lime lovers and their loose adherents, however, tolerate soils that are neutral to slightly or even markedly acidic. In practice, therefore, it is gardeners on alkaline soils that have to be most particular in choosing plants, and this section is focused on their needs. Other sections of this book cover woodland gardens on acidic soils (see "Shrubs in Woodland," pp. 70–71) and acid-loving plants (see "Heather and Peat Gardens," pp. 80–81).

Some gardeners are so besotted with rhododendrons and other calcifuges that even on strongly alkaline soils they will contrive conditions to suit them. Far better, though, to embrace lime-tolerant plants with enthusiasm and to delight in their very varied ornamental qualities. Most of the plants that give gardens on lime their distinctive character belong to families that are enthusiastic lime lovers or are so easygoing that it makes no difference. Wildflowers in grassland on chalky soil, a model for meadow gardening (see p. 65), give an idea of their beauty. Others come from families that show a mixture of responses to lime, some genera and species implacable in their hatred of it, others often tolerant to a remarkable degree.

LIME ENTHUSIASTS AND EASYGOING PLANTS

The genus *Dianthus*, which includes pinks, carnations, and sweet Williams, is among the pick of the lime-loving families. Many have an old-world charm, but their ornamental value in borders and raised beds, as well as in many other open positions where the soil is free draining, does not depend on mere sentimental association. The peonies (*Paeonia*), shrubby and herbaceous, have also long been in cultivation, their sumptuous beauty appreciated in China and Japan long before the Asiatic species and hybrids were added to those grown for centuries in Europe and then North America. The winter- and spring-flowering hellebores (*Helleborus*), currently riding on a crest, have a subdued beauty, most exciting in the Lenten roses (*H. orientalis*), with white, green, pink, and plum flowers, some heavily speckled. Clematis do not need lime to make healthy vigorous growth, as was once often asserted, but the fact remains that the genus as a whole is a great success where there is lime in the soil. In the temperate garden, there are no climbers to match them for seasonal and color variation.

These few genera are the tip of an iceberg. There are also trees, on the large scale beeches (*Fagus*), on a smaller scale most species and hybrids of *Prunus* (the ornamental cherries from Japan being something of a surprise, since many plants from this region are lime hating). The dove or handkerchief tree (*Davidia involucrata*), breathtaking when it hangs out its large white bracts, is representative of the

numerous plants from western China that grow readily on alkaline soils. Shrubs include buddleias, viburnums, and a vast number from the Mediterranean, where limestone formations are common. There are, too, climbers like the jasmines and numerous perennials. Most or all of the following genera flourish where there is lime in the soil: *Acanthus*, *Agapanthus*, campanulas, euphorbias, gypsophilas, kniphofias, and scabious. To these can be added numerous annuals and biennials, including wallflowers (*Erysimum*) and stocks (*Matthiola*). And there is almost the whole gamut of bulbous plants, with the notable exception of lilies (see below).

LIME-TOLERANT PLANTS AMONG THE LIME-HATERS

No group of plants is more notorious for its intolerance of lime than the vast ericaceous family, with its mobs of rhododendrons. It has even given its name to lime-free potting medium. Nonetheless, the winter-flowering ericas, including *Erica carnea* and its numerous cultivars, tolerate lime. The family also contains the evergreen strawberry trees (*Arbutus*), of which *A. andrachne*, *A. unedo*, and the hybrid between them, *A. × andrachnoides*, can be grown on alkaline soils.

Undoubtedly, the majority of lilies do best in neutral to acidic soils. Many, including one of the most spectacular, the golden-rayed lily (*Lilium auratum*), object to the slightest trace of lime. There are, however, glorious lime-tolerant exceptions. In the first rank are two Chinese species, the regal lily (*L. regale*) and the orange-flowered *L. henryi*. The martagon or Turk's-cap lily (*L. martagon*), the most widely distributed of the European species, and the splendid *L. monadelphum* from Turkey and the Caucasus, also tolerate lime, but these, like the Chinese species, are not suitable for dry, chalky soils. The Madonna lily (*L. candidum*) is undeniably capricious, but is certainly found in a wild or semiwild state in the eastern Mediterranean, growing in hot, dry niches among limestone rocks. Lime tolerance has been passed on to the Nankeen lily (*L. × testaceum*), the first of all the lily hybrids and a cross between *L. candidum* and *L. chalcedonicum*.

The magnolias, among the most beautiful of all the flowering trees and shrubs, are best known as plants for acidic to neutral soils, but a surprising number, including some of great ornamental quality, tolerate lime. Few will thrive on the free-draining conditions of chalk, although *Magnolia grandiflora* can succeed even here if nursed through its first years. Others that do well on moist soils containing lime include *M. kobus*, *M. × loebneri*, *M. stellata*, and *M. wilsonii*. Plants that stand out in other genera on account of their lime tolerance include *Acer griseum* among the maples, *Eucryphia cordifolia* and the hardier *E. × nymansensis* in the eucryphias, *Gentiana septemfida* among the autumn-flowering alpine gentians, and *Hydrangea aspera* and the vigorous climbing *H. anomala* subsp. *petiolaris* among the hydrangeas.

The roses are also mixed in their reactions to lime. The least satisfactory are the large-flowered modern bush roses (hybrid teas), but even many of these do reasonably well on a heavy soil that contains lime. The most satisfactory are the climbers and ramblers, the cluster-flowered modern bush roses (floribundas), and vigorous old and modern shrub roses (the Albas, for example, and hybrids such as 'Nevada').

Above Although camellias are said to be slightly more tolerant of lime than rhododendrons, healthy growth can only be expected on moist, lime-free soil. A high broken canopy, as here, helps protect the flowers from frost and wind.

Below The early-flowering hybrid *Clematis* 'Proteus' makes a startling appearance among the variegated leaves of *Actinidia kolomikta*, often with more white to give a distinctive tricolour effect. Both plants tolerate alkaline soils but clematis do not require lime, as is sometimes asserted.

HEATHER AND PEAT GARDENS

Two distinctive and contrasting garden features are associated with plants that prefer or require acidic soils. Heather gardens exploit the capacity of plants of moorland and heath to form a dense, interlocking cover that excludes weeds. As a result, they are usually intended as low-maintenance features over extensive areas. The plants used are heather or ling (*Calluna vulgaris*) and heaths (*Daboecia* and *Erica*), all small-leaved and small-flowered members of the ericaceous family. The great stronghold of ericas in the wild is in South Africa, but these species are excluded from the typical heather garden of temperate regions by their relative tenderness. Several ericas, notably the winter heath (*E. carnea*) and the Darley Dale heath (*E. × darleyensis*), will grow on alkaline soils. Nevertheless, extensive gardening with heaths and heathers is largely confined to acidic soils.

The peat garden, usually on a small scale, is in effect a specialized kind of raised bed or series of raised beds providing growing conditions that suit a number of alpines and small woodland plants that will not tolerate lime. The point of the raised bed is that it insures acidic, moist, and lightly shaded growing conditions, but because it is raised, it can even be constructed in a garden on chalky soil. The perversity of fighting against the growing conditions deserves to fail but can be successful, particularly if the bed is isolated from the underlying soil with a plastic or butyl rubber liner. Despite the name by which these gardens are commonly known, peat is less and less a component of them. Because of the ecological damage done to wetlands by large-scale extraction of peat, growing mediums based on materials such as coir and pulverized wood are increasingly used as peat substitutes.

HEATHER GARDENS

As an allusion to wild heathland and moorland, heather gardens cannot fail to disappoint. The exhilarating scale and openness to the elements of wild landscapes covered with heather is heightened by the poverty of their vegetation and the broad effects of seasonal changes. The model does not translate to the scale of a suburban garden, where the view abruptly ends with a house wall, or a sharp boundary marks an incongruous juxtaposition of heather garden and green lawn or heather garden and colorful border.

The strongest case for planting a heather garden is that it provides reasonably low-maintenance cover. This requires some qualification, however. Ground for planting must first be cleared of weeds. The young plants—set deeply, about 18in (45cm) apart, closer in the case of the less-vigorous kinds—will take several years to knit together as a weed-suppressing groundcover, and during this time some weed

Top **The taller heaths—the Portuguese heath (*E. lusitanica*), the tree heath (*E. arborea*), and *E. a.* var *alpina*—together with shrubs and trees can help to make the heather garden a more interesting association of plants than the conventional mixture of low heaths and dwarf conifers.**

Center **Many dwarf cultivars of heath (*Erica*) and ling (*Calluna vulgaris*) give long-lasting effects in cool temperate gardens. However, real variety in the genus is found in the Cape heaths.**

Bottom **On reasonably moist soils, amelanchiers make good two-season shrubs to back heaths. They are a mass of small flowers in spring and color well in autumn.**

control will be necessary. Fire, the means of rejuvenating heather on grouse moorland, is not an option open to the gardener. Mechanical trimming in spring or after flowering for winter- and spring-flowering heaths will help to keep plants vigorous and bushy, but after 8 to 10 years the cover will become sparse and replanting will be necessary.

One of the few places where a heather garden can hardly be bettered is as a transition to a wild, open landscape. An effect that is too obviously managed would jar, but planting heaths or heathers in groups of 6 or more of the same kind for flower season (including dead flowers that remain in winter), flower color, or foliage color and texture, especially varied among the callunas, can give a pleasing year-round succession. Some in the nursery trade have pushed the idea of introducing conifers, usually dwarf, as incidents in the heather garden, but in most instances the match is ill-fated. A better option, if the garden is large enough, is to plant a small cluster of trees that are tolerant of acidic soils, such as birch (*Betula*) or rowan (*Sorbus aucuparia*).

PEAT GARDENS

An ideal position for a peat bed is on a sheltered sloping site that faces away from the sun and is lightly shaded but not overhung by a deciduous tree. However, peat beds can also be constructed where in summer they are shaded throughout part or most of the day by buildings. Until recently, peat blocks were widely used to construct the walls. One of the best substitutes for them are old railroad ties that have been treated with a preservative that is not toxic to plants. Wood is usually preferable to brick, as lime in the mortar of a brick wall will eventually leach into the soil unless the bed is lined or the inside of the wall is treated with a sealant. A wall height of approximately 10–20in (25–50cm) is adequate. The acid-loving plants suitable for peat gardens can be grown in a mixture of neutral to acidic soil (2 parts), acidic peat substitute (2 parts), and lime-free grit (1 part). This needs to be well mixed, with the addition of a slow-release fertilizer, before being put into the bed. Beds should be watered and then left to settle for a few days before being planted. Once planted, a mulch, say of bark chips, will help to conserve moisture and keep the bed free of weeds.

It is inevitable that to some extent the peat garden has the character of a treasured collection containing less common and in some cases undeniably difficult plants. It is, however, a feature that can be of interest over a long season, particularly if the range it covers goes beyond acid-loving shrubs such as *Cassiope*, *Gaultheria*, and dwarf rhododendrons, and classic perennials such as the autumn-flowering *Gentiana sino-ornata*. Plants that will thrive in the cool, moist conditions of a peat bed include numerous bulbs, among them the erythroniums, and woodland plants such as the trilliums and the harebell poppy (*Meconopsis quintuplinervia*).

Below left Bloodroot (*Sanguinaria canadensis*) is widely distributed in northeast North America, usually growing in moist deciduous forest. In cultivation it is best known for its double form 'Plena', a plant of startling whiteness for a peat bed.

Below Most of the trilliums show a marked preference for neutral to acidic soil, and in gardens, as well as in the wild, thrive in partial, even quite dense shade. The glistening radiance of the wake robin (*Trillium grandiflorum*), with its parts arranged in threes, makes it a choice plant to grow with erythroniums as here.

MOISTURE-RETENTIVE AND HEAVY SOILS

In principle, a soil that has moisture-retaining qualities is a great asset. It will see plants through periods when the natural water supply falters. Even in open sunny borders, it will allow many plants to be grown that are strongly associated with boggy places and the waterside. Astilbes, the ornamental rhubarb (*Rheum palmatum*), globe flowers (*Trollius*), and the arum lily (*Zantedeschia aethiopica*) are just a few of the plants that grow happily in moist soils quite divorced from the specialized conditions in which they are often seen.

In a moist and well-drained soil, there is a balanced supply of water and air; for the majority of plants one is just as important as the other. In soils that have a high clay content, however, there is no happy equilibrium. In their fine-textured stickiness, their particles so small that they do not leave the myriad pockets of air that give buoyant life to soils, they hold onto water with a sullen tenacity. Clay soils are nearly the despair of gardeners. In a sodden state, plants growing in them drown. When they dry out, they bake and crack. They are slow to warm up in spring, so plants make a late start. They fully justify their description as "heavy," being backbreaking to work. They are temperamental about when they can be handled. They are like glue to work on when wet and quickly compact so that what little structure they have is seriously damaged. The best time to dig clay soils is in autumn or early winter; where there are frosts the alternation of freezing and thawing helps to break down large slabs. In spring the gardener has to wait patiently until the clay can be worked. And yet clay soils are redeemed by their fertility and their capacity for improvement, and in moderation their water-retaining qualities are invaluable.

IMPROVING CLAY SOILS

A seriously waterlogged garden on clay soil can only be remedied by the installation of a drainage system in which sloping pipes, laid in a herringbone pattern about 2ft (60cm) below the surface, carry water to a drainage basin or ditch. For the amateur gardener with a less serious problem, the most important method of improving the soil's structure is to incorporate copious quantities of well-rotted organic matter, preferably worked into the soil and also laid as a mulch while the soil is moist but after it has started to warm up. Although the soil will not be transformed overnight, applications over several years will greatly increase the openness of the soil, creating a better balance between moisture retention and aeration. Other measures that help improve the structure include the addition of generous quantities of horticultural grit or coarse sand and liming. Liming helps the clay particles form into crumbs, but inevitably alters the acid-alkaline balance of the soil and is generally advisable only where the conditions are highly acidic.

While overall improvement of clay soils is desirable, it is often better to concentrate resources of time and energy by improving limited areas of the garden. Raised beds that can be worked without being walked on, either loosely mounded or with low walls of board or brick, have a much more general application than the vegetable garden and are particularly appropriate on clay. Even after years of cultivation and the application of generous quantities of organic matter, clay soils will remain heavy, but once they are aerated, a broad range of plants can take advantage of their fertility.

PLANTING ON HEAVY SOILS

Given the labor involved in working heavy soils, it makes sense when planting to aim for broad effects that in the long term will require only low-level maintenance. A large part of the garden can be devoted to mixed plantings, relying heavily on sturdy shrubs and plants that have a good ground-covering capacity. Well-chosen trees, shrubs, and perennials are usually slow to get started but eventually outstrip the same

Top The fat buds of the drumstick primulas (*Primula denticulata*) push through heavy soils in late winter or early spring. Seed-raised plants of this Himalayan species show a color range from pale mauve to deep purple and white.

Above Garden groundsel *Ligularia dentata*, cannas, and dahlias make a hot color scheme for the second half of summer on heavy, moist soils where they do well.

Right Joe-pye weed (*Eupatorium purpureum*) is impressive in scale and has a long autumn season. This clump is at least 8ft (2.5m) high and dwarfs a knotwood (*Persicaria*) and coneflower (*Rudbeckia*).

Opposite A mauve tradescantia and Bowles' golden sedge (*Carex elata* 'Aurea') are key plants in a cluster thriving in moisture-retentive soil.

plants growing on free-draining soils. Some of the best hedging plants, including hornbeam (*Carpinus betulus*), hawthorn (*Crataegus*), holly (*Ilex*), and yew (*Taxus*) do well on heavy soils. Major genera of ornamental trees in temperate gardens, among them maples (*Acer*), crab apples (*Malus*), oaks (*Quercus*), and *Sorbus* species thrive on, or are adaptable to, these conditions. There are many popular shrubs, from the solid spotted laurel (*Aucuba japonica*) to the more showy flowering quinces (Chaenomeles) and forsythias, that can be relied on as well as shrubs or small trees of real class, including the witch hazels (*Hamamelis*), magnolias, and roses. Roses do not need a clay soil, but they usually flourish on one that is well-drained. Smaller plants with good ground-covering capacity—*Alchemilla mollis*, bergenias, and ivies (*Hedera*)—greatly reduce heavy work on a clay soil. They can be used extensively or in combination with more distinguished but hearty perennials such as monkshood (*Aconitum*), day lilies (*Hemerocallis*), heleniums, many primulas, and coneflowers (*Rudbeckia*). Almost all of these plants, woody and herbaceous, will benefit if soil mixed with grit or coarse sand is worked around the roots in the planting hole.

Plants that cannot be expected to do well on heavy soils unless special provision is made for them include those of marginal hardiness, and broad categories that thrive in free-draining soils. These include most rock garden plants, almost all plants with silver foliage, many Mediterranean plants (*Euphorbia characias* is an exception), and numerous annuals. It must be expected that bulbs, too, are ill-suited to heavy soils, but there are in fact a number that are successful. These include snowdrops (*Galanthus*), daffodils (*Narcissus*), and a sprinkling of other bulbs, including camassias, bluebells (*Hyacinthoides*), and the summer snowflake (*Leucojum aestivum*). Few lilies can be added to these, but the Caucasian *Lilium monadelphum* is a distinctive exception. Any measures that improve the drainage of heavy soils will greatly increase the choice of bulbs that can be grown. Even on an improved clay soil, it is worth planting individual bulbs, especially lilies and fritillarias, on a bed of grit or coarse sand.

WATER AND WATERSIDE GARDENS

Mirror reflections, cascades of splintered light, the splash of fountains, or the gentle murmur of a quiet current all add a dimension to the garden that has an age-old fascination. While it is uncommon for a garden to contain natural bodies of water, whether still or moving, the ready availability of flexible and rigid liners and simple pumps to circulate water have made it easy to install ponds, streams, and fountains. Even a tiny paved garden has space for a tub or pot.

These water features provide opportunities for a range of different plantings but, even with the fringe of plants that thrive in shallow water, the water garden itself is much less important as an area for planting than the moist ground that sometimes lies close to streams, ponds, and lakes. The combination of fertile soil and an unfailing supply of moisture produces rapid growth in trees and shrubs, and prodigious size and lushness in perennials.

The wonderful exuberance of plants that can plug into a dependable supply of moisture means that water and waterside gardens demand regular maintenance and vigilance. Weeds thrive in the same conditions and can romp away in spring before they are crowded out by dense growth. During and after the growing season, the gardener almost certainly has to step in and reestablish a balance of forces that has tilted in favor of the most aggressively vigorous plants. And initial caution about what to introduce is well justified, for the beguiling can turn into monsters.

DEEP WATER AND SUBMERGED PLANTS

Water lilies (*Nymphaea*) are by far the best known and most varied of aquatics for planting in the deepest water, with species and hybrids that thrive in tropical and temperate conditions. The most vigorous are suitable for lakes, but many thrive in ponds less than 2ft (60cm) deep. All, however, are best suited to still water. Their many-petaled starry flowers are of ravishing beauty, but it is the shade cast by their foliage and that of other plants with floating leaves that is of critical importance to the ecological balance of a pool. A combination of light, warmth, and nutrients encourages the growth of aquatic algae, which can make the water of a pond as turbid as pea soup or fill it with blankets of green filaments. These unsightly although perfectly natural growths are only temporarily and ineffectually checked by chemical control. A much more certain, long-term solution is to plant so that about a third of the water surface is covered by leaves. The inclusion of submerged plants such as hornwort (*Ceratophyllum demersum*) or curled pondweed (*Potamogeton crispus*) also helps, for these compete for the salts that encourage the growth of algae. They also play an important role as oxygenators, and they provide cover and breeding

Top left Water irises, such as the plain-leaved and variegated yellow flag iris (*Iris pseudacorus*), give double value with their reflections when planted in the shallow margins of ponds.

Above Water lilies (*Nymphaea*) vary greatly in their vigor, some tolerating a depth of almost 10ft (3m). Some of the pygmy water lilies will happily thrive in less than 1ft (30cm) of water.

sites for fish. Keeping nutrients to a minimum will help to control algal growth. If at all possible, ponds should be topped up with rainwater instead of more nutrient-rich tap water, and fertilizers should not be used with the planting medium. Small pools are more likely to suffer from the problem of algal growth than larger bodies of water, the rapid fluctuations in the temperature making it difficult to establish a steady balance and the water level requiring more frequent topping up.

In natural bodies of water and in clay-puddled pools, water lilies and other aquatics can be planted directly in the soil on the bottom. In pools made from flexible or rigid liners, it is best to plant in micromesh or lined baskets that are topped with a layer of gravel so the soil particles do not make the water dirty.

Top In the southeastern states of America, the swamp cypress (*Taxodium distichum*) lives up to its name, stands of it draped with Spanish moss (*Tillandsia usneoides*) being found in alluvial valleys. This deciduous conifer, however, makes an adaptable waterside tree.

Above A small stream and pool allow scope for the imaginative use of waterside and floating plants.

THE WATER MARGINS

Plants that tolerate their feet plunged in water are a godsend to the gardener who wants to create a natural-looking pond. The challenge in establishing such a pond is to make it sit in its setting so that it seems to have always been there. Marginals help the eye slip over the give-away seam where land and water meet, particularly when they are backed by planting that is all of a piece with the waterside setting. With their reflections, they can provide a continuous line that extends from the heart of a pool to a distant backing of shrubs and trees. An over-exuberant planting of marginals would spoil the outline of a formal body of water, but even here they have a role, and when planted in ordered groups they can discreetly underline the geometry of a pool.

The succession observable in natural bodies of water, where reeds and other swamp lovers that colonize shallow water trap debris and silt until they eventually extend the shoreline, serves as a warning to gardeners planting the shallow margins of their ponds. Many marginals are extremely vigorous; some, such as the common reed (*Phragmites australis*), form large stands that exclude all other plants and are limited in their extent only by lack of moisture on the land side and by deep water on the other side. These aggressive colonizers have a place in landscape planting, but are not suitable for a garden pond. They inevitably include plants that are well suited to ponds that are intended to attract wildlife, giving particularly valuable cover to birds and insects. There is, however, an irony in the degree of management required if they are planted in a small-scale pond. Even less vigorous marginals need to be controlled, and their roots are best contained by planting them in baskets, which can be positioned on ledges that are an intrinsic part of the design of many ponds. Where ledges do not exist, stacked bricks can be used as an underwater base.

Many marginals are plants with striking foliage, among the most distinctive being several with linear or strap-shaped leaves with vertical variegation. The leaves of *Iris laevigata* 'Variegata' are stiffly upright, while the blades of the grass *Glyceria maxima* var. 'Variegata' arch gracefully. But marginals also include plants from many corners of the world with flowers of great distinction. Among them are the kingcup or marsh marigold (*Caltha palustris*), the arum lily (*Zantedeschia aethiopica*), and the cultivars of the Japanese iris (*I. ensata*).

WATERSIDE AND BOG PLANTINGS

An area of naturally moist soil is the ideal place to create a waterside or bog garden as background to a pond or stream, but it cannot be taken for granted that there will be such an area adjacent to a natural body of water. It may have to be created by diverting water from a stream or channeling an overflow from a dam. Because of its impermeable lining, an artificial water feature, unless specially constructed with an overflow, does not provide moisture to replenish the reserves of a bog garden. However, a bog garden can be created as an integral part of a pond or as an independent feature using a flexible liner laid in an excavated hole. The hole needs to be at least 18in (45cm) deep so that it does not dry out too quickly. The liner should be sparingly pierced to let excess water seep away and filled with soil that is rich in organic matter and free of perennial weeds. Bog gardens can also be created in naturally moist areas that are unrelated to open water.

Although the divide is not clearcut, a workable distinction can be made between marginals that thrive in shallow water and those that

require wet conditions but do not tolerate indefinite flooding of their roots. This second category of plants, catered for by the dependably moist conditions of a bog garden, includes some of the most sensational giants among herbaceous plants. There is nothing in the temperate garden that can quite match the scale and splendor of *Gunnera manicata*, with its handsome, rough, rhubarblike leaves thrust out on prickly stalks and its floral cones lurking within the massive clump. Other impressive perennials include species of *Ligularia*, *Rheum*, and *Rodgersia*, plants with superb foliage and flowers that are by no means insignificant, those of *L.* 'The Rocket' sparking into life as if to launch the tall, dark stems. Combined with such plants as the skunk cabbages (*Lysichiton*), clumps of the royal fern (*Osmunda regalis*), and tall grassy plants, they create a rich pattern of shapes and textures that can be infinitely varied with the addition of light fronds, broad leaves such as those of the large hostas, and erect or lax straps and blades. The bog garden can, of course, be given a much more strongly floral character, and for this purpose few plants surpass the candelabra primulas and astilbes, the finest of the astilbes providing a superior combination of elegant, longlasting flowers and superb foliage.

Above left Like the yellow skunk cabbage (*Lysichiton americanum*) of North America, the species from Kamchatka (*L. camtschatcensis*), thrives in bog, but it is a most refined plant and its flowers are sweet smelling.

Above The candelabra primulas, which have their flowers arranged distinctively in whorls up the stems, will seed themselves freely in moisture-retentive soil.

Left *Miscanthus sinensis* 'Gracillimus' is an elegant waterside plant, but the species and its cultivars adapt to a wide range of conditions.

Opposite top Moisture and nutrient-rich soil fuel the growth of gunneras and skunk cabbages (*Lysichiton*).

Opposite bottom Even the narrowest channel can be planted with moisture lovers, such as these water irises.

WATERSIDE TREES AND SHRUBS

Most moisture-loving trees grow rapidly and, when mature, take up enormous quantities of water in summer, drying out small areas of bog and ponds to which their roots have access. They create shade and shed leaves that accumulate at the bottom of ponds. Although shade is needed to discourage the growth of algae, that cast by a high canopy is indiscriminate. There is little opportunity for the successful planting of tall, moisture-loving trees except on the margins of large ponds and lakes in a landscape setting. In such a context, the large alders (*Alnus*), poplars (*Populus*), willows (*Salix*), and two deciduous conifers, the American swamp cypress (*Taxodium distichum*) and the Chinese dawn redwood (*Metasequoia glyptostroboides*), come into their own.

Even small trees such as the snowy mespilus (*Amelanchier*) are best kept back from the edges of medium-sized garden ponds, for which the most suitable woody framework is provided by moisture-loving shrubs. Among the most elegant of the evergreens are bamboos, but nonrunning kinds must be chosen or the waterside will become a thicket. The smaller willows are among the most useful of the deciduous shrubs. Some, like *Salix hastata* 'Wehrhahnii', are slow growing. Others, such as *S. alba* subsp. vitellina 'Britzensis', can be kept to a moderate size by regular cutting back, which insures a succession of young stems that become brilliant orange-red in winter.

DRY AND DESERT GARDENS

Many gardens are predictably dry. They lie, for example, in areas of seasonal or consistently low rainfall and low humidity. An additional or separate problem may be that the soil is fast-draining sand, gravel, chalk, or limestone. Even when the overall picture of a garden does not suggest problems of drought, there will inevitably be areas within it that are drier than others. Buildings, walls, and trees, just to mention the most conspicuous features, all create their own microclimates, often exaggerated by differences of level and steepness of slope.

Low or seasonal rainfall and fast-draining soils are familiar norms, but more and more gardeners are having to cope with relatively dry conditions. Patterns of climate seem to be changing in many regions of the world, in part at least as a consequence of human activity. Irregularities in rainfall have coincided with accelerating demand for water. Rationing and substantial increases in the cost of supply have shocked gardeners into recognizing the extent to which the plants they grow rely on watering and irrigation. By taking measures to conserve moisture and by choosing drought-tolerant plants, many of the problems posed by dry gardens can be solved in a way that is aesthetically pleasing. Even in true desert conditions, the garden can bloom without the lavish use of scarce water reserves.

CONSERVING MOISTURE

Quite simple measures can help to reduce water loss in vulnerable gardens. Shelter belts and hedges (see also p.96) reduce the amount of water lost through evaporation. Building up the level of organic matter content in the soil makes it more efficient at retaining moisture. Various materials can be used, the most practical being garden waste composted on site. A mulch covering the soil helps to hold in moisture and discourages the growth of weeds, which compete with plants for available moisture and nutrients. Mulches also help to maintain an even temperature and protect the soil from violent deluges. One of the most useful general-purpose organic mulches is pulverized bark, which should be laid about 4–6in (10–15cm) deep. Gravel and pebbles are effective as mulches in dry gardens, especially around succulents and other plants that resent moisture accumulating around the collar. Newly planted trees and shrubs are especially vulnerable. Black plastic sheeting or strips of old carpet are effective mulches around newly planted trees and shrubs but, as with all mulches, should only be laid on ground that has been well watered.

In using scarce water resources, gardeners have to rank priorities according to their own judgment. The lawn, a great guzzler if it is to attain velvety perfection and unsightly as a parched dust bowl, is the first feature to consider axing. It can be replaced with paving, decking, or a less-thirsty kind of planting consisting of drought-tolerant plants, perhaps growing in beds of gravel or pebbles. Vegetables and fruit may have to take precedence over ornamentals, for they are unlikely to produce worthwhile crops unless they have a regular supply of moisture. Young plants of all kinds need more regular watering than those that are established. Planting in a slight depression means that the maximum amount of water gets to the roots and the minimum is lost through runoff. Although not without their disadvantages, low-level drip or trickle systems of irrigation in conjunction with timing devices

are generally considered the most efficient way of directing scarce water to the plants that need it most. As a general rule, watering little and often can be harmful and certainly less effective than less-frequent soaking that is long and slow.

PLANTS FOR DRY GARDENS

Desert gardens are a special case deserving their own discussion (see pp. 90–91). For less extreme conditions, the astonishing range of plants that are in varying degrees drought tolerant must be selected according to their hardiness. It has already been acknowledged that the choice of plants for dry shade is relatively limited (see p. 75), but the case is quite different where the site is open. Those who garden in the Mediterranean and roughly comparable climates such as parts of coastal California come off extremely well. Many plants of great ornamental value are native to these regions, and they translate easily from one geographical area to another. A surprising number of these adapt well to cool climates. Their greatest problems result from low temperatures combined with winter wet, compounded sometimes by insufficient sun and warmth in summer to ripen the tissues of woody plants and bulbs.

The pick of the trees, climbers, and large shrubs suitable for wall training—including acacias or wattles, bougainvilleas, coral trees (*Erythrina*), and the showiest of the eucalypts—need a mild climate to succeed. There are, however, reasonably hardy plants among the evergreens, including the strawberry tree (*Arbutus unedo*), California lilac (*Ceanothus*), other eucalypts, the almost leafless Mount Etna broom (*Genista aetnensis*), the holm oak (*Quercus ilex*), and numerous conifers. Among deciduous trees are the Judas tree (*Cercis siliquastrum*) and the oleaster (*Elaeagnus angustifolia*).

The gray and silver theme introduced by the oleaster can be extended with many shrubs and perennials. The felted or hairy foliage of artemisias, *Convolvulus cneorum*, lavenders (*Lavandula*), salvias, and santolinas, in some cases powerfully aromatic, is pleasing aesthetically and successfully reduces loss of moisture through the leaves. These gray- and silver-leaved plants look at home mixed with airy and tufted grasses, such as species of *Pennisetum* and *Stipa*, globe

Above Annuals, including pretty selections of the field poppy (*Papaver rhoeeas*) and love-in-a-mist (*Nigella damascena*), add an airy touch to beds planted with drought-tolerant perennials, bulbs, and shrubs, among which the candles of mulleins (*Verbascum*) are conspicuous. The planting and design is by Beth Chatto, one of the foremost British exponents of imaginative planting to suit the growing conditions.

Below The crown imperial (*Fritillaria imperialis*) looks at home with drought-tolerant plants, as here, and is reasonably tolerant of dry conditions. However, it grows most vigorously in moderately heavy soil.

Above The Canary Island date palm (*Phoenix canariensis*) is often planted as an ornamental where frosts are rare or non-existent, but its dates, although edible, do not have the succulence of the fruits of the date palm (*P. dactylifera*). Once established, the Canary Island date palm tolerates considerable drought.

Above right Yuccas and a flowering *Agave* are major plants in a French Mediterranean garden consisting almost entirely of rock. Agaves take many years to reach flowering maturity, but not the 100 years implied in the name "century plant" sometimes applied to *A. americana*.

Opposite top *Aeonium arboreum* is a succulent subshrub with leaf rosettes that have a flowerlike symmetry. In frost-prone areas it is best grown as a container plant so that it can be given protection during the winter.

Opposite center and bottom Small succulents, barrel and columnar cacti, and specimens of the Joshua tree (*Yucca brevifolia*) form part of an impressive collection of North American desert plants at the Huntington Botanic Garden, Pasadena, California. Although primarily botanical, it is an inspiration to those who garden in conditions of extreme drought.

thistles (*Echinops*), and sea hollies (*Eryngium*), as well as towering spires of mulleins (*Verbascum*). Ideas can be borrowed from the desert garden with the inclusion of impressive succulents such as the agaves.

Summer can be a colorful season with a generous use of annuals and long-flowering plants. There are few that can match pelargoniums, often treated as annuals but shrubby in character. Even in areas with a cool climate, easily overwintered under glass. It is not surprising that they have become such popular container plants, for they are remarkably tolerant of neglect, but more should be made of those with aromatic leaves. But summer in the dry garden never quite matches the blithe freshness of spring, echoed faintly in autumn, when bulbs detonate in a series of colorful explosions. Those of Mediterranean origin are supplemented by a rich selection from western North America, South Africa, and even Central Asia, where spring is a brief interlude between a cruelly cold winter and a parched summer.

DESERT GARDENS

The Koranic vision of the paradise garden, with running water and cool shade, presents an idealized contrast to the dusty rigors of a harsh desert landscape. The Islamic tradition of gardenmaking which elaborates this theme has had a profound influence in arid regions. It presupposes, however, a plentiful supply of water with which to create fountains and pools and to irrigate ground for ornamental flowers and fruit. Another landscape approach is represented by the work of the great American architect Frank Lloyd Wright, whose own house and studio at Taliesen West was designed to harmonize with the austere beauty of the desert. Xeriscaping, to use the fashionable term, has taken off, and gardenmaking or landscaping in arid regions increasingly rejects the oasis effect in favor of open, rocky surfaces with carefully grouped specimens of true desert plants.

As in the ungardened desert a stone's throw away, plants in desert gardens have to keep a decent distance from one another if they are to find enough water to survive. Plants are spread out horizontally, not arranged in integrated layers as they are in temperate regions. Trees are rare. The few that tolerate low, irregular rainfall and might be considered include several Australian desert gums (*Eucalyptus* species) and the spiny deciduous mesquite (*Prosopis* species) of North and South America. The honey mesquite (*P. glandulosa*) has weeping branches and bright green leaves, but most of this genus must be treated with caution, for they can be aggressive weeds.

The supremely successful plants of desert conditions are, however, the succulents. A bald statement of the principal way they survive long periods of drought, by storing water in the fleshy tissues of leaves, stems, and the base of stems, is an inadequate preparation for their variety of scale and sculptural form. To achieve their stark beauty, they must have sharp drainage. They quickly succumb in the misery of a cold, wet climate, but a few are surprisingly hardy and most will tolerate a few degrees of frost, as they do in the cold nights of the desert, provided their growing conditions are dry.

Of all plant families, the cacti from the Americas have most whole-heartedly embraced succulence as a way of life, jettisoning leaves and carrying out photosynthesis through the skin of their swollen stems. Their range includes the treelike saguaro cactus (*Carnegiea gigantea*), up to 60ft (18m) high with columnar stems that are often branched, its gaunt presence lending authenticity to countless old western films. The cylindrical shapes of other cacti, single or in familylike huddles, are equally familiar. The vertical ribbing and clusters of spines that ensure that part of the barrel cactus (*Ferocactus cylindraceus*) is always in shade make a characteristic pattern in the desert garden. A shaggy coat of hairs, another self-shading device, gives several cacti a highly distinctive appearance. This feature has earned *Cephalocereus senilis*, a columnar Mexican species up to 40ft (12m) high, the common name old man cactus. Among the most widespread of all cacti in cultivation are the prickly pears and chollas (*Opuntia* species). Their almost 2-dimensional oval extensions root with great ease when they fall, accounting for their dismaying proliferation in many desert landscapes. Their cultivation is prohibited in Australia, where their outrageous success in covering miles of desert was checked only by the introduction of a biological control. Where they can be grown, they make interesting contrasts of scale and form, and *O. macrocentra* is unusual for the violet-gray coloring of its pads. Their remarkable durability in harsh conditions is undoubtedly the principal reason for growing the very varied members of the cactus family, but their flowers, sadly short-lived, are of such sheeny magnificence that it is worth much patient waiting to see them in their sumptuous fullness.

Other treelike giants that seem to mirror cactus forms include several spurges, the grandest, *Euphorbia candelabrum*, found wild from Somalia to South Africa, growing to 50ft (15m) or more. Just as important in the desert garden, where contrasts of scale, form, and texture count for so much, are the numerous succulents with fleshy leaves. The rosettes in the Mexican *Agave americana* are on a monumental scale and strikingly handsome in the plain-leaved and variegated forms. One of the most important groups of African succulents are the aloes, the pokerlike spikes of flowers being a distinctive feature of many, including the treelike *Aloe ferox*. Many succulents have leaf rosettes of almost flowerlike quality. Those of one of the hardiest aloes, *A. aristata*, are speckled with soft white spines; *Aeonium* 'Zwartkop' has burnished purple leaves arranged like the petals of a sinister bloom. Spiky leaves, such as those of the Joshua tree (*Yucca brevifolia*), introduce a very different graphic quality, as do the strange tufts of the Australian grass trees (*Xanthorrhoea* species). Like many plants that survive in arid conditions, these are for the patient gardener, the clump of narrow grassy leaves rising on a trunk made up of old leaf bases gummed together with resin and erratically producing spears of creamy flowers, in the wild commonly after bush fires.

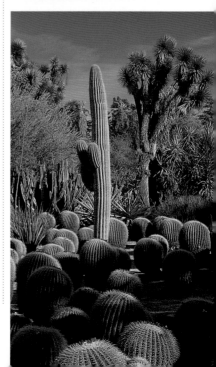

PLACES FOR ROCK PLANTS

Despite the windswept harshness of the environment above the tree-line, often blanketed in snow for months of the year, the alpine zone is astonishingly rich in plants of refined beauty. The plants of high rocky crevices and the screes beneath them, composed of rock shattered by a constant cycle of freezing and thawing, first entered gardens on a large scale in the 19th century. Sometimes they were a mere adjunct of grandiose although miniaturized alpine scenery. The ridiculed excesses of the 19th century have been swept away, but the manmade rock garden, which attempts to convey a natural geological formation, continues to be used as a setting for these small plants. The emphasis has shifted to providing the free-draining growing conditions that most of them need and a range of settings—small pockets, crevices, vertical cracks, overhangs, and slopes of rocky debris—that allow alpines to be grown in a natural way. These plants have been augmented by numerous small shrubs and perennials from lower altitudes, usually from harsh rocky environments, which also need to be grown in open free-draining conditions. All of these compact or trailing perennials and small shrubs, and sometimes, too, the dwarf bulbs that go so well with them, are commonly bundled together in the term "rock plants."

Left Where alpines and rock garden plants are to be grown on relatively flat sites, initial preparation of the ground must ensure good drainage.

Right *Geranium dalmaticum* clambers over the dark and densely clustered rosettes of a houseleek (*Sempervivum*).

Below Rock can be used to create terraces to be planted generously with low-growing campanulas, geraniums, and the like.

Bottom A ferny tuft of pasque flowers (*Pulsatilla*) is set against the rock rose *Helianthemum* 'Wisley Primrose'.

Far left A low dry-stone wall can be planted at various levels with houseleeks (*Sempervivum*), pinks (*Dianthus*), sisyrinchium, and thymes (*Thymus*).

For many gardeners, the true alpines are the elite among the rock plants. Not all of these plants adapt well to outdoor conditions in lowland gardens. The snow that covers them for months of the year in mountainous country is a surprisingly protective mantle, keeping them dry and ensuring a relatively stable temperature, without sudden highs that might start plants into premature growth. When the snows melt and the short growing season begins, there is plenty of moisture, but it is constantly on the move and well oxygenated, draining quickly through a soil that is low in nutrients and organic matter. In lowland areas, where the atmosphere is sluggish and the winters wet rather than snowy, with temperatures fluctuating from well below freezing to springlike highs, they are like uprooted sherpas, pining for the clear air of the Himalayas. The alpine house in which they are sometimes grown is in effect an unheated but well-ventilated greenhouse where the conditions are never allowed to become soggy. The plants are usually potted individually, with the pots sometimes sunk in a bed of sand.

The rock garden still has its adherents, but the recognition that rock plants, including the less-temperamental alpines, do not have to be associated with the imitation of a geological form is a substantial advance. Raised beds are much more flexible components of gardens, especially those that are small, and allow a very wide range of plants to be grown in conditions that can be tailored to their needs. Although they may not have the cachet of the true alpines, many robust rock plants have the great virtue of adaptability and can be fitted into many positions in the garden where there is good drainage.

ROCK GARDENS AND SCREE BEDS
The conventional rock garden is usually designed as a stratified outcrop and is commonly combined with a pool or flowing water. The advice generally given is to use local rather than imported rock and large rather than small pieces. Choice, however, is often limited, partly the consequence of measures to conserve natural rock landscapes that have already been heavily exploited. The most popular readily available materials are various stratified sandstones, which absorb moisture and are relatively cool in summer. Weathered limestones are sometimes available secondhand. The scale of a rock garden may well be determined by the high cost of the rock and its transportation. It is a good idea from the outset to consider if there are better ways to provide the growing conditions that rock plants need. A meager modern rock garden can be as absurd in its way as the rock follies of the 19th century.

93

The position for a rock garden should be open and sheltered, with unimpeded drainage, and preferably sloping to catch the sun. In constructing a rock garden, the aim should be to establish a free-draining base of coarse rubble and to set the rock pieces tipped back so that they are at least half covered by soil, with the strata forming more or less continuous lines. A suitable soil consists of equal parts of garden loam, grit, and, peat substitute. A rock garden can be partly planted during construction but the final planting should be left until the soil has settled. A topping of stone chippings is an attractive finish and is a weed-suppressing mulch that keeps the soil cool and moist.

A scree bed made of very free-draining material can be formed as an integral part of a rock garden but is also an alternative, as it requires less rock and is more easily adapted to a small space. The essential requirement is a foundation of rubble or graded rock providing perfect drainage, over which is laid soil having the same constituents as for a rock garden but with the quantity of grit doubled or tripled, then topped with a layer of stone chippings or coarse gravel. Provided there is a good supply of freely moving water beneath the apparently dry surface layer of stones, this provides ideal conditions for carpeting and cushion plants such as *Dianthus alpinus* and several other pinks.

RAISED BEDS AND DRY STONE WALLS

Raised beds are particularly suitable for difficult sites where the soil is heavy and slow-draining. The raised level of the beds has the advantage of making gardening possible even from a wheelchair. A wide range of materials can be used, including mortared brick, unmortared stone, sawn logs, and railroad ties. A more or less flat surface, suitable for bulbs as well as low perennials and shrubs, and dry (that is, unmortared) stone walls is a winning combination. The crevices in the walls, sunny and shaded, according to the bed's orientation, provide planting sites and a cool root run for trailing plants, such as many of the campanulas, and niches well suited to plants that resent moisture around the crown. The individual stones, usually 4–8in (10-20cm) thick, need to be set so that they slope back gently to ensure stability and good drainage. The maximum height should be 30in (75cm); higher walls may need to be

Above left Logs leaning into a bank form an unusual retaining wall that is not without drawbacks. The weathered grey of the wood shows off the plants climbing from the top.

Above Tulipa saxatilis and the grape hyacinth (*Muscari armeniacum*) grow freely in a garden that has levels defined by large lumps of chalk.

Opposite top A highly finished dry-stone wall has openings at the base so that excess water behind the wall can drain off easily. Although the stones are closely set, there is still space for a few rock garden plants. There is additional space for planting along the top.

Opposite center Low-growing geraniums and rock roses (*Helianthemum*) are the sort of rock garden plants that are suitable for frontal positions in borders.

Opposite bottom Rock garden plants, including the vigorously spreading *Campanula portenschlagiana*, play an important role in this garden, which has freestanding retaining walls.

reinforced. The same soil mixture can be used as for rock gardens, modified if necessary to suit the special requirements of selected plants, and topped with stone chippings.

On a sloping site, retaining walls for terracing can be constructed in much the same way as the walls of raised beds and planted with equally pleasing mixtures of trailing and rosette-forming plants. It is important to get professional advice before constructing retaining walls on a steep site, where the strength of the wall must match the potential pressures of water and soil.

Small collections of rock plants can be gathered together in containers, in effect miniature raised beds. Stone sinks and troughs are very appealing visually, but they are difficult to obtain and expensive. Furthermore, they tend to be shallow, so that plants do not have a cool root run. To some extent this can be overcome by positioning rocks on the surface and using a dressing of stone chippings or gravel. Tufa is often used with them. This form of water-deposited lime is soft and porous. Small plants can be established directly in drilled holes that are topped up with soil once the plant has been inserted. The surprising thing is that plants that usually dislike lime, as well as those that are lime lovers, will extend their roots into the tufa and grow happily.

Troughs made of hypertufa, a mixture of concrete and peat or peat substitute, and glazed sinks with a hypertufa coating simulate stone containers reasonably well once they have weathered. Terracotta containers stand in their own right and are much less trouble. Whatever the material of the container, good drainage is essential. Because of their weight when filled, position containers while still empty, setting them in an open position raised on bricks or similar supports to ensure that water can get away. Drainage holes should be covered with broken crocks or wire gauze and the bottom 2–3in (5–8cm) filled with gravel, stone chippings, or other fast-draining material before the compost is added. A suitable mixture consists of equal parts of a soil-based potting medium, peat substitute, and coarse grit.

FREE-RANGE ROCK PLANTS

The toughest of the rock plants are suitable for planting in cracks or larger gaps between paving in paths and other areas of hard surface, sometimes merging with other low plants in front positions in borders. The combination of very free-draining conditions and cool, moist areas under paving slabs provides a good balance. It is important that the planting cover should not be overdone, partly because many plants will not stand the wear and tear but partly because firm, clean areas are needed for access and often, too, for placing tables and chairs. It is sometimes recommended that gaps should be left in paving to make planting easier, but even at the edges of a path or paved area they can present an ankle-cracking hazard. Tough, low plants such as the aromatic thymes are the most suitable plants for general use in paving, but in out-of-the-way corners it is worth introducing contrasting shapes, including the uprights of spring bulbs, summer-flowering sisyrinchiums, and, particularly good in shade, large-leaved bergenias. The planting can extend from paving on the flat to steps. The free-draining conditions suit many plants to perfection and, running along in cracks between treads and risers, they have the effect of bedding the steps in the planting.

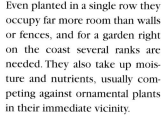

Above The hybrid pelargoniums, often thought of as a Mediterranean speciality, are mainly drived from South American species. They do extraordinarily well in sunny coastal areas, either in mountains or in the open garden, and flower for many months.

Below The Isles of Scilly, off the southwest tip of Britain, are windswept, but the careful planting of shelter belts around the gardens of Tresco Abbey has created an environment in which many plants of the world thrive.

GARDENS NEAR THE SEA

At its bright and sunny best, the seaside seems a perfect place for relaxed gardening. Coastal conditions do, however, present real challenges. The great tyrant in seaside gardens is wind, not just a pleasant on-shore breeze but roaring gales, which come laden with salt picked up over miles of open water and, from the shoreline, an abrasive mixture of small pebbles and sand. Wind breaks brittle stems and branches, drags moisture out of the ground and from leaves, and damages young shoots and tender foliage. Salt drift scorches plants, and when washed into the ground creates difficult growing conditions. The soil is likely to present additional problems. There is a good chance of it being sandy, holding water only briefly, and being leached of nutrients. Even more difficult is pure rock with a negligible layer of soil except for shallow accumulations in small pockets.

Happily, there are plants wellsuited to these conditions. There are, also, advantages in gardening near the sea. The proximity of a vast body of water has a moderating influence on temperature, seaside gardens often escaping the worst effects of frost. Warm currents have a benign effect, as can be seen in some of the remarkable coastal gardens of western Scotland that benefit from the Gulf Stream.

CREATING SHELTER

Buildings and people as well as plants benefit if the seaside garden can be sheltered from prevailing winds. Walls and fences are not the ideal way of creating a calmer microclimate, for on the leeward side of these solid defenses there are wild and damaging downdrafts and eddies. Shelter belts and hedges are much more effective baffles, filtering wind and sapping it of its force without creating turbulence. The plants used for these living screens must themselves be tolerant of the growing conditions. The range is surprisingly extensive, including numerous conifers and tough and sinewy broad-leaved trees and shrubs. Until a living barrier becomes established, a temporary windshield, such as brushwood or openwork fencing, will almost certainly be necessary. Trees and shrubs used as shelter belts or hedging are space-consuming. Even planted in a single row they occupy far more room than walls or fences, and for a garden right on the coast several ranks are needed. They also take up moisture and nutrients, usually competing against ornamental plants in their immediate vicinity.

IMPROVING THE SOIL AND MULCHING

Sandy soils warm up quickly in spring and provide conditions in which many annuals germinate freely, but they are less successful at sustaining mature and long-lived plants. It is naive to hope that sandy soils can be totally transformed. Nonetheless, it is worth taking trouble to improve them, giving plants more leeway during dry weather and broadening the range of ornamentals that can be grown. Organic matter can be used as a mulch, but other materials are gravel or pebbles. These stone mulches are not a

source of nutrients for the soil as organic mulches are, but they are highly effective at keeping the ground cool and moist. Where a garden is being created on almost bare rocky ground, the addition of brought-in topsoil makes feasible the establishment of key plants. Without major importations, the ground will probably have to remain sparsely planted.

THE STRENGTHS OF SEASIDE GARDENS

Those that are new to seaside gardening often feel that they are getting a raw deal when they recognize the large number of familiar ornamentals that cannot be grown successfully in their robust conditions. And it is true that only heartbreak can follow if gardeners near the sea persist with plants that are of brittle character, that have lush and delicate foliage, or that are highly bred and carry large flowers on tall, upright stems. Once reconciled to their lot, however, seaside gardeners will discover that there is ample material with which to create planted havens of great character.

Where space is adequate, there is a choice of distinctive trees, predominantly evergreen with leathery leaves, such as the holm oak (*Quercus ilex*) and strawberry trees (*Arbutus*). There is hardly a more distinctive tree of the Mediterranean than the wide-crowned umbrella pine (*Pinus pinea*). The Canary Island palm (*Phoenix canariensis*) and other highly ornamental members of this group are also a feature of Mediterranean and similarly favored gardens.

The tough shrubs and perennials that relish the full glare of seaside light provide a pleasing mixture of compact rounded shapes and jagged outlines. Much of their ornamental value derives specifically from characteristics that allow them to survive the onslaught of salty desiccating winds. Some, like sea thrift (*Armeria maritima*), form low clumps of narrow leaves. Others, like seakale (*Crambe maritima*), have handsome foliage protected by a waxy coating. Many have leathery or glossy leaves (*Phormium tenax* and *Griselinia littoralis*). Even more are gray with a covering of fine hairs (*Santolina chamaecyparissus*). And some, such as the aloes, are spectacular succulents.

In the most successful seaside gardens, such distinctive plants combined with sun roses (*Cistus*), brooms (*Cytisus* and *Genista*), and other free-flowering shrubs form close associations that defy the wind. When these are given a skirt of California poppies (*Eschscholzia californica*) and other bright annuals, or even tender shrubs such as pelargoniums (which in favored coastal areas can be left in the open garden year-round), the garden acquires dazzling color.

Above Evergreen shrubs and small trees in a French Mediterranean garden give an impression of the maquis. Some have been simply shaped, almost, it seems, as though they were browsed by goats.

Below An impressive example of planting in coastal conditions is provided by the famous Scottish garden in Inverewe, where the first attempts at making a garden on a bare rocky site at the edge of the sea loch began in the 1860s. The warming influence of the Gulf Stream allows a very wide range of plants to be grown.

Tropical and Subtropical Gardens

Mention of tropical gardens summons up an image of a seasonless hot and steamy environment in which dense foliage and a profusion of brightly colored and bizarrely shaped flowers provide an endless display. Not surprisingly, this stereotype is misleading. The broad equatorial belt bounded by the tropics of Cancer and Capricorn, covering about 40 per cent of the earth's surface, includes areas that are enormously varied in their natural vegetation, reflecting considerable differences in climate, geography, geology, and altitude. In many areas there are more or less dramatic alternations of wet and dry seasons, and in some regions the rainfall is so low that semidesert or desert conditions prevail. Gardens in the subtropical zone, extending to about the 35th parallel north and south, and taking in places with an equable climate such as Madeira, have their tropical character diluted by a high proportion of temperate plants.

The Character of Tropical and Subtropical Gardens

Tropical and subtropical gardening does not represent a style, but reflects a choice of plants for particular conditions. Nevertheless, the way plants are used does draw on old traditions of palace and temple landscaping, especially in parts of Southeast Asia; sometimes shows the strong influence of traditional European gardens, this a legacy of colonial rule, and is increasingly dominated by modern trends in town planning and design, as can be seen in the gardens of many large international hotels. From a very early stage, plants were brought together from many parts of the world, points at the intersections of sea routes (such as Tenerife in the Canaries), acting as botanical entrepôts. Selection of plants on the basis of their economic and ornamental value has almost invariably been at the expense of native species.

Shade trees are an important feature of almost all tropical gardens, creating places of refreshing retreat, supports for epiphytes and climbers, and providing, too, an environment that suits shade-tolerant plants that grow at ground level. Among the most impressive of the shade trees are species of fig (*Ficus*), some making vast buttressed

Above In the tropics, as in the temperate world, plants of different origins but similar requirements are brought together in an imaginative way to make successful gardens.

Below The cycas—including species of genera such as *Cycas*, *Dioon* and *Encephalartos*—have proved successful survivors of a distant geological past. Some are of economic importance, the stems being used to make sago, and the seeds, although toxic, being treated to make a flour.

Below left In the intensity of their foliage color, some cultivars of *Cordyline fruticosa* are the equal of many tropical flowers. The flowers of *Anthurium* clearly show that they belong to the arum family.

structures dangling curtains of aerial roots. The prominence of flowering trees is perhaps even more striking. Those from regions with a high and evenly distributed rainfall are evergreen, and in many cases flower spasmodically throughout the year. One of the most handsome of these is the African tulip tree (*Spathodea campanulata*), a native of tropical West Africa. Leaf loss often makes trees that are geared to an alternation of dry and wet seasons particularly conspicuous. The jacarandas of tropical America—the best known, *Jacaranda mimosifolia*, being much used as a street tree—drop their leaves during the dry period and produce their clouds of violet-blue flowers shortly before the new leaves emerge. The same pattern can be seen in the flamboyant or flame tree (*Delonix regia*) from Madagascar, valued for its light shade and the brilliance of its flowers massed in a broad umbrella-like dome.

There are shrubs and climbers that, like some of the trees, follow a clear seasonal cycle. Frangipani (*Plumeria alba*), a plant native to the West Indies, loses its leaves at the beginning of the dry season, the richly fragrant flowers being borne on a stark and almost leafless shrub. The success of bougainvilleas in Mediterranean climates is an indication of their tolerance of dry periods. It is a common practice in the tropics to withhold water from these climbers as a way of bringing them into flower. There are, of course, many other shrubs and climbers where there seems to be no conventional seasonal rhythm. Common shrubs such as the Chinese hibiscus (*Hibiscus rosa-sinensis*), from tropical Asia, and flame of the woods (*Ixora coccinea*), from India and Sri Lanka, are in flower for much of the year. The vigor of the numerous climbers expresses the surging energy of the tropical garden. There is hardly a pause in the flowering of some, like the blue trumpet vine (*Thunbergia grandiflora*) from northern India.

The palms that are such a distinctive feature of tropical and subtropical gardens come from widely separated geographical regions and demonstrate a considerable range in growing requirements and tolerances. A large number thrive in open positions in full sun. Of these, one of the most remarkable is the coconut palm (*Cocos nucifera*). As might be guessed from the tropical holiday brochures, it is tolerant of salt-laden winds. Others include the drought-tolerant Canary Island date palm (*Phoenix canariensis*), one of the most widely planted palms in subtropical regions. In contrast to these, the royal palm (*Roystonea regia*), a magnificent Cuban species much planted as an avenue tree, thrives in moist soil. So, too, does the fish-tail palm (*Caryota mitis*), an unusual species from Southeast Asia that in the wild is part of the forest understory and does best in partial shade. The contrasts in requirements extend to several palmlike trees. The traveller's tree of

Right top Shade has a special importance in tropical and subtropical gardens, as do plants such as ferns that grow in it.

Right center Crotons (*Codiaeum*) have insignificant flowers but, due to their startling foliage, they are among the most widely planted tropical perennials.

Right bottom The flowers that have given angel's trumpets (*Brugmansia*) their fanciful common name are often highly fragrant. The species from which the hybrids are derived are mainly from tropical South America, as is the climber golden shower (*Pyrostegia venusta*).

Above The most important bromeliad economically is the pineapple (*Ananas comosus*), and the bromeliad with the widest natural distribution is Spanish moss (*Tillandsia usneoides*). In this large and varied family, with a distribution almost entirely confined to the New World, many of the mainly epiphytic species and their hybrids are distinctive ornamentals, often, for their foliage as well as their flowers. There is a sinister side to the water tank formed in the leaf bases of many that live in the dry tropics. Malaria-carrying mosquitos can use these small bodies of water to breed.

Below The terrestrial orchid *Phaius tankervilleae*, an early species to be cultivated under glass in the West, is widely distributed in lowland and lower montane forest from Sri Lanka to China. It is difficult to think of orchids as weeds, but in Australia and tropical conditions this species spreads almost too freely, and it is naturalized in Florida.

Below right The tropical water lilies fall into two main categories according to the time of day the flowers are open. Some bloom from sundown to mid-morning, others from mid-morning to early evening. Most have highly fragrant flowers.

Madagascar (*Ravenala madagascariensis*), with its symmetrical fan of banana-like leaves (it is a banana relative), is a plant for full sun in areas of high rainfall. The cycads or fern palms—neither ferns nor palms but an ancient group lying somewhere between conifers and true flowering plants—are, in the wild, mainly plants of open, dry woodland or semidesert.

The epiphytic dimension of humid tropical gardens is on a scale far beyond anything imaginable in the temperate garden, the piled and cascading foliage and flowers creating an impression of fullness and luxuriance. The most numerous of the flowering epiphytes are orchids (see below), but other important groups include waxy, flowered anthuriums, rosette-forming bromeliads (species of *Aechmea* and *Guzmania,* for example) and epiphytic climbers such as the Swiss cheese plant (*Monstera deliciosa*). Competing with them for space are numerous ferns, including large species such as the staghorn fern (*Platycerium grande*), the fronds of which form massive bracts.

Foliage often counts for as much as flowers in the low shrubs and perennials that make up the floor of the tropical garden. Plants for shade in the humid tropics include caladiums and dieffenbachias, both widely grown as houseplants, species of *Spathiphyllum*, which tolerate deep shade, and various gingers, among them species of *Alpinia*. Foliage plants for more open positions include the vividly colored cordylines and crotons (*Codiaeum*), almost a match in their coloring for the extraordinary heliconias, plants producing zigzag arrangements of brightly colored boatlike bracts that cradle the flowers. Luxuriant growth is inevitably a problem in water gardens. Isolation is sometimes the best course, appropriately so in the case of the sacred lotus (*Nelumbo nucifera*), worthy of veneration for its beauty alone.

ORCHIDS

Even in the context of the tropical garden, with its bewildering variety of plant form and flower color, orchids stand out as an exceptionally diverse family. It is one of the largest among flowering plants, with a total of about 20,000 species. Far from all of these species are tropical or subtropical. Orchids are found in almost every geographical region except for Antarctica and a few isolated islands and in all but the most extreme environments. About half are terrestrial, growing in soil, from

which the roots extract nutrients. The other half, all tropical or subtropical, are epiphytes, not parasitic but perching on other plants or rocks. Although there are many terrestrial orchids in tropical and subtropical regions, it is the epiphytes and lithophytes (to use the correct term for those that grow on rocks), with their curiously coarse and tangled aerial roots, that are the most conspicuous. The green root tips absorb moisture and nutrients, while the active tissues within are protected by a grayish layer of dead cells.

There are many intriguing characteristics of orchids. A large number of those growing in the tropics and subtropics are surprisingly well equipped for extreme conditions. The leaves are very varied but in many cases are strap shaped and leathery. The pseudobulbs possessed by most tropical terrestrial and epiphytic species are swollen stems that store water and nutrients. The tissues in these as well as in other parts of the plants apart from the leaves are actively involved in photosynthesis. The seeds of orchids are minute but usually produced in prodigious quantities. Successful germination depends on a mycorrhizal association of orchid and fungus, a symbiotic relationship that appears to continue throughout the life of an orchid. Inevitably, however, it is the flowers of orchids that grab attention.

The variety of their form and color is so extraordinary that it is difficult to take in the essential structure that most share. This consists of a whorl of 3 sepals and an inner whorl of 3 petals that surrounds the sexual organs, united to form a single structure, the column. The confusing and fascinating feature of these flowers is that while the 2 lateral petals are often similar to the sepals, the dorsal petal has a character all its own. The lip or labellum, as this petal is known, is usually much larger than the other segments and of highly distinctive shape and sometimes color and texture. The apparently fantastic and whimsical character of the flowers is, of course, deceptive. Their business is to ensure pollination. The spectacular variety that has made tropical orchids so attractive to collectors and growers is an indication of the highly specific relationship between an individual species and its pollinator. "Various contrivances," as Charles Darwin called them, ensure a precise match between flower and pollinating agent, be it insect, hummingbird, bat, or even frog.

In his study of orchids Darwin demonstrated that the flowers were structured to ensure cross-pollination. Even in the wild, hybrids sometimes occur; orchids have more naturally occurring hybrids than any other plant family. Since the first artificially produced orchid hybrid was flowered in 1856 numerous deliberate crosses have been made, resulting in tens of thousands of different hybrids. The ease with which many orchids hybridize even extends to crosses between different genera. Plants have been bred combining as many as 20 species and 5 genera. The promiscuity of these plants is the basis of a major orchid growing and breeding industry, with its center in the USA but with other countries, including Germany, Malaysia, Singapore, and Thailand, playing an active part.

Far from all the tropical and subtropical species and their hybrids can be grown in the same conditions. They have different temperature, light, and humidity requirements, as might be expected when the species are found in so many different habitats, from equatorial lowland to mountainous, mist-shrouded jungle north of the tropic of Cancer and south of the tropic of Capricorn. Their sheer numbers mean, however, that in most tropical and subtropical regions where the climate is reasonably humid a large selection can be grown outdoors, just as in temperate regions there are numerous orchids for cool, medium, and warm greenhouses.

Above left While trees in the tropical garden can be ornamental they also provide essential shade and support galleries of epiphytic plants, including orchids. The largest orchid genus is *Dendrobium*. Numerous hybrids such as those grown here adding to a species total of 900 to 1,400, most of them epiphytic.

Above and below The Singapore Botanic Gardens, on the present site since 1859, played a key role in the development of the Malayan rubber industry. In the 20th century the gardens became less concerned with economic botany, but initiatives in orchid breeding in the 1920s led to several southeast Asian countries playing an active role in the modern orchid business. A major orchid garden, displaying orchids among other tropical plants, offers a wealth of ideas for ambitious gardeners.

A–Z DIRECTORY

Using the Directory

The "A-Z Directory" is divided into nine plant categories: Trees; Shrubs; Conifers; Climbers; Roses; Perennials; Bulbs, Corms, and Tubers; Annuals and Biennials; Bamboos, Grasses, Grasslike Plants, and Ferns.

In every category, there is an introduction to each genus describing its main qualities. Each introduction is accompanied by concise information on Cultivation; Propagation; Potential Problems; and a Warning for any plant that can be dangerous. This is followed by a selection of plant entries organized alphabetically according to their internationally accepted botanical name.

A plant entry might be a species, a hybrid or group of hybrids, a variant, or a cultivar, although these also appear within other entries. Some more complicated genera are further subdivided into species and hybrids. In addition to a brief description, information is given on a plant's natural origins; height and spread; best time of interest for flowers, foliage, and fruits/berries/ hips; and zones. Brief descriptions of other plants that are relevant in some way may appear within a genus introduction or a plant entry.

Genera that appear in more than one category, such as *Acer*, which appears both in "Trees" and "Shrubs," are cross-referenced within the Directory. However, botanical and common names and synonyms are cross-referenced in the Plant Index (pp. 342-351).

Family name
This is the botanical family (group of related genera) to which the genus belongs.

Genus introduction
This is a general description of the genus and gives the number of species, some indication of preferred conditions and natural habitat, and sometimes advice on how the plants can be used in the garden.

Additional plants
A plant that has not been given its own entry is often described within the genus introduction. In the same way, additional plants are sometimes described under the main plant entry when they have similar characteristics as the entry. In both cases, the plant is in bold.

Propagation
Only the main methods of propagation are given, with the most likely appearing first followed by any other methods. The season for each method is also given.

Potential Problems
This lists the most common pests to which a plant is susceptible followed by the most common diseases. These are given in order of susceptibility. "Usually none" is used to describe genera that are not really susceptible to any problems.

Warning
This states whether any part of a plant may cause sickness or stomach upset if swallowed, or skin irritations or allergies if touched.

Main plant entry
This gives the current botanical name of the plant in bold. Occasionally, there is one entry for a group of hybrids. For example, **H. hybrids** is used to denote *Hemerocallis* hybrids in "Perennials."

Flowers; Foliage; Fruits; Berries; Hips
Where appropriate, these headings indicate when a plant has interesting, attractive foliage; the period when it flowers; and when any fruits or berries appear. An evergreen plant is denoted by "year-round."

Height and spread
This gives a range of heights and spreads to show the difference in growth rates that gardeners may experience, depending on location and conditions. If the height and the spread are the same, then only one measurement is given. There is no spread given for "Climbers" or for climbing or rambling roses in "Roses." Standard measurements always precede metric measurements.

Variants and cultivars
The descriptions of cultivars, forma, subspecies, and varieties appear within the main plant entry. Heights and spreads are only included if they differ from those of the main plant entry.

RUTA

RUTACEAE Rue

The best-known species in this small genus of 8 aromatic shrubs and subshrubs has long been cultivated for its supposed medicinal properties. In the wild it is found in sunny stony places. Fringed rue (*R. chalepensis*), which is a subshrub, also has blue-green aromatic leaves.

CULTIVATION Require full sun or partial shade and well-drained soil. Cut back old stems to fresh growth.

PROPAGATION From seed, sown in spring. From semiripe cuttings, in mid-summer.

POTENTIAL PROBLEMS Phytophthora root rot.

WARNING Swallowing will cause severe stomach discomfort; photodermatitis occurs with foliage contact.

Ruta graveolens 'Jackman's Blue'

R. graveolens S.E. Europe
Common rue
Flowers: mid- to late summer.
Foliage: year-round. H: 2–3ft (60–90cm), S: 24–30in (60–75cm). Z: 5–9.
The pungently aromatic blue-green leaves make a low bush bearing greenish-yellow flowers in summer. The form usually seen in gardens is 'Jackman's Blue', with very dense and glaucous foliage.

Genus name
This gives the botanical name for a group of related species.

Common name or names
These apply to the whole genus and are not intended to be exhaustive. Where a genus is monotypic (there is only one species in the whole genus), any common name appears with the genus heading rather than the main entry heading.

Cultivation
This section gives the aspect (level of sun or shade) that the plants described in the selection either require or tolerate, followed by the type of soil in which they should be grown. Reference to acidity or alkalinity is only made if a plant definitely requires those conditions. If one particular plant in a genus requires slightly different growing conditions to the norm, this is also described here. The planting-out time is given only for "Bulbs, Corms, and Tubers"; the planting times for the other categories are given in each category introduction. Where appropriate, there is also advice on pruning for "Shrubs," "Climbers," and "Roses" (for each different category of rose). A brief reference to the pruning for "Trees" and "Conifers" is made in the introductions to these categories.

Caption
A full botanical name is given with each photograph.

Country or countries of origin
The geographical origins of the plant are given in alphabetical order. If no origin is given, then the plant is of garden origin. This means that it has been cultivated and does not occur naturally in the wild.

Common name or names
This gives the common name or names for the main plant entry.

Zones
Zones are based on the average annual minimum temperature for each zone; the smaller number indicates the northernmost zone it can survive in and the higher number the southernmost zone the plant will tolerate. See the endpapers for details of zones and a zone map.

Z   Zone

An   Annual

Bi   Biennial

trees

A tree is a woody perennial plant, growing from a single stem or from several stems. The growth rates and habits of trees are modified to a great extent by factors such as pruning or climatic conditions. The leaves of deciduous trees provide shade in summer, while their bare branches present an intricate tracery in winter. At other times of the year, flowers, fruit, and colorful leaves may ornament the branches. Evergreen trees are a constant backdrop in the garden, giving year-round privacy and color.

Trees give a sense of permanence and maturity in a garden, providing height, depth, and a framework for even the simplest garden design. Interest in trees has increased steadily since the first exotic species were introduced in the 19th century. Today, the number of cultivars are legion and are added to all the time as new forms of existing trees are noticed, selected, and become available, or new cultivars are bred. Trees grown in containers are available for transplanting throughout the year. Root-balled trees should be planted in autumn or spring and bare-rooted trees in autumn.

Most young trees benefit from pruning to train them to grow in a desired way. As they grow, pruning is necessary to remove dead, damaged, or diseased wood, and to balance growth where plants compete for space.

Top *Ilex* × *altaclerensis* 'Belgica Aurea'
Center *Cordyline australis* 'Variegata'
Bottom *Cornus controversa* 'Variegata'

ACER

ACERACEAE Maple

The maples are an important genus
of ornamental trees and shrubs,
with about 150 evergreen and
deciduous species found in the
temperate Northern Hemisphere.
A few maples are canopy trees of
woodland, but the majority are
plants of the understory. Several
species have interesting and
attractive flowers and winged
fruits, and a number have
handsomely patterned bark, but it
is the lobed leaves, often coloring
brilliantly in autumn, that make the
maples so outstandingly beautiful.
See also SHRUBS.
CULTIVATION Tolerate sun or partial
shade and fertile, moist, well-
drained soil.
PROPAGATION From seed, sown as
soon as ripe; plants raised this way
are variable. By grafting, in late
winter or budding in summer
(cultivars).
POTENTIAL PROBLEMS Aphids, scale,
borers, caterpillars; leaf scorch,
anthracnose, other fungal diseases.

A. griseum *C. China*
Paper-bark maple
Foliage: autumn. Flowers: spring.
H and S:20–30ft (6–9m). Z:5–8.
For the quality of its deciduous
foliage alone, this is an outstanding
small tree. The dark green leaves,
divided into 3 leaflets, are dark
green with blue-green undersides
during the summer months, and
turn scarlet in autumn. The buff-
colored bark, peeling to reveal
orange-brown layers beneath, is
intriguing at all seasons.

Acer negundo 'Variegatum'

A. negundo *North America*
Ash-leaved maple, box elder
Foliage: spring to autumn. Flowers:
spring. H:40–50ft (12–15m),
S:20–30ft (6–9m). Z:3–9.
The bright green leaves of this

deciduous maple turn clear golden
yellow in autumn. In spring, bright
golden yellow flowers grow in
broad flat clusters before the
leaves emerge. 'Flamingo' has
pink-edged leaves that turn white
in summer, while 'Variegatum'
(Z:5–8) has pink shoot tips in
spring and medium green leaves
marbled with creamy flecks.

Acer pensylvanicum

A. pensylvanicum *E. North
America*
Moosewood, striped maple
Foliage: autumn. Flowers: spring.
H:40ft (12m), S:30ft (9m). Z:4–7.
An especially striking maple by
virtue of its green-and-white-striped
bark and green leaves which turn
yellow in autumn. The greenish
yellow flower panicles are also an
attractive feature. Other species
with conspicuously striped bark
and good autumn color, several
going under the common name
snake-bark maple, include
A. capillipes (Z:5–7), *A. grosseri*
var. *hersii* (Z:5–7), and *A. rufinerve*
'Hatsuyuki' (Z:5–7), the last having
leaves with bold white mottling. All
grow eventually to 30ft (9m).

A. platanoides *Europe*
Norway maple
Foliage: autumn. Flowers: spring.
H:100ft (30m), S:50ft (15m). Z:4–7.
Flat clusters of conspicuous golden
yellow flowers emerge before the
leaves on this vigorous deciduous
maple. 'Crimson King' produces
red-purple foliage and yellow
flowers tinged red. It reaches 50ft
(15m) in height. 'Drummondii'
has green leaves with a broad
creamy white margin and grows
to 40ft (12m). *A. pseudoplatanus*
'Brilliantissimum' (Z:5–7) is
another strikingly variegated tree,
with foliage that unfolds pink, then
turns yellow before becoming
green. The tree slowly grows to
a height of 20ft (6m).

A. rubrum *E. North America*
Red maple, scarlet maple, swamp
maple
Foliage: autumn. Flowers: spring.
H:70ft (22m), S:30ft (9m). Z:4–9.
The dark green leaves, which turn
vivid red in autumn, are 5-lobed,
the center lobe being the longest.
An acid soil will give optimum
autumn color. 'October Glory' has
shiny leaves that turn dark orange-
red or bright crimson in autumn,
while the columnar, dense
'Scanlon' has a show of deep red
autumn foliage.

A. saccharinum *E. North America*
Silver maple
Foliage: autumn. Flowers: spring.
H:80ft (25m), S:50ft (15m). Z:5–8.
A light breeze ruffling the pale
green leaves shows the silvery
underside that gives this fast-
growing spreading maple its
common name. Autumn color is of
variable quality.

AESCULUS

HIPPOCASTANACEAE

These woodland deciduous trees
and shrubs, with all 15 species in
the genus from the Northern
Hemisphere, have fingered leaves
and flowers arranged in upright
panicles. Glossy brown seeds
ripen and burst out of spiny
or smooth capsules in autumn.
Among the most magnificent
species are the common horse
chestnut (*A. hippocastanum*,
Z:4–7), decked with candlelike
white flower panicles in late
spring, and the yellow buckeye
(*A. flava*, Z:4–8), which displays
yellow flowers and rich autumn
colors. But since they reach a
height of 80ft (25m) or more, they
are too large for most gardens.
CULTIVATION Require sun or partial
shade and fertile, moist but well-
drained soil.
PROPAGATION From seed, sown as
soon as ripe in autumn (species
and natural varieties).
POTENTIAL PROBLEMS Leaf blotch.
WARNING All parts of the trees are
poisonous.

Aesculus hippocastanum

A. × *carnea*
Red horse chestnut
Foliage: autumn. Flowers: early
to mid-summer. H:70ft (22m),
S:50ft (15m). Z:4-7.
Dark green leaves set off red or
deep pink flowers. Spiny fruits
contain the seeds. '**Briotii**' has dark
rose flower candles and glossy
leaves that turn gold in autumn.

Aesculus × *carnea* '**Briotii**'

A. *indica* *N.W. Himalayas*
Indian horse chestnut
Foliage: autumn. Flowers: summer.
H and S:50ft (15m). Z:7-8.
The leaves open bronze and turn
dark green, then yellow in autumn.
The flowers are white or pinkish.
Pear-shaped smooth fruit contains
almost black shiny nuts.

A. × *neglecta* *S.E. USA*
Foliage: autumn. Flowers: mid-
summer. H:30ft (9m), S:25ft (7.5m).
Z:5-8.
Smooth fruit capsules follow
yellow or yellow-flushed red
flowers. The green leaves are richly
colored in autumn. The sunrise
horse chestnut, '**Erythroblastos**',
has bright pink leaves, which turn
yellow, then green, and finally
golden in autumn.

ALNUS

<small>BETULACEAE</small> Alder

The alders are deciduous trees of
the Northern Hemisphere; many
of the 35 species tolerate wet
growing conditions. The Italian
alder (**A. *cordata***, Z:6-7), a fast-
growing conical tree with bright
green glossy leaves, is remarkably
tolerant of a wide range of soils,
thriving even on dry, thin soils on
lime. The drooping male catkins
and the shorter female catkins,
which later become seed-bearing
cones, are borne on the same tree.
CULTIVATION Require full sun
and moist but well-drained soil.
A. cordata tolerates dry soil;
A. glutinosa (Z:4-7) tolerates
wet soil.
PROPAGATION From seed, sown as
soon as ripe.
POTENTIAL PROBLEMS Canker.

Alnus glutinosa '**Imperialis**'

A. *glutinosa* *Europe, N. Africa,
W. Asia*
Common alder
Flowers: late winter to early spring.
H:80ft (25m), S:30ft (9m). Z:4-7.
The dark yellow male catkins, 4in
(10cm) long, make a distinctive
winter display before the dark
green leaves. '**Imperialis**', a light,
graceful tree, has deeply cut leaves.

ARBUTUS

<small>ERICACEAE</small>

Evergreen foliage, distinctive bark,
and clusters of small bell-shaped
flowers followed by strawberrylike fruits are outstanding features
of several species of this genus.
There are about 14 in all, which
are found in North and Central
America, the Mediterranean, and in
the case of the Killarney strawberry
tree (**A. *unedo***, Z:7-9), also in
Ireland. The madrone (**A. *menziesii***,
Z:7-9) is conspicuous among
California evergreens for its smooth,
reddish brown bark. All need
protection from cold wind.

Arbutus unedo

CULTIVATION Require full sun
and fertile well-drained soil.
A. menziesii will only flourish
on acid soil.
PROPAGATION From seed, sown
fresh. From semiripe cuttings,
taken in late summer.
POTENTIAL PROBLEMS None serious.

A. × *andrachnoides* *S.E. Europe,
S.W. Asia*
Foliage: year-round. Flowers: late
spring to early summer. H and
S:20-25ft (6-7.5m). Z:7-9.
The fully hardy Killarney strawberry
tree and the frost-hardy Grecian
strawberry tree (**A. *andrachne***,
Z:8-9) are the parents of this lime-
tolerant hybrid. It has leathery
leaves, orange-red peeling bark,
clusters of white bell-shaped
flowers, and orange-red fruits.

BETULA

<small>BETULACEAE</small> Birch

The 60 or so species of birch are
deciduous trees and shrubs that
are found in a wide variety of
habitats in the Northern
Hemisphere. The genus includes
a number of elegant small to
medium-sized trees with attractive
bark and delicate foliage, which
usually turns shades of yellow in
autumn. Male and female catkins
are borne on the same tree.
CULTIVATION Require full sun and
well-drained neutral to acid soil.
PROPAGATION From seed, sown in
early spring. By grafting, under
protection in early spring.
POTENTIAL PROBLEMS Leaf miner,
bronze birch borer; mildew.

Betula pendula

B. *pendula* *Europe, N. Asia*
Silver birch
Foliage: autumn. H:70-80ft
(22-25m), S:20-30ft (6-9m). Z:3-7.
The silver birch takes its common
name from its white bark, but the
base of the trunk becomes darkly
fissured as the tree ages. It is a
lightly elegant tree with pendant
branchlets and diamond-shaped
leaves that turn yellow in autumn.
'**Laciniata**' has deeply divided,
mid-green leaves; '**Youngii**'
(Young's weeping birch) grows
to about 30ft (9m) and hangs
down to the ground.

Betula utilis var. jacquemontii

B. utilis *China, Himalayas*
Himalayan birch
Foliage: autumn. H:50–60ft
(15–18m), S:25–30ft (7.5–9m).
Z:5–7.
The tree is variable but the bark is
beautiful, whether copper-brown,
pink-gray, or white. The long leaves
are dark green, turning butter-
yellow in autumn. The graceful **var.
jacquemontii** has pure white bark;
var. jacquemontii 'Jermyns' has
white bark and large catkins.

CARPINUS

CORYLACEAE Hornbeam

The 35–40 species are deciduous
trees and occasionally shrubs of
woodland in the temperate
Northern Hemisphere. The
prominently veined leaves are
borne on zigzag twigs. Flowers are
produced in catkins, male and
female on the same plant, followed
by clusters of fruit; the nuts have
winglike bracts. The American
hornbeam (*C. caroliniana*, Z:4–9),
a small tree to 40ft (12m) tall with
blue-green leaves, is sometimes
known as ironwood, an allusion
to the hardness of the wood.
CULTIVATION Require sun or partial
shade and well-drained soil. Clip
hedges annually in mid-summer.
PROPAGATION From seed, sown in
autumn.
POTENTIAL PROBLEMS Usually none.

Carpinus betulus

C. betulus *Europe*
Common hornbeam
Foliage: autumn. Flowers: spring.
H:70–80ft (22–25m), S:60–70ft
(18–22m). Z:5–8.
The trunk of this conical, later
more rounded, tree is gray, and the
dark green toothed leaves turn
yellow in autumn. As a hedge, it
holds onto brown leaves in winter.

CATALPA

BIGNONIACEAE

The 11 species of *Catalpa* are
deciduous and usually spreading
trees from E. Asia and North
America, which in their native
habitat are plants of woodland and
the banks of streams and rivers.
They produce dramatically large
heart-shaped leaves and upright
clusters of bell-shaped flowers,
which are followed by long,
slender, beanlike pods. The seeds
eventually released from the pods
are winged at both ends.
CULTIVATION Prefer full sun and
fertile, moist, free-draining soil and
shelter from strong winds. Can be
regularly cut back to near the base
in early spring to produce extra-
large leaves.
PROPAGATION From seed, sown in
autumn. From softwood cuttings,
taken in spring or summer. From
hardwood cuttings, taken in
winter. By grafting (winter) or
budding (summer).
POTENTIAL PROBLEMS Usually none.

Catalpa bignonioides 'Aurea'

C. bignonioides *S.E. USA*
Indian bean tree, Southern catalpa
Flowers: summer. H and S:40–50ft
(12–15m). Z:6–9.
The magnificent heart-shaped
leaves, tinged purple before
turning light green, are late to
develop on the open, spreading
tree. The frilled foxglovelike
flowers are white with yellow and
purple markings. These are
followed by long drooping pods
that turn black and remain on the
tree throughout winter. **'Aurea'**,
which grows to 30ft (9m), has
yellow leaves, which are bronze
when young.

CERCIS

CAESALPINIACEAE

The half dozen species are shrubs
or trees of woodland and more
open rugged terrain in C. and E.
Asia, North America, and the
Mediterranean. They have heart-
or kidney-shaped leaves and pretty,
pealike flowers, which are followed
by flat pods. The E. Mediterranean
Judas tree (*C. siliquastrum*, Z:6–9),
which grows to 30ft (9m), fizzes
with an abundance of purple-pink
flowers, even on the trunk, before
the leaves open.
CULTIVATION Require full sun and
fertile, moist, free-draining soil.
PROPAGATION From seed, sown in
a cold frame in autumn. From semiripe cuttings, taken in summer. By
budding in summer (cultivars).
POTENTIAL PROBLEMS Scale;
verticillium wilt, canker.

Cercis canadensis 'Forest Pansy'

C. canadensis *North America*
Eastern redbud
Foliage: autumn. Flowers: late
spring. H and S:25–30ft (7.5–9m).
Z:4–9.
This large shrub or small tree
needs hot summers to produce
bright pink flowers in profusion.
The heart-shaped leaves are bronze
when young, yellow in autumn.
'Forest Pansy' (Z:5–9) has rich
purple leaves, which turn red and
orange in autumn.

CORDYLINE

AGAVACEAE

Leathery straplike leaves held in
tufts or rosettes give several of the
cordylines a palmlike appearance.
The 15 species are widely
distributed in India and the
Southern Hemisphere, most being
found in tropical and subtropical
zones. They are grown mainly as
foliage plants, outdoors and under
glass, but the mass of sweetly
scented flowers can be impressive
in its abundance. The flowers are
followed by round berries.
CULTIVATION Tolerate full sun or
partial shade and require fertile
well-drained soil.

PROPAGATION From suckers, taken in spring. From stem-section cuttings, taken in early summer. From seed, sown in spring.
POTENTIAL PROBLEMS Usually none outdoors; mealybugs, scale, red spider mites under glass.

Cordyline australis

C. australis *New Zealand*
New Zealand cabbage palm or cabbage tree
Foliage: year-round. H:20–30ft (6–9m), S:6–9ft (1.8–2.7m). Z:9–10.
This small upright tree usually forms a single trunk with short stout branches that are topped with a large dense mass of sword-like gray-green leaves. After 8–10 years they produce large plumes of fragrant creamy white flowers in early summer. The **Purpurea Group** has purple-flushed leaves.

CORNUS

CORNACEAE Cornel, dogwood

These decorative deciduous small trees and multistemmed shrubs contribute flowers and showy bracts, berry clusters, and colorful stems to the yard at different seasons. The 45 or so species are found in a wide range of habitats in the temperate Northern Hemisphere. See also SHRUBS.
CULTIVATION Require full sun and fertile well-drained soil. Prune plants grown for their colored stems in alternate years in spring.
PROPAGATION From seed, sown in autumn. From hardwood cuttings, taken in winter.
POTENTIAL PROBLEMS Borers; anthracnose, canker.

C. alternifolia *E. North America*
Green osier, pagoda dogwood
Foliage: autumn. Flowers: late spring to early summer. Fruits: autumn.
H and S:20–25ft (6–7.5m). Z:4–7.
Tiered branches carry alternate, oval, green leaves that color red in autumn. The clusters of small white flowers are followed by black berries. **'Argentea'** is an outstanding variegated shrub or small tree, 15ft (4.5m) tall, with white-margined bright green leaves.

C. controversa *China, Himalayas, Japan*
Foliage: autumn. Flowers: early summer. H and S:40–50ft (12–15m). Z:5–8.
The tiered tree has dark green leaves, glossy above and glaucous on the underside, which turn purple in autumn. Flat clusters of white flowers are followed by bluish-black fruits. **'Variegata'** has leaves edged creamy white. It is half the size of the species.

Cornus controversa 'Variegata'

C. florida *E. North America*
Flowering dogwood
Foliage: autumn. Flowers: late spring to early summer. Fruits: autumn. H and S:20–30ft (6–9m). Z:5–9.
The clusters of greenish flowers are inconspicuous, but the white bracts surrounding them make this large shrub or small tree highly ornamental. There are red fruits in autumn, and the leaves turn red and purple. **'Cherokee Chief'** has deep pink bracts, and **'Rainbow'**, growing to 10ft (3m), has white bracts and yellow variegated leaves coloring vividly in autumn. The bracts of **f. rubra** are pink.
'Eddie's White Wonder' (Z:7–9), with white bracts and brilliant autumn foliage, grows to 20ft (6m).

Cornus florida f. rubra

C. mas *Europe, W. Asia*
Cornelian cherry
Foliage: autumn. Flowers: late winter. Fruits: late summer. H and S:15–20ft (4.5–6m). Z:5–7.
Clusters of small yellow flowers are followed by dark green glossy leaves. Bright red fruits form in late

summer. The slow-growing **'Variegata'**, which grows to 8ft (2.5m) tall, is distinguished by its white-edged leaves.

CRATAEGUS

ROSACEAE Hawthorn

These deciduous, sometimes evergreen, trees produce clusters of white to vivid pink flowers followed by mostly red berries (haws) in winter. The foliage of some species provides rich autumn color. The 200 or more species, found in woodland and more open habitats, are widely distributed in the temperate zone of the Northern Hemisphere. Because of their ornamental qualities, moderate size, adaptability, and hardiness, hawthorns are ideal for specimen planting in yards. Thorny branches make many species suitable as sturdy hedging plants, among them the common hawthorn, **C. monogyna** (Z:5–7).
CULTIVATION Tolerate full sun or partial shade and any garden soil that is not waterlogged. Trim hedges in autumn.
PROPAGATION From seed (which may take 18 months to germinate), sown in early spring. By grafting (cultivars).
POTENTIAL PROBLEMS Rust, fire blight.

Crataegus laevigata 'Rosea Flore Pleno'

C. laevigata *Europe to India, N. Africa*
May, Midland hawthorn
Flowers: late spring. Fruits: autumn. H and S:25ft (7.5m). Z:5–7.
Clusters of white flowers, sometimes tinted pink and followed by red haws, brighten a rounded thorny tree with glossy green leaves. **'Paul's Scarlet'** has double red flowers, and **'Rosea Flore Pleno'** has double pink flowers. All have a cloying scent.

C. × **lavalleei** 'Carrierei'
Foliage: autumn. Flowers: early summer. Fruits: late autumn to early winter. H:15–25ft (4.5–7.5m), S:20–25ft (6–7.5m). Z:5–7.
The tree is lightly thorned, and it often holds its glossy dark green leaves until early winter. The vivid orange-red fruits that follow the clusters of white flowers are long lasting.

Crataegus persimilis 'Prunifolia'

C. persimilis 'Prunifolia'
Foliage: autumn. Flowers: early summer. Fruits: autumn. H:25ft (7.5m), S:30ft (9m). Z:5–7.
The broad-headed thorny tree has distinctive glossy dark green foliage that colors well in autumn, and round bright red haws, which follow dense clusters of white flowers and persist into winter.

DAVIDIA

DAVIDIACEAE Dove tree, ghost tree, handkerchief tree

The single deciduous species is a woodland tree from China, rare in the wild and with a scattered distribution. The adventurous search for it by E. H. Wilson, culminating in large-scale introduction to the West at the beginning of the 20th century, has added glamour to an already remarkable tree.
CULTIVATION Require full sun or partial shade, and fertile moist but well-drained soil.
PROPAGATION From seed, sown in autumn. From semiripe cuttings, taken in early summer.
POTENTIAL PROBLEMS Usually none.

Davidia involucrata

D. involucrata *S.W. China*
Foliage: autumn. Flowers: late spring. H:50ft (15m), S:30ft (9m). Z:6–8.
When in flower, the tree, improbably, seems decked with drooping handkerchiefs. The flowers themselves are small and clustered in a rounded head, each of which is surrounded by an unequal pair of white bracts. The leaves are heart shaped and vivid green with a coating of dense hairs on the underside; in autumn they turn bright golden-yellow with a red tinge around the margin. The greenish-brown fruits are ridged and egg shaped. The leaves of **var. vilmoriniana** (Z:5–8) are hairless.

EUCALYPTUS

MYRTACEAE Gum, gum tree

The eucalypts, a large genus of more than 500 species of evergreen trees and shrubs, most native to Australia, are notable for their bark, their foliage, and for their petalless but showy flowers. These are usually creamy white, but the half-hardy species (**E. ficifolia**, Z:8–10) has red flowers. Juvenile and mature leaves often differ in shape, size, and arrangement on the stems, changing from opposite to alternate as they age. Plants are usually fast growing, and many are heat and drought tolerant. Only a few are hardy enough to grow in a cool temperate climate. The spreading Tasmanian blue gum (**E. globulus**, Z:8–10) makes a splendid large tree where the climate is mild enough, but is also grown as a bedding plant for its silvery blue-green juvenile leaves.
CULTIVATION Require full sun and fertile, well-drained, neutral to acid soil. Some shelter may be necessary while plants are young.
PROPAGATION From seed, sown in spring.
POTENTIAL PROBLEMS Silver leaf, edema.

E. gunnii *Tasmania*
Cider gum
Foliage: year-round. Flowers: summer. H:60–80ft (18–25m), S:20–40ft (6–12m). Z:8–10.
The rounded blue leaves of the young plant give way to sickle-shaped gray-green leaves, although the plant can be pruned hard each year to maintain the blue juvenile foliage. On mature trees, the older green-white bark is shed in summer, revealing new gray-green bark, sometimes with a pink or orange flush. Clusters of small cream-white flowers are borne in summer.

Eucalyptus gunnii

E. pauciflora subsp. **niphophila** *S.E. Australia, Tasmania*
Alpine snow gum, snow gum
Foliage: year-round. Flowers: summer. H:20–40ft (6–12m), S:20–30ft (6–9m). Z:7–10.
The bark, likened to the skin of a python, is marked in shades of green, gray, and cream. The gray-green leaves are long and leathery. The flowers are creamy white.

Eucalyptus pauciflora subsp. *niphophila*

EUCRYPHIA

EUCRYPHIACEAE

The 5 or 6 deciduous and evergreen trees and shrubs of this genus from Chile and S.E. Australia bear white cup-shaped flowers with golden stamens from late summer until early autumn. The medium- to dark green leaves are leathery with a crinkled margin.
CULTIVATION Require full sun and shelter from cold winds with the roots kept cool and damp.
PROPAGATION From semiripe cuttings with a heel, taken in early autumn.
POTENTIAL PROBLEMS Usually none.

E. × *nymansensis* *South America*
Leatherwood
Foliage: year-round. Flowers: late summer to early autumn. H:36ft (11m), S:6-8ft (1.8-2.5m). Z:7-9. This is a small columnar evergreen tree, and the hardiest, most lime-tolerant of the eucryphias. It bears both simple and compound leaves, reflecting the leaf shapes of its parents, **E. *cordifolia*** (Z:9-10) and **E. *glutinosa*.** E. × **'Nymansay'** spreads to between 8-15ft (2.5-4.5m) and grows and matures quickly, producing pure white flowers that are 2¼in (6cm) across and are more numerous than on the species.

Eucryphia × nymansensis

FAGUS

FAGACEAE Beech

The 10 species of woodland trees, all from the temperate Northern Hemisphere, produce foliage that colors well in autumn. The inconspicuous flowers are followed by woody fruits, which contain nuts (mast). Their size and the shade they cast limit their use in small to medium-sized yards.
CULTIVATION Tolerate full sun or partial shade and well-drained soil. Trim hedges in late summer.
PROPAGATION From seed, sown in autumn. By grafting (cultivars).
POTENTIAL PROBLEMS Beech bark disease, powdery mildew.

Fagus sylvatica 'Dawyck'

Fagus sylvatica 'Purpurea Pendula'

F. *sylvatica* *C. Europe*
Common beech
Foliage: autumn. H:80–100ft (25–30m), S:40–60ft (12–18m). Z:5-7.
Oval leaves emerge clear green, then turn dark green and golden and finally copper and brown on this gracefully spreading deciduous tree. The bark is silver-gray in maturity. As a specimen tree, the species and upright purple-leaved forms such as **'Riversii'** are too large for most yards but are excellent hedging plants, holding their leaves in winter. There are cultivars of more manageable size. **'Dawyck'** is columnar with copper leaves in autumn. The narrow leaves of **var. *heterophylla*** **'Aspleniifolia'** are deeply cut. The branches of the weeping beech (**'Pendula'),** which is up to 60ft (18m) tall, hang to the ground. **'Purpurea Pendula'**, with purple foliage, rarely exceeds 15ft (4.5m).

FRAXINUS

OLEACEAE Ash

There are about 65 species of ash, all but a few deciduous trees and the majority woodland plants of the temperate Northern Hemisphere. The common ash (**F. *excelsior*,** Z:6-7) is a fast-growing tree eventually reaching about 100ft (30m) and has far-reaching surface roots, making it unsuitable for all but large yards. **F. *excelsior*** 'Pendula' (Z:6-7), known as the weeping ash, rarely exceeds 50ft (15m), and its hanging branches form a curtained bower.
CULTIVATION Require full sun and neutral to alkaline moist but well-drained soil.
PROPAGATION From seed, stratified over winter, sown in autumn or spring.
POTENTIAL PROBLEMS Borers, scale; canker.

F. *ornus* *S. Europe, S.W. Asia*
Manna ash
Foliage: autumn. Flowers: late spring to early summer. H and S:50ft (15m). Z:6-8.
This bushy rounded species, the best known of the "flowering ashes," produces clustered plumes of fluffy cream-white flowers that are heavily scented. The pinnate dark green leaves turn purple-red in autumn.

Fraxinus ornus

GENISTA

PAPILIONACEAE Broom

The graceful Mount Etna broom (*G. aetnensis*) rises above most of the 90 or so species in this genus to form an open and airy small deciduous tree. It is drought tolerant and, despite its green appearance, nearly leafless. See also SHRUBS.
CULTIVATION Requires full sun and well-drained light sandy soil. Tolerates acid and alkaline soils.
PROPAGATION From seed, sown in spring. From semiripe cuttings with a heel, taken in early autumn.
POTENTIAL PROBLEM Aphids.

Genista aetnensis

G. *aetnensis* *Italy (Sardinia, Sicily)*
Mount Etna broom
Flowers: summer. H and S:18–25ft (5.5-7.5m). Z: 9-10.
This is an elegant large shrub or small tree with a large number of slender, drooping, bright green branches. Large quantities of heavily fragranced, golden-yellow pealike flowers are produced from mid- to late summer. It casts only light shade.

GLEDITSIA

CAESALPINIACEAE

The 14 or so species of this deciduous spiny tree, distantly related to the garden pea, are grown for their attractive leaves, which are pinnate or bipinnate with up to 32 leaflets. The flowers are greenish white and give rise to long brown pods in autumn.
CULTIVATION Require full sun, fertile well-drained soil, and shelter from wind in spring. Tolerant of atmospheric pollution.
PROPAGATION From seed, sown in spring (species). By grafting, in early spring (named cultivars).
POTENTIAL PROBLEMS Borers, webworm; canker.

G. triacanthos C. and E. North America
Honey locust
Foliage: autumn. Flowers: mid-summer. H:60–80ft (18–25m), S:30–50ft (9–15m). Z:4–9.
A formidably armored tree with frondlike foliage that turns clear yellow in autumn. Where summers are warm enough, the insignificant flowers are followed by seedpods. '**Sunburst**', thornless and growing to 40ft (12m), has yellow foliage, which turns lime green before coloring yellow again in autumn. It does not produce seedpods.

Gleditsia triacanthos '**Sunburst**'

ILEX

AQUIFOLIACEAE Holly

In a genus of over 400 species of mainly evergreen trees and shrubs distributed in woodlands and forests in temperate, subtropical, and tropical regions, the best-known hollies are species and hybrids with spiny evergreen leaves and berries in autumn. Male and female flowers usually grow on separate trees (the sex is indicated following plant names in the entries), although some plants are self-fertile. Tolerant of wind and pollution, hollies are valuable hedging plants. Fully hardy shrubby evergreen hollies include the Japanese holly (*I. crenata*, Z:5–7), often with black berries, and the blue holly (*I.* × *meserveae*, Z:5–9) with blue-green leaves. The American holly (*I. opaca*, Z:-9), also fully hardy, is treelike, with matte green leaves.
CULTIVATION Tolerate full sun or partial shade and prefer moist well-drained soil.
PROPAGATION From seed, sown in autumn (seed may not germinate for 2–3 years). From semiripe cuttings, taken in late summer or early autumn.
POTENTIAL PROBLEMS Scale, leaf miner.

Ilex × *altaclerensis* '**Camelliifolia**'

I. × *altaclerensis*
Highclere holly
Foliage: year-round. Flowers: spring to early summer. Berries: autumn to winter. H:50–70ft (15–22m), S:25–50ft (7.5–15m). Z:7–9.
These fast-growing hollies, useful for hedging, have glossy, sparsely spiny leaves that set off the red berries. Cultivars include '**Belgica Aurea**' (f), with gray-green mottled leaves edged cream; '**Camelliifolia**' (f), purple stemmed and with large berries and deep green, almost spineless leaves; and '**Golden King**' (f), with yellow leaf margins.

Ilex aquifolium '**Madame Briot**'

I. aquifolium W. and S. Europe, N. Africa, W. Asia
Common holly, English holly
Foliage: year-round. Flowers: spring to early summer. Berries: autumn to winter. H:50–70ft (15–22m), S:15–25ft (4.5–7.5m). Z:6–9.
As a young tree, this forms a loose dark green pyramid of glossy and prickly leaves. Mature foliage is only spine tipped. The long-lasting berries are red, occasionally orange or yellow. Cultivars include '**Ferox Argentea**' (m), dark green cream-margined leaves covered in spines; '**Golden Milkboy**' (m), spiny leaves with irregular yellow centers; '**Handsworth New Silver**' (f), purple stems and white-margined spiny leaves; '**Madame Briot**' (f), spiny leaves with yellow margins; '**Pyramidalis**' (f), lightly spined green leaves, self-fertile, and fruiting freely; and '**Silver Queen**' (m), purple-stemmed and dense with spiny leaves, their creamy edges tinged pink on emerging.

Ilex aquifolium '**Ferox Argentea**'

KOELREUTERIA

SAPINDACEAE

Showy seedpods follow sprays of small flowers on the 3 species of these spreading deciduous trees and shrubs from dry valley woodlands in Asia. The leaves are long and decorative.
CULTIVATION Require full sun and well-drained soil.
PROPAGATION From seed, sown under glass in autumn. From root cuttings, taken in autumn.
POTENTIAL PROBLEMS None serious.

K. paniculata China, Korea
Golden-rain tree, Pride of India
Foliage: autumn. Flowers: mid- to late summer. Fruits: late autumn. H:30–50ft (9–15m), S:20–30ft (6–9m). Z:5–9.
The long, elegant, pinnate leaves are reddish when they emerge, medium green in summer, and yellow in autumn. The prominent seedpods that follow sprays of small yellow flowers are green flushed red. Hot summers are needed for a good display.

Koelreuteria paniculata

LABURNUM

PAPILIONACEAE Golden chain tree

The genus contains 2 similar deciduous species, **L. alpinum** (Z:5-7) and **L. anagyroides** (Z:6-7), from south and central Europe, which make small trees that produce graceful trailing clusters of yellow pealike flowers during late spring or early summer. The plant described is a hybrid between them.
CULTIVATION Require full sun and reasonably fertile, well-drained soil. L. × watereri 'Vossii' has a brittle root system and must be permanently staked.
PROPAGATION From seed, sown in spring. By grafting in spring (cultivars).
POTENTIAL PROBLEMS Aphids; twig blight.
WARNING All parts of the plant are poisonous.

Laburnum × watereri 'Vossii'

L. × watereri 'Vossii'
Flowers: late spring. H:20-30ft (6-9m), S:18-25ft (5.5-7.5m). Z:6-7.
In late spring the tree drips with clusters of deep yellow flowers, to 24in (60cm) long, followed by gray-brown pods filled with black seeds (the most poisonous part of the plant). The gray-green leaves have a glossy upper surface and a paler underside.

LIQUIDAMBAR

HAMAMELIDACEAE

The 4 species are deciduous woodland trees from Asia, North America, and Mexico, the best known being remarkable for the complex coloring of the foliage in autumn. The leaves are maplelike, with 3-7 lobes. The flowers are inconspicuous.

L. styraciflua E. USA, Mexico
Sweet gum
Foliage: autumn. Flowers: late spring. H:70-80ft (22-25m), S:25-30ft (7.5-9m). Z:5-9.
The palmate leaves of this conical-shaped tree are glossy with 5-7 lobes. In autumn, their color changes from orange and red to purple. **L. formosana** (Z:7-9), from China and Japan and usually less than 40ft (12m) in height, has foliage that is purplish red in spring and colors brilliantly in autumn.

Liquidambar styraciflua

LIRIODENDRON

MAGNOLIACEAE Tulip tree

The 2 fast-growing deciduous trees in this genus make fine specimen plants where there is adequate space. Green cup-shaped flowers appear on trees after 15 years. The leaves are almost straight across the top.
CULTIVATION Require full sun or partial shade and reasonably fertile, moist, well-drained soil.
PROPAGATION From seed, sown in autumn (species). By grafting in early spring (cultivars).
POTENTIAL PROBLEMS Aphids; canker.

Liriodendron tulipifera

L. tulipifera E. North America
Tulip tree
Foliage: autumn. Flowers: mid-summer. Fruits: autumn. H:80-100ft (25-30m), S:40-50ft (12-15m). Z:5-9.
The pale green tulip-shaped flowers have orange markings at the base and enclose long crowded stamens. The leaves are dark green, turning yellow in autumn. In the slow-growing '**Aureomarginatum**', the leaves have gold-green edges, and the tree grows to 70ft (22m).

MAGNOLIA

MAGNOLIACEAE

Magnolia campbellii

This genus of 125 deciduous and evergreen species, from Asia and the Americas, includes some of the most splendid flowering trees and shrubs that can be grown in temperate yards. The flowers, usually borne prolifically on mature plants, are beautifully formed—sometimes saucer, bowl, or goblet-shaped, sometimes starry with numerous petals—and in some cases fragrant. See also SHRUBS.
CULTIVATION Require sun or partial shade, with protection from winds, and moist, well-drained, fertile soil.
PROPAGATION From green wood cuttings, taken in early summer (deciduous plants). From semiripe cuttings, taken in late summer (evergreens). From seed, sown in spring.
POTENTIAL PROBLEMS Usually none.

M. campbellii India, Nepal, S.W. China
Flowers: late winter to spring. H:50-70ft (15-22m), S:25-33ft (7.5-10m). Z: 6-7.
Large goblets appear on the bare branches of this deciduous tree after 20 or more years. The usual color is deep pink, but the range extends from white to pink.
'**Charles Raffill**' has flowers that are deep pink on the outside, white with a pinkish flush inside. It and **subsp. mollicomata** (Z:7-8), which usually has purple-pink flowers, reach flowering age in 10-15 years.

M. denudata *China*
Lily tree, yulan
Flowers: spring. H and S:20–30ft
(6–9m). Z:5–8.
The cup-shaped white flowers are
lemon scented and open before the
leaves on this spreading deciduous
tree, which comes into flower in
3–5 years. Primrose-yellow flowers
appear on **M. 'Elizabeth'** (Z:5–8)
before and at the same time as the
coppery leaves unfurl, once the
tree is 2–3 years old.

Magnolia grandiflora

M. grandiflora *S.E. USA*
Bull bay
Foliage: year-round. Flowers: late
summer to autumn. H:20–60ft
(6–18m), S:20–40ft (6–12m). Z:7–9.
This evergreen magnolia is often
wall-trained but makes a handsome
free-standing specimen. The
scented creamy white flowers,
up to 10in (25cm) across, nestle
among large, dark green, glossy
leaves. **'Exmouth'**, with narrower
paler leaves, and **'Goliath'**, with
very large flowers up to 12in
(30cm) across, come into flower at
a relatively young age.

**Magnolia × loebneri
'Leonard Messel'**

M. × loebneri 'Leonard Messel'
Flowers: mid-spring. H:20–25ft
(6–7.5m), S:15–20ft (4.5–6m).
Z:5–9.
Crosses between **M. kobus** (Z:4–7),
a Japanese species that is slow to
come into flower, and **M. stellata**
have produced small deciduous
trees or large shrubs of great
quality that flower when young.
'Leonard Messel' has pink flowers
tinged with mauve. **M. × loebneri**

'Merrill' can grow to 33ft (10m)
and produces white goblets that
are fragrant and starry when open.

M. salicifolia *Japan*
Willow-leaved magnolia
Flowers: mid-spring. H:30–40ft
(9–12m), S:15–25ft (4.5–7.5m).
Z:6–9.
The white star-shaped flowers are
faintly fragrant, and open before
the long lance-shaped leaves on
this deciduous tree.

MALUS

ROSACEAE Apple, crab apple

The thousands of eating and
cooking apples are very ornamental.
There are about 35 species, all
deciduous and found in woodland
or more open habitats in Europe,
Asia, and North America. They and
some of their hybrids include
relatively small trees valuable for
their blossom, colorful fruits, and
in some cases, autumn foliage.
CULTIVATION Best in full sun, but
tolerate partial shade. Require
moist but well-drained soil.
PROPAGATION From seed, sown in
autumn. Trees are propagated
commercially by budding in late
summer or grafting in mid-winter.
POTENTIAL PROBLEMS borers;
canker, apple scab, fire blight, cider
apple rust. (Crab apples are less
prone to disease than orchard
apples.)

M. coronaria var. **dasycalyx
'Charlottae'**
Foliage: autumn. Flowers: late
spring to early summer. Fruits:
autumn. H:20–30ft (6–9m),
S:15–20ft (4.5–6m). Z:4–7.
Clustered semidouble fragrant
flowers of palest pink are followed
by yellowish fruit. The leaves turn
scarlet in autumn.

Malus floribunda

M. floribunda *Japan*
Japanese crab apple
Flowers: mid- to late spring. Fruits:
autumn. H and S:20–30ft (6–9m).
Z:4–7.
Clustered crimson buds open to
pale pink blossoms, which are

followed by tiny yellow fruits.
Another Japanese crab apple,
M. toringo subsp. **sargentii** (Z:4–7),
which rarely exceeds 12ft (3.7m),
bears white flowers followed by
long-lasting deep red fruits.

M. 'John Downie'
Flowers: late spring. Fruits: autumn.
H:20–30ft (6–9m), S:15–20ft
(4.5–6m). Z:5–7.
The tree is narrowly upright when
young but broadens with age. The
display of white flowers opening
from pink buds is generous, but
even more outstanding is the crop
of orange and red conical fruits.

M. × robusta 'Red Sentinel'
Flowers: late spring. Fruits: autumn
to winter. H and S:20–25ft
(6–7.5m). Z:3–7.
A heavy crop of long-lasting, glossy,
deep red fruits follows the white
flowers. The foliage is dark green.
'Yellow Siberian', which
eventually may grow to 40ft (12m),
bears clusters of yellow fruits,
which are still hanging in winter.

Malus × schiedeckeri 'Red Jade'

M. × schiedeckeri 'Red Jade'
Flowers: late spring. H:12–18ft
(3.7–5.5m), S:8–15ft (2.5–4.5m).
Z:4–7.
Pink buds open to white blossoms
on weeping branches. Red fruits
follow.

M. tschonoskii *Japan*
Foliage: autumn. Flowers: late spring.
Fruits: autumn. H:30–40ft (9–12m),
S:18–23ft (5.5–7m). Z:6–7.
This species, upright at first, later
spreading, is one of the best crab
apples for autumn color, turning
shades of red, orange, yellow, and
purple. Yellow-green fruits follow
the pink-flushed white blossoms.

M. × zumi 'Golden Hornet'
Flowers: spring. Fruits: autumn to
winter. H:18–25ft (5.5–7.5m),
S:12–18ft (3.7–5.5m). Z:5–7.
Long-lasting bright yellow fruits
hang thickly from the branches of
this small rounded tree in autumn
and winter. The flowers open
white from pink buds.

MORUS

MORACEAE

The genus contains about 10 species of shrubs and trees from a variety of habitats in Africa, Asia, and the Americas. Two species have long been cultivated—the white mulberry (**M. alba**, Z:5-8), the leaves of which were used to feed silkworms, and the species described, which produces edible loganberry-like fruits and is a characterful tree with a rounded crown when mature.
CULTIVATION Require full sun, well-drained soil, and shelter. Any pruning should be carried out in late winter or early autumn; at other times, wounds are likely to ooze.
PROPAGATION From hardwood cuttings, taken in the early winter and rooted out in the open ground.
POTENTIAL PROBLEMS Bacterial blight, canker.

M. nigra S.W. Asia
Black mulberry
Foliage: autumn. Flowers: early spring. H and S:25-40ft (7.5-12m). Z:5-8.
The purplish-red fruits are delicious but the deciduous tree is also a distinctively gnarled ornamental when mature, with large, heart-shaped, dark green leaves that turn yellow in autumn. The flowers are inconspicuous.

Morus nigra

NYSSA

NYSSACEAE Tupelo

Vivid coloring of the foliage in autumn marks out the best of the nyssas, a genus of about 5 deciduous species, which are plants of woodland and swampy conditions in China and North America. The Chinese species *N. sinensis* (Z:7-9), usually a large shrub rather than a tree, colors brilliantly in autumn.
CULTIVATION Require sun or partial shade and moist lime-free soil.
PROPAGATION From seed, sown in early spring. By layering, in autumn.
POTENTIAL PROBLEMS Usually none.

Nyssa sylvatica

N. sylvatica E. North America
Black gum, sour gum, tupelo
Foliage: autumn. Flowers: spring to early summer. H:50-70ft (15-22m), S:25-30ft (7.5-9m). Z:4-9.
This is a handsome, slow-growing, medium to large tree with a broadly conical to columnar habit. The dark glossy green leaves turn a rich red, orange, and yellow in autumn. The flowers and fruits are inconspicuous.

PARROTIA

HAMAMELIDACEAE

The single species of this genus is a deciduous forest tree with ornamental bark and foliage that colors well in autumn.
CULTIVATION Tolerates full sun or light shade and alkaline conditions, but requires a well-drained soil.
PROPAGATION From softwood cuttings, taken in summer. By layering in autumn. From seed, sown in autumn.
POTENTIAL PROBLEMS Usually none.

P. persica Caucasus, N. Iran
Persian ironwood
Foliage: autumn. Flowers: late winter to early spring. H and S:20-30ft (6-9m). Z:5-8.
The flaking bark on the older branches of this spreading shrub or tree creates a random patchwork of cream, gray, and fawn. The flowers, which appear before the leaves, are mere tufts of crimson stamens. They easily go unnoticed, but not so the rich tints of the leaves in autumn. '**Pendula**' is a weeping form.

Parrotia persica

PLATANUS

PLATANACEAE Plane

This genus of about 6 species of deciduous trees includes the American sycamore, **P. occidentalis** (Z:5-9), native to E. and S. North America, and the Oriental plane, **P. orientalis** (Z:7-9), found from Europe to W. Asia. Generous proportions, bright green leaves, multicolored bark, and long-lasting fruits are common to all species.
CULTIVATION Require full sun and well-drained soil.
PROPAGATION From hardwood cuttings, taken in early winter.
POTENTIAL PROBLEMS Anthracnose, canker stain.

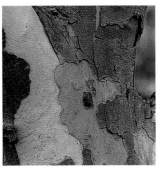

Platanus × hispanica

P. × hispanica
London plane
Foliage: autumn. Fruits: summer to the following spring. H:80-100ft (25-30m), S:50-70ft (15-22m). Z:5-8.
This columnar tree, which has large leaves with 5 to 7 lobes, is widely planted in towns because it tolerates atmospheric pollution and heavy pruning. The bark of the trunk and branches is mottled brown, cream, and gray. Strings of 2 to 6 ball-like fruit clusters hang during autumn and winter.

POPULUS

SALICACEAE Poplar

This genus of some 35 species of deciduous trees and shrubs, which are distributed throughout the Northern Hemisphere, includes some of the most rapidly growing trees. The balsam poplars, including **P. balsamifera** (Z:2-6), have aromatic young buds. Trees are single sex. The decorative male catkins are borne on bare branches in spring. Female catkins are followed by small fruits carried in a white mass of threads. All plants have a wide-spreading root system that takes up large quantities of water in the growing season. The leaves of **P. × candicans** 'Aurora' (Z:2-7) have splashy green, cream, and pink variegation.

CULTIVATION Require sun or partial shade and moist well-drained soil.
PROPAGATION By hardwood cuttings, taken in winter; instant young trees can be created by rooting cuttings up to 6ft (1.8m) in length.
POTENTIAL PROBLEMS Aphids, borers, caterpillars; canker.

P. alba *Asia, C. Europe*
Abele, white poplar
Flowers: spring. H:80ft (25m), S:30ft (9m). Z:4–8.
A broad spreading habit, dark gray-green fissured bark, and young shoots covered with a thick white felt are all appealing, but the main attraction is the fluttering foliage, the leaves dark green with a silvery and downy underside, turning yellow in autumn. '**Raket**' is narrow and conical in shape with erect branches.

Populus alba

P. tremula 'Pendula' *France*
Weeping aspen
Flowers: spring. H:20–30ft (6–9m), S:18–25ft (5.5–7.5m). Z:3–5.
This small female tree of pendulous habit produces grayish-green catkins before the almost circular leaves emerge. It is one of the best and most robust weeping trees for the garden. The American aspen (*P. tremuloides*, Z:1–7), similar to *P. tremula* but with yellow bark and finely toothed leaves, also has a weeping form '**Pendula**'.

PRUNUS

ROSACEAE

The genus includes about 200 species of deciduous and evergreen trees and shrubs, most of which are native to the temperate Northern Hemisphere, with a few found in South America. It is horticulturally important for the large number of plants—including almonds, apricots, cherries,

peaches, and plums—that are grown for their edible fruits. Their ornamental value, sometimes considerable, is eclipsed by that of several species and numerous hybrids that are grown for their prolific displays of flowers and, in some cases, colorful autumn foliage. Many have bark circled with glossy bands, the most outstanding for its coppery luster being *P. serrula* (Z:5–6). See also SHRUBS. The plants are listed under "Species" and "Hybrids."
CULTIVATION Require full sun or partial shade and moist but well-drained fertile soil. Trim hedges after flowering.
PROPAGATION From seed, sown in autumn. From greenwood cuttings, taken in early summer.
POTENTIAL PROBLEMS Aphids, borers, caterpillars, scale; leaf spot.

SPECIES

P. avium *Europe, N. Africa, S.W. Asia, Russia*
Gean, wild cherry
Foliage: autumn. Flowers: mid-spring. H:60–75ft (18–23.5m), S:30–40ft (9–12m). Z:4–8.
The trunk of this spreading tree has red-banded bark, and the leaves open bronze, turn dark green, then crimson in autumn. The clusters of white flowers are followed by reddish fruits. '**Plena**', to 40ft (12m), has double white flowers.

P. cerasifera *S.E. Europe, S.W. Asia*
Cherry plum, myrobalan
Flowers: early spring. H and S:25–33ft (7.5–10 m). Z:5–8.
The bare shoots of this deciduous tree bear small white flowers in profusion. These may be followed by yellow or red edible fruits. Purple-leaved forms include '**Nigra**', with pink flowers, and '**Pissardii**', with very pale flowers. All make a dense hedge.

P. dulcis *N. Africa, C. and S.W. Asia*
Common almond
Flowers: early spring. H:25–40ft (7.5–12m), S:25–30ft (7.5–9m). Z:7–9.
An erect, later spreading, deciduous tree bears early pink blossoms. The green fruits contain edible nuts.

P. mume *China, Korea*
Japanese apricot
Flowers: late winter to early spring. Foliage: deciduous. H and S:20–30ft (6–9m). Z:6–9.
This small deciduous tree has long been cultivated in Japan for its almond-scented pink or white

flowers, which are borne on bare shoots. They are followed by sour edible fruits. The flowers of '**Beni-chidori**' are deep pink and double, those of '**Omoi-no-mama**' white with a pink flush and semidouble. Both of these cultivars are shrubby, growing to about 8ft (2.5m).

Prunus × subhirtella 'Autumnalis Rosea'

P. × subhirtella 'Autumnalis'
Foliage: autumn. Flowers: late autumn to early spring. H and S:20–30ft (6–9m). Z:4–8.
The clusters of semidouble white flowers are tinged pink and appear intermittently over a long period. The leaves turn yellow in autumn. '**Autumnalis Rosea**' has pinkish flowers. *P. pendula* '**Pendula Rosea**' (Z:6–8) has weeping branches and pink flowers that rarely appear before early spring.

HYBRIDS

Foliage: autumn. Flowers: early spring to early summer. H and S:12–30 ft (3.7–9 m). Z:5–7.
This group includes the Japanese ornamental cherries. Cultivars include '**Accolade**', deep pink buds opening to semidouble pink flowers; '**Chôshû-hizakura**', bronze-red young leaves and pink blossoms; '**Kiku-shidare-zakura**', compact, weeping, and with crowded pink double blossoms; '**Kursar**', dark pink flowers preceding the leaves; '**Shirofugen**', large, scented, double white flowers and leaves that turn from bronze to green to red; '**Shirotae**' (Z:6–7), scented white flowers on arched branches and rich autumn foliage; '**Shôgetsu**', (Z:6–8) hanging clusters of pink and white flowers, and orange and red autumn foliage; '**Spire**', pale pink flower clusters and orange and red autumn leaves; and '**Taihaku**' with clusters of large white single blossoms.

Prunus 'Shirofugen'

PYRUS

ROSACEAE Pear

Clusters of decorative white spring blossoms characterize these deciduous trees and shrubs, found in woodland and on hillsides in Europe, Asia, and N. Africa. There are about 30 species as well as many cultivars of the dessert and culinary pears, which are ornamental in their own right.
CULTIVATION Require full sun and fertile well-drained soil.
PROPAGATION From seed, sown in autumn.
POTENTIAL PROBLEMS Aphids, caterpillars; powdery mildew.

P. salicifolia 'Pendula'
Flowers: spring. H:20–30ft (6–9m), S:12–20ft (3.7–6m). Z:5–7.
Dense creamy white blossoms are clustered on weeping branches with the attractive gray-felted foliage, which is narrow and willowlike, and turns gray-green in summer months.

Pyrus salicifolia 'Pendula'

QUERCUS

FAGACEAE Oak

The oaks constitute a major genus of about 600 species of deciduous to evergreen trees and shrubs, which are widely distributed in woodland and more open habitats, mainly in the temperate Northern Hemisphere. The grand presence of many oaks, including the fast-growing Turkey oak (*Q. cerris*, Z:6–7), can be appreciated only when they are given generous space. Leaf size and shape vary enormously, but the foliage is often ornamental, particularly on several species that color well in autumn. The insignificant male and female flowers, borne separately on the same tree, are followed by egg-shaped brown nuts (acorns) in basal cups.
CULTIVATION Tolerate sun or partial shade and require deep well-drained soil. The evergreen *Q. ilex* is best grown in full sun. *Q. rubra* and *Q. coccinea* need lime-free soil.
PROPAGATION From seed, sown as soon as ripe under glass or in a seedbed.
POTENTIAL PROBLEMS Borers; powdery mildew, anthracnose, canker, galls.

Quercus coccinea 'Splendens'

Q. coccinea E. North America
Scarlet oak
Foliage: autumn. Flowers: late spring to early summer. Fruits: autumn. H:65–80ft (20–25m), S:40–50ft (12–15m). Z:5–9.
This fast-growing, eventually broad deciduous tree has deeply cut glossy leaves that in autumn turn from dark green to bright red. The bark is gray-brown. '**Splendens**' has red-purple foliage in autumn.

Q. ilex S.W. Europe
Holm oak
Foliage: year-round. Flowers: late spring to early summer. Fruits: autumn. H:70–80ft (22–25m), S:60–70ft (18–22m). Z:7–8.
The broad rounded head is dense with glossy dark green leaves that are gray on the underside. Branches on mature specimens of this evergreen are pendulous. Acorns are small and roundish and are borne singly or in clusters.

Q. palustris E. USA
Pin oak
Foliage: autumn. Flowers: late spring to early summer. Fruits: autumn. H:60–80ft (18–25m), S:40–50ft (12–15m). Z:5–8.
This fast-growing tree has weeping lower branches and deeply cut glossy green leaves that turn red-brown in autumn.

Quercus robur

Q. robur Europe
Common oak, English oak, pedunculate oak
Flowers: late spring to early summer. Fruits: autumn. H:120ft (35m), S:80ft (25m). Z:5–8.
The broad and often irregularly domed head of this deciduous species is heavily branched. The almost stalkless deep green leaves have rounded lobes. Acorns are carried singly or in clusters of 2 or 3. The smaller '**Concordia**', H and S:30ft (9m), has golden young foliage. The sessile oak, *Q. petraea* (Z:5–8), bears stalkless acorn cups.

Q. rubra E. North America
Red oak
Foliage: autumn. Flowers: late spring to early summer. Fruits: autumn. H:80ft (25m), S:70ft (22m). Z:5–8.
On this fast-growing tree, long dark green leaves with pointed lobes turn reddish and yellow-brown in autumn.

Quercus rubra

ROBINIA

PAPILIONACEAE

The fast-growing and generally suckering trees and shrubs in this genus (about 20 species, according to some authorities) are all from North America. Most are plants of wooded or more open dry habitats. The green leaves are divided into many small leaflets along a central rib up to 18in (45cm) long, held on thorny, very brittle branches. The pealike flowers are carried in long hanging racemes; where the summers are hot enough, these are often followed by long brown seed-pods. The shrubby and fully hardy rose acacia (*R. hispida*, Z:6–8), usually about 8ft (2.5m) tall and bearing deep pink flowers,can be grafted and grown as a small tree.
CULTIVATION Require full sun and thrive in moist well-drained soils but tolerate drier conditions.
PROPAGATION From seed, sown in spring (species). By grafting in early spring (cultivars).
POTENTIAL PROBLEMS Borers, leaf miner.

Robinia pseudoacacia 'Frisia'

R. pseudoacacia E. USA
Black locust, false acacia, locust
Foliage: autumn. Flowers: late spring to early summer. H:70–80ft (22–25m), S:40–50ft (12–15m). Z:4–8.
This elegant upright tree has an open habit and slightly arching thorny branches that break easily. The dark green leaves consist of up to 13 oval leaflets and turn butter yellow in autumn. The scented flowers are creamy white. **'Frisia'** is a small tree up to about 50ft (15m) tall with bright yellow foliage.

SALIX

SALICACEAE Willow

About 300 deciduous trees and shrubs are widely distributed, mainly in temperate regions but in a wide variety of different habitats. Willows have tiny seeds, each with a tangle of long hairs that aid wind dispersal, and require moist conditions to germinate. Most of the ornamental tree willows are plants of moist lowlands and riversides. Several with weeping shoots are shown to best effect planted near water. These include the weeping willow (*S. babylonica*, Z:5–8) and the golden weeping willow, *S.* × *sepulcralis* **var. chrysocoma** (Z:6–8). Their roots travel far, however, and these trees are not for planting near buildings or within striking distance of drains. The shape and poise of the trees, the elegance of the foliage and the catkins, male (usually the more showy) and female on separate trees, are all attractive features. There are some, too, with young stems that are colorful or that have a distinctive bloom in winter. Pollarding and coppicing are traditional methods of pruning that maintain a supply of young growths. See also SHRUBS.
CULTIVATION Require full sun and moist well-drained soil. To insure crops of colorful young stems on *S. alba*, cut back to a framework of permanent branches annually in early spring.
PROPAGATION From greenwood cuttings, taken in summer. From hardwood cuttings, taken in winter.
POTENTIAL PROBLEMS Aphids; gall, canker, powdery mildew.

S. alba Europe, N. Africa, C. Asia
White willow
Catkins: spring. Stems: winter. H:65–80ft (20–25m), S:30–40ft (9–12m). Z:2–8.
As a landscape tree, it quickly provides a mass of silvery foliage, the reverse of the leaves being blue-green and silky. The metallic luster of the silver willow (**var. sericea**),which grows to 50ft (15m), is even more pronounced. Young stems of some cultivars are strongly colored in winter. Those of **subsp. vitellina 'Britzensis'** are orange-red.

Salix alba **var. sericea**

S. babylonica var. pekinensis 'Tortuosa'
Catkins: late winter to early spring. H:40–50ft (12–15m), S:20–25 ft (6–7.5m). Z:5–8.
The twisted branches and contorted bright green leaves of this upright fast-growing willow make it a tree of character at all seasons. Yellow-green catkins precede the leaves.

SOPHORA

PAPILIONACEAE

In a genus of about 50 species widely distributed in temperate and tropical regions, there are deciduous and evergreen shrubs and trees of woodland and dry, more open, habitats. The flowers are pealike, and the division of the pinnate leaves gives the foliage a light ferniness. The frost-hardy New Zealand kowhai (*S. tetraptera*, Z:8–9), an evergreen that grows to 30ft (9m), produces dense clusters of golden flowers in late spring.
CULTIVATION Require full sun and fertile well-drained soil. They perform best in hot dry conditions.
PROPAGATION From seed, sown in early spring under protection.
POTENTIAL PROBLEMS Canker, powdery mildew.

Sophora japonica

S. japonica China, Korea
Japanese pagoda tree
Flowers: late summer to early autumn. H:60–80ft (18–25m), S:40–60ft (12–18m). Z:5–8.
This deciduous species, although not native to Japan, long cultivated there, has leaves about 12in (30cm) long composed of up to 15 leaflets. It is slow to reach flowering age, but in maturity produces masses of creamy white pea flowers when grown in regions with hot, dry summers. The seedpods, 2–4in (5–10cm) long, often stay on the tree all winter.

SORBUS

ROSACEAE

About 100 species of these deciduous trees and shrubs are found in the temperate Northern Hemisphere, many of them in woodland, but some in more open, sometimes mountainous, habitats. The genus includes several ornamental trees of moderate size, with elegant foliage that usually colors well in autumn, conspicuous berries that are sometimes long lasting, and flowers that attract attention despite being soberly unshowy.
CULTIVATION Require full sun or partial shade and well-drained soil.
PROPAGATION From seed, sown in autumn. From greenwood cuttings, taken in early summer.
POTENTIAL PROBLEMS Aphids, scale; fire blight, canker.

S. aria Europe
Whitebeam
Foliage: spring to autumn. Flowers: late spring. Berries: autumn. H:50–80ft (15–25m), S:30–40ft (9–12m). Z:6–7.
In the wild this rounded tree is commonly seen on lime-rich soils and is sensational when silvered with young spring foliage. Although the gray felt persists on the back of the simple leaves, the upper surface becomes bright green. The clusters of berries that follow white flowers become crimson before the leaves turn gold and brown. 'Lutescens', rarely more than 30ft (9m) tall, is exceptionally silvery in spring and later gray-green. 'Majestica' has large leaves and fruit.

Sorbus aria

S. aucuparia Europe, Asia
Mountain ash, rowan
Foliage: autumn. Flowers: late spring. Berries: late summer to autumn. H:40–50ft (12–15m), S:15–25ft (4.5–7.5m). Z:4–7.
On an open elegant tree, bright red berries, which follow scented white flowers, stand out against still green pinnate leaves. The foliage colors well in autumn.

'Aspleniifolia' has distinctively cut leaflets. Cultivars growing 25–30ft (7.5–9m) tall include 'Fructu Luteo', with yellow berries, and the narrowly upright 'Sheerwater Seedling'.

Sorbus cashmiriana

S. cashmiriana W. Himalayas
Foliage: autumn. Flowers: late spring. Berries: autumn to early winter. H:20–25ft (6–7.5m), S:15–20ft (4.5–6m). Z:5–7.
Clusters of white or pink flowers are succeeded by long-lasting white berries on this open tree. The long pinnate leaves are dark green. The Hubei rowan (*S. hupehensis*, Z:6–7) from China, of similar size, has blue-green foliage that turns red in autumn and white berries with a pink tinge.

S. 'Joseph Rock'
Foliage: autumn. Flowers: late spring. Berries: autumn to winter. H:25–30ft (7.5–9m), S:15–20ft (4.5–6m). Z:5–6.
Bright green pinnate leaves that turn orange, red, and purple in autumn and long-lasting yellow to orange-yellow berries are features of this highly ornamental upright tree. Unfortunately, it is prone to fire blight.

S. vilmorinii S.W. China
Foliage: autumn. Flowers: late spring to early summer. Berries: autumn. H and S:12–18ft (3.7–5.5m). Z:6–7.
The elegant ferny foliage of this shrub or small tree turns red to purple in autumn. The berries, drooping in clusters from arching branches, change from red to pink and eventually pink-tinged white.

STEWARTIA

THEACEAE

The 15–20 species include deciduous and evergreen woodland trees and shrubs growing on acid soils in E. Asia and S.E. USA. Several of the deciduous species have colorful autumn foliage as well as summer flowers and attractive peeling bark.

CULTIVATION Require partial shade, well-drained neutral to acid soil, and protection from strong winds.
PROPAGATION From seed, sown in autumn. From greenwood cuttings, taken in early summer. From semi-ripe cuttings, taken in mid- to late summer.
POTENTIAL PROBLEMS Usually none.

S. pseudocamellia Japan
Foliage: autumn. Flowers: mid- to late summer. H:50–70ft (15–22m), S:20–25ft (6–7.5m). Z:5–7.
Good reasons for growing this open tree as a specimen if space allows include cup-shaped white flowers with prominent stamens, leaves that turn yellow-orange to red-purple in autumn, and pink to red-brown flaking bark.

Stewartia sinensis

S. sinensis C. and E. China
Foliage: autumn. Flowers: mid-summer. H:20–30ft (6–9m), S:15–20ft (4.5–6m). Z:6–7.
This large shrub or small tree has peeling red-brown bark, fragrant cup-shaped white flowers, and foliage that turns rich crimson in autumn.

STYRAX

STYRACACEAE

Among the 100 or so species of this genus of deciduous and evergreen trees and shrubs, widely distributed in temperate and tropical regions of the Northern Hemisphere, several are woodland plants producing graceful displays of pendulous white flowers in spring or summer.
CULTIVATION Tolerate full sun or partial shade and require moist well-drained soil and shelter from cold winds.
PROPAGATION From seed, sown in a cold frame in autumn. From semi-ripe cuttings, taken in mid-summer.
POTENTIAL PROBLEMS Usually none.

Styrax japonicus

S. japonicus *China, Korea, Japan*
Japanese snowbell
Foliage: deciduous. Flowers:
summer. H:30ft (9m), S:9ft (2.7m).
Z:6-8.
This attractive large shrub or small
tree has a loose, open habit. The
spear-shaped leaves are dark green
on the upper surface with a silver-
white underside. Short drooping
clusters of large, fragrant, white,
bell-shaped flowers are carried on
the undersides of the shoots in
early summer. Other notable
species that are fully hardy and
deciduous include **S. hemsleyanus**
(Z:7-8), from China, which grows
to 30ft (9m), and the more shrubby
S. obassia (Z:5-8), from N. China
to Japan, which has fragrant
flowers and peeling bark.

TILIA

TILIACEAE Lime, linden

The limes are deciduous woodland
trees of the temperate Northern
Hemisphere, different authorities
giving a total of between 20 and
45 species. Several, including the
common lime (**T. × europaea**,
Z:4-7), have been much planted as

Tilia × europaea

stately avenue trees or pleached,
having pliable stems and being
tolerant of heavy pruning. The
magical fragrance of the small
creamy white to yellow flowers
has understandably inspired much
poetry and song.
CULTIVATION Require full sun or
partial shade and moist well-drained
soil. *T. × euchlora* and *T.* 'Petiolaris'
do not sucker strongly, but their
flowers are narcotic to bees.
PROPAGATION From seed, sown as
soon as ripe in autumn. From semiripe cuttings, taken in summer.
POTENTIAL PROBLEMS Aphids, except
T. × euchlora and *T.* 'Petiolaris', gall
mites, borers; anthracnose, canker.

T. × euchlora
Flowers: mid-summer. H:60-70ft
(18-22m), S:40-50ft (12-15m).
Z:4-7.
Unlike many limes, this is free of
aphids and therefore does not shed
honeydew. The arching branches
bear dark green rounded, toothed
leaves, paler on the underside, and
clusters of wonderfully fragrant
yellow-green flowers that are
narcotic to bees.

T. 'Petiolaris'
Pendulous silver lime
Flowers: late summer. H:80-100ft
(25-30m), S:50-70ft (15-22m).
Z:5-7.
Weeping branches, dark green
rounded leaves with silvery
undersides, and strongly scented
pale yellow flower clusters
distinguish this handsome
deciduous tree. The flowers are
narcotic to bees.

Tilia platyphyllos 'Rubra'

T. platyphyllos *Europe*
Large-leaved lime
Flowers: early to mid-summer.
H:80-100ft (25-30m), S:50-70ft
(15-22m). Z:5-7.
Drooping branchlets give the
columnar tree a weeping character.

The leaves are heart shaped, on
the underside downy and pale
green, and the yellow-green flowers,
which are narcotic to bees, exhale
a scent of summer contentment.
This species suckers less freely
than the common lime, but, like it,
attracts aphids that shed
honeydew. The shoots of the red-
twigged lime ('**Rubra**') are
conspicuous in winter.

TRACHYCARPUS

ARECACEAE

The 6 species of evergreen palms
comprising this genus are forest
trees from the Himalayas and
E.Asia. The only species that is
commonly grown, the Chusan
palm *T. fortunei*, is the hardiest of
the palms and notable for the size
of its fan-shaped leaves.
CULTIVATION Tolerate full sun or
light shade and require well-
drained soil and protection from
strong winds.
PROPAGATION By division, removing
basal growths with 2 or more
leaves in late spring. From seed,
sown under glass in spring.
POTENTIAL PROBLEMS Usually none.

Trachycarpus fortunei

T. fortunei *China*
Chusan palm
Foliage: year-round. Flowers: late
spring to early summer. H:30-50ft
(9-15m) S:8-10ft (2.5-3m). Z:7-10.
The medium green leaves are about
3ft (90cm) across and are pleated
and split at the ends, giving a
jagged, toothlike appearance. They
are held on sharply toothed
leafstalks up to 3ft (90cm) long
that arch out from the top of an
upright stem that is covered with
the fibrous remains of dead
leaves. Small yellow flowers appear
in large, dense bunches that can be
24in (60cm) long. Where summers
are hot enough, they produce
small, black, datelike fruits.

shrubs

The term shrub covers an enormous range of plants, originating all over the world, which have given rise to numerous cultivars and hybrids. The proportion of this book devoted to these perennial woody plants reflects their importance in the modern garden and the interest shown in them by gardeners. They often provide a structural framework within the garden, as well as interest for every season of the year. Some have attractive leaves year-round or during one season; others have colorful bark that is noticeable after the leaves have fallen. Flowers or fruits are produced by numerous shrubs. Size and habit within this vast group of plants cover a wide range, from tall erect subjects to prostrate but spreading plants, so there is likely to be a shrub for every situation in the garden.

Most shrubs are available for sale in containers, which facilitates transplanting throughout the year, provided the soil conditions are suitable. Deciduous shrubs grown in the open should be transplanted when they are dormant, from late autumn to early spring. Evergreen shrubs can be planted in early autumn or late spring.

For most of these plants, the best time for pruning is immediately after flowering, although some shrubs require no regular pruning at all.

Top Pyracantha 'Golden Charmer'
Center Viburnum tinus 'Gwenllian'
Bottom Camellia japonica 'Gloire de Nantes'

ABELIA

CAPRIFOLIACEAE

About 30 species, from Asia and Central America, are represented in gardens by a small number of semievergreen and deciduous shrubs with neat foliage. They bear small foxglovelike flowers in great profusion. Abelias do well in a sunny bed. In temperate gardens, the most colorful species, the half-hardy Mexican *A. floribunda* (Z:8-11), which is an evergreen shrub, dangles tubular flowers of reddish pink. To flourish it needs a special position at the foot of a warm wall. Here it can then grow to a height of 10ft (3m) or more.

CULTIVATION Require full sun and fertile well-drained soil. Prune out old, straggly stems in mid-spring. In frost-prone areas, grow plants against a south- or west-facing wall or fence.

PROPAGATION From cuttings, in the summer.

POTENTIAL PROBLEMS Usually none.

Abelia × grandiflora

A. × grandiflora

Flowers: mid-summer to autumn. H:6-9ft (1.8-2.7m), S:4-7ft (1.2-2.2m). Z:6-9.

The slightly fragrant pink and white flowers of this shrub, densely clustered above the glossy semi-evergreen foliage, are undramatic but the season is long and late. 'Francis Mason', which has dark-green leaves with a yellow margin, is attractive as a foliage plant but the variegation is ill at ease with the flowers. The semievergreen *A.* 'Edward Goucher' (Z:7-9), of which *A. × grandiflora* is a parent, is more compact, and the glossy bronze of its young leaves is a lovely prelude to the mauve flowers.

ABUTILON

MALVACEAE

The genus, with well over 100 species, is widely distributed in tropical and subtropical regions. Several shrubby species and a number of hybrids are notable for their bell-shaped flowers and maplelike leaves. In cool temperate regions, the tender species need greenhouse conditions, but in milder areas the hardiest abutilons can be grown outdoors, preferably with the backing of a warm wall. The handsomely shaped leaves of *A. pictum* 'Thompsonii' (Z:9-10) can look unhealthy with their yellow and green mottling. However, because of this, rather than despite it, the shrub is a favorite to include in subtropical planting schemes.

CULTIVATION Require full sun and well-drained soil. Prune weather-damaged shoots in early spring and prune crossing shoots after flowering.

PROPAGATION From seed, sown in spring at 59-64°F (15-18°C). From cuttings, taken in spring and summer.

POTENTIAL PROBLEMS Under glass: red spider mites, whiteflies, mealybugs, scale.

A. megapotamicum Brazil

Trailing abutilon

Flowers: summer to autumn. H and S:4-6ft (1.2-1.8m). Z:8-10.

Vivid heart-shaped buds dangle from flopping slender stems, which are improved by wall training. The crimson calyces open just enough to allow yellow petals and purple stamens to protrude. Among several hybrids that owe some of their character to this species, *A.* 'Kentish Belle' features larger pale apricot petals, which have striking reddish veins.

Abutilon vitifolium
'Veronica Tennant'

A. vitifolium Chile

Flowers: early summer. H:12-15ft (3.7-4.5m), S:6-8ft (1.8-2.5m). Z:8-10.

Almost treelike when it romps away, this fast-growing deciduous shrub has downy, vinelike leaves and clusters of large saucer-shaped mauve flowers. 'Veronica Tennant' is very pale, edging toward the purity of 'Tennant's White'. The species is a parent of the hybrid *A. × suntense*, a smaller shrub with colors from white to violet blue.

ACER

ACERACEAE Maple

Their poise as shrubs or small trees, the elegant cut of their foliage, and their color variations, with spectacular transformations in autumn, have earned for a small group of deciduous Asiatic maples a special place in Japanese gardens. In the West this genus of about 150 species has been grown for well over 100 years, most impressively as a shrub layer in woodland glades where the soil is moist and there is shelter from cold winds. Autumn color is most brilliant on acid soils. Their qualities are also easily appreciated in small gardens, even those in no way inspired by a Japanese aesthetic. Acers are easily accommodated, being slow growing and of moderate size. They do not rely on a passing display of flowers to grab attention, but are, at the least, pleasing. They are sometimes superbly ornamental when in leaf, and remain interesting when reduced to an intricate pattern of twigs and stems. See also TREES.

CULTIVATION Require sun or partial shade, well-drained, moist, fertile soil, and shelter from late spring frosts; temperatures below 25°F (-4°C) will kill new foliage. Prune out crossing and unsightly shoots in late autumn to mid-winter.

PROPAGATION From seed, sown as soon as ripe. By grafting, in late winter. By budding, in late summer.

POTENTIAL PROBLEMS Aphids, mites, scale, caterpillars; tar spot, verticillium wilt, leaf scorch, honey fungus.

A. japonicum Japan

Full-moon maple, Japanese maple

Foliage: mid-spring to autumn. Flowers: early to mid-spring. H:20-30ft (6-9m), S:10-20ft (3-6m). Z:5-8.

In spring, the clusters of purplish-red flowers are an attractive feature. However, the species and its named cultivars are grown mainly for their rounded outline and their many elegant leaves. The large deeply lobed leaves of 'Aconitifolium' and the broader fans of 'Vitifolium' turn from soft green to rich shades of orange-red in autumn.

A. palmatum China, Japan, Korea

Japanese maple

Foliage: mid-spring to autumn. Flowers: spring. Fruits: late summer. H:15-25ft (4.5-7.5m), S:10-20ft (3-6m). Z:5-8.

In the wild, the Japanese maple is said to make a tree as much as 40ft

Acer palmatum Dissectum Atropurpureum Group

(12m) in height, but in cultivation its numerous forms are better known as slow-growing bushes. These eventually form large shrubs or small trees of rounded outline. The Japanese fascination with this species over many centuries accounts for the extraordinary range of leaf color and shape, all variations on a 5- to 7-lobed green pattern with bronze to red coloring in autumn. The flowers are insignificant but in some of the cultivars the red-winged fruits are conspicuous in late summer. Many cultivars, not only the deeply lobed **f. atropurpureum**, have dark purplish or bronze foliage in summer, turning red in autumn. **'Bloodgood'**, for example, has rich purple leaves with 5 deeply divided lobes, and is richly colored in autumn with bright red fruits. Deep division of the leaves in **var. dissectum** gives them a soft ferny texture, the effect of which is heightened by the growth of mounded shrubs rarely more than 6ft (1.8m) tall. The leaves have as many as 11 lobes, each finely cut and toothed. Some of the cultivars with finely divided foliage have copper-red or purplish foliage. In summer, the **Dissectum Atropurpureum Group** make mushroom shapes of bronze red. **Var. d. 'Inaba-shidare'** is a more open bush, with large, red-stalked, dark leaves that become intense crimson in autumn. The larger-leaved forms include the treelike **'Osakazuki'**, the 7-lobed leaves, more than 4in (10cm) long, turning in autumn from mid-green to incandescent reds. Also treelike, **'Sango-kaku'** (Z:6–8), sometimes known as the coral bark maple, makes a beautiful transition from green to soft yellow in autumn. It has remarkable red stems in winter.

A. shirasawanum 'Aureum'
Foliage: mid-spring to autumn. Flowers: spring. H and S:12–20ft (3.7–6m). Z:6–8.
Prettily fan-shaped leaves, with 7 to 11 elegant points, are carried in overlapping tiers on a compact bush that is slow to reach treelike proportions. Its lime green turns to orange and red in autumn.

Acer shirasawanum 'Aureum'

AMELANCHIER

ROSACEAE Service berry

White starry flowers in spring and foliage that colors brilliantly in autumn are the winning ornamental characteristics of a mainly North American genus of deciduous shrubs and small trees. It also has representatives in Asia and Europe. There are altogether about 25 species, some of which have proven difficult to distinguish one from another, and because of this have been much confused in commerce.
CULTIVATION Require sun or partial shade and well-drained, moist, fertile, acid soil. In winter, remove any branch that spoils the shape of the plant.
PROPAGATION From seed, sown as soon as ripe. From cuttings, taken in summer. Also by sucker removal of stoloniferous species, in autumn.
POTENTIAL PROBLEMS Fire blight.

Amelanchier lamarckii

A. lamarckii
Foliage: autumn. Flowers: mid-spring. Fruits: mid-summer. H and S:10–25ft (3–7.5m). Z:5–8.
The 5-petaled white flowers are massed among young foliage that is copper red and silky. This large shrub or small tree is spectacular again in autumn, when the leaves color red and orange. The purple-black berrylike fruits, which ripen in summer, are edible. Two similar North American species with which it is confused are the shadbush (**A. canadensis**, Z:4–8) and the Allegheny service berry (**A. laevis**). The latter is a parent of a fine hybrid, **A. × grandiflora** **'Ballerina'**, which has large flowers that are borne in great profusion.

ARALIA

ARALIACEAE

This very mixed genus of about 40 species, distributed in Asia and the Americas, includes several deciduous shrubs or small trees that are notable for their compound leaves. Variegation refines the already elegant foliage of the species described.
CULTIVATION Require sun or partial shade and organic-rich, moist soil. Prune unwanted stems in autumn and winter.
PROPAGATION From seed, sown as soon as ripe or in spring after stratification. From root cuttings, in winter. By removal of suckers, in autumn or winter. By grafting **A. elata** variegated cultivars in winter.
POTENTIAL PROBLEMS Aphids.

A. elata E. Asia
Japanese angelica tree
Foliage: late spring to autumn. Flowers: late summer to early autumn. H and S:20–30ft (6–9m). Z:4–9.
The species, usually an upright tree, has spiny sparsely branching stems topped by magnificent leaves, which are up to 4ft (1.2m) long, doubly divided and with about 80 leaflets. The frothy clusters of tiny cream flowers appear just as the leaves begin to turn red and yellow.
'Aureovariegata', with leaflets margined yellow to cream, and the paler **'Variegata'** are less vigorous, usually making large shrubs about 10–15ft (3–4.5m) in height and spread. The tendency to sucker needs to be watched, particularly on variegated cultivars, which are oftengrafted on plain-leaved stocks.

Aralia elata 'Aureovariegata'

123

AUCUBA

CORNACEAE

The fate of the Japanese aucuba
(*A. japonica*) is to be taken for
granted, for it has long been used as
a shrub of last resort, expected to
tolerate heavy pollution and to
flourish in those dismal corners of
the garden where other plants
would certainly fail. The 3 or 4
species in the genus are all
evergreen and they bear male and
female flowers on different plants.
For female clones to produce
berries, there must be a male
situated close by.
CULTIVATION Require full sun or
partial or full shade, and tolerate
most soil conditions. Remove
unwanted stems during dormancy.
PROPAGATION From seed, sown in
autumn. From semiripe cuttings, in
mid-summer.
POTENTIAL PROBLEMS Usually none.
WARNING Mild stomach upsets can
result if the plant is eaten.

A. japonica *Japan*
Japanese aucuba
Foliage: year-round. Flowers: mid-
spring. Fruits: autumn to spring
(female plants only). H and S:6–10ft
(1.8–3m). Z:7–9.
Even in dense shade, this is a bushy
shrub that is well covered with
large glossy leaves. The small
purplish flowers are easily
overlooked, but the long-lasting
berries, when they eventually
color, are a lustrous scarlet. There
are numerous plain-leaved and
variegated cultivars. The female
f. longifolia and the male **'Lance
Leaf'** have narrow plain leaves.
'Crotonifolia' (female) is brightly
splashed and speckled with yellow.
The plain-leaved and compact
'Rozannie', about 3ft (90cm) in
height, is self-pollinating and bears
some heavy crops of berries. The
original spotted laurel, and once
widely planted **'Variegata'**
(female), have toothed leaves that
are densely spotted with gold.
Reverted growths that appear on
variegated cultivars should be
removed promptly.

Aucuba japonica **'Variegata'**

BALLOTA

LAMIACEAE

Among the 30 to 35 species are
several evergreen subshrubs of
Mediterranean origin that thrive in
hot stony places. Their wooly gray
mounds become whiter the drier
the conditions.
CULTIVATION Require full sun and
poor, dry, well-drained soil or
potting media. Cut the plant back
in the mid-spring.
PROPAGATION From cuttings, in
summer.
POTENTIAL PROBLEMS Usually none.

Ballota pseudodictamnus

B. pseudodictamnus *Crete, Greece, W. Turkey*
Foliage: mid-spring to late autumn
(year-round in frost-free zones).
Flowers: late spring to early
summer. H and S:18–24in
(45–60cm). Z:7–9.
Erect white-felted stems carry
rounded yellow-green leaves
silvered with a covering of gray
wool. The small purplish-pink
flowers, carried in whorls, are much
less important ornamentally than
the foliage. *B. acetabulosa* is a
similar plant with greener leaves,
and the flowers have larger calyces.

BERBERIS

BERBERIDACEAE Barberry

Many of the barberries seem rather
gauche plants. But in this large
genus comprising about 450
species of deciduous and evergreen
shrubs are numerous plants of
ornamental value, grown for their
flowers, foliage, and large crops of
berries. The spininess of many
makes them difficult to work
among, but this is an asset when
they are used for hedging. They are
found in a wide range of habitats
throughout the Northern
Hemisphere and also in Africa and
South America.
CULTIVATION Require sun and any
well-drained soil. Prune only to
maintain a balanced shape. Prune
evergreen shrubs and trim
evergreen hedges after flowering;
prune and trim deciduous

specimens and hedges during the
late winter.
PROPAGATION From seed, sown in
winter; from cuttings, taken in
summer.
POTENTIAL PROBLEMS Aphids;
powdery mildew.
WARNING All parts may cause
stomach upset if eaten. The spines
may irritate the skin.

Berberis × stenophylla

B. darwinii *Argentina, Chile*
Flowers: mid- to late spring. Fruits:
autumn. H and S:8–10ft
(2.5–3m). Z:6–8.
Clusters of small, cup-shaped,
orange-yellow flowers hang in
great profusion among the glossy
spiny leaves and are followed by
blue berries. This evergreen
species makes a highly ornamental
informal hedge. It is a parent of
B. × stenophylla, another spiny
evergreen of similar height but
making a wider thicket. It is one of
the most graceful barberry, putting
out arching stems that in late spring
have deep yellow, strongly fragrant
flowers. The crop of berries that
follows is sparse. **B. × s. 'Corallina
Compacta'**, a dwarf usually under
1ft (30cm) in height, has yellow
flowers from coral buds.

Berberis darwinii

B. julianae *China*
Flowers: late spring. Fruits: autumn.
H and S:8–10ft (2.5–3m). Z:6–8.
A hedge of this spiny- stemmed and
spiny-leaved evergreen is almost
impenetrable. The leaves are
coppery when young, and the
scented yellow flowers, which
have a red tinge, are followed by
blue-black berries.

B. × ottawensis

Flowers: late spring. Fruits: autumn. H and S:6-8ft (1.8-2.5m). Z:6-8.
The plain-leaved hybrid is a pleasing deciduous shrub with arching stems that give it a rounded outline. The yellow flowers, which have a red tinge, are followed by dangling clusters of red berries. 'Superba' has purplish-red leaves that turn bright crimson in autumn.

B. 'Rubrostilla'

Flowers: late spring. Fruits: autumn. H:4-6ft (1.2-1.8m), S:6-8ft (1.8-2.5m). Z:6-8.
The glaucous leaves of this gracefully arching deciduous shrub color well in autumn. Clustered pale yellow flowers are followed by some distinctively pear-shaped coral-red berries that are broadest at their base.

B. thunbergii Japan

Flowers: early summer. Fruits: autumn. H:4-5ft (1.2-1.5m), S:6-8ft (1.8-2.5m). Z:5-8.
The straw-colored flowers have a warm tint, and the leaves of this spiny deciduous species color bright red and orange in autumn at the same time as the small ovoid berries turn scarlet. The plain-leaved form is useful for hedging, but it is the numerous purple-leaved variations that are most commonly grown. The full-scale **f. atropurpurea** has bronze purple foliage. Less vigorous is '**Rose Glow**', with pale pink or white streaking of the leaves. Dwarf purple-leaved forms include '**Atropurpurea Nana**', up to 2ft (60cm) tall, and the even more compact '**Bagatelle**'.

Berberis thunbergii 'Rose Glow'

BRACHYGLOTTIS

ASTERACEAE

Daisy flowerheads and leaves that are usually gray or white felted on the underside are characteristic of a group of about 30 evergreen shrubs, native to New Zealand and Tasmania, that have been moved from *Senecio* to this genus. They are found in a wide range of habitats, but most species, like the hybrid that is described, are lovers of the sun and will tolerate well the wind and salt conditions of oceanside gardens. Other species grow well in a shrub border.
CULTIVATION Require full sun and well-drained soil. Prune the older straggly stems back to new lower growths in mid-spring.
PROPAGATION From semiripe cuttings, in mid-summer.
POTENTIAL PROBLEMS Usually none.

Brachyglottis Dunedin Group 'Sunshine'

B. Dunedin Group 'Sunshine'

Foliage: evergreen. Flowers: mid-summer to autumn. H:4-5ft (1.2-1.5m), S:4-6ft (1.2-1.8m). Z:8-10.
The sprawling mound looks silvery when covered by young hairy leaves and felted buds. The mature leaves are gray-green, but their wavy margins are outlined in silver-gray. The brash yellow daisies are borne in great profusion. '**Moira Read**' (Z:9-10) has an irregular yellow and pale-green variegation.

BUDDLEJA

BUDDLEJACEAE

Self-sown seedlings of the common butterfly bush (*Buddleja davidii*), apparently thriving in the cracks of old walls or on rubbly waste ground, show the resilience of these plants in dry conditions. This is a large and very mixed genus of about 100 species, from Asia, Africa, and the Americas, but all the shrubs in general cultivation share a preference for open, sunny positions and well-drained soils, and are tolerant of lime. They generally grow well (except climbers) in a shrub border. The individual tubular flowers, which are sweetly scented, are small, but their densely clustered arrangements are conspicuous. Buddlejas that flower in late summer are highly attractive to butterflies and other insects.
CULTIVATION Require full sun and fertile well-drained soil. Prune buddlejas that flower in late summer and autumn in early spring, cutting back to a low framework of stems. Prune *B. alternifolia* after flowering, cutting the flowered shoots back to lower young growths and removing about a quarter of the old shoots. Prune *B. globosa* lightly after it has flowered.
PROPAGATION From semiripe cuttings, in summer; *B. davidii* from hardwood cuttings, in autumn.
POTENTIAL PROBLEMS Capsid bugs, caterpillars, figwort weevils, mullein moths, red spider mites.

B. alternifolia China

Flowers: early summer. H:12-15ft (3.7-4.5m), S:10-15ft (3-4.5m). Z:5-9.
The long arching branches, generously covered along their length with clusters of small purplish-mauve flowers, are seen to best effect when specimens are trained on a main stem to form a weeping standard. The flowers are borne on growths made in the previous season. The species is unusual in having alternate leaves.

Buddleja alternifolia

B. crispa Himalayas

Foliage: mid-spring to autumn. Flowers: mid- to late summer. H and S:6-10ft (1.8-3m). Z:8-9.
This deciduous white-felted shrub is a study in soft tones. It has scented flowers that are white centered and pale mauve. These are borne in cylindrical spikes. Where the shrub's hardiness is borderline, it is best to train it up onto a warm wall. The flowers are produced on the wood of the current season.

Buddleja 'Pink Delight'

B. davidii *China, Japan*
Butterfly bush
Flowers: mid-summer to early autumn. H and S:8-12ft (2.5-3.7m). Z:5-9.
The nectar-rich flowers, lilac to purple in color, densely cluster in arching plumes up to 20in (50cm) long. Their glorious scent draws butterflies to the garden over a long season. The fast-growing broad bushes have lance-shaped gray-green leaves, felted on the underside. The flower color in the wild and of most self-sown seedlings is pale purple. The many white and richly colored forms in cultivation include the following: **'Dartmoor'**, with short magenta plumes; **'Empire Blue'**, violet blue with orange eye; **'Royal Red'**, purplish red; and **'White Profusion'**, white with a yellow eye. **'Nanho Blue'**, with pale mauve flowers, is an example of several of slender build. The pink flowers of **B. 'Pink Delight'**, a hybrid of this species, have orange eyes.

B. fallowiana *W. China*
Flowers: late summer to early autumn. H:6-8ft (1.8-2.5m), S:10ft (3m). Z:6-9.
This species, which is less vigorous and more tender than the better known *B. davidii*, produces mauve-blue flowers with an orange eye against felted gray foliage. The young foliage of **B. 'Lochinch'**, probably a hybrid between this species and *B. davidii*, is silvery gray, and the orange-centered flowers are violet blue in color.

B. globosa *Argentina, Chile*
Orange ball tree
Flowers: early summer. H and S:10-15ft (3-4.5m). Z:6-9.
The arrangement of the yellow flowers, which are clustered together in tight balls, is unique among the buddlejas. The balls are about ¾in (2cm) across, 8 to 10 balls standing above the partially evergreen foliage in a branched arrangement at the end of each stem. It can be deciduous or semievergreen.

BUXUS

BUXACEAE BOX, boxwood

Of about 70 species, all evergreen, several are remarkably tolerant of regular clipping and as a consequence have long been grown as hedging plants and as subjects for topiary. The leaves can be rather leathery and are round to oval shaped. In southern Europe *B. balearica* is used in much the same way as the most widely grown of the species, the common box (*B. sempervirens*). The flowers, with male and female carried on the same plant, are shaped like stars and are yellow-green in color, but are a bit inconspicuous.
CULTIVATION Tolerate full sun or partial shade and a wide range of well-drained soils but best in light shade and fertile conditions. Clip hedges and topiary species in mid- to late summer; prune old hedges in late spring.
PROPAGATION From semiripe cuttings, in mid-summer.
POTENTIAL PROBLEMS Box suckers, red spider mites.
WARNING Sap contact may irritate the skin.

B. sempervirens *Europe, N. Africa, Turkey*
Common box
Foliage: year-round. Flowers: mid-spring. H and S:10-15ft (3-4.5m). Z:6-8.
The glossy dark-green leaves of this species are its main attraction and on unclipped specimens form dense sprays on untidy bushes or small trees. Clipping results in even denser growth that holds its shape well. The many cultivars of this species, including several that are variegated, show a considerable range of vigor and in leaf size. An irregular creamy margin on the leaves of **'Elegantissima'** give this slow-growing box a silvery look. Bearing plain leaves **'Handsworthiensis'**, which is vigorous and of upright growth, is much favored for hedges. It can even reach heights of 6ft (1.8m)

Buxus sempervirens 'Elegantissima'

or more. In marked contrast, **'Suffruticosa'**, which is compact and very slow growing, is mainly used in formal gardens for edging flower beds. Dense slow-growing clones of the small-leaved box (**B. microphylla**, Z:5-8), such as **'Green Pillow'**, can be used in the same way and only need to be clipped occasionally.

CALLICARPA

VERBENACEAE

In a genus of well over 100 species, many are tropical and subtropical shrubs and trees. The beauty berry is one of the hardiest and makes a startling autumn discovery in temperate gardens when thinning leaves expose clustered fruits of unusual coloring. Several plants of different clones need to be grown together to guarantee good crops.
CULTIVATION Require sun or partial shade and well-drained fertile soil. Prune in early spring, cutting back to new shoots.
PROPAGATION From seed, sown in autumn or spring. From cuttings, in spring and summer.
POTENTIAL PROBLEMS Usually none.

Callicarpa bodinieri var. giraldii

C. bodinieri var. giraldii
C. and W. China
Beauty berry
Flowers: mid-summer. Fruits: autumn. H:6-10ft (1.8-3m), S:5-8ft (1.5-2.5m). Z:6-8.
In summer this bushy deciduous shrub with its dark-green leaves does not attract much attention, although later in the season it does carry numerous tiny flowers that are mauve pink in color. However, when its small round fruits start to change color, it is transformed. Beautiful clusters of shiny violet-purple berries encrust the stems before leaf-fall and remain afterward on the bare stems. **'Profusion'** freely produces violet fruit, and its foliage has a purplish tint to it in the spring that then turns an attractive reddish-purple color during the autumn months.

CALLISTEMON

MYRTACEAE Bottlebrush

The "bottlebrushes" of these Australian evergreens bristle with colorful stamens, the other flower parts being insignificant. In the wild, the long-lasting seed capsules that cluster along the stems only open after bush fires. These shrubs or small trees are curious in that the stems continue to grow beyond the faded flowers. There are about 25 species, most of which are plants of open or lightly forested land where the soil is reasonably moist. They can be grown at the foot of house walls or in shrub beds.
CULTIVATION Require full sun and well-drained soil, which is neutral or slightly acid. Prune back any unsightly shoots to lower new growths in early spring.
PROPAGATION From seed, sown in spring at 61–64°F (16–18°C). From semiripe cuttings, in late summer.
POTENTIAL PROBLEMS Red spider mites, mealybugs, scale.

C. citrinus *Australia (Victoria, New South Wales)*
Crimson bottlebrush
Flowers: late spring to early summer. H and S:4–20ft (1.2–6m). Z:9–10.
The specific name of this shrub refers to the lemon scent of the bruised leaves. This species must stand as representative of several very beautiful half-hardy callistemons. It is especially impressive in the form **'Splendens'**, when the arching branches carry numerous crimson flower spikes. **'White Anzac'** is 3–10ft (1–3m) tall and produces white flowers, which can have attractive touches of pink when they are fully open. The fully hardy Tonghi bottlebrush (*C. subulatus*, Z:8–10) reaches a height of 5ft (1.5m) and has red flowers. The alpine bottlebrush (*C. alpina*, Z:8–10) is about the same size, but has pale yellow flowers. Both are good alternatives to the more tender species.

Callistemon citrinus

CALLUNA

ERICACEAE Scotch heather

In the Northern Hemisphere vast stretches of mountainside, boggy and peaty areas, and heathland are transformed in late summer and autumn by the dense clusters of purple bell-shaped flowers produced by the single species in this genus. The leaves are generally dark green in color. The soils on which this low evergreen shrub is found in the wild are acidic and usually of low fertility. As garden plants, the hundreds of cultivars are restricted to being grown in areas where the soil is lime-free.
CULTIVATION Requires full sun and well-drained, acidic, organic-rich soil. Trim annually after flowering or in early spring.
PROPAGATION From semiripe cuttings, in mid-summer. By layering, in spring.
POTENTIAL PROBLEMS Gray mold (*Botrytis*), phytophthora root rot, rhizoctonia.

Calluna vulgaris

C. vulgaris *Azores, N. and W. Europe to Russia (Siberia), Morocco, Turkey*
Flowers: mid-summer to late autumn. H:4–24in (10–60cm), S:4–30in (10–75cm). Z:4–6.
Few plants of such intrinsic beauty so defeat the gardener. Heather has a way of looking alien in the domesticated order of a garden with beds and lawn. It needs a setting on the wild side. The many cultivars include singles and doubles in white, mauve, pink, purple, and ruby. Even the dead flowers can look attractive in winter. There are differences in height and spread, and also great variations in foliage color (admittedly, not always matching the flowers), often with seasonal changes that make their strongest effects in winter. The following selection, flowering in late summer to early autumn unless stated otherwise, is a mere sample of the range. **'Allegro'**, 20 by 24in (50 by 60cm), has mid- to dark-green foliage and deep red flowers in

Calluna vulgaris 'County Wicklow'

autumn; **'Anthony Davis'**, 18 by 24in (45 by 60cm), has gray-green foliage and white flowers; **'County Wicklow'**, 10 by 12in (25 by 30cm), has dark-green foliage and double pink flowers in mid- to late summer; **'Darkness'**, 10 by 14in (25 by 35cm), has bright green foliage and crimson flowers; **'Firefly'**, 18 by 24in (45 by 60cm), has red-brown foliage turning orange-red in winter and purplish-pink flowers; **'Foxii Nana'**, 6 by 12in (15 by 30cm), has foliage that makes a bright green tight mound with only a few mauve flowers; **'Gold Haze'**, 18 by 24in (45 by 60cm), has foliage yellow-green to gold with white flowers; **'H.E. Beale'**, 18 by 24in (45 by 60cm), has mid- to dark green foliage and double pink flowers in autumn; **'Inshriach Bronze'**, 10 by 14in (25 by 35cm), has yellow-gold leaves and lilac-pink flowers; **'Robert Chapman'**, 10 by 24in (25 by 60cm), has yellow-green foliage in spring, strongly tinted orange and red in winter, and purple flowers; **'Sister Anne'**, 4 by 10in (10 by 25cm), has silver foliage bronzing in winter and mauve-pink flowers; **'White Lawn'**, 2 by 16in (5 by 40cm), has bright green foliage and white flowers; and **'Tib'**, 12 by 16in (30 by 40cm), has dark green foliage and purple flowers from mid-summer to mid-autumn.

Calluna vulgaris 'Robert Chapman'

CAMELLIA

THEACEAE

This Asiatic genus of evergreen shrubs and small trees contains about 250 species, of which relatively few are widely grown, but the cultivated forms are numbered in the thousands. The attention of breeders and selectors over a long period accounts for the curious contrasts of simple grace and formal artifice that make such striking contrasts in the many cultivars. The color range is relatively limited, covering white and shades of pink and red, as well as a number of bicolors. Admittedly, there is the yellow-flowered *C. nitidissima* (Z:8-9) from South China and Vietnam, but the color has yet to make a significant mark among the hardier hybrids. In flower form, however, the choice includes singles and semidoubles, with the stamens forming a prominent central boss. Others have anemone and peony centers, in which some of the stamens are petallike, making very full flowers in the peony forms. There are also doubles, and these sometimes show stamens at the center, surrounded by numerous tiers of petals, but in the case of the formal doubles the numerous petals overlap symmetrically right to the center. The striking leaves are shiny, dark green in color and oval shaped. Being in essence woodland plants of moist neutral to acid soils, camellias do well under a light deciduous canopy, which protects the flowers from frost and reduces the risk of any bruising caused by rapid thawing in the early morning sunshine. Many of the cultivated camellias have traveled so far from their origins that they look out of place in a wild garden and are much more plants to be included in sheltered town gardens. Here they do well when planted in the shade of walls and buildings, even as container-grown specimens. They are also very suitable as plants for hedges and screens.

CULTIVATION Require partial shade and organic-rich, moist, well-drained, acid soil (ericaceous potting medium). Mulch annually during late winter. Prune any straggly shoots from plants in early spring.

PROPAGATION From leaf bud and semiripe cuttings, in late summer to late winter. Also by grafting, in late winter.

POTENTIAL PROBLEMS Aphids, scale, vine weevils; sooty mold, viruses, leafy gall, leaf spot, honey fungus.

Camellia japonica 'Adolphe Audusson'

C. japonica China, Japan, Korea
Japanese camellia
Flowers: late winter to late spring. H:6-25ft (1.8-7.5m), S:6-20ft (1.8-6m). Z:7-9.
These plants have handsome glossy foliage. They exhibit the whole gamut of camellia flower form and considerable differences in growth, some being compact and upright, others spreading wide. Even when flowers are caught by frosts, the season is usually long enough for some flowers to attain perfection. A drawback, however, is that blooms do not fall when they are over, so that, unless they are picked off, the browned flowers vie for attention with those that are pristine. There is a great deal of duplication of qualities in the many cultivars available. The following selection merely gives an idea of the range. '**Adolphe Audusson**', vigorous but compact and free-flowering, with semidouble, large, blood-red flowers; '**Alba Plena**', upright but slow growing, with white formal double flowers of medium size; '**Bob Hope**', upright and compact, with very dark red, large, semi-double flowers, sometimes peonylike in form; '**Bob's Tinsie**', upright and compact, with small bright red flowers of anemone form; '**Elegans**', spreading, with large, anemone-form, deep pink flowers; '**Gloire de Nantes**', upright and medium sized, with large, semi-double and red-pink flowers; '**Hagoromo**', upright and medium sized, with semidouble pale pink flowers; '**Jupiter**', vigorous

Camellia japonica 'Jupiter'

and upright, with medium-sized single flowers, the bright red petals cradling yellow stamens; and '**Lavinia Maggi**', vigorous and open, with medium-sized, formal, double flowers that are white with pink or crimson streaks and spots.

C. reticulata China
Flowers: early spring. H:10-50ft (3-15m), S:5-15ft (1.5-4.5m). Z:7-9.
The species, long cultivated in China, was first known in the West as a sumptuous semidouble, an early introduction being '**Captain Rawes**', with carmine flowers that can be more than 6in (15cm) across. The dark-green leathery leaves are not glossy. Only in mild climates can this and other cultivars be grown outdoors, but some magnificent hybrids, of which *C. reticulata* is a parent, are hardier. *C.* '**Leonard Messel**', which makes a rounded shrub to about 12ft (3.7m), is fully hardy and has large, clear pink flowers that are semidouble or of peony form.

Camellia 'Leonard Messel'

C. sasanqua Japan
Flowers: mid- to late autumn. H:10-20ft (3-6m), S:10-15ft (3-4.5m). Z:7-9.
The shrub is hardy, but the small scented flowers are often damaged by frost. They can be single and white in the wild but often semi-double or double and in shades of pink or red in the cultivars. Plants need moisture but California sun does wonders for their performance. '**Crimson King**' is a bright red single and '**Narumigata**' a pink-tinged single white.

C. × williamsii
Flowers: late autumn to mid-spring. H:6-15ft (1.8-4.5m), S:3-10ft (90-300cm). Z:7-9.
This name covers a range of hybrids raised from crosses between *C. japonica* and *C. saluenensis*, the latter a leafy shrub from Yunnan in China that has single flowers in white or shades of pink. The hybrids, hardier than *C. saluenensis* and very free-flowering, have the great merit of dropping their

Camellia saluenensis

blooms once they fade. The foliage is glossy and the flowers, white to deep pink, are single or semidouble, occasionally of anemone or peony fullness. **'Brigadoon'**, dense and upright, has semidouble flowers of lovely form and deep pink. **'Donation'**, upright and compact, also has semidouble soft pink flowers that are darkened by carmine veining. It is a magnificent and free-flowering camellia, but it is too widely planted to seem the treasure it undeniably is. Among the finest of the singles are the white **'Francis Hanger'** and also the pale pink **'J.C. Williams'**.

Camellia × williamsii **'Donation'**

CARYOPTERIS

VERBENACEAE Blue spirea

The half dozen plants in this genus include several small aromatic shrubs that are Asiatic in origin. One of these, *C. mongolica* (Z:5–9), a plant that in the wild experiences hot dry summers and very cold winters, is a parent of the widely grown hybrid described below.
CULTIVATION Require full sun and light well-drained soil. Prune to a low woody framework annually in early spring.
PROPAGATION From seed, sown in autumn. From cuttings, in late spring to early summer.
POTENTIAL PROBLEMS Capsid bugs.

C. × clandonensis
Flowers: late summer to early autumn. H:2–3ft (60–90cm), S:30–48in (75–120cm). Z:5–9.
The bushy plants have gray-green

leaves, silvered with fine hairs on the underside, and clusters of small tubular flowers in shades of blue. **'Heavenly Blue'** is a compact upright cultivar that has dark blue flowers.

Caryopteris × clandonensis **'Heavenly Blue'**

CASSIOPE

ERICACEAE

The dozen dwarf evergreen shrubs of this genus are heatherlike plants originating from the arctic and alpine regions of N. Europe, N. Asia, and North America. The stems seem leafless, but are in fact tightly clasped by overlapping green or gray scalelike leaves. The small bell- or urn-shaped flowers dangle prettily on fine stalks, but to achieve their exquisite best these little shrubs need to be grown in cool acid conditions. Several species are prostrate. *C. lycopodioides* (Z:3–6), for example, makes a wiry mat that rarely reaches more than 3in (7.5cm) in height but grows as much as 18in (45cm) across. It is topped by nodding creamy flowers in late spring. Some of the more upright plants include 'Edinburgh' and other hybrids that are usually much easier to maintain as garden plants than the more demanding species.
CULTIVATION Require sun or partial shade and organic-rich, moist, acid soil.
PROPAGATION From seed, sown in autumn. From cuttings, in summer. Also by layering prostrate species, in autumn or early spring.
POTENTIAL PROBLEMS Usually none.

Cassiope lycopodioides

Cassiope **'Edinburgh'**

C. **'Edinburgh'**
Flowers: late spring. H and S:10in (25cm). Z:3–6.
The upright clump of dark-green stems is enlivened in spring by white bells with green-red calyces.

CEANOTHUS

RHAMNACEAE California lilac

Ceanothus × veitchianus

The common name is a misleading introduction to a genus of deciduous and evergreen shrubs with dense heads of very small flowers, usually in shades of blue or white. There are about 55 species, all from North America and many from California, where they are an important constituent of the dense scrub known as chaparral. The deciduous kinds are generally hardier than the evergreens. Plants are fast growing and come into flower when young. A number of ceanothus are low growing and dense enough to make ground-cover. Others are treelike, with bushy growth developing above a short trunk to a height of 20ft (6m) or more. *C. arboreus* (Z:8–10) and its cultivar **'Trewithen Blue'** (Z:8–10), which has deeply tinted flowers, are notable. Some hybrids occur naturally such as *C. × veitchianus* (Z:6–8), an evergreen shrub about 10ft (3m) tall, with dark blue flowers in late spring.
CULTIVATION Require full sun and well-drained fertile soil. Prune straggly stems from evergreens after flowering. Prune deciduous plants in early spring by cutting old shoots back close to the wood.

PROPAGATION From seed, sown in autumn. From cuttings, in mid- to late summer.
POTENTIAL PROBLEMS Honey fungus.

C. 'Autumnal Blue'
Flowers: late summer to early autumn. H:8–10ft (2.5–3m), S:6–10ft (1.8–3m). Z:7–10.
The hardiness of this evergreen hybrid and its long season in late summer or autumn, sometimes, too, with flowers in spring, are great assets. The flowers are sky blue, the leaves glossy green.
C. 'A.T. Johnson' (Z:8–10), a slightly smaller evergreen hybrid, produces rich blue flowers in 2 distinct seasons, in spring and then again in late summer and autumn.

Ceanothus 'Cascade'

C. 'Cascade'
Flowers: late spring to early summer. H:10–15ft (3–4.5m), S:10–12ft (3–3.7m). Z:8–10.
The arching branches, loaded with bright blue flowers, really show to good effect when this vigorous evergreen is trained up a wall.

C. × delileanus 'Gloire de Versailles'
Flowers: mid-summer to autumn. H and S:5–6ft (1.5–1.8m). Z:7–8.
The deciduous hybrids include some of the hardiest ceanothus. 'Gloire de Versailles' bears large panicles of soft blue flowers, but the darker indigo tint of 'Topaze' makes more point. C. × pallidus 'Perle Rose' (Z:8–10) is of similar character but has pink flowers.

Ceanothus × delileanus 'Gloire de Versailles'

C. griseus var. horizontalis
Flowers: late spring to early summer. H:2–3ft (60–90cm), S:7–10ft (2.2–3m). Z:8–10.
This is a low-growing variant of the Carmel ceanothus, itself a medium-sized to large evergreen shrub. In 'Yankee Point' bright blue flowers stand out against glossy dark-green leaves. C. 'Blue Mound', an evergreen hybrid of which C. griseus is a parent, also flowers in late spring and summer, when the sprawling pile of glossy foliage, up to 5ft (1.5m) tall, is almost hidden by heads of dark blue flowers.

C. impressus USA (California)
Santa Barbara ceanothus
Flowers: mid- to late spring. H:5–6ft (1.5–1.8m), S:8ft (2.5m). Z:8–10.
Deep veining of the small leaves is a distinctive feature of this densely branched evergreen species. The small clusters of deep blue flowers are borne in great profusion. This species is a parent of several medium-sized to large hybrids that flower from mid-spring to early summer. C. 'Concha', with a height and spread of up to 10ft (3m), has purplish-red buds opening to dark blue flowers. C. 'Puget Blue', of similar size, makes a dense shrub covered for a long season with flowers of a rich and deep blue.

C. thyrsiflorus var. repens
USA (N. California)
Creeping blueblossom
Flowers: late spring. H:3–4ft (90–120cm), S:6–8ft (1.8–2.5m). Z:8–10.
One of the hardiest of the evergreen species, C. thyrsiflorus is a large shrub or small tree with dark-green leaves and pale-blue flowers. The creeping blueblossom, a low-growing variant found in coastal areas, makes a wide-spreading mound well covered in spring with clustered heads of light blue flowers.

CERATOSTIGMA

PLUMBAGINACEAE

The blue flowers of a few Asiatic species are great fresheners of the garden in late summer and early autumn. In cool temperate gardens, even C. willmottianum, the most widely grown shrub in this small genus, is commonly cut to the ground in winter. The autumn-flowering C. plumbaginoides (Z:5–9), with brilliant blue flowers in autumn on a spreading plant about 16in (40cm) tall, is a woody-based perennial.
CULTIVATION Require full sun and light, moist, well-drained soil. Prune in early spring.

PROPAGATION From cuttings, in summer.
POTENTIAL PROBLEMS Powdery mildew.

Ceratostigma willmottianum

C. willmottianum W. China
Flowers: late summer to early autumn. Foliage: autumn. H:2–3ft (60–90cm), S:3–5ft (90–150cm). Z:7–10.
Small clusters of rich blue flowers, tubular and opening to 5 lobes, are sprinkled generously among diamond-shaped leaves that have red tints in autumn. The Himalayan C. griffithii is a more tender evergreen or semievergreen species with dark blue flowers and leaves that turn scarlet in autumn.

CHAENOMELES

ROSACEAE Flowering quince, Japanese quince

The 3 species of this genus, all early-flowering, thorny, deciduous shrubs, are natives of mountain woodland in China and Japan. In the wild they are found in high wooded country. The fresh beauty of their saucer-shaped flowers, especially when clustered thickly on bare stems, is their chief interest. These flowers appear before and with the simple leaves. The green or yellow-green fruits that follow are not highly ornamental but are aromatic, and delicious jellies can be made from them. These shrubs, which make dense and tangled bushes when they are grown as specimens in the open garden, are also suitable for hedging. They can also be grown well on a bank and trained against walls.
CULTIVATION Tolerate full sun or partial shade and require well-drained soil. Trim hedges and cut back most of the previous year's growth on wall-trained specimens after flowering.
PROPAGATION From semiripe cuttings, in mid-summer. By layering, in autumn. Also from seed, sown in autumn.
POTENTIAL PROBLEMS Aphids, scale; canker.

C. speciosa *China*
Japonica
Flowers: late winter to early spring.
Fruits: autumn. H:6–8ft (1.8–2.5m),
S:8–12ft (2.5–3.7m). Z:5–9.
In mild weather, clusters of single
red flowers are sometimes
produced on this plant as early as
mid-winter, and the season can
continue until well after the leaves
have developed. Eventually this
species makes a large spreading
shrub that is tallest when it is wall
trained. There is a good color range
in the cultivated forms, the best
including **'Moerloosei'**, a mixture
of pink and white, and **'Nivalis'**,
which has pure whiteflowers.
'Simonii' has semidouble blood-
red flowers on a low shrub, and
grows to about 3ft (90cm) in
height.

Chaenomeles speciosa **'Simonii'**

C. × superba
Flowers: mid-spring to early
summer. Fruits: autumn. H:3–6ft
(90–180cm), S:5–6ft (1.5–1.8m).
Z:5–9.
The free-flowering hybrids going
under this name are the result of
crosses between *C. speciosa* and the
shorter-growing Japanese species
C. japonica. Most are low-
spreading shrubs with cup-shaped
flowers that are white, pink,
crimson, or scarlet. **'Crimson and
Gold'** owes its name to the contrast
of yellow anthers and dark red
petals. Other cultivars include
'Knap Hill Scarlet', with orange-red
flowers; **'Nicoline'**, with single to
semidouble scarlet flowers; and
'Pink Lady', a low-spreading bush
with clear pink flowers.

Chaenomeles × *superba* **'Nicoline'**

CHIMONANTHUS

CALYCANTHACEAE Wintersweet

Only one of the half dozen species
in this Chinese genus is widely
cultivated, but as its common name
suggests, the wintersweet holds its
place in temperate gardens
because of its winter flowers and
beguiling scent. The wood ripens
more fully and produces flowers
more freely when the shrub is
trained against a warm wall.
CULTIVATION Requires full sun and
fertile well-drained soil. Prune
immediately after flowering.
PROPAGATION From seed, sown
when ripe.
POTENTIAL PROBLEMS Usually none.

Chimonanthus praecox

C. praecox *China*
Wintersweet
Flowers: late winter. H:10–12ft
(3–3.7m), S:8–10ft (2.5–3m). Z:7–9.
Out of its flowering season the
shrub is a nonentity, and even the
flowers themselves are more
curious than ornamental, being
almost stalkless and with dull,
almost translucent outer segments
surrounding the small maroon
inner segments. The scent, though,
is invigorating even in a cold
garden, and when the flowers are
brought into a warm room, the
spicy fragrance becomes even
more expansive.

CHOISYA

RUTACEAE

The choisyas are aromatic
evergreen shrubs from Mexico and
southern USA. Of about 8 species,
one has a surprisingly strong
foothold in cool temperate
gardens, making a densely leafy
bush pleasing for its year-round
dark-green glossiness and for its
citrus-scented flowers.
CULTIVATION Require full sun and
fertile well-drained soil. Prune after
first flush of flowers has finished.
Cut back frost-damaged stems
in spring.
PROPAGATION From semiripe
cuttings, in summer.
POTENTIAL PROBLEMS Snails.

C. ternata *Mexico*
Mexican orange blossom
Foliage: year-round. Flowers: late
spring and late summer to autumn.
H:5–8ft (1.5–2.5m), S:6–8ft
(1.8–2.5m). Z:7–9.
Rounded bushes are covered to the
ground with shining leaves, which
are divided in threes and pungently
aromatic when crushed. Single and
clustered white fragrant flowers
spangle the bushes in spring,
usually with a second flush in
autumn, and there are often
flowers at other times of the year,
even in winter. An unblemished
plant is a splendid sight, but except
where the climate is mild this is
only achieved in a sheltered
position. There is inexplicable
enthusiasm for **Sundance**, a form
with yellow or greenish yellow
leaves. *C.* **'Aztec Pearl'** is smaller,
usually less that 6ft (1.8m) tall, and
carries leaves that are divided into
5 to 10 linear leaflets and almond-
scented white flowers that are
pink in bud.

Choisya **'Aztec Pearl'**

CISTUS

CISTACEAE Rock rose, sun rose

These are among the most
common medium-sized shrubs of
the Mediterranean region and the
Iberian peninsula, where they bask
in hot sun and survive months with
negligible rainfall. Their saucer-
shaped flowers, crumpled and
silky, shatter within a day, but a
shrub carries many at a time and
the season lasts for many weeks.
The color range covers white, often
with dark blotches at the bases of
the petals, and various shades of
pink, extending to bright magenta.
These are among the first
evergreen shrubs for dry sunny
gardens, and do well near the
ocean. However, in cool regions,
there is a risk of losses in winter.
CULTIVATION Require full sun and
well-drained soil. Prune after
flowering.
PROPAGATION From seed, sown
when ripe and in spring. From
cuttings, in summer.
POTENTIAL PROBLEMS Usually none.

C. × *hybridus* *S. Europe*
Flowers: late spring to early
summer. H:3–4ft (90-120cm), S:5-
6ft (1.5–1.8m). Z:7–9.
The dark-green leaves of this
naturally occurring hybrid are a
good foil for the reddish buds and
white flowers, which are stained
yellow at the center. It has one of
the best records among cistuses for
surviving hard winters.

C. *ladanifer* *S.W. Europe to*
N. Africa
Common gum cistus, laudanum
Flowers: late spring to early summer.
H:5–6ft (1.5–1.8m), S:4–5ft (1.2-
1.5m). Z:7–9.
The large flowers, white with
chocolate blotches around a yellow
center, are borne on a leggy shrub
with narrow, dull green leaves that
are slightly sticky and aromatic.
This species is a parent of some of
the most important hybrids.
C. × aguilarii, a cross with
C. populifolius that is found wild
in the Iberian peninsula and North
Africa, is a smaller plant with a
height and spread of 4ft (1.2m).
Its leaves have a wavy margin; the
flowers are white with a yellow
center and, in the case of
C. × a. **'Maculatus'**, have bold
crimson blotches. *C. × cyprius*, a
hybrid of *C. ladanifer* and
C. laurifolius, is one of the hardiest
of the cistuses, making an upright
shrub, with a height and spread of
about 5ft (1.5m). Its attractive large
white flowers have dark crimson
blotches situated around the
yellow stamens.

Cistus ladanifer

C. *laurifolius* *S.W. Europe*
Flowers: early to late summer.
H and S:5–6ft (1.5–1.8m). Z:7–9.
Yellow-centered white flowers
are produced freely on an upright
bush with leathery dark-green
leaves. The relative hardiness of
this species is a character also
found in *C.* **'Silver Pink'**, a
sprawling hybrid that reaches up to
30in (75cm) tall, of which it is a
parent. The cross is well named for
the cool pink color of the plant's
crumpled flowers.

C. × *purpureus* *S. Europe*
Flowers: late spring to mid-summer.
H and S:3–4ft (90–120cm). Z:7–9.
Yet again the popular *C. ladanifer* is
credited as a parent, but this hybrid
probably owes the deep pink of its
flowers to *C. creticus*, a frost-hardy
species from the eastern
Mediterranean. The flowers of the
hybrid, a small shrub with reddish
stems, are distinguished by the
deep crimson blotches around the
yellow center.

Cistus × purpureus

CONVOLVULUS

CONVOLVULACEAE Bindweed

This large family of bindweeds is
best known for its climbers and
scramblers. There are also some
shrubby species. *C. cneorum* is
described as a Mediterranean plant
with hairy gray leaves, a clear
indication of its preference for
well-drained soils and sun. It is
short-lived, often succumbing in
cold clammy winter weather, but it
is worth having rooted cuttings of
this lightweight charmer in
reserve.
CULTIVATION Require full sun and
well-drained gritty soil. Cut back to
new growths in spring.
PROPAGATION From seed, sown
in spring at 55–64°F (13–18°C).
From cuttings, in late spring and
summer.
POTENTIAL PROBLEMS Under glass:
red spider mites, aphids.

Convolvulus cneorum

C. *cneorum* *C. and W.*
Mediterranean
Flowers: spring to summer. H and
S:2–3ft (60–90cm). Z:8–10.

The silvery silkiness of the foliage
of this plant is the perfect
complement to the funnel-shaped
flowers. These are meticulously
folded when in bud, which are
pink, but yellow centered when
open, and produced in succession
for months.

CORNUS

CORNACEAE Dogwood, cornel

The dogwoods are plants of various
habitats that grow throughout the
northern temperate regions. They
demonstrate an enormous diversity
in their ornamental qualities.
Almost all of the approximately 45
species are deciduous shrubs or
trees, but the creeping dogwood
(*C. canadensis*) is a low-creeping
perennial notable for the white
bracts surrounding its insignificant
flowers. See also TREES.
CULTIVATION C. kousa tolerates full
sun and partial shade, but requires
a fertile well-drained soil that is not
alkaline. Those grown for their
winter stems require full sun and
moist soil but they are tolerant of
lime. *C. canadensis* requires moist
acid soil.
PROPAGATION From cuttings, in
summer. From hardwood cuttings,
in winter of winter stems (for
dogwoods grown for winter stem
color). From seed, sown under glass
in autumn.
POTENTIAL PROBLEM Anthracnose.

Cornus alba 'Elegantissima'

C. *alba* *N. China to Korea, Siberia*
Red-barked dogwood
Flowers: late spring to early
summer. H and S:8–10ft (2.5–3m).
Z:2–7.
The real interest of this deciduous
suckering shrub does not lie in its
modest white flowers or the bluish-
white berries that follow, but in the
lush foliage and colored stems.
Regular coppicing ensures a supply
of young wood, which is a lustrous
scarlet in winter. Outstanding for its
brightness is **'Sibirica'**, usually under
8ft (2.5m) tall. Of several forms with
yellow to white variegated foliage,
the first choice must be the
vigorous **'Elegantissima'**, with a

creamy white variegation brightening the gray-green leaves. It, too, makes a thicket of vivid young stems if coppiced. A sobering contrast to these is **'Kesselringii'**, with purple stems and leaves that turn purplish red in autumn. *C. stolonifera* **'Flaviramea'** (Z:2–8), a form of the red osier dogwood of eastern North America that has greenish yellow young wood, also needs cutting back regularly to maintain a supply of well-colored stems.

Cornus kousa var. *chinensis*

C. kousa *Japan, Korea*
Kousa dogwood
Foliage: autumn. Flowers: early summer. Fruits: late summer. H:10– 20ft (3–6m), S:9–15ft (2.7–4.5m). Z:5–8.
The flowers are insignificant but the large white bracts surrounding them make this a dazzling large shrub or small tree in early summer. The pointed bracts stand upright along the spreading branches, the general effect being of unevenly tilted broad tiers. As the bracts age, they often take on a pink tint. There are strawberrylike fruits, and the foliage colors well in autumn. In **'Satomi'** the bracts are a strong pink and the autumn foliage reddish purple. **Var. *chinensis*** is a more treelike shrub, with its growth less obviously tiered.

CORONILLA

PAPILIONACEAE

The shrubby species in this genus of about 20 species are mainly sun-loving plants from southern Europe. The plant described is an easy-going self-seeder where the climate is mild, but at the limit of its range it also needs a sheltered position at the base of a warm wall.
CULTIVATION Require full sun and well-drained soil. Prune the plant after the main flowering season in spring.
PROPAGATION From seed, sown as soon as ripe or in spring at 50-55°F (10–13°C) after stratification. From cuttings, in summer.
POTENTIAL PROBLEMS Usually none.

Coronilla valentina subsp. *glauca*

C. valentina subsp. *glauca*
Flowers: late winter to early spring, also in late summer. H and S:24–30in (60–75cm). Z:8–9.
Although it is flimsy and likely to succumb to hard frosts, this is an easy plant where the weather is mild enough, cheerfully producing a profusion of pea flowers in spring and a trickle at almost all times of the year. Their yellow goes well with the hint of blue in the foliage; even better is the lemon-yellow of **'Citrina'**.

CORYLOPSIS

HAMAMELIDACEAE Winterhazel

The genus is Asiatic, and the species, of which there are about 10 in all, are deciduous woodland shrubs or small trees that flower in spring. They are not showy or attention seeking, but a leafless plant hung with catkin-like racemes of small fragrant flowers is a very lovely sight.
CULTIVATION Require partial shade and well-drained, moist, fertile, acid soil.
PROPAGATION From cuttings, in summer. By layering, in autumn. From seed, sown in autumn.
POTENTIAL PROBLEMS Usually none.

Corylopsis sinensis

C. pauciflora *Japan, Taiwan*
Buttercup winterhazel
Flowers: early to mid-spring. H:5–6ft (1.5–1.8m), S:6–8ft (1.8–2.5m). Z:6–8.
Numerous racemes of primrose yellow flowers hang from a densely branching shrub with twiggy stems. The leaves, hornbeamlike but small, are copper or tinged with pink when they first open but then become bright green. *C. sinensis* is a taller shrubs, growing to 10ft (3m), with scented pale yellow flowers on racemes up to 3in (7.5cm) long.

CORYLUS

CORYLACEAE Hazel, filbert

The hazels and filberts belong to a small genus of about 15 species of deciduous shrubs and trees, mainly woodland plants of the temperate Northern Hemisphere. The Turkish hazel (*C. colurna*, Z:4–8) is a handsome pyramidal tree that thrives where there is a marked contrast between hot summers and cold winters. The shrubs that are grown for their nuts include several that are ornamental ones.
CULTIVATION Tolerate full sun or partial shade and well-drained fertile soils. Coppice colored foliage in spring to encourage new growth with large leaves. Remove suckers from grafted plants.
PROPAGATION By layering, in autumn. From seed, sown as soon as ripe. By grafting, in winter.
POTENTIAL PROBLEMS Aphids, caterpillars, mites, sawflies; honey fungus, powdery mildew, silverleaf.

Corylus maxima 'Purpurea'

C. avellana *Europe, Turkey*
European filbert
Flowers: late winter to early spring. H:15–20ft (4.5–6m), S:5–20ft (1.5–6m). Z:4–8.
As a nut-bearing shrub or small tree, this is appealing when the male catkins hang from the bare branches and again in autumn, when the leaves turn soft yellow. **'Aurea'**, not a vigorous grower and rarely more than 6ft (1.8m) in height, has yellow-green leaves, that are greener in late summer. **'Contorta'** grows slowly to about 10ft (3m). The leaves are puckered but the writhing twigs and branches are graphic in winter. A vigorous purple-leaved form of the filbert, *C. maxima* **'Purpurea'**, grows to 20ft (6m) and is a brooding shrub, even down to its tinted catkins.

COTINUS

ANACARDIACEAE Smoke bush

Curious wispy plumes surrounding the tiny flowers and fruits, and the rich colors of the foliage in autumn, are the main features of the 2 species included in this genus, both of which are deciduous shrubs occurring in poor stony ground and open positions. *C. obovatus* (Z:4–8), originating from southern USA, often develops into a small tree. It is less ornamental in flower than the European species, but outclasses it in the brilliance of its autumn foliage color.
CULTIVATION Require full sun or partial shade and well-drained soil. Autumn foliage color is less intense on rich soils. Prune only lightly; coppicing in spring produces the maximum foliage effect, but few or no inflorescences at all develop.
PROPAGATION From seed, sown in autumn. By layering, in spring. From cuttings, in summer.
POTENTIAL PROBLEMS Verticillium wilt, powdery mildew.

C. coggygria *S. Europe to C. China*
Smoke bush, Venetian sumac
Foliage: autumn. Flowers: midsummer. H and S:10–15ft (3–4.5m). Z:4–8.
The shrub is often almost enveloped by the smoky plumes of the inflorescences, which sometimes have a pink tint before they turn gray in late summer. The oval green leaves color well in autumn. **'Notcutt's Variety'** features dark red leaves, which have purplish-pink panicles. The light green leaves of **f. *purpureus*** are orange red in autumn. The plant also produces purplish-pink inflorescences. **'Royal Purple'** carries red-purple leaves that turn scarlet in autumn. Even more spectacular in autumn are the vigorous treelike hybrids *C.* **'Flame'**, which displays purple-pink plumes, and *C.* **'Grace'**, with leaves that are purple throughout spring and summer, and turn scarlet in autumn.

Cotinus coggygria f. *purpureus*

COTONEASTER

ROSACEAE

Many of the cotoneasters bear masses of flowers, usually pink in bud and white on opening, but they are small and they make nothing like the effect of the fruits that follow, which enrich the garden for weeks and sometimes months in autumn and winter. There are more than 200 species, most of them from the temperate regions of Europe and Asia. In the wild, some are shrubs of open rocky places, but many are plants of woodland fringes. They are found on a wide range of soils, but in cultivation their tolerance extends to stiff clays and sandy and alkaline soils. There are deciduous, semievergreen, and evergreen species and in scale they range from compact low mounds and prostrate carpets to treelike large shrubs.
CULTIVATION Require full sun (dwarf evergreens and deciduous species); medium and large evergreens require sun or partial shade and shelter from cold winds. All require well-drained soil.
PROPAGATION From seed, sown as soon as ripe in autumn. From cuttings, in summer.
POTENTIAL PROBLEMS Webber moth caterpillars, wooly aphids, scale, aphids; honey fungus, fire blight.
WARNING The seeds can cause slight stomach upset if eaten.

C. conspicuus *S.E. Tibet*
Flowers: early summer. Fruits: late summer to mid-winter. H:5–6ft (1.5–1.8m), S:5–8ft (1.5–2.5m). Z:7–8.
The plant usually grown is **'Decorus'**, which makes a dense mound closely covered with glossy evergreen leaves. The white flowers that crowd the stems are followed by rounded and lustrous orange-red fruits that are usually ignored by birds and therefore last well into winter.

C. dammeri *China (Hubei)*
Flowers: early summer. Fruits: all autumn. H:5–8in (12.5–20cm), S:5–7ft (1.5–2.2m). Z:6–8.
The creeping stems, which root rapidly as they spread, make an evergreen carpet that is bright with scarlet berries in autumn. Other evergreen cotoneasters that are useful as low groundcover include *C. salicifolius* **'Gnom'**, which may make a mound up to 2ft (60cm) tall but quickly spreads as much as 6ft (1.8m). The bright red berries show up well against glossy dark-green leaves.

Cotoneaster frigidus

C. frigidus *Himalayas*
Flowers: early summer. Fruits: late summer to late winter. H:15–25ft (4.5–7.5m), S:12–25ft (3.7–7.5m). Z:6–8.
A small tree can be made of this deciduous species by training up a main stem. Great crops of pea-sized crimson fruits are borne. The semi-evergreen **'Cornubia'**, loaded with bright red fruits among its dark leaves, is one of the most spectacular of all large berrying shrubs. *C. frigidus* is a parent of several large semievergreen hybrids, including those listed under *C.* × *watereri*. One of these, **'John Waterer'**, has a height and spread of about 15ft (4.5m), and its arching branches seem weighed down by its red fruits. Two large evergreens that are sometimes grouped with these hybrids are *C. salicifolius* **'Exburyensis'** and *C. s.* **'Rothschildianus'**; both have a height and spread of about 15ft (4.5m) and produce heavy crops of long-lasting yellow fruits.

Cotoneaster × *watereri* **'John Waterer'**

C. horizontalis *W. China*
Foliage: autumn. Flowers: late spring. Fruits: late summer to late winter. H:2–4ft (60–120cm), S:5–6ft (1.5–1.8m). Z:5–7.
The herringbone pattern of the stems is distinctive, especially when set with small bright red fruits. This is a deciduous shrub, with tiny, glossy, dark-green leaves that turn red when the fruits are already ripe. *C. atropurpureus* **'Variegatus'** has white margins on the leaves giving it a silvered look.

C. lacteus *China (Yunnan)*
Flowers: early to mid-summer.
Fruits: mid-autumn to late winter.
H:10-15ft (3-4.5m), S:8-12ft
(2.5-3.7m). Z:6-8.
The milky white flowers of this
shrub are borne in great profusion
but its chief seasons are autumn
and winter. At this time the broad
clusters of egg-shaped fruits stand
out bright red against the dark-
green leaves, which are felted on
the underside.

CYTISUS

PAPILIONACEAE Broom

The brooms, including those that
belong to other genera (see also
Genista), are mainly sun-loving
shrubs with pealike flowers. These
are often fragrant and usually
yellow, and are produced with
great prodigality. The flowers are
followed by green, often hairy,
seedpods. The genus, which
contains about 50 species, has its
center of gravity in Europe, but it is
also represented in northern Africa
and western Asia. Most of the
species are found on free-draining,
even poor soils, the common
broom (*C. scoparius*, Z:6-8), for
example, being a common shrub of
sandy heathland. The fact that they
are fast-growing shrubs makes
them particularly useful in newly
established gardens.
CULTIVATION Require full sun and
well-drained soil.
PROPAGATION From seed, sown in
autumn or spring. From cuttings,
in summer.
POTENTIAL PROBLEMS Gall mites.
WARNING Stomach upsets may
occur if any part is eaten
(particularly the seeds).

Cytisus battandieri

C. battandieri *Morocco*
Pineapple broom
Flowers: mid- to late summer.
H:12-15ft (3.7-4.5m), S:10-15ft
(3-4.5m). Z:8-9.
The common name refers to the
fruity scent of the yellow flowers,
which are clustered in conelike
spikes. This is a large lax shrub
with laburnum-like leaves that are

divided into 3, the fine hairs giving
them a silky gray finish. Where it is
of marginal hardiness, this is a
shrub worth wall training.

Cytisus × kewensis

C. × beanii
Flowers: late spring. H:18-24in
(45-60cm), S:36in (90cm). Z:6-8.
The sprawling *C. ardoinoi* from
the Maritime Alps, itself a pleasing
miniature for a raised bed or rock
garden, is a parent of this hybrid,
which is at its best when its stems,
well set with dark-yellow flowers,
arch over from the top of a
retaining wall. *C. × kewensis* is a
larger shrub, up to 2ft (60cm) tall
but spreading as much as 6ft
(1.8m), that also owes its semi-
prostrate habit to *C. ardoinoi*. It
needs a raised position to show off
its cascades of creamy flowers.

C. hybrids
Flowers: late spring to early
summer. H and S:3-5ft (90-150cm).
Z:7-9.
The complex hybrids by which
brooms are best known in yards
owe much to the common broom
of western Europe, *C. scoparius*,
an upright deciduous shrub 5-6ft
(1.5-1.8m) tall, commonly seen in
summer brightening wasteland and
heathland with a profuse display
of large rich yellow flowers. The
flowers of many of the hybrids
are bicolored or two-toned. The
following is a small selection:
'**Hollandia**', has cream and dark
pink flowers; '**Lena**', yellow and
reddish brown; '**Windlesham
Ruby**', dark crimson; and '**Zeelandia**'
creamy white and mauve-pink.

C. × praecox
Flowers: mid- to late spring. H:4-6ft
(1.2-1.8m), S:5-6ft (1.5-1.8m).
Z:7-9.
The free-flowering *C. multiflorus*
from the Iberian peninsula and
northern Africa is a parent with
C. purgans of several compact
deciduous hybrids, the first of
which, '**Warminster**', bears masses
of creamy yellow flowers. The
arching stems of '**Allgold**' are
loaded with bright yellow flowers.

DABOECIA

ERICACEAE

The 2 evergreen species are low
shrubs of coastal and mountain
heathland in western Europe, the
half-hardy *D. azorica* (Z:6-8) being
confined to the Azores. In
appearance they are close to the
ericas and, like many of them,
require a neutral to acid soil. The
flowers are not retained as they are
by other heaths, but fall when they
are spent. The flowering season is,
however, exceptionally long.
CULTIVATION Require full sun and
well-drained acid soil. Shear off the
previous year's flowers in early to
mid-spring.
PROPAGATION From semiripe
cuttings, in mid-summer.
POTENTIAL PROBLEMS Phytophthora
root rot.

D. cantabrica *W. Europe*
Cantabrian heath, St. Dabeoc's
heath
Flowers: early summer to mid-
autumn. H:10-24in (25-60cm),
S:2-3ft (60-90cm). Z:6-8.
The urn-shaped flowers are carried
on one-sided spikes above glossy
dark-green foliage. The flower color
is usually purplish pink, but can
include white and magenta. The
eccentric '**Bicolor**' can have white,
pink, red, or striped flowers on the
same plant, even on the same stem.
D. × scotica is a frost-hardy hybrid
between the 2 species.

Daboecia cantabrica

DAPHNE

THYMELAEACEAE

The scented flowers are the great
delight of this genus, which
includes about 50 Asiatic and
European species. Many are
woodland plants, the European
spurge laurel (*D. laureola*, Z:7-8)
being tolerant of heavy shade and
making a pleasing mound of glossy
evergreen leaves up to 5ft (1.5m)
tall. Others are of more open
habitats and in cultivation need
positions in full sun. Even the
easiest in cultivation tend to be
unpredictable, and some of the

dwarf species provide the sort of challenge that sets the pulse of alpine specialists racing. Triumph for them is a flower-studded hummock less than 6in (15cm) tall of **D. petraea** 'Grandiflora' (Z:7–8), an evergreen that originates from the European Alps.
CULTIVATION Require sun or partial shade and organic-rich, moist, well-drained soil that is neutral to slightly acid or slightly alkaline.
PROPAGATION From seed, sown as soon as ripe. From cuttings, in summer. By grafting, in winter. By layering, in spring.
POTENTIAL PROBLEMS Aphids; leaf spot, gray mold (*Botrytis*), viruses.

Daphne cneorum 'Eximia'

WARNING Swallowing any part will cause poisoning. Sap contact can cause skin irritations.

D. cneorum *Mountains of C. and S. Europe*
Rose daphne
Flowers: late spring. H:6–8in (15–20cm), S:2–5ft (60–150cm). Z:5–7.
The scent of many low plants often goes unnoticed, but not this lovely evergreen garland flower. The sprawling 'Eximia' bears crimson buds opening to deep pink flowers. Semievergreen hybrids between this species and the larger deciduous **D. caucasica** are very easy to cultivate. **D. × burkwoodii** 'Somerset' has purple flowers.

Daphne mezereum

D. mezereum *Caucasus, Europe, Siberia, Turkey*
Mezereon
Flowers: late winter to early spring. H:4–5ft (1.2–1.5m), S:2–4ft (60–120cm). Z:4–7.
The small scented flowers of this deciduous species are stemless and cluster densely along the upper portions of the bare stems making a mauve- to purple-pink or white sleeve. The flowers are followed by fleshy red berries. Plants with white flowers, such as **f. alba**, have yellow fruits.

D. odora *China, Japan*
Flowers: mid-winter to early spring. H:and S:5–6ft (1.5–1.8m). Z:7–9.
Tight posies of starry flowers at the tips of twiggy stems on this shrub exhale an incomparable fragrance. They are surrounded by ruffs of glossy leaves, and the combination of purplish-red reverse and crystalline white interior to the flowers gives the clusters a bicolored effect. This is a compact rounded evergreen for a sheltered position. 'Aureomarginata' has irregular yellow margins to the leaves.

DEUTZIA

HYDRANGEACEAE

The deutzias, mainly plants of woodland and scrub in the Himalayas and farther east in Asia, are free-flowering shrubs that are easily grown in a wide range of conditions. Of about 60 species, most are deciduous and of medium height. A large number are hardy enough for gardens in cool temperate regions, although those that flower in spring are sometimes damaged by frost. Among the largest is **D. scabra** (Z:5–8), which grows up to 10ft (3m), and has white or pink-tinted fragrant flowers in dense upright clusters. Like many deutzias, it has peeling bark.
CULTIVATION Require full sun and well-drained soil. Cut one-fifth of the oldest branches back to ground level and the flowered shoots down to new strong growths annually after flowering.
PROPAGATION From seed, sown in autumn. From cuttings, in summer. From hardwood cuttings, in autumn.
POTENTIAL PROBLEMS Usually none.

D. × elegantissima
Flowers: late spring to early summer. H and S:4–5ft (1.2–1.5m). Z:5–8.
The medium-sized Chinese species **D. purpurascens**, with fragrant

purple-tinted flowers, is a parent of this and several other hybrids. The cross is an upright shrub with arching stems carrying loose heads of starry flowers that are pink or, in 'Rosealind', white with carmine tips. Another hybrid of similar size, with **D. purpurascens** in its genetic make-up, is **D. × rosea**, which produces graceful sprays of pink or white bell-shaped flowers in early summer; 'Carminea' has deep pink flowers that open from purplish-pink buds.

D. longifolia *W. China*
Flowers: early to mid-summer; H:4–6ft (1.2–1.8m), S:6–10ft (1.8–3m). Z:5–8.
The comparatively large flowers arching out in graceful clusters put this in the top flight of deutzias. The star-shaped flowers are white with purple reverse; 'Veitchii' has mauve pink flowers outlined in white. *D. longifolia* and the small Chinese species **D. discolor** are the parents of several shrubs, listed under **D. × hybrida**, that flower freely in early summer. 'Magicien' has mauve-pink flowers that are edged with white, displaying a purple reverse; 'Mont Rose' has purplish buds that open out to pink flowers. The hybrids are generally 4–5ft (1.2–1.5m) in height and spread.

Deutzia × hybrida 'Mont Rose'

ELAEAGNUS

ELAEAGNACEAE

The bell-shaped flowers, in several cases deliciously scented, are inconspicuous, and it is largely for their foliage that these shrubs are grown. Silvery or bronzy scaliness is a feature of the young foliage, often persisting on the underside of leaves, and sometimes showing also on stems and flowers. There are about 45 species altogether, the majority of Asiatic origin, some deciduous and some which are evergreen. They are found in a variety of habitats, but all the shrubs are remarkably tolerant of dry conditions.
CULTIVATION Require full sun

SHRUBS

(deciduous), full sun or partial
shade (evergreens), and well-
drained soil. Prune reverted
shoots on variegated cultivars.
PROPAGATION From seed, sown
in autumn. From cuttings, in
summer. By grafting, in late winter.
From rooted suckers of deciduous
species, in autumn.
POTENTIAL PROBLEMS Coral spot.

Elaeagnus angustifolia

E. angustifolia *S. Europe to
C. Asia, Himalayas, China*
Russian olive
Foliage: spring to autumn. Flowers:
early summer. Fruits: late summer.
H and S:12–20ft (3.7–6m). Z:2–9.
The tiny pale yellow flowers would
go unnoticed among the silvery
willowlike leaves, were it not for
their penetrating fruity scent. This
is a spreading, deciduous shrub or
small tree, to some extent spiny,
that tolerates shaping. The amber-
colored fruits are edible.
E. 'Quicksilver' is a more compact
silvery shrub in the same mold.

E. × ebbingei
Foliage: year-round. Flowers: early
to mid-autumn. Fruits: spring.
H and S:10–12ft (3–3.7m). Z:6–9.
Fast-growing, although not very
shapely, this evergreen hybrid is
most useful for creating shelter in
coastal gardens. The leaves are large
and silver on the underside, and
the tiny flowers, which declare
themselves by their rich spicy
fragrance, also have a silvery
quality. The leaves of **'Gilt Edge'**
have a splendid golden margin to
the dark center.

E. pungens *Japan*
Foliage: year-round. Flowers: early
to mid-autumn. Fruits: late winter.
H:8–12ft (2.5–3.7m), S:10–15ft
(3–4.5m). Z:6–9.
Glossy dark-green leaves, which are
gray-white on the underside and
have wavy margins, hide the small
scented flowers of this shrub,
which are sometimes followed by
red berries. This usually spiny plant
is much used for hedging and
shelter in gardens, and is most
commonly seen in its variegated

forms. The leaves of **'Maculata'** have
yellow centers outlined in green.

ENKIANTHUS

ERICACEAE

Subtle beauty in flower and
brilliance of leaf color in autumn
distinguish the deciduous shrubs
or small trees in this Asiatic genus
of about 10 species. These are
predominantly woodland plants,
and like most of the members of
the heath family, the ericaceous
plants, they need a lime-free soil.
CULTIVATION Require full sun or
partial shade and organic-rich,
moist well-drained, neutral to
acid soil.
PROPAGATION From seed, sown in
late winter or early spring at
64–70°F (18–21°C). From semiripe
cuttings, taken in mid-summer. By
layering, in autumn.
POTENTIAL PROBLEMS Usually none.

E. campanulatus *Japan*
Foliage: autumn. Flowers: late
spring to early summer. H:8–12ft
(2.5–3.7m), S:5–10ft (1.5–3m).
Z:4–7.
The reserve of this shrub in flower
is as appealing as the brilliance of
its foliage in autumn. Red veining
usually adds a warm tinge to the
creamy yellow of small bells, which
hang closely and profusely in
pretty clusters. There is, in fact,
considerable variation in flower
color, the range including white
and pale yellow-green. Another
Japanese species, **E. perulatus**,
about 6ft (1.8m) in height and
spread, has white urn-shaped
flowers and foliage that outdoes in
intensity most autumn scarlets.

Enkianthus campanulatus

ERICA

ERICACEAE Heath

A handful of mainly European
species provides the large number
of low-growing heaths that are
widely grown, especially on lime-
free soils, in cool temperate
regions. The genus is, however, a
very large one, and a high
proportion of the 700 or more

Erica vagans 'Saint Keverne'

evergreen species are from South
Africa. It is only because of their
relative tenderness that beautiful
plants such as **E. bauera**,
E. cerinthoides, **E. perspicua** (all
Z:9–10), and many others do not
relieve the monotonous effect of
the most familiar heaths, which,
like ling (**Calluna vulgaris**, Z:4–6),
are rarely as beautiful in cultivation
as they are in the wild. Although
most heathers need a neutral to acid
soil, some including the Cornish
heath (**E. vagans**, Z:5–7) and its
cultivars, such as **'Saint Keverne'**,
tolerate mildly alkaline conditions.
Their greatest value is when they are
planted in groups away from the
lushest areas of the yard.
CULTIVATION Require full sun and,
although there are some
exceptions that tolerate lime, well-
drained acid soil (ericaceous media
and sharp sand). Clip off spent
flowers after flowering.
PROPAGATION From semiripe
cuttings, in mid- to late summer.
POTENTIAL PROBLEMS Fungal diseases.

E. arborea *N. Africa, mountains
of central E. Africa, Mediterranean,
S.W. Europe*
Tree heath
Flowers: late spring. H:12–20ft
(3.7–6m), S:6–10ft (1.8–3m). Z:7–9.
The bell-shaped flowers that cover
tall upright plants with gray-white
snow have a honeyed scent. As
specimens age, they become
lanky but can be pruned back into
old wood. The more compact
var. alpina grows to about 6ft
(1.8m). The Portuguese heath
(**E. lusitanica**, Z:8–9) is a frost-
hardy species that grows to about
10ft (3m). From late autumn to
early spring, the feathery stems are
crowded with white tubular
flowers that open from pink buds.

E. carnea *C. Alps, E. Europe,
N.W. Balkans, N.W. Italy*
Winter heath, alpine heath
Flowers: late winter to early spring.
H:8–12in (20–30cm), S:15–24in
(38–60cm). Z:5–7.
The species, a dwarf evergreen
alpine shrub, is represented in

137

gardens by numerous cultivars, some of which are prostrate while many others are generally more upright. In the wild, the flowers are usually purplish pink and the foliage mid- to dark green, but there is considerable variation in the cultivars. The following is a small selection from those that are well established, but new additions are always being made: **'Ann Sparkes'** has foliage golden with bronze tips in spring, and pink flowers that darken to purple; **'Myretoun Ruby'**, foliage deep green, with pink flowers deepening to crimson; **'Springwood White'**, foliage bright green on a vigorous spreading shrub, with a great profusion of white flowers; and **'Vivellii'**, foliage bronzed in winter and pink flowers that darken to carmine.

Erica carnea 'Myretoun Ruby'

E. cinerea *Europe*
Bell heather
Flowers: early summer to early autumn. H:1-2ft (30-60cm), S:15-30in (38-75cm). Z:5-7.
The bell heather, typical of the genus in being intolerant of lime, has deep-green leaves that curl back along their margins. The wild bells, usually purplish red, fade to a pleasing russet. Cultivars include: **'C.D. Eason'**, with vibrant magenta-pink flowers; **'Pink Ice'**, compact, growing to about 6in (15cm), with clear pink flowers and bronze winter foliage; and **'Velvet Night'**, with deep purple bells. The cross-leaved heath (**E. tetralix**, Z:4-7), another hardy species from western Europe that flowers from early summer to early autumn, is found wild in boggy, lime-free ground. It grows up to about 1ft (30cm), and the hairy leaves seem gray-green. The flowers are usually pink, but the white ones of **'Alba Mollis'** complement the gray foliage.

E. × darleyensis
Darley Dale heath
Flowers: late winter to early spring. H:18-24in (45-60cm), S:24-30in (60-75cm). Z:6-8.
Like *E. carnea*, one of its parents, this hybrid is reasonably lime-

tolerant and makes calf-high groundcover with a long flowering season. **'Darley Dale'**, the original plant, has pale pink flowers. **'Arthur Johnson'** has long dense sprays of bright purplish-pink flowers. **'Silberschmelze'** has white flowers and dark-green foliage tinted red in winter.

ESCALLONIA

ESCALLONIACEAE

Glossy evergreen foliage and a long flowering season are attractive characteristics of many escallonias, which are invaluable shrubs or small trees for hedging and shelter belts in coastal areas where the climate is reasonably mild. The 50 or so species in this South American genus are mainly plants of scrubland and are found on a wide range of soils, most of them tolerating lime. In gardens the hybrids are in general more widely grown than the species. However, one of the finest escallonias for hedging is undoubtedly *E. rubra* **'Crimson Spire'** (Z:7-9), a vigorous upright shrub with deep crimson flowers. Where they are of borderline hardiness, escallonias are best when grown against a warm wall.
CULTIVATION Require full sun and fertile well-drained soil.
PROPAGATION From cuttings, in summer. From hardwood cuttings, in late autumn.
POTENTIAL PROBLEMS Usually none.

Escallonia 'Iveyi'

E. hybrids
Flowers: early summer to autumn. H:6-10ft (1.8-3m), S:8-10ft (2.5-3m). Z:7-9.
Although in their overall appearance they are reasonably homogenous, these escallonias vary somewhat in hardiness, vigor, growth, and flowering season. The following small selection samples the range. **'Apple Blossom'**, a frost-hardy, bushy, evergreen shrub about 6ft (1.8m) in height and spread, with pink and white flowers in early to mid-summer; **'Edinensis'**, a fully hardy evergreen

shrub up to 10ft (3m) in height and spread, with arching stems bearing red buds opening to dark pink flowers in early to mid-summer; **'Iveyi'**, a frost-hardy tall evergreen shrub, up to 10ft (3m) in height and spread, with white flowers in late summer and autumn; and **'Langleyensis'**, a fully hardy evergreen or semievergreen shrub, about 6ft (1.8m) in height but spreading, with pink flowers among small leaves in the first half of summer.

EUONYMUS

CELASTRACEAE

The ornamental qualities of the shrubs and trees in this large genus of around 175 species are very mixed. The flowers count for little, but at their best the evergreens are variegated shrubs of bright effect, and the deciduous species include several with foliage that colors vividly in autumn, at the same time as the intriguing round-shaped fruits ripen. In the wild, the few European species, as well as the Asiatic majority, are found in woodland and scrubland on a wide range of soils, including those containing lime. To get good crops on species that bear colorful fruits, it is advisable to grow several specimens of different clones in close proximity. Several evergreen species can also make useful hedging shrubs. The Japanese spindle (*E. japonicus*, Z:7-9), for example, with its dense foliage, which is in some forms variegated, is particularly good when cultivated in coastal areas where the climate is mild enough.
CULTIVATION Require full sun or partial shade and also well-drained soil.
PROPAGATION From seed, sown as soon as ripe. From cuttings, taken in summer.
POTENTIAL PROBLEMS Scale, caterpillars, vine weevils; powdery mildew, leaf spot.
WARNING Stomach upsets may occur if any part of the plant is swallowed.

E. alatus *China, Japan*
Winged euonymus
Foliage: autumn. Flowers: late spring. Fruits: autumn. H:6-7ft (1.8-2.2m), S:8-10ft (2.5-3m). Z:4-9.
The corky wings to the branches are almost obscured by dense growth when the plant is in leaf. The reliable brilliance of its pink and crimson foliage in autumn is exceptional and far more important ornamentally than the purple-red fruits, which burst to

show orange-coated seeds. **'Compactus'** is of very dense growth and rarely exceeds 3ft (90cm) in height.

Euonymus alatus **'Compactus'**

E. europaeus *Europe, W. Asia*
European euonymus
Foliage: autumn. Flowers: late spring. Fruits: autumn. H and S:6-10ft (1.8-3m). Z:5-8.
What might be despised as a dull deciduous shrub or small tree in spring and summer is transformed in autumn. At this time rich leaf colors coincide with the ripening of purplish-pink fruits that split to show orange-coated seeds. **'Red Cascade'** is sensational, bearing heavy crops among scarlet leaves weighing down the branches.
E. hamiltonianus subsp. sieboldianus, a Japanese plant sometimes more than 20ft (6m) in height, is in the same mold, but the exterior color of the fruits is a strong pink.

Euonymus fortunei **'Silver Queen'**

E. fortunei *Japan*
Wintercreeper euonymus
Foliage: year-round. H as shrub: 2-4ft (60-120cm), H as climber: 8-15ft (2.5-4.5m), S:4-6ft (1.2-1.8m). Z:4-9.
Given support, what is usually seen as a prostrate or mound-forming evergreen shrub becomes a self-clinging climber. There are juvenile and adult stages, and it is the juvenile foliage of the non-flowering stage that is of prime value ornamentally. It is a very variable plant and has numerous variegated forms, usually seen as bushy shrubs. These include

Emerald Gaiety, with an irregular white outline surrounding the dark green center of the leaves; **Emerald 'n' Gold**, the margins of the dark-green leaves bright gold; and **'Silver Queen'**, with a striking contrast between dark green and a white outline to the leaves. In most cases the yellow or white variegation becomes pinkish in winter.

EXOCHORDA

Rosaceae Pearl bush

Their profusion of pure white flowers makes these deciduous shrubs a dazzling, although short-lived, spectacle in late spring or early summer. The 4 species, all Asiatic, are plants of woodland margins that flower most freely in full sun. More common in cultivation is the hybrid described below, but a lovely alternative to it is **E. giraldii var. wilsonii** (Z:5-8), a bush up to 10ft (3m) tall and wide, covered in late spring with flowers up to 2in (5cm) across.
CULTIVATION Require full sun and well-drained, moist, fertile soil. Cut back flowered shoots to lower, new, strong growth after flowering. Each year remove about a fifth of the oldest shoots to the base.
PROPAGATION From seed, sown in autumn. From cuttings, in summer.
POTENTIAL PROBLEMS Usually none.

E. × macrantha 'The Bride'
Flowers: late spring to early summer. H and S:3-6ft (90-180cm). Z:5-8.
Arching branches become white garlands that coincide with late spring bulbs. This is a lower growing plant than the species, but its growth is so lax that it may need some support.

Exochorda × macrantha **'The Bride'**

FATSIA

Araliaceae

Of the 2 or 3 species in this genus, one is widely grown, most commonly as an evergreen houseplant. It is a woodland plant and tolerant of shade; more surprisingly, it also stands up well

to coastal conditions and the pollution of urban gardens. Where the climate is mild enough, the plant's deeply lobed glossy leaves are a great asset in the open garden. The tree-ivy (× **Fatshedera lizei**, Z:7-10), a hybrid between it and ivy (*Hedera*), with 5- to 7-lobed leaves, is another handsomely glossy foliage plant, but it tends to be less hardy.
CULTIVATION Require full sun or partial shade and well-drained, moist, fertile soil or potting media. Variegated cultivars all require partial shade.
PROPAGATION From seed, sown in autumn or spring at 59-70°F (15-21°C). From cuttings, in early or mid-summer. By air layering, in spring or late summer.
POTENTIAL PROBLEMS Under glass: mealybugs, scale.

Fatsia japonica **'Variegata'**

F. japonica *Japan, S. Korea*
Foliage: year-round. Flowers: mid-autumn. H and S:5-12ft (1.5-3.7m). Z:7-10.
The shining dark green leaves, up to 16in (40cm) across and wavy at the edges, are thrust out on long stems from a spreading shrub. In autumn, stiff sprays composed of numerous globular clusters of tiny creamy flowers stand above the bold foliage. These are followed by small black berries. **'Variegata'** (Z:8-10) is a very striking variegated plant, with the tips of the lobes splashed creamy white.

FORSYTHIA

Oleaceae

If they were seen less often, forsythias would be splendid shrubs. Perhaps the secret of enjoying their uncompromising radiance is to observe them in a neighbor's yard, so avoiding the problem of masking the dullness of forsythias for much of the year. There are about 7 species in the genus, usually deciduous, and with the exception of a single European example, they are all Asiatic. The species are plants of open woodland, but like the hybrids, which are more commonly seen, they are adaptable to a wide range of conditions. All have yellow flowers. The species have their merits. *F. giraldiana* (Z:5–9), which eventually reaches about 12ft (3.7m), often starts to bear its solitary flowers on arching stems in late winter. Its fault is lankiness, but the relative sparseness of its flowers can be thought a point in its favor. Golden bell (*F. suspensa*, Z:4–9) is usually a lax shrub, but can grow to 10ft (3m) when trained on a wall, which is the best way to show off its pendulous flowers.

CULTIVATION Require full sun or partial shade and well-drained, moist soil. Each year, after flowering, remove about a fifth of the oldest shoots on established plants and cut back the remaining flowered shoots to strong lower shoots or buds.

PROPAGATION From cuttings, taken in summer.

POTENTIAL PROBLEMS Birds eating buds; forsythia gall, honey fungus.

F. × intermedia

Flowers: early to mid-spring. H and S:5–7ft (1.5–2.2m). Z:5–9. Numerous hybrids have been raised, most of them medium to large shrubs, the stems crowded with starry flowers in spring. **'Lynwood'** bristles with large, rich yellow flowers. Those of **'Spectabilis'** are only marginally smaller. These are large shrubs but even **'Minigold'** grows to 6ft (1.8m). **'Spring Glory'** is of similar size, but its paler yellow flowers are less assertive.

***Forsythia* × *intermedia* 'Spectabilis'**

FOTHERGILLA

HAMAMELIDACEAE

The fothergillas have 2 high seasons, but in between these they are inconspicuous shrubs. The 2 species, deciduous woodland shrubs of acidic soils in the south-eastern USA, bear bottlebrush spikes of creamy white flowers in spring, and in autumn their foliage has a good color. The dwarf fothergilla (*F. gardenii*) is similar to the plant

described but in height and spread rarely exceeds 3ft (90cm).

CULTIVATION Require full sun or partial shade and organic-rich, moist, well-drained acid soil.

PROPAGATION From seed, sown in autumn or winter. From cuttings taken in summer. By air layering, in summer.

POTENTIAL PROBLEMS Usually none.

F. major *USA (Allegheny Mountains, Virginia to South Carolina)*

Large fothergilla
Foliage: autumn. Flowers: late-spring to early summer. H:6–8ft (1.8–2.5m) S. 4–6ft (1.2–1.8m). Z:5–8.
The stems are bare or just breaking into leaf when the fragrant flower spikes open. The flowers are without petals, the bottlebrush consisting of a mass of stamens. Before falling, the leaves turn a stunning bright orange-yellow and red color in a long-lasting display.

Fothergilla major

FREMONTODENDRON

STERCULIACEAE Flannel bush

Although the shrubs themselves are somewhat coarse, they bear magnificent yellow flowers over a long season. These are petalless, but have a large and waxy calyx. The few species, which are evergreen or semievergreen, are plants that exist on dry and scrubby terrain in northern Mexico and southern USA. Where they are of borderline hardiness, fremontodendrons will fare best planted at the bottom of a warm wall.

CULTIVATION Require full sun and also well-drained neutral to alkaline soil.

PROPAGATION From seed, sown in spring at 55–64°F (13–18°C). From cuttings, in summer.

POTENTIAL PROBLEMS Phytophthora root rot.

WARNING Inhalation of the leaf and stem hairs may cause severe asthmatic attacks. Skin irritations can also be caused by having some contact with the shoots and the foliage.

***Fremontodendron* 'California Glory'**

F. 'California Glory'

Flowers: late spring to mid-autumn. H:12–20ft (3.7–6m), S:8–12ft (2.5–3.7m). Z:8–9
This free-flowering hybrid and its parents, *F. californicum* and *F. mexicanum*, all show a strong family resemblance. 'California Glory', marginally the hardiest, makes rapid growth vertically and then becomes more spreading, but at an early age starts producing large flowers more than 2in (5cm) across. The leaves of all of these plants are backed with a rusty felting, and the stems, too, are hairy; the warning given above should be noted.

FUCHSIA

ONAGRACEAE

Relatively few of the evergreen and deciduous species, about 100 in all, are widely grown. However, the hybrids, numbered in the thousands, are enormously popular and are often grown as half-hardy perennials that are overwintered under glass. Some make erect and bushy plants; others have lax and trailing stems. The flowers of the hybrids, borne very freely over a long season, dangle with a balletic charm inherited from their parents. The typical flower consists of a waxy tube that opens out into 4 sepals, which curl back from or partly cover a bell (the corolla) of 4 overlapping petals. It is, however, the protruding stamens and style that give the flowers their special poise, and without them the dancing blooms would seem like amputees. The color range is largely restricted to mauve, purple, pink, red, and white but in many cases there is a pleasing contrast between the body and overskirt, composed of tube and sepals, and the bell-like skirt itself. Semidouble hybrids have 5 to 7 petals, the doubles sometimes many more than 8, making a very full, even cluttered corolla. Some species, including the deciduous trailing fuchsia from New Zealand (*F. procumbens*, Z:8–10), have erect flowers. Where the weather is mild enough, this is an appealing frost-hardy rock-garden plant, but it is more interesting when it is bearing plumlike red fruits than when it is in flower. In the following selection of shrubs, the species are then followed by the hybrids that are grouped broadly according to their hardiness.

CULTIVATION Require full sun or partial shade and soil that is fertile and moist but well drained. Under glass, plants require loam-based soil.

PROPAGATION From seed, sown in spring at 75°F (24°C). From softwood cuttings, in spring. From semiripe cuttings, in late summer.

POTENTIAL PROBLEMS Whiteflies, capsid bugs, aphids; rust.

Fuchsia magellanica

SPECIES

F. magellanica *Argentina, Chile*
Flowers: summer. H and S:5–10ft (1.5–3m). Z:7–9.
The hardiest species and the parent of many hybrids is a shrub of rare refinement. The arching stems carry neat pointed leaves and have small crimson flowers, their long sepals almost hiding the short purple corolla. Its numerous forms, some variegated and usually less hardy, are all graceful shrubs. The narrow leaves and slender scarlet and violet flowers give **var. *gracilis*** an added delicacy. **'Versicolor'** is one of the loveliest of variegated shrubs. The foliage, pink tinted when young, becomes gray-green, making a soft foil for the crimson flowers. *F.* **'Riccartonii'** is like a particularly vigorous version of the species, the flowers with broader sepals of a darker red. Where the climate is mild enough, it makes a good, although rather broad, informal flowering hedge.

HYBRIDS

Frost hardy
Flowers: summer. H:6–60in (15–150cm), S:12–36in (30–90cm). Z:7–9.
Some of the hybrids are surprisingly

Fuchsia **'Tom Thumb'**

tough and, where frost does not penetrate the ground deeply, are often grown in the open garden. They vary considerably in size, but are usually erect and bushy, and their flowers are much larger than those of *F. magellanica*. The following selection is no more than a sample: **'Alice Hoffman'**, up to 2ft (60cm) in height and spread, has bronze and purple-tinted foliage and single flowers with a deep pink tube and sepals above a pink-veined white corolla; **'Genii'**, an upright bush reaching 3ft (90cm), has yellow-green foliage, red shoots, and small single flowers that are red with a violet corolla; **'Mrs. Popple'**, a vigorous bush up to 4ft (1.2m) tall, has large single flowers that have a scarlet tube and sepals and violet petals, from which protrude conspicuous crimson stamens and style; **'Phyllis'**, a fast-growing bush reaching 3ft (90cm), has semi-double flowers, the tube and sepals reddish pink, with the corolla a deeper shade; and **'Tom Thumb'**, a compact bush up to 1ft (30cm) tall, with small single flowers that have scarlet sepals and a mauve corolla.

Fuchsia **'Jack Shahan'**

Half hardy
Flowers: summer. H:6–30in (15–75cm), S:12–24in (30–60cm). Z:9–10.
The half-hardy hybrids, the most varied of the fuchsias, are widely used for summer bedding and container gardening, those with trailing stems being popular for tall pots and hanging baskets. The following all make upright bushes:

'Annabel', up to 2ft (60cm) in height and spread, has double white flowers, the tube and sepals flushed pink, the corolla veined pink, and the stamens pink; **'Dollar Princess'**, up to 18in (45cm) tall, has double flowers, the tube and sepals red, the corolla deep purple; **'Flash'**, 2–3ft (60–90cm) in height, has large numbers of small uniformly red single flowers; and **'Royal Velvet'**, up to 30in (75cm) tall, has double flowers, with the tube and sepals crimson, and the corolla deep purple. The following have lax or trailing stems, unless stated otherwise, growing up to 18in (45cm) tall with a spread of 2ft (60cm). They are suited to growing in tall pots or hanging baskets. **'Bicentennial'** has double flowers, with the tubes near white, the sepals pale orange, and the corolla orange and magenta; **'Golden Marinka'**, 1ft (30cm) tall and as much as 18in (45cm) across, has variegated green and yellow foliage and single red flowers, the corolla slightly darker than the sepals; **'Jack Shahan'** has large single pink flowers, with the corolla darker than the tubes and sepals; **'La Campanella'** has many small semidouble flowers, with the tube pink, the sepals white with pink flush, and the corolla purple. **'Red Spider'**, up to 1ft (30cm) tall and almost twice this in spread, bears long, narrow, single flowers, with the tube and sepals crimson, and the corolla reddish pink.

Fuchsia **'Thalia'**

Frost tender
Flowers: summer. H:24–30in (60–75cm), S:18–36in (45–90cm). Z:9–10.
These include a group derived from *F. triphylla*, a species native to Haiti and Santo Domingo. This parent bears long-tubed orange-scarlet flowers with small sepals at the tips of arching stems and the leaves, in threes, are purple on the underside. **'Gartenmeister Bonstedt'** and **'Thalia'** are 2 similar hybrids with velvety bronze-red leaves and long-tubed flowers of uniform orange-red.

GARRYA

GARRYACEAE

A small genus of a dozen or so evergreen shrubs from western USA, Central America, and the West Indies is mainly of interest to gardeners on account of the long and slender catkins. Male and female catkins are borne on separate plants, the male catkins usually being the more ornamental. The species are found in a wide range of habitats. The plant described flowers best in full sun and where it planted in areas is of borderline hardiness it should be placed at the base of a warm wall.

CULTIVATION Require full sun or partial shade and well-drained soil.
PROPAGATION From seed, sown in autumn or spring. From semiripe cuttings, in mid-summer.
POTENTIAL PROBLEMS Fungal leaf spot.

G. elliptica W. USA
Silk-tassel bush
Flowers: mid-winter to early spring. H:8-13ft (2.5-4m), S:6-12ft (1.8-3.7m). Z:7-9.
For much of the year this is a plodding evergreen with rather dull, gray-green, leathery leaves. The winter transformation of the male plants is dramatic, the whole shrub being draped with pliant gray-green catkins swaying gently. In the male clone 'James Roof', the sea green catkins can be as much as 8in (20cm) long. The plainer catkins that grow on the female plants are followed by clusters of purplish fruits.

Garrya elliptica 'James Roof'

GAULTHERIA

ERICACEAE Wintergreen

The lustrous berries are the chief interest of these ericaceous shrubs, but their evergreen foliage is an asset in the lime-free conditions on which they exist. There are about 170 species, which are found in woodland and more open rocky habitats in the Americas, Asia, including the Himalayas, and Australasia. They spread readily by suckers, and some, such as the salal or shallon (G. shallon, Z:5-8) from western North America, can become a nuisance. G. cuneata (Z:6-8) and G. miqueliana (Z:5-8) are less troublesome, low but spreading plants about 1ft (30cm) tall, with white or pink-tinted fruits, and are suitable for a peat bed. The plant described is, however, by far the showiest.

CULTIVATION Require partial shade and moist, peaty, acid, or neutral soil.
PROPAGATION From seed, sown in autumn. From semiripe cuttings, in mid-summer. By sucker removal, in spring.
POTENTIAL PROBLEMS Usually none.
WARNING Stomach upsets may occur if any part (except the fruit) is swallowed.

Gaultheria mucronata 'Indian Lake'

G. mucronata Argentina, Chile
Flowers: late spring to early summer. Fruits: mid-autumn to late winter. H and S:2-4ft (60-120cm). Z:7-9.
A thicket of wiry stems is densely covered with glossy spiny leaves, but plants become leggy with age. The white urn-shaped flowers, often tinged pink, are less conspicuous nestling among the foliage than the marblelike fruits that follow and remain on the plants through autumn and winter. In color the fruits range from white and pink through to purplish red. Male and female flowers are usually borne on separate plants, a male plant, such as the compact and free-flowering 'Thymifolia', being needed to make sure female plants carry good crops. Many, such as 'Indian Lake' and 'Mulberry Wine', have red to purple fruits. Those of 'Parelmoer' are light pink, while those of 'Sneeuwwitje' are white flecked with pink. 'Bell's Seedling' is hermaphroditic, and its fruits are dark red.

GENISTA

PAPILIONACEAE Woadwaxen

Genista lydia

The brooms in this genus, like those in the closely related genus Cytisus, are valued for their profusion of pea flowers. Almost all are deciduous, but their green stems give the impression they are in leaf year-round. Most of the species, about 90 in all, are from Europe and W. Asia, and almost all are plants of dry open habitats. In some areas, such as parts of Australia, they are so successful in dry conditions that they have become weeds. Their adaptability is, however, a big asset in gardens with hot dry banks and stony free-draining ground. See also TREES.

CULTIVATION Require full sun and light well-drained soil.
PROPAGATION From seed, sown in autumn or spring.
POTENTIAL PROBLEMS Aphids.

G. lydia E. Balkans
Flowers: early summer. H:2-3ft (60-90cm), S:3-4ft (90-120cm). Z:7-9.
The gray-green hummock of slender arching stems becomes a mound of bright yellow flowers, which looks effective when cascading over a retaining wall.

G. pilosa var. minor W. and C. Europe
Flowers: late spring to early summer. H:18in (45cm), S:2-3ft (60-90cm). Z:6-8.
The overlapping stems of this prostrate shrub make a tangled

Genista pilosa 'Vancouver Gold'

mat, in **'Procumbens'** not more than 8in (20cm) tall and thickly sprinkled with yellow flowers. The taller **'Vancouver Gold'** also flowers generously.

G. sagittalis
Flowers: early summer. H:6–8in (15–20cm), S:3–4ft (90–120cm). Z:4–8.
The real leaves are small, but the color and broad wings of the stems give this shrub a very leafy appearance. The yellow flowers are clustered in dense heads. A diminutive version from the Pyrenees, **subsp. *delphinensis***, makes a sunny little mound rarely more than 6in (15cm) tall.

G. tinctoria *Europe, Turkey*
Dyer's greenwood, woadwaxen
Flowers: early summer to early autumn. H:18–36in (45–90cm), S:3–4ft (90–120cm). Z:5–7.
Slender short spires of bright yellow flowers stand out against dark green leaves and stems over a long season in this shrub. Especially noticeable is the double-flowered **'Flore Pleno'**. The free-flowering **'Royal Gold'** is richly colored.

HAMAMELIS

HAMAMELIDACEAE Witch hazel

The winter encrustation on bare branches of fragrant spidery flowers in shades of yellow and dull red is the principal ornament of most of the half dozen species. However, the autumn coloring of the foliage is also an asset of some of these deciduous shrubs and small trees from Asia and North America. The moisture-loving Ozark witch hazel (**H. vernalis**, Z:5–8) from central USA has an outstanding form, **'Sandra'**, with leaves that are purplish when they first open and which turn vivid shades of orange, scarlet, and red before falling. All the witch hazels are woodland plants of neutral to acid soils.
CULTIVATION Require full sun or partial shade and well-drained, moist, neutral to acid soil.
PROPAGATION From seed, sown as soon as ripe. By grafting, in late winter. By budding, in late summer.
POTENTIAL PROBLEMS Honey fungus, coral spot.

H. × intermedia
Foliage: autumn. Flowers: early to mid-winter. H and S:10–12ft (3–3.7m). Z:5–8.
Crosses between the Japanese witch hazel (**H. japonica**) and the Chinese witch hazel (**H. mollis**), strongly stamped with the family characteristics, have produced a

Hamamelis × intermedia 'Pallida'

varied range of hybrids. All have flowers consisting of 4 narrow crimpled petals that are to some extent scented. **'Arnold Promise'**, upright when young but spreading with age, has large yellow flowers in thick clusters from mid- to late winter. **'Diane'** has dark-red flowers at the same time, **'Jelena'** copper-red flowers a little earlier; both have colorful autumn foliage. The refined ultimate in these shrubs is, however, the cool yellow of **'Pallida'**, in mid- to late winter, a supreme woodland garden shrub. The hybrids are commonly grafted onto stocks of the Virginia witch hazel (**H. virginiana**, Z:4–8), and any suckers should be removed.

HEBE

SCROPHULARIACEAE

About 100 species of evergreen shrubs or, rarely, trees are the woody versions of the veronicas. A very high proportion are natives of New Zealand, where they are found among other shrubs in a range of habitats, many in coastal regions, some in gravelly river valleys and others in high country and mountainsides. The foliage is usually dense, but the size of the leaves varies considerably, those with small leaves being the hardiest. The white-flowered **H. rakaiensis** (Z:7–9), which makes a spreading dome about 3ft (90cm) tall, has leaves under 1in (2.5cm) long and is frost hardy to fully hardy. The "whipcord hebes" have closely overlapping scalelike leaves so that superficially they resemble some of the dwarf conifers. The flowers are tubular, opening out to 4 lobes, and are usually tightly packed in spikelike arrangements. Where the weather is mild enough, and especially in coastal and exposed gardens, these are very useful shrubs, but where

they are growing at the margins of their hardiness, losses are common.
CULTIVATION Require full sun or partial shade and moist, well-drained neutral or alkaline soil.
PROPAGATION From seed, sown as soon as ripe. From semiripe cuttings, in late summer.
POTENTIAL PROBLEMS Aphids; phytophthora root rot, leaf spot, downy mildew.

Hebe rakaiensis

H. cupressoides *New Zealand (South Island)*
Foliage: year-round. Flowers: early to mid-summer. H:3–4ft (90–120cm), S:3–4ft (90–120cm). Z:8–9.
The closely packed tiny leaves give this whipcord hebe the appearance of a cypress. Mature plants are studded with short spikes of pale blue flowers. **'Boughton Dome'**, a dwarf and very dense form that makes a pleasing green mound about 1ft (30cm) tall, seldom flowers.
H. ochracea 'James Stirling', which is fully hardy, is another whipcord type, with tiered sprays of ocher-yellow foliage tinted orange in winter. It makes a low mound about 16in (40cm) tall with white flowers in late spring and summer.

H. 'Midsummer Beauty'
Foliage: year-round. Flowers: mid-summer to late autumn. H:4–6ft (1.2–1.8m), S:4–5ft (1.2–1.5m). Z:8–9.
A large number of hybrids, many with **H. speciosa** as a parent, bear tapering or bottlebrush spikes of flowers over a long period in summer, the colors including blue, violet, pink, purplish red, and pure white. **'Midsummer Beauty'** has lance-shaped leaves, purplish red on the underside, and its mauve spikes, fading to white, can be as much as 6in (15cm) long. Other hybrids in the same mold are **'Alicia Amherst'**, with dark-green leaves and violet-blue flowers; **'Great Orme'**, flowers pink turning to white; and **'La Séduisante'**, usually no more than 3ft (90cm) in height, with purple-tinted foliage and wine-red flowers.

Hebe pinguifolia 'Pagei'

H. 'Pewter Dome'

Flowers: late spring to early summer. H:12-18in (30-45cm), S:18-24in (45-60cm). Z:8-9. Several dwarf hebes that make low mounds of gray-green foliage are appealing plants for rock gardens, raised beds, and edging. 'Pewter Dome' has short spikes of white flowers. *H.* 'Red Edge', a similar plant in size and hardiness but with blue-gray leaves veined and margined with red, is particularly conspicuous in winter. It has mauve-blue flowers that fade to white. Hardier than these is *H. pinguifolia* 'Pagei' (Z:7-9), a blue-green sprawling plant about 1ft (30cm) tall but making a mat up to 3ft (90cm) wide. It has short spikes of white flowers in late spring or early summer. Slightly more compact and equally hardy is *H.* 'Youngii' (Z:7-9), but its foliage is dark green and it bears its violet flowers in early to mid-summer.

HELIANTHEMUM

CISTACEAE Rock rose, sun rose

The genus contains about 100 species, which are found in many parts of the world, including parts of Asia, Europe, and North Africa, as well as North and South America. They are best known in gardens by their hybrids that are derived from crosses of European species such as *H. nummularium* (Z:6-8), a low-spreading plant with bright yellow flowers that is an ardent sun lover and thrives on poor dry soils. *CULTIVATION* Require full sun and well-drained neutral or alkaline soil. Cut back to the woody clump in early spring. *PROPAGATION* From seed, sown as soon as ripe or in spring. From softwood cuttings, in late spring or early summer. *POTENTIAL PROBLEMS* Usually none.

H. hybrids

Flowers: early to mid-summer. H:6-12in (15-30cm), S:10-20in (25-50cm). Z:6-8. Sprawling shrubs with variable foliage but often gray-green carry masses of single or double papery flowers in a wide range of colors. The individual flowers are short-lived, but there are a few dwarf shrubs that reliably give a long display in sunny well-drained positions, particularly in raised beds and rock gardens. The color range includes many shades of pink, red, and orange, as well as yellow and white. Three singles with gray or silver-gray foliage from a range in which almost all are worth growing are **'Rhodanthe Carneum'**, soft pink flowers with a yellowish center; **'The Bride'**, milky white flowers with a yellow center; and **'Wisley Primrose'**, pale yellow flowers with a deeper colored center.

Helianthemum 'The Bride'

HIBISCUS

MALVACEAE

This very varied genus of about 200 species, including annuals and perennials as well as trees and shrubs, is best known for one of the most popular tropical and subtropical shrubs, the Chinese hibiscus (*H. rosa-sinensis*, Z:9-11). The numerous cultivars of this evergreen species produce single or double flowers in a color range including crimson, yellow, and white over a very long season. The species described is the most reliable in cool temperate gardens. *CULTIVATION* Require full sun and organic-rich, moist, well-drained, neutral or slightly alkaline soil. *PROPAGATION* From seed, sown in spring at 55-64°F (13-18°C). From cuttings, in late spring and mid-summer. By layering, in spring or summer. *POTENTIAL PROBLEMS* Aphids, scale, mealybugs, whiteflies; powdery mildew.

H. syriacus *China to India*
Rose of sharon
Flowers: late summer to mid-autumn. H:6-10ft (1.8-3m), S:4-6ft (1.2-1.8m). Z:5-9.
The penalty of being so late into leaf and late into flower is that the blooms are sometimes damaged by frost, despite the shrub's relative hardiness. The mallowlike flowers are borne on an upright shrub, the single cultivars being of much more pleasing shape than the doubles. **'Oiseau Bleu'** has violet-blue flowers with purplish veining; **'Red Heart'** has white flowers with magenta blotches and veining; and **'Woodbridge'** has rich pink flowers, a darker pink center, and veining.

Hibiscus syriacus 'Oiseau Bleu'

HYDRANGEA

HYDRANGEACEAE

The main ornamental value of the hydrangeas lies in their flattened or dome-shaped flowerheads. These generally consist of fertile flowers that are small but numerous, surrounded by sterile flowers or ray flowerets, usually much less numerous but of greater size. Flower color is affected by the alkalinity or acidity of the soil. The best blues are produced on neutral to acid soils; on alkaline soils an otherwise blue hydrangea becomes purplish or pink in color. Almost all the 80 or so species of hydrangea are climbers or shrubs from moist woodlands in eastern Asia or North and South America. All the shrubs described are deciduous and the leaves of some are richly colored during the autumn months. See also CLIMBERS.
CULTIVATION Require sun or partial shade and organic-rich, moist, well-drained soil. Cut a third of the oldest stems of *H. macrophylla*, *H.* 'Preziosa', and *H. serrata* down to the base in early spring. Cut out any weak crossing stems and prune the previous year's flowered shoots down to the next pair of healthy buds.
PROPAGATION From seed, sown in spring. From softwood cuttings, taken in early summer. From hardwood cuttings, taken in winter (deciduous shrubs). From semiripe cuttings, taken in mid-summer (evergreens).
POTENTIAL PROBLEMS Aphids, red spider mites, vine weevils, capsid bugs, scale; gray mold (*Botrytis*),

powdery mildew, honey fungus, leaf spot, hydrangea virus. **WARNING** Swallowing any parts may cause stomach upsets. Skin allergies may be aggravated by foliage contact.

H. aspera E. Asia
Foliage: early summer to autumn. Flowers: mid- to late summer. H and S:8-10ft (2.5-3m). Z:6-9. Several shrubs, sometimes treelike, previously regarded as separate species, are grouped under this name. All have flattened flowerheads consisting of mauve to purplish-blue fertile flowers surrounded by a broken ring of sterile flowers that are white, usually with a pink or mauve tint. The roughly hairy leaves and flowerheads of *H. macrophylla* are very large. Coming into flower slightly earlier is **subsp. sargentiana**, with large leaves that are bristly on the underside. The most refined of these hydrangeas are those of the **Villosa Group**, in which the foliage has a soft velvety texture.

Hydrangea macrophylla 'Madame Emile Mouillère'

H. macrophylla Japan
Common hydrangea
Flowers: mid- to late summer. H:4-6ft (1.2-1.8m), S:4-8ft (1.2-2.5m). Z:6-9. By far the best known of the hydrangeas are the numerous mophead cultivars of this species, with large rounded flowerheads composed almost entirely of single or double sterile flowerets. They can be criticized for their graceless excess, but they give value for a very long period and are even beautiful when they have faded. They are, not surprisingly, popular in town gardens and as container plants. '**Générale Vicomtesse de Vibraye**' flowers early and carries good pale blue or pink flowers in large flowerheads. '**Madame Emile Mouillère**' is a handsome white that flowers well into autumn. The flowers become pink tinged with age. More adaptable than these are the lacecap cultivars, with flat

heads of fertile flowers ringed by sterile flowerets. On acid soils '**Mariesii Perfecta**' is rich blue with paler flowerets. The fertile flowers of '**Lanarth White**' are often mauve or pink tinted, but the flowerets are white. *H.* '**Preziosa**', a particularly fine mophead, grows to about 5ft (1.5m). The young leaves are purplish and the flowers are strong pink, darkening to purplish red. *H. serrata* '**Bluebird**' is like a compact lacecap, up to 4ft (1.2m) tall, displaying rich blue flowers over a long summer and autumn season.

Hydrangea paniculata

H. paniculata Russia (Sakhalin), China, Japan
Flowers: late summer to early autumn. H:10-20ft (3-6m), S:8-10ft (2.5-3m). Z:4-8. Large conical flowerheads are made up of small creamy white sterile flowers and large ray flowerets, white at first but pink as they age. '**Grandiflora**' has flowerheads up to 1ft (30cm) tall.

H. quercifolia S.E. USA
Oak-leaved hydrangea
Foliage: autumn. Flowers: mid- to late summer. H:5-6ft (1.5-1.8m), S:4-8ft (1.2-2.5m). Z:5-9. The boldly lobed "oak" leaves turn shades of purple and bronze just as the white ray flowerets in the cone-like flowerheads take on pink tints.

Hydrangea quercifolia

HYPERICUM

CLUSIACEAE St. John's wort

In a genus of over 400 species, the numerous shrubs, evergreen and deciduous, are widely distributed and found in a variety of habitats, including woodland and open rocky places. Most of those in cultivation produce their bright yellow flowers, which have prominent stamens, in the second half of the summer. In some cases the flowers are followed by ornamental fruits. The St. John's wort (*H. calycinum*, Z:6-7), a low semievergreen shrub growing to about 2ft (60cm), spreads by runners to the point of becoming a weed. However, it is a useful shrub for covering ground in dry, shady places. Its cup-shaped yellow flowers are filled with several long stamens.
CULTIVATION Require sun or partial shade and moist well-drained soil (large species), full sun and very well-drained soil (dwarf species). The small alpine species require protection from winter wet. Prune deciduous species and *H. calycinum* down to woody base in early spring.
PROPAGATION From seed, sown in autumn. From cuttings, in summer.
POTENTIAL PROBLEMS Rust (*H. calycinum* and *H. × inodorum*).

H. 'Hidcote'
Flowers: mid-summer to early autumn. H and S:3-5ft (90-150cm). Z:6-7.
This semievergreen and aromatic shrub bears saucer-shaped yellow flowers over a long season, but its great popularity has rather blunted its effect. The deciduous and fully hardy *H. forrestii*, which originates from southwestern China, is a pleasing alternative which has a long season of clustered yellow flowers and good foliage color in autumn.

H. × inodorum
Flowers: mid-summer to mid autumn. H:3-4ft (90-120cm), 4-6ft (1.2-1.8m). Z:6-7.
The small, starry, yellow flowers are produced freely on a semi-evergreen shrub with dark-green aromatic leaves. They are followed by clusters of conical fruits. '**Elstead**' has copper-tinted autumn foliage and coral-red fruits but is prone to rust. The compact Chinese species, *H. kouytchense*, which grows to a height of about 3ft (90cm), also has bright red fruits following a long season of yellow flowers.

Hypericum olympicum

H. olympicum *N. Greece, N.W. Turkey*
Flowers: late summer. H:9–12in (23–30cm), S:1ft (30cm). Z:6–7. Bright yellow flowers are scattered over a loose blue-green hummock in this shrub. It is deciduous with attractive, pointed leaves that are gray-green. Even more beautiful as a rock-garden miniature is the **f. *uniflorum* 'Citrinum'**, which has lemon-yellow flowers.

H. 'Rowallane'
Flowers: late summer to early autumn. H:4–6ft (1.2–1.8m), S:3–5ft (90–150cm). Z:6–7. Where the climate is mild enough, this semievergreen hybrid, with its tall arching branches, is the pick of the hypericums. The dark-green leaves make a good background to the bowl-shaped golden flowers, sometimes 3in (7.5cm) across.

KALMIA

Ericaceae Laurel

The kalmias are firmly in the same lime-intolerant camp as the rhododendrons. One species is found in Cuba, the other half dozen in North America, always on acid soils and usually in woodland or swamp. They do well in a shrub border or a woodland garden. The large species described below is the pick of these shrubs, but the sheep laurel (**K. angustifolia**, Z:2–6) makes pleasing low thickets 2–3ft (60–90cm) tall that are brightened by crowded clusters of reddish-pink flowers in early summer. It is also fully hardy.
CULTIVATION Require full sun or partial shade and organic-rich acid soil. Mulch in late winter with leaf mold.
PROPAGATION From seed, sown in spring at 45–54°F (6–12°C). From cuttings, in late spring and mid-summer. By layering, in late summer.
POTENTIAL PROBLEMS Usually none but tends to resent continued containerization.
WARNING Swallowing any part may cause severe discomfort.

K. latifolia *E. USA*
Mountain laurel
Flowers: late spring to mid-summer. H:6–10ft (1.8–3m), S:8–10ft (2.5–3m). Z:4–9. Bushes are densely clothed with dark-green leathery leaves, but these can be nearly obscured when the large flower clusters are open. The bowl-shaped flowers are pink, although there is great variation in the precise shade. They are prettily detailed, with conspicuous stamens and a ring of darker color. There are numerous slight variations on this very beautiful theme. **'Ostbo Red'** has bright red buds opening to pale pink flowers.

Kalmia latifolia

KOLKWITZIA

Caprifoliaceae Beauty bush

The single species, from rocky mountainous slopes in western China, is a graceful deciduous shrub that is grown for its wonderful profusion of bell-shaped flowers.
CULTIVATION Requires full sun and fertile well-drained soil. Cut about a fifth of the oldest stems down to ground level after flowering. Prune flowered shoots down to strong, healthy growths.
PROPAGATION From cuttings, taken in late spring or early summer. By removal of suckers, in spring.
POTENTIAL PROBLEMS Usually none.

K. amabilis *China (Hubei)*
Flowers: late spring to early summer. H and S:6–12ft (1.8–3.7m). Z:4–9.
Masses of pink flowers, yellow in

Kolkwitzia amabilis

the throat, cover a densely twiggy arching bush. **'Pink Cloud'** is a particularly good selection with flowers of deep coloring.

LAURUS

Lauraceae Laurel

The crown of laurels that was the accolade of classical heroes was fashioned from the foliage of the bay laurel (*L. nobilis*). This and one other species, from the Canary Island, and the Azores, *L. azorica*, are aromatic evergreens that are capable of developing into small trees. The culinary value of the bay laurel is enough to justify its place in the garden.
CULTIVATION Require full sun or partial shade, soil that is fertile and moist but well-drained, and shelter from wind.
PROPAGATION From seed, sown in autumn. From semiripe cuttings, in summer.
POTENTIAL PROBLEMS Bay suckers; powdery mildew.

Laurus nobilis

L. nobilis *Mediterranean*
Bay laurel, sweet bay
Flowers: spring. H:10–30ft (3–9m), S:8–16ft (2.5–5m). Z:8–10.
The glossy leaves are this shrub's feature. Untrained, the shrub is of irregular growth, but it is very tolerant of trimming and, shaped as a standard, cone, or pyramid, makes a splendid container plant, easily moved under cover when it becomes vulnerable to winter cold outdoors. The flowers are small and greenish yellow, with male and female on separate plants. Female plants bear purple-black berries.

LAVANDULA

Lamiaceae Lavender

The lavenders are strongly associated with southern Europe and the Mediterranean region, but the distribution of about 25 species extends from the Canary Islands in the west to India in the east. Almost everywhere, however, these evergreen shrubs or subshrubs are plants of dry and sunny habitats.

They have long been grown for their spikes of small 2-lipped flowers, which are strongly scented and loved by bees. The gray-green of their aromatic foliage is also appealing and has made them popular as dwarf hedging. The most interesting of the lavenders for foliage, such as the white wooly *L. lanata* (Z:8–9) from southern Spain, abhor wet weather.
CULTIVATION Require full sun and well-drained soil. Shear off spent flower spikes immediately after flowering. Prune straggly plants in late spring down to buds that have just broken.
PROPAGATION From seed, sown in spring. From semiripe cuttings, in mid-summer.
POTENTIAL PROBLEMS Froghoppers; honey fungus, gray mold (*Botrytis*).

L. angustifolia W. Mediterranean
Flowers: mid- to late summer. H:2–3ft (60–90cm), S:2–4ft (60–120cm). Z:5–8.
Many of the plants that have been grown under this name are now recognized as hybrids (see *L. × intermedia*). The aromatic gray-green shrub is represented in gardens by several clones, typically with violet-blue spikes but some have pink or white flowers. **'Hidcote'** and **'Twickel Purple'**, broader in leaf, are compact, growing to about 2ft (60cm), with dark purple flowers. **'Munstead'** is a useful dwarf about 18in (45cm) tall, but less intense in coloring.

Lavandula angustifolia 'Hidcote'

L. × intermedia
Flowers: mid- to late summer. H and S:1–2ft (30–60cm). Z:5–7.
These crosses between *L. angustifolia* and *L. latifolia* (Z:7–9) often have spoon-shaped leaves, like the latter species. **The Dutch Group** with silver-gray leaves and gray-blue flowers belongs here.

L. stoechas Mediterranean
French lavender
Flowers: late spring to mid-summer. H and S:20–30in (50–75cm). Z:8–9.
Bushy, strongly aromatic plants

Lavandula stoechas 'James Compton'

with gray-green leaves are topped by short spikes of dark purple flowers with a showy bract as finial. The flower stalks of **subsp. pedunculata** are longer, and the earlike bracts can reach 2in (5cm) long. The bracts of **'James Compton'** can be 1½in (3cm) long.

LAVATERA

MALVACEAE Tree mallow

In this mixed genus of about 25 species, there are several shrubby species that are plants of open and dry habitats. The plants that are most commonly grown are fast-growing and vigorous subshrubs that produce a long succession of funnel-shaped flowers among downy lobed leaves. They are often short-lived, but are good on light soils and do well in coastal gardens.
CULTIVATION Require full sun and well-drained light soil. Cut the previous year's growth down to woody base stems in early spring.
PROPAGATION From seed, sown in mid- to late spring. From softwood cuttings, in spring.
POTENTIAL PROBLEMS Rust, stem rot, fungal diseases.

L. 'Barnsley'
Flowers: mid- to late summer. H and S:5–6ft (1.5–1.8m). Z:5–8.
Throughout summer airy branches carry innumerable funnel-shaped flowers that are pale pink animated by a darker center. Others in the same mold include **'Burgundy Wine'**, with deep pink flowers darkened by rich veining.

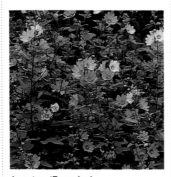

Lavatera 'Barnsley'

LEUCOTHOE

ERICACEAE

Several shrubs in this widely distributed genus of about 50 species are grown for their foliage as much as for their flowers. Most are plants of woodland and swampy ground, and all show the heath family's dislike of lime.
CULTIVATION Require partial or deep shade and organic-rich, moist, acid soil.
PROPAGATION From seed, sown in spring. From semiripe cuttings, in mid-summer. By division of suckering species, in spring.
POTENTIAL PROBLEMS Usually none.

Leucothoe walteri

L. walteri S.E. USA
Drooping leucothoe, fetterbush
Foliage: autumn and winter.
Flowers: late spring. H:4-6ft (1.2–1.8m), S:4–5ft (1.2–1.5m). Z:5–8.
Few evergreens color so dramatically in autumn and winter, but in spring it is the numerous clusters of white urn-shaped flowers dangling all along the arching stems that offer the main ornamental value. The leathery leaves, which are lance shaped and narrow to a sharply pointed tip, color most strongly when the plant is grown in exposed positions, taking on purplish to beet-red tints. *L. Scarletta*, usually not more than 2ft (60cm) tall, is similar to the species, but has young reddish-purple leaves that turn green and later bronzy purple.

LEYCESTERIA

CAPRIFOLIACEAE

The half dozen species in the genus are deciduous shrubs of rugged and wooded country in India and China. The arrangement of the flowers in tassellike racemes is unusual, as are the hollow stems.
CULTIVATION Require full sun or partial shade and well-drained soil. Cut back flowered shoots to strong lower buds in spring.
PROPAGATION From seed, sown in autumn. From cuttings, in summer.
POTENTIAL PROBLEMS Usually none.

Leycesteria formosa

L. formosa *Himalayas, W. China*
Himalayan honeysuckle
Flowers: mid-summer to early autumn. Fruits: winter. H and S:5–8ft (1.5–2.5m). Z:7–9.
In winter the thicket of upright stems, at first covered with a glaucous bloom, later polished and dark green, are highly ornamental in this shrub. However, in summer they are obscured by the elegant foliage. Dangling among the pointed leaves are racemes about 4in (10cm) long of funnel-shaped white flowers set among wine-red bracts. The round berries that follow are purplish black.

LIGUSTRUM

OLEACEAE Privet

The adaptability of the privets to a wide range of conditions is their major asset, but from about 50 species of evergreen, semi-evergreen, and deciduous shrubs, there are few to choose that are notable ornamentals. The nearest to a plant of distinction is the Asiatic **L. lucidum** (Z:8–10), an evergreen large shrub or tree, which may reach 30ft (9m) in height. It has splendidly glossy, dark evergreen leaves, and in late summer or early autumn there are sprays of creamy flowers, followed by blue-black fruits. Even more striking is the yellow variegated **'Excelsum Superbum'** (Z:8–10). The shrub described below is a humdrum plant but it is useful for hedging purposes.
CULTIVATION Require full sun or partial shade and well-drained soil.
PROPAGATION From seed, sown in autumn or spring. From semiripe cuttings, in mid-summer. From hardwood cuttings, in winter.
POTENTIAL PROBLEMS Thrips, aphids, scale, leaf miners; leaf spots, honey fungus, wilt.
WARNING Swallowing any part can cause severe discomfort.

L. ovalifolium *Japan*
California privet
Flowers: mid-summer. H and S:10–15ft (3–4.5m). Z:8–10.

This species is usually seen as an evergreen or semievergreen hedge but untrimmed it makes a large, open shrub. Its creamy flowers are followed by round black fruits. **'Aureum'**, the golden privet, is bright, with leaves edged with a broad yellow margin.

Ligustrum ovalifolium 'Aureum'

LITHODORA

BORAGINACEAE

The star of the genus, a low evergreen subshrub with flowers of ravishing blue, is a lime-hater, but about half a dozen other species with less arresting blue or white flowers tolerate alkaline conditions. They are plants of the Mediterranean region, including parts of North Africa and east to Greece and Turkey, and are found in a variety of habitats, including the margins of woodland and sandy coasts.
CULTIVATION Require full sun and well-drained neutral or alkaline soil (equal parts loam, leaf mold, and sharp sand). *L. diffusa* 'Heavenly Blue' requires organic-rich acid soil. Cut back flowered shoots down to strong lower growths. Plant in spring.
PROPAGATION From semiripe cuttings, taken in mid-summer.
POTENTIAL PROBLEMS Under glass: aphids, red spider mites.

L. diffusa *S. Europe*
Flowers: late spring to early summer. H:6–12in (15–30cm), S:18–24in (45–60cm). Z:7–9.
The sprawling mat of intricately branched stems, so ordinary when

Lithodora diffusa

merely covered with narrow hairy leaves, is transformed by all the blue flowers. In **'Heavenly Blue'** they are of a piercing azure intensity. This subshrub is at its loveliest spilling over a raised edge or trailing from a rock-garden ledge.

LONICERA

CAPRIFOLIACEAE Honeysuckle

The twining plants in this genus of over 150 species are certainly more showy than most of the evergreen and deciduous shrubs. The dense, glossy, dark green leaves of **L. nitida** (Z:7–9), a fully hardy evergreen that can grow to more than 6ft (1.8m), qualify it and the yellow-leaved form **'Baggesen's Gold'** as a hedging plant. Another hardy evergreen, **L. pileata** (Z:7–9), makes good groundcover up to 2ft (60cm) tall in almost any conditions. More decorative are some of the deciduous species, like the pink-flowered **L. tatarica** (Z:4–8), which have red berries to follow the late spring or early summer floral display. Where there is space, however, the shrubby honeysuckles to include are those that flower in winter and make their point with scent. See also CLIMBERS.
CULTIVATION Require full sun or partial shade and organic-rich, moist, well-drained soil. After flowering, cut flowered shoots down to strong lower growths. Remove about a fifth of old stems down to ground level.
PROPAGATION From seed, sown when ripe. From semiripe cuttings, in mid-summer (evergreens). From semiripe cuttings, in summer or hardwood cuttings, in autumn (deciduous plants).
POTENTIAL PROBLEMS Aphids.
WARNING Swallowing berries can cause mild stomach upsets.

Lonicera × purpusii

L. × purpusii
Flowers: mid-winter to early spring. H:5–6ft (1.5–1.8m), S:6–8ft (1.8–2.5m). Z:5–8.
Two very similar Chinese species, **L. fragrantissima** and

L. standishii, are the parents, but their hybrid is freer flowering, especially in the form **'Winter Beauty'**. The creamy flowers on the bare stems can easily go unnoticed so that the fragrance is a delicious mystery. The parent species produce red berries, the hybrid only rarely.

MAGNOLIA

MAGNOLIACEAE

The magnolias are in the first rank of flowering trees and shrubs. A high proportion of their evergreen and deciduous species, about 125 in total, as well as numerous hybrids, bear flowers of exceptional quality. The color range is limited, but in many cases individual blooms are of superb form and texture, and on mature plants they are borne in profusion. The species are mainly plants of woodland and scrub, with a distribution ranging from the Himalayas to southeast Asia and from North to South America. The foliage, although generally pleasing, does not match the distinction of the flowers. In many cases the clusters of fruits are a curious, even moderately colorful feature in autumn. See also TREES.
CULTIVATION Require sun or partial shade and organic-rich, moist, well-drained, acid soil.
PROPAGATION From semiripe cuttings, in late summer.
POTENTIAL PROBLEMS Honey fungus.

M. liliiflora *China*
Flowers: mid-spring to mid-summer. H:8–10ft (2.5–3m), S:6–12ft (1.8–3.7m). Z:5–9.
This rather open deciduous shrub has slender tuliplike flowers that are mauve pink on the outside, white inside. More commonly seen is the more compact **'Nigra'**, which has upright purplish-red flowers, white with purple staining on the inside. This shrub is a parent of many fully hardy deciduous hybrids that flower freely in mid- to late spring. **M. 'Susan'**, one of these, is of upright growth, bearing long buds, often rather crescent shaped, opening to fragrant flowers with long reddish-purple segments that twist slightly to show the paler inside.

M. sieboldii *China, Korea, Japan*
Flowers: late spring to late summer. H:15–25ft (4.5–7.5m), S:20–40ft (6–12m). Z:5–9.
The white bowl-shaped flowers, up to 4in (10cm) across and refined in fragrance as well as in form, are borne among dark green foliage.

They look out or down, showing their conspicuous wine-red anthers. The shrub is deciduous, and its leaves are downy and gray-green on the underside.

Magnolia × soulangeana

M. × soulangeana
Saucer magnolia
Flowers: mid- to late spring. H:12–15ft (3.7–4.5m), S:15–20ft (4.5–6m). Z:5–9.
Despite their profusion, the large goblet-shaped flowers have a dignified eloquence matched by the flowers of few other spring shrubs and trees. Although this deciduous hybrid can make a spreading tree, it is most often seen as a large rounded shrub. The sculpted blooms, which can be as much as 6in (15cm) across, are seen at their best before the young leaves develop. Several fine forms, some of which produce a few flowers in autumn as well as the main flush in spring, vary in color from the familiar white with a purple stain at the base. The fragrant flowers of the treelike **'Alba Superba'** are almost pure white. **'Lennei'** has purplish-pink goblets, **'Rustica Rubra'** has goblets of a deeper reddish purple, but in both cases the flowers are milky white on the inside.

Magnolia stellata **'Royal Star'**

M. stellata *Japan*
Star magnolia
Flowers: early to mid-spring. H:8–10ft (2.5–3m), S:8–12ft (2.5–3.7m). Z:5–9.
Twigs of gray-green flower buds have a somber beauty of their own but the shrub's great moment is when the narrow snowy segments,

spill out to make fragrant, slightly limp stars up to 4in (10cm) across. **'Royal Star'**, pink in bud, and **'Waterlily'** have slightly larger flowers, with about 30 segments.

MAHONIA

BERBERIDACEAE

Handsome evergreen foliage and yellow flowers in winter or early spring, followed in many cases by blue-black berries, are important ornamental features of shrubs that adapt well to a wide range of conditions. There are about 70 species, which are found in woodland and more open rugged country in Asia, from the Himalayas to China, as well as in North and Central America.
CULTIVATION Require partial or full shade and organic-rich, moist, well-drained soil. **M. fremontii** (Z:8–9) and **M. nevinii** (Z:7–9) require full sun and very well-drained soil.
PROPAGATION From seed, sown as soon as ripe or in autumn. From semiripe or leaf-bud cuttings, in mid- to late summer.
POTENTIAL PROBLEMS Mildew, rust.

M. aquifolium *W. North America*
Oregon grape
Flowers: early spring. Fruit: late spring. H:2–3ft (60–90cm), S:3–5ft (90–150cm). Z:5–8.
Although never in the first rank of shrubs, this performs astonishingly well, forming dense suckering thickets even in the least favored corners of the garden. The pinnate leaves are shiny green, often turning red-purple in winter. The yellow flowers are densely clustered and are followed by grapelike blue-black berries.

M. japonica *China*
Foliage: year-round. Flowers: early winter to early spring. H:5–9ft (1.5–2.7m), S:8–12ft (2.5–3.7m). Z:6–8.
The evergreen foliage has a severe and graphic boldness, the large leaves, arranged at the end of branches in whorls, consisting of paired spiny leaflets. The leaflets are dark green but in full sun sometimes turn red. In winter, clustered flower sprays spill from the center of the leaf rosettes. They are crowded with lemon-yellow bells that provide one of the best scents in the winter garden, carrying well when the weather is mild. Inexplicably, the laxness of the flower sprays is sometimes considered a failing, but is a concession to gracefulness lacking in most of the hybrids. After the flowers have finished, there are blue-black berries.

M. × *media*

Foliage: year-round. Flowers: late autumn to late winter. H:12–15ft (3.7–4.5m), S:10–12ft (3–3.7m). Z:7–9.

The hybrids that go under this name are the result of crosses between *M. japonica* and another winter-flowering Chinese species, *M. lomariifolia* (Z:8–9). This is an often leggy shrub to 10ft (3m), with erect sprays of yellow flowers. The hybrids lean toward one or other parent. '**Charity**' has numerous sprays of yellow flowers that at first are upright, later spreading; on the long sprays of '**Lionel Fortescue**' the yellow flowers open early. The flowers of these 2 hybrids are faintly scented; those of '**Winter Sun**', which has erect sprays, are more fragrant.

Mahonia × *media* 'Charity'

MYRTUS

MYRTACEAE Myrtle

The 2 evergreen shrubs that remain after their close relatives have been shunted off to other genera are Mediterranean, thriving most in hot dry conditions. The common myrtle (*M. communis*), which has been long in cultivation, is a happy horticultural connection with the classical world of Roman and Greek mythology.

CULTIVATION Require full sun and moist well-drained soil.

PROPAGATION From seed, sown in autumn. From semiripe cuttings, taken in mid-summer.

POTENTIAL PROBLEMS Usually none.

M. *communis* *Mediterranean*

Common myrtle

Flowers: mid- to late summer. Fruits: autumn. H and S:8–10ft (2.5–3m). Z:9–10.

These bushy plants are dense with small glossy leaves that are spicily aromatic when they are bruised between the fingers. The plants can be trimmed to shape very much like box (*Buxus sempervirens*). The fragrant white flowers, which are carried in profusion, have 5 petals and a central puff of stamens. Where the

climate is warm enough, there are dark purple berries to follow. The compact **subsp. *tarentina***, with a height and spread of up to 5ft (1.5m), has narrow leaves, flowers that are tinted pink, and gray-white berries. Where these shrubs are grown at the margins of their hardiness, they are best planted at the foot of a warm wall.

Myrtus communis

NANDINA

BERBERIDACEAE Heavenly bamboo

The single species of this genus, bamboolike but really an evergreen *Berberis* relative, is a streamside and woodland shrub of mountainous country in many parts of Asia.

CULTIVATION Requires full sun and moist well-drained soil.

PROPAGATION From seed, sown as soon as ripe. From semiripe cuttings, taken in mid-summer.

POTENTIAL PROBLEMS Viruses.

Nandina domestica

N. *domestica* *China, India, Japan*

Heavenly bamboo

Foliage: early spring to late autumn. Flowers: mid-summer. Fruits: autumn and winter. H:4–6ft (1.2–1.8m), S:3–5ft (90–150cm). Z:7–9.

The unbranched stems of this evergreen or semievergreen shrub carry large leaves consisting of many narrow segments. They are purplish red when young and color well again in autumn. Where the climate is warm enough, the clusters of starry white flowers with long yellow anthers are followed by red berries.

OSMANTHUS

OLEACEAE

Although relying simply on their polished leaves and small but fragrant flowers, several shrubs in this genus have an irresistible appeal. There are about 15 species, all of them evergreen woodland shrubs or trees. Some are natives of southern USA and the Pacific Islands, but the best known are Asiatic. When the shrubs have flowered, bluish-black fruits usually follow. The plants described all respond well to clipping and can be used to advantage for hedges and topiary.

CULTIVATION Require sun or partial shade and well-drained fertile soil.

PROPAGATION From seed, sown as soon as ripe. From semiripe cuttings, in mid-summer. By layering, in autumn or spring.

POTENTIAL PROBLEMS Usually none.

Osmanthus delavayi

O. *delavayi* *W. China (Sichuan, Yunnan)*

Flowers: mid- to late spring. H:6–15ft (1.8–4.5m), S:6–12ft (1.8–3.7m). Z:8–10.

The slow-growing dark-green bush has neat glossy leaves, which set off to perfection the clusters of tubular white flowers. Their scent is sweet and refined. There are sometimes blue-black fruits to follow. A fully hardy hybrid of which this is a parent, *O.* × *burkwoodii* (Z:7–9), is more compact, slightly coarser, and less well scented, but it is being measured against a paragon.

O. *heterophyllus* *Japan, Taiwan*

Holly tea olive

Flowers: late summer to early autumn. H:8–15ft (2.5–4.5m), S:8–12ft (2.5–3.7m). Z:7–9.

Its green glossy leaves are toothed and prickly so that the shrub seems to be a fake holly. Tiny white flowers, rather lost among the leaves, are sweetly scented. They are sometimes followed by blue-black berries. There are variegated forms; '**Variegatus**' features a pale yellow edging on the leaves.

PACHYSANDRA

BUXACEAE

This small genus of 4 species of evergreen or semievergreen woodland plants includes a subshrub that is useful for carpeting bare ground under trees.
CULTIVATION Require partial or full shade and any soil.
PROPAGATION By division, in spring. From softwood cuttings, in early summer.
POTENTIAL PROBLEMS Slugs, snails.

P. terminalis *N. China, Japan*
Flowers: mid- to late spring. H:8–12in (20–30cm), S:18–24in (45–60cm). Z:5–8.
The small glossy dark green leaves clustered at the tips of the short stems are the plant's principal asset. The upper portion of the leaves is often toothed. The overlapping rosettes make very dense cover, and the plants spread freely at the roots, especially in moist soils rich in organic matter. Male and female flowers, which are borne on separate plants, are small, greenish white or white, and without petals.

Pachysandra terminalis

PAEONIA

PAEONIACEAE Tree peony

The common name "tree peony" is misleading for the woody plants in this genus, which are shrubby and usually of short stature. In the sumptuous beauty of their flowers, many of these deciduous shrubs rank with the finest of the more numerous herbaceous peonies, and the foliage of some is of a very high order. With such qualities, they can be forgiven for the gauntness of their bare stems out of season. There are about 30 peony species in all, the tree peonies coming from lightly wooded country or more open terrain in western China and bordering areas of Tibet. The current interest in the tree peonies may make them seem a novelty, but they have long been cultivated in China and Japan. See also PERENNIALS.

CULTIVATION Require full sun or partial shade plus organic-rich, deep, moist, well-drained soil.
PROPAGATION From seed, sown in autumn or winter. From semiripe cuttings, in mid-summer. By grafting, in winter.
POTENTIAL PROBLEMS Swift moth larvae, eelworms; viruses, honey fungus, peony wilt.
WARNING Swallowing any part of the plant may cause mild stomach upsets.

Paeonia delavayi

P. delavayi *China*
Foliage: late spring to autumn. Flowers: late spring. H:5–6ft (1.5–1.8m), S:4–5ft (1.2–1.5m). Z:4–8.
The nodding flowers are short-lived and rather lost in the foliage, but combine splendidly sober maroon-red petals and yellow stamens. The large leaves are composed of jagged leaflets with a hint of blue on the underside. The Tibetan **var. ludlowii**, with a height and spread of about 8ft (2.5m), is also impressive in its foliage, and its single flowers, as much as 5in (12.5cm) across, are rich yellow.
P. × lemoinei 'Souvenir de Maxime Cornu', one of the best and most fragrant of several good hybrids raised between *P. delavayi* and *P. suffruticosa*, has very double ruffled flowers with orange-yellow petals edged red.

Paeonia delavayi var. ludlowii

P. suffruticosa *China*
Moutan peony
Flowers: late spring to early summer. H:6–7ft (1.8–2.2m), S:5–7ft (1.5–2.2m). Z:4–8.
This species is represented in

Paeonia suffruticosa subsp. rockii

gardens by a range of single to double cultivars, many of which are fragrant. They compensate by their magnificence for the shortness of their flowering season. The leaves, deeply cut and with pointed lobes, set the flowers off well. The following 4 are selected from a court of near equals: **'Hana-daijin'**, a violet-purple double; **'Mrs. William Kelway'**, a white double; **subsp. rockii**, a semidouble white with maroon touches; and **'Yae-zakura'**, a soft pink double.

PHILADELPHUS

HYDRANGEACEAE Mock orange

The best of the mock oranges produce masses of heavily scented pure white or tinted flowers in early to mid-summer. At their peak they are highly seductive, so their dullness out of flower is inevitably disappointing. This shortcoming is not such a disadvantage in a large garden or when the more compact mock oranges are grown, and one compensation is the way these shrubs tolerate a wide range of conditions. There are about 40 species, mainly deciduous, and they are found in Europe, Asia, and North and Central America, usually in scrub or lightly wooded country. The species have been displaced in cultivation by numerous hybrids, but the yellow-leaved form of a fully hardy European species, **P. coronarius** 'Aureus' (Z:5–8), is widely grown as a foliage plant. The yellow burns in full sun, and the shrub is better seen as a lime-green accent, as much as 10ft (3m) tall, in partial shade.
CULTIVATION Require full sun or partial shade and well-drained soil. Cut out about a fifth of the oldest growths down to ground level after flowering. Cut back the flowered shoots to new strong shoots lower down the stems.
PROPAGATION From cuttings, taken in summer. From hardwood cuttings, in autumn or winter.
POTENTIAL PROBLEMS Aphids; powdery mildew.

P. hybrids
Flowers: early to mid-summer.
H and S:4–10ft (1.2–3m). Z:5–8.
Some gardeners will insist on pure
white in the flowers, but good
fragrance and suitable size are
more to the point. The following
small selection includes compact
and large hybrids: **'Beauclerk'**,
single, very fragrant white flowers
with a mauve stain on an arching
shrub up to 8ft (2.5m) tall; **'Belle
Etoile'**, single, strongly scented
creamy flowers with a purplish
center on a bushy plant up to 8ft
(2.5m) tall; **'Dame Blanche'**,
semidouble, scented, pure white
flowers on an arching shrub up to
6ft (1.8m) tall; **'Manteau
d'Hermine'**, double, very fragrant,
milk-white flowers on a spreading
bush only 30in (75cm) tall;
'Sybille', strongly scented pure
white single flowers with purple
centers on a broad shrub about
4ft (1.2m) tall; and **'Virginal'**,
double pure white flowers with
rich scent on a shrub that at 10ft
(3m) can be gawky.

Philadelphus 'Dame Blanche'

PHOTINIA

ROSACEAE

The photinias, an Asiatic genus
found in the Himalayas and farther
east, are shrubs and trees of
woodland and scrub. There are
about 60 species, mainly evergreen,
some of which have bright-colored
young leaves in spring. For those
with alkaline soils, they are a
substitute for the colorful forms of
Pieris that are intolerant of lime.
CULTIVATION Require full sun or
partial shade and fertile, moist,
well-drained soil.
PROPAGATION From seed, sown in
autumn. From semiripe cuttings, in
mid-summer.
POTENTIAL PROBLEMS Fire blight,
leaf spot, powdery mildew.

P. davidiana *China, Vietnam*
Foliage: late summer to autumn.
Flowers: mid-summer. Fruits:
autumn. H:12–20ft (3.7–6m),
S:10–18ft (3–5.5m). Z:7–9.
The main ornament of this large

evergreen shrub or small tree is the
crop of matt red berries, hanging in
loose bunches. The hawthornlike
flowers that precede them have an
unpleasant smell. Odd leaves can
turn scarlet with age. **'Palette'** is
slow growing, and its leaves are
streaked with cream and pink.

Photinia × *fraseri* **'Red Robin'**

P. × fraseri
Red tips
Foliage: late spring to early summer.
Flowers: mid- to late spring.
H:12–15ft (3.7–4.5m), S:10–15ft
(3–4.5m). Z:8–9.
The small white flowers are of little
importance, but the intense
copper red of the young leaves
makes this evergreen shrub or small
tree an arresting plant in spring.
The young foliage of **'Red Robin'** is
exceptionally vivid in color.

PIERIS

ERICACEAE

The connection with the heath
family shows not only in botanical
characteristics but also in a dislike
of lime. There are 7 species, all
evergreen. The sprays of small
pitcher-shaped flowers are borne
in great profusion, but even in
winter, long before they open, the
buds look attractive against the
glossy leaves. More dramatic on
some *Pieris* is the young foliage
that is lustrous red.
CULTIVATION Require full sun or
partial shade and organic-rich,
moist, acid, well-drained soil.
PROPAGATION From seed, sown in
spring or autumn. From cuttings,
in summer.
POTENTIAL PROBLEMS Leaf spot,
phytophthora root rot.
WARNING Swallowing leaves can
cause severe stomach upsets.

P. formosa *China, Himalayas*
Foliage: late spring to early
summer. Flowers: mid to late
spring. H:6–15ft (1.8–5m),
S:10–12ft (3–3.7m). Z:7–8.
Where the climate is mild enough,
this makes a large dark green bush
loaded with drooping sprays of
waxy flowers. The young foliage is

usually tinted copper but in **var.
forrestii 'Wakehurst'** is spectacular
scarlet. **P. japonica** (Z:6–8), a more
compact species than *P. formosa*
and equally good in foliage and
flower, is probably a parent with it
of several hybrids, including
P. 'Forest Flame' (Z:6–8). This
bears masses of fragrant flowers,
and the young leaves in spring are
bright before changing color
through pink and cream to green.

Pieris formosa **var. forrestii**
'Wakehurst'

PITTOSPORUM

PITTOSPORACEAE

Good foliage and scented flowers
distinguish several of the evergreen
shrubs and small trees in this large
genus of about 200 species. A high
proportion of those in cultivation
are Australasian, but plants are also
found in regions as far apart as
Japan and South Africa.
CULTIVATION Require full sun and
well-drained, moist, fertile soil or
potting media.
PROPAGATION From seed, sown as
soon as ripe or in spring. From
semiripe cuttings, in mid-summer.
By layering or air-layering, in
spring.
POTENTIAL PROBLEMS Under glass:
red spider mites. Leaf spot,
powdery mildew.

Pittosporum tenuifolium **'Irene
Patterson'**

P. tenuifolium *New Zealand*
Kohuhu
Foliage: year-round. Flowers: late
spring to early summer. H:12–30ft
(3.7–9m), S:6–15ft 91.8–4.5m).
Z:9–10.

Light-green leaves with wavy margins contrast with very dark stems and as a consequence the shrub, sometimes a small tree, is savaged by flower arrangers. The small fragrant flowers are maroon. In a mild climate, it is an attractive shelter or hedge plant. There are forms with purple and variegated leaves; those of **'Irene Patterson'** are almost white but speckled and mottled with gray and green.

P. tobira *China, Japan, Korea*
Japanese mock orange
Foliage: year-round. Flowers: late spring to early summer. H:6–33ft (1.8–10m), S:5–10ft (1.5–3m). Z:8–10.
In warm air a luxurious scent spreads from the clusters of small creamy flowers, which are surrounded by dark green leaves. The capsules split to show orange seeds. This slow-growing species can be used for hedging, but, at the margins of its hardiness, needs the protection of a warm wall. The leaves of **'Variegatum'** have an irregular creamy white margin.

POTENTILLA

Rosaceae Cinquefoil

Small 5-petaled flowers, like miniature single roses, liberally decorate the shrubby potentillas over a long season. They, like the perennials, annuals, and biennials in this large genus of about 500 species, are found in a range of habitats throughout the Northern Hemisphere. The most important species for gardeners, *P. fruticosa*, has an astonishing distribution in the wild, so its adaptability in the garden is not surprising. See also PERENNIALS.
Cultivation Require full sun and well-drained soil. Cut off the tips of the flowered shoots after they have flowered.
Propagation From seed, sown in autumn or spring. From cuttings, in early summer.
Potential problems Usually none.

P. fruticosa *Europe, N. Asia, North America*
Flowers: late spring to mid-autumn. H:3–4ft (90–150cm), S:4–5ft (1.2–1.5m). Z:3–7.
This deciduous species is represented in yards by numerous cultivars with flower colors that include white and shades of yellow, pink, red, and orange. Bushes are usually compact, with dark green to gray-green leaves, but there is variation in scale, as can be seen in the following selection: **'Abbotswood'**, up to 4ft (1.2m) tall,

has dark gray-green leaves and white flowers; **'Manchu'**, a spreading plant but only about 1ft (30cm) tall, has white flowers over gray-green foliage; **'Primrose Beauty'**, about 3ft (90cm) tall, has soft yellow flowers over gray-green foliage; **'Red Ace'**, up to 30in (75cm) tall, has vermilion flowers, the petals having a yellow reverse; and **'Vilmoriniana'**, a tall plant up to 4ft (1.2m) tall, has creamy flowers and silvery foliage.

Potentilla fruticosa **'Abbotswood'**

PRUNUS

Rosaceae Ornamental cherry

The genus contains over 200 species, and there are numerous hybrids of the flowering cherries. Most of the fruit-bearing and flowering cherries are treelike, but the Fuji cherry (**P. incisa**, Z:6–8) is one of several lovely deciduous shrubs that are laden with blossoms on bare stems in winter or spring. **'Kojo-no-mai'** is a gnarled form, ancient in appearance even in youth, which has pale pink flowers and slowly reaches 6ft (1.8m). The main interest of the evergreen shrubs described here is their foliage, but their flowers and fruit are far from insignificant. See also TREES.
Cultivation Require full sun (deciduous) or full sun or partial shade (evergreens) and moist well-drained soil.
Propagation From seed, sown in autumn. From cuttings, in summer. By budding cultivars, in summer or grafting, in early spring.
Potential problems Bullfinches, aphids, caterpillars; silverleaf, honey fungus, blossom wilt.
Warning The leaves and fruits of some plants may cause severe discomfort if swallowed.

P. laurocerasus *E. Europe, S.W. Asia*
English laurel, cherry laurel
Foliage: year-round. Flowers: mid- to late spring. H:15–25ft (4.5–7.5m), S:20–30ft (6–9m). Z:7–9.
The cherry laurel is so widely planted and naturalized that it is

Prunus laurocerasus

hard to appreciate the splendid glossiness of its dark-green leaves and to give it full credit as an evergreen shelter and hedging plant. The sprays of white flowers are followed by small "cherries," which turn from red to black. Regrettably, the scent of the flowers is tainted. It is worth seeking out a distinctive clone, such as the compact **'Otto Luyken'**, which grows to about 3ft (90cm).

P. lusitanica *S.W. Europe*
Portugal laurel
Foliage: year-round. Flowers: early summer. H and S:15–40ft (4.5–12m). Z:7–9.
As a dense shrub or small tree, this is a very satisfying evergreen, its dark glossy foliage given class by the red leafstalks. Slender sprays of scented white flowers are followed by red fruits that blacken as they start to ripen.

PYRACANTHA

Rosaceae Firethorn

The firethorns come into their own in autumn and winter, for it is then that these more or less spiny evergreen shrubs are laden with prodigious quantities of colorful berries. There is a corresponding mass of hawthornlike white flowers in early summer, but they rely for effect on quantity rather than refinement. There are 7 species, some such as the fully hardy and red-berried *P. coccinea* (Z:6–9), from southern Europe and southwestern Asia. Others are from the Himalayas and farther east, one of the finest, *P. rogersiana* (Z:6–9), coming from China. This species has fragrant flowers and orange-red or, in the case of **'Flava'**, yellow berries. The species have been overtaken in popularity by the hybrids, which show resistance to fire blight and scab, to which some of these shrubs are particularly prone. All can be wall-trained or grown as hedges.
Cultivation Require full sun or partial shade and fertile, well-drained soil.

PROPAGATION From seed, sown in autumn. From semiripe cuttings, in mid-summer.
POTENTIAL PROBLEMS Aphids, caterpillars, scale, leaf miners; fire blight, scab, coral spot.
WARNING Mild stomach upsets may be caused by swallowing the seeds.

P. hybrids

Flowers: early summer. Fruits: late summer to early spring. H:8–15ft (2.5–4.5m), S:10–15ft (3–4.5m). Z:6–9.
Despite various species being involved in the crosses, the family resemblance among these hybrids is strong. The following 4 are fully hardy and among the best: **'Golden Charmer'**, up to 10ft (3m), has orange-red berries; **'Orange Glow'**, up to 10ft (3m), has long-lasting orange or orange-red berries; **'Soleil d'Or'**, up to 10ft (3m), has rich yellow berries; and **'Teton'**, up to 15ft (4.5m), has yellow-orange berries and resistance to fire blight.

Pyracantha 'Golden Charmer'

RHAMNUS

RHAMNACEAE Buckthorn

Although the genus contains over 100 species, relatively few of these evergreen and deciduous shrubs or trees find a place in gardens. *R. alaternus*, widely found in the wild, is an adaptable plant that is usually found with sun-loving shrubs in dry stony terrain.
CULTIVATION Require full sun and well-drained soil. Prune out reverted shoots on *R. alaternus* 'Argenteovariegata' as they appear.
PROPAGATION From seed, sown as soon as ripe. From semiripe cuttings of evergreen species, in summer. From greenwood cuttings of deciduous species, in autumn.
POTENTIAL PROBLEMS Usually none.

R. alaternus 'Argenteovariegata'

Foliage: year-round. Flowers: late spring to early summer. H:10–15ft (3–4.5m), S:8–12ft (2.5–3.7m). Z:8–9.
The plain-leaved plant is a fast-growing evergreen with glossy green foliage. Small yellow-green flowers are followed by red berries, which ripen to black. It is, however, variegation that transforms this shrub into a distinguished plant. The gray-green leaves of 'Argenteovariegata' are irregularly outlined in a creamy white color.

Rhamnus alaternus 'Argenteovariegata'

RHODODENDRON

ERICACEAE

Even those who disparage rhododendrons and azaleas for the color crudities and funereal dullness of the foliage, which are sometimes the lasting impression of massed plantings, must acknowledge the extraordinary importance of this genus. Well over 500 species are found in various parts of the world, although not in the African continent. A high proportion of those used most extensively in horticulture come from the Himalayas and farther east in Asia.
The species vary vastly in scale from tiny shrublets to small or medium-sized trees, and they are found in a very wide range of habitats where the soil is neutral to acidic. Hybridizing, once almost exclusively a pastime of dignified rivalry between aristocrats but increasingly plebeian, has resulted in countless crosses. Some of these are large and only suitable for woodland gardens, but many are small enough and sufficiently shade tolerant to find a place in tiny urban gardens or rock gardens. A particularly useful compact group is derived from *R. yakushimanum*. A very large number of species, as well as the hybrids, carry flowers of remarkable beauty. Many are bell- or funnel-shaped, but there is considerable variation from tubular to an open saucer shape. The leaves of many rhododendrons also have ornamental value. In some species they are of impressive size, and in many the underside has a feltlike hairiness, the nap being referred to as the indumentum. Most rhododendrons are evergreen, but among the azaleas, a group that is popular for producing abundant displays of small flowers on small to medium-sized shrubs, some are deciduous. In the following selection of shrubs, which provides only a small glimpse of the genus, the plants usually distinguished as rhododendrons and azaleas are listed separately and in both cases the species that are described precede all the hybrids.
CULTIVATION Require dappled shade (in a sheltered woodland area for larger species) and well-drained, moist, acid soil (ericaceous media). Deadhead immediately after flowering.
PROPAGATION From seed, sown as soon as ripe or in spring on ericaceous media. From semiripe cuttings, in mid-summer. By layering, in autumn. By grafting, in late winter or late summer.
POTENTIAL PROBLEMS Vine weevils, lacebugs, scale, caterpillars, aphids, leafhoppers, rhododendron and azalea whiteflies; bud blast, honey fungus, leafy gall, powdery mildew, petal blight, rust, silverleaf, phytophthora root rot.
WARNING Severe stomach upsets may occur if the nectar of some rhododendron flowers is swallowed by mistake.

Rhododendron yakushimanum

RHODODENDRON SPECIES

R. augustinii *China*

Flowers: mid to late spring. H:6–10ft (1.8–3m), S:6–8ft (1.8–2.5m). Z:6–7.
At its best this is a startling evergreen shrub when it bears clusters of violet-blue flowers among its dark leaves. The throat is spotted olive green. Forms that have mauve flowers are definitely inferior.

R. falconeri *E. Himalayas*

Foliage: year-round. Flowers: mid- to late spring. H:25–40ft (7.5–12m), S:10–20ft (3–6m). Z:8–9.
Whether growing as a large shrub or as a small tree, this is

magnificent for its foliage as well as for its flowers. Thick-textured bells, creamy or yellow, usually with purple marks on the inside, stand in bold trusses above large, paddle-shaped leaves that are deeply veined and felted brown on the underside.

R. moupinense W. China
Flowers: late winter to early spring. H and S:3–4ft (90–120cm). Z:7–8.
As a parent of many fine hybrids, this is an important species, but it is also a fine dwarf evergreen shrub in its own right, provided it can be sheltered from early frosts. The rounded shiny leaves, paler and scaly on the reverse, are a quiet background for funnel-shaped pale to dark-pink funnel-shaped flowers, spotted with purple, that are usually borne in clusters of 2 or 3.

R. orbiculare W. China
Flowers: mid- to late spring. Foliage: year-round. H:8–10ft (2.5–3m), S:8–10ft (2.5–3m). Z:7–8.
The domed outline of this evergreen shrub and its heart-shaped pale green leaves, blue-green on the underside, are very pleasing. The bell-shaped flowers, borne in clusters of 7 to 10, are deep pink with a bluish tinge.

R. sinogrande Burma, China, Tibet
Foliage: year-round. Flowers: mid- to late spring. H:25–40ft (7.5–12m), S:25–35ft (7.5–10.5m). Z:8–9.
Just for the scale of its leaves, sometimes more than 30in (75cm) long and as much as 1ft (30cm) across, this is an impressive evergreen tree or large shrub. The upper surface is lustrous deep green, the underside downy with a silver or buff indumentum. The flowers are cream or yellow bells, usually stained purple inside, and they are borne in clusters of 20 or 30.

R. williamsianum W. China
Flowers: mid- to late spring. H and S:3–5ft (90–1.5cm). Z:5–7.
The spreading evergreen dome has bronze-tinted young growth, the mature leaves, often kidney shaped, becoming dark green and blue-green on the underside. The bell-shaped flowers borne singly or in small clusters are red in bud, paling to soft pink on opening.

R. yakushimanum Japan
(Yakushima Island)
Foliage: mid-summer. Flowers: late spring to early summer. H and S:6–7ft (1.8–2.2m). Z:4–7.

This parent of many very fine dwarf hybrids makes a compact evergreen dome, the leaves with a thick brown indumentum on the underside and, when young, with a fawn indumentum on the upper surface. Trusses of up to 10 deep-pink buds open to paler pink, later white, funnel-shaped flowers.

RHODODENDRON HYBRIDS

R. 'Anna Baldsiefen'
Foliage: winter. Flowers: early spring. H and S:30–36in (75–90cm). Z:7–8.
The leaves of this dwarf evergreen turn bronze in winter. It has bright pink flowers with wavy darker margins, borne in dense clusters.

Rhododendron 'Anna Baldsiefen'

R. Bow Bells Group
Foliage: late spring to early summer. Flowers: late spring. H and S:6–7ft (1.8–2.2m). Z:6–8.
Long-stalked bell-shaped flowers are borne in loose clusters on this plant. They are deep pink when in bud, and a paler pink on opening fully. The foliage is a copper-tinted color when young. The name applies to a group of plants and also to a clone.

R. Cilpinense Group
Flowers: early spring. H and S:3–4ft (90–120cm). Z:6–8.
This evergreen rounded bush, which is one of the loveliest of the compact hybrids, carries numerous loose trusses of bell-shaped white flowers that are lightly tinged with pink.

R. 'Curlew'
Flowers: mid-spring. H and S:20–24in (50–60cm). Z:6–8.
This dwarf spreading evergreen shrub has small leaves and pale yellow flowers, which feature grayish-brown markings inside. They cluster together in twos or threes.

R. 'Dopey'
Flowers: late spring. H and S:5–6ft (1.5–1.8m). Z:6–8.
The deep red bells carried in

rounded trusses on this plant fade slightly as they age, but they normally last for a long time. This is a free-flowering and compact evergreen shrub.

Rhododendron 'Dopey'

R. 'Fastuosum Flore Pleno'
Flowers: late spring to early summer. H and S:10–12ft (3–3.7m). Z:5–7.
This "iron-clad" rhododendron is of exceptional hardiness. It bears semidouble flowers that are mauve blue in color.

R. 'Hydon Dawn'
Flowers: mid-spring to early summer. H and S:5–6ft (1.5–1.8m). Z:6–8.
Like one of its parents, *R. yakushimanum*, the upper surface of the young leaves of this compact shrub is covered by a pale indumentum. It is very easy to grow and bears ruffled pale pink flowers that fade almost to white. They are carried in numerous trusses among the evergreen leaves.

Rhododendron 'Loderi King George'

R. 'Loderi King George'
Flowers: late spring to early summer. H and S:10–12ft (3–3.7m). Z:7–8.
The large evergreen rhododendrons of the Loderi group include several large shrubs or small trees that bear very large trusses of fragrant trumpet-shaped flowers. The pink-tinged buds of '**King George**' open to white flowers with delicate pale green markings. The leaves display yellow veining.

R. 'Mrs. G.W. Leak'

Flowers: mid-spring. H and S:10–12ft (3–3.7m). Z:7–8.
The funnel-shaped flowers, borne in loose trusses on this large dark evergreen shrub, are pink with some deep brown and crimson interior markings.

Rhododendron 'Mrs. G.W. Leak'

R. 'Pink Pearl'

Flowers: mid- to late spring. H and S:10–12ft (3–3.7m). Z:6–8.
Although tending to become lanky, especially if grown in shade, this tall large-leafed evergreen bears funnel-shaped pink flowers in splendid conical trusses. Brown markings give an attractive accent to the center of the flowers.

R. 'Sappho'

Flowers: early summer. H:10–12ft (3–3.7m), S:8–10ft (2.5–3m). Z:5–7.
Although long in cultivation, this stands up well to the competition offered by other large hybrids. The funnel-shaped flowers, which are tightly clustered in dome-shaped trusses, are white with conspicuous purple and black markings in the throats.

AZALEA SPECIES

R. *luteum* E. Europe to Caucasus
Flowers: late spring to early summer. Foliage: autumn. H:8–12ft (2.5–3.7m), S:7–10ft (2.2–3m). Z:6–8.
Funnel-shaped yellow flowers, sticky in bud and borne in trusses of up to 12, are strongly scented. The deciduous foliage often colors richly in autumn.

R. *schlippenbachii* China (N. Manchuria), Korea
Foliage: autumn. Flowers: mid- to late spring. H:8–13ft (2.5–4m), S:8–10ft (2.5–3m). Z:5–7.
This deciduous species is the perfect answer to those who find fault with the brash colors of many azaleas. The flowers, saucer shaped and borne up to 6 in a cluster, are pink or white, spotted with red. The leaves are purple, tinted when young, and color well in autumn.

AZALEA HYBRIDS

R. 'Gibraltar'
Flowers: mid-spring. H and S:4–5ft (1.2–1.5m). Z:4–8.
This deciduous azalea is one of the numerous Knap Hill-Exbury crosses. The flowers, deep colored in bud, are frilly and orange-red with a yellow flash. Another from the same background is 'Klondyke', with vibrant orange-yellow flowers of large size. The young foliage has copper tints.

R. 'Hino-mayo'
Flowers: mid-spring to early summer. H and S:24–30in (60–75cm). Z:7–9.
The evergreen Kurume azaleas, of which this is a particularly fine example, originated in Japan. They flower prolifically and in colors that can sometimes hurt the eye. 'Hinode-giri' is bright crimson. 'Hino-mayo' is clear pink.

Rhododendron 'Narcissiflorum'

R. 'Narcissiflorum'
Flowers: late spring to early summer. H and S:5–8ft (1.5–2.5m). Z:4–8.
This deciduous shrub is a lovely representative of the **Ghent hybrids**, a group producing clusters of fragrant flowers. Those of 'Narcissiflorum' are pale yellow with darker shading on the outside and at the center.

Rhododendron 'Spek's Orange'

R. 'Spek's Orange'
Flowers: late spring to early summer. H and S:6–8ft (1.8–2.5m). Z:6–8.
This bushy deciduous shrub has dense clusters of bright orange-red flowers. It is scentless, like other **Mollis hybrids** but is untypical in flowering so late; most bloom just after mid-spring.

RHUS

ANACARDIACEAE Sumac

Most of the sumacs in cultivation are deciduous and are grown for the brilliant coloring of their foliage in autumn. However, this is a large genus of about 200 species of shrubs, trees, and climbers, some of which are evergreen. Species are found in many parts of the temperate and tropical world. The poison ivy of North America (*R. radicans*, Z:4–9) also belongs to this genus.
CULTIVATION Require full sun and moist well-drained soil. In early spring, coppice prune *R. typhina*.
PROPAGATION From seed, sown in autumn. From semiripe cuttings, in mid-summer. From root cuttings, taken in winter. From removal of suckers, when dormant.
POTENTIAL PROBLEMS Verticillium wilt, coral spot.
WARNING The skin may react allergically on contact with the foliage of some species of *Rhus*.

R. *glabra* North America
Scarlet sumac, smooth sumac
Foliage: early to mid-autumn. Flowers: summer. Fruits: autumn. H and S:6–12ft (1.8–3.7m). Z:3–9.
The smooth leaflets turn dashing shades of red and yellow in autumn when the scarlet and hairy fruit clusters are also conspicuous.

R. *typhina* E. North America
Stag's horn sumac, Velvet sumac
Foliage: autumn. Fruits: autumn to winter. H:10–15ft (3–4.5m), S:12–20ft (3.7–6m). Z:4–9.
This shrub or small tree makes a striking appearance at most times of the year. The large pinnate leaves, with lance-shaped paired leaflets, are impressive throughout summer and magnificent when they turn brilliant yellow, orange, and purplish red in autumn. Male and female flowers are borne on separate plants. On female plants the dense clusters of dark crimson hairy fruits stand out as the leaves fall and remain as dark brown accents throughout winter. The sparsely branched irregular shape of the shrub also shows in winter, but it is only young stems that have a velvet coating of red-brown hairs. 'Dissecta' is a female form with much-divided leaves that are especially vivid in autumn. Another fully hardy ferny-leaved shrub

coloring sensationally in autumn is *R.* × *pulvinata* 'Red Autumn Lace', a female plant with smooth stems.

Rhus typhina

RIBES

GROSSULARIACEAE Flowering currant

In addition to the culinary currants and gooseberries, this genus of about 150 mainly deciduous species contains a number of ornamental flowering shrubs. A few species come from South America, but these are mainly plants of temperate regions of the Northern Hemisphere, many of them growing in woodland or scrub. Their main use is in mixed borders but *R. sanguineum* can make an informal hedge.
CULTIVATION Require full sun and well-drained soil. After flowering, cut about a fifth of the oldest stems down to ground level and reduce the flowered shoots down to lower, strong, new growths.
PROPAGATION From hardwood cuttings, in winter (deciduous). From semiripe cuttings, in mid-summer (evergreens).
POTENTIAL PROBLEMS Aphids; coral spot, honey fungus, leaf spot, powdery mildew.

R. sanguineum *W. North America*
Flowering currant, winter currant
Flowers: mid-spring. H:6–7ft (1.8–2.2m), S:5–6ft (1.5–1.8m). Z:6–9.
This deciduous shrub has very upright growth and in spring is covered with numerous sprays of bright red flowers, their color often being forced to fight it out with the bright yellows of forsythias and daffodils. At first the flower sprays droop, later they stand more erect. 'Pulborough Scarlet' is a vigorous cultivar with dark red white-centered flowers and 'Tydeman's White' displays pure white flowers. The strong coarse smell of the flowers is one of the shortcomings, but this is not the case with the clove-scented *R. odoratum* (Z:4–9), a fully hardy species from central North America that grows

to a height and spread of about 6ft (1.8m). In mid- to late spring it carries small sprays of bright yellow flowers.

R. speciosum *USA (California)*
Fuchsia-flowered currant
Flowers: mid- to late spring. H:6–8ft (1.8–2.5m), S:4–6ft (1.2–1.8m). Z:7–9.
Slender, bright red flowers dangling in clusters of 3 or 4 give this plant a fuchsialike grace. It is semi-evergreen and upright, the lobed leaves dark green and glossy and the stems thickly covered with reddish bristles. It is worth a place on a warm wall.

Ribes speciosum

ROSMARINUS

LAMIACEAE Rosemary

Common rosemary is one of the happiest transfers from the physic to the ornamental garden. In a genus of 2 species, it is the one that is known and loved for its evergreen aromatic foliage and usually pale blue flowers. In its Mediterranean homeland, it is usually found growing with other sun-loving shrubs in stony dry ground. They are ideal scented plants to grow in a herb garden, as part of a shrub or mixed bed, or up against a sun-drenched wall.
CULTIVATION Require full sun and well-drained soil. Cut back any straggly stems to strong, lower, new growths in spring.
PROPAGATION From seed, sown in the spring. From semiripe cuttings, in the summer.
POTENTIAL PROBLEMS Honey fungus.

R. officinalis
Rosemary
Foliage: year-round. Flowers: mid-spring to early summer (often again in autumn and mild winters). H:5–6ft (1.5–1.8m), S:5ft (1.5m). Z:6–10.
Stems densely clothed with gray-green needlelike leaves, gray-white on the underside, are upright, but the shrub is of irregular shape and often sprawls. When the usual color form produces its small

flowers, the effect is of a gray-blue shrub. 'Severn Sea' is one of several rosemaries with bright blue flowers. 'Miss Jessopp's Upright' is very erect, at least when young, a contrast to the **Prostratus Group**, regrettably the first to succumb in cold weather, with trailing stems.

Rosmarinus officinalis

RUBUS

ROSACEAE

The best-known plants in this large genus of about 250 species are the blackberries and raspberries grown for their edible fruits. There are, however, several species that are ornamental on account of their flowers, fruits, or stems. They are often plants of woodland, but species are found in a very wide range of habitats almost worldwide.
CULTIVATION Require sun or partial shade (species grown for winter stem color require full sun) and well-drained fertile soil. Cut stems of *R. cockburnianus* in early spring down to near ground level. Prune *R.* 'Benenden' after flowering, cutting about a fifth of old stems down to ground level and reducing the flowered shoots down to strong new growths.
PROPAGATION From greenwood cuttings, in summer (deciduous). From semiripe cuttings, in summer (evergreens).
POTENTIAL PROBLEMS Gray mold (*Botrytis*).

R. 'Benenden'
Flowers: late spring to early summer. H:7–10ft (2.2–3m), S:8–10ft (2.5–3m). Z:5–8.
The large, saucer-shaped white flowers, with a boss of bright yellow stamens, are radiant. They are borne in profusion, but are beautifully spaced on arching thornless stems. Crowding can spoil the superb effect of this very large deciduous shrub.

R. cockburnianus *China*
Flowers: early summer. H:7-9ft
(2.2-2.7m), S:6-8ft (1.8-2.5m).
Z:6-9.
The small purplish flowers do not
count for much, but in winter this
arching deciduous species has a
ghostly charm, its purplish ground
color being overlaid by an unusual
white bloom.

Rubus cockburnianus

RUTA

RUTACEAE Rue

The best-known species in this
small genus of 8 aromatic shrubs
and subshrubs has long been
cultivated for its supposed
medicinal properties. In the wild it
is found in sunny stony places.
CULTIVATION Require full sun or
partial shade and well-drained soil.
Cut back old stems to fresh growth.
PROPAGATION From seed, sown in
spring. From semiripe cuttings, in
mid-summer.
POTENTIAL PROBLEMS Phytophthora
root rot.
WARNING Swallowing will cause
severe stomach discomfort;
photodermatitis occurs with
foliage contact.

Ruta graveolens 'Jackman's Blue'

R. graveolens *S.E. Europe*
Common rue
Flowers: mid- to late summer.
Foliage: evergreen. H:2-3ft (60-
90cm), S:24-30in (60-75cm).
Z:5-9.
The pungently aromatic blue-green
leaves make a low bush bearing
greenish-yellow flowers. The form
usually seen in yards is **'Jackman's
Blue'**, with dense, glaucous foliage.

SALIX

SALICACEAE Willow

Many of the tree willows are fast
growing and far too large for
modern gardens, but this important
genus, with about 300 species,
contains a number of compact,
even dwarf shrubs. The genus is
represented in many parts of the
world, but the deciduous shrubs
that are grown for their ornamental
value are essentially from the more
temperate regions of the Northern
Hemisphere. In the wild, however,
they are found in a surprising range
of habitats. The willows produce
male and female catkins, the male
catkins usually being the more
ornamental. See also TREES.
CULTIVATION Require full sun and
moist well-drained soil. Alpine and
dwarf species require very well-
drained gritty soil. Cut stems of
Salix grown for winter stems down
to about 6in (15cm) above ground
level in early spring annually or
according to the desired dimensions
of the shrub.
PROPAGATION From hardwood
cuttings, in winter. From cuttings,
in early summer.
POTENTIAL PROBLEMS Aphids,
sawflies, caterpillars, leaf beetles;
rust, anthracnose, honey fungus.

S. 'Boydii'
Foliage: late spring to autumn.
Flowers: early spring. H:1-2ft (30-
60cm), S:8-12in (20-30cm). Z:4-9.
Only a few dull catkins are
produced, but the gnarled slow
growth and small gray-green leaves
that are deeply veined make this a
useful little shrub to combine with
alpines. It is a female clone.

S. caprea *Europe, W. Asia*
Goat willow
Flowers: early spring. H:25-30ft
(7.5-9m), S:20-25ft (6-7.5m). Z:4-8.
The goat willow is usually a large
shrub or small tree, the female with
silver catkins ("pussy willow"), the
male with large yellow catkins. The
weeping male form **'Kilmarnock'**
is grafted to make a miniature tree
about 6ft (1.8m) tall.

Salix hastata 'Wehrhahnii'

S. hastata 'Wehrhahnii'
Flowers: early spring. H and S:3-4ft
(90-120cm). Z:4-8.
The species is represented in
gardens by a slow-growing shrub,
which is decked in spring with
upright silver catkins that later turn
yellow. This is a male clone.

S. irrorata *S.W. USA*
Flowers: early spring. H:8-10ft
(2.5-3m), S:8-12ft (2.5-3.7m).
Z:5-8.
The catkins appear before the
green leaves, the male having red
anthers that turn yellow. The
shrub, though, is most interesting
in winter, when the purplish stems
are covered with a white bloom.

S. lanata *N. Europe*
Wooly willow
Foliage: late spring to autumn.
Flowers: late spring. H:2-4ft (60-
120cm), S:2-5ft (60-150cm). Z:3-5.
In a rock garden the slow growth
rate of this willow is an advantage.
It gets its common name from its
felted gray-white leaves. The male
catkins are yellow, the longer
female catkins gray-yellow.

SALVIA

LAMIACEAE Sage

It is difficult to draw a sharp line
between the shrubs and subshrubs
in this very large genus of about
900 species, including annuals,
biennials, and perennials. Several of
the Mediterranean species,
aromatic plants of sunny dry
habitats, do well in open positions
where there is good free drainage.
See also PERENNIALS.
CULTIVATION Require full sun and
organic-rich, moist, light, well-
drained soil. Protect frost-hardy
species from too much winter rain.
Cut straggly shoots back to lower
new growth in spring.
PROPAGATION From seed, annuals at
61-64°F (16-18°C) in mid-spring;
biennials in summer; perennials in
spring.
POTENTIAL PROBLEMS Slugs, snails.

S. officinalis *N. Africa,
Mediterranean*
Common sage
Flowers: early to mid-summer.
H:24-30in (60-75cm), S:2-3ft
(60-90cm). Z:5-9.
Its value as a culinary herb ensures
a place for this in the yard, but its
gray-green aromatic leaves are also
ornamental. The color variations in
the foliage can be used for contrast.
The variegated **'Icterina'** has
yellow and green leaves. In purple
sage (**Purpurascens Group**), the
purple color is particularly

pronounced in young foliage. The leaves of the frost-hardy and less vigorous '**Tricolor**' are gray-green with an irregular cream margin and are tinged with purplish pink. The frost- to fully hardy *S. lavandulifolia*, which grows to a height of about 20in (50cm), has narrow lavender-scented leaves and bears generous sprays of violet-blue flowers.

Salvia officinalis Purpurascens Group

SAMBUCUS

CAPRIFOLIACEAE Elder

The common elder (*S. nigra*, Z:5–7) is such a weed that most gardeners would not be happy on being advised to plant it. Some of its forms are, however, really handsome. '**Guincho Purple**' (Z:5–7) is exceptional when the dark purple leaves, which turn red in autumn, provide a background for heads of dark pink buds and pale pink flowers. The American elder (*S. canadensis*, Z:4–9) also has striking forms, the yellow-leaved '**Aurea**' having red berries. These fully hardy plants, like many other shrubs and trees in this genus of about 25 species, are admittedly coarse, but will tolerate a wide range of conditions.
CULTIVATION Require full sun or partial shade and organic-rich, moist, well-drained soil. Colored leaved kinds require dappled shade and should be cut down to within 1ft (30cm) of ground level in early spring.
PROPAGATION From seed, sown in autumn. From cuttings, in summer. From hardwood cuttings, in winter.
POTENTIAL PROBLEMS Blackflies; verticillium wilt.
WARNING Severe discomfort can occur if swallowed. Skin problems can occur from foliage contact.

S. racemosa Europe, Russia (W. Siberia)
Red-berried elder
Flowers: mid-spring. Fruits: mid to late summer. H and S:8–10ft (2.5–3m). Z:4–8.
In the plain green plant, the

Sambucus racemosa 'Sutherland Gold'

pinnate leaves, divided into 5 to 7 leaflets, are a relatively subdued feature, the creamy flowers and especially the scarlet berries being more conspicuous. The picture changes when the leaflets are deeply cut and are bright yellow, as they are in '**Sutherland Gold**'. '**Tenuifolia**' makes a ferny green mound only about 3ft (90cm) tall.

SANTOLINA

ASTERACEAE

The santolinas are aromatic evergreen shrubs of dry stony habitats in the Mediterranean. There are about 18 species in all, many of which have tightly packed gray leaves. These species tolerate heat and drought to a remarkable degree, and even the green-leaved santolinas, such as the frost-hardy *S. rosmarinifolia*, do well in dry conditions. The foliage is topped in summer by buttonlike flowerheads.
CULTIVATION Require full sun and well-drained soil. Clip off spent flower stems in early spring. Older plants can be renovated by hard pruning.
PROPAGATION From seed, sown in autumn or spring. From cuttings, in summer.
POTENTIAL PROBLEMS: Usually none.

Santolina chamaecyparissus

S. chamaecyparissus C. and W. Mediterranean
Cotton lavender
Foliage: year-round. Flowers: mid- to late summer. H and S:18–24in (45–60cm). Z:6–9.
The stems are gray-white and

felted, and the the leaves are silvery and finely dissected. Plants lose their distinctive tight shape when they produce their yellow button flowerheads.

S. pinnata subsp. *neapolitana*
Foliage: evergreen. Flowers: mid-summer. H:24–30in (60–75cm), S:2–3ft (60–90cm). Z:7–9.
The foliage is very feathery and silvery white in very dry conditions and the flowerheads are lemon yellow in color.

SARCOCOCCA

BUXACEAE Christmas box, sweet box

These small bushy evergreens appear modest in every way, but in winter their refined character reveals itself in the sweet scent wafting from the numerous little tassellike flowers covering the plant. They are also grown for their leaves and fruits, which are similar to berries. The dozen or so species, which are mainly distributed from the Himalayas eastward, are usually plants of rich moist woodland. In gardens they will tolerate a wide range of conditions and make no distinctions between acid and alkaline soils.
CULTIVATION Require partial or deep shade and moist well-drained soil.
PROPAGATION From seed, sown in autumn or spring. From semiripe cuttings, taken in mid-summer. By sucker removal, in late winter.
POTENTIAL PROBLEMS Usually none.

Sarcococca hookeriana var. digyna

S. hookeriana var. *digyna*
W. China
Flowers: late winter. H and S:3–4ft (90–120cm). Z:7–9.
The erect bush is filled with narrow glossy leaves, which almost hide the small creamy flowers. There are sometimes a few dark berries to follow. In '**Purple Stem**' the young stems and even the leaf-stalks have a purplish color.
S. confusa, also fully hardy, is a slightly taller plant and carries heavy crops of purplish-black berries into summer.

SKIMMIA

RUTACEAE

It is the gardener's good fortune that birds seem to dislike the brilliant red berries produced by female plants of the best-known species of this small evergreen genus, *S. japonica*. In the wild the plants exist in woodland in the Himalayas and eastern Asia. Its shade tolerance, neat growth and long-lasting berries have made it a favorite of town gardeners.
CULTIVATION Require partial or full shade and organic-rich, moist, well-drained soil.
PROPAGATION From seed, sown in autumn. From semiripe cuttings, in mid-summer.
POTENTIAL PROBLEMS Scale.
WARNING Swallowing fruits can cause mild stomach upsets.

Skimmia japonica

S. japonica China, Japan, S.E. Asia
Flowers: mid- to late spring. Fruits: late summer to autumn. H:20–48in (50–120cm), S:20in (50cm). Z:7–9.
The species is variable, but is usually a compact dome-shaped bush dense with oval leathery leaves, sometimes tinted on the reverse. The male plant 'Rubella', which grows to about 4ft (1.2m), has red stalks and a thin red rim to its dark green leaves. The tint is picked up in the numerous clusters of red-brown buds that stand through winter before opening in spring to sweetly scented white flowers. 'Nymans' is a free-fruiting dwarf female clone that grows to about 3ft (90cm). The fragrant hermaphrodite flowers of **subsp. reevesiana** 'Robert Fortune', which forms a low mound up to 3ft (90cm) tall, do not need male flowers to produce colorful berries. 'Veitchii', also female, is more vigorous. It needs a male plant nearby in order to produce berries.

SPARTIUM

PAPILIONACEAE Spanish broom

The single species of this genus brightens dry hillsides, open woodland, and waste ground throughout the Mediterranean region. In the garden it is useful for dry sunny banks and as a fast-growing filler in new plantings.
CULTIVATION Requires full sun and well-drained soil. Coppice poor specimens in early spring to give them a new lease on life.
PROPAGATION From seed, sown in autumn or spring.
POTENTIAL PROBLEMS Usually none.

Spartium junceum

S. junceum N. Africa, S. Europe, Syria, Turkey, Ukraine (Crimea)
Flowers: early summer to early autumn. H:8–10ft (2.5–3m), S:7–10ft (2.2–3m). Z:7–9.
This shrub is deciduous, but the green of its upright stems lasts throughout the year. The pea flowers, rich yellow and fragrant, are borne very freely. The seed-pods that follow are brownish black in color.

SPIRAEA

ROSACEAE

The best of the spiraeas are graceful deciduous or semi-evergreen shrubs with good foliage, but it is for their flowers that most are grown. There are about 80 species found throughout temperate regions of the Northern Hemisphere and as far south as Mexico. Many are plants of moist woodland or woodland margins, but several species are found in more open habitats. As garden plants they can be roughly divided into 2 main groups according to their season of flowering. Those that flower in spring do so on growths that are made in the previous year. Those that flower in summer bloom on the current season's shoots.
CULTIVATION Require full sun and moist, fertile, well-drained soil. Cut down the flowered stems of plants that flowered on the previous year's stems to strong lower growths or buds. Cut down the stems of plants that flowered on the current season's shoots to within a few inches of ground level after flowering.

PROPAGATION From cuttings, in summer. By dividing suckering species, in late autumn.
POTENTIAL PROBLEMS Usually none.

S. 'Arguta'
Foam of May, bridal wreath
Flowers: mid- to late spring. H and S: 6–8ft (1.8–2.5m). Z:4–9.
Wiry arching stems are crowded with small white flowers, a reliable display being maintained provided the twiggy growths are cut back annually after flowering.

Spiraea 'Arguta'

S. japonica China, Japan
Flowers: mid- to late summer. H:4–6ft (1.2–1.8m), S:4–5ft (1.2–1.5m). Z:3–9.
There are numerous cultivars of this variable summer-flowering species, usually with small pink flowers borne in flattish heads. **'Anthony Waterer'**, which grows to about 5ft (1.5m), has dark pink flowers, and there are random shoots with cream or bronze-red leaves. The popularity of **'Goldflame'** (Z:4–9) is a puzzle; the mound of bronzed orange foliage, about 30in (75cm) tall, clashes with the pink flowers. **'Shirobana'** (Z:4–9), only about 2ft (60cm) tall, has a bicolored effect, with white and pink flowers in the same head.

Spiraea japonica 'Goldflame'

S. × vanhouttei
Flowers: early summer. H:6–7ft (1.8–2.2m), S:4–5ft (1.2–1.5m). Z:4–9.
This earns a place in early summer with its snowy mass of tiny white flowers that are borne in dense clusters on every twig of the shrub.

STACHYURUS

STACHYURACEAE

The best-known species of *Stachyurus* are grown for their flowers in late winter or early spring. The individual flowers are small, but the short, catkinlike racemes are pretty hanging stiffly from bare stems and are conspicuous from late autumn, when the flowers are still in bud. The half dozen species of deciduous and semievergreen shrubs and small trees in the genus are mainly woodland plants that originate from the Himalayas and from eastern Asia.

CULTIVATION Require full sun or partial shade and well-drained, moist, organic-rich soil. Cut about a fifth of the oldest stems down to ground level annually.

PROPAGATION From seed, sown in autumn. From semiripe heel cuttings, taken in mid-summer.

POTENTIAL PROBLEMS Usually none.

Stachyurus praecox

S. praecox *Japan*
Flowers: late winter to early spring. H:6–12ft (1.8–3.7m), S:6–10ft (1.8–3m). Z:7–8.
Small pale yellow bells are closely set in short racemes about 4in (10cm) long and contrast well with purplish-brown bare twigs. Another fully hardy species, **S. chinensis**, has slightly longer racemes, and the flowers open slightly later. **'Magpie'** is a variegated form that has oval, finely tapered leaves that are gray-green with a broad, creamy margin that often shows pink tints.

STEPHANANDRA

ROSACEAE

The flowers are pleasing enough, but it is for their general character as graceful shrubs that stephanandras are grown. The 4 species, all from eastern Asia, are plants of woodland margins or shrubby thickets with moist conditions.

CULTIVATION Require full sun or partial shade and well-drained, moist, fertile soil. Cut the flowered stems down to strong lower growths or buds after flowering.

PROPAGATION From cuttings, in summer. By rooted sucker separation, in autumn. From hardwood cuttings, in late autumn.

POTENTIAL PROBLEMS Usually none.

Stephanandra tanakae

S. tanakae *Japan*
Foliage: autumn. Flowers: early to mid-summer. H:5–8ft (1.5–2.5m), S:6–8ft (1.8–2.5m). Z:6–7.
This suckering shrub forms a thicket of arching stems that are bright greenish or orange-brown in color. The broad leaves, sharply toothed and tapering to a point, turn rich shades of yellow and orange in autumn. Airy clusters of yellow-green flowers are a diversion in summer. **S. incisa** **'Crispa'** (Z:4–7), also fully hardy, makes a low dense thicket of arching stems to a height of about 2ft (60cm) with a good showing of greenish-white flowers and splendid foliage colors in autumn.

SYMPHORICARPOS

CAPRIFOLIACEAE Snowberry

The best-known species and hybrids are valued for their white berries, which are shunned by birds and therefore long lasting. However, the berry color varies among the 15 or so species, all deciduous and found in a range of woodland and more open habitats, mainly in North and Central America. The coral berry or Indian currant (**S. orbiculatus**, Z:3–7), best known in its variegated forms, has purplish-red fruits. Their tolerance of shade and adaptability to a number of soils make the snowberries useful, but to produce heavy crops of berries they need sun and good growing conditions.

CULTIVATION Require full sun or partial shade in well-drained soil. Cut straggly stems down to ground level in early spring.

PROPAGATION From cuttings, in summer. From hardwood cuttings, in autumn. By division of suckering specimens, in autumn.

POTENTIAL PROBLEMS Usually none.

WARNING Swallowing fruits can result in mild stomach upsets. Skin irritations can occur through contact with the fruits.

S. × doorenbosii
Flowers: mid- to late summer. Fruits: early autumn to mid-winter. H:6–7ft (1.8–2.2m), S:6–20ft (1.8–6m). Z:5–8.
Several of the best snowberries go under this name. **'Mother of Pearl'** is a bushy dense shrub with heavy crops of white berries that are flushed pink. **'White Hedge'**, usually no more than 5ft (1.5m) tall, is compact and erect with marblelike white berries. In the background of these hybrids is another hybrid, **S × chenaultii** (Z:5–7), often grown in its own right, especially in the dwarf form **'Hancock'**. This makes good groundcover at about 3ft (90cm) tall but produces rather thin crops of pink berries.

Symphoricarpos × doorenbosii 'White Hedge'

SYRINGA

OLEACEAE Lilac

When the period bridging spring and summer is spoken of as "lilac time," what people have in mind is the common lilac (*S. vulgaris*) and its numerous cultivars, with their fragrant flowers densely clustered in cone-shaped panicles. But it is, too, the season of several other graceful and somewhat neglected lilacs. Some of these are large but there are also several more compact shrubs that are suitable for small gardens. There are about 20 species of lilac, all of them deciduous shrubs and trees, most of them found in woodland and scrub. Many are Asiatic in origin; some come from eastern Europe.

CULTIVATION Require full sun and well-drained neutral to alkaline soil, rich in organic matter.

PROPAGATION From greenwood cuttings, in early summer. By layering, in early summer. By grafting or budding, in mid-summer.

POTENTIAL PROBLEMS Leaf miners, thrips; lilac blight, honey fungus.

S. komarovii subsp. reflexa
C. China

Flowers: late spring to early summer. H:10-14ft (3-4.3m), S:6-10ft (1.8-3m). Z:5-7. Where there is space, this justifies inclusion with its long drooping panicles, the flowers purplish pink in bud, paler on opening. It is a parent of a fine fully hardy hybrid of similar size, *S.* × **josiflexa** 'Bellicent', with large panicles of fragrant clear pink flowers, and the **Canadian Hybrids** (*S.* × *prestoniae*, Z:2-7), large, though less elegant shrubs that have been bred for hardiness. One of the best of these is *S.* × *p.* 'Elinor', with erect panicles of mauve-pink flowers opening from darker buds.

Syringa pubescens subsp. microphylla 'Superba'

S. pubescens subsp. microphylla *W. China*

Flowers: early summer, often in autumn. H:6-10ft (1.8-3m), S:5-8ft (1.5-2.5m). Z:5-7. The form most widely grown is 'Superba', a twiggy bush with small rounded leaves, which at its main flush bears numerous panicles of small fragrant flowers that are rich pink in bud, paler on opening. It continues to flower intermittently until autumn, especially if encouraged with watering and feeding. Another small twiggy lilac is *S. meyeri* var. *spontanea* 'Palibin' (Z:4-7). It grows slowly to a height of 4-5ft (1.2-1.5m), and the bushes are well covered in early summer with numerous panicles of mauve-tinted, sweetly scented pink flowers.

Syringa vulgaris 'Primrose'

S. vulgaris *E. Europe*

Flowers: late spring to early summer. H and S:22ft (7m). Z:3-9. In gardens, numerous cultivars have taken the place of the species, a vigorous large suckering shrub or small tree bearing small mauve flowers. They are clustered in cone-shaped panicles when the leaves, more or less heart shaped, are well developed. The flowers of the cultivars have retained the refined scent of the parent but are larger and the panicles are more densely packed. There are singles and doubles, and the color range includes white and cream as well as various shades of mauve and purple, some leaning to blue, others to pink and red. Well-established cultivars include 'Andenken an Ludwig Späth', with slender panicles of single wine-red flowers on a spreading shrub; 'Firmament', with panicles of single mauve-blue flowers; 'Katherine Havemeyer', with double flowers mauve-pink in bud, making dense purplish-blue panicles; 'Madame Lemoine', with creamy buds opening to make dense white panicles; 'Mrs. Edward Harding', with long panicles of red-purple double flowers; and 'Primrose', with single pale yellow flowers.

TAMARIX

TAMARICACEAE Tamarisk

Several of the tamarisks are astonishing survivors of extreme conditions. In the deserts of North Africa and the Middle East, for instance, the shade tree, *T. aphylla*, survives great heat and drought and tolerates high levels of salinity. There are just over 50 species of these deciduous trees and shrubs, and several are good for gardens, especially in coastal areas. Despite the light feathery foliage, they make useful windbreaks. If grown freely, they can become angular trees, and it can be better to prune them down to shrubs.
CULTIVATION Require full sun and well-drained soil. Require protection from drying winds in inland gardens.
PROPAGATION From semiripe cuttings, in summer. From hardwood cuttings, in winter.
POTENTIAL PROBLEMS Usually none.

T. ramosissima *S.E. Europe to Asia*

Flowers: late summer to early autumn. H and S:12-15ft (3.7-4.5m). Z:2-8. The arching red-brown stems carry pale gray-green foliage, and plumes of soft pink flowers, more richly

Tamarix ramosissima

colored in 'Pink Cascade', are carried on growths made in the current year *T. tetrandra* (Z:6-8) has greener foliage and carries sprays of pink flowers on growths made the year before.

TEUCRIUM

LAMIACEAE

Only a few species are widely grown, and these are mainly shrubs or subshrubs from southern Europe and the Mediterranean area. The genus, however, has about 300 species, distributed worldwide.
CULTIVATION Require full sun and well-drained soil.
PROPAGATION From softwood cuttings, in early summer with bottom heat. From semiripe cuttings, in mid-summer with bottom heat.
POTENTIAL PROBLEMS Usually none.

Teucrium fruticans

T. fruticans *W. Mediterranean*
Shrubby germander

Flowers: summer. H:24-39in (60-100cm), S:12ft (3.7m). Z:8-9. The stems and undersides of the leaves are covered with a white, silvery felt. The long-lipped flowers of this aromatic evergreen are pale blue and borne over a long season. Where it is of borderline hardiness, grow it at the foot of a warm wall.

THYMUS

LAMIACEAE Thyme

The common thyme (*T. vulgaris*) was long ago brought into gardens so that its aromatic foliage could be gathered fresh for medicinal and culinary purposes. Other thymes also please with the piquant scent of their crushed leaves, particularly when planted among paving stones. Some have attractive golden or variegated foliage and most flower freely. Thymes are sun lovers, most cultivated species coming from the Mediterranean region. The genus is large with 300 to 400 species of evergreen shrubs and subshrubs distributed in Europe and Asia.

CULTIVATION Require full sun and well-drained neutral to alkaline soil.

PROPAGATION From seed, sown in spring. From semiripe cuttings, in mid- to late summer.

POTENTIAL PROBLEMS Usually none.

T. × citriodorus
Lemon thyme
Flowers: summer. H:8-12in (20-30cm), S:10-18in (25-45cm). Z:6-9.
The leaves are broad and valued for their lemon scent; the flowers are mauve-pink. There are numerous golden-leaved and variegated forms. The leaves of **'Silver Queen'** have cream variegation.

T. serpyllum *Europe*
Flowers: summer. H:2-3in (5-8cm), S:12-18in (30-45cm). Z:4-9.
Purple flower spikes cover mats of hairy leaves on this species. There are numerous named forms. **'Pink Chintz'** bears masses of pink flowers.

Thymus serpyllum

T. vulgaris *W. Mediterranean*
Flowers: late spring to early summer. H:6-12in (15-30cm), S:16in (40cm). Z:6-9.
Bushes are variable in size, but at least when young, the wiry stems are densely covered with dark green leaves. The flowers are pink or white. **'Silver Posie'** has leaves with a cool white variegation.

VIBURNUM

CAPRIFOLIACEAE

The viburnums are mainly shrubs and trees of woodland and thickets in the temperate regions of the Northern Hemisphere, but the genus extends into southeast Asia and South America. Among the 150 or so species, there are several very fine deciduous and evergreen shrubs for temperate gardens, several of which are outstanding for their winter flowers.

CULTIVATION Require full sun or partial shade, and fertile moist but well-drained soil. Shelter evergreen plants from wind in cold areas.

PROPAGATION From seed, in autumn. From greenwood cuttings, in summer (deciduous); semiripe cuttings, in summer (evergreens).

POTENTIAL PROBLEMS Aphids, viburnum beetles; honey fungus.

V. × bodnantense
Flowers: late autumn to spring. H:8-12ft (2.5-3.7m), S:5-8ft (1.5-2.5m). Z:6-8.
Two winter-flowering deciduous species, the Chinese *V. farreri* (Z:7-8) and the Himalayan *V. grandiflorum* (Z:7-8), are the parents of this upright shrub, which gets more arching as it ages. Dense clusters of pink-tinged white flowers that hang from bare stems open over several months. **'Charles Lamont'** and **'Dawn'** are rich pink.

Viburnum carlesii 'Charis'

V. carlesii *Japan, Korea*
Korean spice viburnum
Flowers: mid- to late spring. H and S:5-6ft (1.5-1.8m). Z:5-7.
The rounded bush is in leaf when pink buds open to fragrant white flowers. The fruits that follow are deep black. **'Aurora'** has pink flowers opening from red buds. The flowers of the compact form **'Diana'** are similar, but fade to near white, and its young foliage is purple tinted. This deciduous species is a parent of several fine fully hardy hybrids with fragrant flowers in mid- to late spring. Those going under the name *V. × burkwoodii* are semievergreen with clusters of pink buds opening to white flowers. **'Anne Russell'** (Z:4-9) is a compact shrub about 6ft (1.8m) tall; **'Charis'** (Z:4-9) has a profusion of white flowers; and **'Park Farm Hybrid'** (Z:4-9) can reach 8ft (2.5m) in height and spread. By unfair comparison *V. × carlcephalum* (Z:5-9) is less refined, but its foliage is tinted in autumn and it is handsome when pink buds open to white flowers. It is an upright plant to about 8ft (2.5m). *V. × juddii* (Z:5-8) is bushy and compact, with a height and spread of 5ft (1.5m), and has pink-tinged white flowers.

Viburnum davidii

V. davidii *W. China*
David viburnum
Flowers: late spring. H and S:3-5ft (90-150cm). Z:8-9.
The glossy oval leaves, 3 nerves boldly cutting into their surface, create low tiers of dark-green foliage on this shrub. The flat heads of small white flowers are followed by long-lasting egg-shaped berries of turquoise blue. Several specimens must be planted close together to make sure of a good crop of berries.

V. opulus *Europe, N. Africa, C. Asia*
European cranberry viburnum
Flowers: late spring to early summer. H:10-15ft (3-4.5m), S:8-12ft (2.5-3.7m). Z:4-8.
This is a large shrub of many parts. Its maplelike deciduous foliage colors well in autumn. Its heads of white flowers are ringed by sterile flowerets and the bunches of red fruits gleam enticingly. **'Compactum'**, with a height and spread of 5ft (1.5m), flowers and fruits freely. **'Xanthocarpum'** (Z:4-9) bears yellow fruits. The snowball tree (**'Roseum'**, Z:4-9) carries rounded heads of sterile white flowers, often tinted pink.

Viburnum opulus

163

V. plicatum

Japanese snowball bush
Flowers: late spring. H:8–12ft (2.5–3.7m), S:10–15ft (3–4.5m). Z:5–8.
This deciduous shrub is variable in its growth, most forms being spreading, but some having a markedly tiered arrangement of horizontal branches that is easily spoiled by crowding. In its various forms, there are differences also in the flowerheads, some consisting entirely of crowded white infertile flowerets, others with small creamy white fertile flowers surrounded by a ring of infertile flowerets. 'Grandiflorum' has large heads of sterile flowers that are tinged pink. The branches of 'Mariesii' are in tiered layers, and the flowerheads consist mainly of infertile flowerets. The compact 'Nanum Semperflorens', which slowly reaches 5ft (1.5m) or so, bears small white flowers from late spring to early autumn.

V. tinus Mediterranean

Laurustinus
Flowers: late winter to spring. H and S:8–12ft (2.5–3.7m). Z:8–10.
Municipal planting has made the laurustinus seem dull, but a dense evergreen bush of dark foliage flowering generously from autumn through to spring is not to be despised. The flat heads of pink buds open to small white flowers, which are followed by blue-black fruits. 'Eve Price' and 'Gwenllian' are both compact and have flowers that are strongly pink tinted in bud. 'Gwenllian' fruits freely.

WEIGELA

CAPRIFOLIACEAE

The weigelas most commonly seen in gardens are hybrids that are valued as reliable and easy shrubs. The dozen species are plants of woodland margins or more open scrub in temperate east Asia. The flowers, borne on growth made in the previous year, are bell or funnel shaped. The predominant colors are pinks and reds.
W. middendorffiana (Z:6–8) has soft yellow flowers, with orange spots accenting the throat. This is a lovely and reasonably hardy shrub growing to about 5ft (1.5m), but its precocious early shoots are sometimes damaged by frost.
CULTIVATION Require full sun or partial shade and fertile well-drained soil.
PROPAGATION From hardwood cuttings, in autumn to winter.
POTENTIAL PROBLEMS Leaf and bud eelworms.

Weigela florida 'Foliis Purpureus'

W. florida N. China, Korea

Flowers: late spring to early summer. H and S:6–8ft (1.8–2.5m). Z:5–8.
This is a vigorous bush with arching stems well covered with light green leaves and in its season numerous clusters of reddish-pink flowers with a pale interior. 'Foliis Purpureis', a compact plant about 3ft (90cm) tall, combines purplish foliage and soft pink flowers. The attractive leaves of 'Variegata', with a creamy yellow margin, contrast with the pink flowers.

W. hybrids

Flowers: late spring to early summer. H and S:6–8ft (1.8–2.5m). Z:5–8.
The family resemblance of these is very strong, even though some may show characteristics hinting at one or other parent. 'Abel Carrière' is a spreading bush with purplish-red buds opening to deep pink flowers with a gold spot in the throat. 'Bristol Ruby' is vigorous with erect dark red flowers. 'Candida' is compact with green buds opening to white flowers, and 'Newport Red' is erect with dark red flowers and contrasting off-white anthers.

YUCCA

AGAVACEAE

Impressive spikes of bell-shaped flowers contrast with rosettes of evergreen swordlike leaves. The yuccas, some stemless, others tree-like, are plants of dry or desert habitats in North and Central America and the West Indies. There are about 40 species in this genus, some which are of great value in desert gardens, and several add a jagged exoticism when planted in sunny positions in temperate gardens. The heights given in the head information are for foliage rosettes.
CULTIVATION Require full sun and well-drained soil.
PROPAGATION From seed, sown in spring with bottom heat. From rooted suckers, in spring.
POTENTIAL PROBLEMS Aphids; leaf spot.

Y. filamentosa USA (New Jersey to Florida)

Adam's needles
Flowers: mid- to late summer. H:5–6ft (1.5–1.8m), S:3–4ft (90–120cm). Z:4–10.
The stiff gray-green leaves forming a stemless rosette are edged with threadlike hairs. The compact flowering spike of creamy bells reaches 5ft (1.5m). The leaves of 'Bright Edge' have yellow margins. Our Lord's Candle (Y. whipplei, Z:8–10) is magnificent but less hardy. A spiked narrow gray-blue rosette has massive clusters of lemon-scented ivory bells, over 10ft (3m) tall. Plants take years to flower and then die.

Y. flaccida USA (North Carolina to Alabama)

Flowers: mid- to late summer. H and S:4–5ft (1.2–1.5m). Z:4–10.
The rosettes on this almost stemless shrub have narrow, limp, gray-green leaves that arch at the tips. The leaves, like those of Y. filamentosa, have threads along their margins. The graceful flower spikes, up to 5ft (1.5m) tall, have many creamy bells. 'Golden Sword' has yellow variegated leaves; 'Ivory' is impressive in flower.

Y. gloriosa USA (North Carolina to Florida)

Spanish dagger
Flowers: late summer to autumn. H:6–8ft (1.8–2.5m), S:4–6ft (1.2–1.8m). Z:6–9.
The woody trunk bears rosettes of blue-green to dark-green leaves. The spike of bell-shaped flowers, creamy white with a pink tinge, can be more than 6ft (1.8m) tall. 'Variegata' has leaves with a yellow edge. The fully hardy Y. recurvifolia (Z:8–10) has dark gray-green foliage. The flower spikes of creamy white bells, up to 6ft (1.8m) tall, often appear in late summer.

Yucca gloriosa

conifers

Some of the most economically important trees in the world are conifers. This group of trees and shrubs includes junipers (*Juniperus*), firs (*Abies*), pines (*Pinus*), and many others. The greater part of the vast range of ornamental garden cultivars are smaller versions of these important lumber trees. Many forms of these plants have developed, with foliage in shades of blue, golden yellow, or green, variegated with flecks of other colors. Variegated plants are often useful in the smaller garden, as they grow much more slowly than their green counterparts. Conifers provide a foil for flowering plants and are adaptable to a wide range of soil types. Most are extremely hardy. Some grow in near desert conditions; others thrive in a swamplike environment. Although nearly all conifers are evergreen, *Ginkgo*, *Larix*, *Metasequoia*, and *Taxodium* display attractive autumn tints before shedding their leaves. Conifers reproduce by means of catkinlike male flowers and conelike female flowers called strobili.

Most conifers are available in containers. The ideal time for planting conifers is just before one of their 2 main surges of growth, in late spring and early autumn. Young conifers require formative pruning to train them, or to thicken growth. Regular pruning is unnecessary for many conifers.

Top **Cedrus deodara**
Center **Juniperus horizontalis 'Blue Chip'**
Bottom **Larix decidua**

ABIES

PINACEAE Silver fir

There are more than 50 species of fir trees distributed throughout the Northern Hemisphere. Many grow to a prodigious size; the giant fir (*A. grandis*, Z:6–8) of western North America can exceed 300ft (90m). Most species have compact or dwarf forms. Some of them are of considerable garden value, although they lack the majestic conical shape and tiered horizontal branches that make these trees so impressive in the wild.
CULTIVATION Tolerate full sun or partial shade, and require moist soil that is neutral to acid.
PROPAGATION From seed, sown outdoors in late winter. From grafting, under glass in early autumn or late winter to early spring (cultivars).
POTENTIAL PROBLEMS None serious.

A. balsamea f. *hudsonia*
C. and E. Canada, E. USA
Foliage: year-round. H and S:2–3ft (60–90cm). Z:3–8.
The balsam fir (*A. balsamea*) grows to 80ft (25m), but this curiosity makes a compact spherical mound. It does not produce cones.

Abies balsamea f. hudsonia

A. concolor *S.W. USA to N. Mexico*
White fir
Foliage: year-round. H:50–100ft (15–30m), S:15–25ft (4.5–7.5m). Z:4–8.
An alternative to the handsome but tall upright species, which has blue or gray foliage, '**Compacta**' grows to 6ft (1.8m) and can have a spread of 10ft (3m). It seldom produces cones, and its short leaves are steely blue. *A. lasiocarpa* '**Arizonica Compacta**' (Z:5–8), a slow-growing form of the Rocky Mountain fir, is another moderate blue-gray tree, reaching 15ft (4.5m).

A. koreana *S. Korea*
Korean fir
Foliage: year-round. H:20–30ft (6–9m), S:10–20ft (3–6m). Z:4–8.
This very hardy and slow-growing fir is exceptional in producing its

Abies koreana

violet-blue cones when only 5 to 10 years old and as small as 3ft (90cm) tall. It makes a broad pyramid, the spiky foliage dark green on the upper surface and bright silver underneath. Even slower in growth is '**Silberlocke**' (Z:5–8). This has a silvery sheen caused by the leaves as they twist on themselves to show silvery undersides. Pale green cones ripen to dark yellow.

ARAUCARIA

ARAUCARIACEAE

Most of the 18 species of this genus from the Southern Hemisphere need a warm, temperate climate. The curiously symmetrical Norfolk Island pine (*A. heterophylla*, Z:9–11) is sometimes grown as a house plant. The hardiest is the monkey puzzle (*A. araucana*), which is best grown as a specimen, uncluttered by close planting.
CULTIVATION Require an open position and moist but well-drained soil. Water young plants well.
PROPAGATION From seed, sown in a propagator or greenhouse with a temperature of 68°F (20°C).
POTENTIAL PROBLEMS Usually none.

Araucaria araucana

A. araucana *Argentina, Chile*
Chilean pine, monkey puzzle
Foliage: year-round. H:50–80ft (15–25m), S:20–30ft (6–9m). Z:6–9.
On the highly distinctive mature specimens, the long branches, which are densely clothed with darkly glossy spine-tipped leaves, sweep downward, sometimes almost to ground level. The spiky cones take 3 years to mature.

CALOCEDRUS

CUPRESSACEAE Incense cedar

The hardiest of the 3 species of evergreen conifers in this genus, the North American *C. decurrens* makes a handsome specimen tree for parks and large gardens. Other species are Asiatic.
CULTIVATION Require an open sheltered position and a well-drained, preferably acid, soil.
PROPAGATION From seed, sown outdoors in late winter. From hardwood cuttings, in early autumn (essential for variegated forms).
POTENTIAL PROBLEMS Heart rot fungus.

Calocedrus decurrens

C. decurrens *W. North America*
Foliage: year-round. H:40–130ft (12–39m), S:2–10ft (60–300cm). Z:5–8.
The dark green column is tightly packed with sprays of aromatic scalelike leaves, which are carried on short horizontal branches. The cylindrical cones, rust colored when mature, are about 1in (2.5cm) in length.

CEDRUS

PINACEAE Cedar

Mature cedars are among the most magnificent trees. The 4 species, all evergreens from the Himalayas and the Mediterranean region, are conical when young, but with age, they become broad and irregular in

outline. The needlelike leaves grow in dense clusters, and the barrel-shaped cones ripen slowly from purplish green to brown.
CULTIVATION Require full sun and well-drained soil.
PROPAGATION From seed, sown outdoors in spring. From grafting, in a propagator in late winter to early spring. From cuttings, in late summer (cultivars).
POTENTIAL PROBLEMS weevils; root rot, stem rot.

Cedrus deodara

C. deodara *W. Himalayas*
Deodar cedar
Foliage: year-round. H:60–120ft (18–35m), S:15–30ft (4.5–9m). Z:6–9.
Drooping branches give this fast-growing blue conifer a languid air. The yellow '**Aurea**' slowly attains a height of 15ft (4.5m).

Cedrus libani subsp. atlantica

C. libani subsp. atlantica *Asia Minor, Syria*
Atlas cedar
Foliage: year-round. H:80–130ft (25–39m), S:15–30ft (4.5–9m). Z:6–9.
The ascending branches and upright leader are distinctive, but

eventually, specimens usually develop the flat-topped outline associated with the cedar of Lebanon. The foliage is green or gray-green but in the blue cedars (**Glauca Group**) it is a startling silvery blue. '**Glauca Pendula**' has weeping branches and glaucous leaves and rarely exceeds 15ft (4.5m) tall; the branches may need to be staked. *C. libani* (cedar of Lebanon) has tiered arching branches with dense flat layers of gray-green foliage. The cones are gray-green with just a hint of pink. *C. libani* '**Sargentii**' is slow growing, to 5ft (1.5m), but the gracefully weeping branches can ultimately have a spread of more than 20ft (6m).

CHAMAECYPARIS

CUPRESSACEAE False cypress

Although there are only 7 species of these natives of eastern North America, Japan, and Taiwan, the false cypresses are represented in gardens by numerous cultivars, offering a vast choice in shape, size, growth rate, and foliage color, often at its best during the coldest winters. A standard feature is the broad frondlike foliage, which has a flattened appearance. Young plants are usually conical in outline but spread with age.
CULTIVATION Tolerate full sun or partial shade and a wide range of soils, but best on neutral to acid soils. Trim hedges between late spring and early autumn.
PROPAGATION From seed, sown outdoors in late winter. From semi-ripe cuttings, taken in late summer to early autumn. By grafting, under cover in early spring (cultivars).
POTENTIAL PROBLEMS No serious problems.

C. lawsoniana *North America*
Lawson cypress
Foliage: year-round. H:50–130ft (15–39m), S:6–15ft (1.8–4.5m). Z:5–8.
This elegant and narrow columnar tree, with its characteristic drooping leading shoot, will quickly outgrow all but the largest of yards. The dense dark green leaves are arranged in pairs along shoots, which are a rich reddish brown when young, aging to a dull gray-brown. The cones are small and round. '**Green Hedger**', vigorous and upright, with light green leaves, makes a good hedge when clipped. Columnar forms that usually grow to 15–25ft (4.5–7.5m) tall include '**Alumnii**', with upright branches and large sprays of blue-gray foliage; the

narrow 30ft (9m) tall '**Ellwoodii**', with dense sprays of gray-green leaves, which are bluer in winter; and the slow-growing '**Fletcheri**', dense and erect with gray-green foliage. Dwarf cultivars include '**Minima Aurea**', compact and very hardy, making an oval mound some 3ft (90cm) tall of 2-tone foliage, golden on the upper surface and yellow underneath; and '**Minima Glauca**', which forms a 6ft (1.8m) ball of sea-green sprays.

Chamaecyparis obtusa 'Crippsii'

C. obtusa *Japan*
Hinoki cypress
Foliage: year-round. H:50–70ft (15–22m), S:15–20ft (4.5–6m). Z:4–8.
This cone-shaped tree has spreading branches with shiny, aromatic, dark green leaves, the undersides white and the leaf tips blunt. The small cones ripen from green to brown. '**Crippsii**', slow growing to 50ft (15m), has bright golden new growth that fades to yellow-green. It reaches a height of around 30ft (9m). Semidwarf cultivars include '**Nana Gracilis**', which grows to 8ft (2.5m) with glossy dark green foliage, and '**Tetragona Aurea**', which reaches twice this height, with gold foliage at its best in full sun. '**Kosteri**', one of several dwarf cultivars, makes a tight cone of bright green, eventually reaching 4ft (1.2m).

Chamaecyparis obtusa 'Kosteri'

C. pisifera *Japan*

Sawara cypress
Foliage: year-round. H:50–70ft
(15–22m), S:12–15ft (3.7–4.5m).
Z:4–8.
The species is conical, with sharply
pointed, scalelike, aromatic leaves
that are bright green with a white
line on the underside. Its cultivars
include one of the most popular
of all conifers, '**Boulevard**',
outstanding for its soft steely blue
foliage, tinged purple in winter.
It grows to 30ft (9m). '**Filifera
Aurea**', which is slow to exceed
10ft (3m) but commonly spreads to
15ft (4.5m), has slender, elongated,
yellow foliage on drooping stems.

Chamaecyparis pisifera
'Filifera Aurea'

CRYPTOMERIA

TAXODIACEAE Japanese cedar

The single species is an elegant,
fast-growing evergreen that is
generally represented in gardens
by its compact cultivars.
CULTIVATION Tolerates full sun or
partial shade and a wide range of
soils, but performs best on those
that are moist and slightly acid.
PROPAGATION From semiripe
cuttings with a heel, taken in early
autumn and placed in a cold frame
over winter.
POTENTIAL PROBLEMS None serious.

C. japonica *Japan*

Foliage: year-round. H:50–80ft
(15–25m), S:15–20ft (4.5–6m).
Z:6–9.
Attractive orange-red bark shreds
into fine strips as the tree ages. The
thin, needlelike, evergreen leaves
are mid-green, deepening to dark
green, and densely packed in
spirals along the extended lateral
branches. '**Elegans**', which forms
a small tree 20–30ft (6–9m) tall,
retains its soft and feathery juvenile
foliage, although this changes color
through the year, from silver in
spring and green in summer, to
blue-red in autumn and bronze-red
in winter. '**Elegans Compacta**',
slower growing to 12ft (3.7m), has
even softer, more feathery foliage,
which turns dark purple in winter.

'**Vilmoriniana**', with a height and
spread of only 3ft (90cm), has
dense light green foliage that turns
reddish brown in winter.

Cryptomeria japonica 'Vilmoriniana'

× CUPRESSOCYPARIS

CUPRESSACEAE

Leyland cypresses are fast growing
with dense, resilient, scalelike
foliage, which makes them suitable
for shelter belts, even in coastal
areas. However, their rapid growth
counts against them as hedging
plants since they require frequent
cutting.
CULTIVATION Tolerate full sun or
partial shade and a wide range of
soils, although prefer moist neutral
to acid soils. Trim hedges several
times annually between late spring
and early autumn.
PROPAGATION From semiripe
cuttings, taken in spring or autumn.
POTENTIAL PROBLEMS None serious.

× *Cupressocyparis leylandii*

× C. leylandii

Leyland cypress
Foliage: year-round. H:100–120ft
(30–35m), S:15–20ft (4.5–6m).
Z:5–9.
This cypress forms a dense column
of dark green or gray-green foliage
held in flat dense sprays. The small
cones are round and dark brown.
The bronze-yellow '**Castlewellan**'
is less vigorous, forming a straighter
column with a flatter crown.

CUPRESSUS

CUPRESSACEAE Cypress

The true cypresses, of which there
are 20 or so species, are plants of
dry landscapes. They have scalelike
aromatic leaves, and the cones,
which are green when new and
woody from the second year, often
remain on the tree for years.
Included among them are the
Monterey cypress (*C. macrocarpa*,
Z:8–10), which is columnar when
young but cedarlike when mature;
the weeping Kashmir cypress
(*C. torulosa* '**Cashmeriana**',
Z:8–9); and the Arizona cypress
(*C. arizonica*, Z:6–8).
CULTIVATION Require full sun, well-
drained soil, and protection from
cold winds.
PROPAGATION From semiripe
cuttings with a heel, taken in early
to mid-autumn and placed in a cold
frame or with bottom heat.
POTENTIAL PROBLEMS Phytophthora,
canker, but usually trouble-free.

Cupressus sempervirens

C. sempervirens *Mediterranean,
W. Asia*

Italian cypress, Mediterranean
cypress
Foliage: year-round. H:30–60ft
(9–18m), S:3–15ft (90–450cm).
Z:7–9.
This narrow tree, evocative of the
landscape of Tuscany, has upward-
pointing branches and erect sprays
of dark green leaves. The leaves are
short, stubby, and closely packed
together, completely covering the
twigs. Young plants may be
damaged by freezing winter winds.
'**Stricta**' (pencil pine) is a narrower
tree with flaking gray-brown bark.

GINKGO

GINKGOACEAE Maidenhair tree

To use Charles Darwin's term, the
single species in this genus is a
"living fossil," an astonishing
survivor of a primitive plant group.
It is thought to be unknown in the
wild, but was widely grown in
imperial and temple gardens of
China. Its tolerance of pollution
makes it a useful city tree.

CULTIVATION Requires sun or partial shade and well-drained soil.
PROPAGATION From seed, sown in spring. From semiripe cuttings, taken in summer.
POTENTIAL PROBLEMS Usually none.

Ginkgo biloba

G. biloba

Foliage: spring to autumn. H:80–100ft (25–30m), S:15–25ft (4.5–7.5m). Z:4–8.
This upright deciduous conifer spreads with age. The bright green leaves, which form a notched fan up to 3in (7.5cm) across, turn clear yellow in autumn. If fertilized, the female trees produce fruits with edible kernels in late summer and autumn; the outer coating has a rank smell. **'Pendula'** is smaller than the species and has spreading or weeping branches.

JUNIPERUS

CUPRESSACEAE Juniper

This important genus of evergreen conifers includes 50 to 60 species that are native to dry forests and hillsides of the Northern Hemisphere, and hundreds of ornamental varieties. Nearly all the plants are hardy, and they show remarkable tolerance of heat and considerable resistance to drought. There are forms for almost every situation, and the full conifer foliage color palette of greens, blues, yellows, and grays is covered. Sharp, needlelike, young leaves mature into fleshy stem-hugging scales. Juvenile and mature foliage are present at the same time on some junipers. As the plants mature, the attractive reddish bark peels and flakes.
CULTIVATION Tolerate full sun or light shade (the gold forms are best in full sun) as well as a wide range of soils.
PROPAGATION From semiripe cuttings with a heel, taken in early autumn. From seed, placed in a cold frame in late winter (species).
POTENTIAL PROBLEMS Bagworm mites; cedar apple rust, twig blight.
WARNING Young needles can cause skin irritation.

J. chinensis *China, Japan*
Chinese juniper
Foliage: year-round. H:60–80ft (18–25m), S:15–20ft (4.5–6m). Z:4–8.
In Chinese gardens, this is a tall columnar tree of imperial solemnity, but in the wild it is very variable. The aromatic foliage is gray-green, composed of needlelike juvenile leaves and scalelike adult leaves. Male and female strobili are borne on separate plants. The fruits on female plants are berrylike and blue-black when ripe. The dull brown bark peels away in strips as the tree ages. Some of the smaller cultivars are very popular. **'Aurea'** is about half the size of the species, making a tall slender tree with green juvenile foliage and golden adult foliage. A male form, it is slow to establish, but grows quickly thereafter. The golden foliage has a tendency to scorch when the plant is grown in full sun. The shrub **'Blue Alps'** has a vigorous and spreading habit although, compared to other junipers, it is quite modest, reaching a height of 12ft (3.7m). The shoots arch over at the tips when young and the foliage is silver-blue to steel-blue. **'Obelisk'** is a tall narrow shrub growing to 8ft (2.5m) with bluish-green dense foliage. **'Pyramidalis'** (pyramidal juniper) slowly makes a dense blue-green column, about 6½ft (2m) tall.

J. communis
Common juniper
Foliage: year-round. H:2–25ft (60–750cm), S:3–20ft (90–600cm). Z:3–8.
The common juniper ranges from a small spreading shrub to a large upright tree. The needlelike, glossy, and aromatic leaves are mid-green or yellow-green with silver undersides. The rounded fleshy fruits, which are sometimes used as

Juniperus communis **'Hibernica'**

a flavoring, for example in gin, are black with a glaucous bloom. The slow-growing **'Compressa'** will reach a height of 3ft (90cm) after a number of years, and is covered in sharp gray-green or green needles. **'Hibernica'** (Irish juniper) is similar but more vigorous, eventually making a silver-blue column about 10ft (3m) tall. **'Hornibrookii'** is a low, creeping plant that molds itself to the contours it covers. Its blue-green needles are silvery on the underside.

Juniperus conferta

J. conferta
Shore juniper
Foliage: year-round. H:10–12in (25–30cm), S:3–4ft (90–120cm). Z:5–8.
The creeping stems with raised tips are clothed with needlelike leaves to make gray-green to bright green mats. The berrylike fruits are purplish black with a light bloom.

Juniperus horizontalis **'Blue Chip'**

J. horizontalis *North America*
Creeping juniper
Foliage: year-round. H:12–20in (30–50cm), S:6–10ft (1.8–3m). Z:3–7.
This juniper eventually forms a large mat of blue-green or blue-gray aromatic needles. The berries are pale blue but are rarely produced in cultivation. Dwarf cultivars, none growing more than 1ft (30cm) tall, include **'Blue Chip'** (Z:4–7), with bright blue foliage throughout the year; **'Emerald Spreader'** (Z:4–7), with bright green foliage; and the vigorous **'Hughes'** (Z:4–7), with upward pointing branches and gray-green leaves.

Juniperus × pfitzeriana

J. × pfitzeriana

Foliage: year-round. H:6–10ft
(1.8–3m), S:8–15ft (2.5–4.5m).
Z:4–8.
The long branches of this juniper
rise at an angle of about 45° from
a short trunk and have drooping
tips. The green scalelike leaves are
carried in tiered sprays, among
which there is a scattering of more
glaucous juvenile leaves. The
spherical fruits are purple. 'Aurea'
is a golden version that becomes
yellow-green in winter. 'Old Gold',
which is a sport of it, is more
compact and remains bronzed
yellow through the year. 'Mint
Julep', another of the numerous
junipers covered by this hybrid,
resembles *Pfitzeriana*, but has
bright green foliage.

Juniperus sabina 'Tamariscifolia'

J. sabina C. Europe to N. China
Savin
Foliage: year-round. H and S:6–15ft
(1.8–4.5m). Z:3–8.
The savin shows considerable
variation over its wide natural
distribution but is usually a
spreading shrub and only rarely
treelike. Its flaking red-brown bark
is, therefore, generally obscured.
The foliage, which consists mainly
of adult scalelike leaves, is gray-
green and produces a rank smell
when bruised. Low, spreading
cultivars include the very hardy
'Blaue Donau', which has light
gray-blue foliage and spreads to
around 6ft (1.8m); and the form it
is best known by, 'Tamariscifolia',
which grows to 4ft (1.2m) across
and carries bright green needlelike
leaves arranged in tiers.

J. scopulorum North America
(British Columbia; Arizona; Texas),
N. Mexico
Rocky Mountain juniper
Foliage: year-round. H:30–50ft
(9–15m), S:12–15ft (3.7–4.5m).
Z:3–8.
The species is a cypresslike conical
tree, sometimes with several main
stems. Although the foliage can
vary in color, it is often blue-green,
while the bark, which shreds, is
red-brown. The garden cultivar
'Skyrocket' is a column of feathery
blue-gray foliage, which reaches
20ft (6m) in height but not much
more than 1ft (30cm) in diameter.

Juniperus squamata 'Blue Star'

J. squamata Asia
Singleweed juniper
Foliage: year-round. H:3–30ft
(90–900cm), S:3–25ft (90–750cm)
Z:4–9.
This prostrate or bushy juniper
has rusty brown bark that flakes off
the trunk as the plant ages. All
forms have short triangular-shaped
leaves, which are silvery blue to
green with a white or pale green
line on the upper surface, and
drooping tips to each shoot.
Spreading branches carry the blue-
gray foliage of 'Blue Carpet', which
grows to 8–12in (20–30cm) by
5–6½ft (1.5–2m). The densely
bushy 'Blue Star' makes a mound
of silvery blue foliage, 12–16in
(30–40cm) by 18–36in (45–90cm).
'Meyeri' has angular branches
with densely packed glaucous blue
foliage. Although usually seen as a
shrub with a height and spread of
about 5ft (1.5m), it can reach to
over 20ft (6m).

Juniperus virginiana 'Grey Owl'

J. virginiana E. USA
Eastern red cedar
Foliage: year-round. H:50–100ft
(15–30m), S:15–25ft (4.5–7.5m).
Z:4–9.
The eastern red cedar is a slow-
growing columnar or conical tree
that resembles the Chinese juniper.
The foliage is gray-green, with
patches of glaucous juvenile leaves
among the scalelike adult leaves.
The brown bark comes away in
shreds. The brown-blue fruits are
like berries, with a white bloom.
'Grey Owl' is a wide-spreading
open shrub, eventually growing to
more than 8ft (2.5m) tall and as
much as 12ft (3.7m) across, with
tiered sprays of gray-green foliage.
Its fruits are a glaucous purple.

LARIX

PINACEAE Larch

The larches make up a small genus
of 10 to 14 species, all deciduous
and all belonging to temperate
regions of the Northern
Hemisphere. Most are fast growing
and tolerant of a wide range of
conditions. Several, including the
European larch (L. decidua, Z:3–7),
are widely used in commercial
forestry. Although their size may
count against them as garden trees,
the green of the young foliage and
their brilliant autumnal colors,
especially the yellow, make them
highly ornamental. Pretty strobili,
sometimes pink or red, are
followed by small neat cones that
persist long after they have shed
their seeds.

Larix kaempferi 'Pendula'

CULTIVATION Require full sun and
well-drained soil.
PROPAGATION From seed, sown
from late winter to mid-spring. By
grafting (cultivars).
POTENTIAL PROBLEMS Wooly aphids,
larch case-bearer; stem canker
(especially L. decidua cultivars).

L. kaempferi *Japan*
Japanese larch
Foliage: autumn. H:80–100ft
(25–30m), S:15–25ft (4.5–7.5m).
Z:4–8.
Purplish-red twigs make this
columnar larch distinctive in winter.
The needlelike leaves are gray-green,
occasionally with a bluish tinge; the
light pink, sometimes light lime-
green, strobili are followed by small
oval cones with scales that turn
outward and downward at the tips.
'**Pendula**' is a tall elegant cultivar
with long weeping branches that
are particularly telling in autumn.

METASEQUOIA

TAXODIACEAE Dawn redwood

The genus was first described in
1941, based on the fossil specimens
of 3 species. Remarkably, a fourth
living species was found in 1945
in N.E. Sichuan in western China.
Seed gathered from this deciduous
conifer and distributed in Europe
and North America germinated
freely, and the tree has grown
vigorously in a wide variety of
conditions, shooting to stardom
after millennia of obscurity.
CULTIVATION Requires fertile,
preferably acid, moist soil.
PROPAGATION From seed, sown in
autumn. From cuttings, taken in
mid- to late autumn, with bottom
heat.
POTENTIAL PROBLEMS None serious.

Metasequoia glyptostroboides

M. glyptostroboides
Foliage: autumn. H:60–120ft
(18–35m), S:12–20ft (3.7–6m).
Z:4–9.
In summer this fast-growing
conical tree has bright green
feathery leaves, which turn rusty
pink and gold before falling. Male
and female strobili are borne on
the same tree, the females
developing into small cones on
long stalks. The bark is red-brown.

PICEA

PINACEAE Spruce

Between 30 and 40 species of
spruce are distributed in the
temperate Northern Hemisphere,
many in rugged mountainous
country. The typical arrangement of
the main branches in tiered whorls
on an erect trunk gives the trees
their conical or columnar shape;
the pendulous branchlets of some
give them their weeping character.
The needlelike leaves are borne on
stubby projections. Male and
female strobili are carried on the
same tree, and the cones, which are
ovoid or cylindrical and pendant,
usually fall late in the second year.
Several handsome species,
including the Serbian spruce
(**P. omorika**, Z:4–8) and the
oriental spruce (**P. orientalis**,
Z:4–8), both capable of growing to
100ft (30m), are too large for most
yards. The compact cultivars do not
usually produce cones.
CULTIVATION Require a sunny
sheltered site and a deep moist but
well-drained soil, preferably neutral
to acid.
PROPAGATION From seed, sown
under glass in late winter. Grow
on seedlings for 2 to 3 years before
planting out.
POTENTIAL PROBLEMS Red spider
mites (particularly on dwarf
spruces), agelgids, bagworms.

P. abies *S. Scandinavia to C. and
S. Europe*
Common spruce, Norway spruce
Foliage: year-round. H:70–130ft,
(22–39m), S:15–25ft (4.5–7.5m).
Z:2–8.
Much used in parts of Europe as a
Christmas tree, this fast-growing
pyramidal conifer has needles that
are shiny dark green above and a
lighter green underneath. Dark red
strobili are followed by conspicuous
cigar-shaped glossy cones, 4–8in
(10–20cm) long, ripening from
green flecked with purple to light
brown. '**Little Gem**' (Z:4–8) is a
slow-growing dwarf cultivar with
spreading branches that form a
neat nest-sized mound. Its new

Picea abies 'Nidiformis'

spring needles are light green; the
older ones are dark. '**Nidiformis**'
(Z:3–8), a low-growing bush,
eventually reaching up to 5ft
(1.5m) tall but more than twice
this across, has a nestlike
depression in the center.

Picea breweriana

P. breweriana *USA (N. California,
S. Oregon)*
Brewer's weeping spruce
Foliage: year-round. H:30–50ft
(9–15m), S:10–15ft (3–4.5m).
Z:6–8.
Although the main branches dip
slightly before turning up, the tree
gets its weeping character from
hanging shoots that create a blue-
green curtain of foliage. The
morinda spruce (**P. smithiana**) of
the western Himalayas is another
species of weeping habit, although
its foliage is dark green. Green
cones, 4in (10cm) long and pointed
at both ends, mature to purple.

Picea glauca var. *albertiana*
'Conica'

P. glauca *Canada, N.E. USA*
White spruce
Foliage: year-round. H:80–120ft
(25–35m), S:10–20ft (3–6m). Z:3–7.
This large cone-shaped tree, with
down-turned branches lifting at
the tips, has glaucous green leaves
that produce a fetid smell when
bruised. The light brown oval
cones grow to 2in (5cm) in length.
Although slow to reach its ultimate
size, it will be too large for most
yards. The compact **var. albertiana**
'Conica' very slowly makes a
bright green cone up to 6ft (1.8m)
tall and ultimately it can exceed
10ft (3m).

Picea pungens 'Koster'

P. pungens N. USA
Colorado spruce
Foliage: year-round. H:50–100ft
(15–30m), S:12–18ft (3.7–5.5m).
Z:2–8.
The species, a handsome, medium
to large, conical tree with blue-
green foliage, has been neglected in
favor of the blue spruce (**f. glauca**),
with its glaucous leaves and
numerous compact forms with
blue foliage. '**Globosa**' makes a
bright blue flattened mound, 30in
(75cm) tall and wide, while, in
contrast, the light blue '**Hoopsii**' is
a narrow conical tree reaching 15ft
(4.5m) tall with a spread of 5ft
(1.5m). '**Koster**' is a similar shape
but smaller and slow growing. It
has curved silver-blue needles.

PINUS

PINACEAE Pine

Over 100 species of pine are
distributed in the Northern
Hemisphere, and several are found
farther south in mountainous
country. These evergreen conifers
range in size from tall trees to low
shrubs. They include some of the
oldest living trees—specimens of
the bristle cone pine (**P. aristata**,
Z:5–8) of the Southwest USA are
said to be more than 4,000 years
old—and also some very fast-
growing trees that are widely
planted for forestry. The needlelike
leaves are bundled in clusters of
2 to 5. Male and female strobili are
borne on the same tree, the females
developing into woody cones that
are usually conical, although they
can be spherical or banana shaped.
In most species the nutlike seeds
are winged.
CULTIVATION Require full sun
and well-drained soil. Species
with needles in fives, such as
P. parviflora, do best on acid soils.
PROPAGATION From seed, sown
under glass in late winter or in the
open in late spring. Plant out when
at least 2 years old. By grafting
(cultivars).
POTENTIAL PROBLEMS Sawflies, pine
shoot moth caterpillars, weevils;
phytophthora, rust.

P. mugo C. Europe
Dwarf mountain pine
Foliage: year-round. H:10–15ft
(3–4.5m), S:15–25ft (4.5–7.5m).
Z:2–9.
This spreading conifer, which
grows along the ground and then
bends upward, has curved, dark
green paired leaves and oval brown
cones. '**Gnom**' makes a dense
rounded mound about 6ft (1.8m)
tall. Dwarf cultivars include the
slow-growing dense '**Mops**',
eventually about 3ft (90cm) tall,
and the creeping but bushy
var. pumilio, up to 6ft (1.8m) tall
but with a spread of 10ft (3m).

Pinus mugo var. pumilio

P. parviflora Japan
Japanese white pine
Foliage: year-round. H:30–70ft
(9–22m), S:20–25ft (6–7.5m).
Z:5–9.
This slow-growing pine is conical
when young but develops a flat
top. A popular bonsai tree, it has
abundant needles with a blue-
white stripe on the underside,
purple-brown smooth bark, and
blue-green oval cones 2–4in
(5–10cm) long. '**Adcock's Dwarf**' is
slow growing, to about 8ft (2.5m),
and has closely packed gray leaves.

P. sylvestris British Isles
Scots pine
Foliage: year-round. H:50–100ft
(15–30m), S:25–30ft (7.5–9m).
Z:2–9.
Easily recognized by its attractive
reddish-brown young bark, this
upright conifer, which develops a
tall clean trunk, is sometimes seen as
a low-spreading tree. Only then is
this natural forest tree suitable for
the average yard. The twisted paired
leaves are gray- or blue-green; the
green cones, which ripen to pale
gray- or red-brown, are 3in (7.5cm)
long. '**Aurea**' has blue leaves, which
turn golden yellow in winter. The
miniature '**Beuvronensis**' makes a

compact blue-green dome 3ft
(90cm) tall. '**Watereri**' is a slow-
growing blue-gray bush or small
tree that reaches 12ft (3.7m).

Pinus sylvestris 'Beuvronensis'

P. wallichiana Himalayas,
from Afghanistan to N.E. India
Bhutan pine, blue pine
Foliage: year-round. H:70–120ft
(22–35m), S:20–40ft (6–12m). Z:6–9.
Conical young specimens develop
into tall trees with blue-green
foliage, the needles arranged in
fives. The cones are banana shaped.

Pinus wallichiana

PSEUDOLARIX

PINACEAE Golden larch

Like the larches (*Larix*), from
which it is distinguished by small
botanical differences, the single
species is deciduous and colors
magnificently in autumn. This is an
excellent specimen tree, but it is
slow growing, especially in areas
where the growing tips are caught
by late frosts.
CULTIVATION Requires a warm
sheltered site in full sun and deep,
well-drained, slightly acid soil.
PROPAGATION From seed, sown
under protection in spring.
POTENTIAL PROBLEMS Usually none.

P. amabilis S. and E. China
Foliage: autumn. H:50–70ft
(15–22m), S:20–40ft (6–12m). Z:5–7.
On mature specimens, the conical
shape often gives way to a flatter
profile and an open crown. The
long, larchlike leaves are light
green in summer but turn clear
yellow, orange, and then reddish
brown in autumn before falling.

The erect cones, which are up to 3in (7.5cm) long, go through similar color changes, from pale green to light orange.

Pseudolarix amabilis

TAXODIUM

TAXODIACEAE Swamp cypress

The 2 species of deciduous conifers in this genus form columnar trees with frondlike foliage that turns orange in autumn. In the wild, they are found in the shallows of lakes and on waterlogged ground. On wet sites the trunks, flared at the base, are usually surrounded by numerous kneelike stumps, which are aerial roots (pneumatophores).
CULTIVATION Tolerate sun or partial shade. Require moist, preferably acid soil, thriving even in waterlogged conditions.
PROPAGATION From seed, sown in spring; plant outside in autumn the following year. From hardwood cuttings, taken in autumn.
POTENTIAL PROBLEMS Mites; twig blight.

T. distichum North America
Swamp cypress
Foliage: autumn. H:70–130ft (22–39m), S:20–30ft (6–9m). Z:4–10.
This strikingly beautiful, slow-growing, and large deciduous cypress is one of the most typical trees of the Old South of the USA. It has fibrous, reddish-brown,

Taxodium distichum

peeling bark and a broadly conical habit. The branches are bright orange-brown with gray-green young shoots, producing small narrow leaves, which are a vivid yellow-green, turning russet-brown in autumn. Var. *imbricatum* '**Nutans**' (Z:5–10) makes a narrow column of short branches.

TAXUS

TAXACEAE Yew

The common yew (*T. baccata*), widely grown in temperate regions as a superlative plant for hedges and topiary, is one of half a dozen or so evergreen species, distributed in the Northern Hemisphere and extending to Central America and the Philippines. Plants are male or female, the females carrying red or orange fruits, each with a single seed. The seed, like most parts of the plant, is poisonous.
CULTIVATION Tolerate a wide range of conditions, provided the soil is well drained. Trim hedges in summer or early autumn. Yews tend to respond well to heavy renovative pruning.
PROPAGATION From cuttings with a heel, taken in early to mid-autumn.
POTENTIAL PROBLEMS Weevils; blight.
WARNING All parts of yew, except the flesh of the fruits, are highly poisonous. They should never be planted where animals graze.

Taxus baccata

T. baccata Asia Minor, Europe
Common yew, English yew
Foliage: year-round. H:30–70ft (9–22m), S:25–30ft (7.5–9m). Z:5–9.
Whether grown as a bushy, often multistemmed specimen, or clipped as a fine-textured hedge, the common yew is a tree of dark steadfastness, tolerant of a wide range of conditions. There is an unexpectedly jaunty side to this evergreen; the fleshy red covering of the seeds is gaily translucent when seen against the light. The numerous forms include several with yellow foliage. One of the best for hedging is '**Elegantissima**', which matures from rich gold to light green. It is female, as is

'**Standishii**', which slowly makes a narrow golden column to a height of 5ft (1.5m). '**Fastigiata**', the Irish yew, another female clone, makes a dark green column, 30ft (9m) tall.

Taxus baccata '**Standishii**'

T. × *media*
Foliage: year-round. H and S:10–25ft (3–7.5m). Z:4–9.
This vigorous, very wide-spreading but variable shrub has stiff, needle-like, flattened leaves held on olive-green stems. Female plants bear bright red fruits. '**Hicksii**', which makes a broad dark green column, like a more open *T. baccata* '**Fastigiata**', is suitable for hedging.

THUJA

CUPRESSACEAE Arbor vitae

Pleasing dense foliage, extending to the ground, and a neat conical or columnar form are the chief attractions of these hardy evergreen trees and shrubs. The juvenile foliage is soft and feathery; the mature leaves are scalelike and held in flat sprays. Both leaves and cones are aromatic. A small genus of 6 species, thujas are native to temperate regions of the Northern Hemisphere. They can be long-lived and make useful screen or hedge plants, and attractive freestanding specimens. Several of the species have numerous cultivars, some of which are slow-growing or dwarf.
CULTIVATION Prefer a sheltered position in full sun and deep, moist, well-drained, acid soil. Young plants may be damaged by cold winds. Trim hedges in late spring or early autumn.
PROPAGATION From semiripe cuttings, taken in spring or autumn.
POTENTIAL PROBLEMS Bagworms; honey fungus, canker rot, leaf blight.
WARNING Contact with the sap may aggravate skin allergies.

Thuja occidentalis 'Rheingold'

T. occidentalis *E. North America*
American arbor vitae
Foliage: year-round. H:30–70ft
(9–22m), S:9–15ft (2.7–4.5m).
Z:5–9.
This slow-growing columnar
conifer has leaves that are glossy
light green above and matt below,
turning bronze in winter. When
crushed, they give off a scent of
apples. The peeling bark is reddish
brown; the small cones are yellow,
ripening to brown. '**Holmstrup**'
(Z:3–9), an upright tree, grows to
12ft (3.7m) and has rich green
foliage all year. '**Rheingold**' (Z:2–9)
with golden-yellow foliage, bronze
in winter, makes a cone shape 3–6ft
(90–180cm) tall.

T. orientalis *N. and W. China*
Chinese arbor vitae
Foliage: year-round. H:30–50ft
(9–15m), S:10–15ft (3–4.5m). Z:6–9.
This slow-growing large shrub or
small tree has an irregularly
rounded crown. Erect branches
carry scentless pale acid-green
leaves in flattened vertical sprays.
The bark is fibrous and the egg-
shaped cones a glaucous gray,
ripening to brown. At only 2ft

Thuja orientalis

(60cm), '**Aurea Nana**' makes a
dwarf globe-shaped bush with
yellow-green foliage that turns
bronze in winter. The foliage of the
small columnar '**Elegantissima**',
which grows to 15ft (4.5m), is
golden yellow, developing bronze
tinges and turning green in winter.

T. plicata *North America*
Western red cedar
Foliage: year-round. H:70–120ft
(22–35m), S:20–30ft (6–9m). Z:5–9.
This is a vigorous long-lived tree
with a neat conical shape. The bark
is light to reddish brown and peels
and flakes as the tree ages. The
bright green leaves have a white
cross on the underside. Flat and
made up of numerous small scalelike sections, they release a strong
pineapple-like aroma when
crushed. It is an excellent plant
for growing as a freestanding
specimen, but is also easily
controlled to make a dense hedge
or screen. '**Atrovirens**' (Z:5–8),
very upright and suitable for
hedging, has exceptionally dark
and glossy leaves. '**Rogersii**'
(Z:5–8) slowly forms a compact
cone 3–4ft (90–120cm) tall with
gold and bronze foliage. '**Stoneham
Gold**' (Z:5–8), with a height and
spread of 6ft (1.8m), is green with
coppery shoots. '**Zebrina**' makes a
conical tree up to 50ft (15m) tall,
with yellow banding to the leaves
that is particularly marked on
specimens grown in full sun.

Thuja plicata 'Zebrina'

TSUGA

PINACEAE Hemlock

Elegant sweeping branches and a
broadly conical outline are typical
of the 10 or 11 species of these
evergreen conifers, which originate
from North America and northern
and eastern Asia. The needles are
blunt and short, often white
underneath against the dark or

blue-green upper surface. The small
cones are pendulous and remain
on the tree for as long as 3 years.
CULTIVATION Tolerate partial shade.
Require moist but well-drained soil,
preferably neutral to acid, and
shelter from cold winds. Trim
hedges during summer. Can be
pruned.
PROPAGATION From seed, sown in
spring. From ripe cuttings, in
autumn (cultivars).
POTENTIAL PROBLEMS Wooly adelgid,
scale, mites; cankers; sensitive to
environmental pollution.

Tsuga canadensis 'Pendula'

T. canadensis *E. North America*
Canada hemlock, eastern hemlock
Foliage: year-round. H:50–80ft
(15–25m), S:20–30ft (6–9m). Z:3–7.
The gray shoots of this broadly
conical conifer produce dark green
leaves, which are often inverted to
reveal silver lines beneath. The oval
cones are light brown and up to
1in (2.5cm) long. '**Jeddeloh**', up to
5ft (1.5m) tall and as much as 6ft
(1.8m) across, makes a light green
bush with branches arching out
from a very low center. '**Pendula**'
slowly builds into a mound up to
6ft (1.8m) tall of drooping
branches.

T. heterophylla *W. North
America (Alaska to California)*
Western hemlock
Foliage: year-round. H:70–100ft
(22–30m), S:20–30ft (6–9m). Z:6–9.
In addition to being an extremely
valuable and fast-growing lumber
tree with light straight-grained
wood and tannin-rich bark that is
used in the leather industry, the
western hemlock is one of the
most graceful of all conifers. This
narrowly conical tree, displaying
cracked purple-brown bark, has
slender branches, the lower ones
drooping. The flattened needlelike
leaves are dark green with silvery
bands underneath and the small
shoots are slightly pendulous.
The oval pale green cones ripen
to dark brown. Tolerant of shade,
this makes a handsome specimen
tree and is also an excellent
hedging plant.

climbers

True climbers are plants that are able to support themselves by grasping onto their surroundings. A wall, fence, arch, arbor, trellis, or even other plants are among the objects that may accommodate their progress. The range of modifications that enables climbers to cling and grow over a large area includes sucker pads, aerial roots, twining stems, thorns, and tendrils.

Climbers introduce a vertical dimension to the garden. Many of the plants available make living screens to cover or camouflage areas or objects in the garden or to ornament trees or shrubs. Deciduous species, such as the familiar Virginia creeper (*Parthenocissus tricuspidata*), display vivid color in autumn, while evergreens, including the various forms of ivy, are verdant or variegated throughout the year.

A range of figures is given for the heights of climbers in the information that heads each entry, but it is important to bear in mind that the ultimate height will depend on the type of support provided. No spread is given for the plants because this depends on the method of training.

Climbers are grown in containers and can be transplanted throughout the year, although the best time to transplant them is in spring, once the danger of severe frosts has passed and as new growth is starting.

Top *Clematis viticella* **'Purpurea Plena Elegans'**
Center *Jasminum polyanthum*
Bottom *Campsis* × *tagliabuana* **'Madame Galen'**

ACONITUM

RANUNCULACEAE Aconite, monkshood

This genus of 100 species consists of hardy herbaceous perennials, including some twining climbers, occurring throughout the Northern Hemisphere, often in grassland or scrub. They have slender spires of usually blue or purple, helmet-shaped or hooded blooms, and glossy dark green leaves with deeply divided lobes. See also PERENNIALS.
CULTIVATION Prefer partial shade but tolerate full sun. Require fertile, moist but well-drained soil.
PROPAGATION From seed, sown in spring. By division, in autumn.
POTENTIAL PROBLEMS Aphids, slugs; fungal stem rot, verticillium wilt.
WARNING All parts of the plant are toxic if consumed. Contact with the foliage may irritate skin.

A. hemsleyanum C. and W. China

Flowers: mid-summer to early autumn. H:6-10ft (1.8-3m). Z:5-8. This twining climber's scrambling habit makes it ideal for growing through shrubs. It bears racemes of soft lilac-purple flower spikes.

Aconitum hemsleyanum

ACTINIDIA

ACTINIDIACEAE

This genus contains 40 species of mostly deciduous twining climbers, native to light forests in eastern Asia. They are highly valued for their striking ornamental foliage. Male and female flowers, generally less interesting than the foliage, are usually carried on separate plants, although hermaphrodite plants do occur. The vigorous Chinese gooseberry, also known as kiwi fruit (*A. deliciosa*, Z:8-9), mainly grown as a fruiting climber, has impressively large, heart-shaped leaves that are carried on hairy shoots. Tara vine (*A. arguta*, Z:5-8) is another vigorous species that is capable of clambering high into tall trees; its leaves are light green

and heart shaped, with toothed margins, and turn a rich golden color in autumn. It bears edible but insipid fruits. Some species, including Chinese gooseberry (*A. deliciosa*) and *A. kolomikta*, induce rapture in cats, who chew and rub against the stems.
CULTIVATION Require full sun, shelter from strong winds, and moist but well-drained soil. Thin out overcrowded growth in spring.
PROPAGATION From semiripe cuttings, in late summer. From seed, sown in autumn or spring.
POTENTIAL PROBLEMS Usually none.

Actinidia kolomikta

A. kolomikta E. Asia

Foliage: early summer. Flowers: early summer. H:10-15ft (3-4.5m). Z:5-8.
This deciduous twining climber is grown for the striking variegation of its dark green leaves; the tips or sometimes even the whole leaf may be white with a pink tinge. The coloration is most marked early in the season, and in leaves that are in full sun. On female plants, the fragrant but insignificant white flowers may be followed by edible, yellow-green fruits in autumn.

AKEBIA

LARDIZABALACEAE Chocolate vine

The genus comprises about 5 deciduous and semievergreen twining climbers from forest margins in east Asia. They are valued both for their elegant foliage, with compound leaves composed of 3 or 5 leaflets, and for their ornamental, spicily fragrant flowers. These are borne in pendant racemes, with small male flowers at the tip, and larger, cup-shaped female flowers near the base. If different clones are grown together, attractive violet, sausage-shaped seedpods may form in early autumn. *A trifoliata* (Z:6-8) is similar to *A. quinata*, except it is fully deciduous and its leaves have 3 radiating leaflets.
CULTIVATION Tolerate light shade or full sun, preferably in a sheltered

site and fertile, moist but well-drained soil. To fruit well, need warm springs and hot summers.
PROPAGATION From semihardwood cuttings, taken in summer. By layering, in winter. From seed, as soon as ripe.
POTENTIAL PROBLEMS Usually none.

Akebia quinata

A. quinata China, Japan, Korea

Foliage: year-round in mild winters. Flowers: mid-spring. Fruits: early autumn. H:20-30ft (6-9m). Z:5-8.
The leaves of this semievergreen twining climber are usually made up of 5 rounded, untoothed, dark green leaflets; when young, they are suffused with bronze-purple. The stems are dark purple-red. Vanilla-scented, cup-shaped female flowers have large, dark maroon sepals. If fertilized, they produce long, gray-violet, sausage-like pods, which split open when ripe to reveal white pulp and black seeds.

AMPELOPSIS

VITACEAE

Like the vines in the closely related genus *Vitis*, the 20 or so species of *Ampelopsis* have twining stem tendrils. They are deciduous woodland plants of Asia and North America, mainly grown for their foliage, although the fruits that follow the insignificant flowers are also of ornamental value.
A. aconitifolia (Z:5-7) is a slender species with pea-sized orange fruits.
CULTIVATION Tolerate full sun or partial shade (they fruit best in full sun) and require moist but well-drained soil.
PROPAGATION From softwood cuttings, in summer. From seed, sown in autumn or spring.
POTENTIAL PROBLEMS Usually none.

A. glandulosa var. *brevipedunculata* N.E. Asia

Foliage: autumn. Flowers: late spring. Fruits: autumn. H:15-25ft (4.5-7.5m). Z:5-8.
The hoplike leaves, with 3 or 5 lobes, are dark green and hairy on the undersides. If grown against a

warm wall, this climber will bear attractive, near-spherical, bright blue fruit in autumn. **'Elegans'** is a less vigorous form of the species, with irregular, agitated variegation in white, pink, and green.

Ampelopsis glandulosa **var. brevipedunculata 'Elegans'**

BERBERIDOPSIS

FLACOURTIACEAE

Although rare in cultivation, this single species, an evergreen twining climber from moist forests in Chile, is now thought to be extinct in the wild.
CULTIVATION Requires partial shade and neutral to acid, moist but well-drained soil.
PROPAGATION From semiripe stem cuttings, in late summer. By layering, in autumn.
POTENTIAL PROBLEMS Usually none.

Berberidopsis corallina

B. corallina Chile
Coral plant
Foliage: year-round. Flowers: late summer to early autumn.
H:12–18ft (3.7–5.5m). Z:7–9.
The dark green, oblong leaves have spiny margins and are leathery in texture. They form a striking contrast to the drooping clusters of near-spherical, deep red flowers, dangling on red stalks.

BOUGAINVILLEA

NYCTAGINACEAE

Among the 14 species in the genus, all native of forest and scrub in South America, are several scrambling, sometimes thorny climbers. They may be evergreen

or partly deciduous. Bougainvilleas seem to be covered for months by vivid, showy flowers. However, it is the bracts surrounding the flowers that are so colorful and long lasting; the true flowers are insignificant. **'Scarlett O'Hara'** (Z:9–10) is a vigorous climber, with bright crimson to scarlet bracts. The hybrids of *B. glabra*, *B. peruviana*, and *B. spectabilis* (all Z:9–10) should be grown under glass in frost-prone areas.
CULTIVATION Require full sun and fertile, well-drained soil. In early spring, remove all thin weak growths and shorten the main stems to about two-thirds.
PROPAGATION From semiripe cuttings, from mid- to late summer.
POTENTIAL PROBLEMS Red spider mites, mealybugs, scale.

Bougainvillea **'Scarlett O'Hara'**

B. × *buttiana*
Flowers: mid-summer to autumn.
H:25–40ft (7.5–12m). Z:9–10.
This strong, vigorous, evergreen climber, a hybrid of *B. glabra* and *B. peruviana*, has purple, red, or rich yellow floral bracts. Oval, dull green leaves conceal small sharp spines on the stems. **'Mrs Butt'** has crimson-magenta bracts. Numerous newer hybrids of *B.* × *buttiana* are now available.

CAMPSIS

BIGNONIACEAE Trumpet creeper, trumpet vine

Both of the 2 species in this genus are deciduous climbers, found in woodland in China and North America, usually climbing by aerial roots. They produce trusses of trumpet-shaped flowers in shades of orange and scarlet, and the leaves are pinnate, composed of about 7 leaflets. The Chinese trumpet creeper or vine (*C. grandiflora*, Z:7–9) has larger flowers, which are orange and red veined in the throat, with paler lobes. Its aerial roots are less secure than those of the common trumpet creeper (*C. radicans*, Z:5–9), from S.E. USA. Where summers are cool, they tend to flower poorly unless

the wood is ripened by exposure to full sun.
CULTIVATION Require full sun, although they will tolerate partial shade in warm climates, and fertile but well-drained soil.
PROPAGATION From semiripe cuttings, in late summer or early autumn. By layering or from rooted suckers, in spring.
POTENTIAL PROBLEMS Red spider mites, mealybugs, scale; powdery mildew.

Campsis × *tagliabuana* **'Madame Galen'**

C. × *tagliabuana* **'Madame Galen'**
Foliage: autumn. Flowers: late summer to early autumn.
H:20–40ft (6–12m). Z:5–9.
This hybrid freely produces trusses of up to 12 salmon-red, trumpet-shaped flowers. In autumn, the light to mid-green leaves turn yellow and the young, light gray-green stems age to creamy brown.

CELASTRUS

CELASTRACEAE Bittersweet, staff vine

There are about 30 species of shrubs and twining climbers in the genus, most of which are deciduous and native to thickets and woodland in tropical or subtropical regions. These climbers are particularly attractive when trained into sturdy trees. The flowers are inconspicuous, and in some species male and female flowers are borne on separate plants. Several hardy species are grown for their brightly colored autumn fruits. American bittersweet (*C. scandens*, Z:4–8) bears pea-sized fruits containing scarlet seeds, but both a male and female plant are required. It is fully hardy, but only fruits well in a warm climate.
CULTIVATION Tolerate full sun or partial shade and most soils. Remove up to one-third of the old branches in spring, but leave plants growing in trees unpruned.
PROPAGATION By layering, in spring. By seed, sown as soon as ripe.
POTENTIAL PROBLEMS Usually none.

C. orbiculatus *E. Asia*

Oriental bittersweet, staff vine
Foliage: autumn. Flowers: early
summer. Fruits: autumn. H:25–40ft
(7.5–12m). Z:5–9.

The almost rounded, scalloped to
toothed mid-green leaves of this
vigorous often invasive climber
have pointed tips and turn yellow
in autumn. When the
inconspicuous green flowers are
fertilized, they are followed in
autumn by beadlike, yellow fruits.
These split open when ripe to
reveal scarlet-coated seeds. Male
and female flowers are usually
borne on separate plants, but a
single plant of the **Hermaphrodite
Group** will bear crops of fruits.

Celastrus orbiculatus

CLEMATIS

RANUNCULACEAE

In this large genus of about 250
deciduous and evergreen species,
a high proportion are subshrubby
climbers. Most are plants of forest
and woodland, widely distributed
in both hemispheres, mainly in
temperate regions. The climbing
species attach themselves to
supports by means of twining leafstalks. The flowers are often very
showy, particularly those of the
numerous hybrids, and they vary
greatly in shape, size, color, and
flowering season. The petallike
segments, which are in fact sepals,
are often of contrasting color to
the conspicuous central stamens.
Some clematis also carry stamens
that are petallike, giving a double
effect. Feathery seeds are an
attractive feature of many species
at the end of the season.

In addition to the climbing
species and hybrids, there are a
few clematis that are lax or semi-
climbing perennials or subshrubs;
they all need supports when
grown in beds. These include
C. × durandii (Z:4–9) with large,
single, indigo-blue flowers, and
C. × jouiniana (Z:4–9), with small
flowers that are creamy white and
gray-blue. The climbing clematis
described here are all deciduous,
unless otherwise stated.

Clematis × durandii

CULTIVATION Tolerate full sun or
partial shade, with the roots and
base in shade. Require moist but
well-drained soil. Tie in securely
initially. Pruning depends on
flowering time, according to these
categories:
(i) Early-flowering species that
flower winter to early spring:
prune immediately after flowering,
removing dead or damaged
growth; most require only light
trimming to restrict size.
(ii) Large-flowered hybrids that
flower late spring to early summer,
in some cases flowering again
later: prune in early spring, before
growth starts, removing dead or
damaged growth and cutting back
stems at the topmost strong buds.
(iii) Large- and small-flowered
species and hybrids, including
herbaceous clematis, that flower
mid-summer to autumn: prune in
late winter, before growth starts,
cutting back the previous season's
stems to a height of about 6in
(15cm), making the cut above a
pair of strong buds.
PROPAGATION From softwood
cuttings, in early spring. From
semiripe cuttings, in mid-summer
(climbing species only). By
division, in early spring
(herbaceous clematis only).
POTENTIAL PROBLEMS Aphids,
earwigs, slugs; powdery mildew,
clematis wilt.

SPECIES

C. alpina *Europe*

Alpine clematis
Flowers: spring. H:6–8ft (1.8–2.5m).
Z:4–8. Pruning group (i).
The early nodding flowers, usually
mauve-blue, are carried singly on
brownish green stems. The pale to
mid-green leaves are broadly oval
and end in a pointed tip. Silky
seedheads are produced in the
autumn and last well into the
winter. '**Frances Rivis**' is larger
and more vigorous, and is grown
for its deep blue, white-centered
flowers. Also larger, **subsp.
sibirica** '**White Moth**' bears
creamy white double flowers.

C. armandii *China*

Foliage: year-round. Flowers: early
spring. H:20–30ft (6–9m). Z:7–9.
Pruning group (i).
The evergreen, glossy, dark green
leaves, each with 3 leathery
leaflets with 3 veins, are copper
tinted when young. The shiny
green stems are slightly tinged
with red when young, but turn
dull green with age. The densely
clustered fragrant flowers, each
with 5 or 6 sepals, are white or
occasionally, as in '**Apple
Blossom**', pink and white.

C. cirrhosa *Europe*

Foliage: year-round. Flowers: early
to late winter. H:8–12ft (2.5– 3.7m).
Z:7–9. Pruning group (i).
This evergreen clematis has dainty,
fernlike, light to mid-green foliage.
The small, creamy white flowers,
spotted with pink inside, are bell
shaped and nodding, and borne
singly or in pairs. '**Freckles**' has
sepals with maroon-pink markings.

Clematis florida '**Sieboldii**'

C. florida '**Flore Pleno**'

Flowers: late spring to early
summer. H:8–10ft (2.5–3m). Z:6–9.
Pruning group (ii).
Flowering in late spring to early
summer, this clematis carries an
abundance of large, double,
greenish cream flowers, up to 5in
(12.5cm) across. A less vigorous
but striking plant, '**Sieboldii**', has
deep purple-red, petallike stamens
at the center of its large, creamy
white flowers.

C. macropetala *China (Gansu),
Mongolia, Russia (Siberia)*

Flowers: late spring to early
summer. H:8–10ft (2.5–3m). Z:5–9.
Pruning group (ii).
The slender stems carry fernlike
foliage and nodding blue flowers.
The 4 sepals surround numerous
petallike stamens, which are
usually creamy white, creating a
double effect. The flowers of
'**Maidwell Hall**' are deep blue on
the outside, with lighter blue,
petallike stamens. '**Markham's
Pink**' bears rich mauve-pink
flowers.

C. montana *C. and W. China, Himalayas*
Flowers: early summer. H:30–40ft (9–12m). Z:6–9. Pruning group (i). Deservedly popular for its vigor, tolerance of a wide range of conditions, and its prodigious display of white flowers, this species is best planted where it can grow unchecked. '**Elizabeth**' bears large, pale pink, vanilla-scented flowers, which make an attractive contrast to the bronze-green foliage. The flowers of **var. rubens** are mauve-pink, becoming paler with age, and the foliage is purple flushed.

Clematis montana var. rubens

C. tangutica *W. China*
Flowers: late summer to early autumn. H:15–20ft (4.5–6m). Z:3–8. Pruning group (iii). Balloon-shaped buds open to nodding, solitary, bell-shaped yellow flowers, with pointed sepals and a prominent central boss of stamens. The flowers are borne above the light green, fern-like foliage, and are followed by silvery white, silky seedheads.

C. tibetana subsp. **vernayi**
Nepal, Tibet
Flowers: autumn. H:20–25ft (6–7.5m). Z:6–9. Pruning group (iii). The finely divided leaves are bluish-green, with a waxy texture to the upper sides. The nodding, bell-shaped flowers range in color from orange-yellow to greenish yellow with purple flecks. When the flowers open, the thick, spongy sepals curl outward to reveal purple stamens. It is the color and texture of the sepals that give '**Orange Peel**' its name. The hybrid *C.* '**Bill MacKenzie**' is similar, with yellow flowers.

C. viticella *Central S. Europe*
Flowers: autumn. H:8–12ft (2.5–3.7m). Z:3–8. Pruning group (iii).
The numerous small, nodding flowers, usually violet-blue or purple, make this a delightful late-season climber. It is a parent of many very fine, small-flowered

hybrids. They are listed here under *C.* hybrids (small-flowered), under their cultivar names. '**Purpurea Plena Elegans**' has double, violet-purple flowers, 3in (7.5cm) across.

HYBRIDS

C. hybrids (large-flowered)
Flowers: late spring to early autumn. H:6–12ft (1.8–3.7m). Z:5–8. Pruning group (ii) or (iii), depending on flowering time (see Cultivation).
The large-flowered hybrids come in various shades of white, cream, pink, red, purple, and blue, often with contrasting stamens. The color, size, and form of the flowers are greatly influenced by temperature and other weather conditions during bud development. Some cultivars have a few, quite separate, pointed sepals, while others with a larger number of rounded sepals make an almost circular or saucer-shaped bloom. The following is a small selection of the large-flowered cultivars available:
'**Comtesse de Bouchaud**', mauve-pink flowers with cream anthers in summer; '**Countess of Lovelace**', deep mauve-blue flowers in early summer (double) to early autumn (single); '**Duchess of Edinburgh**', short growing, to 10ft (3m), with double, creamy white flowers faintly tinged with green, in early to late summer; '**Edith**', large white flowers with prominent red-brown anthers, in late spring to early autumn; '**Elsa Späth**', deep violet-blue flowers with large sepals and reddish-purple anthers, in early summer to early autumn (early flowers are large, later flowers are smaller and better formed); '**Général Sikorski**', mid-blue flowers with overlapping sepals, purple tinged at the base, and a central boss of golden yellow anthers, in early summer to early autumn; '**Henryi**', with creamy white sepals and a central boss of light brown anthers, in early to late summer; '**Huldine**', pure white flowers with mauve undersides

Clematis '**Lasurstern**'

and creamy white stamens, in early to mid-autumn; '**Jackmanii Superba**', deep purple flowers with large, rounded sepals, in mid-summer to early autumn; '**Lady Caroline Nevill**', mauve-blue flowers with a darker central stripe on the 8 sepals, in summer to autumn; '**Lasurstern**', large flat flowers, purple-blue to mauve-blue, the sepals with ruffled edges, appear in 2 flushes: early spring to early summer, and late summer to early autumn; '**Marie Boisselot**', very large, pure white flowers with broad, overlapping sepals and light brown anthers, in early and late summer; '**Miss Bateman**', pale cream flowers with deep brown anthers, in mid-spring to early summer; '**Niobe**', deepest velvet-red flowers with 6 sepals with ruffled edges, and a central boss of cream stamens, throughout summer; '**Perle d'Azur**', light blue flowers, faintly tinted mauve-pink, with creamy green centers, in mid-summer to autumn; '**Proteus**', mauve-pink with cream stamens, in mid-summer (double) and autumn (single); '**Rouge Cardinal**', deep crimson-red flowers with a tuft of cream stamens, in early summer to early autumn; '**The President**', saucer-shaped flowers in deep blue-purple with a paler stripe, and red-purple anthers, in late spring to early autumn; '**Vyvyan Pennell**', double, subtly shaded flowers, purple-carmine with mauve-blue inner sepals, and a central boss of yellow stamens, in late spring to mid-summer.

Clematis '**Abundance**'

C. hybrids (small-flowered)
Flowers: mid-summer to early autumn. H:8–12ft (2.5–3.7m). Z:4–8. Pruning group (iii). Many small-flowered clematis (cultivars or hybrids of *C. viticella*) revive the garden in late summer and autumn with masses of nodding flowers. Their many merits include a long and reliable flowering period relatively late in the season, ease of pruning, and resistance to wilt. Some of the best cultivars include '**Abundance**',

Clematis 'Alba Luxurians'

deep red to pink flowers with darker veins and 4 sepals; '**Alba Luxurians**', white flowers with dark stamens and 4 twisted, green-tipped sepals; '**Étoile Violette**' (Z:6–9), violet-purple flowers with 5 or 6 sepals and creamy stamens; '**Kermesina**' (Z:6–9), crimson-red flowers; '**Pagoda**' (Z:5–8), dainty, nodding, bell-shaped flowers of pale mauve-pink; '**Royal Velours**' (Z:5–8), royal-purple, velvety flowers with black anthers.

Clematis 'Étoile Violette'

COBAEA

COBAEACEAE

About 20 species of these evergreen climbers are found in forests and thickets in tropical America. Only 1, *C. scandens*, is widely grown. In the wild, this can reach 50ft (15m) or more, but it produces long-stalked, bell-shaped flowers in its first year and is commonly treated as a shorter-growing annual.
CULTIVATION Require full sun and moist but well-drained soil.
PROPAGATION From seed, sown under glass at 64°F (18°C) in spring.
POTENTIAL PROBLEMS Usually none.

C. scandens *Mexico*
Cathedral bell, cup and saucer vine
Foliage: year-round. Flowers: early summer to mid-autumn. H:12–20ft (3.7–6m). Z:9–11.
The leaves, composed of 4 to 6 rich green leaflets, terminate in branched tendrils, which hook on to supports and then tighten their grip. The honey-scented,

bell-shaped flowers are yellow-green at first, then purple, and grow from the upper leaf axils; they are backed by a 5-lobed, saucerlike calyx. In the case of **f. *alba***, white flowers age to creamy white.

Cobaea scandens

CODONOPSIS

CAMPANULACEAE

This genus includes 30 or so species of perennials, some of which are twining or scandent climbers, and annuals. All are Asiatic and mainly plants of scrub in mountainous areas. The climbers look best when their slender stems are allowed to work their way through or over a supporting shrub. The flowers are intricately marked on the inside.
CULTIVATION Tolerate full sun or partial shade. Require a sheltered site, particularly *C. convolvulacea*, and fertile, moist but well-drained soil rich in organic matter.
PROPAGATION From seed, sown in autumn or spring. From basal cuttings, between mid- and late spring.
POTENTIAL PROBLEMS Slugs, snails.

Codonopsis convolvulacea

C. convolvulacea *Himalayas, W. China*
Flowers: mid-summer. H:3–6ft (90–180cm). Z:5–8.
This slender-stemmed species bears star-shaped, pale blue to violet flowers, up to 2in (5cm) across. The shorter-growing *C. clematidea* has pale blue flowers with dark veining, and gold, black, and dark blue markings inside.

CUCURBITA

CUCURBITACEAE

The 25 species in this genus are trailing or climbing annuals and perennials of the Americas, the majority native to tropical and subtropical regions. They include pumpkin and squash, both of which are grown primarily for their edible fruits, but also for their ornamental qualities, such as their attractive large, lobed leaves. Other species are grown just for their ornamental gourds, since their flesh is bitter and inedible. Some of the plants in this genus make useful short-term groundcover, but they can also can be encouraged to climb. The ornamental gourds, with their smaller, lighter fruit, are more appropriate for climbing than the heavier pumpkins and squashes.
CULTIVATION Require full sun and fertile, moist soil heavily enriched with organic matter.
PROPAGATION From seed, sown under glass in mid-spring or where plants are to grow in late spring.
POTENTIAL PROBLEMS Slugs, snails; cucumber mosaic virus, gray mold (*Botrytis*), powdery mildew.

Cucurbita pepo

C. pepo *Mexico and S.W. USA*
Ornamental gourd
Flowers: summer to autumn.
Fruits: late summer to autumn.
H:8–16ft (2.5–5m). An.
Cultivars of this species include ornamental gourds and the summer squash. Their floppy yellow flowers are followed by smooth or warty fruits, which vary greatly in size, shape, and color. They may be dramatically striped or bicolored yellow and green.

ECCREMOCARPUS

BIGNONIACEAE

Of this genus of 5 climbers from forest margins and scrub in western South America, only a single species is widely grown. The Chilean glory flower (*E. scaber*) is a short-lived evergreen perennial, but is often grown as an annual. It

climbs by tendrils at the leaf tips, producing tubular flowers.
CULTIVATION Requires full sun and fertile, well-drained soil.
PROPAGATION From seed, sown under glasss at 61–66°F (16–19°C) in spring.
POTENTIAL PROBLEMS Red spider mites, whiteflies (under glass).

Eccremocarpus scaber

E. scaber *Chile*
Chilean glory flower
Flowers: early summer to mid-autumn. Fruits: autumn. H:10–15ft (3–4.5m). Z:7–9.
This is easily raised from seed in warmth, and flowers profusely in its first year. The narrow mouths of the orange-red tubular flowers are surrounded by 5 lobes. The fruit pods are bladderlike.

FALLOPIA

POLYGONACEAE

The 7 species in this genus are scrambling and climbing perennials native to moist habitats in temperate regions of the Northern Hemisphere. The climbing species are ideal for training through trees and on pergolas; the fast-growing species, such as Russian vine (*F. baldschuanica*), are particularly useful in larger gardens for quickly concealing eyesores.
CULTIVATION Tolerate full sun or partial shade and require moist but well-drained soil.
PROPAGATION From semiripe cuttings, in summer. From hardwood cuttings, in autumn. From seed, sown as soon as ripe.
POTENTIAL PROBLEMS Leaf miners.

F. baldschuanica *C. China, Tajikistan to W. China*
Mile-a-minute plant, Russian vine
Flowers: mid-summer to early autumn. H:40–50ft (12–15m). Z:4–9.
Highly vigorous and attractive, this climber is ideal for quickly concealing unsightly structures. However, it must be used with caution, particularly in a small garden, where its rampant growth may well be cause for regret.

Frothy sprays of tiny, pink-tinted flowers are followed by small pinkish white fruits. The foliage is dark green and heart shaped.

Fallopia baldschuanica

HEDERA

ARALIACEAE Ivy

Ivies are highly adaptable plants, either growing as climbers, when they attach themselves to surfaces by aerial roots, or trailing along the ground, making thick cover and rooting as they go. There are about 10 species, all evergreen and found chiefly in woodland from North Africa and Europe to Japan. There are 2 distinct phases of growth. In the juvenile stage, the ivy creeps or climbs by its roots. The leaves are usually 3- or 5-lobed, and all grow in the same direction. In the adult phase, the leaves are usually unlobed and arranged spirally on woody stems that do not have aerial roots. The stems bear rounded clusters of small, pale green flowers in autumn, followed by usually black fruits.
CULTIVATION Tolerate full sun or partial or dense shade (some variegation may scorch in full sun, and gold variegation generally becomes green in shade). Tolerate a wide range of soils.
PROPAGATION From softwood cuttings, from mid- to late summer. By layering, in late summer.
POTENTIAL PROBLEMS Red spider mites, scale, aphids.
WARNING All parts of ivy may cause great discomfort if eaten. The sap may irritate skin.

H. canariensis *Algeria, Tunisia*
Canary Island ivy, North African ivy
Foliage: year-round. Flowers: winter to early spring. H:15–20ft (4.5–6m). Z:8–10.
The purplish stalks of this ivy carry roughly triangular leaves that are heart shaped at the base. Their glossy, bright green color usually turns bronze in winter. '**Gloire de Marengo**', which is a popular houseplant, has silver-green leaves with irregular creamy white margins.

H. colchica *Caucasus, N. Iran*
Bullock's heart ivy, Persian ivy
Foliage: year-round. Flowers: winter to early spring. H:20–30ft (6–9m). Z:6–9.
Dark green, leathery leaves, almost heart shaped and lemon scented when crushed, are as much as 10in (25cm) long. It is highly vigorous, but '**Dentata**', with thinner leaves, slightly toothed at the margins, grows even more rapidly. '**Dentata Variegata**', about 15ft (4.5m) tall, has gray-green leaves with irregular yellow, later creamy white margins. '**Sulphur Heart**', of similar height, has light green or yellow splashes in the center of each leaf.

Hedera colchica 'Dentata Variegata'

H. helix *Europe*
Common ivy, English ivy
Foliage: year-round. Flowers: winter to early spring. H:30–40ft (9–12m). Z:5–9.
The common ivy, with glossy, dark green 3- or 5-lobed leaves, is vigorous and tough, both as a climber and trailing plant. It has produced many fine, highly variable cultivars. '**Congesta**' and '**Erecta**' are shrubby, nonclimbing forms, with upright stems and leaves arranged in 2 ranks. The cultivars are usually less vigorous than the species, but many grow as tall as 15–25ft (4.5–7.5m). In the selection below, approximate heights are given for shorter-growing cultivars only: '**Adam**', neat, 3-lobed leaves, gray-green with irregular creamy white margins and tinged pink in winter; '**Buttercup**', 5-lobed leaves, yellow-green in sun but pale green in

Hedera helix 'Duckfoot'

shade, 6ft (1.8m); '**Cavendishii**', gently lobed, gray-marbled leaves with a broad, irregular creamy white margin; '**Duckfoot**', small, green, shallow-lobed leaves with wedge-shaped bases, 30in (75cm); '**Glacier**' (Z:6–9), small, 3- to 5-lobed, gray-green leaves with silver-gray patches and irregular creamy white margins, 8ft (2.5m); '**Green Ripple**', glossy, elegantly jagged leaves, with forward-pointing lobes and prominent pale veins, 6ft (1.8m); '**Ivalace**', glossy dark green leaves with paler veins, the 5 shallow lobes with frilly margins, 3ft (90cm); '**Kolibri**' (Z:6–9), neat, very bright, white-splashed leaves with 5 lobes, the center lobe long and pointed, 4ft (1.2m); '**Königers Auslese**', slender 5-lobed leaves, the center lobe very elongated, 6ft (1.8m); '**Oro di Bogliasco**', pink stems and glossy dark green leaves with 3 lobes and a conspicuous yellow splash in the center; '**Pedata**' (bird's foot ivy), dark green leaves with paler veins and 5 lobes, the center one long, the basal lobes pointing backward.

Hedera helix '**Glacier**'

H. hibernica *W. Europe*
Irish ivy
Foliage: year-round. Flowers: winter to early spring. H:20–30ft (6–9m). Z:5–9.
Although once classified as a form of common ivy (*H. helix*), this plant has larger leaves with broader, less well-pronounced lobes. '**Anne Marie**', which rarely exceeds 4ft (1.2m), has dainty, 5-lobed, gray-green leaves with creamy white margins. '**Deltoidea**', the shield or sweetheart ivy, reaches 15ft (4.5m) and has heart-shaped, glossy, dark green leaves, up to 4in (10cm) long, with overlapping basal lobes.

HUMULUS

CANNABACEAE Hop

The 2 species in this genus are perennial twining climbers of uncertain origin, but widely distributed in woodland, scrub, and hedgerows in the temperate Northern Hemisphere. *H. lupulus* is widely grown as a crop; the overlapping bracts that cover the female flowers provide the hops used in brewing. The species is grown mainly for its foliage, but the bracts are also attractive.
CULTIVATION Tolerate full sun or partial shade and prefer moist but well-drained soil.
PROPAGATION From semiripe cuttings, from early to mid-summer.
POTENTIAL PROBLEMS Hop mildew.

Humulus lupulus '**Aureus**'

H. lupulus *North America, W. Asia*
Hop
Flowers: spring to summer. Fruits: autumn. H:15–25ft (4.5–7.5m). Z:5–9.
The deeply lobed, light green leaves, 4–6in (10–15cm) long, are bristly with toothed margins. They are carried on square, thin twining stems. Yellow-leaved '**Aureus**' is useful for brightening dark corners.

HYDRANGEA

HYDRANGEACEAE

Of the 80 or so species usually considered to belong to this genus, most are deciduous or evergreen shrubs and small trees that are widely distributed in the temperate Northern Hemisphere and Central and South America. However, a few are vigorous climbers that cling to supports by means of aerial roots. They produce flat-topped flower clusters, which are composed mainly of small, fertile flowers. In the most showy species, larger sterile flowers orbit the cluster, as in the shrubby "lacecap" hydrangeas. The frost-hardy evergreen **H. serratifolia** (Z:7–9) can grow more than 50ft (15m) into trees, and produces fluffy white flower clusters of usually fertile flowers only. See also SHRUBS.
CULTIVATION Tolerate full sun or partial shade and require fertile, moist but well-drained soil.
PROPAGATION From cuttings, in late summer. By layering, in spring.
POTENTIAL PROBLEMS Aphids, red spider mites; gray mold (*Botrytis*), hydrangea virus, powdery mildew, leaf spot, honey fungus.
WARNING Eating any part of the plant can cause stomach upset. Contact with foliage can irritate skin allergies.

H. anomala subsp. petiolaris
Japan, Korea, Russia (Sakhalin), Taiwan
Climbing hydrangea
Foliage: autumn. Flowers: summer. H:30–50ft (9–15m). Z:5–8.
In the wild, this deciduous climber is capable of growing 80ft (25m) into the canopy of tall trees, but it is slow to get started and to attach itself to its support. The flower clusters consist of tiny, creamy green fertile flowers surrounded sparingly by sterile flowers, 1in (2.5cm) or more across. When the dark green leaves yellow and fall in autumn, the lattice of red-brown stems is revealed. This species can also be grown without supports to make a wide-spreading shrub.

Hydrangea anomala **subsp. petiolaris**

IPOMOEA

CONVOLVULACEAE Morning glory

This large genus of about 500 species, almost all plants of warm temperate to tropical regions from a wide range of habitats, contains numerous annual and perennial trailing or twining climbers. The relatively small number that are cultivated have elegant, tubular or funnel-shaped flowers and, in some cases, very intense coloring. Among the most striking of these are the blue dawn flower (*I. indica*), a vigorous, frost-tender perennial with purplish-blue flowers, and the red morning glory (*I. coccinea*), a frost-tender annual with yellow-throated scarlet flowers.
CULTIVATION Require full sun and light, moist but well-drained soil or potting media.
PROPAGATION From seed, sown under glass at 64°F (18°C) in mid-spring.
POTENTIAL PROBLEMS Aphids, whiteflies (under glass), slugs; viruses, powdery mildew.

I. purpurea Mexico
Common morning glory
Flowers: summer to autumn.
H:10–15ft (3–4.5m). An.
The bristly stems of this vigorous
annual climber carry heart-shaped,
sometimes 3-lobed leaves and
single or clustered flowers, which
unfurl from elegant buds. Their
color range includes white, purple-
blue, and pink, and they are
sometimes striped.

Ipomoea purpurea

I. tricolor Tropical Central and
South America
Morning glory
Flowers: summer to autumn.
H:8–12ft (2.5–3.7m). An.
This short-lived perennial is best
grown as an annual. The leaves are
heart shaped, and the delicate,
funnel-shaped flowers, usually
blue or purple and produced in
succession, fade within a day.
I. 'Heavenly Blue' has azure flowers
with contrasting white throats.

JASMINUM

OLEACEAE Jasmine, jessamine

A high proportion of the 200 to
300 evergreen and deciduous
shrubs and climbers in this genus
are tropical, found in a variety of
habitats. The climbers have
twining stems, and their tubular
flowers, opening to 5 petallike
lobes, are borne singly or in
clusters. The best-known species
have white flowers, but some
of the climbers, including
J. beesianum (Z:7–10) are pink
flowered, and many of the shrubby
species bear yellow flowers. An
essential oil extracted from the
fine-scented flowers has been
much used in perfumery. The
flowers of most species are
followed by black, berrylike fruits.
CULTIVATION Prefer full sun (but
tolerate light shade in warm
climates) and moist but well-
drained soil.
PROPAGATION From cuttings, taken
from summer to early autumn. By
layering, in autumn.
POTENTIAL PROBLEMS Aphids; gray
mold (*Botrytis*).

J. officinale Afghanistan,
Caucasus, Himalayas, N. Iran,
W. China
Common jasmine
Flowers: early summer to early
autumn. H:30–40ft (9–12m).
Z:8–10.
The beguiling scent of this deciduous
to semievergreen climber,
combined with its extended display
of white, star-shaped flowers set
against dark green foliage, has for
centuries delighted gardeners,
poets, and travelers throughout its
wide area of natural distribution. In
f. affine, the buds are tinged pink.
Variegated, less vigorous cultivars
include '**Argenteovariegatum**',
with white-edged, gray-green
leaves, and '**Aureum**', in which the
leaves are irregularly splashed
yellow.

Jasminum officinale

J. polyanthum W. and S.W. China
Foliage: year-round. Flowers: late
spring to early autumn. H:8–16ft
(2.5–5m). Z:9–10.
This evergreen climber, with its
pink- or red-tinted buds in large
clusters opening to strongly
fragrant, usually white flowers,
closely resembles *J. officinale*
f. *affine*. However, it is significantly
less hardy, and in many temperate
gardens is only suitable for a
conservatory or greenhouse.

Jasminum polyanthum

LAPAGERIA

PHILESIACEAE Chilean bellflower

This single species, the national
flower of Chile (known there as
"copihue"), clambers through
trees and shrubs in moist forests.

CULTIVATION Requires partial shade
in a warm site, and fertile, well-
drained, neutral to slightly acid soil
or lime-free (ericaceous/acid)
potting media.
PROPAGATION From seed, in spring.
By layering, in spring or autumn.
POTENTIAL PROBLEMS Aphids,
mealybugs, scale (under glass).

Lapageria rosea

L. rosea Chile
Foliage: year-round. Flowers:
summer to late autumn. H:12–16ft
(3.7–5m). Z:9–11.
The wiry, twining stems of this
climber carry leathery, pointed,
dark green leaves and a succession
of waxy, narrow, bell-shaped
flowers, up to 3in (7.5cm) long,
which hang singly or in groups of
2 or 3. The color range includes
pink, light crimson, and pink-
tinged white. '**Flesh Pink**' is
delicately colored, and '**Nash
Court**' has soft pink flowers lightly
marbled with a darker shade.

LATHYRUS

PAPILIONACEAE

This genus of approximately 150
species comprises annuals and
herbaceous or evergreen
perennials. They are found in a
wide range of habitats in the
temperate Northern Hemisphere,
North and eastern Africa, and
temperate South America. Their
flowers are pealike, often scented,
and available in a range of colors.
These climbers have leaves
composed of 2 leaflets and a
branched tendril. Lord Anson's
blue pea (*L. nervosus*, Z:8–9),
with fragrant, purplish blue
flowers, is a climbing herbaceous
species, which originates from the
Straits of Magellan.
CULTIVATION Require full sun and
well-drained soil. *L. odoratus*
requires plenty of organic matter
added.
PROPAGATION From seed, sown
under cover in autumn or early
spring.
POTENTIAL PROBLEMS Slugs.
WARNING Seeds may cause
stomach upset if eaten.

L. latifolius *S. Europe*
Everlasting pea, perennial pea
Flowers: summer to early autumn.
H:5–10ft (1.5–3m). Z:5–8.
The winged stems of this
herbaceous perennial climber
carry blue-green leaves and clusters
of purplish-pink flowers. '**White
Pearl**' bears lustrous, pure white
flowers. The Persian everlasting
pea (**L. rotundifolius**) is also fully
hardy, but is more slender and
carries pink flowers.

Lathyrus odoratus

L. odoratus *Italy (including Sicily)*
Sweet pea
Flowers: summer to early autumn.
H:6–10ft (1.8–3m). An.
The pealike flowers of this annual
climber, which can be prone to
powdery mildew, have a delicate
beauty and sweet fragrance. There
are numerous cultivars. "Old-
fashioned" sweet peas, the earliest
cultivars, have highly scented
flowers in red, pink, blue, and
white. Modern sweet peas
(Spencer cultivars) have larger
flowers, with graceful, wavy-edged
petals, and have a wider color
range; they are available in single
colors and mixtures. There are
numerous dwarf forms of sweet
peas; cultivars of the bushy **Bijou
Group** grow to approximately
18in (45cm); those of the **Jet Set
Group** and the **Knee-hi Group**
reach about 4ft (1.2m).

LONICERA

CAPRIFOLIACEAE Honeysuckle

Honeysuckles are widely distributed
in the Northern Hemisphere,
occurring in a range of habitats
from woodland to rocky terrain.
Of the 180 or so species, which
include some shrubs, the most
ornamental are the evergreen and
deciduous twining climbers. Their
flowers are tubular or bell shaped,
either 2-lipped or with 5 equal
lobes at the mouth, and borne in
pairs or in small whorls. The pale
to mid-green leaves in opposite
pairs vary in shape from broadly
oval to almost circular, and in some
species and hybrids the topmost

pair of leaves unites to form a
collar beneath the flowers. Honeysuckles are noted mainly for their
heady fragrance, but some of the
climbers are valuable simply for
the profusion of their flowers.
The most magnificent of all the
species is the half-hardy, giant
Burmese honeysuckle
(**L. hildebrandiana**, Z:10–11),
capable of growing to 60ft (18m),
with its sweetly scented, creamy
white flowers. Out of their natural
habitats, some species have become
serious weeds, as is the case with
Japanese honeysuckle (*L. japonica*,
Z:4–9) in parts of the USA. See also
SHRUBS.
CULTIVATION Tolerate full sun or
partial shade and a wide range of
soil types. Thin out old wood after
flowering.
PROPAGATION From semiripe
cuttings, in summer or hardwood
cuttings, in mid-autumn.
POTENTIAL PROBLEMS Aphids;
mildew.
WARNING Berries may cause
stomach upset if eaten.

L. × americana
Flowers: summer to early autumn.
Berries: autumn. H:20–30ft
(6–9m). Z:5–9.
This vigorous, deciduous twining
climber, which flowers prolifically
from summer to early autumn, is
strongly fragrant. The tubular
flowers are 2-lipped and yellow,
tinged with purple. The flowers
are followed in the autumn by
red berries.

Lonicera × *brownii* '**Dropmore
Scarlet**'

L. × brownii
Scarlet trumpet honeysuckle
Flowers: mid- to late summer.
H:10–15ft (3–4.5m). Z:2–9.
This deciduous or semievergreen
twining climber has orange-scarlet,
tubular, slightly 2-lipped flowers,
unfortunately without scent. The
blue- to mid-green leaves are
almost circular and carried in pairs
on thin, twiggy stems. One of the
parents of this hybrid, the coral
or trumpet honeysuckle
(**L. sempervirens**, Z:3–9), of the

eastern and southern USA, is
splendidly vivid, with tubular,
orange-scarlet, unscented flowers
opening to 5 equal lobes at the
mouth. It is frost hardy to fully
hardy. Cultivars of the hybrid
L. × brownii include the long-
flowering and richly colored
'**Dropmore Scarlet**' (Z:3–9).

L. caprifolium *Europe, W. Asia*
Italian honeysuckle
Flowers: summer. Berries: autumn.
H:15–20ft (4.5–6m). Z:5–9.
One of the most seductively
scented of all honeysuckles, this
deciduous species produces
creamy white to yellow flowers,
flushed with pink. The flowers are
cupped by the blue-green,
uppermost leaves, which are
united in pairs. Orange-red berries
appear in autumn.

L. japonica *E. Asia*
Japanese honeysuckle
Flowers: spring to late summer.
Berries: autumn. H:25–30ft
(7.5–9m). Z:4–9.
The foliage is evergreen, the leaves
sometimes lobed, and fragrant,
tubular white flowers, with soft
purple staining, are produced over
a long season. They are followed in
autumn by blue-black berries.

Lonicera periclymenum '**Graham
Thomas**'

L. periclymenum *Europe,
Caucasus, North Africa, Turkey*
Common honeysuckle, woodbine
Flowers: mid- to late summer.
Berries: autumn. H:20–25ft
(6–7.5m). Z:5–9.
Long cultivated, this plant of
woodland and hedgerows is prized
for the sweet fragrance of its
flowers; in the evening, the scent
is particularly strong. The tubular,
white and yellow flowers are
flushed pink and red, and followed
by red berries in autumn. '**Belgica**'
(early Dutch honeysuckle) has
reddish purple flowers, fading to
white and yellow in late spring and
sometimes again in late summer.
'**Graham Thomas**', which flowers
throughout summer, is white in
bud, becoming yellow when open.

'Serotina' (late Dutch honey-suckle) is similar to 'Belgica' (early Dutch honeysuckle), but blooms from mid-summer to mid-autumn.

L. × tellmanniana
Flowers: late spring to mid-summer. H:12–18ft (3.7–5.5m). Z:6–8.
The striking appearance of the flowers of this deciduous hybrid more than compensates for its lack of scent. Carried in whorls cupped by the topmost pair of leaves, the flowers are large, 2-lipped, and glowing amber-colored, flushed scarlet in bud. The foliage is dark green, with blue-white undersides.

PARTHENOCISSUS

VITACEAE Virginia creeper

This is a small genus of vines, comprising about 10 species of deciduous climbers equipped with tendrils, which in most cases are tipped with adhesive suckers. They are mainly tree-climbing plants of forest and woodland in the Himalayas, east Asia, and North America; however, those with suckerlike pads are ideal for climbing walls. Virginia creeper is grown mainly for its lobed or entirely divided, layered leaves, which provide a luxuriant display in summer and are usually brightly colored in autumn. The flowers are insignificant and are followed by grapelike berries.
CULTIVATION Tolerate full sun or partial shade and a fertile, well-drained soil.
PROPAGATION From softwood or greenwood cuttings, in summer. From hardwood cuttings, in winter. From seed, sown under glass in autumn.
POTENTIAL PROBLEMS Usually none.
WARNING Berries can cause mild stomach upset if eaten.

P. henryana China
Silvervein creeper
Foliage: autumn. H:20–30ft (6–9m). Z:7–8.
Attaching itself by disklike suckers, this handsome species quickly climbs walls and trees. The adult leaves consist of 3 to 5 coarsely toothed leaflets, which achieve their finest coloration in shade. The upper sides are velvety green, sometimes lightly bronzed, with silvery gray veins; the undersides, like the leafstalks, are reddish. In autumn, the leaves turn vivid red.

P. quinquefolia E. North America
Virginia creeper
Foliage: autumn. Flowers: late spring to early summer. H:40–60ft (12–18m). Z:4–9.

Whether growing into lofty trees or on walls, this vigorous, self-clinging vine becomes a vision of glowing crimson in autumn. The leaves are composed of 3 or 5 coarsely serrated leaflets.

P. tricuspidata China, Japan, Korea
Boston ivy
Foliage: autumn. Flowers: spring to summer. H:40–60ft (12–18m). Z:5–8.
This is a secure, self-clinging vine of great vigor, although growth may be slow to start. The lustrous leaves are very variable in size and shape: in young plants, they are often indistinctly lobed, while in mature plants they are usually 3-lobed and up to 8in (20cm) across. In autumn, the leaves turn reddish purple to scarlet; the young purple shoots retain their striking color after the leaves have dropped. Cultivars include 'Beverley Brook', with purple-tinted summer foliage that turns bright red in autumn, and 'Veitchii', with dark reddish purple foliage in autumn. Both grow to about 23ft (7m) tall.

Parthenocissus tricuspidata

PASSIFLORA

PASSIFLORACEAE Passion flower

Tropical South America is the home of many of the 400 or so species in this genus, which are predominantly evergreen climbers that attach themselves to supports with twining tendrils. The common name is a reference to Christ's suffering: the parts of the highly distinctive flowers are interpreted as representing his own attributes and the instruments of his Passion. Each flower has a tubular base and 10 segments, which usually spread out flat. A stalk in the center of each flower holds a distinctive organ bearing the ovary and stamens, and is surrounded by a ring of filaments, known as the corona (interpreted as the crown of thorns). The flowers, in many species pendant, are followed by egg-shaped or spherical fruits, some of which are highly valued

for their flavorsome pulp. The best known of these is the frost-tender passion fruit (*P. edulis*, Z:10–11), which has white flowers and yellow to purple fruit.
CULTIVATION Tolerate full sun or partial shade and require fertile, moist but well-drained soil in a sheltered site. Remove frost-damaged growth in mid-spring. Trim out one-third of the main growths each year, and cut back side-shoots to 6in (15cm).
PROPAGATION From semiripe cuttings, from mid- to late summer. From seed, sown under glass at 55–64°F (13–18°C) in spring.
POTENTIAL PROBLEMS Viral infections.

Passiflora caerulea

P. caerulea C. and W. South America
Blue passion flower
Flowers: mid- to late summer. Fruits: H:20–30ft (6–9m). Z:7–9.
If cut down in winter, this fast-growing species will shoot up again in the spring to make a fresh tangle of new growth. The divided, fingerlike leaves are dark green, and the large, lightly scented flowers contain purplish blue filaments, which stand out against the white segments. Egg-shaped orange-yellow fruits, edible but not flavorsome, sometimes follow. 'Constance Elliot' is less vigorous, with white flowers.

RHODOCHITON

SCROPHULARIACEAE

This very small genus consists of only 3 species of perennial climbers from woodland in Mexico. They are grown for their attractive pendant flowers, each consisting of a 5-lobed, hatlike calyx, protecting the long-tubed corolla, which opens out into 5 petallike lobes.
CULTIVATION Require full sun and fertile, moist but well-drained soil or potting media.
PROPAGATION From seed, sown under glass at 59–64°F (15–18°C) or as soon as ripe, in spring.
POTENTIAL PROBLEMS Red spider mites, whiteflies (under glass).

R. atrosanguineus *Mexico*
Flowers: summer to autumn.
H:8–10ft (2.5–3m). Z:9–11.
In mild conditions, this slender-
stemmed perennial is extremely
fast growing. Also quick to reach
flowering maturity, it can be
grown as an annual. It has heart-
shaped, rich green leaves and
small showers of purple-red
flowers, and climbs by means of
twining leaf and flower stalks.

Rhodochiton atrosanguineus

SCHISANDRA

SCHISANDRACEAE

There are about 25 species of
woody, deciduous, and evergreen
climbers in this genus; all are
native to east Asia, except for 1
plant from North America. They
are twining stem climbers of
woodland and open scrub. The
small, drooping blooms appear in
clusters at the leaf joints, male and
female flowers usually on separate
plants. Provided the female
flowers are fertilized, which
generally means having male and
female plants in close proximity to
each other, they are followed by
zigzagging, trailing strings of
luscious red fruits. The broad
green leaves give good autumn
color. They may take up to 5 years
to make substantial growth and to
flower well. **S. grandiflora**
(Z:8–9) is a rare species from the
Himalayas, with conspicuously
veined, leathery leaves and pale
pink hanging blooms in late spring
to early summer.
CULTIVATION Tolerate full sun or
light shade. Require fertile,
preferably neutral to acid, moist
but well-drained soil.
PROPAGATION From greenwood or
semiripe cuttings, from early to
mid-summer. From seed, sown in
spring.
POTENTIAL PROBLEMS Usually none.

S. chinensis *E. Asia*
Flowers: late spring. Fruits:
summer to autumn. H:20–30ft
(6–9m). Z:5–9.
With adequate support, this
deciduous climber is a tall-growing

species, although it can be trained
sideways or allowed to sprawl at
the top of a framework. Small,
fragrant, white- or pink-flushed
flowers in drooping clusters
appear in late spring. Where males
and females are planted together,
the flowers are followed by long-
lasting strings of fleshy red fruits.

S. rubriflora *Burma, India,
W. China*
Flowers: late spring to early
summer. Fruits: summer to autumn.
H:15–25ft (4.5–7.5m). Z:8–9.
Deep red, slightly fragrant flowers,
up to 1in (2.5cm) across, open
widely when mature. Long skeins
of red currantlike fruits sometimes
follow in summer to autumn. The
deciduous foliage is bold, dark
green, and glossy, with oval to
lance-shaped blades, up to 2in
(5cm) across.

Schisandra rubriflora

SCHIZOPHRAGMA

HYDRANGEACEAE

The 2 species in this genus are
woody-stemmed deciduous
climbers native to damp, shady
woodland in Japan, China, and
Korea. The elegant flowerheads,
which resemble those of a
hydrangea, are made up of many
tiny fertile flowers, and a few large
sterile bracts (actually modified
sepals). These climbers, with
broadly oval leaves, are self-
clinging, supporting themselves
with aerial roots. They are slow to
become established, but once they
begin flowering in earnest they are
ideal for climbing on walls or
through trees.
CULTIVATION Tolerate full sun or
partial shade (although flower best
in sun) in a sheltered site to
protect from winds. Prefer moist
but well-drained, neutral to slightly
acid soil, rich in organic matter.
PROPAGATION From greenwood
cuttings, from early to mid-summer
or from semihardwood cuttings,
in late summer. By layering, in
autumn. From seed, sown in
spring.
POTENTIAL PROBLEMS Usually none.

S. hydrangeoides
Flowers: summer to early autumn.
H:30–40ft (9–12m). Z:5–9.
The flat, "lacecap" flowerheads
have a scattering of sterile flowers
around the rim. Surrounding these
is a single, conspicuous, oval- to
heart-shaped creamy white bract.
The bracts remain on the plant for
some time after flowering,
prolonging interest. '**Roseum**' has
pale pink bracts.

Schizophragma integrifolium

S. integrifolium
Flowers: summer to late autumn.
H:30–40ft (9–12m). Z:5–9.
The large, flat "lacecap" flowerheads measure up to 12in (30cm)
across. They are white and
composed of fertile flowers and a
few marginal bracts. They are long
lasting and still attractive in
autumn and early winter when
they turn the color of parchment.
The leaves are large, broad, and
oval, with finely serrated margins.

SOLANUM

SOLANACEAE

This very large and highly varied
genus, with about 1,400 species
widely distributed throughout the
world in a range of habitats,
includes important vegetables,
such as potatoes (**S. tuberosum**,
An.), and several ornamental
plants. Among these are several
woody-stemmed climbers and
shrubs that can be wall trained.
CULTIVATION Require full sun and
moist but well-drained soil. Thin
out or remove overcrowded or
damaged growth in mid-spring.
PROPAGATION From stem cuttings,
in late summer.
POTENTIAL PROBLEMS Gray mold
(*Botrytis*).
WARNING Eating the fruits may
cause severe stomach upset.

S. crispum *Chile, Peru*
Chilean potato tree
Flowers: summer. H:12–18ft
(3.7–5.5m). Z:7–9.
This evergreen or semievergreen,
bushy scrambling climber has oval-
shaped leaves, with dark green

upper sides and paler green undersides, borne on green woody stems. The star-shaped flowers are purple-blue and have prominent yellow centers. **'Glasnevin'** is hardier than the species, with dark purple-blue flowers that last into autumn.

S. jasminoides *Brazil*
Potato vine
Flowers: summer to early autumn. H:10–15ft (3–4.5m). Z:8–10.
The glossy, pale green leaves of this slender, evergreen or semi-evergreen twining climber are oval to lance shaped, occasionally lobed. The star-shaped, slate-blue flowers have prominent golden anthers, and are produced in large, delicate clusters. **'Album'**, with white flowers and yellow anthers, is more widely grown.

Solanum jasminoides 'Album'

THUNBERGIA

ACANTHACEAE

The genus comprises about 100 species of twining climbers, shrubs, evergreen perennials, and annuals, a high proportion native to tropical Africa and Asia. Those of ornamental value are grown for their tubular flowers with 5 petal lobes at the mouth. One of the most splendid climbers of tropical gardens is the frost-tender, evergreen Bengal clock or blue trumpet vine (*T. grandiflora*, Z:10–11). This produces clusters of pale purple-blue flowers over a long season.
CULTIVATION Require full sun and a moist but well-drained soil.
PROPAGATION From seed, sown under glass at 61–64°F (16–18°C) in early spring.
POTENTIAL PROBLEMS Red spider mites (under glass).

T. alata *Tropical Africa*
Black-eyed Susan
Foliage: year-round. Flowers: summer to autumn. H:5–10ft (1.5–3m). An.
This twining climber, widely naturalized in the tropics and subtropics, is quick to flower when grown from seed, and makes a cheerful half-hardy annual in temperate gardens. The leaves are triangular and heart shaped at the base, and the flowers are usually orange-yellow with dark purplish-brown eyes.

Thunbergia alata

TRACHELOSPERMUM

APOCYNACEAE

Found in woodland in China, Japan, and Korea, this genus consists of 30 evergreen twining or self-clinging climbers. The small, leathery, lance-shaped leaves make dense cover on established plants, clothing the woody stems to the ground. The small, white, 5-petalled flowers, produced in clusters, are highly fragrant. Their habits become bushier with age, provided they do not suffer from severe winter damage. Plants may remain virtually dormant for the first 2 or 3 years after planting, and are generally slow to establish.
CULTIVATION Require full sun to light shade and fertile, moist but well-drained soil, rich in organic matter. The site must be sheltered from wind and cold—a warm, sunny wall is ideal.
PROPAGATION From seed, sown in spring. By layering, in summer. From semihardwood cuttings, in late summer or autumn.
POTENTIAL PROBLEMS Aphids (on young growth).

T. asiaticum
Foliage: year-round. Flowers: mid- to late summer. H:15–20ft (4.5–6m). Z:7–10.
This is a highly fragrant climber, with masses of small white, cartwheel-shaped flowers, creamy white aging to yellow. The dark, glossy, oval-shaped leaves are relatively small, up to 2in (5cm) long, providing attractive, dense cover. The stems reach about 12ft (3.7m) at maturity.

T. jasminoides
Confederate jasmine, star jasmine
Foliage: year-round. Flowers: mid-summer. H:20–30ft (6–9m). Z:7–9.
This beautiful, scented, evergreen climber is the most widely available species in the genus. With proper training and extra protection from cold and wind, especially in the early years, the confederate jasmine will make a superb year-round feature; wrap it with insulation from late autumn to mid-spring, and mulch to protect the root system. The small white flowers, up to 1in (2.5cm) wide, look at first sight like those of common jasmine (*Jasminum officinale*), hence the common name, but on closer inspection, you can see that the 5 petals are swirled like a cartwheel. They are carried in clusters at the ends of the shoots. The handsome glossy green, oval- to lance-shaped leaves are large, measuring up to 4¼in (11cm) in length. **'Variegatum'** (Z:8–9) is less vigorous. It has glossy gray-green leaves, variegated creamy white, and attractive pinkish red tints in winter.

Trachelospermum jasminoides

TROPAEOLUM

TROPAEOLACEAE

The 80 to 90 species of annual and herbaceous perennials in this genus are mostly trailing or climbing. They are plants of Central and South America, many of them from the Andes. The Canary creeper (*T. peregrinum*), which acquired its common name while being acclimatized in the Canary Islands, is an annual with feathered yellow flowers from Ecuador and Peru. All species have short, broadly trumpet-shaped flowers, some with petals of differing sizes, and a prominent spur at the base of each individual bloom. They usually flower from mid-summer to mid-autumn. One of the most familiar annuals, the nasturtium (*T. majus*), is typical of the genus in climbing by means of a coiling action of the leafstalks. However, many of its cultivars, such as **'Empress of India'**, with semidouble scarlet flowers, are compact plants for bedding and container gardening.

CULTIVATION Tolerate full sun or partial shade, and most soils.
PROPAGATION From seed (annuals), sown where plants are to flower in mid-spring or under glass at 55-61°F (13-16°C) and planted out when the risk of spring frosts is over. By division of the rootstock, in early spring (*T. speciosum*).
POTENTIAL PROBLEMS Aphids.

T. speciosum Chile
Flame creeper, flame nasturtium
Flowers: summer to autumn. Fruits: autumn. H:10-15ft (3-4.5m). Z:7-9.
With its spurred, scarlet flowers, this climber is particularly striking set against the backdrop of a dark green yew hedge in cool, moist gardens. The slender, twining stems grow from a creeping rhizome and carry pretty leaves with 6 lobes. The bright blue fruits that sometimes follow the flowers are set against deep red calyces.

Tropaeolum speciosum

VITIS

VITACEAE Vine

Most of the 60 to 70 species in the genus *Vitis* are deciduous tendril climbers from temperate regions of the Northern Hemisphere. Many of them grow vigorously into trees, particularly at the margins of woodland. Some have superbly ornamental foliage, the leaves coloring brilliantly in autumn. The flowers of the majority of species are small, green, and insignificant, but the fruits (grapes) of some species can be ornamental, edible, or used to make wine. The grape vine (*V. vinifera*) is of great economic and cultural importance, but its origins are not known for certain.
CULTIVATION Tolerate full sun or partial shade and prefer a fertile, well-drained soil. Thin out old growths and shorten young growths in late summer.
PROPAGATION From hardwood cuttings, from late autumn to winter. From vine eyes, in mid-winter.
POTENTIAL PROBLEMS Scale, vine weevils.

Vitis coignetiae

V. coignetiae Japan, Korea
Foliage: autumn. Flowers: late spring. Fruits: autumn. H:50-70ft (15-22m). Z:5-9.
The vigor and splendor of this vine put it in a class of its own. The dark green, heart-shaped leaves, up to 12in (30cm) long and wide, have 3 to 5 lobes, deeply sunken veins, and felted rust-red undersides. The foliage is attractive in autumn, turning orange, purplish brown, and scarlet. The bluish black fruits are inedible.

V. vinifera Probably Asia Minor and the Caucasus
Grape vine
Flowers: late spring to early summer. H:20-30ft (6-9m). Z:5-9.
The characteristic leaf of the grape vine is leathery, with 3 to 5 lobes and toothed margins in a broadly rounded outline. A few cultivars have been selected for their ornamental qualities: *V.* '**Brant**', which is similar to *V. vinifera*, with leaves that turn bronze and purple in autumn, although the veins remain green; '**Ciotat**' (parsley vine) has finely cut leaves; '**Purpurea**' has young leaves that are white and downy, becoming claret red and, in autumn, turning deepest purple.

WISTERIA

PAPILIONACEAE

Well known for their beautiful cascades of white, pink, blue, or mauve pealike flowers, this genus consists of 10 hardy deciduous climbers, all of which support themselves with twining stems. The usual flowering season is late spring through to mid-summer, although small flushes of flowers are often produced until early autumn. The 2 most commonly grown species are Japanese wisteria (*W. floribunda*) and Chinese wisteria (*W. sinensis*), both of which are ideal for covering walls, fences, and trellises and growing into large trees, twining anticlockwise around the support. The flowers of the fully hardy

silky wisteria (*W. venusta*, Z:5-9), which comes from Japan, are the largest of all the wisterias, reaching up to 1½in (3cm) in diameter. The fragrant flowers, which appear in early summer, are produced on short, drooping racemes with all the flowers opening at the same time. The young foliage has a silvery sheen.
CULTIVATION Require full sun to flower well and a deep, moist but well-drained soil. Prune side-shoots to 2 or 3 buds in late winter, and prune gently in mid-summer to keep size in check.
PROPAGATION From heel or nodal cuttings, in late summer. By layering, in late spring.
POTENTIAL PROBLEMS Aphids, brown scale, red spider mites; fungal leaf spot, honey fungus.
WARNING All parts can cause stomach upset if eaten.

W. floribunda Japan
Japanese wisteria
Flowers: early summer. H:20-30ft (6-9m). Z:4-9.
The light to mid-green leaves, composed of up to 19 leaflets, open at the same time as the fragrant violet-blue flowers. These are produced in drooping racemes, 12in (30cm) long, which open successively from the base downward. Named cultivars of this vigorous species include '**Alba**' (Z:5-9), with white flowers, flushed with lilac at the keel and borne in racemes up to 2ft (60cm) long; and the spectacular '**Multijuga**', with mauve and blue-purple flowers, borne in large racemes, up to 4ft (1.2m) long.

W. sinensis China
Chinese wisteria
Flowers: early summer. H:40-60ft (12-18m). Z:5-9.
This classic wisteria produces dense racemes of fragrant mauve flowers, up to 1ft (30cm) long, on small, spurlike growths. They open almost simultaneously, before the dark to mid-green leaves start to develop. Other forms include the white-flowered '**Alba**'.

Wisteria sinensis

roses

Although roses are found wild throughout the Northern Hemisphere, from the arctic down to the tropics, they are unknown naturally in the Southern Hemisphere. Roses are tolerant of cold, but most are able to thrive in hot, dry conditions as well. Due to the extensive breeding programs used to provide many of the more popular hybrid roses, some of the more traditional rose categories have tended to merge, particularly with the interbreeding of Large-flowered Bush Roses (Hybrid Teas) and Cluster-flowered Bush Roses (Floribundas). Over recent years, there has been a huge increase in low-growing cultivars and miniature patio roses, which reflect the changing tastes of gardeners and constraints imposed by the shrinking size of gardens. A greater range of habits than ever before has resulted, with low-growing roses that reach only 12–18in (30–45cm) in height, and some older rambling roses that achieve 20–30ft (6–9m) of growth in a season. No spread is given for climbers and ramblers.

Roses grown in containers can be transplanted at any time of year. Roses raised in the field should be transplanted when they are dormant, from late autumn to early spring. Autumn planting achieves the best results, because the soil is warm and moist and new roots develop quickly.

Top Rosa glauca
Center Rosa 'New Dawn'
Bottom Rosa 'Albertine'

ROSA

ROSACEAE ROSE

The finest roses are plants of superlative quality and ranked behind them are thousands that are only slightly inferior. And yet the awful fact must be faced that there is a high cost to pay for the dominant role roses so often play in gardens. The most popular look unspeakably dreary and unattractive in winter, and a very high proportion of roses require the regular use of chemicals to control pests and diseases.

There are about 150 species of rose, which are widely distributed throughout the Northern Hemisphere. Most of them are thorny shrubs or climbers, and they are found in a variety of habitats. In themselves the species are relatively unimportant as garden plants, representing only a tiny proportion of the roses in cultivation. A few, however, have played an enormously important role in the breeding of the old roses and the extraordinary output of the modern rose industry.

The following selection is so small that it risks trivializing a much-loved group of plants, but it does make an attempt to reflect variety and valued qualities such as scent. According to a standard horticultural classification, the roses are grouped into 6 categories: Species and closely related hybrids; Old Shrub Roses; Modern Shrub Roses; Modern Bush Roses; Modern Miniature and Patio Roses; and Climbers and Ramblers.

General information on cultivation, propagation, and potential problems follows, but advice on pruning is given at the end of the introduction to each section. In addition to following the recommended pruning regimes, gardeners should always remove all dead, diseased, and damaged growths and, as a general principle, prune to outward-facing buds so that air can move freely through a more open center.
CULTIVATION Most roses require full sun (a few will tolerate the absence of direct sunlight but need an open well-lit position) and moist well-drained soil. Many hybrid roses, especially the modern bush roses, perform well only in fertile soil containing plenty of organic matter. Avoid planting in soils where roses have grown recently.
PROPAGATION Most hybrid roses are raised commercially by grafting. Species, Modern Shrub Roses, and Ramblers from semi-ripe cuttings after flowering or hardwood cuttings in winter; true species from seed, sown in autumn.
POTENTIAL PROBLEMS Aphids, caterpillars, leafhoppers, red spider mites, scale; black spot, canker, honey fungus, powdery and downy mildews, rose "replant sickness," rust, viruses.

SPECIES AND CLOSELY RELATED HYBRIDS

The small number grown usually have only one flush of flowers in a season, but they deserve to be judged by their overall character. The best are well-shaped, arching shrubs with attractive foliage, usually single flowers and often highly ornamental hips. They include some of the most disease-resistant roses available.
PRUNING Little required except for the removal at ground level, after flowering, of up to one-quarter of the oldest stems.

Rosa 'Geranium'

R. 'Geranium'
Flowers: mid-summer. Berries: autumn. H:6-8ft (1.8-2.5m), S:5-6ft (1.5-1.8m). Z:4-9.
The Chinese species **R. moyesii** makes a large open bush as much as 10ft (3m) tall that is spangled in summer with pink or red single flowers and laden in autumn with flagon-shaped scarlet hips. **R. 'Geranium'** is a slightly smaller shrub very much in its parents' mold. Creamy stamens brighten the blood-red single flowers, which are followed by heavy crops of the highly distinctive and long-lasting hips.

R. glauca *Mountains of C. and S. Europe*
Flowers: mid-summer. Berries: autumn. H:5-7ft (1.5-2.2m), S:4-6ft (1.2-1.8m). Z:4-9.
The pink starry flowers, borne in clusters, are of fleeting interest, but there are splendid clusters of red hips to follow. However, what makes this a rose of great distinction is the cool purple-blue of the foliage.

Rosa glauca

R. xanthina 'Canary Bird'
Flowers: mid- to late spring. H:8-10ft (2.5-3m), S:6-12ft (1.8-3.7m). Z:5-9.
The species, a graceful arching shrub from China and Japan, is usually represented in gardens by '**Canary Bird**'. Its high season comes early, with single clear yellow flowers nestling thickly among ferny gray-green leaves. The fragrance is fairly light, and flowering is sparse after early summer. **R. 'Cantabrigiensis'**, flowering in spring and early summer, bears a resemblance but the prickly bush is more compact and the sweetly scented flowers are creamy yellow.

Rosa xanthina 'Canary Bird'

OLD SHRUB ROSES

The hybrid roses that existed before the development of the modern Large-flowered Bush Roses (Hybrid Teas) are very mixed in character, but they are consistent in their color range, which excludes yellow and orange. Each of the main groups—Alba, Bourbon, Centifolia, China, Damask, Gallica, Hybrid Perpetual, Moss, and Portland—is now often represented in gardens by a relatively small cluster of survivors, but these include some of the most memorably beautiful of all roses. Many do not repeat.
PRUNING With the exception of Hybrid Perpetuals, cut back stems by a third, and on established plants cut out at ground level up to a quarter of the oldest stems, pruning once-flowering roses as

soon as flowering has finished, repeat-flowering roses in late winter or early spring. Prune Hybrid Perpetuals more drastically, cutting back main stems to about 10in (25cm) above ground level and removing completely up to a third of the oldest stems in late winter or early spring.

R. 'Cécile Brünner'

Flowers: repeat, summer/autumn. H:30–36in (75–90cm), S:18–24in (45–60cm). Z:4–9.
Although introduced in the 1880s, this is usually listed with the more modern Polyanthas, which are low-growing with clusters of small flowers. The pale pink buds of the twiggy '**Cécile Brünner**' are exceptional for their miniature elegance. The open flowers are lightly scented. There is a climbing form that can grow to 20ft (6m), but it flowers only once. '**Perle d'Or**' has lightly fragrant flowers in shades of apricot and cream.

Rosa 'Céleste'

R. 'Céleste'

Flowers: early summer. H:5–6ft (1.5–1.8m), S:4–5ft (1.2–1.5m). Z:3–9.
From their name, it might be thought that the Albas are united in having white flowers. Some of these tough hybrids do, including one of the oldest, the so-called Jacobite rose or White Rose of York (*R.* × *alba* '**Alba Maxima**'), a sweet-scented double up to 7ft (2.2m). '**Céleste**', however, is an Alba rose with fragrant, double, pink flowers with gray leaves.

R. 'Charles de Mills'

Flowers: early summer. H and S:4–5ft (1.2–1.5m). Z:4–9.
The Gallicas, one of the oldest groups of roses, include several examples that have a distinctive personality. '**Charles de Mills**', like many Gallicas almost thornless, produces flowers that seem to have been sliced through to show their crimson and purple tones. '**Cardinal de Richelieu**' grows to 3ft (90cm) and has very double flowers of deep purplish red.

Rosa 'Complicata'

'**Complicata**', up to 7ft (2.2m) tall, is a more vigorous alternative carrying hot-pink single blooms with showy yellow stamens.

Rosa 'Fantin-Latour'

R. 'Fantin-Latour'

Flowers: early summer. H:4–6ft (1.2–1.8m), S:4–5ft (1.2–1.5m). Z:4–9.
The Centifolia roses—also known as the "cabbage" or "Provence" roses—so lovingly rendered by 17th-century Dutch and Flemish painters, originated in Holland during the late 16th century. They are distinguished by their large, usually pink, sweetly scented double blooms, which often droop with their own weight. '**Fantin-Latour**', named after the famous 19th-century French painter, makes a strong, spreading bush that benefits from support, and whose fully double, flat, rose-pink flowers have a delicate scent. '**De Meaux**' produces an abundance of small clear pink flowers on arching stems. This is a more compact shrub only 3ft (90cm) tall. Nearly twice its size is '**Tour de Malakoff**', which carries sumptuous flowers blending magenta, purple, and mauve-gray.

R. 'Madame Hardy'

Flowers: early summer. Berries: autumn. H:5–7ft (1.5–2.2m), S:4–5ft (1.2–1.5m). Z:4–9.
The Damasks are a very old group of roses and their fragrant flowers have long been used in the commercial production of attar of roses. '**Madame Hardy**' is a white of incomparable beauty with a

distinctive lemon scent. Its strong shrubby form bears pure white double-petaled flowers, each petal perfectly folded around a central green "button eye." '**Celsiana**', bears pale-pink yellow-eyed blooms with crinkled petals. It has a heavy perfume. '**Ispahan**' is a vigorous Damask bearing large, fragrant, blush-pink blooms over a long period. The abundant foliage is gray-green.

Rosa 'Madame Isaac Pereire'

R. 'Madame Isaac Pereire'

Flowers: repeat, summer/autumn. H:7–15ft (2.2–4.5m), S:4–6ft (1.2–1.8m). Z:5–9.
Some detect a hint of raspberries in the flowers of this and other Bourbons. '**Madame Isaac Pereire**', which can be grown as a climber as well as a shrub, like several Bourbons, has deep purple-pink double flowers. The flowers of '**Boule de Neige**', creamy white, and '**Louise Odier**', pink with mauve tints, are almost camellia-like. '**Reine Victoria**' is lax and needs support to carry its scented, beautifully cupped, rose-pink double flowers.

Rosa 'Louise Odier'

R. 'Madame Knorr'

Flowers: repeat, summer/autumn. H:4–5ft (1.2–1.5m), S:3–4ft (1–1.2m). Z:4–9.
The Portlands were popular roses in the 19th century, valued because they repeated well and had good scent. '**Madame Knorr**' has mauve-pink double flowers, flushed a deeper pink at the center, and remarkable disease resistance for an old rose.

Rosa 'Nuits de Young'

R. 'Nuits de Young'
Old black rose
Flowers: early summer. H:4-5ft
(1.2-1.5m), S:30-36in (75-90cm).
Z:4-9.
Moss roses are typified by the soft
down or "moss" of glands on the
flower buds and upper stems,
which give off a resinous scent
and add to their fragrance. 'Nuits
de Young'—said to be the darkest
of all the old roses—makes an
erect but compact bush. The dark
brownish-green moss encloses the
double scented flowers, which are
deep purple-maroon with a central
boss of yellow stamens. 'Gloire
des Mousseuses', another Moss
rose, is similar in habit, with
scented flowers in pale sugar-pink,
flushed darker at the center. An
occasional bloom in autumn is an
added bonus.

Rosa 'Reine des Violettes'

R. 'Reine des Violettes'
Flowers: repeat, summer/autumn.
H:5-6ft (1.5-1.8m), S:3-4ft
(1-1.2m). Z:4-9.
The Hybrid Perpetuals were
immediate forerunners of the
modern Large-flowered (Hybrid
Tea) roses, their color range
representing a stage before the
introduction of yellow. The well-
scented double flowers of 'Reine
des Violettes' show, however, the
richness of the old palette. The
blooms, set against gray-green
foliage, are velvet purple, aging
to lilac. 'Paul Neyron', although
unfortunately carrying little scent,
makes a more vigorous shrub,
with enormous ruffled flowers in
pink, flushed lilac. 'Mrs. John

Laing' carries fully double silvery-
pink flowers with a very good
scent. It makes a compact shrub
about 3ft (90cm) tall.

MODERN SHRUB ROSES

These roses, which have been
developed since the end of the
19th century, are very varied, but
differ from the Modern Bush Roses
in having a more graceful
character. Many add to the
qualities of the Species or the Old
Shrub Roses a repeat-flowering
habit. Some are generously
described as "groundcover" roses.
PRUNING Carry out pruning of
repeat-flowerers in late winter or
early spring. Those that flower
only once should be pruned in late
summer. Cut back main shoots by
up to a third and shorten laterals
to about 4in (10cm); cut out at
ground level 1 or 2 of the oldest
stems of mature plants.

Rosa Bonica

R. Bonica
Flowers: continuous, summer/
autumn. H:34-36in (85-90cm),
S:3½-5ft (1.1-1.5m). Z:4-9.
With dense, glossy-green, disease-
resistant foliage and large sprays of
scented, double, pink flowers
borne over a long season, **Bonica**
is too good to be pigeonholed
merely as a groundcover rose.
Other roses marketed under this
name include the slightly smaller
Rosy Cushion (Z:5-9), with single
to semidouble bright pink flowers
with a white eye, and several in
the County Series, among them
Kent, only 18in (45cm) tall but
spreading to 36in (90cm) and well
covered in summer with semidouble white flowers.

R. 'Buff Beauty'
Flowers: mid-summer, with flushes
on into autumn. H and S:4-5ft
(1.2-1.5m). Z:6-9.
The Hybrid Musks, most of which
were bred in the 20th century
before World War II, make
substantial but graceful shrubs
with remarkable disease resistance
and copious dark green leaves.

Rosa 'Buff Beauty'

They flower prodigiously in their
first flush and often impressively
later in the year. 'Buff Beauty'
carries large double flowers that
are buff colored with a subtle
tinge of apricot. 'Cornelia'
(Z:5-9) has summer flowers that
are pale sugar-pink and autumn
blooms that are deeper pink with
a copper tint. The light pink
flowers of 'Felicia' are flushed
apricot. All three are fragrant.

R. 'Frau Dagmar Hastrup'
Flowers: mid- to late summer.
Berries: autumn. H and S:3-5ft
(1-1.5m). Z:3-9.
The Rugosa roses are only one
stage removed from the rugged
wild *R. rugosa*, an exceedingly
tough suckering species often
found on sand dunes in China,
Siberia, Japan, and Korea. Rugosas
have inherited the constitution of
their wild parent, making disease-
resistant thorny shrubs that endure
drought better than most roses.
They come into leaf early, produce
scented flowers with fine-textured
petals throughout summer, and the
singles and semidoubles bear
impressive crops of tomato-shaped
hips in autumn. 'Frau Dagmar
Hastrup', one of the most
compact, bears single pink
flowers. The ripening hips
coincide with the late blooms.
'Roseraie de l'Häy', carrying
double purple-red flowers, and
'Blanche Double de Coubert', a
double of purest white, can both
grow to a height of 6ft (1.8m) or
more. Both can be grown as
informal hedges.

Rosa 'Frau Dagmar Hastrup'

R. 'Frühlingsmorgen'
Flowers: late spring. Berries: autumn. H:5–6ft (1.5–1.8m), S:4–5ft (1.2–1.5m). Z:5–9.
The roses bred from the wild Scotch rose or Burnet rose (**R. pimpinellifolia**) inherit that plant's tough constitution and so can adapt to a wide range of conditions. '**Frühlingsmorgen**', with sweetly scented peach-pink flowers that have pale yellow centers, is one of the first roses to flower each year, and has a graceful arching habit. There is usually a small second crop of flowers. **Frühlingsgold** bears a magnificent display of soft lemon-yellow blooms that fade to creamy white, but there is no follow-on after the first display.

R. 'Golden Wings'
Flowers: continuous, summer/autumn. H and S:4–6ft (1.2–1.8m). Z:6–10.
Single saucer-shaped flowers, up to 5in (12.5cm) across, are carried on an elegantly arching shrub, a cluster of red stamens contrasting with the yellow petals. The sweetly scented blooms are borne in profusion throughout the summer. **Sally Holmes** (Z:5–9) is another impressive modern shrub with single scented flowers that have a pink flush to the margins of ivory-white petals.

Rosa Constance Spry

R. Heritage
Flowers: continuous, summer/autumn. H and S:3–4ft (1–1.2m). Z:5–9.
In the English Roses, a new group that came to notice in the 1970s, some of the qualities of the old roses, in particular flower shape and fragrance, have been combined with the ability to flower repeatedly throughout summer and the wide color range of modern bush roses. English roses that repeat-flower well include **Heritage**, with cup-shaped fragrant flowers in soft pink, and **Graham Thomas**, a bushy plant with pure yellow fragrant flowers. **Constance Spry**

disappoints by flowering only once, but the soft pink fragrant blooms, up to 6in (15cm) across, have a luminous beauty. This rose can be grown as a shrub or trained as a climber.

R. 'Nevada'
Flowers: early summer with occasional autumn blooms. H and S:7–9ft (2.2–2.7m). Z:5–9.
Arching red-brown stems carry masses of large, semidouble, creamy white blooms that are slightly scented. The sparse autumn flowers are often much pinker in color. '**Marguerite Hilling**' is its equal but produces an abundant display of deep-pink scented flowers.

Rosa 'Marguerite Hilling'

R. 'Nymphenburg'
Flowers: continuous, summer/autumn. H:8–9ft (2.5–2.7m), S:5–6ft (1.5–1.8m). Z:4–9.
The size and vigor of many modern shrub roses allow them to be trained as climbers as well as grown more conventionally. '**Nymphenburg**', a vigorous Hybrid Musk that lends itself to either treatment, has scented, semidouble, peach-pink flowers. **Dortmund**, an equally versatile rose, has single, cherry-red, white-eyed flowers.

Rosa Jacqueline du Pré

R. Pearl Drift
Flowers: continuous, summer/autumn. H and S:3–4ft (1–1.2m). Z:5–9.
Semidouble pale pink flowers are borne above dark green glossy foliage on a spreading shrub.

Jacqueline du Pré, a taller shrub growing to 6ft (1.8m), has semi-double flowers with a musklike scent. The flowers are ivory-white with a hint of pink.

R. 'White Pet'
Flowers: continuous summer/autumn. H:18–32in (45–80cm), S:18–24in (45–60cm). Z:5–10.
Small white pompon flowers open from tight pink buds to provide a succession of dainty clusters on a compact little bush. This variety can be grown as a small standard. The blooms of this Polyantha are very faintly scented. '**The Fairy**', sometimes described as a groundcover rose, is another pretty Polyantha with sprays of pale pink pompons. It is usually less than 30in (75cm) in height and spread and comes into flower late but continues into autumn. The pink, semidouble, lightly scented flowers of '**Mevrouw Nathalie Nypels**' (Z:4–9) are carried in abundant clusters.

Rosa 'The Fairy'

MODERN BUSH ROSES

In bloom, the Modern Bush Roses are wonderfully free-flowering or neurotically hectic, depending on your point of view; out of bloom they are undeniably stiff and gawky. Within this broad category are 2 important groups. The Large-flowered Bush Roses (Hybrid Teas) produce high-centered, usually double, flowers that are borne either singly or in small clusters in several flushes between early summer and autumn. The Cluster-flowered Bush Roses (Floribundas) bloom more continuously and have smaller flowers carried in larger clusters.
PRUNING In late winter or early spring, cut back stems of Large-flowered roses to 6–10in (15–25cm) above ground level. Cluster-flowered roses should have their stems cut back to 10–18in (25–45cm). Established bushes of both types should have 1 or 2 of the oldest stems cut out at ground level.

R. Alexander

Flowers: continuous, summer/autumn. H:6–7ft (1.8–2.2m), S:24–32in (60–80cm). Z:5–9. This very vigorous, erect, long-stemmed rose is ideal for cutting. It is also considered a great improvement on its parent **Super Star**, a Large-flowered Bush Rose, which has a less regular habit and a less consistent flower color. The dark green foliage of **Alexander** shows good disease resistance, and the lightly scented double flowers are of unfading vermilion.

Rosa Amber Queen

R. Amber Queen

Flowers: continuous, summer/autumn. H:20–24in (50–60cm), S:18–24in (45–60cm). Z:5–9. The dark bronze-green foliage of this Cluster-flowered Bush Rose, tinted red when young, makes an attractive foil for the fully double, fragrant, amber-yellow flowers. This is a compact spreading rose that is more suitable for bedding than '**Glenfiddich**', which is slightly taller but with flowers of a similar color. Both roses offer good continuity of flowering.

Rosa 'Arthur Bell'

R. 'Arthur Bell'

Flowers: continuous, summer/autumn. H:2–3ft (60–90cm), S:24–30in (60–75cm). Z:5–9. With shiny bright green leaves and double, fragrant, creamy yellow flowers, this spreading Cluster-flowered rose is useful for bedding. **Mountbatten** is taller with a slender upright habit and is less prone to fading. It has slightly larger flowers of a deeper yellow.

R. Chicago Peace

Flowers: continuous, summer/autumn. H:4–6ft (1.2–1.8m), S:2–3ft (60–90cm). Z:5–9. This sport of the famous **Peace** rose has inherited the robust character and glossy dark green foliage of its Large-flowered parents, but in the blooms it shows a stronger pink than in the original gentle mixture of soft pink and creamy white.

R. Double Delight

Flowers: continuous, summer/autumn. H:2–3ft (60–90cm), S:18–24 (45–60cm). Z:5–9. With a more compact habit than most Large-flowered cultivars, this is an unusually good bedding rose for a plant of this group. The highly fragrant double flowers are pale pink, with the edges painted deep carmine-red, but unfortunately it is susceptible to mildew. **Blessings**, similar in size, is another good Large-flowered bedding type. It has scented, double, salmon-pink flowers, although mildew can also be a problem.

R. Elina

Flowers: continuous, summer/autumn. H:3–3½ft (1–1.1m), S:24–30in (60–75cm). Z:5–9. The ivory-white flowers have the classic shape of a Large-flowered bush rose, and they are shown off well by the foliage. **Pascali**, with sparse foliage, also has white flowers. Both are doubles and are only lightly fragrant.

R. Escapade

Flowers: continuous, summer/autumn. H:30–36in (75–90cm), S:24–30in (60–75cm). Z:5–9. This Cluster-flowered rose has unusual and sweetly scented semi-double flowers, which are white centered and pink with violet tints. **Eye Paint** has little scent but is a bolder color choice, its white eye making a startling contrast with the brilliant scarlet petals of the single flowers. It is taller at 3½ft (1.1m).

Rosa Escapade

R. Fragrant Delight

Flowers: continuous, summer/autumn. H:2–3ft (60–90cm), S:24–30in (60–75cm). Z:5–9. The double salmon-pink blooms have a good scent, but uneven growth counts against this Cluster-flowered rose. Pink doubles of neater habit include '**Dearest**' and '**English Miss**'.

R. 'Gruss an Aachen'

Flowers: in flushes, summer/autumn. H and S:24–30in (60–75cm). Z:4–9. Many of the Polyantha roses were interbred with the Large-flowered roses to produce the freer, more perpetually flowering Cluster-flowered roses. As such, the oldest varieties are truly "parents" to the modern Cluster-flowered roses that have largely supplanted them. Polyanthas are often smaller flowered and without scent, however, which gives fragrant '**Gruss an Aachen**', with its creamy white to pale pink sprays of double blooms, a special attraction. **Yesterday** (Z:5–9), a spreading, very free-flowering, rather shrubby modern Polyantha type, is similarly scented. The single to semidouble flowers are pink to violet. It has a height and spread of 3–5ft (1–1.5m).

Rosa Iceberg

R. Iceberg 'Korbin'

Flowers: continuous, summer/autumn. H:3–4ft (1–1.2m), S:30–36in (75–90cm). Z:5–9. Despite its susceptibility to black spot, **Iceberg** has remained a popular Cluster-flowered bush rose because of the graceful way it carries lightly scented double flowers over a long season. '**Margaret Merril**' is a more compact white with better scent.

R. Mister Lincoln

Flowers: continuous, summer/autumn. H:3–5ft (1–1.5m), S:24–30in (60–75cm). Z:5–9. The velvet texture of the shapely buds gives an added depth to their deep crimson. This is an upright

Large-flowered bush rose with leathery dark green foliage. **Royal William** is more compact and carries fragrant flowers with similar coloring.

Rosa Royal William

R. 'National Trust'
Flowers: continuous, summer/ autumn. H and S:24–30in (60–75cm). Z:5–9.
The high-centered buds open to bright red double flowers with elegantly pointed petals, displaying the classic form of the Large-flowered bush roses. The scent, however, is disappointing. The double flowers of **Silver Jubilee**, which are pink with shades of peach and cream, are also of elegant form and only lightly scented.

Rosa 'National Trust'

R. Oranges and Lemons
Flowers: continuous, summer/ autumn. H and S:24–30in (60–75cm). Z:5–9.
The scarlet striping of orange-yellow double flowers gives this novelty value, even among the highly variable Cluster-flowered roses. Another orange-flowered bicolor, **Tango** is a deeper reddish color, fading to yellow at the petal margins, with each petal yellow on the reverse.

R. 'The Queen Elizabeth'
Flowers: continuous, summer/ autumn. H:6–7ft (1.8–2.2m), S:3–4ft (1–1.2m). Z:5–9.
This, one of the most vigorous of the Cluster-flowered bush roses, carries double, well-shaped, clear pink flowers on long stems.

Chinatown, less vigorous but capable of growing to 6ft (1.8m) if lightly pruned, produces double scented flowers that are yellow with a hint of pink.

MODERN MINIATURE AND PATIO ROSES

Miniature roses and the Patio roses, which are intermediate between Miniatures and the Cluster-flowered bush roses, need an intimate setting in the open garden or in a container. *PRUNING* Trim Miniatures lightly and reduce stems of Patio roses by about a third in late winter or early spring.

R. Baby Masquerade
Flowers: continuous, summer/ autumn. H and S:12–18in (30–45cm). Z:5–9.
This Miniature has flowers that are similar to those of the well-known Cluster-flowered rose **'Masquerade'**—slightly scented, yellow-pink, flushed deeper red—but they are only 1in (2.5cm) wide. It makes a dense twiggy bush, unlike the more erect **'Little Buckaroo'** with semidouble orange-red flowers. **Orange Sunblaze** (Z:4–9) has fully double bright orange-red blooms.

R. Gentle Touch
Flowers: continuous, summer/ autumn. H:15–20in (38–50cm), S:16–20in (40–50cm). Z:5–9.
This is a slightly scented dwarf Cluster-flowered rose, with perfectly cup-shaped, semi-double, pale apricot-pink flowers, which are large for this group—as much as 2in (5cm) across. **Sweet Magic** makes a smaller bush at 14in (35cm), carrying double flowers in a deeper apricot-orange and yellow.

Rosa Gentle Touch

R. Sweet Dream
Flowers: continuous, summer/ autumn. H:14–20in (35–50cm), S:12–16in (30–40cm). Z:5–9.
The well-proportioned double flowers, lightly scented and a

melting blend of apricot and peach shades, are carried on an upright bushy plant. Other Patio roses include **Anna Ford**, which carries semidouble orange-red flowers, **Little Bo-peep**, with semidouble pale pink flowers and a more spreading habit, and **Sweet Magic**, which has well-formed, double, orange flowers that pale to rich yellow.

CLIMBERS AND RAMBLERS

Most Ramblers are roses of exceptional vigor, producing long flexible stems that can be directed to streak into the branches of a tree or trained on a sturdy support such as a pergola. They do not repeat, but they produce masses of small flowers, which are usually well scented. Climbers lack the carefree energy of the Ramblers but in most cases the stiff growths carry flowers either in a couple of flushes or more continuously between early summer and autumn. The spread depends on the method of training used, so measurements have not been given here.
PRUNING Cut out up to a third of flowered shoots from established Ramblers as soon as flowering is over; shorten side-shoots of Climbers to 3 or 4 buds between autumn and spring, and reduce main shoots, if necessary, to keep the plant within available space.

R. 'Albertine'
Flowers: early to mid-summer. H:15–20ft (4.5–6m). Z:4–9.
For a Rambler, **'Albertine'** has large flowers in a distinctive shade of copper-pink. In mid-summer this vigorous rose provides a deliciously scented mass of blooms, looking most at ease when its stiff arching stems are allowed to sprawl over a fence. Another vigorous Rambler, the semievergreen **'Albéric Barbier'** bears rather drooping creamy white flowers, which are lightly scented of apples. Both roses have shiny foliage.

Rosa 'Albertine'

Rosa banksiae 'Lutea'

R. *banksiae* 'Lutea'
Yellow Banksian rose
Flowers: mid-spring. H:20–30ft (6–9m). Z:7–9.
The Banksian roses, which are vigorous, finely branching Ramblers of Chinese origin, need a warm wall and shelter if they are to be grown in frost-prone areas. The yellow Banksian, said to be the hardiest, bears numerous clusters of small fully double flowers exceptionally early in the rose year. The flowers have little scent. '**Paul's Himalayan Musk**' (Z:5–9), another vigorous Rambler displaying clusters of small double flowers, in this case pale pink and scented, is hardier and more conventional in its summer flowering.

R. 'Bobbie James'
Flowers: early to mid-summer. H:20–30ft (6–9m). Z:5–9.
Large clusters of semidouble creamy white flowers shed a far-reaching scent. '**Wedding Day**', bearing single, creamy white, scented flowers opening from apricot buds, is another vigorous Rambler suitable for training up a sturdy tree.

Rosa Golden Showers

R. Golden Showers
Flowers: continuous, summer/autumn. H:8–10ft (2.5–3m). Z:5–9.
This rose is a stiff, upright, almost thornless climber, which can also be grown as a shrub. The well-shaped buds open to scented, loose double, yellow blooms. **Breath of Life**, another of the short Climbers sometimes known as "pillar roses," produces double peach-pink flowers, which have a light scent.

R. 'Madame Alfred Carrière'
Flowers: in flushes, mid-summer to autumn. H:15–20ft (4.5–6m). Z:5–9.
Old Noisette Climbers such as this are very vigorous, producing volumes of new soft stems in a season and a succession of flowers, not carried continuously but in prolonged flushes. '**Madame Alfred Carrière**' is a particularly lovely, delicately scented rose with very disease resistant pale green foliage. It carries double ivory-white flowers flushed palest pink. It is best grown on a large wall or heavy pergola support. Other old Noisette types with a good scent include '**Gloire de Dijon**', with rosette-shaped double flowers in an unusual buff-yellow, tinged pink, and '**Alister Stella Gray**' (Z:7–10), with apricot buds opening to buff to creamy white flowers with a yellowish center.

R. 'Meg'
Flowers: continuous, summer/autumn. H:12–13ft (3.7–4m). Z:5–9.
The large fragrant flowers, semi-double and nearly flat when fully open, are pink-apricot to pink, with conspicuous reddish amber stamens. Another stiff-stemmed Climber with semidouble flowers, **Parkdirektor Riggers** makes a more flamboyant statement with large clusters of scarlet blooms that have wavy petals.

R. 'New Dawn'
Flowers: continuous, summer/autumn. H:10–20ft (3–6m). Z:4–9.
Even on walls that get little direct sun, this vigorous Climber can produce good displays of salmon-pink, lightly scented, double flowers, which are borne in small sprays. The dark green glossy foliage shows good disease resistance. '**New Dawn**' is the parent of a number of healthy repeat-flowering Climbers such as

Rosa 'New Dawn'

'**Parade**' (Z:5–9), which carries carmine-pink double flowers. The dark glossy leaves have a reddish tinge. Unfortunately, this rose has not inherited its parent's scent.

R. 'Veilchenblau'
Flowers: mid-summer. H:10–12ft (3–3.7). Z:5–9.
A compact, easily controlled, thornless Rambler with healthy, disease-resistant, light green foliage, '**Veilchenblau**' is especially remarkable for the curious beauty of the clusters of apple-scented, rosettelike double blooms. They open dusky magenta-purple before fading to soft gray-mauve. With long pliable stems, this rose is admirably suited to training on most moderately sized supports and can tolerate shade. A taller compact Rambler '**Félicité Perpétue**' (Z:6–10), reaching a height of 15ft (4.5m), covers itself with a snowstorm of small double flowers carried in clusters, opening from pink-edged buds to a final gentle white, blushed pink. Although remarkable for its evergreen to semievergreen foliage, it is unlikely to prove hardy in the very coldest areas. '**The Garland**' has sprays of small, light salmon-pink flowers and a rich orange fragrance.

Rosa 'Veilchenblau'

R. 'Zéphirine Drouhin'
Thornless rose
Flowers: continuous, summer/autumn. H:9–15ft (2.7–4.5m). Z:5–9.
Despite being prone to mildew, this old Bourbon remains a favorite. Its almost thornless stems are easily trained, and in early summer it produces an extravagant and vivid display of loose bright pink flowers that are strongly scented. There are more flowers later, but never in such profusion. '**Blairii Number Two**', another climbing Bourbon, has few flowers after its main flush but its full and shapely blooms are of exceptional quality, with deep pink centers shading delicately to the palest pink at the edges.

perennials

In a broad sense, the term perennial covers all nonwoody flowering plants that live for more than two years, that is to say they have a life expectancy longer than annuals or biennials, but do not have the durable framework of shrubs and trees. A large proportion of these plants are herbaceous, their seasonal cycle consisting of annual growth that dies down in autumn before a period of winter dormancy. To these can be added long-lived nonwoody evergreens and semievergreens, such as bergenias, and those plants that have a woody base and fall somewhere between the typical herbaceous perennials and shrubs. There is no difficulty in letting out of the perennial net plants such as hybrid petunias that are almost invariably grown from seed annually in all climatic regions. More problematic are plants such as *Salvia patens* that are treated as annuals where they are too tender to survive winters outdoors but in warmer climates can be reasonably long-lived. The solution adopted here may not always seem consistent. When a plant cannot be found, the first step should be to consult the index. Planting times are spring or autumn.

The generous space devoted to perennials in this book reflects the revived interest of gardeners in the many roles they can play in a relaxed kind of gardening.

*Top **Euphorbia griffithii** 'Fireglow'*
*Center **Hemerocallis lilioasphodelus***
*Bottom **Houttuynia cordata** 'Chameleon'*

ACAENA

ROSACEAE Bidi bidi, New Zealand burr

Good foliage, topped in summer by attractive spiny burrs, makes many among the 100 or so vigorous, mat-forming plants from the Southern Hemisphere useful as groundcover. Most of the best-known species, including *A. buchananii* (Z:5-9) and *A. novae-zelandiae* (Z:5-9), come from New Zealand, where they are usually found in open terrain, including high country. It is ironic that the introduction to New Zealand of domesticated animals, especially sheep, should have provided the perfect means of seed distribution.
CULTIVATION Tolerate full sun or partial shade and fertile well-drained soil.
PROPAGATION From self-layered stems in autumn or spring. From softwood cuttings in late spring. From seed, sown in autumn.
POTENTIAL PROBLEMS Usually none.

A. microphylla New Zealand
Foliage: year-round. Flowers: summer. H:1-2in (2.5-5cm), S:18-24in (45-60cm). Z:5-9.
This evergreen species is generally represented by the cultivar '**Kupferteppich**', with ground-hugging compound leaves of bronzy green, spherical flowerheads and an encrustation of bright red burrs in late summer.

A. saccaticupula '**Blue Haze**'
Foliage: year-round. Flowers: mid-summer. H:4-6in (10-15cm), S:3-4ft (90-120cm). Z:5-9.
The evergreen compound leaves, the paired leaflets with finely toothed edges, are a metallic blue-green tinged with purple. Bronzed stems carry spherical flowerheads that turn to reddish-brown burrs.

Acaena saccaticupula '**Blue Haze**'

ACANTHUS

ACANTHACEAE Bear's breeches

In the dry, stony landscapes of the Mediterranean basin, which is the home of several among the 30

species, their foliage is conspicuously handsome, forming bold clumps from which rise stiff spikes of tubular flowers encased in prickly bracts. It is said that acanthus leaves inspired the classical decorative motif of Corinthian capitals, but which species provided the model is subject to debate. In their combination of foliage and flowers, the latter produced most freely in full sun, several species are among the most impressive perennials and worthy of growing in isolated groups. However, the planting site must be well chosen from the start, since the fleshy roots are almost ineradicable. The cut flower spikes, although awkward to handle when dry, are highly decorative.
CULTIVATION Tolerate full sun or partial shade and require well-drained soil.
PROPAGATION By division, in spring. From seed, sown in spring. From root cuttings, taken in winter.
POTENTIAL PROBLEMS Powdery mildew.

A. mollis N.W. Africa, S. Europe
Foliage: spring to autumn. Flowers: late summer. H:4-5ft (1.2-1.5m), S:3-4ft (90-120cm). Z:7-9.
A large clump of the dark green leaves, which are glossy and generously lobed, produces several spikes of purplish-veined white flowers hooded by long-lasting purple bracts. In the **Latifolius Group**, the leaves are easily 8in (20cm) across.

A. spinosus Mediterranean, S. Europe
Foliage: spring to autumn. Flowers: late summer. H:4-5ft (1.2-1.5m), S:2-3ft (60-90cm). Z:6-10.
The spiny, arching leaves, up to 3ft (90cm) long and deeply cut, form a splendid base for tall stems bristling with tiers of white flowers hooded by purple bracts. The very finely cut leaves of the **Spinosissimus Group** are gray-green with silvered midribs and points.

Acanthus spinosus

ACHILLEA

ASTERACEAE Yarrow

The 85 or so species from temperate parts of the Northern Hemisphere and several hybrids provide a range of tough, sun-loving plants. These are suitable for borders and for small-scale planting in rock gardens and among paving stones. The flowerheads, predominantly but not exclusively yellow and densely packed with small daisy flowers, are long lasting outdoors and are highly decorative when dried. The foliage is often ferny (*A. ptarmica*, Z:4-9, is an exception) and in some cases silvered. Those with invasive roots need careful positioning but even the common yarrow (*A. millefolium*, Z:3-8) has bright forms, such as '**Cerise Queen**', that have a place in plantings on rough ground.

Achillea millefolium '**Cerise Queen**'

CULTIVATION Require full sun and well-drained soil.
PROPAGATION By division in spring (advisable every third year, particularly for *A*. '*Moonshine*'). From seed, sown in spring.
POTENTIAL PROBLEMS Aphids; powdery mildew.
WARNING The skin may react allergically on contact with foliage.

A. '**Coronation Gold**'
Foliage: year-round. Flowers: summer. H:30-36in (75-90cm), S:18-24in (45-60cm). Z:3-9.
Although owing much to *A. filipendulina*, this is a more compact plant with grayer leaves and flatter, less densely packed yellow flowerheads.

A. filipendulina Caucasus
Flowers: early summer to early autumn. H:3-4ft (90-120cm), S:18-30in (45-75cm). Z:3-9.
Cultivars of this species, with their stiff stems bearing broad flowerheads in shades of yellow over a long period, are classic tall border plants, providing a contrast to perennials with more flowing lines. The densely packed,

mushroom-shaped heads of **'Gold Plate'** can be up to 6in (15cm) across. The rich golden color is retained if the flowerheads are dried properly.

Achillea filipendulina 'Gold Plate'

A. 'Lachsschönheit'
Flowers: summer. H:30–36in (75–90cm), S:20–24in (50–60cm). Z:3–8.
Hybrids of *A. millefolium* and *A.* 'Taygetea' run freely like common yarrow, but the best of them have heads of delicately tinted flowers. In 'Lachsschönheit', the coral of the opened flowers fades to peach, the 2 colors often present at the same time. *A.* **'Hoffnung'**, a **Galaxy Hybrid**, up to 30in (75cm) tall, has flowers that change from cream to biscuit.

A. × lewisii 'King Edward'
Foliage: spring to mid-autumn. Flowers: early and mid-summer. H:4–6in (10–15cm), S:9–12in (23–30cm). Z:3–9.
This scaled-down version of the border achilleas is a long-flowering plant for the rock garden. The heads are buff yellow and the ferny leaves gray-green.

A. ptarmica 'Boule de Neige'
Flowers: early to late summer. H:1–3ft (30–90cm), S:12–18in (30–45cm). Z:4–9.
They are invasive, but the blithe brightness of the double forms of sneezewort, with their profusion of white button flowerheads nearly obscuring the indifferent foliage, makes it worth taking trouble to position them well. **The Pearl Group** covers seed-raised doubles.

A. 'Taygetea'
Foliage: spring to early autumn. Flowers: mid- to late summer. H:18–24in (45–60cm), S:12–18in (30–45cm). Z:3–8.
This has its own cool scheme with pale yellow flowerheads, flat and up to 4in (10cm) across, and ferny evergreen leaves that in reality are a soft gray-green. *A.* **'Moonshine'** (Z:3–9), up to 2ft (60cm), is like a larger version with silvery foliage.

Achillea 'Moonshine'

ACONITUM

RANUNCULACEAE Aconite, monkshood

Despite the fascination of their curious hooded flowers, a color range that includes wonderfully rich blues, and lobed leaves well above the average in quality, these plants are less widely grown than they deserve. They are highly poisonous in all their parts, a fact that may have contributed to their neglect. There are over 100 species from the Northern Hemisphere, of which the dozen or so that are grown and which are the parents of some fine hybrids are mainly natives of alpine pastures and thin woodland where there is a good supply of moisture. Many, including the common monkshood or helmet flower (*A. napellus*, Z:5–8), are sturdy erect plants, suitable for borders or planting in light shade beneath shrubs or trees, but the tallest may need staking. The rootstock of many is tuberous. As cut flowers, aconites are statuesque.

Aconitum napellus

CULTIVATION Tolerate full sun or shade and require moist soil. To maintain vigor, divide plants every third year.
PROPAGATION By division, during autumn. From seed, sown in spring.
POTENTIAL PROBLEMS Aphids; verticillium wilt, fungal stem rot.
WARNING Long recognized as plants of sinister potency. Contact may cause allergic skin reactions and all parts of the plant, but especially the roots, are poisonous.

A. × cammarum 'Bicolor'
Foliage: spring to autumn. Flowers: mid- to late summer. H:4–5ft (1.2–1.5m), S:12–18in (30–45cm). Z:5–8.
One of the most striking of the old hybrids, this has bicolored flowers in blue and white arranged in loose clusters up the stem.

A. carmichaelii China
Flowers: early autumn. H:3–4ft (90–120cm), S:12–18in (30–45cm). Z:3–8.
The late flowering season is a bonus in a sturdy plant with rich leaves that give body to a bed throughout summer. Violet flowers are borne in branched spires; in **'Arendsii'** the color is exceptionally rich. **Wilsonii Group 'Kelmscott'** has purplish blue flowers.

Aconitum carmichaelii 'Arendsii'

A. 'Ivorine'
Flowers: late spring to early summer. H:2–3ft (60–90cm), S:12–18in (30–45cm). Z:5–8.
Short spires, closely set with cream helmetlike flowers, provide a cool foretaste of the monkshood season.

A. 'Newry Blue'
Flowers: mid- to late summer. H:4–5ft (1.2–1.5m), S:12–18in (30–45cm). Z:5–8.
The range of blues in the hybrids is impressive. The branches of this tall aconite are densely packed with mid-blue helmets. Other hybrids flowering in the second half of summer include the violet-blue *A.* **'Bressingham Spire'**, about 3ft (90cm) tall, and the deeper colored, taller *A.* **'Spark's Variety'**.

Aconitum 'Spark's Variety'

ACORUS

ARACEAE

The 2 species in this genus are
waterside plants that are more
valuable for their bladelike leaves
than for their curious flowers.
They are widely distributed in the
Northern Hemisphere. Their
rhizomes may need to be lifted and
divided after several years if they
have become congested.
CULTIVATION Require full sun and
moist or wet soil (especially pond
margins).
PROPAGATION By division, in spring
(establish in a pot before planting
out).
POTENTIAL PROBLEMS Usually none.

Acorus calamus 'Variegatus'

A. calamus 'Variegatus'
Foliage: spring to autumn. H:2-3ft
(60-90cm), S:18-24in (45-60cm).
Z:4-9.
The swordlike leaves of *A. calamus*,
the sweet flag, emit a slightly spicy
scent when crushed. 'Variegatus' is
a much more distinguished
marginal for planting in shallow
water along the edge of ponds or
streams, its longitudinal striping
making an intriguing play of green
and cream verticals.

A. gramineus E. Asia
Japanese rush
Foliage: spring to autumn.
H:6-12in (15-30cm), S:6-8in
(15-20cm). Z:6-9.

Acorus gramineus 'Ogon'

The relatively short fans of semievergreen linear leaves, beautifully
striped cream and yellow in
'Variegatus' and with a broad

yellow stripe in 'Ogon', make all of
these rushlike plants invaluable
marginals for small ponds.

ACTAEA

RANUNCULACEAE Baneberry

The 8 baneberry species, natives
of moist woodland in temperate
regions of the Northern
Hemisphere, are grown more for
their late summer display of
enticing but poisonous berries
and pleasing divided foliage than
for their clusters of small white
flowers.
CULTIVATION Require partial shade
and moist fertile soil.
PROPAGATION By division, in early
spring. From seed, sown in autumn.
POTENTIAL PROBLEMS Usually none.
WARNING The berries are very
poisonous.

A. alba E. North America
Doll's eyes, white baneberry
Flowers: late spring and early
summer. Fruits: late summer.
H:2-3ft (60-90cm), S:18-24in
(45-60cm). Z:3-9.
The light green leaves, usually
composed of 5 irregularly toothed
leaflets, make a pleasing mound of
foliage. The fluffy white flowers are
followed by mesmerizing clusters
of white berries, each with a black
eye and on a stalk that thickens
and turns red. The red baneberry,
A. rubra, is a shorter-growing
plant, reaching a height of about
18in (45cm), and the berries that
follow the white flowers are
glistening scarlet.

Actaea alba

ADONIS

RANUNCULACEAE

Most of the perennials among the
20 species from Europe and Asia
are alpine plants from open grassy
slopes or the edges of mountain
woodland. The widely distributed
European species *A. vernalis* is
suitable for growing in a rock
garden or the front of a bed.
CULTIVATION Require full sun and
well-drained fertile soil. The
European species tolerate alkaline

conditions, but the Asiatic species
do best in moist acid soils
containing plenty of organic matter.
PROPAGATION By division, after
flowering. From seed, sown in
autumn.
POTENTIAL PROBLEMS Slugs.

Adonis amurensis 'Fukujukai'

A. vernalis Europe
Flowers: mid- to late spring.
H:10-16in (25-40cm), S:12-18in
(30-45cm). Z:3-8.
The bright green leaves, ferny with
narrow linear leaflets, are topped
by anemone-like yellow flowers
that are up to 3in (7.5cm) across.
The Japanese species, *A. amurensis*
(Z:4-8), has similarly bowl-shaped
flowers in yellow, but it requires
shadier and more moist growing
conditions in an acid soil. The semidouble 'Fukujukai' is one of many
selected forms cultivated in Japan.

AGAPANTHUS

ALLIACEAE African blue lily

There are about 10 species of
Agapanthus found in southern
Africa. Some of them are
deciduous, mainly from
mountainous grasslands; others are
evergreen, mainly plants of coastal
areas where the rainfall is lower.
In addition there are numerous
hybrids, which, like the species,
are remarkably consistent in their
flower color, straying into white
but otherwise keeping to shades
of blue. The hybrids as well as the
species are fleshy-rooted plants
that usually produce clumps of
strap-shaped leaves and stout
stems culminating in umbels of
trumpet-shaped or tubular flowers.
The stalks and their flowers often
radiate out from the end of the
stem to form a rounded head, but
sometimes the flowers are more or
less loosely pendulous, as in the
deciduous and frost hardy
A. inapertus (Z:7-10). Where the
climate is mild enough, they make
well-anchored border plants, with
flowers that are good for cutting
and seedheads that are also
decorative. Agapanthus are
excellent container plants, and in

areas where it is too cold to grow them outdoors, or even where a thick mulch might help to get them through the winter, container-growing is the solution for the more tender evergreen species such as *A. africanus* (Z:8–11) and *A. praecox* subsp. *orientalis* (Z:9–11). They can be positioned outdoors in summer and given protection in a greenhouse or conservatory during the coldest months. Plants need plenty of moisture throughout summer, but should be kept dry in winter.

CULTIVATION Require full sun and moist, fertile, well-drained soil.

PROPAGATION By division, in spring. From seed, sown when ripe or in spring and kept at a temperature of 55–59°F (13–15°C). Plants flower after 2–3 years.

POTENTIAL PROBLEMS Slugs and snails; viruses.

***Agapanthus campanulatus* 'Isis'**

A. campanulatus *South Africa* (*Natal, Northern Cape*)

Flowers: late summer. H:2–4ft (60–120cm), S:16–20in (40–50cm). Z:8–10.

The flowers, which are nearly bell shaped and variable in the depth of their blue, are carried in rounded umbels above narrow gray-green deciduous leaves. It is a fine plant in its own right and a parent of many hybrids. The flowers of **var. *albidus*** are white, and 'Isis' is a dark blue version.

A. hybrids

Flowers: late summer. H:12–48in (30–120cm), S:10–20in (25–50cm). Z:7–10.

The umbrella term **Headbourne Hybrids**, used to describe blue- and white-flowered seedlings noted for their hardiness and floral qualities raised and distributed by the Hon. Lewis Palmer, has been cavalierly applied to mixed seedlings, giving no guarantee of quality. For this reason, unless you buy plants in flower, it is better to seek out named hybrids, most of which are deciduous. One of the

most substantial is **'Blue Giant'** (Z:7–11), with flower stems about 4ft (1.2m) tall and dense umbels of blue flowers. At 12–16in (30–40cm), **'Lilliput'** (Z:7–11), with deep blue flowers, is small enough to be planted in narrow beds with other sun-loving plants. **'Bressingham White'** (Z:7–11), about 3ft (90cm) tall, is one of the best white hybrids.

***Agapanthus* 'Lilliput'**

AGASTACHE

LAMIACEAE

Among the aromatic, sun-loving plants in this genus of about 30 species are several that are natives of dry hilly country in North America and Mexico. The half-hardy plant *A. mexicana* (Z:9–10) produces spikes of small tubular red-pink flowers and can be grown as an annual.

CULTIVATION Require full sun and well-drained fertile soil.

PROPAGATION By division, in spring. From semiripe cuttings, taken in late summer and protected from frosts. From seed, sown in early spring at 55–64°F (13–18°C).

POTENTIAL PROBLEMS Powdery mildew.

Agastache foeniculum

A. foeniculum *North America* Anise hyssop

Foliage: spring to early autumn. Flowers: mid-summer to early autumn. H:3–5ft (90–150cm), S:12–18in (30–45cm). Z:6–9.

The bruised leaves, downy on the underside, are pleasantly aromatic, and the erect stems are topped by long-lasting dense spikes of tiny violet-blue flowers.

AGAVE

AGAVACEAE

The agaves are among the most useful plants for frost-free gardens in hot, dry areas, their rosettes of fleshy leaves retaining their sculptural and jagged appeal even during long periods of drought. In cooler climates, they make magnificent container plants but need protection under glass during winter. There are more than 200 species, most of them found wild in areas of low rainfall, sometimes at high altitudes, from North to South America and in the West Indies. Many species are slow to reach maturity, and when they have flowered, the main rosette dies but usually leaves offsets.

CULTIVATION Require full sun and fertile, free-draining soil, preferably neutral to acid (add grit to potting media).

PROPAGATION From offsets, in spring or autumn. From seed, sown in early to mid-spring at 70°F (21°C).

POTENTIAL PROBLEMS Scale insects and, particularly under glass, mealy bugs.

WARNING Leaves of many species are sharp tipped.

***Agave americana* 'Variegata'**

A. americana *Mexico*

Foliage: year-round. Flowers: (when mature) late summer. H:5–6ft (1.5–1.8m), S:6–8ft (1.8–2.5m). Z:9–11.

Impressive rosettes are composed of pointed gray-green leaves imprinted on the reverse with the spiny margins of the outer leaves. When the plant eventually produces its yellow-green tubular flowers, the stem may be more than 20ft (6m) tall. The variegated cultivars include **'Mediopicta'**, with yellow streaks on the leaf centers, and **'Variegata'**, with cream-edged blue-green leaves.

AJUGA

LAMIACEAE Bugle

The 40 or so plants are shade-loving natives of temperate Europe and Asia. *A. reptans* has a close spreading habit, which makes it useful as groundcover, especially in the variants with distinctively colored foliage. The glossy green leaves of the pyramidal bugle (*A. pyramidalis*, Z:3-9) are less effective for this purpose, but the eye is strongly drawn to spikes of intense blue flowers in late spring.
CULTIVATION Require partial shade and moist soil.
PROPAGATION By division, in early summer. From softwood cuttings, taken in early summer.
POTENTIAL PROBLEMS Powdery mildew.

A. reptans *Europe, Iran*
Flowers: late spring to early summer. H:4-10in (10-25cm), S:2-3ft (60-90cm). Z:3-9.
The glossy green species is irrepressible, colonizing in all directions, but in late spring a carpet of the blue flowers carried in short spikes makes a wonderfully bright effect in shade. The forms with colored foliage, generally less vigorous, provide groundcover year-round. The bronzy purple of 'Atropurpurea' is at its best with the flowers, but with the variegated forms such as 'Burgundy Glow', a mixture of deep red, pink, and cream, the flowers are a distraction.

Ajuga reptans 'Atropurpurea'

ALCHEMILLA

ROSACEAE Lady's mantle

Alchemilla mollis, the best-known species, is a native of woodland margins, especially on moist soils, but the genus is a large one and representatives of the 250 or so species are found in many different parts of the world. After *A. mollis*, the most useful as garden plants are small species that follow its formula in combining attractive foliage with showers of frothy lime-green flowers.

CULTIVATION Tolerate full sun or partial shade, and moist but reasonably well-drained soil that is rich in organic matter.
PROPAGATION By division, in spring or autumn. From seed, sown in spring. From self-sown seedlings. Transplant these when small.
POTENTIAL PROBLEMS Usually none.

Alchemilla erythropoda

A. erythropoda *Carpathians, Caucasus, Turkey*
Foliage: spring to autumn. Flowers: late spring to late summer. H and S:8-12in (20-30cm). Z:3-7.
The sprays of greenish-yellow flowers fall across green, hairy leaves with a blue tint that are rounded but divided into 7 to 9 lobes. The alpine lady's mantle (*A. alpina* Z:3-8) and *A. conjuncta* (Z:3-7) are other compact species; both have the underside of the leaves covered with silky hairs.

A. mollis *Caucasus, Turkey*
Lady's mantle
Foliage: spring to autumn. Flowers: early summer. H:16-24in (40-60cm), S:20-30 in (50-75cm). Z:3-7.
The downy softness of the rounded gray-green leaves traps droplets of water and turns them to quicksilver. The intricately branched sprays of tiny greenish-yellow flowers remain attractive for weeks. The mounds of sympathetic greenery and the casual looseness of the flower sprays in a related color are a combination that makes this species one of the best plants to use around shrubs and other perennials that are bare at the

Alchemilla mollis

base. The main fault of this very beautiful plant is that it can self-seed too freely, but the prompt removal of spent flowers avoids this and in any case unwanted seedlings are easy to remove.

ALOE

ALOEACEAE

This large genus of African succulents, with about 300 species, includes a number of rosette-forming plants of jagged character that are suitable for desert gardens. In frost-prone areas they make interesting container plants that can be moved outdoors during the summer months.
CULTIVATION Require full sun and free-draining soil (potting media with added grit). Under glass, need ventilation and full light.
PROPAGATION From offsets, removed in late spring or early summer. From seed, sown in spring.
POTENTIAL PROBLEMS Scale, mealybugs, particularly when grown under glass.

Aloe aristata

A. aristata *South Africa (Cape Province)*
Foliage: year-round. Flowers: late spring to early summer. H:4-6in (10-15cm), S:6-8in (15-20cm). Z:9-11.
The stemless rosettes are composed of densely packed gray-green leaves with toothed margins and a liberal covering of spinelike white eruptions. The cylindrical flowers are orange. This species produces numerous offsets.

A. variegata *South Africa (Cape Province)*
Partridge-breasted aloe
Foliage: year-round. Flowers: early to mid-spring. H:8-12in (20-30cm), S:6-10in (15-25cm). Z:9-11.
The common name refers to the irregular white banding on the dark green leaves, which are V-shaped, arranged in 3 ranks, and have white-toothed edges. A thick stem carries scarlet flowers.

ALSTROEMERIA

ALSTROEMERIACEAE Peruvian lily

The 50 or so species in this South American genus are plants with running fleshy roots that are mostly natives of high open country. Relatively few species are grown as garden plants, the best-known being 3 that are frost hardy, the orange-yellow *A. aurea* (Z:7–10), *A. ligtu* (Z:7–10), with flowers dominated by shades of purple and pink, and the curious *A. psittacina* (Z:7–10), in an arresting combination of green and deep red with maroon marks. The hybrids are better known as a result of breeding for the cut-flower trade, and the amateur gardener stands to benefit from their beautifully marked trumpet flowers, their wiry stems, and their long period in flower (when grown commercially, they give a year-round performance). Some of these new alstroemerias go under the name **Princess hybrids** (Z:7–10). In frost-prone areas, deep planting, with the tubers covered by 9in (23cm) of soil, and mulching in autumn protect plants in winter.
CULTIVATION Require sun or partial shade and moist, well-drained soil.
PROPAGATION By division, in early spring. From seed, sown as soon as ripe.
POTENTIAL PROBLEMS Slugs, red spider mites under glass; viruses.
WARNING Contact with foliage may irritate the skin.

Alstroemeria ligtu hybrids

A. ligtu hybrids
Flowers: summer. H and S:2–3ft (60–90cm). Z:7–10.
Until recently these have been the most widely grown of the hybrids and have proved themselves more hardy than the species. The wide range of colors includes strong oranges and coral reds as well as softer shades of cream, yellow, and pink. The markings of the topmost segments are an appealing feature of these flowers, clustered at the tops of wiry stems. These hybrids can be invasive and in exposed positions may need support.

ANACYCLUS

ASTERACEAE

There is an excellent perennial daisy in this Mediterranean genus of only 9 species. It grows wild in open and stony mountainous country and makes an easy rock-garden plant, flowering prettily above feathery foliage, but is adaptable to any sunny position in the garden where the drainage is sharp.
CULTIVATION Require full sun and well-drained, light soil (potting medium with added grit). Require protection from winter wet.
PROPAGATION From cuttings, taken in spring to early summer. From seed, sown in autumn.
POTENTIAL PROBLEMS Usually none.

Anacyclus pyrethrum var. depressus

A. pyrethrum var. *depressus*
N. Africa (Atlas Mountains)
Foliage: spring to early winter. Flowers: summer. H:2–4in (5–10cm), S:6–12in (15–30cm). Z:6–10.
The finely cut evergreen foliage is ground hugging, but the stems turn up to present the flowerheads. Seen from above, these seem to be white daisies with yellow centers, but the outside of the ray flowerets is crimson.

ANAPHALIS

ASTERACEAE Pearl everlasting

In this genus of about 100 plants, the species cultivated have gray-green, often wooly, leaves and produce "everlasting" flowerheads. They come from a wide range of habitats and, surprisingly for plants with gray foliage, tolerate moisture and shade. Erect *A. margaritacea* (Z:4–8) and the more silvery *A. margaritacea* var. *yedoensis* (Z:6–8) are useful in planting schemes but can be invasive.
CULTIVATION Require full sun or partial shade and moist soil.
PROPAGATION By division, in spring. From cuttings, in spring and early summer. From seed, sown in spring.
POTENTIAL PROBLEMS Usually none.

Anaphalis triplinervis

A. triplinervis *Himalayas to S.W. China*
Foliage: spring to autumn. Flowers: mid- to late summer. H and S:18–24in (45–60cm). Z:3–9.
The 3 veins running down the gray-green leaves, which are wooly on the underside, give this species its name. The small ball-like flowerheads, which remain conspicuous for a long season, are clustered at the ends of stems, a yellow center just showing among the stiff bracts. It demands a plentiful supply of moisture.
'Sommerschnee' is laundry white and compact, rarely more than 10in (25cm) tall.

ANCHUSA

BORAGINACEAE

Anchusa cespitosa

The herbaceous plants in this genus of about 35 species, in the wild found growing in full sun on dry soils, are rather coarse, but the best are saved from being commonplace by the blue of their flowers. Intense blue flowers are also a feature of a few alpine species, including the Cretan *A. cespitosa* (Z:5–7), a plant that is adamant about sharp drainage. It can be grown as a crevice plant or in screelike conditions, or in deep pots as an alpine house plant.
CULTIVATION Require full sun and moist but well-drained soil. Trim after flowering.
PROPAGATION From root cuttings, taken in winter. From seed, sown in spring.
POTENTIAL PROBLEMS Mildew.

A. azurea *N. Africa, W. Asia,*
S. Europe
Flowers: early summer. H:18–48in
(45–120cm), S:18–24in (45–60cm).
Z:3–8.
This hairy-leaved plant is not long-
lived and tall cultivars often need
staking, but the erect stems carry
numerous saucer-shaped flowers
that are bright blue. '**Little John**' is
short growing, up to 18in (45cm)
tall, and has deep blue flowers;
'**Loddon Royalist**', usually twice as
tall but rarely needing staking, has
flowers of deep purplish blue.

ANDROSACE

PRIMULACEAE Rock jasmine

About 100 species are distributed
in alpine regions throughout the
Northern Hemisphere, and of
these the high alpine species, tiny
cushions delectably flower-studded
in season, present an exquisite
challenge to specialist gardeners.
High alpine species include several
from the Pyrenees. *A. pyrenaica*,
A. cylindrica, and *A. vandellii*
(from mountains of Spain and also
the Alps, all Z:4–7) have white
flowers; *A. ciliata* (Z:4–7) has
yellow-throated pink flowers.
Winter wet is a lethal enemy, and
success with them is rare outside
the alpine house. Other easier
species can be grown in rock
gardens and scree beds.
CULTIVATION Require full sun and
moist, gritty, very well-drained soil
(potting media with added grit
under glass). Outdoors, protect
from excessive water.
PROPAGATION From rooting rosette
cuttings, taken in summer. From
seed, sown in autumn.
POTENTIAL PROBLEMS Aphids; fungal
diseases.

A. lanuginosa *Himalayas*
Flowers: mid- to late summer.
H:2–4in (5–10cm), S:9–12in
(23–30cm). Z:4–8.
This mat-forming evergreen looks
best when the stems of silky gray-
green leaves trail from a rocky
chink, the clusters of 5-lobed pink
flowers brightening a small swag.

Androsace sarmentosa

A. sarmentosa *Himalayas to*
W. China (Sichuan)
Flowers: late spring to early
summer. H:2–4in (5–10cm),
S:12–15in (30–38cm). Z:3–8.
Rosettes of hairy leaves form dense
mats topped by tight clusters of
deep pink flowers with lime-green
eyes. *A. sempervivoides* (Z:4–8)
also has rosettes and pink flowers.

ANEMONE

RANUNCULACEAE Windflower

The fibrous-rooted species among
the 120 or so are mainly plants of
glades and woodland fringes on
moist soils, and often the mainstays
of gardens in late summer and
autumn. The basal leaves, usually
3-lobed, are good throughout the
summer, and the saucer-shaped
flowers, cradling a central knob
and its surround of yellow
stamens, are zestful just at the
moment when many other
perennials are beginning to look
tired. Even tall cultivars do not
need staking. Although tolerating
partial shade, all of the following
flower most freely in reasonably
open positions. These anemones
are often slow starters but once
established they spread freely and
can be invasive. A combination of
A. hupehensis and *A. × hybrida*
cultivars gives a flowering season
from mid-summer into autumn.

Anemone hupehensis

See also BULBS, CORMS, AND
TUBERS for tuberous and
rhizomatous anemones.
CULTIVATION Require varying
culture. *A. hupehensis* and *A. ×*
hybrida, described, tolerate full sun
and partial shade and require moist
soil rich in organic matter. Require
protection from winter wet.
PROPAGATION By division, in spring.
From root cuttings, taken in late
autumn or winter. From seed, sown
when ripe.
POTENTIAL PROBLEMS Nematodes,
caterpillars, slugs; leaf spot,
powdery mildew.
WARNING Contact with the sap of
some anemone species can cause
skin reactions.

Anemone hupehensis '**Hadspen**
Abundance'

A. hupehensis *W. and C. China*
Flowers: mid- to late summer.
H:2–3ft (60–90cm), S:16–20in
(40–50cm). Z:5–8.
The species itself, with white or
pink flowers carried on wiry stems
above the dark green, 3-lobed basal
leaves, is rarely seen. The free-
flowering '**Hadspen Abundance**'
has alternating small and large
segments, their reddish pink paling
at the edges. '**September Charm**'
is a uniform pale pink; **var.**
japonica '**Bressingham Glow**' and
var. ***japonica*** '**Prinz Heinrich**' are
semidouble and dark pink, with
longer often twisted segments.

A. × hybrida
Japanese anemone
Flowers: late summer to early
autumn. H:4–5ft (1.2–1.5m),
S:2–4ft (60–120cm). Z:5–8.
The pink-flowered Japanese
anemone is commonly seen in
old gardens and is a beautiful sight
when the numerous semidouble,
soft-toned flowers float above the
base of mid-green leaves. An old
favorite among pink cultivars is the
semidouble '**Königin Charlotte**'.
'**Kriemhilde**' is a purplish-pink
semidouble and '**Max Vogel**' a
single pink. The freshness of the
whites places them in a class of
their own; they look their best
when seen against a dark
background such as a yew hedge.
The vigorous '**Géante des**
Blanches' and '**Whirlwind**' are
both semidouble, but the single
'**Honorine Jobert**' is the
undisputed queen.

Anemone × hybrida '**Whirlwind**'

ANEMONOPSIS

RANUNCULACEAE

The single species is a woodland plant of shy charm, and opens its gently nodding pale violet flowers in summer. It is only happy in conditions that match the cool, moist shade of its mountain habitat in Japan.

CULTIVATION Requires partial shade and moist, deep, fertile, acid soil that is rich in organic matter. Requires shelter from wind.
PROPAGATION By division, in spring. From seed, sown as soon as ripe.
POTENTIAL PROBLEMS Usually none.

Anemonopsis macrophylla

A. macrophylla *Japan*
Foliage: spring to autumn. Flowers: mid- to late summer. H:24–30in (60–75cm), S:16–20in (40–50cm). Z:5–8.
From a mound of fresh green leaves, the leaflets irregularly toothed and lobed, rise dark stems with purplish buds nodding at the tips. The demure stance does not change when the 3 waxy sepals spring open, releasing the pale violet petals, white at the center around a boss of stamens.

ANTHEMIS

ASTERACEAE

Radiant daisy flowers are produced in great quantity and usually over a long period by several among the 100 or so sun-loving species. As wild plants they are found on very well-drained, often poor stony soils in North Africa, Europe, and eastward to the Caucasus and Iran. Their cheerful, straightforward qualities show up well when set against more sophisticated plants in sunny beds or rock gardens, but they have the disadvantage of being short-lived. In addition to cutting plants back after flowering to encourage fresh growth and prolong their life span, replace them with newly propagated plants on a regular basis.
CULTIVATION Require full sun and light, well-drained soil. These plants should be cut back after flowering.

PROPAGATION By division, in spring. From cuttings, taken in spring. From seed, sown in spring.
POTENTIAL PROBLEMS Aphids, slugs; powdery mildew.

A. punctata subsp. *cupaniana*
Sicily
Flowers: early summer to autumn. H:8–12in (20–30cm), S:2–3ft (60–90cm). Z:5–7.
The tireless flowering and the sprawling aromatic gray-green foliage transform a simple daisy, white with a yellow center, into a valuable plant for a large rock garden or path edging. The Caucasian *A. marschalliana*, which is lower growing and has yellow daisies over silvery, finely cut foliage, can be planted in gritty soil among paving.

A. sancti-johannis *S.W. Bulgaria*
Flowers: summer. H:24–30in (60–75cm), S:18–24in (45–60cm). Z:4–9.
The vibrant orange-yellow of these daisies, the stubby ray flowerets circling a dense convex center, can be described as brassy without any pejorative overtones. The gray-green foliage is delicately cut.

Anthemis tinctoria 'E. C. Buxton'

A. tinctoria *Europe and E. to Iran*
Golden marguerite, ox-eye chamomile
Foliage: year-round. Flowers: summer. H and S:2–3ft (60–90cm). Z:4–8.
Stiff-stemmed daisies, the cultivars providing a range of yellows, are crowded above the ferny green leaves. 'E. C. Buxton', with pale

Anthemis tinctoria 'Kelwayi'

lemon ray flowerets around a brighter yellow disk, lends itself to subtle color schemes. 'Sauce Hollandaise' and 'Wargrave', both creamy yellow, are also good for incorporation into cool color schemes. 'Grallach Gold' is bright yellow and makes a splash in a border; so do the bold yellow flowers of 'Kelwayi'.

AQUILEGIA

RANUNCULACEAE Columbine

Aquilegia vulgaris

The columbines are too readily pigeonholed as old-fashioned flowers, even when this is meant as a compliment. It is true that the European granny's bonnet (*A. vulgaris*) has been grown for centuries, but it does not require a nostalgic gloss to make it a very good plant, as are others among about 70 species found in woodland and more open habitats, in some cases alpine, in the temperate Northern Hemisphere. There are also numerous hybrids, most species crossing with indiscriminate freedom. Almost all combine good foliage, with prettily divided leaflets, in some cases in a beautiful gray-blue tone, and graceful, distinctively spurred flowers in a broad color range. The taller columbines are ideal in dappled shade and among shrubs, where they can be allowed to self-seed freely. In highly regulated gardens their generous self-seeding might be thought a nuisance, but it is compensation for the tendency of aquilegias to be short-lived. The alpine species described, which do better in more open positions, can be planted in rock gardens, raised beds, or between paving stones.
CULTIVATION Tolerate full sun or partial shade and require moist but well-drained soil.
PROPAGATION From seed, sown as soon as ripe. By division, in spring.
POTENTIAL PROBLEMS Aphids, leaf miners, caterpillars, sawflies; powdery mildew.
WARNING Contact with sap may irritate the skin.

205

A. alpina *Switzerland*
Alpine columbine
Flowers: late spring. H:2–3ft
(60–90cm), S:12–14in (30–35cm).
Z:3–8.
Blue or blue and white flowers
hover above soft green leaves. The
flowers have short spurs. **A. 'Hensol
Harebell'** (Z:5–9) is a fine blue
hybrid between *A. alpina* and
A. vulgaris. A species from S. France
and Italy, **A. bertolonii**, is like a
dwarf form of *A. alpina*, each stem
carrying a single purplish flower.

Aquilegia 'Hensol Harebell'

A. canadensis *E. Canada to
S. USA (Florida, Texas, and New
Mexico)*
Flowers: mid-spring to mid-
summer. H:2–3ft (60–90cm),
S:12–14in (30–35cm). Z:3–9.
The long-spurred species are much
less widely grown than the hybrids
derived from them, but their airy
lightness makes them highly
distinctive. *A. canadensis* has lemon-
yellow flowers with red spurs.
Other long-spurred species from
N. America, both yellow flowered,
are **A. chrysantha** and
A. longissima, the latter with
slender spurs up to 6in (15cm) long.

A. flabellata var. pumila
Flowers: early summer. H and
S:4–6in (10–15cm). Z:3–9.
This does not require coaxing
from an enthusiast as do some of
the alpine species. The blue-green
foliage with neatly lobed leaflets is
itself very beautiful, and the blue
and white flowers are large for the
size of the plant.

A. McKana Group
Flowers: late spring to early
summer. H:2–3ft (60–90cm),
S:18–24in (45–60cm). Z:5–9.
The promiscuity of aquilegias is
tiresome if you are trying to
maintain pure populations, but it
has resulted in some fine hybrids.
In the McKana hybrids, the mid-
green leaves are topped by
showers of long-spurred flowers,
up to 15 per stem, in a color range
that includes white and shades of
blue, yellow, and red. Some of the

Aquilegia Biedermeyer Group

flowers in the group are bicolored.
A. Biedermeier Group are shorter-
growing hybrids, rarely taller than
18in (45cm), the hosts of upturned
flowers usually having blue sepals
and short-spurred white petals.
Their confectionary prettiness,
however, owes little to the light
grace of the species.

A. viridiflora *E. Siberia and
W. China*
Flowers: late spring to early
summer. H:8–12in (20–30cm),
S:6–8in (15–20cm). Z:3–7.
The color is in itself a surprise, the
2 or 3 nodding flowers having
greenish sepals and purplish-
brown spurred petals, from which
protrude the clustered stamens. In
addition, this is one of the sweetly
fragrant species.

A. vulgaris *Europe*
Granny's bonnet
Flowers: late spring to early
summer. H:2–3ft (60–90cm),
S:18–24in (45–60cm). Z:4–9.
The short-spurred flowers that float
in profusion above the pretty
foliage are in shades of violet, blue,
pink, and plum or white. In so
many of its variations, this is a very
beautiful plant, the white **'Nivea'**,
with light green foliage, being an
irresistible woodland enchantress.
It seems perverse, therefore, that
2 curiosities, the double **'Nora
Barlow'**, which has flowers
reduced to cluttered tufts of pink
and green, and the **Vervaeneana
Group**, with gold variegated leaves
and mixed flower colors, should be
so popular.

Aquilegia vulgaris Vervaeneana Group

ARENARIA

CARYOPHYLLACEAE Sandwort

Among the 150 or more species in
this genus are many low-growing
evergreen perennials and subshrubs
found wild in mountainous or
arctic regions of the Northern
Hemisphere, the common name
indicating the kind of free-draining
terrain on which some are found.
The dense cushion-forming species
such as
A. tetraquetra are most easily
pleased in an alpine house, but the
prostrate stems of several easy
species readily drape themselves
over rocks or the edge of a raised
bed.
CULTIVATION Require full sun and
moist but well-drained, poor, sandy
soil.
PROPAGATION By division, in spring.
From basal cuttings, taken in early
summer. From seed, sown in
autumn.
POTENTIAL PROBLEMS Usually none.

Arenaria tetraquetra

A. montana *S.W. Europe*
Flowers: early summer. H:2–4in
(5–10cm), S:12–18 (30–45cm).
Z:4–9.
The saucer-shaped white flowers
nestle among narrow leaves that
cover a mat of wiry stems. The
pink sandwort (**A. purpurascens**),
from N. Spain, has starry flowers,
deep pink in bud, pale on opening.

ARMERIA

PLUMBAGINACEAE Sea pink, thrift

The thrifts are perennials and
subshrubs of rocky mountains and
seashore in Europe, N. Africa, and
the Americas, most forming tight
cushions or hummocks of
evergreen grassy leaves. Of about
80 species, a few are widely grown
in rock gardens and as edging for
their round heads of small flowers.
CULTIVATION Require full sun and
well-drained soil.
PROPAGATION By division, in early
spring. From semiripe cuttings,
taken in summer. From seed, sown
in spring or autumn.
POTENTIAL PROBLEMS Usually none.

A. juniperifolia Mountains of
C. Spain
Flowers: late spring. H:2–3in
(5–7.5cm), S:4–6in (10–15cm).
Z:4–7.
In a rock garden, this makes a tight
hummock of dark green leaves
well covered by almost stemless
heads of pink flowers. The reddish
pink of **'Bevan's Variety'** makes a
very bright miniature.

Armeria maritima

A. maritima Europe, including
Britain
Sea thrift
Flowers: late spring to summer.
H and S:6–12in (15–30cm). Z:4–8.
This widely distributed plant is
found wild near the coast and also
in mountainous terrain in many
parts of the Northern Hemisphere.
The flowerheads, up to 1in (2.5cm)
across and held well above the
linear dark green leaves, are often a
washed-out pink in the wild but
the color range includes darker
shades of pink and red as well as
white. Strongly colored cultivars
include **'Bloodstone'**, with deep
red flowerheads on short stems;
'Dusseldorfer Stolz', wine-red
flowerheads on short stems; and
'Vindictive', deep pink.

Armeria **'Dusseldorfer Stolz'**

ARTEMISIA

ASTERACEAE Mugwort, sagebrush,
wormwood

Most of the perennial species in
this genus of around 300 species,
found in the Northern Hemisphere,
have insignificant flowers, but the
aromatic gray, pewter, or silver
foliage of several is outstanding.

Tarragon (*A. dracunculus*, Z:4–7),
in the first rank of culinary herbs,
has green leaves, as does
A. lactiflora (Z:3–9), its dark green
foliage being heavily cut and its
creamy flowerheads suitable for
drying. In the wild, the species are
plants of open dry country. It is
difficult to overstate their value as
a calming influence where sunny
well-drained beds have been
planted with vivid color schemes,
in their mediating role, easing
tensions in what is often described
with approval as a riot of color.
Their silky or felted texture is
appealing to the eye and to the
touch, and adds another dimension
of contrasts. Although many are
evergreen, they look bedraggled in
cold wet winters. See also SHRUBS.
CULTIVATION Require full sun and
well-drained fertile soil. Cut back in
spring to keep plants compact.
PROPAGATION By division, in spring.
From cuttings, in summer. From
seed, sown in spring or autumn.
POTENTIAL PROBLEMS Aphids; gall
(*A. absinthium* and *A.* 'Powis Castle').

A. absinthium Temperate Asia,
Europe
Absinth, wormwood
Foliage: spring to mid-winter.
Flowers: late summer. H:2–3ft
(60–90cm), S:20–24in (50–60cm).
Z:5–8.
This perennial has fine silver leaves
and sprays of yellow flowers. As a
foliage plant it achieves distinction
in **'Lambrook Silver'**.

A. ludoviciana W. North America
to Mexico
Western mugwort, white sage
Foliage: spring to autumn. Flowers:
mid-summer to autumn. H:2–4ft
(60–120cm), S:2–3ft (60–90cm).
Z:4–8.
Roots run freely in well-drained
soil, producing numerous upright
stems clothed in clean gray leaves,
which become almost white in a
hot summer. The plumes of tiny
flowers do not compete with the
foliage. The leaves of **var. *latiloba***
(Z:5–7) and **'Valerie Finnis'**
(Z:5–7) have jagged margins.

Artemisia ludoviciana

A. **'Powis Castle'**
Foliage: spring to late autumn.
Flowers: late summer. H:24–30in
(60–75cm), S:2–3ft (60–90cm).
Z:5–8.
This woody-based perennial may
owe some of its character to the
shrubby *A. arborescens* (Z:8–9),
itself a good foliage plant with
finely divided silver leaves. The
mound of soft, fine, silver-green
foliage has the quality of a pelt, a
light breeze bringing to life its
texture and subtle coloring.

Artemisia **'Powis Castle'**

A. schmidtiana Japan
Foliage: year-round. Flowers:
summer. H:8–12in (20–30cm),
S:12–18in (30–45cm). Z:5–8.
The silky texture of the finely cut
leaves is an invitation to touch. The
very compact **'Nana'** makes silky
cushions of soft thread.

A. stelleriana N.E. Asia, E. North
America
Dusty miller
Foliage: spring to mid-winter.
Flowers: late summer and early
autumn. H:18–24in (45–60cm),
S:2–3ft (60–90cm). Z:3–8.
The intricately cut outline of the
gray-green, almost silver leaves and
their felted texture make this a
remarkable foliage plant.
'Boughton Silver', which sprawls
on prostrate stems, is a superb
edging and container plant. The
yellow flowerheads are
insignificant.

ARUNCUS

ROSACEAE Goat's beard

The 2 or 3 species tolerate a wide
range of conditions but grow wild
in high moist woodlands of the
Northern Hemisphere. In sun, they
need fertile moist soil to achieve
the full splendor of their foliage
and plumy flowers. The low-
growing *A. aethusifolius* (Z:3–9),
with astilbelike cream flowers over
finely cut leaves, is an appealing
plant for a wodland edge.
CULTIVATION Tolerate full sun or
partial shade and require fertile
moist soil.

PROPAGATION By division, in early spring or autumn. From seed, sown in spring or autumn.
POTENTIAL PROBLEMS Usually none.

A. dioicus *Europe to E. Siberia, E. North America*
Foliage: spring to autumn. Flowers: early to mid-summer. H:4–6ft (1.2–1.8m), S:3–4ft (90–120cm). Z:3–9.
In full flower, this is a commanding plant, the broad clump of light green, compound leaves perfectly balancing the long plumes of tiny flowers. Male and female flowers are carried on separate plants, the male flowers being cleaner white, but the creamy female flowers are followed by attractive seedheads. It is often consigned to the wild garden (female plants may self-seed to excess), but is undeniably a splendid plant for borders and waterside. **'Kneiffi'**, about 3ft (90cm) tall, has cream plumes over foliage cut away to a ferny lace.

Aruncus dioicus

ASPHODELINE

ASPHODELACEAE Jacob's rod

In dry stony landscapes from the Mediterranean eastward through Turkey to the Caucasus, king's spear (*A. lutea*) and the related 19 species make conspicuous clumps, with spikes of starry flowers followed by long-lasting seedpods. An asphodel (**Asphodelus albus**, Z:6–8), from a closely related genus, survives in similarly parched and stony conditions, in early summer producing spikes of white flowers warmed by pink central

Asphodelus albus

veins. Both this and the species described are bold plants for dry, sunny borders or wild plantings in open positions where the soil is free draining. They may need to be mulched where winters are severe.
CULTIVATION Require full sun and well-drained light soil.
PROPAGATION By division, in late summer or early autumn. From seed, sown in spring.
POTENTIAL PROBLEMS Slugs, snails, aphids.

Asphodeline lutea

A. lutea *C. and E. Mediterranean, W. Turkey*
King's spear, yellow asphodel
Flowers: late spring. H:3–5ft (90–150cm), S:10–12in (25–30cm). Z:6–8.
The fleshy roots produce tall stems with whorls of blue-green, grassy leaves, culminating in a spike of fragrant starry yellow flowers. These are followed by rounded green seedpods that dry to brown.

ASTER

ASTERACEAE

Representatives of this large genus —it contains about 250 species— are found in such a wide range of habitats throughout the Northern Hemisphere and so many of the plants grown are hybrids that the only useful generalization to make is that there are asters for most situations in the garden. Their relationship is evident in the daisy-like flowerheads, which are solitary or clustered, but in scale and color there is an impressive choice, valuable for reviving borders in late summer and autumn.
CULTIVATION Require varying conditions, but the plants described need a moist but well-drained soil.
PROPAGATION By division, in spring. From cuttings, taken in spring and early summer. From seed, sown in spring or autumn.
POTENTIAL PROBLEMS Aphids, nematodes, earwigs, slugs, snails; leaf spot, fusarium wilt, gray mold (*Botrytis*). *A. novi-belgii* cultivars are very prone to mildew.

A. alpinus *Alps*
Flowers: early to mid-summer. H:7–10in (17–25cm), S:18–24in (45–60cm). Z:4–8.
The leaves are often spoon shaped and the flowerheads a pale mauve. The deep-colored selections, such as the rich purple **'Dunkle Schöne'**, are the most attractive.

A. amellus *C. and E. Europe*
Flowers: late summer to autumn. H:1–2ft (30–60cm), S:14–18in (35–45cm). Z:5–7.
The species, which has gray-green leaves that are rough to the touch and mauve-blue flowerheads with yellow centers, has been displaced in gardens by cultivars mainly in shades of blue. **'King George'** has large, mauve-blue flowerheads, but a more refined plant is the purplish blue **'Veilchenkönigin'**.

Aster amellus 'King George'

A. ericoides *C. and E. North America*
Flowers: late summer to late autumn. H:2–3ft (60–90cm), S:12–18in (30–45cm). Z:5–8.
The slender twiggy bush carries a late profusion of tiny white flowerheads. The cultivars include pale blues, the creamy **'Brimstone'**, with strong yellow centers, and pinks such as **'Pink Cloud'**.

Aster ericoides 'Pink Cloud'

A. × frikartii 'Mönch'
Flowers: late summer and early autumn. H:24–30in (60–75cm), S:18–24in (45–60cm). Z:5–8.
This early hybrid deserves the praise that has been heaped on it. It is a long-flowering and refined plant with yellow-centered

flowerheads in a lovely shade of purplish blue. Furthermore, it does not require support and is resistant to disease.

A. × frikartii 'Mönch'

A. novae-angliae *E. North America*
New England aster
Flowers: late summer to mid-autumn. H:4–5ft (1.2–1.5m), S:18–24in (45–60cm). Z:5–8.
The stiff-stemmed plants have dull foliage, and some of the cultivars that represent the species in gardens are indifferent plants. Reddish pink **'Andenken an Alma Pötschke'** is, however, superbly vibrant. Other good cultivars are the softer **'Harrington's Pink'** and the white **'Herbstschnee'**.

Aster novae-angliae 'Herbstschnee'

A. novi-belgii *North America*
Michaelmas daisy, New York aster
Flowers: late summer to mid-autumn. H:tall 2–4ft (60–120cm), short 12–18in (30–45cm), S:18–36in (45–90cm). Z:4–8.
This species, which has tough rhizomatous roots, is represented in gardens by several hundred cultivars in a wide range of heights and with flowerheads in white or shades of blue, pink, mauve, and purple. Despite being nondescript out of flower and prone to disfiguring diseases, these plants have remained popular for their late display of daisy flowerheads. The following selection gives only a glimpse of the choice available from a specialized nursery. Two short-growing examples, about 1ft (30cm) in height, are **'Heinz Richard'**, a large semidouble with

Aster novi-belgii 'Heinz Richard'

bright pink rays surrounding the yellow center, and **'Kristina'**, a double white. Taller examples, about 3ft (90cm) tall, include the pale blue double **'Marie Ballard'** and **'Winston S. Churchill'**, a deep red double.

Aster novi-belgii 'Marie Ballard'

A. pilosus var. demotus *North America*
Flowers: mid- to late autumn. H:30–36in (75–90cm), S:18–24in (45–60cm). Z:5–8.
This is one of the last perennials of autumn, with constellations of small white daisies caught in its wiry stems. *A. pringlei* **'Monte Cassino'** is like a more slender version, up to 2ft (60cm) tall.

ASTILBE

SAXIFRAGACEAE

The best of the astilbes combine to perfection densely ground-covering but highly ornamental foliage and graceful, long-lasting airy plumes of tiny flowers, the vestiges of which remain a decorative etching in winter. The

Astilbe hybrids

species, from S.E. Asia and North America, are about 12 in number. They are plants of moist ground, often growing in shade near water. The numerous hybrids are versatile plants, growing equally well in sun and shade, relishing moisture, but tolerant of drier conditions in beds. The short-growing hybrids deserve frontal positions; the large need generous spacing. Their parentage is complex, and those described are listed according to their cultivar name. Plants should be divided every 3 to 4 years.
CULTIVATION Tolerate full sun or partial shade and require a moist fertile soil, thriving even in boggy conditions.
PROPAGATION By division, in late winter.
POTENTIAL PROBLEMS Leaf spot, powdery mildew.

A. × arendsii 'Brautschleier'
Flowers: mid-summer. H and S:2–3ft (60–90cm). Z:4–9.
Open sprays, white changing to cream, froth over bright green leaves. The appealing lightness of form and color of many astilbes is sacrificed in some of the hybrids with dense, strong-colored plumes. **'Fanal'**, which grows to about 2ft (60cm), has dark green foliage and rich red flowers.

Astilbe × arendsii 'Fanal'

A. 'Bronze Elegans'
Foliage: spring to autumn. Flowers: late summer. H and S:10–12in (25–30cm). Z:4–9.
This short-growing astilbe is for a frontal position, its dark foliage, tinted bronze, making a beautiful base for sprays of salmon pink and cream flowers. *A.* **'Sprite'** (Z:4–8), slightly shorter and later flowering, has more ferny dark green leaves and airy pink sprays.

A. chinensis var. pumila *China*
Flowers: late summer. H:12–18in (30–45cm), S:1–2ft (30–60cm). Z:3–8.
Although dwarf, this makes good groundcover. It is more welcome for its reddish-green foliage than its mauve-pink flower spikes.

209

A. × *crispa* 'Perkeo'

Foliage: spring to late summer.
Flowers: summer. H and S:8–12in
(20–30cm). Z:4–8.
Bronzed finely cut leaves turn dark
green as the tight pyramids of
bright pink flowers develop.

A. 'Deutschland'

Flowers: late spring. H:20–24in
(50–60cm), S:1–2ft (30–60cm).
Z:4–9.
Sprays of white flowers toss about
over decorative bright green leaves.

Astilbe 'Professor van der Wielen'

A. 'Professor van der Wielen'

Flowers: mid-summer. H and S:18–
36in (45–90cm). Z:4–8.
The pick of the large whites has
arching sprays of creamy flowers
over a large mound of mid-green
leaves. Its match in pink but late
flowering is *A.* 'Straussenfeder'.

ASTILBOIDES

SAXIFRAGACEAE

E. Asia is the place of origin of the
single species, which grows wild
in shaded areas near lakes and
streams but with its roots above
the water level. In a cool waterside
position, particularly in a
woodland setting, it is a foliage
plant of rare quality.
CULTIVATION Requires partial shade
and fertile moist soil.
PROPAGATION By division, in early
spring. From seed, sown in
autumn.
POTENTIAL PROBLEMS Slugs in
autumn and spring.

A. *tabularis* N.E. China, N. Korea

Foliage: spring to autumn. Flowers:
early and mid-summer. H:5ft
(1.5m), S:4ft (1.2m). Z:5–7.
The broad satisfying clump of
foliage consists of light green
leaves of soft texture, rounded but
with a wandering edge making
slight lobes, and supported at the
center by the leafstalks. If the soil
is reliably moist and fertile, leaves
can be up to 3ft (90cm) across. The
drooping sprays of small cream
flowers are carried on strong stems
well above the foliage base.

Astilboides tabularis

ASTRANTIA

APIACEAE Masterwort

The masterworts, a genus of about
10 species, are found wild in
woodland and alpine meadows
from Europe to W. Asia. They
produce sprays of intriguing
flowerheads, with posies of tiny
flowers surrounded by rufflike
bracts, usually pale green, giving a
cool finish to the clusters of little
pincushions. The base from which
these sprays rise is a good clump
of attractively divided leaves.
Provided the soil is reasonably
moist, the plants described can be
grown in a wide range of conditions
and in beds as well as in wilder
parts of the garden.
CULTIVATION Tolerate full sun or
partial shade and require a fertile,
moist but well-drained soil. *A.
major* tolerates drier soils.
PROPAGATION By division, in spring.
From seed, sown as soon as ripe.
POTENTIAL PROBLEMS Aphids, slugs;
powdery mildew.

**Astrantia major subsp. involucrata
'Shaggy'**

A. *major* Austria

Flowers: early and mid-summer.
H:2ft (60cm), S:18in (45cm). Z:5–7.
The greenish-white flowerheads
with tints of pink and stronger
green make a wonderfully subtle
plant for a shady corner that far
exceeds its common brief to
please in a cottage garden. The rich
colored cultivars—'**Hadspen
Blood**' is dark red and '**Rubra**' is
wine red—are undoubtedly useful
in strong color schemes but look
mournful, especially in shade. An
amusing extravagance is displayed
by **subsp. *involucrata* 'Shaggy'** in
the length of its bracts, the tips of
which are strong green. The yellow
and cream markings on the foliage
of '**Sunningdale Variegated**' make
it a distinctive foliage plant, but the
leaves are at odds with the flowers.

A. *maxima* Europe

Flowers: early and mid-summer.
H:18–24in (45–60cm), S:12–15in
(30–38cm). Z:5–7.
The broad fringed bracts clasp a
dense cluster of tiny flowers, the
whole flowerhead pink but tinged
green at first.

AUBRIETA

BRASSICACEAE

The 12 or so species in this genus
of European and Asian origin are
rarely grown, but the hybrids
derived from them share their taste
for rocky ground, especially on
alkaline soil. They produce vivid
splashes of color in the garden in
spring, never better than when
cascading over low walls or from
crevices. Trimming plants after
flowering keeps them compact.
CULTIVATION Require full sun and
fertile well-drained soil that is
neutral or alkaline.
PROPAGATION From cuttings, taken
in summer. From seed, sown in
autumn or spring.
POTENTIAL PROBLEMS Aphids,
eelworms, flea beetles; white
blister.

A. hybrids

Flowers: spring. H:2–3in
(5–7.5cm), S:15–28in (38–70cm).
Z:4–7.
The evergreen mounds of small
hairy leaves are often almost totally
obscured by the cross-shaped
flowers in shades of blue, purple,
pink, and red and also in white.
Singles include '**Doctor Mules**', a
strong purple; '**Greencourt Purple**',
rich purple; and '**Red Carpet**', deep
red. '**Bressingham Pink**' is a
double pink. Among those with
variegated leaves is '**Silberrand**',
which has blue flowers.

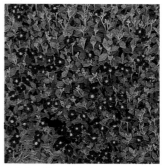

Aubrieta 'Doctor Mules'

AURINIA

BRASSICACEAE

Changes in nomenclature have brought into this small genus of 7 species the familiar gold dust, better known as *Alyssum saxatile*. The 2 genera are closely allied, and both include sun-loving plants of mountainous and rocky habitats in C. and S. Europe. Gold dust itself is best suited to a position in a rock garden or raised bed where in lazing about it softens hard lines and beams with a sunny radiance. The same could also be said of the yellow-flowered and fragrant *Alyssum montanum* 'Berggold' (Z:4-9). Trimming plants after flowering keeps them compact.
CULTIVATION Require full sun and very well-drained soil.
PROPAGATION From cuttings, taken in early summer. From seed, sown in autumn.
POTENTIAL PROBLEMS Aphids.

Aurinia saxatilis

A. saxatilis C. and S.E. Europe
Gold dust
Flowers: late spring to early summer. H:8-12in (20-30cm), S:12-18in (30-45cm). Z:3-7.
Stems densely clustered with 4-petaled bright yellow flowers sprawl from clumps of hairy gray-green leaves. 'Citrina' is lemon-yellow, and 'Dudley Nevill' has distinctive apricot-orange flowers.

BAPTISIA

PAPILIONACEAE False or wild indigo

Most of the 20 or so species of this North American genus have white or yellow pea flowers, but the best known has flowers in a wonderful shade of blue. *B. australis* makes a large border plant, and its position should be well chosen from the outset as it is deep rooting and resents disturbance.
CULTIVATION Require full sun and moist but well-drained and preferably acid soil.
PROPAGATION By division, in early spring. From seed, sown as soon as ripe.
POTENTIAL PROBLEMS Usually none.

Baptisia australis

B. australis E. USA
Foliage: summer to late autumn. Flowers: early summer. Fruits: autumn. H:2-4ft (60-120cm), S:18-24in (45-60cm). Z:4-9.
The blue-tinted foliage and the slender spires of deep blue, lupine-like flowers have an unusually soft quality. Dark seedpods remain when frost has blackened and cut down the leaves.

BERGENIA

SAXIFRAGACEAE Elephant's ears

It is difficult with this genus of about 8 Asiatic species to strike a balance between the enthusiasm of its overgenerous advocates and the skepticism of those who find the formula of hard flower color and coarse leafage repeated to excess. The great virtue of several species and most hybrids is that they make dense groundcover in a wide range of conditions, even including shady dry areas, reflecting the diversity of their origins in woodland and boggy and peaty areas. The boldness of the large leaves is indisputable, and their glossiness enhances the rich mahogany and purple tones that often develop in winter, especially on plants grown in open positions. The flowers, clustered at the tip of heavy stems, are in themselves beautifully bell shaped; even those of piercing magenta are not impossible to place and are perhaps best left to scream in isolation. The bergenias described are all suitable as groundcover, but some of the smaller species and

Bergenia cordifolia

hybrids are also worth growing. *B. strachyi* (Z:4-8), for example, usually less than 8in (20cm) tall, has tight clusters of fragrant pink flowers in early spring.
CULTIVATION Tolerate full sun or partial shade and a wide range of soil conditions but best in well-drained soil rich in organic matter.
PROPAGATION By division, in autumn or early spring. By rooting leafy rhizomes, in autumn.
POTENTIAL PROBLEMS Slugs, snails, caterpillars, vine weevils; leaf spot, dry brown rot.

B. 'Abendglut'
Foliage: year-round. Flowers: mid-to late spring. H:8-12in (20-30cm), S:18-24in (45-60cm). Z:4-8.
The clumps of rounded small leaves color strongly in winter, the reverse becoming a rich purplish red. The semidouble flowers are a vivid reddish pink. The leaves of the **Ballawley Hybrids**, nearly twice the size of those of 'Abendglut', are also richly colored in winter, becoming glossy maroon and purple. The purplish-red flowers are borne in the second half of spring.

Bergenia 'Bressingham White'

B. 'Bressingham White'
Foliage: year-round. Flowers: mid-to late spring. H:12-18in (30-45cm), S:18-24in (45-60cm). Z:4-8.
The leaves do not take on purplish tones in winter, but out of their deep green rise sprays of white flowers. The flowers of another white of similar dimensions but early flowering, *B.* 'Silberlicht', take on pink tinges as they age.

B. ciliata N. India, Nepal, W. Pakistan
Foliage: spring to mid-autumn. Flowers: early spring. H:12-14in (30-35cm), S:18-20in (45-50cm). Z:7-9.
The large rounded leaves are hairy, quite different in their soft texture from the run of bergenias. Frost may damage the light pink flowers, and this species is sometimes deciduous.

Bergenia cordifolia 'Purpurea'

B. cordifolia *Siberia*
Foliage: year-round. Flowers: late winter to early spring. H:18–24in (45–60cm), S:24–30in (60–75cm). Z:4–8.
The species itself is an impressive evergreen, with large, almost heart-shaped, deep green leaves that take on purple tints in winter. The dark pink flowers are carried on reddish stems. In **'Purpurea'** the purplish red of the foliage is intensified in winter, the flower stem is vivid red and the flowers bright magenta.

Bergenia 'Morgenröte'

B. 'Morgenröte'
Foliage: year-round. Flowers: mid- to late spring and early summer. H:12–18in (30–45cm), S:18–24in (45–60cm). Z:4–8.
Red flower stems emerge from the rosettes of large deep green leaves carrying reddish-pink flowers on this good ground-covering hybrid.

B. purpurascens *N. Burma, W. China, E. Himalayas*
Foliage: year-round. Flowers: mid- to late spring. H and S:12–18in (30–45cm). Z:5–8.

Bergenia 'Wintermarchen'

In winter the dark green narrow leaves turn purplish red and an even brighter red on the reverse. The flowers, which dangle stiffly from a red-brown stem, are purplish pink. **B. 'Wintermarchen'** is a narrow-leaved hybrid, slightly more compact, with early flowers in reddish pink. The leaves are slightly twisted, showing both the richly colored reverse and purple-tinged glossy surface in winter.

BLETILLA

ORCHIDACEAE

This small genus of about 10 Asiatic terrestrial orchids includes 1 well-known woodland species that can form large colonies in lightly shaded borders provided the climate is mild enough. The pseudobulbs, which are tuberlike, resent deep planting.
CULTIVATION Tolerate full sun or partial shade. Require shelter and well-drained moist soil rich in organic matter. In frost-prone areas, lift and store over winter. If left outdoors, mulch with potting medium and bark or leaf mold.
PROPAGATION By division, in spring.
POTENTIAL PROBLEMS Aphids. Under glass, red spider mites, whiteflies, mealybugs.

Bletilla striata

B. striata *China, Japan*
Flowers: spring to early summer. H and S:1–2ft (30–60cm). Z:6–9.
In well-established colonies of these vivacious plants, sinuous stems carry sprays of bell-shaped, light magenta orchid flowers over sheaves of pleated, sword-shaped leaves.

BRUNNERA

BORAGINACEAE

Forget-me-not flowers are a vivid attraction of the commonly grown species in this genus of 3 plants from woodland in E. Europe and N. W. Asia. The large, heart shaped leaves, slightly coarse companions for the dainty flowers, make good groundcover and in the variegated forms are beautifully marked.

CULTIVATION Tolerate full sun but grow most successfully in partial to full shade and require a moist but well-drained soil that is rich in organic matter.
PROPAGATION By division, in early spring. From root cuttings, taken in late autumn. From seed, sown in spring.
POTENTIAL PROBLEMS Usually none.

Brunnera macrophylla

B. macrophylla *Caucasus*
Foliage: early summer to early autumn. Flowers: mid- to late spring. H:12–18in (30–45cm), S:2ft (60cm). Z:3–9.
The plain-leaved form will thrive in sun or shade, provided the soil is reasonably moist, producing abundant sprays of tiny blue flowers as the foliage develops. The variegated forms tend to burn in full sun. **'Dawson's White'**, with nearly white margins, is the most vulnerable. **'Hadspen Cream'** has an irregular margin of palest yellow, and **'Langtrees'** has metallic-gray markings.

CALTHA

RANUNCULACEAE Kingcup, marsh marigold

The buttercup relatives that make up this genus of about 10 species are all moisture-loving plants, and those described are most beautiful when their rich foliage has fed on fertile boggy ground and their golden flowers, caught in direct sunlight, are also lit by reflections from water. They are possible in borders but need an unfailing supply of moisture.
CULTIVATION Require full sun and water's edge planting but will tolerate fertile, very moist soil.
PROPAGATION By division, in early spring or after flowering. From seed, sown as soon as ripe.
POTENTIAL PROBLEMS Powdery mildew.

C. palustris *Europe, North America*
Foliage: spring to late summer. Flowers: early spring. H:6–15in (15–38cm), S:18–24in (45–60cm). Z:3–9.

Caltha palustris

The cup-shaped flowers of richest yellow shine above kidney-shaped deep green leaves. A hardier version of the species, **var. palustris**, supports waxy golden cups on rafts of its long stems floated over water. The knob of greenish gold in the double **var. radicans 'Flore Pleno'** (Z:3–9) unfolds in an ordered but ravishing sunburst.

CAMPANULA

CAMPANULACEAE Bellflower

The genus, which contains about 300 species from temperate parts of the Northern Hemisphere, is astonishingly rich in material for the garden. Some species are compact alpines, while others are tall woodland and meadow plants. The nodding or upward-facing flowers, predominantly in shades of blue, can be starry, cup shaped, or tubular but almost all have a shapely elegance. The taller perennial bellflowers are important components of summer borders, shaded as well as sunny. There are, too, many exquisite compact or low-spreading plants ideal for raised beds and rock gardens or for edging paths. Some of the alpine species are, admittedly, difficult plants, but a large percentage of the genus are easy to grow and a few representatives are beautiful but invasive weeds. Canterbury bells (**C. medium**), from S. Europe, is a true biennial, producing single, double, or cup-and-saucer flowers in blue, pink, or white. The short-lived frost-hardy chimney bellflower (**C. pyramidalis**, Z:7–8), which is native to Italy and the Balkans and has fragrant clusters of cup-shaped flowers, is usually grown as a biennial.
CULTIVATION The perennial species described below flower most freely in full sun but tolerate partial shade. They require a well-drained soil, particularly the compact rock-garden campanulas, and a good supply of moisture. Tall species may need staking.

PROPAGATION By division, in spring or autumn. From cuttings, taken in spring or summer. From seed, sown in spring or, for rock-garden campanulas, in autumn.
POTENTIAL PROBLEMS Slugs, snails; rust.

C. alliariifolia *Caucasus, Turkey*
Ivory bells
Flowers: mid-summer to early autumn. H:15–24in (38–60cm), S:18in (45cm). Z:4–8.
Toppling spires of nodding creamy tubular flowers rise on wiry stems from a mound of heart-shaped, gray-green leaves.

C. 'Birch Hybrid'
Flowers: summer. H:4–6in (10–15cm), S:18–24in (45–60cm). Z:4–8.
This vigorous evergreen hybrid has arching prostrate stems and ivy-shaped green leaves almost submerged by deep violet flowers. Its parents are the vigorous **C. portenschlagiana** and the even more invasive **C. poscharskyana**. It is difficult not to be taken in by something so beautiful.

Campanula 'Birch Hybrid'

C. 'Burghaltii'
Flowers: mid-summer. H:2ft (60cm), S:1ft (30cm). Z:4–8.
Dark purplish-blue buds contrast with large pale blue open bells that dangle from slender stems.

C. carpatica *C. Europe (Carpathian Mountains)*
Flowers: summer. H:8–12in (20–30cm), S:1–2ft (30–60cm). Z:4–8.
The myriad up-turned saucer-shaped flowers breaking open from fluted buds are attractive in all the permutations of this variable species, one of the easiest and most appealing for the rock garden. The named selections such as **'Blaue Clips'** and **'Weisse Clips'** cover a color range that includes white as well as shades of blue and violet. Pale blue **var. turbinata**, usually less than 6in (15cm) tall, is more compact. Even more compact is **C. raineri** (Z:5–9) with

similarly up-turned blue flowers, but this, like several alpine species that are covered by snow in winter in their natural environment, is a much more difficult plant, demanding very sharp drainage.

C. garganica *S. Europe*
Adriatic bellflower
Flowers: summer. H:2–4in (5–10cm), S:12–18in (30–45cm). Z:4–8.
This looks its best when the stems, clothed with toothed heart-shaped leaves, radiate from a rock crevice. The pale blue starry flowers are borne in great profusion.

Campanula garganica

C. glomerata 'Superba'
Flowers: summer. H:18–24in (45–60cm), S:2–4ft (60–120cm). Z:4–8.
The rather tubular flowers clustered at the ends of erect leafy stems are a deep violet-purple, their quality making up for the invasiveness of the species.

C. lactiflora *Caucasus, Turkey*
Milky bellflower
Flowers: early summer to early autumn. H:4–5ft (1.2–1.5m), S:18–24in (45–60cm). Z:4–8.
Although it may need staking, the milky bellflower is still one of the finest tall perennials. The sturdy leaf stems are crowned with great heads of powder blue bellflowers. There is also a beautiful white and the pink **'Loddon Anna'**. **'Prichard's Variety'**, about 30in (75cm) tall, has violet-blue flowers, and **'Pouffe'**, under 12in (30cm), is a mound of light blue.

Campanula lactiflora 'Loddon Anna'

C. latifolia *Europe eastward to Iran and Kashmir*
Flowers: summer. H:4ft (1.2m), S:2ft (60cm). Z:4–8.
The leafy stems that emerge straight and stiff from a clump of rich green leaves bear spikes of large blue or white tubular flowers, the topmost being the smallest. In borders, remove the spent flowers, but in the wild garden this species can be allowed to self-seed.

Campanula persicifolia 'Alba'

C. persicifolia *N. Africa, W. and N. Asia, S. Europe, C. and S. Russia*
Peach-leaved bellflower
Flowers: early to mid-summer. H:3ft (90cm), S:1ft (30cm). Z:4–8.
The wiry stems that rise from rosettes of narrow evergreen leaves carry open bells that are outward facing or nodding. The white 'Alba' is, if anything, more beautiful than the usual blue form, and both self-seed freely without making a nuisance of themselves in the garden. It is a winning plant in all its forms, including doubles such as 'Fleur de Neige' and 'Telham Beauty' with large pale blue flowers. *C. latiloba* is similar in character to *C. persicifolia* except that the shallowly cup-shaped flowers are stalkless.

Campanula takesimana

C. takesimana *Korea*
Flowers: summer. H:18–24in (45–60cm), S:18–36in (45–90cm). Z:5–8.
Above toothed and heart-shaped leaves rise numerous stems hung with narrow white bells that are flushed purplish pink, darker on the inside and with maroon spots. The position for this great beauty needs to be well chosen for it is invasive, as is the shorter-growing *C. punctata*, with flowers of similar color.

CANNA

CANNACEAE Indian shot plant

The hybrid cannas, large in leaf and flamboyant in flower, are among the most popular bedding plants in tropical and subtropical countries. Various species have played a role in the breeding of the hybrids, but almost all of the 50 or so that are distributed in Asia and North and South America are plants of damp forest glades and margins. In temperate gardens that are not frost-free, a tropical effect can be achieved with cannas, either in lavish bedding schemes or by combining a smaller number with other bold plants, but they must be planted annually, and the rhizomes need to be lifted as soon as the foliage has been cut down by frost. In these conditions, cannas flower less freely than in warmer climates, but their foliage, as in the dark-leaved *C. indica* 'Purpurea' (Z:7–10), can be superb. They also make an impact in containers.
CULTIVATION Require full sun, moist fertile soil, and a sheltered position. In cold areas, mulch in autumn. In frost-prone areas, lift plants in early autumn, remove the stems and leaves, and store in slightly moist leaf mold or peat over winter in a frost-free place.
PROPAGATION By division of rhizomes, in early spring. From seed, sown in spring at 70°F (21°C) after soaking in warm water for about a day.
POTENTIAL PROBLEMS Slugs, snails, caterpillars; under glass, red spider mites.

C. hybrids
Foliage: summer to autumn.
Flowers: mid-summer to early autumn. H:5–6ft (1.5–1.8m), S:2–3ft (60–90cm). Z:7–10.
Most have paddlelike leaves, prominently veined and often bronzed or tinted purple. Stout stems carry spikes, usually somewhat cluttered, of asymmetrical flowers, which are predominantly in shades of red and yellow, sometimes in bold combinations. The following is a mere sample of the great choice available from specialized nurseries: 'King Midas', plain green leaves and bright yellow flowers lightly marked with orange; 'Roi Humbert', purple

Canna 'Roi Humbert'

foliage and flowers of vivid red; and 'Wyoming', purple leaves with darker veining and flowers in shades of apricot and orange.

CATANANCHE

ASTERACEAE Cupid's dart

One species of this small Mediterranean genus containing 5 perennials and annuals has long been cultivated in sunny well-drained gardens. The daisy flowerheads, with their "everlasting" bracts, are good for cutting and will also dry well.
CULTIVATION Require full sun and well-drained soil.
PROPAGATION By division, in spring. From root cuttings, taken in winter. From seed, sown in spring.
POTENTIAL PROBLEMS Powdery mildew.

C. caerulea *S.W. Europe, Italy*
Flowers: mid-summer to autumn. H:18–30in (45–75cm), S:12–18in (30–45cm). Z:4–8.
From a clump of grassy gray-green leaves rise branching wiry stems that terminate in silvered buds. The papery bracts open to reveal dark-centered blue daisies, their strap-shaped ray flowerets neatly fringed at their square ends. 'Alba' has white flowerheads with a creamy center, 'Bicolor' white with a purple center, and in 'Major' the blues are exceptionally rich.

Catananche caerulea

CENTAUREA

ASTERACEAE

The genus includes the knapweed, or hardhead (*C. nigra*) of alkaline soil grassland in Europe, but the annual bachelor's buttons (*C. cyanus*) is probably the best-known example of this large genus, with 400 to 500 species distributed in a wide range of habitats in many parts of the world. Many of the species show a preference for well-drained alkaline soils, and almost all are found in open positions. The flowerheads consist of a central disk, often thistly in appearance, ringed by tubular or trumpet-shaped flowerets that in the showiest species are usually much dissected. Papery bracts around the flowerheads can be a conspicuous feature, as in the yellow-flowered *C. macrocephala*.

Centaurea macrocephala

See also ANNUALS AND BIENNIALS.
CULTIVATION Require full sun and a reasonably fertile well-drained soil. *C. macrocephala* and *C. montana* are the least tolerant of drought. *PROPAGATION* By division, in spring or autumn. From seed, sown in spring (*C. montana* in late summer). *POTENTIAL PROBLEMS* Powdery mildew.

Centaurea hypoleuca 'John Coutts'

C. hypoleuca *Turkey, Caucasus, Iran*
Flowers: summer. H and S:18-24in (45-60cm). Z:4-7.
The deeply cut leaves form a gray-green clump through which thrust a succession of pink flowerheads over a long season. It is usually represented in cultivation by '**John Coutts**', with deep mauve-pink flowers. A similar but flopping species is **C. dealbata**, (Z:4-8). It makes a clump up to 3ft (90cm).

C. macrocephala *Caucasus, Turkey*
Flowers: early to mid-summer. H:3-5ft (90-150cm), S:20-24in (50-60cm). Z:3-7.
The plant is undeniably coarse in foliage and thick stemmed, but its brawny solidity is justified by the flowerheads. For a short period it is bright in the garden when the large globes of brown papery bracts are topped by bright yellow tufts. The flowerheads dry well.

C. montana *Europe to Poland and N.W. Balkans*
Flowers: late spring to mid-summer. H:18-24in (45-60cm), S:12-18in (30-45cm). Z:3-8.
The stems have a tendency to flop, but this species, which has been in cultivation for centuries, presents its reddish-violet flowerheads in the gap between spring and high summer. There are several cultivars in a range in shades of pink and violet, and '**Alba**' is a lovely white.

Centaurea montana

CENTRANTHUS

VALERIANACEAE Valerian

Red valerian, the single plant in a genus of about 10 species that is in general cultivation, is found far from its Mediterranean home as a handsome weed colonizing old walls and sidings, never happier than when growing on chalky rubble in full sun. Its enthusiastic self-seeding is a drawback in the garden, but this easy plant is a welcome filler on rough banks and even in sunny borders that parch in summer, and it is a good plant for the seaside.
CULTIVATION Require full sun and poor alkaline soil that is well drained.
PROPAGATION By division, in early spring. From seed, sown in spring.
POTENTIAL PROBLEMS Usually none.

C. ruber *S. Europe, N. Africa to Turkey*
Red valerian
Flowers: late spring to late summer. H and S:2-3ft (60-90cm). Z:4-9.
Erect stems carry dense heads of small starry flowers over a clump of fleshy leaves. The flowers are usually in shades of red or pink; '**Albus**' is a clean white.

Centranthus ruber

CEPHALARIA

DIPSACACEAE

Few of the 65 or so species, mainly plants of moist meadows and high pastures from Europe to Asia, are in cultivation, but 1, the giant scabious, is remarkable for its height and the soft primrose-yellow of its flowerheads.
CULTIVATION Require sun or partial shade and moist soil.
PROPAGATION By division, in early spring. From seed, sown in spring.
POTENTIAL PROBLEMS Usually none.

C. gigantea *Caucasus, N. Turkey*
Giant scabious, yellow scabious
Flowers: early summer. H:6-8ft (1.8-2.5m), S:2-4ft (60-120cm). Z:4-8.
The divided leaves form a substantial dark green clump, above which hover the pale yellow scabious flowerheads. The butterfly liveliness of these as they move in a breeze is compensation for the gawky branching of the plant. *C. alpina*, about half the height of the giant scabious, is a more compact alternative with flowerheads of a similar color.

Cephalaria gigantea

CHELONE

SCROPHULARIACEAE Turtlehead

The 6 or so species in this North American genus have their origins in mountainous terrain or moist woodland. They include several late-flowering plants, one of which, the intriguingly named turtlehead (*C. obliqua*), provides a long display of tubular pink flowers, in contrast with the predominant yellow of the season. The common and generic name is not so fanciful, given the flower shape.
CULTIVATION Require sun or partial shade and moist, deep, fertile soil. Tolerate heavy clay and can be grown in boggy conditions.
PROPAGATION By division, in spring. From tip cuttings, taken in late spring to early summer. From seed, sown in spring.
POTENTIAL PROBLEMS Slugs, snails.

Chelone obliqua

C. obliqua *C. and S.E. USA*
Turtlehead
Flowers: late summer to early autumn. H:18–36in (45–90cm), S:12–18in (30–45cm). Z:3–9. Erect stems forming a dense thicket have prominently veined dark green leaves their whole length and terminate in spikes of pink "turtleheads." These 2-lipped tubular flowers, each about 1in (2.5cm) long, have a yellow beard on the inside.

CHIASTOPHYLLUM

CRASSULACEAE

In cultivation, as in the wild, the single species in this genus is a plant for a cool and shady rocky niche or crevice.
CULTIVATION Requires partial shade and moist well-drained soil.
PROPAGATION From side-shoot cuttings, taken in early summer. From seed, sown in autumn.
POTENTIAL PROBLEMS Slugs, snails.

C. oppositifolium *Caucasus*
Foliage: year-round. Flowers: late spring to early summer. H and S:6–8in (15–20cm). Z:5–8. Creeping rosettes are composed of

Chiastophyllum oppositifolium

fleshy rounded leaves that are coarsely toothed. Branching reddish stems carry drooping sprays of small yellow flowers.

CHRYSANTHEMUM

ASTERACEAE

The following groups of chrysanthemums, in this genus of about 20 species, are the result of complex hybridization, the process starting in China and Japan long before the main introductions to Europe began at the end of the 18th century. As with other florists' flowers that have been popular on the show bench, there are numerous categories, partly reflecting the astonishing range of form in the flowerheads. The direction the ray flowerets curve is something to note in the large doubles, some being incurved, others reflexed. Other curiosities are flowerheads with spoon- or quill-shaped ray flowerets (in the latter case they are tubular) and even some that are spider form, looking like bizarre toupees combining thin and long dangling ray flowerets with curled shorter ones at the top. After discounting the more extreme and tender plants, there is still a wealth of material here for beds and borders. *C. carinatum* is a striking annual with bold banding of the purple-eyed flowerheads.
CULTIVATION Require full sun and well-drained fertile soil, preferably containing lime.
PROPAGATION By division, in spring. From basal cuttings, taken in spring. From seed of perennial mixtures, sown in late winter or early spring at 55–61°F (13–16°C).
POTENTIAL PROBLEMS Aphids, earwigs, eelworms; gray mold (*Botrytis*), viruses.

HYBRIDS

Korean
Flowers: late summer to mid-autumn. H:1–3ft (30–90cm), S:1–2ft (30–60cm). Z:4–9. This type of spray chrysanthemum

produces many flowers—single, semidouble, or double. The choice includes: **'Brown Eyes'**, small double pompon, 2-tone orange-brown; **'Ruby Mound'**, double, deep ruby; and **'Wedding Day'**, single, white with a green center.

Chrysanthemum 'Ruby Mound'

Pompon
Flowers: late summer to early autumn. H:1–2ft (30–60cm), S:18–24in (45–60cm). Z:4–9. Dwarf bushes produce dense sprays of small, double flowers with recurved ray flowerets. Popular examples of these are: **'Anastasia'** , pale pink; **'Peterkin'**, orange; **'Mei-Kyo'**, warm pink; and **'Purleigh White'**, white.

Rubellum
Flowers: late summer to mid-autumn. H:30–36in (75–90cm), S:20–24in (50–60cm). Z:4–8. The free-flowering bushy chrysanthemums that take their name from the plant *C. rubellum* are among the most valuable of the hybrids for garden use. The flowerheads, usually single, have yellow centers and ray flowerets in a wide color choice: **'Clara Curtis'**, single, mauve-pink; **'Duchess of Edinburgh'**, single, copper-red; **'Emperor of China'**, double with quilled petals, silver-pink; and **'Mary Stoker'**, single, yellow to apricot with a green tint to center.

Chrysanthemum 'Wendy'

Spray
Flowers: late summer to mid-autumn. H:3–4ft (90–120cm), S:2–3ft (60–90cm). Z:4–8. Whether lined out for cutting or

incorporated in general planting schemes, the great value of these hybrids is in the amount of flowers produced, generally 5 to 6 blooms to a stem in a wide color variation, not including blue, with each bush having about 5 stems. Examples include '**Enbee Wedding**', single, pink; '**Salmon Margaret**', reflexed double, apricot-pink; and '**Wendy**', reflexed double, bronzed orange, darker in the center.

Chrysanthemum 'Salmon Margaret'

CIMICIFUGA

RANUNCULACEAE Bugbane

The common and the generic botanical name refer to the use of *C. foetida*, a graceful species but rarely cultivated as an ornamental, as an insect repellent. Other tall species in the genus of 18 plants from temperate areas grow in cool moist conditions in the wild. They produce wands of bottlebrush flowers that jostle elegantly over a base of ferny leaves.
CULTIVATION Require partial shade and moist fertile soil that is rich in organic matter.
PROPAGATION By division, in spring. From seed, sown as soon as ripe.
POTENTIAL PROBLEMS Usually none.

C. racemosa E. North America
Black snakeroot
Flowers: mid- to late summer.
H:4–6ft (1.2–1.8m), S:2–3ft (60–90cm). Z:4–8.
Of those species in general cultivation, this is the first to flower, the base of deeply cut leaves topped by branching stems ending in slender white bottlebrushes.

Cimicifuga racemosa

C. simplex Russia, China
Foliage: mid-spring to mid-autumn. Flowers: early to mid-autumn.
H:3–4ft (90–120cm), S:20–24in (50–60cm). Z:3–8.
The sinuous narrow spires of white flowers swaying gently or waving wildly add dramatic movement to the autumn garden. Purple-tinted buds open white on **var.** *matsumurae* '**Elstead**'. Most striking of all are the forms with dark foliage, the creamy bottlebrushes of the **var.** *simplex* **Atropurpurea Group** rising from a dark purple base.

CIRSIUM

ASTERACEAE

There are many more weeds than attractive ornamentals in this thistle genus of about 200 species, which are found in a wide range of habitats in the Northern Hemisphere. The one described is not a spectacular plant, but the unusual coloring of the flowerheads, carried on branching stems above dark green leaves, adds an unexpected tone to sunny, reasonably moist borders.
CULTIVATION Require full sun and moist well-drained soil.
PROPAGATION By division, in autumn or spring. From seed, sown in spring.
POTENTIAL PROBLEMS Mildew.

Cirsium rivulare 'Atropurpureum'

C. rivulare '**Atropurpureum**'
Flowers: early to mid-summer.
H:3–4ft (90–120cm), S:18–24in (45–60cm). Z:4–8.
The clump of slightly spiny dark green leaves, with spreading roots, produces branching stems with glowing ruby-crimson soft thistles.

CONVALLARIA

CONVALLARIACEAE Lily-of-the-valley

The deliciously scented single species, by some authorities considered 3, is found throughout the Northern Hemisphere, usually in damp woodland. It can be quirkish in the garden, in some situations extending its ground-covering role by thonglike rhizomes to invade areas that should be off-limits, elsewhere just holding its ground. It is a good candidate for shady wild gardens where the soil is moist.
CULTIVATION Tolerates full sun, but best in shade, even full shade, and a wide range of soils, provided there is a good supply of moisture.
PROPAGATION From seed, sown as soon as ripe. By division, in autumn.
POTENTIAL PROBLEMS Gray mold (*Botrytis*).
WARNING The seeds of *C. majalis* may cause a stomach upset if swallowed.

Convallaria majalis

C. majalis Europe, Asia, North America
Flowers: late spring. H:8–12in (20–30cm), S:12–16in (30–40cm). Z:2–9.
Stems dangling fragrant white bells are nursed between paired oval leaves. The best of the named selections are '**Albostriata**', the leaves of which have longitudinal creamy stripes, and '**Fortin's Giant**', vigorous with large flowers.

COREOPSIS

ASTERACEAE Tickseed

This North and Central American genus of about 100 species is represented in gardens by several annuals and a few perennials, some of which, like *C. grandiflora*, are short-lived and usually grown as annuals. Yellow is the predominant color, but in the annual *C. tinctoria* the single to double flowerheads are darkened by varying proportions of mahogany and deep crimson. These bright daisies, mainly of open grassland, are easy plants that thrive in sunny gardens, especially on light soils.
CULTIVATION Require full sun or partial shade and well-drained soil.
PROPAGATION By division, in early spring. From seed, sow perennials in a nursery bed in mid-spring, and annuals where they are to flower.
POTENTIAL PROBLEMS Slugs, snails; mildew.

Coreopsis verticillata 'Grandiflora'

C. verticillata *S.E. USA*
Flowers: summer. H:18–30in
(45–75cm), S:12–18in (30–45cm).
Z:3–9.
Relays of starry flowerheads make
a dense yellow cover over green,
needlelike foliage. **'Grandiflora'** is
richly colored, but the lemon
'Moonbeam' is more versatile.

CORYDALIS

PAPAVERACEAE

The generic name of this large
genus, which includes about 300
species, is from the Greek for a
lark, a fanciful allusion to the
tubular spurred flowers, the lark
having spurred feet. Species in
cultivation are mainly plants of
cool woodland or rocky
mountainous terrain in temperate
areas of the Northern Hemisphere.
They are grown principally for
their highly distinctive flowers,
although in most cases their divided
foliage is of very great beauty. No
weed is more beguiling than the
yellow-flowered evergreen *C. lutea*
(Z:5–7), which is widely distributed
in Europe. *C. ochroleuca* (Z:5–7),
also European but from farther
south and east, is another species
that self-seeds freely. It resembles
C. lutea, but the flowers are creamy
with a yellow throat. Some species
are tuberous or fleshy rooted,
including the temperamental
Himalayan *C. cashmeriana*
(Z:5–8), with flowers of ravishing
blue, but all are grouped together
here.
CULTIVATION The species have
varying requirements, but many
tolerate full sun or partial shade
and require well-drained but
moisture-retentive soil. Of those
described, *C. solida* is suitable for a
free-draining position in a sunny
rock garden. *C. flexuosa* thrives
best in soil that is rich in organic
matter. *C. cashmeriana* needs lime-
free soil that is cool and leafy.
PROPAGATION By division, in
autumn and from offsets of
tuberous species in spring. From
seed, sown as soon as ripe.
POTENTIAL PROBLEMS Slugs, snails.

C. cheilanthifolia *China*
Foliage: year-round. Flowers: early
spring to summer. H and S:8–12in
(20–30cm). Z:5–8.
The lightly bronzed leaves make a
ferny clump, and as a bonus there
is a long succession of yellow,
spurred flowers, crowded onto the
stems.

Corydalis flexuosa 'Pere David'

C. flexuosa *China (W. Sichuan)*
Foliage: spring to summer. Flowers:
late spring to summer. H:9–12in
(23–30cm), S:8–10in (20–25cm).
Z:5–8.
The impact this species has made
since its introduction from W.
China in 1989 owes almost
everything to real virtues. It is easy
to grow in the open garden or in
containers, provided the medium
is moist and rich in organic matter.
The soft divided foliage is a calm
blue-green, sometimes marked
reddish brown or tinged purple.
The flowers, like darting schools of
little blue fish, are produced over
many weeks in spring and
sometimes again later. The named
selections, including **'Pere David'**,
with their slight variations in tone
or intensity of blue or in the tint of
their foliage, are beautiful and
deserve to remain popular.

**Corydalis solida f. transsylvanica
'George Baker'**

C. solida *Asia, N. Europe*
Flowers: mid- to late spring.
H:10–12in (25–30cm), S:6–8in
(15–20cm). Z:5–8.
This ferny-leaved tuberous species
produces upright spikes of tilted
flowers that have down-turned
spurs. The color varies

considerably, from near white to
mauve and reddish purple. The
pink terra-cotta shade of
f. transsylvanica 'George Baker',
usually grown in the alpine house,
is a rare color in flowers.

CRAMBE

BRASSICACEAE

Most of the species, about 20 in
number, are plants of dry country
in Europe, Asia, and Africa, sometimes coastal, as in the case of sea
kale (**C. maritima**, Z:6–9). When
the leaf shoots are blanched, this is
a spring vegetable delicacy, but it
also offers large blue-green leaves
of waxy texture and wavy margin.
In flower, the airy open heads of
the plant described have a
miraculously weightless quality.

Crambe maritima

CULTIVATION Require full sun and
deep, fertile, well-drained soil.
PROPAGATION By division, in early
spring. From root cuttings, taken in
winter. From seed, sown in spring
or autumn.
POTENTIAL PROBLEMS Usually none.

C. cordifolia *Caucasus*
Foliage: spring to mid-summer.
Flowers: late spring to mid-
summer. H:6–8ft (1.8–2.5m),
S:4–5ft (1.2–1.5m). Z:6–9.
The puckered and lobed large
leaves are hairy and coarse, but a
crisscross of branched stems is the
almost invisible support for a
cloud of small white flowers.

CYNARA

ASTERACEAE

About 10 species make up the
genus. No perennial can match the
cardoon for the jagged splendor
of its silvery leaves. In the same
mold, but smaller and less silvered,
is the globe artichoke. This is not
so surprising; what was once
considered a separate species
(**C. scolymus**, Z:6–8) is, the pundits
assert, the same Mediterranean
thistle in another guise
(**C. cardunculus** Scolymus Group,
Z:6–8).

CULTIVATION Require full sun, fertile well-drained soil, and shelter from strong winds. For best foliage effects, remove the flowers as they emerge.
PROPAGATION By division, in spring. From root cuttings, taken in winter. From seed, sown in spring.
POTENTIAL PROBLEMS Slugs, aphids; gray mold (*Botrytis*).

Cynara cardunculus

C. cardunculus *Morocco, S.W. Mediterranean*
Cardoon
Foliage: spring to mid-autumn. Flowers: early summer to early autumn. H:5-6ft (1.5-1.8m), S:4-5ft (1.2-1.5m). Z:6-8.
Blanching young leaves produces a connoisseur's vegetable, but this treatment is incompatible with the development of the great fountain of silvery foliage. Massive stems carry thistle flowerheads, which are up to 3in (7.5cm) across, the heavy prickly base topped by a tuft of violet-purple.

CYNOGLOSSUM

BORAGINACEAE Hound's tongue

Few of the 50 to 60 species, which occur in temperate zones and tropical uplands, are in general cultivation and of these several, including the Chinese forget-me-not (*C. amabile*), are annuals or biennials. These as well as the perennial described are plants of open ground or dappled shade. In the garden, plants may need twiggy supports.
CULTIVATION Require sun or partial shade and moist, well-drained soil of moderate fertility.
PROPAGATION From seed, sown in autumn or spring. By division, in autumn or spring.
POTENTIAL PROBLEMS Mildew.

C. nervosum *Himalayas*
Flowers: mid-spring to mid-summer. H and S:18-24in (45-60cm). Z:4-7.
Over several weeks the intense azure of the forget-me-not-like flowers transforms a nondescript clump of narrow hairy leaves.

Cynoglossum nervosum

DARMERA

SAXIFRAGACEAE Umbrella plant

The rounded clusters of flowers rise naked on tall stately flower stems before the impressive mound of umbrella leaves develops. In the mountainous woodlands of the western USA where it grows wild, the single species in this genus is a waterside plant. In the garden it thrives in a bog garden but tolerates drier conditions in shade.
CULTIVATION Requires sun or partial shade and moist or, if growing in full sun, very wet soil.
PROPAGATION By division, in spring. From seed, sown in spring or autumn.
POTENTIAL PROBLEMS Usually none.

Darmera peltata

D. peltata *USA (S.W. Oregon to N.W. California)*
Foliage: early summer to late autumn. Flowers: late spring. H:3-6ft (90-180cm), S:2-4ft (60-120cm). Z:6-8.
The thick rhizomes throw up sturdy stems terminating in dense heads of 5-petaled pink or white flowers. The dark green leaves that follow are up to 2ft (60cm) across, with a scalloped margin and prominent radiating veins. In autumn they often take on red tints.

DELPHINIUM

RANUNCULACEAE

The tall narrow spires of the hybrid delphiniums represent a phenomenal achievement of plant breeding. The main species used is

D. elatum (Z:3-7). Each spire is densely packed with single, semidouble, or double spurred flowers in white, cream, gray, and even red, as well as every shade of blue. For the last 100 years, hybrid delphiniums have been a mainstay of the traditional herbaceous border. Their popularity has been at the expense of the species themselves, of which there are about 250, including annuals and biennials, well distributed throughout the world. Among the most commonly grown species is *D. grandiflorum* (Z:3-7), itself important in the breeding of the hybrids, but cultivars such as '**Blue Butterfly**' (Z:3-7), an open plant

Delphinium hybrids

about 2ft (60cm) tall with small sprays of bright blue flowers, are short-lived and often grown as annuals. *D. tatsienense* (Z:3-7), another, but slightly smaller, airy plant with deep blue flowers, violet-purple at the tips, is also short-lived. Like many other species, these are not fussy about soil, provided it is free-draining, but the magnificent perfection of the hybrids requires generous feeding. A liquid fertilizer every 2 weeks during the growing season and thinning of shoots help boost flower size. Furthermore, plants need staking, attention to control pests and disease (slugs view young growths as the ultimate delicacy), and frequent propagation.
CULTIVATION Require full sun, fertile well-drained soil, and shelter from strong winds. Require staking when plants are over 1ft (30cm) tall.
PROPAGATION Belladonna and Elatum Group hybrids from sturdy basal cuttings, taken in early spring. From seed, sown in early spring at 55°F (13°C).
POTENTIAL PROBLEMS Slugs, snails, leaf miners, delphinium moth caterpillars; leaf blotch, powdery mildew, crown rot, cucumber mosaic virus.
WARNING All parts will cause stomach upsets if eaten. Contact with foliage may cause skin irritation.

HYBRIDS

Belladonna Group
Flowers: summer. H:3–4ft (90–120cm), S:18–24in (45–60cm). Z:3–7.
Since their development in the late 19th century, these have been popular as cut flowers and in the garden. Their loose spikes branch above fingered leaves, following in succession over a long period, provided the old spikes are removed. Examples include '**Casa Blanca**', white; '**Cliveden Beauty**', sky blue; '**Völkerfrieden**', deep blue; '**Wendy**', violet blue.

Delphinium 'Völkerfrieden'

Elatum Group
Flowers: early to mid-summer. H:5–7ft (1.5–2.2m), S:2–3ft (60–90cm). Z:2–7.
This range of short, medium, and tall hybrids produces attractive clumps of soft green leaves, from which rise stiff spikes, crowded with evenly spaced flowerets, as the flowers are generally known, some of them with a dark eye known as a "bee," others with a light center. The largest flowerets are usually at the bottom of the

Delphinium 'Faust'

spike and can be 3in (7.5cm) across. Cutting back the main spikes when they are spent encourages the development of laterals that give a lesser late display. Many of these delphiniums are short-lived, as are the **Pacific Hybrids**, which are similar in character but grown as annuals or biennials. Among the most compact are '**Mighty Atom**', semidouble, violet-blue with brown-streaked "bees"; '**Rosemary Brock**', semidouble, soft pink with brown eyes; '**Sandpiper**', semidouble, white with dark-brown eyes; and '**Sungleam**', semidouble, cream with yellow eye. Examples of medium height include '**Blue Nile**', semidouble, medium blue with a white eye; and '**Loch Leven**', semidouble, light blue with white eye. Among the tallest are '**Bruce**', semidouble, violet-purple with dark brown eye; '**Fanfare**', semidouble, mauve with white eye; and '**Faust**', semidouble, rich blue with purple overlay and dark eye.

Delphinium 'Sungleam'

DIANTHUS

CARYOPHYLLACEAE Carnation, pink

Few genera are held in such deep affection by gardeners. About 300 species are widely distributed in the Northern Hemisphere and southern Africa, many of them tough dwarf plants found in mountainous country. The perennial species, including compact plants suitable for rock gardens, raised beds, and edging are, however, overwhelmed by the thousands of hybrid pinks and carnations. These flower in great profusion and are long lasting when cut. Some have a rich clove scent. What has also fascinated gardeners during their long history in cultivation is the form of the flower—single or double, fringed or smooth in outline—and the variety of markings, for which a special vocabulary is employed. Picotee carnations, for example, usually white, have petals outlined in a darker color; laced pinks, such as 'Gran's Favourite', have the

margin and center in 1 color contrasting with the body color of the flower while in fancies irregular flakes and streaks contrast with the ground color. The sentimental attachment to these plants is explained in part by the important role they have played in humble gardens, in part by their status as florists' flowers, one of the group of plants devotedly cultivated for perfection of bloom and competitive showing, particularly in the 18th and 19th centuries. As with all the florists' flowers, the hybrids are complex and their categories sometimes confusing. The entry on hybrids covers the main categories usually grown outdoors, but omits the half-hardy perpetual-flowering carnations, grown commercially under glass on a large scale for cut flowers, and the Malmaison carnations, also half-hardy and grown under glass for their large flowers and penetrating fragrance. Propagate all plants frequently as many deteriorate after 2 or 3 years. The short-lived Chinese or Indian pink (*D. chinensis*) is grown as an annual or biennial, sweet william (*D. barbatus*), with clusters of white to red flowers, often prettily marked, as biennials.

Dianthus 'Gran's Favourite'

CULTIVATION Require full sun and well-drained soil, with few exceptions preferring neutral to alkaline soils. (*D. pavonius* is among those that are best on acid soil). Alpine species need very sharp drainage.
PROPAGATION From cuttings of nonflowering shoots in summer. From seed, sown from autumn to early spring (alpine species).
POTENTIAL PROBLEMS Aphids, slugs; rust.

SPECIES

D. alpinus *Europe (S.E. Alps)*
Alpine pink
Flowers: all summer. H:3–4in (7.5–10cm), S:4in (10cm). Z:4–8.
The single flowers overlap like interlocking shields to hide tight

dark green cushions of foliage. The fringed petals are variable in coloring, the range extending from pale pink to crimson. There is often a white eye and some degree of spotting. **'Joan's Blood'** is bright magenta with a dark red center.

D. deltoides *Asia, Europe*
Maiden pink
Flowers: all summer. H:6–9in (15–23cm), S:12–15in (30–38cm). Z:3–8.
The single flowers are small but profuse on plants with narrow foliage with a purplish tinge. The color range includes pink, bright crimson in **'Leuchtfunk'**, among others, and white in **'Albus'**.

D. gratianopolitanus *N.W. and C. Europe*
Cheddar pink
Flowers: mid-summer. H:4–10in (10–25cm), S:10–16in (25–40cm). Z:5–8.
Above a carpet of gray leaves, single pink flowers with fringed petals exhale a carrying fragrance.

D. pavonius *Europe (S.W. Alps)*
Flowers: summer. H:3–5in (7.5–12.5cm), S:6–8in (15–20cm). Z:4–8.
Although the single flowers, which have fringed and overlapping petals, are variable in their shade of pink, they are consistent in the biscuit color of the underside.

D. superbus *Mountains of Asia and Europe*
Flowers: mid-summer to autumn. H and S:8–12in (20–30cm). Z:4–8.
The untidy sprawl of lax stems counts against it, but the sprays of mauve-pink flowers, green-eyed and ragged, are bewitchingly fragrant. The hybrid **'Loveliness'** is a more substantial version.

Dianthus 'Pike's Pink'

HYBRIDS

Alpine
Flowers: summer. H:3–4in (7.5–10cm), S:6–8in (15–20cm). Z:4–8.
Compact cushions or tufted mats of narrow gray-green leaves are

covered by short-stemmed flowers, usually fragrant and large in proportion. The singles include the greenish-white **'Dewdrop'**, the dark-eyed **'Inshriach Dazzler'**, which is a vivid reddish pink, and **'La Bourboule'**, a clear pink. The double **'Pike's Pink'** has darker markings in the muddled center, giving a focus to the prettily fringed pale pink flowers.

Border carnations
Flowers: mid-summer. H:18–24in (45–60cm), S:12–16in (30–40cm). Z:4–8.
The earliest examples were the delight of 16th- and 17th-century gardeners. They are lax plants with gray-green leaves and need staking to hold up sprays of fragrant double flowers. Modern kinds have unfringed petals giving a rounded outline about 2in (5cm) across. The small-flowered, crimson **'Fenbow Nutmeg Clove'** and a few others are said to date from the 17th century. More modern examples include **'Bookham Fancy'**, yellow flecked and outlined in purplish red; **'Irene Della-Torré'**, white with pink streaking; and **'Sandra Neal'**, rich yellow with irregular dark pink streaks.

Dianthus 'Doris'

Modern pinks
Flowers: early summer to autumn. H:10–18in (25–45cm), S:10–16in (25–40cm). Z:4–8.
The usually compact plants produced by hybridizing old-fashioned pinks and perpetual-flowering carnations give a long-flowering display of rather crisp-textured flowers. Some, but far from all, are well scented. Examples of laced doubles include **'Becky Robinson'**, with red-pink markings on soft pink, and the more muddled **'Gran's Favourite'**, white with fine edging and central markings in purplish pink. **'Doris'**, a double bicolor well known as a cut flower, has pale pink flowers that are soft coral at the center, and the very full **'Houndspool Ruby'** is a sharp pink with darker tints. All of these are clove scented.

Dianthus 'Sops-in-wine'

Old-fashioned pinks
Flowers: early summer. H:10–18in (25–45cm), S:10–14in (25–35cm). Z:4–8.
Their season is short, and some make untidy gray-green clumps of narrow leaves, but these pinks hold pride of place in gardeners' affections. The spiced scent of **D. plumarius**, said to be one of the parents, is a hallmark of the best. Some have been in cultivation for a very long time, but others, although in the old style, are relatively modern. Singles include **'Brympton Red'**, of marbled crimson, the white but green-eyed **'Musgrave's Pink'**, and **'Sops-in-wine'**, with a white patch on each purplish crimson petal. Many are laced, among them the semidouble **'Dad's Favourite'**, white with crimson edging and a dark red center. The creamy white **'Mrs. Sinkins'** is renowned for its scent but the double flowers are untidy, the petals spilling out of the calyces.

Dianthus 'Mrs. Sinkins'

DIASCIA

SCROPHULARIACEAE

About 50 species, annuals as well as perennials, are native of southern Africa, where most grow in open positions with a good supply of moisture. Although they are not fully hardy, the perennial species and a growing number of hybrids are enjoying a vogue. The elegant spikes of pink flowers, varying in shade according to species and cultivar, are borne in quantity over a long season. The individual flowers, which resemble

nemesias, are tubular with 5 lobes, the common name referring to the 2 spurs extending behind the top paired lobes. An attractive feature of diascias is the ease with which they combine with other plants, either at the front of a bed or in a container. The flowering season is agreeably long. To keep up the display, old stems should be sheared off as soon as the flowers are spent. Diascias are easily propagated, which partly explains their popularity among specialized growers. In frost-prone areas it is a sensible precaution to over-winter rooted cuttings under glass.
CULTIVATION Require full sun and fertile, moist, well-drained soil.
PROPAGATION By division, in spring. From cuttings, taken in summer. From seed, sown at 61°F (16°C) in spring.
POTENTIAL PROBLEMS Slugs, snails.

Diascia 'Salmon Supreme'

D. barberae 'Ruby Field'
Flowers: summer to early autumn. H:10–12in (25–30cm), S:18–24in (45–60cm). Z:7–9.
Sprays of rich pink flowers sway lightly over a low mat of mid-green leaves. **D. barberae 'Blackthorn Apricot'**, a more recent hybrid of the same height, produces loose spires of apricot-pink flowers. The paler apricot **D. 'Salmon Supreme'** is only 6in (15cm) tall.

Diascia barberae 'Ruby Field'

D. rigescens *South Africa*
Flowers: summer. H:12–18in (30–45cm), S:16–20in (40–50cm). Z:7–9.
Although a trailing plant, the branching angular stems are stiff

and more or less upright. They are clothed in toothed heart-shaped leaves and dense spikes of dusty purple-pink flowers.

D. vigilis *South Africa (Drakensberg Mountains)*
Flowers: all summer to autumn. H:12–18in (30–45cm), S:18–24in (45–60cm). Z:7–9.
This erect, small-leaved species has spikes of clear pink flowers.
D. fetcaniensis, a similar plant but slightly smaller and sticky to the touch, has flowers of bright pink.

DICENTRA

PAPAVERACEAE

The fanciful common names used to describe several species suggest quaintness rather than beauty. Dutchman's breeches is, admittedly, remarkably descriptive of the unconventional flowers of the E. North American **D. cucullaria** (Z:4–8) with up-turned white pantaloons that are yellow at the waist, but most of the species and hybrids in cultivation are refined plants, far from grotesque in their flowers and with exceptionally beautiful foliage. Most of the 20 or so species are natives of moist woodland in North America and in Asia from the western Himalayas to eastern Siberia. Apart from *D. spectabilis*, one of the supreme herbaceous perennials for dappled shade, those described have rhizomatous roots by which colonies expand.
CULTIVATION Require partial shade and well-drained but moist soil that is rich in organic matter. *D. spectabilis* tolerates full sun, provided the soil does not dry out.
PROPAGATION By division, in early spring. By root cuttings of *D. spectabilis*, taken in winter. From seed, sown in spring.
POTENTIAL PROBLEMS Slugs, snails.
WARNING The skin may react allergically on contact with foliage. Stomach upsets may occur if any part of the plant is swallowed.

D. 'Adrian Bloom'
Foliage: spring to autumn. Flowers: late spring and early autumn. H:12–14in (30–35cm), S:18–24in (45–60cm). Z:3–8.
After its main flowering, this hybrid continues to produce odd stems dangling bright red lockets over gray-green foliage. There is little to choose in quality between the short-growing hybrids, but 2 others outstanding for their blue-gray foliage are **D. 'Langtrees'**, with pinkish-white flowers, and **D. 'Stuart Boothman'**, deep pink.

Dicentra formosa

D. formosa *W. North America*
Wild bleeding heart
Foliage:spring to autumn. Flowers: late spring to early summer. H:12–18in (30–45cm), S:2–3ft (60–90cm). Z:3–8.
Pink-tinted stems rise from dense low clumps of ferny leaves to dangle pretty clusters of mauve-pink lockets. The wide-spreading hummocks of finely textured foliage contrast well with other large-leaved perennials of shady places. The coolness of white lockets in **var. alba** is matched by the pale green of the foliage.

Dicentra spectabilis

D. spectabilis *Korea, N. China, Siberia*
Bleeding heart, Dutchman's breeches, lady's locket, lyre flower
Foliage: spring to autumn. Flowers: late spring to early summer. H:2–4ft (60–120cm), S:18–24in (45–60cm). Z:3–8.
Due to its peerless elegance, this species stands out during the interval between spring and summer, but at any season it would be a plant of the first rank. A sheltered position should be reserved for it as it is brittle, down to its roots. When they arch out from the gray-green divided leaves, the gently sinuous stems are lightly weighed down by dangling deep pink hearts, from which protrude flashes of white petals. **'Alba'**, with pure white lockets, is if anything more beautiful than the species and appears to be a more vigorous plant. For those who can steel themselves to plunder, it is also good as a cut flower.

DICTAMNUS

RUTACEAE

Children of all ages are momentarily
delighted by the know-it-all's trick
of lighting the volatile oil the
plant gives off on a hot day in late
summer. Miraculously, the plant is
undamaged. The single species,
which has a wide distribution in
Europe and Asia, is found mainly
in open positions on dry, stony
ground.
CULTIVATION Requires full sun and
well-drained, preferably alkaline,
soil.
PROPAGATION From seed, sown as
soon as ripe. By division, in spring
or autumn.
POTENTIAL PROBLEMS Usually none.
WARNING Stomach upsets may
occur if any part of the plant is
swallowed. Contact with foliage
may cause dermititis.

D. albus C. and S. Europe to
N. China, Korea
Burning bush, dittany
Flowers: early summer. H:18–36in
(45–90cm), S:18–24in (45–60cm).
Z:2–8.
When bruised between the fingers,
the divided leaves give off a strong
lemon scent. Tall spires of white
flowers are followed by star-
shaped seedpods. The flowers of
var. purpureus are purplish pink
with darker veins.

Dictamnus albus

DODECATHEON

PRIMULACEAE American cowslip,
shooting star

The dartlike flowers, halted in
their plunging descent, are
characteristic of the 14 species,
all of which are found in North
America. The majority are
woodland plants, growing in areas
where there is an abundance of
moisture during spring months,
although often much drier later in
the year; their leaves die down
immediately after flowering. The
flower color of the plants in
cultivation ranges from palest pink
to a vivid carmine, with, in
addition, some beautiful albinos.

The species described is the most
widely grown, but the Californian
D. hendersonii (Z:4–8), with
reddish pink petals, and
D. pulchellum (Z:3–8), from
W. North America, especially the
bright magenta **'Red Wings'**, are
no less appealing and convey the
same sense of arrested drama.
CULTIVATION Tolerate full sun but
best in partial shade, and require
well-drained but moist soil rich in
organic matter.
PROPAGATION From seed, sown
as soon as ripe (after prechilling).
By division, in spring.
POTENTIAL PROBLEMS Slugs, snails.

Dodecatheon meadia f. album

D. meadia N.W. USA
Shooting star
Flowers: mid- to late spring.
H:15–24in (38–60cm), S:10–12in
(25–30cm). Z:3–8.
The stems that rise from a rosette
of green leaves are charged at their
tip with up to 15 toy missiles, the
mauve petals swept back from a
white base, from which protrude
reddish-yellow anthers. The creamy
f. album has yellow anthers.

DORONICUM

ASTERACEAE Leopard's bane

Of about 35 species, several are
grown for their spring show of
cheerful yellow daisies. These
include **D. austriacum** and
D. orientale (both Z:4–8), plants of
woodland margins in mountainous
country in southern Europe and
farther east. They may be the
parents of the plant described,
which is best suited to the wilder
corners of the garden.
CULTIVATION Require partial shade
and moist soil that is rich in
organic matter.
PROPAGATION By division, in
autumn. From seed, sown in spring.
POTENTIAL PROBLEMS Leaf spot, root
rot, powdery mildew.

D. 'Miss Mason'
Flowers: late spring. H and S:
18–24in (45–60cm). Z:4–8.
Yellow flowerheads, about 3in
(7.5cm) across, are carried well

Doronicum 'Miss Mason'

above heart-shaped, green leaves.
D. × excelsum 'Harpur Crewe'
has flowerheads about 4in (10cm)
across and stems 2ft (60cm) tall.

DRABA

BRASSICACEAE Whitlow grass

The plants that excite interest in
this genus of about 300 species
are compact perennials from
mountainous screes and rocky
outcrops in temperate regions.
Their closely packed rosettes of
leaves form tight hummocks or
mats that in spring or early
summer are covered by small,
cross-shaped flowers. Some of the
greatest alpine treasures, such as
D. mollisima (Z:6–8), in flower a
tiny cushion of bright yellow, are
definitely for the committed
specialist.
CULTIVATION Require full sun and
very well-drained soil. The cushion
types require protection from
winter wet and are usually grown
in an alpine house (equal parts of
loam, leaf mold, and grit).
PROPAGATION From rosette cuttings,
taken in late spring. From seed,
sown in autumn after prechilling.
POTENTIAL PROBLEMS Aphids and
red spider mites under glass.

D. aizoides Europe
Yellow whitlow grass
Flowers: late spring. H:4in (10cm),
S:6–10in (15–25cm). Z:5–8.
The alpine cognoscenti may sneer,
but this easy-going rock-garden
plant makes a cheerful show of
lemon-yellow flowers clustered
over rosettes of bristly leaves.

Draba aizoides

223

ECHINACEA

ASTERACEAE Coneflower

The central cone, which gives these plants their common name, is a conspicuous, sometimes glistening, feature of the daisy flowerheads. There are about 9 species, all found in North America, most in prairielike conditions. The species in general cultivation is usually a plant of reasonably moist fertile soils. The flowering season can be prolonged by removing flowerheads as soon as they fade.
CULTIVATION Require full sun and well-drained fertile soil rich in organic matter.
PROPAGATION By division, in autumn or spring. From root cuttings, taken in winter. From seed, sown in spring.
POTENTIAL PROBLEMS Usually none.

Echinacea purpurea

E. purpurea *North America (Ontario S. to Georgia)*
Flowers: mid-summer to early autumn. H:3–4ft (90–120cm), S:18–24in (45–60cm). Z:3–9.
As compensation for the coarseness of the plant, with its bristly dark green leaves and heavy stems, the large flowerheads consist of a splendidly textured orange-brown cone, around which radiate the purplish red ray flowerets. The flowerheads of **'Magnus'** can be well over 6in (15cm) across. In **'White Lustre'** the greenish white ray flowerets hang down from a brassy cone.

ECHINOPS

ASTERACEAE Globe thistle

Bees and butterflies throng to feast from the spherical flowerheads, which in the most ornamental are steely blue. There are more than 100 species, widely distributed in the Northern Hemisphere and parts of Africa, many found wild among grass on dry stony ground, but those cultivated do best in reasonably fertile borders. Flowers can be dried but lose their color unless cut promptly.

CULTIVATION Require full sun and well-drained soil, tolerating even poor soils.
PROPAGATION By division, in autumn, winter, or spring. From root cuttings, taken in winter. From seed, sown in mid-spring.
POTENTIAL PROBLEMS Aphids.

Echinops ritro 'Veitch's Blue'

E. ritro *S. central and S.E. Europe to C. Asia*
Flowers: late summer. H:2–4ft (60–120cm), S:18–24in (45–60cm). Z:4–8.
Tall stems rise above prickly green and silver leaves carrying metallic-blue maces that soften in color as the flowers open. **'Veitch's Blue'** is darker in color and grows to 3ft (90cm). A plant of similar character is **E. bannaticus** **'Taplow Blue'**, with flowers of a brighter hue.

EPIMEDIUM

BERBERIDACEAE Barrenwort, bishop's miter

Above a thicket of thin wiry stems, a low canopy of overlapping, heart-shaped leaflets, often bronze tinted in spring and richly colored again in autumn, makes a distinctive and superior kind of groundcover. There are over 30 species of these rhizomatous perennials distributed in the Northern Hemisphere, most growing in shady moist conditions but some, including **E. alpinum** (Z:4–8), a deciduous, fully hardy species from southern Europe, tolerant of drier soils. The light sprays of small flowers, in many cases extravagantly spurred, are an appealing feature in late spring or

Epimedium alpinium

early summer, but for these to be viewed well, it is generally necessary to trim back the tattered foliage that has overwintered. The flower color is usually white, yellow, pink, or crimson but the evergreen fully hardy **E. × warleyense** (Z:4–8) is unusual with its combination of dull orange and pale yellow.
CULTIVATION Tolerate full sun but best in partial shade and require well-drained but moist soil that is rich in organic matter. See also under entries.
PROPAGATION By division, in autumn. From rhizome cuttings, taken in winter and kept under glass. From seed, which may take 18 months to germinate, sown as soon as ripe.
POTENTIAL PROBLEMS Mosaic virus.

Epimedium 'Rose Queen'

E. grandiflorum *China, Korea, Japan*
Foliage: spring to autumn. Flowers: mid- to late spring. H:8–12in (20–30cm), S:12–16in (30–40cm). Z:4–8.
In spring, when mauve-pink spurred flowers hover above them, the immature leaflets are coppery brown but later change to light green. The foliage of **'Rose Queen'** is more purplish when young, and the deep pink flowers have white-tipped spurs. **'White Queen'** shows a hint of mauve in the flowers.
E. grandiflorum is 1 parent of **E. × rubrum**, with deep pink flowers. In spring, green veins run through coppery leaves, which are green in summer but color richly in autumn.

E. perralderianum *Algeria*
Foliage: year-round. Flowers: mid- to late spring. H:10–14in (25–35cm), S:18–24in (45–60cm). Z:4–8.
The slowly spreading evergreen clump has large leaves with 3 toothed leaflets, bronze when young and then glossy green. The flowers are bright yellow. The species is 1 parent of **E. × perralchicum**, which has yellow flowers and foliage with warm tints in spring but maturing to deep green.

Epimedium perralderianum

E. × *versicolor* 'Sulphureum'

Foliage:spring and autumn.
Flowers: mid- to late spring.
H:12-14in (30-35cm), S:1-2ft
(30-60cm). Z:5-8.
The leaves, generally composed of
numerous toothed leaflets, are
exceptional for their coppery
tones in spring and color well in
autumn too. They hide the spurred
yellow flowers unless cut away.

E. × versicolor 'Sulphureum'

E. × *youngianum*

Foliage: spring. Flowers: mid- to
late spring. H:8-12in (20-30cm),
S:12-18in (30-45cm). Z:4-8.
Although less effective as
groundcover than many
barrenworts, this fully deciduous
species has dainty small leaves. The
foliage of 'Niveum' is flushed soft
brown in spring, when the sprays
of white flowers are carried on
reddish stems.

EREMURUS

ASPHODELACEAE Desert candle,
foxtail lily

The flowering of the tallest species
is one of the great events of the
year in a dry garden, but a cold
winter period is necessary for
them to produce their sensational
candles. *E. robustus* (Z:5-8), a
species from the Tien Shan and
Pamir Mountains, can grow to 10ft
(3m), the foxtail flowerhead itself,
densely packed with pink starry
flowers, being up to 4ft (1.2m)
long. In the wild the 50 or so
species are found in near-desert
conditions in Asia. They die down
after their extravagant display.

Inevitably the large species leave
awkward gaps after flowering, a
problem compounding the
difficulties posed by the space
required for the starfish-shaped
crowns of fleshy roots, which need
to be set about 6in (15cm) deep.
The smaller species and a group of
hybrids are more suitable as
dramatic verticals in dry borders.
CULTIVATION Require full sun and
fertile well-drained soil. However,
young growths may be damaged
by frost if touched by early
morning sun.
PROPAGATION By careful division,
after flowering. From seed, sown as
soon as ripe (seedlings may take 5
years to reach flowering maturity).
POTENTIAL PROBLEMS Slugs, snails.

Eremurus × isabellinus Ruiter
Hybrids

E. hybrids

Flowers: early summer. H:3-6ft
(90-180cm), S:18-24in (45-60cm).
Z:5-8.
A number of hybrid cultivars and
their mixed seedlings are sometimes
listed under *E. × isabellinus*.
They have strap-shaped leaves
and stiff stems, the dense
flowerhead bristling with stamens.
Among the tallest are the Ruiter
Hybrids in a color range that
includes bright pink and rusty
shades. The Shelford Hybrids are
slightly shorter, growing to about
4ft (1.2m).

ERIGERON

ASTERACEAE Fleabane

The 200 or so species are found in
many parts of the world. In
gardens the numerous hybrids
between North American species,
plants of prairies and mountainous
areas, predominate. The wide color
range in the daisy flowerheads
makes these useful plants for
sunny beds, especially as they
often flower a second time if cut
back after their first display. The
tall hybrids need staking and all
plants deteriorate unless divided
about every 3 years.
CULTIVATION Require full sun and
fertile well-drained soil.

PROPAGATION By division, in spring.
From cuttings, taken in spring.
From seed, sown in spring.
POTENTIAL PROBLEMS Slugs;
powdery mildew.

E. hybrids

Flowers: early to mid-summer.
H:10-24in (25-60cm), S:12-18in
(30-45cm). Z:2-7.
Leafy stems are topped by single
or semidouble flowers—usually
yellow-centered. The following are
semidouble: 'Dimity', 10in (25cm),
mauve-pink with orangish center;
'Dunkelste Aller', 2ft (60cm), deep
violet; and 'Foersters Liebling',
20in (50cm), reddish pink.

Erigeron 'Dimity'

E. *karvinskianus* Mexico to
Panama
Mexican daisy
Flowers: all summer. H:6-12in
(15-30cm), S:2-3ft (60-90cm).
Z:8-9.
The Mexican daisy has the manners
of a weed, spreading vigorously
and self-seeding indiscreetly. It is,
nonetheless, exceptionally pretty,
and the random airy mixture of
open white flowerheads with the
pink and purple of buds and faded
daisies is most appealing in plants
that have taken chance lodgings in
walls and paving.

ERODIUM

GERANIACEAE Heron's bill, stork's
bill

The 5-petaled flowers, small but
often delicately veined and artfully
blotched, show the genus's kinship
with Geranium. Many of the 60 or
so species, widely distributed, are
compact plants of rocky limestone
country that make neat mounds
of foliage in rock gardens. The
larger species are suitable for the
front of a bed.
CULTIVATION Require full sun and
very well-drained neutral or
alkaline soil.
PROPAGATION By division, in spring.
From basal cuttings, taken in late
spring. From seed, sown as soon as
ripe.
POTENTIAL PROBLEMS Usually none.

Erodium manescaui

E. manescaui *Spain (Pyrenees)*
Flowers: early summer to early
autumn. H:12–20in (30–50cm),
S:1–2ft (30–60cm). Z:5–8.
The best-known large species is
colorful over a long period, the
cluster of bright magenta flowers,
with darker blotches on the upper
2 petals, carried over a clump of
hairy, carrotlike foliage. It self-seeds
freely without being excessively
troublesome. A much more
compact Pyrenean species,
E. glandulosum, has silvery tufted
foliage and mauve-pink flowers
blotched purple.

Erodium reichardii

E. × variabile
Flowers: all summer. H:6–8in
(15–20cm), S:12–16in (30–40cm).
Z:4–7.
The parents of this hybrid,
E. corsicum and **E. reichardii**, are
attractive plants, the former, found
on the rocky coastlines of Corsica
and Sardinia, has downy gray-green
leaves and white to pink flowers
with magenta veining. In the
hybrid, the scalloped leaves are
topped by deep red flowers.
There are several cultivars of
E. × variabile, including a double,
'**Flore Pleno**', and the dark-veined,
pink '**Roseum**'.

ERYNGIUM

APIACEAE Eryngo, sea holly

Flower arrangers will scavenge for
the best of these, the branched
dried stems and the jagged ruffs of
the old conelike flowerheads
retaining the metallic luster of the
living plant. There are 230 species,

some of which have deep taproots
and thrive in dry rocky conditions
in Asia, Europe, and north Africa
and, in the case of the sea holly
(**E. maritimum**, Z:4–8), on pebbly
shorelines. The silver-green
biennial Miss Willmott's ghost
(**E. giganteum**, Z:4–8), the common
name a barbed compliment, as
perhaps the Edwardian gardener
deserved, is of this persuasion. In
contrast, most of the species from
Mexico and Central and South
America, such as **E. agavifolium**
(Z:5–8), which has a rosette of
toothed leaves, are fibrous-rooted
plants of moister, more fertile soils.
CULTIVATION Require full sun and
well-drained soil; the species
described tolerate dry conditions.
PROPAGATION From seed, sown
when ripe. By division, in spring.
From root cuttings, in winter.
POTENTIAL PROBLEMS Slugs, snails;
powdery mildew, root rot.

E. alpinum *Europe (Alps, Jura,
mountains of W. and C. Balkans)*
Flowers: mid-summer to early
autumn. H:24–30in (60–75cm),
S:18–24in (45–60cm). Z:5–8.
The upper part of the branched
stems, and the flowerheads and
their softly lacy ruffs, seem to be
dyed a steely violet-blue. Silvery
'**Slieve Donard**' is one of several
good selections. **E. × oliverianum**,
of which E. alpinum may be a
parent, is large flowered and silvery
blue, with stiffly spiny bracts.

Eryngium alpinum 'Slieve Donard'

E. bourgatii *Spain (Pyrenees)*
Foliage: spring to autumn. Flowers:
mid- to late summer. H:1–2ft
(30–60cm), S:12–18in (30–45cm).
Z:5–8.
Curved and prickly jagged leaves,
veined and spangled with silver,
are the base for their branched
blue stems and silver-spined blue
or gray-green flowerheads.

E. × tripartitum
Flowers: mid-summer to early
autumn. H:2–3ft (60–90cm),
S:20–30in (50–75cm). Z:5–8.
Numerous small blue cones with
sparse but darker and spiny bracts

are supported by a metallic blue
wiry framework. **E. amethystinum**
(Z:6–8) is similar with very blue
flowerheads later in the season.

EUPATORIUM

ASTERACEAE

This very mixed genus of about 40
species, some of them annuals and
evergreen shrubs, is widely
distributed in temperate,
subtropical, and tropical regions.
It contains a few perennials that
are suitable for large-scale planting
in moist soils. The double form of
the European hemp agrimony
(**E. cannabinum** '**Flore Pleno**',
Z:5–8), like the species described,
is an impressive waterside plant.
CULTIVATION Require full sun or
partial shade and moist soil.
PROPAGATION By division, in spring.
From seed, sown in spring.
POTENTIAL PROBLEMS Aphids, slugs,
snails.

Eupatorium purpureum

E. purpureum *E. USA*
Joe Pye weed
Flowers: mid-summer to early
autumn. H:6–8ft (1.8–2.5m),
S:3–4ft (90–120cm). Z:3–8.
Purplish-red stems rise through
coarse leaves bearing soft domes
of pink-purple flowers. In **subsp.
maculatum** '**Atropurpureum**', the
stems are slightly shorter and the
flowers have a brighter pink tone.

EUPHORBIA

EUPHORBIACEAE Milkweed, spurge

The curious structure of the
flowers is a feature shared by
about 2,000 species in this very
large genus, but in other respects
the character of the plants can be
very different, for they include
flimsy annuals, evergreen and
deciduous perennials, and shrubs,
as well as treelike succulents, some
bearing a strong resemblance to
columnar cacti. Representatives
of the genus are found in a very
wide range of habitats in
temperate, subtropical, and
tropical regions. The most useful
perennials as garden plants, at least

in temperate regions, are those with good clumps of foliage and long-lasting clusters or heads of flowers, the conspicuous feature being the bracts surrounding the small cup that cradles the tiny male and female flowers. Some of these are plants of dry rocky terrain, but others are plants of moister woodland conditions.

CULTIVATION Tolerate full sun or partial shade and a wide range of well-drained soils. Many thrive in dry conditions, but of those described the following prefer moist soils in light shade: *E. amygdaloides, E. griffithii, E. polychroma,* and *E. schillingii.*

PROPAGATION By division, in early spring. From cuttings, taken in spring (dip cut surfaces in warm water to stop sap from bleeding). From seed, sown in spring.

POTENTIAL PROBLEMS Aphids; rust, gray mold (*Botrytis*).

WARNING Contact with sap can cause skin problems. Severe stomach upsets may occur if any part is swallowed.

E. amygdaloides *Caucasus, Europe, Turkey*
Wood spurge
Flowers: mid-spring to early summer. H:1–2ft (30–60cm), S:1ft (30cm). Z:5–9.
The evergreen wood spurge is itself an indifferent plant, but '**Purpurea**' combines maroon and purplish red in its stems and young foliage and sharp yellow in the flowerheads. On poor soils in shade, **var. robbiae** makes outstanding evergreen ground-cover, the dark rosettes topped by yellow-green flowers over a long season.

E. characias *Portugal, W. Mediterranean*
Foliage: year-round. Flowers: early spring to early summer. H:3–5ft (90–150cm), S:3–4ft (90–120cm). Z:7–9.
In reality this is shrubby but in character it is not far removed from perennial species thriving in dry conditions. The narrow blue-

Euphorbia characias subsp.*wulfenii*

green leaves densely clothing stiff stems are attractive throughout the year and especially beautiful when beaded with delicate drops of water. The flowering stems carry huge heads dense with acid-green bracts, nearly-black nectar glands creating a dark eye. In **subsp. wulfenii** the nectar glands are greenish yellow.

Euphorbia griffithii

E. griffithii *Bhutan, S.W. China (Yunnan), Tibet*
Foliage: autumn. Flowers: early summer. H:2–3ft (60–90cm), S:20–24in (50–60cm). Z:5–9.
Spreading by questing rhizomes, this native of light moist woodland, most frequently represented by cultivars such as '**Fireglow**', can make large patches vivid with the brick-red or coral of its bracts. The narrow leaves are usually green with red-tinged midribs, but in '**Dixter**' they are darker, with copper tints.

Euphorbia myrsinites

E. myrsinites *C. Asia, S. and E. Europe to Turkey*
Foliage: year-round. Flowers: spring. H:4–6in (10–15cm), S:12–15in (30–38cm). Z:6–8.
At the edge of a rocky outcrop, the prostrate stems of this evergreen seem to writhe with the spiral arrangement of the blue-green fleshy leaves. The long-lasting flowerheads are greenish yellow.

E. polychroma *C. and S. Europe, Turkey*
Flowers: mid-spring to mid-summer. H:18in (45cm), S:18–24in (45–60cm). Z:4–9.

The clump makes a tidy dome of bright greenish yellow in dry as well as moist soils. All the selections are worth growing, including the extra-large '**Major**'.

Euphorbia polychroma

E. schillingii *E. Nepal*
Foliage: spring to autumn. Flowers: mid-summer to mid-autumn. H:30–36in (75–90cm), S:1–2ft (30–60cm). Z:5–8.
The very long season in which the bracts remain an attractive greenish yellow make this clump-forming plant, only described as a new species in 1987, a valuable addition to those that thrive in moist soils. *E. sikkimensis* (Z:6–8) is slightly taller and also does best in moist soils. It is remarkable for the display of pink leaves and red stems in early spring.

FILIPENDULA

ROSACEAE

Except for dropwort (*F. vulgaris*, Z:4–8), best known for the creamy double '**Multiplex**', the 10 or so species in this genus are moisture-loving plants from temperate regions in the Northern Hemisphere. They are well suited to waterside planting in the wilder reaches of the garden, where their plumy flowerheads do not seem oversophisticated. They can be incorporated, too, in beds with a reliable supply of moisture but the giant among them, the queen of the prairies (*F. rubra*, Z:4–8), up to 8ft (2.5m) tall, requires a very generous space, where its spreading clumps may get out of hand.

CULTIVATION Most tolerate full sun or partial shade and require a moist soil, thriving even in boggy conditions. *F. vulgaris* needs sun and well-drained soil and is best in alkaline conditions.

PROPAGATION By division, in autumn or spring. From root cuttings, taken in early spring. From seed, sown in autumn or in spring at 50–55°F (10–13°C).

POTENTIAL PROBLEMS Leaf spot, mildew.

F. palmata *China, Japan, Mongolia, Siberia*
Foliage: spring to autumn. Flowers: mid-summer. H:2–4ft (60–120cm), S:3–4ft (1–1.2m). Z:4–8.
The lobed dark green leaves are hairy and white underneath. They form a good clump through which rise stiff stems with flat heads of pink, fluffy flowers. '**Elegantissima**' has deep pink flowers followed by bronzy red seedheads.

Filipendula purpurea

F. purpurea *Japan*
Flowers: late summer. H:3–4ft (90–120cm), S:18–24in (45–60cm). Z:4–8.
This is a more manageable plant than *F. rubra*, but still makes an impressive mound. The branched purplish-red stems carry reddish-pink flowers that fade as they age.

Filipendula ulmaria

F. ulmaria *Europe, W. Asia*
Meadowsweet, queen of the meadows
Foliage: spring. Flowers: all summer. H:2–3ft (60–90cm), S:1–2ft (30–60cm). Z:3–9.
The specific name is a reference to the elmlike leaves while the common name is a reminder that the creamy flowers are fragrant. The gold-variegated '**Aurea**' is the plant to grow. It tolerates bog conditions, demanding an unfailing supply of moisture, and some shade will prevent the leaves from scorching as they change from yellow through cream to light green. The flowerheads are inferior and should be removed to prevent plain green-leaved seedlings from becoming established.

FOENICULUM

APIACEAE Fennel

The aniseed-scented herb, the single species in this genus of European origin, likes rather moister conditions than its close relative the giant fennel (**Ferula communis**). The latter is another impressive perennial, a plant that grows on dry rough ground in the Mediterranean and farther east, and which can reach a height of 10ft (3m).
CULTIVATION Requires full sun and moist well-drained soil.
PROPAGATION By division, in spring. From seed, sown in spring.
POTENTIAL PROBLEMS Aphids, slugs; mildew.

Foeniculum vulgare

F. vulgare *S. Europe*
Flowers: mid- to late summer. H:6ft (1.8m), S:18in (45cm). Z:4–9.
The feathery foliage of fennel is most beautiful in the tinted '**Purpureum**', emerging as tight coppery plumes and maturing to gray-green, tinged with bronze. The leaves are topped by branched stems carrying heads of small yellow flowers. Remove well before the seeds drop, or you will be cursed with unwanted seedlings with deep taproots.

GAILLARDIA

ASTERACEAE Blanket flower

The perennial blanket flowers in cultivation, hybrids of the North American prairie species, are showy plants with daisy flowerheads that have a domed disk surrounded by ray flowerets in yellow, orange, or red, sometimes banded in combination. Hard cutting back in autumn helps extend their lives. Among the 30 species from North and South America are several annuals and biennials, the annual fully hardy **G. pulchella** being widely grown for single and double flowerheads in red, yellow, or combinations of these colors.
CULTIVATION Require full sun and well-drained soil.

PROPAGATION From seed, sown in spring at 55–64°F (13–18°C). By division, in spring. From root cuttings, taken in winter.
POTENTIAL PROBLEMS Slugs, snails; downy mildew.

Gaillardia 'Kobold'

G. hybrids
Flowers: early summer to early autumn. H:10–34in (25–85cm), S:18in (45 cm). Z:3–9.
An average height is given for each of the following cultivars, which all make bushy plants that produce colorful flowerheads, usually 3–4in (7.5–10cm) across, over a long season: '**Burgunder**', 2ft (60cm), wine red; '**Dazzler**', 30in (75cm), maroon disk and orange-red ray flowerets with yellow tips; '**Kobold**', 1ft (30cm), dark red disk surrounded by a band of bright red ray flowerets with yellow tips; and '**Wirral Flame**', 30in (75cm), deep reddish brown with yellow tips.

GALEGA

PAPILIONACEAE Goat's rue

The genus comprises about 6 species, most from southern Europe to western Asia. A tendency to sprawl, particularly when grown in rich soils, has counted against these plants, once popular in cottage gardens and herbaceous borders. If they are given body with twiggy supports, they make leafy clumps topped with numerous spikes of small pealike flowers. They are pleasingly unpretentious plants suitable for wild gardens and mixed or herbaceous borders.
CULTIVATION Require sun or partial shade and moist soil.
PROPAGATION By division, in late autumn and spring. From seed, sown in spring (soak before sowing).
POTENTIAL PROBLEMS Pea and bean weevils.

G. officinalis *C. and S. Europe, Turkey to Pakistan*
Flowers: late spring to early summer. H:3–5ft (90–150cm), S:3–4ft (90–120cm). Z:3–8.

This bushy plant has pinnate leaves, with as many as 17 narrow leaflets, making a soft green base for flowers of pale mauve-pink or, in '**Alba**', white. Most of the hybrids of which it is a parent are mauve with a pink or blue bias, and a few, such as **G. × hartlandii 'Alba'** (Z:3–8), are white. **G. 'His Majesty'**, a bicolor, has white and mauve flowers. **G. orientalis** is a similar species with violet flowers, but it is rhizomatous and can be invasive.

Galega officinalis

GAURA

ONAGRACEAE

One prairie perennial from a genus of about 20 North American species is a lively component in dry sunny borders late in the season, its long succession of small flowers dancing lightly on a graceful plant.

CULTIVATION Tolerate full sun or partial shade and dry to moist soils, but best in full sun and moist well-drained conditions.
PROPAGATION From seed, sown in spring. By division, in spring. From cuttings, taken in spring and summer.
POTENTIAL PROBLEMS Usually none.

G. lindheimeri USA (Louisiana, Texas)
Flowers: late spring to early autumn. H:4–5ft (1.2–1.5m), S:30–36in (75–90cm). Z:5–9.
The slender stems with willowlike leaves, often dark spotted, sway freely with their light charge of starry 4-petaled flowers, which are pink in bud but open white.

Gaura lindheimeri

GENTIANA

GENTIANACEAE Gentian

The gentians are best known for the alpine species with trumpet-like flowers in a color range extending from pale sky blue to intense lapis lazuli. However, the genus, with about 400 species widely distributed in temperate zones, holds some surprises. Some of the larger species are woodland or meadow plants. The bitterwort (**G. lutea**, Z:4–8), up to 5ft (1.5m) tall, with clustered whorls of star-shaped yellow flowers, is an example that escapes the stereotype in color as well as in scale. These larger plants, including the willow gentian (*G. asclepiadea*), are easy to grow, and even many of the alpine species are less daunting as charges than their status might suggest. The most easygoing is *G. septemfida*; the most insistent on lime-free conditions are the Asiatic autumn-flowering species such as *G. sino-ornata*; and the most vexing is the European trumpet gentian (**G. acaulis**, Z:3–8), which is not difficult to grow but remain impenetrably fastidious about the conditions that will coax it into producing its deep blue, green-throated trumpets.
CULTIVATION Tolerate full sun or partial shade (shade necessary where summers are hot and dry) and require well-drained but moist soil rich in organic matter with added grit and leaf mold. *G. sino-ornata* and its hybrids require lime-free soil.
PROPAGATION By division, in spring. From cuttings, in spring. From seed, sown as soon as ripe.
POTENTIAL PROBLEMS Slugs and snails, aphids and red spider mites under glass; gentian rust fungus, stem-rotting soil fungi.

Gentiana asclepiadea

G. asclepiadea Mountains of C. and S. Europe, Turkey
Willow gentian
Flowers: late summer to early autumn. H:2–3ft (60–90cm), S:18–24in (45–60cm). Z:5–8.
The deep blue gentian flowers are paired on arching stems in the axils of willowlike leaves. The white **var. alba** is equally fine as an autumn-flowering perennial for light shade.

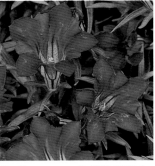

Gentiana × macaulayi '*Kingfisher*'

G. × macaulayi
Flowers: late summer to mid-autumn. H:3–6in (7.5–15cm), S:4–8in (10–20cm). Z:5–8.
G. sino-ornata and *G. farreri* are among the species that have been used in hybridizing autumn-flowering alpine gentians. This hybrid, although a deeper blue, takes after *G. farreri*, a species with narrow pale blue trumpets, white in the throat. *G. × macaulayi* '**Kingfisher**' may be a selected seedling of this hybrid and is like a compact version of *G. sino-ornata*.

G. septemfida Caucasus, Turkey, Iran to C. Asia
Flowers: late summer. H:6–8in (15–20cm), S:10–14in (25–35cm). Z:2–8.
A popular alpine, being easy to grow and producing leafy stems with clusters of blue or purple bells.

G. sino-ornata W. China, Tibet
Flowers: autumn. H:3–6in (7.5–15cm), S:12–14in (30–35cm). Z:5–8.
Subsequent introductions of Asiatic species have not damaged the standing of one of the most splendid autumn-flowering alpines. The azure funnel-shaped flowers with greenish-yellow vertical bands are borne singly on prostrate stems that radiate from overwintering rosettes.

Gentiana sino-ornata

Gentiana verna

G. verna *Mountains in Europe from Ireland to Russia*
Spring gentian, star gentian
Flowers: spring or early summer.
H:2–3in (5–7.5cm), S:4–6in (10–15cm). Z:5–8.
Sky-blue stars, usually white in the throat, are scattered over small rosettes of dark green leaves. This small but startling beauty is regrettably short-lived.

GERANIUM

GERANIACEAE Cranesbill

Few perennials are less in need of an apologist than the cranesbills. The combination of dense and attractive foliage, in many cases prettily cut and lobed, and the generous production of small saucer- or star-shaped flowers has made several species and hybrids enormously popular as groundcover plants. Their good qualities and their tolerance of a wide range of conditions mean that they are suitable for wild and woodland gardens and, more importantly, as a furnishing to gardens that must be managed with the minimum of labor. Many are rhizomatous and are quick to build up colonies. Others, however, are clump forming, with fibrous roots, and a few, including the spring-flowering but summer-dormant **G. tuberosum** (Z:7–9), are tuberous. The genus, which contains about 300 species, is inevitably much more interesting than might be guessed from its stereotyped use. The alpines and some larger species from dry, sunny habitats are good among paving and in gravel as well as in the rock garden. A few of the larger species are impressive in their scale and deportment, none more so than the frost-tender **G. maderense** (Z:9–10), a Madeiran native, with triumphant stands up to 5ft (1.5m) tall of pink-magenta flowers above a podium of beautifully textured dark green leaves. This magnificent plant is, however, short-lived and usually dies after 1 season of flowering.

Almost all of the geraniums are pleasing not only in their general effect, but also when examined in detail, the penciled markings and contrasting eyes in the flowers being an exquisite refinement. Many geraniums will flower a second time if they are cut back as the first crop of flowers fades. An unfortunate source of confusion is the continued but incorrect use of the generic name as a common name for the species and hybrids of Pelargonium (see also SHRUBS).
CULTIVATION Most tolerate full sun or partial shade and require well-drained fertile soil that is reasonably moist. In general the small species and hybrids prefer full sun and sharp drainage (potting media with added grit).
PROPAGATION By division, in spring. By cuttings, rooted with bottom heat, in spring. From seed, sown in spring.
POTENTIAL PROBLEMS Slugs, snails; downy mildew, powdery mildew, viruses.

Geranium maderense

G. cinereum *Pyrenees*
Flowers: late spring to early summer. H:6in (15cm), S:1ft (30cm). Z:4–8.
The cup-shaped white or pink flowers, large for the size of this dwarf species, are held on short stalks above a rosette of gray-green basal leaves. In **'Ballerina'** they are pink veined with darker purplish pink. A slightly larger plant, **var. subcaulescens**, which is from the Balkans and N.E. Turkey, produces black-eyed, bright magenta flowers over a very long season.

Geranium cinereum 'Ballerina'

Geranium endressii

G. endressii *France (Pyrenees)*
Flowers: early summer to early autumn. H:18in (45cm), S:2ft (60cm). Z:4–8.
Rounded mounds of light green leaves, which are 5-lobed and toothed, are covered with pink flowers for months. This rhizomatous species is a parent of **G. × oxonianum**, which has several named selections. **'Claridge Druce'**, height and spread about 3ft (90cm), is the most vigorous and suitable for large-scale planting as groundcover. The lobed leaves are gray-green and the flowers are dark pink and veined.

G. himalayense *Himalayas*
Foliage: autumn. Flowers: early summer to early autumn.
H:12–18in (30–45cm), S:2ft (60cm). Z:4–8.
From running rhizomes this species quickly builds into large colonies, even in full shade. Over a base of deeply lobed leaves, there is a main display of white-eyed, violet-blue flowers in the first half of summer, followed by a steady trickle until autumn.

Geranium 'Johnson's Blue'

G. 'Johnson's Blue'
Flowers: summer. H:12–18in (30–45cm), S:24–30in (60–75cm). Z:4–8.
Saucers of blue flowers that are tinted purple follow in succession over a dense cover of elegantly divided leaves, spreading by rhizomes. One parent is probably the airy meadow cranesbill (**G. pratense**), up to 3ft (90cm) tall, suitable for naturalizing in wilder

parts of the garden. The flowers are usually violet-blue, but in *G. pratense* '**Mrs. Kendall Clark**' are opalescent. Doubles such as *G. pratense* '**Plenum Violaceum**' are better in ordered parts of the yard, singles self-seeding to excess.

Geranium macrorrhizum

G. macrorrhizum *S. Europe*
Foliage: autumn. Flowers: early summer. H:12–20in (30–50cm), S:20–30in (50–75cm). Z:3–8.
The species from which geranium oil is extracted has sticky, aromatic, light green leaves that are rounded but have a prettily scalloped edge. It is rhizomatous and semievergreen, but the foliage often colors well in autumn. Several fine cultivars offer alternatives to the magenta flowers: '**Album**' is pale pink with red calyces, and '**Ingwersen's Variety**' is of a stronger but still soft pink. The species is a parent of *G.* × *cantabrigiense* (Z:5–8), also aromatic but a more compact plant up to 1ft (30cm) tall, which spreads by runners.
G. × *cantabrigiense* '**Biokovo**' (Z:5–8) is a clone forming a mound of deeply divided, smooth leaves with pink-tinged white flowers.

G. × magnificum
Foliage: year-round. Flowers: early to mid-summer. H:18–24in (45–60 cm), S:16–18in (40–45cm). Z:4–8.
The abundant glossy violet-blue flowers are darkly veined. In autumn the deeply cut hairy rounded leaves usually color well on this clump-forming geranium.

Geranium × magnificum

G. psilostemon *S.W. Caucasus, N.E. Turkey*
Armenian cranesbill
Foliage: spring and autumn. Flowers: early to late summer. H:2–4ft (60–120cm), S:2–3ft (60–90cm). Z:4–8.
The riveting dark-eyed magenta of the flowers provides scope for dramatic color schemes in summer. The deeply cut leaves make a large clump, signaling autumn with random red tints. *G.* '**Ann Folkard**', Z:5–8, of which this species is a parent, is a vigorous hybrid remarkable for its long flowering period, but the yellow-green of the foliage is not comfortable with the purple-magenta of the flowers.

Geranium psilostemon

G. renardii *Caucasus*
Foliage: spring to autumn. Flowers: early summer. H and S:1ft (30cm). Z:6–8.
The flowers, white with purple veining, are sometimes only sparingly produced, but the mound of sage-green velvety leaves, which are corrugated, deeply veined, and have a scalloped edge, make this an exceptionally good foliage plant.

Geranium × riversleaianum

G. × riversleaianum
Flowers: summer. H:9–12in (23–30cm), S:3ft (90cm). Z:4–8.
The trailing stems make good groundcover with their gray-green leaves, and the flowers in shades of soft to dark pink are borne over a long season. The flowers of '**Russell Prichard**' are deep magenta.

G. sanguineum *Europe, N. Turkey*
Bloody cranesbill
Foliage: autumn. Flowers: early summer. H:8–12in (20–30cm), S:12–18in (30–45cm). Z:4–8.
The attractive hummock of dark green, finely cut leaves is studded with bright magenta-pink flowers, white eyed and with dark veins, right through summer and into autumn. There are numerous cultivars. '**Glenluce**' has large soft pink flowers. '**Shepherd's Warning**', rarely more than 6in (15cm) across, is deep pink. A similarly compact plant is **var. striatum** (Z:5–8), the pale pink flowers with dark veins nestling among green foliage.

G. sylvaticum *Europe, N. Turkey*
Wood cranesbill
Flowers: late spring to early summer. H:30–36in (75–90cm), S:2ft (60cm). Z:4–8.
The clump-forming wood cranesbill, with violet-blue, white-eyed flowers over soft divided foliage, is transformed into something ethereal in the white-flowered '**Album**'. '**Mayflower**' combines light purple and violet-blue in a prodigal display of large flowers. The color range extends to purplish pink in **subsp. sylvaticum var. wanneri**, the flowers of which are veined red. Another slightly smaller species for planting under a leafy canopy is *G. phaeum* (Z:5–7); the cultivar '**Mourning Widow**' is a pleasingly somber plant with deep maroon flowers; '**Album**' (Z:5–7) is fresh and light enhancing for dark corners.

G. wallichianum
N.E. Afghanistan to Kashmir
Flowers: late summer to early autumn. H:1ft (30cm), S:3–4ft (90–120cm). Z:4–8.
With its trailing stems working their way through other plants, this produces delightful surprises in the form of purplish flowers in late summer and early autumn. It is most commonly represented by '**Buxton's Variety**', with white-eyed blue flowers.

Geranium wallichianum

GERBERA

ASTERACEAE

One of the 40 or so species, a frost-tender daisy from grasslands in southern Africa, is a familiar cut flower as a result of large-scale commercial cultivation under glass. With an astonishing color range, gerberas can complement studied interior decoration well. In frost-free areas and well-drained positions in full sun, they are no mean plants for the garden.
CULTIVATION Require full sun and well-drained soil.
PROPAGATION From seed, sown in autumn or spring at 55–64°F (13–18°C). By division, in early spring. From basal cuttings, taken in summer.
POTENTIAL PROBLEMS Aphids, leaf miners, white flies, tarsonemid mites; leaf spot, root rot.

Gerbera jamesonii

G. jamesonii *South Africa (Northern Transvaal, Eastern Transvaal, KwaZulu/Natal), Swaziland*
Barberton daisy, Transvaal daisy
Flowers: late spring to late summer. H:12–18in (30–45cm), S:18–24in (45–60cm). Z:7–10.
From a deep-rooted rosette of hairy leaves rise a succession of long-rayed, yellow-centered daisies, 1 flowerhead per stem. In the wild plant, the flowerheads are orange-red, but seed-raised selections include singles and doubles, some with heads as much as 4in (10cm) across, in a wide variety of pastel and deep colors. The giants, however, have become a little too worldly and have lost the grace of the species.

GEUM

ROSACEAE Avens

Water avens (**G. rivale**, Z:3–7), widely distributed in the Northern Hemisphere, is a plant of cool moist soils, but many of the species in this genus, about 50 in number, are found in drier, sometimes rocky and mountainous habitats throughout the temperate and arctic regions of the world. The Chilean species **G. chiloense** (Z:4–7) is a parent of several hybrid doubles, the main representatives of the genus in cultivation. Specialized nurseries, however, offer a few rock-garden plants, one of which is described here, and good selections of water avens itself, such as **'Leonard's Variety'**, in which the pendant flowers are a rare shade of copper pink, which is intensified by the maroon of the calyces.
CULTIVATION Tolerate full sun or partial shade and require well-drained soil that is rich in organic matter. *G. rivale* requires moister conditions than most species.
PROPAGATION By division, in autumn or spring. From seed, sown in autumn or spring.
POTENTIAL PROBLEMS Sawh larvae.

G. 'Borisii'
Flowers: early to mid-summer. H:12–20in (30–50cm), S:12–18in (30–45cm). Z:3–7.
Orange-red flowers with conspicuous bosses of yellow stamens show well against the rich green clumps of hairy leaves.

Geum 'Borisii'

G. 'Lady Stratheden'
Flowers: all summer. H and S:18–24in (45–60cm). Z:5–8.
The rounded terminal leaflet of the hairy foliage is a feature of this and other hybrids. The semidouble, clear yellow flowers are saucer shaped, and the notched petals are slightly wavy. *G.* 'Mrs J. Bradshaw', a semidouble scarlet, shows the same good breeding.

Geum 'Lady Stratheden'

Geum montanum

G. montanum *Mountains of C. and S. Europe*
Flowers: spring to early summer. H:6in (15cm), S:1ft (30cm). Z:4–8.
This alpine species makes a dense tuft of hairy leaves from which emerge erect stems carrying rich yellow, saucer-shaped flowers.

GUNNERA

HALORADIGACEAE

The genus, containing more than 40 species of perennials from Australasia, southern Africa, and South America, takes in extremes of scale. There are New Zealand species that make ground-hugging mats and cushions, and even the better-known *G. magellanica* (Z:7–10), with its mats of scalloped leaves, barely reaches 6in (15cm) when in flower. In contrast, the enormous leaves of their large relatives, especially those of *G. manicata*, are among the prodigies of annual foliage growth. Most species are plants of moist soils, and the giants need a rich deep medium and an unfailing water supply to produce their phenomenal leafage. The dead leaves can be used to protect the crowns in winter.
CULTIVATION Tolerate sun or partial shade and permanently moist deep soil that is rich in organic matter. Large-leaved species need shelter from strong winds.
PROPAGATION From seed, sown as soon as ripe and kept frost-free during winter. From basal leaf bud cuttings, taken in spring. By division, in spring.
POTENTIAL PROBLEMS Slugs, snails.

G. manicata *Colombia to Brazil*
Foliage: spring to autumn. Flowers: early summer. H:6–8ft (1.8–2.5m), S:8–12ft (2.5–3.7m). Z:7–10.
In a large garden or landscape, this is the ultimate perennial for waterside or bog. Massive prickly stalks support overlapping dark green leaves, bristly and coarse in texture but magnificent not only for their size—they can be 6ft (1.8m) across—but also for their

lobed and toothed outline and prominent veining. Curious cone-shaped, brownish-green flower spikes, about 2ft (60cm) tall, lurk within the clump. *G. tinctoria*, (Z:8–10) from Chile, still impressive but a slightly smaller plant, has a distinctive knobbly fruit spike composed of small green fruits flushed with red. The deep green leaves are heart shaped to rounded and sharply toothed.

Gunnera manicata

GYPSOPHILA

CARYOPHYLLACEAE

A preference for alkaline conditions is a marked characteristic of most species in a genus composed of more than 100 species of annuals and perennials. Many are compact plants, unlike the best-known species, *G. paniculata*, a florists' cliche in the way its frothy sprays have been used to accompany bolder flowers. In the wild almost all species are found in dry stony or sandy places from the E. Mediterranean to the Caucasus, Asia, and N.W. China, and in general they are most successful in gardens on light soils. The annual *G. elegans* (Z:4–8) is another species much grown for cutting.
CULTIVATION Require full sun and well-drained alkaline soil.
G. 'Rosenschleier' prefers reasonably moist conditions.
PROPAGATION From seed, sown in spring. From root cuttings, taken in late winter (species). By grafting, in late winter (named cultivars).
POTENTIAL PROBLEMS Stem rots.

G. paniculata C. Asia and C. and E. Europe
Baby's breath
Flowers: mid- to late summer. H and S:3–4ft (90–120cm). Z:4–8.
Its vogue as a cut flower may have waned, but baby's breath is an infallible, although often short-lived, charmer in dry borders, the hazy mound of tangled fine stems and tiny white stars masking not only its own grasslike leaves but also untidy remnants of plants that die down early. Most of the

cultivars, including **'Bristol Fairy'**, are double, and some, such as **'Flamingo'**, have a slight pink tint. **G. 'Rosenschleier'**, a hybrid between *G. paniculata* and *G. repens*, makes a low hazy mound about 18in (45cm) tall, the myriad tiny double flowers turning from white to pale pink.

Gypsophila 'Rosenschleier'

G. repens Mountains of C. and E. Europe
Flowers: all summer. H:2–4in (5–10cm), S:10–15in (25–38cm). Z:4–8.
The mat of wiry stems and gray-green leaves nearly obscured by sprays of small white or pink flowers looks its best flowing over a ledge or from a crevice. **'Dorothy Teacher'** carries pale and older dark pink flowers at the same time.

HELENIUM

ASTERACEAE Helen's flower, sneezeweed

Of the 40 or so species, all from North and Central America, few are common garden plants, but the hybrids, mainly derived from *H. autumnale* (Z:3–8), dominate sunny moist beds with profuse displays of daisy flowerheads. They are often disparaged for their lack of subtlety rather than appreciated for the frank mixture of rich mahogany, bronze, and copper with brighter yellows and orange. *H. hoopesii* (Z:3–8), which grows to about 3ft (90cm) and has yellow or orange ray flowerets around a brown center will tolerate drier conditions than the hybrids. All of these plants have distinctive flowerheads; as these mature, the ray flowerets reflex to form a skirt beneath the velvety central knob. The taller hybrids need support, and all deteriorate after 2 to 3 years unless divided.
CULTIVATION Require full sun and moist well-drained soil.
PROPAGATION From seed, sown in spring (species). From basal cuttings, in spring (cultivars). Divide in autumn or spring.
POTENTIAL PROBLEMS Leaf spot.

WARNING Severe stomach upsets occur if any part is eaten. The skin may react allergically on contact with foliage.

H. hybrids
Flowers: early summer to early autumn. H:30–60in (75–150cm), S:16–24in (40–60cm). Z:3–8.
Selecting for season and color will give a display of warm, bright tones over a period of about 4 months. The foliage on the branching clumps is undistinguished, a disadvantage that can be overcome by careful foreground planting for the first half of summer. All of the following have velvety central disks in shades of brown unless stated otherwise. Among the earliest to flower, and both about 30in (75cm) in height, are **'Crimson Beauty'**, red-brown; and **'Goldene Jugend'**, rich yellow with a paler disk. In the next wave is **'Moerheim Beauty'**, copper changing to orange-brown, about 3ft (90cm) in height. Among those still flowering in autumn are **'Butterpat'**, 2ft (60cm) tall, yellow with yellow-brown disk, and **'Coppelia'**, 2ft (60cm) tall, orange and red-brown with brown disk. One of the tallest and also late flowering is **'Sonnenwunder'**, which grows to 5ft (1.5m) and bears yellow flowerheads with greenish-yellow disks.

Helenium 'Moerheim Beauty'

HELIANTHUS

ASTERACEAE Sunflower

The best-known species is certainly the annual sunflower (**H. annuus**), but other species from North and South America include yellow-flowered perennial daisies from soils that are generally alkaline but range from swampy to dry. They are often dismissed as coarse plants and generally have the disadvantage of running roots and need staking, which is best done as plants start to make growth in spring. The tall species and hybrids placed well back give a boost to beds in the second half of summer. *H. salicifolius* (Z:4–9) can even reach 10ft (3m), its sturdy stems carrying drooping narrow leaves that are more important than the small flowerheads. This species does better on dry soils than most of the hybrids, which deteriorate unless divided every 3 years.

CULTIVATION Require full sun and well-drained soil, preferably neutral to alkaline, that is moisture retentive.

PROPAGATION By division, in spring or autumn. From basal cuttings, taken in spring. From seed, sown in spring.

POTENTIAL PROBLEMS Slugs; powdery mildew, *Sclerotinia*.

WARNING The skin may react allergically on contact with foliage.

Helianthus 'Loddon Gold'

H. 'Loddon Gold'

Flowers: late summer to mid-autumn. H:4–5ft (1.2–1.5m), S:30–36in (75–90cm). Z:3–9.
The thin-leaved sunflower (*H. decapetalus*) is a parent of several tall-growing hybrids, sometimes listed under *H.* × *multiflorus*. All are in shades of yellow, 'Loddon Gold' having double flowerheads of rich coloring.

Helianthus 'Monarch'

H. 'Monarch'

Flowers: early to mid-autumn. H:5–6ft (1.5–1.8m), S:3–4ft (90–120cm). Z:5–9.
The dark-eyed sunflower (*H. atrorubens*), which has rough, hairy leaves, has produced this fine plant with semidouble rich yellow flowerheads. The ray flowerets radiate from the deep maroon disk and curl back at the edges.

HELLEBORUS

RANUNCULACEAE Hellebore

The qualities of most of the 15 species transcend the conspiracy of self-conscious good taste that is sometimes apparent in devotees of the genus. The leaves, usually leathery but boldly lobed and divided, are often an attractive feature. Some species are fully herbaceous, losing their leaves in winter. *H. purpurascens* (Z:5–9), for example, produces its slate-tinted green flowers in late winter before the new leaves develop. Other hellebores, among them the Lenten roses (*H. orientalis*), retain the old foliage until spring, when, in a tattered state, it is replaced by new growth. Several, including *H. argutifolius*, are shrublike in character, producing sturdy stems that bear flowers in their second year, which then die back as new stems develop. The flowers are never frivolous, but their sober dignity, often in unexpected shades of green and plum, sometimes softened by delicate shading and freckling, is long lasting at a time of the year when few other perennials are in flower. The thickly textured segments, backed by leafy bracts, often remain long after seed has set. In the wild the species are found in woodland and more open habitats from Europe to Asia, usually on alkaline soils that get a plentiful supply of moisture in winter and spring, although often dry in summer. In the garden they are long-lived plants and are among the most useful and beautiful perennials as an underplanting to shrubs and in shade cast by buildings. In tamed woodland there is little that can match self-seeding drifts of Lenten roses, which are perfect companions for early bulbs.

CULTIVATION Most hellebores tolerate full sun or partial shade and require well-drained, preferably alkaline soil, containing plenty of organic matter. *H. niger* and *H. orientalis* do well on heavy soils. *H. foetidus* is tolerant of deep shade.

PROPAGATION From seed, sown as soon as ripe (dried seed may take 18 months to germinate). Seedlings usually take 3 years to flower. By careful division, as soon as plants have flowered in early spring or in late summer.

POTENTIAL PROBLEMS Snails, slugs; black rot, leaf spot.

WARNING Severe stomach irritation may arise if any part of the plant is swallowed. Contact with sap may cause skin irritation.

Helleborus argutifolius

H. argutifolius *Corsica, Sardinia*

Corsican hellebore
Foliage: year-round. Flowers: late winter, early spring. H:2–3ft (60–90cm), S:3–4ft (90–120cm). Z:6–8.
The jagged, strongly veined leaves, divided into 3 and with a strongly toothed margin, make an impressive mound of foliage. Up to 30 cupped pale green, slightly pendant, flowers cluster at the end of stems in their second year. This superb study in green will remain in good condition for several months. Plants self-seed freely.
H. × *sternii*, a hybrid between this species and the frost-hardy *H. lividus* (Z:7–8) from Majorca, which is remarkable for the silvery veining of its dark evergreen leaves, is also shrublike but only 18in (45cm) in height. Its beauty is partly the effect of the purplish-pink suffusion that tints stalks and creamy green flowers.

Helleborus foetidus Wester Flisk Group

H. foetidus *W. and C. Europe*

Bear's foot, stinking hellebore
Foliage: year-round. Flowers: mid-winter to mid-spring. H and S:18–24in (45–60cm). Z:4–9.
The clump of dark green deeply cut foliage is of somber beauty and the clusters of maroon-rimmed pale green bells are a delightful discovery in winter. The stems and flower stalks are often tinged red in the **Wester Flisk Group**. This plant is often confined to the wild garden, but is worth a place anywhere in the garden, including the flower bed.

H. niger *S. and E. Europe*
Christmas rose
Foliage: year-round. Flowers: early winter to early spring. H and S:12-18in (30-45cm). Z:4-7. Saucer-shaped flowers, white but often tinged pink and with a boss of yellow stamens, face out or nod gently above toothed dark leaflets. The large flowers of '**Potter's Wheel**' are tinged green at the center. Despite its great potential, the Christmas rose often disappoints.

Helleborus niger

H. orientalis *C. and W. Caucasus, N.E. Greece, N. Turkey*
Lenten rose
Foliage: year-round. Flowers: mid-winter to mid-spring. H and S:18-24in (45-60cm). Z:5-9.
The plants that go under this name, apparently of complex hybrid origin, are indisputably perennials of the first rank. The color range of the saucer-shaped nodding flowers is unusual, extending from white and pale yellow through pink and purple to darkest plum. In almost all cases the color is nuanced by shades of green, and many plants have speckled flowers. They are borne on sturdy stems. The dark-fingered foliage makes an attractive clump in summer. After overwintering, it looks tired and is best removed before flowering, a measure that helps to control the spread of gray mold (*Botrytis*). The number of named clones is increasing, many of them remarkable for their spotting or very deep, even blue-black, coloring.

Helleborus orientalis

HEMEROCALLIS

HEMEROCALLIDACEAE Day lily

There are only about 15 species of day lily, all of which are native to China, Korea, or Japan, but plant breeders, especially in the United States, have taken up the genus with such enthusiasm that there are now many thousands of named hybrids. These plants are principally valued for their trumpetlike flowers, which vary considerably in size and shape as well as in their color. Although individual flowers last only a day, the numerous buds on a stem open in succession over several weeks. By planting early- and late-flowering day lilies to extend the main season, it is possible to have a display lasting 4 to 6 months. The foliage is often praised for its lushness and the fact that dense clumps make good groundcover. The new growth in spring is exceptionally beautiful, fresh green and tightly arching. However, in maturity the strap-shaped leaves are often disappointing, forming a rather coarse base to a floral display that in the heavyweight hybrids has moved a long way from the grace of the species. A few day lilies have rhizomes and can spread aggressively. This is true of **H. fulva** (Z:3-9), valued by the Chinese for its edible tawny-orange flowers and cultivated in the West for several centuries. There are several selections with long-lasting double flowers, including the orange and yellow '**Green Kwanso**' (Z:3-9). Most of the species are plants of moist soils and grow in open positions such as meadows or in light shade at the edge of woodland. The hybrids are remarkably tolerant of a wide range of conditions, but they develop to full potential in fertile, moist soils. Plants deteriorate unless divided about every 3 years.
CULTIVATION Require full sun and tolerant of a wide variety of soils but most successful results obtained in well-drained but moist soil conditions.
PROPAGATION By division, evergreen day lilies in mid- to late spring, deciduous kinds in spring or autumn; from seed, sown in spring or autumn.
POTENTIAL PROBLEMS Slugs and snails (young foliage), thrips.

H. dumortieri *Korea, E. Russia, Japan*
Flowers: early summer. H:18-24in (45-60cm), S:16-20in (40-50cm). Z:3-9.
From a clump of stiff narrow leaves rise arching stems bearing red-brown buds that open to rich yellow, starry flowers. This compact species is fragrant.

Hemerocallis '**Pink Damask**'

H. hybrids
Flowers: mid-summer. H:14-36in (35-90cm), S:18-40in (45-100cm). Z:3-9.
The following is an intentionally small and conservative selection. A constant stream of new hybrids will be found in the lists of specialized nurseries; if at all possible, see trial plantings before buying so that foliage and flowers can be judged as a whole. An average height is given for each hybrid while the season of flowering is mid-summer unless stated otherwise. The color range also includes off-whites and bi-colors. Day lilies with cream to rich yellow flowers include '**Cream Drop**', 18in (45cm), scented, creamy yellow flowers over a low clump of foliage; '**Golden Chimes**', 28in (70cm), early to mid-summer, star-shaped, rich yellow flowers, reddish brown on the reverse and in bud; '**Hyperion**', 36in (90cm), finely shaped flowers, clear yellow and deliciously fragrant, over narrow leaves; and '**Stella de Oro**', 16in (40cm), remarkable for its compactness and for producing golden yellow flowers circular in outline, from mid- to late summer. One of the best of the pink day lilies is an old hybrid, '**Pink Damask**', 24in (60cm), mid- to late summer; the starry reddish-pink flowers are yellow in the throat.

Hemerocallis '**Bonanza**'

235

Among hybrids in shades of apricot and orange are **'Bonanza'**, 30in (75cm), pale orange with strong maroon marks; **'Cartwheels'**, 36in (90cm), glowing yellow-orange flowers, sometimes more than 6in (15cm) across; and **'Thumbelina'**, 18in (45cm), numerous small flowers of golden orange. Red, maroon, and purple hybrids include **'Black Magic'**, 36in (90cm), yellow-throated flowers of deep brown; **'Buzz Bomb'**, 28in (70cm), yellow buds open to red-brown flowers that are yellow in the throat; **'Lilac Wine'**, 15in (38cm), a compact hybrid having mauve-purple flowers with darker veins and green throat; and **'Stafford'**, 28in (70cm), mahogany-red flowers with yellow mid-stripe and throat.

Hemerocallis lilioasphodelus

H. lilioasphodelus *China*
Flowers: early summer. H and S:30–36in (75–90cm). Z:3–9.
The first species to find its way to the West provides a standard of elegance that is unflattering to many hybrids. The finely shaped, lemon-yellow flowers are perfectly matched by their sweet scent. The plant is rhizomatous and spreads freely in moist soils.

HEPATICA

RANUNCULACEAE

The 10 or so hepatica species, which are *Anemone* relatives, are woodland plants from temperate regions of the Northern Hemisphere that are usually found on alkaline soils. In the garden they are bright companions for early spring bulbs. The star- to bowl-shaped flowers, which are bluish, pink, or white, usually appear before the new leaves are fully formed. They are useful in shady corners of rock gardens and under shrubs and trees.
CULTIVATION Require partial shade and moist, well-drained soil that is neutral or alkaline.
PROPAGATION From seed, sown as soon as ripe. By division, in spring.
POTENTIAL PROBLEMS Slugs, snails.

H. nobilis *Europe*
Flowers: early spring. H:3–4in (7.5–10cm), S:6–12in (15–30cm). Z:4–8.
The starry flowers, 1 per stem, rise above a tuft of 3-lobed leaves as the old foliage tires and the new shoots. The color is usually purplish, but flowers can also be pink, white, or soft blue. Doubles, once widely cultivated, are now uncommon. **H. transsilvanica** is like a larger version of this plant.

Hepatica nobilis

HEUCHERA

SAXIFRAGACEAE Coral flower

Dense clumps of evergreen or semievergreen foliage, the leaves scalloped or elegantly cut and often richly tinted or marbled, would secure a place for several species and hybrids as groundcover plants of quality even without their numerous spires of dainty flowers. Many of the 55 species are from mountainous woodland in North America, but most of those in cultivation are adaptable, growing well in the open as well as in dappled shade. Replant or apply a topdressing of organic material when plants lift out of the soil. The evergreen hybrid genus × **Heucherella**, the result of crosses between *Heuchera* and *Tiarella* species, is similar in character to *Heuchera*, but the flowers are borne earlier. A pretty example, × **H. alba** **'Bridget Bloom'** (Z:4–8), has sprays of pale pink flowers up to 16in (40cm) tall over lobed leaves with brown tints along the veins.

× **Heucherella alba** **'Bridget Bloom'**

CULTIVATION Require sun or partial shade and moist well-drained soil.
PROPAGATION By division, in autumn. From seed, sown in spring.
POTENTIAL PROBLEMS Leaf eelworms, nematodes.

H. americana *C. and E. North America*
Foliage: spring to autumn. Flowers: early summer. H:12–18in (30–45cm), S:8–12in (20–30cm). Z:4–8.
When young the lobed leaves are glistening fresh but tinted and veined soft brown. They grow to nearly 6in (15cm) in length, forming dark green clumps of satiny texture. Wiry bare stems carry small brown-green flowers.

H. cylindrica *W. North America*
Foliage: spring to autumn. Flowers: mid-spring to mid-summer. H:12–20in (30–50cm), S:12–18in (30–45cm). Z:4–8.
Metallic glints relieve the dark green mound of lobed and scalloped leaves. The flowers are green-brown, but among several selections showing variations is **'Greenfinch'**, which has numerous stiff bare stems up to 36in (90cm) tall, bearing creamy green bells. **'Green Ivory'**, probably a hybrid, is similar but at about 30in (75cm) tall is a smaller specimen.

Heuchera micrantha var. diversifolia 'Palace Purple'

H. micrantha *W. North America*
Foliage: spring to winter. Flowers: early summer. H and S:18–24in (45–60cm). Z:4–8.
Several selections have outclassed the species, which has hairy leaves with gray marbling. Overfamiliarity may yet blunt an appreciation of the foliage qualities of **var. diversifolia 'Palace Purple'**. Jagged, dark bronze-red leaves, with a metallic luster and lighter on the underside, overlap to form dense clusters. Dark stems support a creamy haze of tiny flowers, which are followed by pink seedheads. It contrasts well with lighter colors in containers.

Heuchera 'Snow Storm'

H. 'Snow Storm'

Foliage: spring to mid-autumn.
Flowers: early summer. H and
S:12–14in (30–35cm). Z:4–8.
The rounded leaves, hairy and with
a scalloped edge, resemble in
shape and texture those of coral
bells (**H. sanguinea**), the species
with the most colorful flowers and
the parent of several hybrids, such
as **H. 'Red Spangles'**, notable for
their sprays of small red flowers.
The flowers of 'Snow Storm' are
also red, but the leaves are creamy
white with green edging. In the
garden it can seem a vulnerable
curiosity but it comes into its own
as a container plant.

HOSTA

HOSTACEAE Plantain lily

Hosta lancifolia

Hostas were first introduced to
Western gardens from China and
Japan in the late 18th century, but
their current popularity is a recent
development. Even when the hosta
craze eventually abates and the
ranks of hybrids thin, a core of
really good perennial foliage plants
will remain, including **H. lancifolia**,
with shiny leaves. Some have quiet
but distinguished flowers, in a few
cases sweetly scented. In the wild
the 70 species are found in a wide
range of habitats, mainly in
temperate Asia. In cultivation they
are remarkably versatile. The full
magnificence of their foliage is
usually seen when they are grown
in partial shade on moist but well-
drained soil rich in organic matter.
In full sun they are less lush but

tend to flower more readily, while
many prove remarkably tolerant of
even quite dry conditions. The
dramatic and subtle qualities of
their foliage are shown to good
effect when they are grown in
containers. They are remarkably
little troubled by diseases but their
succulence makes them irresistible
to slugs and snails. Because new
foliage is usually produced only in
spring and early summer, any
damage to young leaves spoils
plants for the whole season. The
following small selection, with the
species described first followed by
the hybrids, is chosen to give a fair
representation of the extraordinary
range of plain and variegated
foliage that is found in the genus.
CULTIVATION Tolerate full sun or
partial shade and require well-
drained but moist soil rich in
organic matter (potting media with
added leaf mold).
PROPAGATION By division, in late
summer or spring. From seed,
sown in spring.
POTENTIAL PROBLEMS Slugs, snails,
nematodes; viruses.

SPECIES

H. fortunei Japan

Flowers: mid-summer. H:2–3ft (60–
90cm), S:18–32in (45–80cm). Z:3–9.
The variegated and yellow-leaved
forms have diverted attention from
the plain plant with long-stalked,
mat, gray-green leaves, and mauve
flowers. Although its variegation
later fades, **var. albopicta** is superb
in spring, the bright yellow leaf
edged with pale green, the balance
gradually changing until there are
2 shades of green. In **var.
aureomarginata**, the edge is
yellow, the leaf color dark green.

Hosta fortunei var. albopicta

H. plantaginea China
Foliage: late spring to autumn.
Flowers: late summer to early
autumn. H:20–30in (50–75cm),
S:2–3ft (60–90cm). Z:3–9.
The heart-shaped, light green
leaves are glossy and
conspicuously veined, the flowers,
a late surprise, pure white and

sweetly fragrant. The relaxed
clumps of **var. japonica** are
composed of narrower and longer
wavy leaves.

H. sieboldiana Japan
Foliage: late spring to autumn.
Flowers: early summer. H:30–36in
(75–90cm), S:3–4ft (90–120cm).
Z:3–9.
The heavily textured and veined
blue-green leaves make an
impressive quilted mound barely
cleared by the dense head of palest
mauve flowers. More commanding
still is **var. elegans**, the puckered
blue-gray leaves, which are thick
and waxy, topped by mauve-white
flowers. The foliage of both these
plants turns tawny gold in autumn.

Hosta sieboldiana var. elegans

H. undulata var. albomarginata
Foliage: late spring to autumn.
Flowers: early to mid-summer.
H and S:20–24in (50–60cm). Z:3–9.
The smooth, dark green leaves
have an irregular white margin
that barely reaches the pointed tip.
The flowers, which appear early,
are mauve. **H. crispula** is a similar
plant but the undulating edge of
the leaves has a broader white
margin. **H. undulata** var.
albomarginata makes good-sized
clumps quickly, is one of the most
adaptable hostas in the garden, and
is handsome enough to isolate in a
container. A dynamic relative, **var.
univittata**, has twisted, rich green
leaves, the spiral movement of
which is emphasized by a bold and
irregular creamy white striping in
the center.

Hosta undulata var. albomarginata

HYBRIDS

H. 'Frances Williams'

Foliage: late spring to autumn. Flowers: early summer. H and S:2–3ft (60–90cm). Z:3–9. Although slow to develop, as a mature clump this is one of the most impressive and subtly variegated of all hostas. Heart-shaped leaves, which are puckered and strongly veined, have a waxy blue center extending fingers into an irregular beige-yellow margin, which later turns yellow-green. The flowers are white. Among hybrids with much stronger contrasts between bright margins and green or blue-green centers are **H.** '**Shade Fanfare**', 18in (45cm) tall, with heart-shaped leaves edged cream changing to near white, and **H.** '**Wide Brim**', which grows to 18–24in (45–60cm) and has a broad yellow margin on puckered blue-green leaves. Both have mauve flowers. Several hybrids provide the contrast in reverse. The oval to heart-shaped leaves of **H.** '**Gold Standard**' start green, but the center changes to greenish yellow or yellow with an irregular green edge. It grows to 26in (65cm) and the flowers are pale mauve.

Hosta 'Gold Standard'

H. 'Ginko Craig'

Foliage: late spring to autumn. Flowers: mid-summer. H:10–12in (25–30cm), S:16–20in (40–50cm). Z:3–9. The white edge to the narrow green leaves is broadest when plants are grown in heavy shade and gives a lively effect to close

Hosta 'Francee'

plantings of tight clumps. The flowers are mauve. The contrast of white margin and dark green is striking in the larger **H.** '**Francee**', superb as a container plant and reaching a height of 22in (55cm) with a spread of 36in (90cm). The elongated heart-shaped leaves are puckered and slightly dished.

Hosta 'Krossa Regal'

H. 'Krossa Regal'

Foliage: late spring to autumn. Flowers: late summer. H:4–5ft (1.2–1.5m), S:30–36in (75–90cm). Z:3–9. The waxy blue-green leaves, pointed and prominently veined, are held on long stems, making a vase-shaped clump that is topped by spires of mauve flowers. Two other outstanding hostas with blue-green leaves are **H. Tardiana Group** '**Hadspen Blue**', 10in (25cm) tall with a spread of 2ft (60cm), with deeply veined, heart-shaped leaves and mauve flowers in mid-summer, and the more upright **H.** '**Halcyon**', 14–16in (35–40cm) tall with a spread of 28in (70cm), with narrow pointed leaves and mauve-blue flowers on purple stems in late summer.

H. 'Royal Standard'

Foliage: late spring to autumn. Flowers: late summer. H:2–3ft (60–90cm), S:2–4ft (60–120cm). Z:3–9. The large, heart-shaped leaves, undulating at the margins and deeply veined, create a bold effect in glossy, light green. This hybrid flowers freely, and the white bells are sweetly scented. Fragrant flowers, in this case mauve, are also a feature of **H.** '**Honeybells**', another plain-leafed hosta that grows to 30in (75cm) with a spread of 4ft (1.2m).

H. 'Sum and Substance'

Foliage: late spring to autumn. Flowers: mid- to late summer. H and S:4–5ft (1.2–1.5m). Z:3–9. The glossy, heavily textured leaves, heart-shaped and up to 20in (50cm) long, are yellow or greenish yellow and the flowers,

carried on tall stems, pale mauve. **H.** '**Zounds**', which slowly reaches 22in (55cm) with a spread of 36in (90cm), is another hosta with large yellow leaves and mauve flowers. The foliage is heavily puckered.

HOUTTUYNIA

SAURURACEAE

In the wild, the single species in the genus, from E. Asia, rampages through damp, shady places with rapidly spreading rhizomes.
CULTIVATION Tolerates full sun or partial shade and requires moisture-retentive soil (potting media with added leafmold).
PROPAGATION From seed, sown as soon as ripe. By division, in spring. From softwood cuttings, in late spring.
POTENTIAL PROBLEMS Slugs, snails.

H. cordata *China, Japan*

Flowers: spring. H:10–12in (25–30cm), S:indefinite. Z:5–7. The heart-shaped leaves of this rampant groundcover smell of oranges when bruised, and the short, conelike spikes of tiny greenish-yellow flowers have 4 white petallike bracts at their base. These features are not reason enough to throw caution to the wind unless you are creating a wild garden on a grand scale. The variegated **H.** '**Chameleon**' is less rampant but so brilliant it is a difficult plant to place in a bed. However, its startling mixture of colors—various shades of red, yellow, and green—make it a useful foliage plant for containers.

Houttuynia cordata 'Chameleon'

INCARVILLEA

BIGNONIACEAE

The flared trumpet flowers of several perennials among the 14 species from mountainous areas of Asia make a show in rock gardens and the front of beds. The plants described have deep taproots and are generally long-lived.
CULTIVATION Tolerate full sun or partial shade and require well-drained soil that is moist and fertile.

Incarvillea mairei

PROPAGATION From seed, sown in spring or autumn. From basal cuttings, taken in spring. By division, in spring.
POTENTIAL PROBLEMS Slugs.

I. delavayi *China (Yunnan)*
Flowers: early to mid-summer. H:18-24in (45-60cm), S:12-18in (30-45cm). Z:5-8.
Above a rosette of divided leaves, sturdy stems carry several yellow-throated, rich pink trumpet flowers up to 3in (7.5cm) across, the lobes wavy in outline. There is a good white, '**Alba**', and the pale '**Bee's Pink**', a slightly shorter plant, has very large flowers. *I. mairei*, rarely more than 1ft (30cm) tall, but in the same mold, carries up to 5 purple flowers per stem.

INULA

ASTERACEAE

A few representatives of this genus of about 100 species are grown ornamentally. They are valued, despite a tendency to coarseness, for their yellow daisy flowerheads. Although most species are plants of open sites, they come from a wide range of habitats in Africa, Asia, and Europe. Several, including *I. ensifolia* (Z:4-8), a bushy plant, about 2ft (60cm) in height, are plants of dry grassland on alkaline soil. The species in cultivation that is most tolerant of shade, *I. hookeri,* rapidly colonizes moist soils.
CULTIVATION Most species, including *I. magnifica*, require full sun and well-drained but moist soil. *I. hookeri* requires partial shade. Stake tall species.
PROPAGATION By division, in autumn or spring. From seed, sown in spring or autumn.
POTENTIAL PROBLEMS Powdery mildew.

I. magnifica *E. Caucasus*
Flowers: late summer. H:5-6ft (1.5-1.8m), S:30-36in (75-90cm). Z:5-8.
Rough, dark green leaves, up to 10in (25cm) long, the largest at the base, are stacked on sturdy stems and topped by rich yellow daisies

up to 6in (15cm) across. This is a blunt-speaking but impressive perennial, if not crowded by other plants, and best near water.
I. royleana (Z:3-7), rarely more than 2ft (60cm) tall, has similarly large flowerheads but of vibrant orange-yellow, which open from dark buds. The flowerheads of *I. hookeri* (Z:4-8) are half the size.

Inula hookeri

IRIS

IRIDACEAE

Even discounting the wonderful riches to be found among the bulbous irises, this genus holds an astonishing number of delectable plants, some as valuable for their foliage as are others for their flowers. The 300 or so species are widely distributed in the Northern Hemisphere. The rhizomatous irises that are described here, like the bulbous species, have distinctive flowers composed of 6 segments. The 3 large outer ones, known as the falls, are in many instances drooping or reflexed, while the standards, the 3 inner segments, are usually smaller and more erect. In addition to these elements, there are petallike style branches or arms that give protection to the stigmas.

For the gardener, the most important group among the rhizomatous irises are those described as bearded. These are plants with thick rhizomes (many of the species are from sunny dry habitats) and swordlike leaves that have flowers with a hairy "beard" on the falls. The classic in this group is the familiar *I. germanica* (Z:4-9), with purple falls, brightened by a yellow beard, and mauve-blue standards. Along with its exquisite and even more fragrant white counterpart **I. 'Florentina'** (Z:4-9), it has long been cultivated and remains desirable, even despite the flood of bearded hybrids in almost every combination of bold and subtle colors imaginable. Numerous irises have been involved in their breeding, with dwarf species such as *I. pumila* (Z:4-9) helping to

extend the range from miniatures less than 8in (20cm) to tall hybrids that can grow to 28in (70cm) or more. For more adventurous gardeners, there are also bearded irises that are dormant in summer, such as the sublime *I. hoogiana* (Z:8-9) of the Regelia group, but these are demanding in their requirements and regretfully have been omitted from this selection.

The beardless irises are a large but mixed bag that includes the water irises (**Laevigatae**, Z:4-9), which thrive in moist soils, in some cases even in shallow water, among these being the numerous Japanese irises, which are the result of hybridization over several centuries. Beardless irises come from a wide range of habitats. Many of the species grow on moist, acid soils, but there are some, including the Algerian iris (*I. unguicularis*), that in the wild are plants of sharply draining alkaline soil.

The crested irises (**Evansia**, Z:8-9) are a smaller group not

Iris 'Florentina'

represented here. In species such as *I. japonica* (Z:7-9) there is a crest instead of a beard on the falls. See also BULBS, CORMS, AND TUBERS.
CULTIVATION Bearded irises require full sun and well-drained soil, preferably neutral to slightly acid. Beardless irises tolerate full sun or partial shade, many preferring well-drained neutral to slightly acid soil, but some having special requirements: *I. sibirica* and the Siberian iris hybrids thrive in sunny positions where the soil is always moist; the water irises, such as *I. ensata* and *I. pseudacorus*, require moist even wet or water-logged soils; *I. foetidissima* tolerates dryness and full shade; and *I. unguicularis* requires full sun and sharp drainage, and prefers alkaline conditions.
PROPAGATION By division of rhizomes or clumps, shortly after flowering or in early autumn.
POTENTIAL PROBLEMS Slugs, snails; viral diseases, fungal diseases, particularly rust and rhizome rot.

SPECIES

I. ensata *Japan, N. China, E. Russia*
Japanese iris
Flowers: mid-summer. H:1–3ft (30–90cm), S:12–18in (30–45cm). Z:4–9.
This species has purple beardless flowers with short standards and broad falls. The color range of its numerous progeny includes white, many shades of blue, mauve, pink, and purple, some flowers having ruffled falls, and some being double. The most beautiful retain the grace of the species despite the size and velvety luxuriance of their flowers. There is a steady stream of new cultivars from Japan as well as the following old favorites: **'Alba'**, a breathtaking white; **'Rose Queen'**, dusky pink; and **'Variegata'** (Z:5–9) with young foliage with vertical white stripes and purple flowers.

Iris foetidissima

I. foetidissima *Azores, Canary Islands, N. Africa, S. and W. Europe*
Stinking gladwyn, stinking iris
Flowers: early summer. H:18–24in (45–60cm), S:1–2ft (30–60cm). Z:6–9.
This beardless iris, burdened with unflattering names (due to the acrid smell of the bruised leaves), is a dull cousin of the plants described here until pods split to reveal orange seeds. The evergreen foliage provides a good contrast to groundcover in shade. The flowers are small and purplish brown, but in **var. citrina** larger and yellow, with purplish-brown markings.

I. innominata *USA (S.W. Oregon, N.W. California)*
Flowers: late spring to early summer. H:6–10in (15–25cm), S:9–12in (23–30cm). Z:6–9.
Beardless flowers, 1 or 2 to a stem and up to 3in (7.5cm) across, are carried above tufts of narrow evergreen leaves. The color is variable, the predominant range being from cream through yellow to orange, with fine veining in purplish brown. The fullest range is seen in the hybrids, which include mauve and purple. This

Iris innominata

species is one of the Pacific Coast irises from North America, which share a number of similarities. Another of these Pacific Coast species, the taller ***I. douglasiana***, has veined flowers in shades of blue-mauve and blue-purple.

Iris laevigata 'Variegata'

I. laevigata *C. Russia to N. China, Korea, Japan*
Flowers: early to mid-summer. H:18–30in (45–75cm), S:9–18in (23–45cm). Z:4–9.
In permanently moist soil or shallow water, this beardless iris produces fans of broad, pale green leaves and stems usually carrying 3 flowers of soft mauve-blue, with a thin white central streak on the falls. **'Alba'** is a very lovely white. **'Variegata'** has soft blue flowers and ivory-white vertical stripes on the leaves.

Iris pallida 'Argentea Variegata'

I. pallida *Croatia*
Sweet iris
Foliage: spring to autumn. Flowers: late spring to early summer. H:3–4ft (90–120cm), S:12–18in (30–45cm). Z:6–9.

This tall bearded iris has soft mauve flowers. In **subsp. pallida** the leaves are exceptionally fine, but more eye-catching are **'Argentea Variegata'**, with white stripes, and **'Variegata'**, with strong yellow stripes.

Iris versicolor 'Kermesina'

I. pseudacorus *Caucasus, Europe to W. Siberia, Iran, N. Africa, Turkey*
Yellow flag
Flowers: mid- to late summer. H:3–5ft (90–150cm), S:12–18in (30–45cm). Z:5–9.
This vigorous beardless iris flourishes in marshy ground and in shallow water, the blue-green leaves making a lush fringe to ponds and lakes. Stems carrying yellow flowers are shorter than the leaves. Plants tolerate drier conditions but do not grow as tall. The vertical yellow stripes of **'Variegata'** stand out in spring but by mid-summer have become green. The blue flag (***I. versicolor***, Z:3–9) from eastern North America, a shorter plant for moist soils, has a distinctive red-purple clone, **'Kermesina'** (Z:3–9), with flowers that are veined white.

Iris sibirica

I. sibirica *C. and E. Europe, Russia, N.E. Turkey*
Siberian iris
Flowers: early summer. H:30–48in (75–120cm), S:18–24in (45–60cm). Z:4–9.
Small blue to white flowers with darker veining hover above clumps of grassy leaves. In the wild this species of beardless iris is found in swamps and damp meadows, but it tolerates drier conditions. It is the

parent of a steadily increasing number of very fine hybrids, which are at their best in reasonably moist soils. Taller hybrids growing to 39in (1m) include **'Caesar's Brother'**, velvety violet-blue; **'Perry's Blue'**, light blue; and **'Sparkling Rose'**, pinkish purple with veined yellow base on the falls. Slightly shorter hybrids include **'Tropic Night'**, violet-blue, and **'White Swirl'**, ruffled white petals and yellow throat.

I. unguicularis *Algeria, Greece, W. and S. Turkey, W. Syria, Tunisia*
Flowers: late winter to early spring. H:1-2ft (30-60cm), S:12-15in (30-38cm). Z:6-9.
The delicacy of the fluttering, scented flowers is a surprise when they emerge from untidy clumps of tough, grasslike, evergreen leaves, the succession lasting over several months, provided plants get a good baking during summer. This is a beardless iris, the color range including white as well as the more usual shades of mauve-blue and purple, with veining and a central yellow band on the falls. **'Mary Barnard'** is a rich violet-purple, **'Walter Butt'**, silvery mauve-blue.

HYBRIDS

Flowers: early spring to early summer. H:6-60in (15-150cm), S:6-24in (15-60cm), but see notes on dimensions under entries. Z:4-9.
The trembling, fine-textured flowers, usually well scented, held above fans of bladelike, gray-green leaves, come in an astonishing range of colors, often combined with breathtaking flair. Ruffling of the falls and standards is a feature of many of the new hybrids, sometimes to such an extent that the essential character of the flower is obscured. This selection gives an idea of the range but even the most ravishing of these plants are often quickly superseded by new introductions from specialized nurseries. The elaborate classification used for exhibition purposes is of limited application to the ordinary gardener, and 3 groups only are distinguished here.

Tall Bearded
Their height, 28-60in (70-150cm), is not always an advantage, but a fluttering display of well-grouped sturdy specimens is a highlight of early summer: **'Frost and Flame'**, pure white with bright red beard; **'Jane Phillips'**, clear pale blue with ruffled falls and white beard; **'Kent Pride'**, red-brown standards

and red-brown margins on yellow falls; **'Party Dress'**, soft pink and heavily ruffled; **'Stepping Out'**, white with dark purple edges; and **'Titan's Glory'**, an even, deep blue-purple.

Iris **'Kent Pride'**

Intermediate Bearded
These range from 15-27in (38-68cm) in height: **'Green Spot'**, white with green veins and spot on falls; **'Rare Edition'**, white with a central streak and broad margins of violet on the standards and narrow violet edge on the falls; and **'Red Orchid'**, dark red with gold beard.

Dwarf Bearded
The standard dwarf bearded irises are 8-16in (20-40cm) in height, but the new classification allows for miniatures that are under 8in (20cm): **'Eyebright'**, yellow with dark brown mark and streaking on the falls; **'Lilli-white'**, pure white with a wavy edge; **'Melon Honey'**, apricot, the falls darker and the orange beard with white tips; **'Pogo'**, strong yellow with rusty markings; and **'Tinkerbell'**, bright blue with darker markings.

KIRENGESHOMA

HYDRANGEACEAE

The 2 species are found in Japan and Korea. It is tempting to see in the refinement of the woodland plant described an expression of traditional Japanese aesthetic values. Where conditions match those of its native habitat, it is not difficult, but it is a plant that would be worth a great deal of trouble.
CULTIVATION Require partial shade and moist neutral to acid soil rich in organic matter.
PROPAGATION By division, in spring. From seed, sown as soon as ripe or in spring.
POTENTIAL PROBLEMS Slugs, snails.

K. palmata *Japan*
Foliage: late spring to autumn.
Flowers: late summer to early autumn. H:3-4ft (90-120cm), S:24-30in (60-75cm). Z:5-8.

In sheltered woodland the clump of vinelike leaves is a dignified quiet presence throughout summer. Fine dark stems eventually arch from the clump bearing loose clusters of rich creamy shuttlecocks. The whole plant has a crafted finish, especially the flowers, which have thick, waxy petals meticulously overlapping at the base.

Kirengeshoma palmata

KNAUTIA

DIPSACACEAE

There are about 40 species of these scabious relatives, mainly plants of open or scrubby limestone country in Europe and N. Africa, but few find their way into gardens. The one described produces a long succession of pincushion flowers in an unusual color among garden plants.
CULTIVATION Require full sun and well-drained, preferably alkaline, soil.
PROPAGATION From seed, sown in spring. From basal cuttings, taken in spring.
POTENTIAL PROBLEMS Aphids.

K. macedonica *C. Balkans to Romania*
Flowers: mid- to late summer. H:24-30in (60-75cm), S:1-2ft (30-60cm). Z:5-8.
Above the basal clump of leaves rise curved and branching stems terminating in domed buds surrounded by green bracts that have soft bristles. The open flowerheads are a dark reddish purple and very attractive to bees.

Knautia macedonica

KNIPHOFIA

ASPHODELACEAE Red-hot poker, torch lily

A base of linear or straplike leaves, upright stems, and a spikelike arrangement of tubular flowers, often strongly colored in shades of yellow, orange, or red, is a formula allowing for a surprising number of variations. There are about 70 species in the genus, all of them coming from southern or tropical Africa, most being plants of soils that are well drained but moist early in the growing season. In addition to the species, there are numerous garden hybrids, which follow their parents in showing a preference for well-drained ground. Although they need a good supply of moisture early in summer, excessive wet in winter, especially in areas that experience low temperatures, spells disaster. The evergreen **K. uvaria** (Z:5–9), which can grow to 5ft (1.5m), is largely responsible for the image of red-hot pokers as coarse plants with untidy leaves, even when they make a bold show of flaming torches in late summer and autumn. Several species, including **K. triangularis** (Z:6–9), which has flame-colored flowers on wiry stems, are much more refined, and these have played a role in the development of lighter and more compact hybrids. As a general rule, the species and hybrids with narrow, grasslike leaves are deciduous, and those with broad, strap-shaped leaves are evergreen.

Kniphofia uvaria

CULTIVATION Require full sun and tolerate a wide range of well-drained soils, preferably moist and rich in organic matter.
PROPAGATION From seed, sown in spring. By division, in late spring.
POTENTIAL PROBLEMS Violet root rot.

Kniphofia 'Goldelse'

K. hybrids

Flowers: summer to early autumn. H:20–60in (50–150cm). S: 9–36in (23–90cm). Z:6–9.
The tallest, 5ft (1.5m) or more in height, include **'Green Jade'**, evergreen, with a spread of 24–30in (60–75cm), and flower color graduating from lime-green to cream and then white; **'Ice Queen'**, autumn flowering, with a spread of 30in (75cm), buds fading from lemon-yellow to ivory on opening; and **'Prince Igor'**, with a spread of 36in (90cm), which brandishes incandescent orange-red torches in autumn. In the middle range, mainly 3–4ft (90–120cm) in height, are: **'Bees' Sunset'**, with a spread of 24in (60cm), flowers in a blend of apricot and yellow throughout summer; **'Royal Standard'**, with a spread of 2ft (60cm), scarlet buds open to yellow flowers in the second half of summer; and **'Sunningdale Yellow'**, with a spread of 18in (45cm), yellow flowers from mid- to late summer. Short hybrids, generally 20–30in (50–75cm) in height, which are slim lined and not dwarfishly

Kniphofia 'Little Maid'

compressed, include: **'Bressingham Comet'**, with a spread of 9in (23cm), orange-red and yellow flowers in early to mid-autumn; **'Goldelse'**, with a spread of 1ft (30cm), yellow spikes in early summer; and **'Little Maid'**, with a spread of 18in (45cm), a hybrid of refinement, with green-yellow buds turning to pale cream when open.

LAMIUM

LAMIACEAE Dead nettle

Many of the 50 or so dead nettles are plants of moist woodland, and the species most commonly seen in gardens are valued as groundcover in shade, their pretty hooded flowers coming second to their foliage, which in many cases is silvered with exquisite variegation. As the common name implies, the leaves are nettlelike in appearance but do not sting. The yellow dead nettle (**L. galeobdolon**, Z:3–9) is so remorseless in its spread that, even with leaves as beautifully frosted as they are in **'Florentinum'** (Z:3–9), it should be kept for large-scale wild planting under trees or shrubs.
CULTIVATION Tolerate full sun or shade, particularly good in shade and require well-drained but moist soil.
PROPAGATION By division, in autumn or early spring. From stem-tip cuttings, in summer. From seed, sown in autumn or spring.
POTENTIAL PROBLEMS Slugs, snails.

Lamium maculatum 'Roseum'

L. maculatum *Europe, N. Africa to W. Asia*
Foliage: spring to mid-autumn. Flowers: summer. H:6–8in (15–20cm), S:1–3ft (30–90cm). Z:4–8.
Flower color that varies from white to reddish pink and degrees of variegation have resulted in numerous selections, all of which, however, spread vigorously, especially in moist shade. Those with yellow leaves, such as **'Aureum'**, are slightly sickly in appearance. The clear pink flowers of **'Roseum'** and silvered leaves are

a happy combination. The leaves of '**White Nancy**' have a narrow green margin to the frosted center and the flowers are icy white.

LEUCANTHEMUM

ASTERACEAE

The 10 species are found in high ground and grassland in Europe and temperate Asia. The Pyrenean *L. maximum* is a parent of numerous single and double white daisies that are good as fillers in beds, although often short-lived, especially the doubles.
CULTIVATION Tolerate full sun or partial shade and require well-drained but moist soil.
PROPAGATION By division, in early spring or late summer. From seed, sown as soon as ripe.
POTENTIAL PROBLEMS Aphids, slugs, chysanthemum eelworm; leaf spot.

Leucanthemum × superbum
'**Wirral Supreme**'

L. × superbum
Shasta daisy
Flowers: early summer to early autumn. H:18–36in (45–90cm), S:18–30in (45–75cm). Z:5–9.
The white daisies, 1 per stem, are borne in long succession over a clump of rather fleshy dark green leaves. Singles include '**Beauté Nivelloise**', which grows to 36in (90cm), and '**Snowcap**', usually less than 20in (50cm). Neither of these need support, but semidoubles such as '**Aglaia**' (Z:4–9) and doubles such as '**Esther Read**', both about 24–30in (60–75cm) in height, should have their clumps stiffened with twiggy sticks. This is even more important with tall doubles such as '**Wirral Supreme**' (Z:4–9), which grows to 36in (90cm). Seed strains are available as an alternative to named clones.

LEWISIA

PORTULACACEAE

In flower, several representatives of this North American genus of about 20 species are among the showiest plants for growing in rock gardens or the alpine house.

They dislike lime and any hint of sluggish drainage, and the reason they are often grown in an alpine house is to protect them from excessive wet in winter. Those, like the peach-pink *L. tweedyi* (Z:5–8) with a rosette of evergreen fleshy leaves, prefer light shade, in the wild lodging in rocky cracks and crevices, while the deciduous species, such as *L. brachycalyx* (Z:5–8), squat and pale pink or white, are plants of more open stony ground. Niches in a retaining wall provide the best position for planting in the open garden.
CULTIVATION Require full sun (deciduous species) or partial shade (evergreen species) and very well-drained soil, rich in organic matter, which is not alkaline (equal parts loam, lime-free sharp sand, and leaf mold).
PROPAGATION From offsets, separated from evergreen species in early summer. From seed, sown in autumn.
POTENTIAL PROBLEMS Slugs, snails; neck rot; under glass: aphids.

L. cotyledon USA (N.W. California)
Flowers: mid-spring to early summer. H:8–12in (20–30cm), S:6–8in (15–20cm). Z:5–9.
The most easily satisfied species is evergreen, with spoon-shaped leaves, often with a wavy edge, making a tight rosette, from which several stems carrying sprays of sumptuous many-petaled flowers emerge. Although pinkish-purple is the usual color, the range includes white, yellow, and soft orange, the petals often penciled with dark stripes. In their size and brilliance, hybrids of *L. cotyledon* are not to all tastes an improvement.

Lewisia cotyledon

LIATRIS

ASTERACEAE Blazing star, gayfeather

Of the 40 species, few are in cultivation. They are mainly plants of prairie or lightly wooded country in eastern and central North America and show a strong family resemblance, one pecularity

being that the dense spikes open from the top down (spikes of flowers usually open from the bottom first). They are carried on stiff stems. The long-lasting effect of the spikes, which are good for cutting as well as for creating vertical accents in sunny borders, is of wispy, vividly colored bottlebrushes.
CULTIVATION Require full sun and well-drained but moist soil.
PROPAGATION By division, in spring. From seed, sown in autumn.
POTENTIAL PROBLEMS Slugs, snails, mice.

Liatris spicata

L. spicata E. and S. USA
Gayfeather
Flowers: late summer to early autumn. H:2–3ft (60–90cm), S:12–18in (30–45cm). Z:3–8.
The stiff stems that emerge from a clump of grassy leaves are clothed in whorls of short linear leaves and in the top two-thirds by tightly packed buds that open to purplish-pink flowerheads. The compact '**Kobold**' is usually less than 20in (50cm), and there are also white cultivars, such as '**Alba**'. The Kansas feather (*L. pycnostachya*) is similar to *L. spicata* in character but slightly taller.

LIGULARIA

ASTERACEAE

Relatively few of the 150 species of this moisture-loving genus are cultivated. Most are found in Asia, but some are European. They and a number of hybrids, although on the coarse side, at their best combine pleasing foliage and tall spires of daisy flowers. The plants are suitable for generous borders where the soil never dries out, but are seen to best effect forming waterside colonies in large-scale semiwild gardens.
CULTIVATION Require full sun or partial shade, deep moist soil, and shelter from strong winds.
PROPAGATION By division, in spring or after flowering. From seed, sown in autumn or spring.
POTENTIAL PROBLEMS Slugs, snails.

Ligularia dentata 'Desdemona'

L. dentata *Japan, China*
Golden groundsel
Foliage: late spring to autumn.
Flowers: mid-summer to early
autumn. H:3–5ft (30–150cm),
S:30–36in (75–90cm). Z:5–9.
The strong stems that rise above
dark green, heart-shaped leaves
break into loose heads of orange-
yellow daisy flowers. 'Desdemona',
rarely more than 36in (90cm) in
height, has flowerheads of a
deeper hue. It is outstanding for its
foliage, but it needs a breeze to
show that the dark bronze-green
leaves are vibrant red-brown on
the underside.

L. 'Gregynog Gold'
Foliage: late spring to autumn.
Flowers: late summer to early
autumn. H: 5–6ft (1.5–1.8m),
S: 30–36in (75–90cm). Z:5–9.
A powerful stem carries the
loosely conical spike of orange-
yellow flowers, which are brown at
the center, well clear of a
handsome clump of heart-shaped
leaves. This plant achieves a
stately height.

Ligularia 'The Rocket'

L. przewalskii
Foliage: late spring to autumn.
Flowers: mid- to late summer.
H:5–6ft (1.5–1.8m), S:30–36in
(75–90cm). Z:4–8.
Slender ebony-dark stems rise from
a clump of fingered dark green
leaves, which have irregularly
jagged lobes. The small
flowerheads are clear yellow.
'**The Rocket**', a hybrid of similar
character, splutters to take off with
a shower of orange-yellow sparks.

LINARIA

SCROPHULARIACEAE Toadflax

The best-known species is the
annual **L. maroccana**, but in this
genus of about 100 plants there
are several short-lived perennials,
mainly plants of dry open habitats
in southern Europe, that are of
ornamental value for their spurred
snapdragon-like flowers, which,
although small, are borne freely
over a long period. The large
species are slender plants that
easily fit between more substantial
perennials and sun-loving shrubs,
and the small species, such as
L. alpina (Z:4–9), with yellow-
lipped violet flowers, are suitable for
planting in rock gardens or paths.
See also ANNUALS AND BIENNIALS.
CULTIVATION Require full and light
well-drained soil.
PROPAGATION From seed, sown in
early spring.
POTENTIAL PROBLEMS Aphids;
powdery mildew.

Linaria purpurea

L. purpurea *S. Europe*
Flowers: early summer to early
autumn. H:30–36in (75–90cm),
S:12–18in (30–45cm). Z:4–9.
The purple-blue flowers are tiny,
but they are closely set on slender
stems that wave nonchalantly
when stirred by a breeze. Variants
include the pale pink '**Canon
Went**' and '**Springside White**'.

L. triornithophora *N. and C.*
Portugal, W. Spain
Flowers: early summer to early
autumn. H:30–36in (75–90cm),
S:18–24in (45–60cm). Z:4–8.
It is not too fanciful to see in the
spurred buds, loosely clustered
above blue-green leaves, a
resemblance to a chattering flock
of parakeets poised for flight. The
flowers are purple or pink with
yellow lips.

LINUM

LINACEAE Flax

The flax grown for linen and
linseed oil (**L. usitatissimum**) is 1
of the annuals in this large genus
of about 200 species. The
flowering flax (**L. grandiflorum**) is
an annual of purely ornamental
value, '**Rubrum**' bearing flowers of
brilliant crimson. The genus
includes several rock-garden
plants, among them the shrubby
yellow-flowered **L. arboreum**
(Z:6–9), and a small number of
short-lived perennials. These are
blithely free-flowering in sunny,
free-draining conditions as found
in the open grasslands and scrub
of the Northern Hemisphere
where they grow wild.
CULTIVATION Require full sun and
light well-drained soil.
PROPAGATION From seed, sown in
spring or autumn. From stem-tip
cuttings, taken in early summer.
POTENTIAL PROBLEMS Slugs, snails,
aphids.

L. flavum *C. and S. Europe*
Golden flax, yellow flax
Flowers: all summer. H:12–18in
(30–45cm), S:8–10in (20–25cm).
Z:5–9.
This woody perennial produces
yellow funnel-shaped flowers, 1in
(2.5cm) across. '**Compactum**' is a
neat edging plant.

L. narbonense *W. and C.*
Mediterranean
Flowers: early to mid-summer.
H:1–2ft (30–60cm), S:12–18in
(30–45cm). Z:5–8.
This is worth replanting regularly
for the rich blue of the satiny,
funnel-shaped flowers, individually
short-lived but borne in succession
on a twiggy plant. '**Heavenly Blue**'
(Z:5–9) is aptly named. **L. perenne**
(Z:5–9) is a similar but smaller
plant that is also short-lived.

Linum narbonense

LIRIOPE

CONVALLARIACEAE Lilyturf

The 5 or 6 species in this Asiatic
genus of woodland plants have
grasslike leaves, and rhizomatous
ones, including **L. spicata** (Z:4–9),
colonize rapidly. The clump-
forming species described flowers
best in an open position, although
the foliage is better in moist shade.

CULTIVATION Tolerate full sun or partial shade and light, well-drained, acid soil.
PROPAGATION By division, in spring. From seed, sown in spring.
POTENTIAL PROBLEMS Slugs.

L. muscari *China, Japan, Taiwan*
Foliage: mid-winter. Flowers: early to late autumn. H and S:12–18in (30–45cm). Z:5–9.
The autumn-flowering period is a compensation for blemishes in the evergreen strap-shaped leaves. Spikes, densely packed with tiny violet flowers that never seem to open fully, bear a resemblance to those of grape hyacinths. Black berries follow.

Liriope muscari

LOBELIA

CAMPANULACEAE

This large genus contains nearly 400 species, showing considerable differences of character and coming from a wide range of habitats in tropical and temperate regions. They are especially well represented in the New World. The species described are plants of moist habitats (some lobelias are desert plants) and their hybrids also need to be in fertile ground where the water supply does not fail. All of the plants described tend to be short-lived, and even those that are fully hardy do not fare well in wet winters unless given a dry mulch. Tall lobelias may need staking. The numerous compact and trailing cultivars of *L. erinus* are grown as annuals, although the species is a half-hardy perennial. They hold their place because of their long flowering season and a delicacy of form that makes them easy companions for other plants.
CULTIVATION Tolerate full sun or partial shade and deep, moist soil.
PROPAGATION By division, in spring. From seed, sown as soon as ripe at 55–64°F (13–18°C).
POTENTIAL PROBLEMS Slugs; leaf blotch.
WARNING Contact with sap may cause skin irritation.

L. cardinalis *E. Canada (New Brunswick) to USA (Michigan to Florida and Texas)*
Cardinal flower
Flowers: late summer to early autumn. H:30–36in (75–90cm), S:12–18in (30–45cm). Z:3–8.
Erect, branching stems, which rise from a basal rosette of glossy, often bronzed leaves, carry flaming spikes of 2-lipped tubular flowers.

Lobelia cardinalis

L. hybrids
Flowers: mid-summer to mid-autumn. H:30–36in (75–90cm), S:12–18in (30–45cm). Z:7–9.
The hybridizing of several species, especially *L. cardinalis*, the less hardy but similar *L. fulgens*, and the blue-flowered *L. siphilitica*, has resulted in a group of upright, moisture-loving plants with flowers of intense coloring. These 3 have deep purplish, red, or maroon leaves and stems: '**Bees' Flame**', bright crimson; '**Dark Crusader**', ruby-red; and, one of the oldest of the hybrids, '**Queen Victoria**', vivid scarlet. See also under *L. siphilitica*.

Lobelia '**Bees' Flame**'

L. siphilitica *E. USA*
Blue cardinal flower
Flowers: late summer to mid-autumn. H:2–4ft (60–120cm), S:12–18in (30–45cm). Z:5–8
The ridged upright stems that rise from rosettes of softly hairy leaves carry numerous flowers that are tubular, 2-lipped, and bright blue.
L. × gerardii '**Vedrariensis**', a hybrid between this species and *L. fulgens*, has narrow spikes with flowers of intense violet-purple.

L. tupa *Chile*
Flowers: late summer to mid-autumn. H:5–6ft (1.5–1.8m), S:3–4ft (90–120cm). Z:7–9.
Gray-green leaves, up to 1ft (30cm) long, form a downy base from which rise purple stems terminating in a spike of tubular flowers that are 2-lipped and curiously curved. The calyces are the same color as the stems, but the flowers are rich red or brick-colored. According to some authorities, even the smell may cause poisoning.

LUPINUS

PAPILIONACEAE Lupine

Lupines are often recommended for cottage gardens as if they had been prized by cottage dwellers in an ill-defined but golden age of rural bliss. There are about 200 species. The familiar hybrid lupines, with magnificent and sturdy spikes, often bicolored and in a wide variety of colors, are, however, hybridizing triumphs of this century. The major parent is the blue-flowered *L. polyphyllus* (Z:3–6), from western North America, but other American species, including the shrubby, yellow-flowered *L. arboreus* (Z:7–9), itself an underrated plant for dry gardens, and *L. perennis* (Z:4–9), have played their part. The hybrids are short-lived, and seed strains offer an alternative to the plants raised from cuttings. The annual *L. nanus*, 20in (50cm) tall, is available in mixtures such as '**Pixie Delight**' that include pinks, blues, purple, and white.
CULTIVATION Require full sun or partial shade and well-drained, slightly acid, sandy soil (equal parts loam, leaf mold and sand).
PROPAGATION From seed (which may need to be soaked for a day or so before sowing), sown in spring. From basal cuttings, in mid-spring.
POTENTIAL PROBLEMS Slugs, snails, aphids; fungal and bacterial rot, gall, mildew, leaf spot, viruses.
WARNING Severe stomach upsets may occur if seeds are swallowed.

Lupinus arboreus

L. hybrids
Flowers: early to mid-summer.
H:3–4ft (90–120cm), S:30–36in
(75–90cm). Z:4–8.
The mounds of soft green foliage
are decorative long before the
flower spikes emerge, the minute
hairs that cover the fanned soft
green leaflets trapping droplets of
moisture. The dense columns of
keeled pea flowers should be cut
back as they fade to encourage a
later display of smaller spikes. As
summer advances, the foliage
becomes untidy so it as well to
have foreground planting that will
mask it. Named selections include
‘Chandelier’, yellow flowers; ‘The
Chatelaine’, pink and white; and
‘The Governor’, deep blue and
white flowers.

LYCHNIS

CARYOPHYLLACEAE Campion

Several species, easy plants that
have long held their place in
gardens, are remarkable for their
unsophisticated but vividly colored
flowers. All 15 or so biennial and
perennial species are from
temperate or arctic regions of the
Northern Hemisphere, but they
come from a variety of habitats,
some preferring moist soils, while
others, especially dusty miller
(*L. coronaria*), flourish in dry
conditions.
CULTIVATION Tolerate full sun or
partial shade and well-drained soil,
L. chalcedonica and *L. viscaria* best
in fertile moist soil.
PROPAGATION By division, in early
spring. From basal cuttings, taken
in early spring. From seed, sown as
soon as ripe or in spring; plants
will flower the following year.
POTENTIAL PROBLEMS Slugs.

Lychnis chalcedonica

L. chalcedonica *European
Russia*
Jerusalem cross, Maltese cross
Flowers: early to mid-summer.
H:3–4ft (90–120cm), S:12–18in
(30–45cm). Z:4–8.
Small scarlet flowers with notched
petals are densely packed in domed
heads up to 5in (12.5cm) across.

L. coronaria *S.E. Europe*
Dusty miller, rose campion
Foliage: year-round. Flowers: late
summer. H:30–36in (75–90cm),
S:12–18in (30–45cm). Z:4–8.
Dusty miller self-seeds prolifically
in compensation for being short-
lived, but it is easy to get rid of
unwanted seedlings. The leaves
forming the basal tuft are silver-
gray and wooly, as are the
wide-branching stems that carry
velvety flowers of vivid red-purple.
The foliage and flowers are a
happy combination and even more
subtle in the white-flowered **Alba
Group** and the **Oculata Group**, in
which white flowers have a deep
pink eye. Flower of Jove (*L. flos-
jovis*) is a shorter plant with less
silvery foliage; the flowers, with
notched petals, are purplish pink.

Lychnis viscaria

L. viscaria *Europe to W. Asia*
German catchfly
Flowers: early to mid-summer. H
and S:12–18in (30–45cm). Z:3–9.
Numerous sticky stems emerge
from a grassy clump of basal leaves
carrying clustered sprays of bright
pink flowers. In **‘Splendens Plena’**
the frilly double flowers are
brilliant magenta pink.

LYSICHITON

ARACEAE Skunk cabbage

The 2 species in this genus are
slow-growing waterside plants
producing large arumlike spathes,
each surrounding an erect spadix
tightly packed with minute
flowers. The huge leaves that
emerge as the flowers are maturing

Lysichiton americanus

remain an impressive feature
throughout the summer, making a
telling contrast to the linear or
strap-shaped foliage of reeds and
irises. The American species,
L. americanus (Z:5–9), wins in
terms of scale, for its glossy leaves
can be up to 4ft (1.2m) long.
However, it has a rank scent, and
the bright yellow of its spathes is
aggressive.
CULTIVATION Tolerate full sun or
partial shade and permanently
damp soil rich in organic matter,
preferably at the water's edge.
PROPAGATION From seed, sown as
soon as ripe in wet potting media.
From offsets, separated in spring or
summer.
POTENTIAL PROBLEMS Usually none.

L. camtschatcensis *N.E. Asia*
White skunk cabbage
Foliage: late spring to autumn.
Flowers: early spring. H and
S:30–36in (75–90cm). Z:5–9.
The pointed white spathe, up to
16in (40cm) tall, looks like a white
napkin furled around the green
spadix. In flower, the plants exhale
a sweet scent. Although it is overall
a smaller plant than *L. americanus*,
individual leaves can be more than
36in (90cm) in length.

LYSIMACHIA

PRIMULACEAE Loosestrife

The common name is confusingly
shared, as is a liking for moist soils,
with the genus *Lythrum*. Relatively
few of about 150 species of
Lysimachia, found in subtropical
regions and temperate parts of the
Northern Hemisphere, are much
used in gardens and even these are
generally relegated to wild areas,
where other vigorous spreaders can
help to keep them in check. One of
the most invasive is *L. punctata*
(Z:4–9), undeniably appealing
when spikes packed with yellow
cup-shaped flowers top clumps of
dark green leaves, but not a plant
for beds and borders.
CULTIVATION Tolerate full sun or
partial shade and require moist
well-drained soil.
PROPAGATION By division, in autumn
or spring. From seed, sown in spring.
POTENTIAL PROBLEMS Slugs, snails.

L. clethroides *China, Japan,
Korea*
Flowers: mid- to late summer.
H:30–36in (75–90cm), S:18–24in
(45–60cm). Z:4–9.
This runs in fertile moist soil, but a
large patch is a lovely sight, the
tapering flower spikes, packed
with white stars, flexing sinuously
above the leafy base.

Lysimachia nummularia 'Aurea'

L. nummularia 'Aurea'

Golden creeping Jenny
Foliage: year-round. Flowers:
summer. H:2–4in (5–10cm),
S:indefinite. Z:4–9.
Where the climate is mild and the
soil moist, this is a plant to treat
with caution in the garden, rooting
stems create large patches dense
with lime-green to yellow heart-
shaped leaves, among which nestle
cup-shaped bright yellow flowers.
It is, however, a useful trailing plant
for container gardening.

LYTHRUM

LYTHRACEAE

Lythrum virgatum 'The Rocket'

The 38 species are found in
temperate parts of the Northern
Hemisphere. The slender spires of
purple loosestrife (*L. salicaria*)
make lightly swaying colorful drifts
over several weeks late in the
season. The similar but slighter *L.
virgatum* (Z:3–9) and its cultivars,
such as 'The Rocket' (Z:3–9),
flower earlier in summer. These
loosestrifes are the only 2 species
with any standing as garden plants
in a genus with a strong preference
for moist growing conditions. The
loosestrifes are happy in a bog
garden or a wild waterside planting
but flourish also in beds where the
water supply does not fail.
CULTIVATION Require full sun and
moist soil.
PROPAGATION By division, in spring.
From basal cuttings, taken in
spring or early summer. From seed,
sown in spring.
POTENTIAL PROBLEMS Slugs, snails.

L. salicaria *Temperate Asia, Europe*

Purple loosestrife
Flowers: mid-summer to early
autumn. H:2–5ft (60–150cm),
S:18–24in (45–60cm). Z:3–9.
The strongly upright stems that
rise from a clump of downy leaves
are closely set with small starry
flowers, pink or purplish red in
color. Among several cultivars the
palest is 'Blush' while 'Robert' is a
brighter pink and 'Feuerkerze' an
intense reddish pink.

Lythrum salicaria

MACLEAYA

PAPAVERACEAE Plume poppy

Colonies of plume poppies, with
tall stems, delicately feathered
above lobed leaves, have a
choreographed beauty when they
flex lightly in a breeze. In the wild,
the 2 or 3 species, found in China
and Japan, form large patches at
the edge of woodland and in
grassy places. In the garden, the
running roots are a minor
drawback of these graceful plants
of real stature.
CULTIVATION Require full sun and
moist, well-drained soil.
PROPAGATION By division, in late
autumn or spring. By separation of
rooted rhizomes, when dormant.
From seed, sown as soon as ripe.
POTENTIAL PROBLEMS Slugs.

Macleaya cordata

M. cordata *China, Japan*

Foliage: summer to autumn.
Flowers: mid- to late summer. H:7–
8ft (2.2–2.5m), S:2–3ft (60–90cm).
Z:4–9.
The leaves, heart shaped in outline

but cut with 5 to 7 lobes, are gray-
green with a downy underside.
The tiny flowers are off-white or, in
'Flamingo', pink. *M. microcarpa*
is similar to it, but in 'Kelway's
Coral Plume' the buds are apricot
pink before opening to buff cream.

MECONOPSIS

PAPAVERACEAE

Meconopsis cambrica

The Welsh poppy (*M. cambrica*,
Z:6–8), the single European plant
among 45 or so species in the
genus, is a sassy but endearing self-
seeder with bright lemon or
orange flowers. It is totally
outclassed, however, by its close
relatives from the Himalayas and
mountainous country farther east,
especially the fabulous blue
poppies. These created a sensation
when first introduced to the West,
and they have retained their power
to command a reverential awe,
especially when seen planted in
quantity to fill a woodland glade.
Some of the species, such as the
yellow-flowered Nepalese *M. regia*
(Z:6–8), are monocarpic, dying
after they have flowered. Another
of this persuasion is *M. horridula*
(Z:6–8), from Nepal, Tibet, and
China, which grows to about 36in
(90cm). It has spiny foliage, but is a
much more appealing plant than
its rather offputting name might
suggest, with blue or reddish-blue
flowers. Those described tend to
be short-lived unless they are
grown in ideal conditions.
The harebell poppy
(*M. quintuplinervia*, Z:6–8) is a
paragon of woodland elegance, with
nodding mauve-blue flowers usually
less than 1ft (30cm) tall. It has
spreading roots and is one of the
most reliably perennial of the genus.
CULTIVATION Require partial shade
and moist well-drained soil that is
neutral or slightly acid and rich in
organic matter.
PROPAGATION From seed, sown as
soon as ripe or in spring. By
division, after flowering. From
offsets, in spring.
POTENTIAL PROBLEMS Slugs, snails.

M. betonicifolia *Burma, S.W. China, Tibet*
Himalayan blue poppy, Tibetan blue poppy
Flowers: early summer. H:3–5ft (1–1.5m), S:12–18in (30–45cm). Z:6–8.
Hairs give a slight rustlike tint to basal and stem leaves. The bright or purplish-blue flowers, growing from the top and also from the leaf axils, open in true poppy fashion with their petals crumpled before they reflex elegantly from the central boss of yellow stamens. **M. × sheldonii**, a hybrid between this species and *M. grandis*, is the most reliably perennial of the large-flowered blue poppies, and its color is free of purple tint.

Meconopsis grandis

M. grandis *Bhutan, E. Nepal to India (Sikkim), E. Tibet*
Himalayan blue poppy
Flowers: early summer. H:3–5ft (90–150cm), S:24–32in (60–80cm). Z:6–8.
There is a rosette of erect, toothed leaves, tinted rust from a sparse pile of reddish hairs, and a whorl of leaves below the nodding flowers. These are up to 6in (15cm) across and usually have 4 petals. At their best, their blue is of heart-stopping brilliance, but they often show a purple tint.

MENTHA

LAMIACEAE Mint

The mints, aromatic plants of moist or wet soils, are mainly grown for their use as culinary herbs, although the Corsican mint (**M. requienii**, Z:7–9) is worth planting to creep among paving just for the peppermint scent released when the minute leaves are bruised. The 25 species are from Africa, Asia, and Europe. Variegation lifts some of the mints into another category, but as foliage plants they need to be treated with caution for they are always in search of *Lebensraum*.
CULTIVATION Require full sun and tolerate a wide range of soils that are moist.

PROPAGATION By division, in spring or autumn. By rooting rhizomes, at any time during the growing season. From tip cuttings, taken in spring or summer. From seed, sown in spring.
POTENTIAL PROBLEMS Powdery mildew, rust.

Mentha suaveolens 'Variegata'

M. suaveolens '**Variegata**'
Flowers: summer. H:10–18in (25–45cm), S:indefinite. Z:5–9.
The brilliant mixture of ivory and green on strongly aromatic leaves shows well in shade and makes this a very good container plant. The contrast of yellow and green in the scented leaves of **M. × gracilis** '**Variegata**' is most remarkable in full sun.

MERTENSIA

BORAGINACEAE

About 50 species of these borage relatives are found in a wide range of habitats in the Northern Hemisphere. Several are true alpines, growing on stony slopes that are fast draining, others are coastal species, surviving in almost pure sand, and an even greater number, including the species described, are plants of moist woodland. These form bright decorative patches in the shade of deciduous trees.
CULTIVATION Require partial shade and well-drained but moist soil that is rich in organic matter.
PROPAGATION By division, in spring. From cuttings, taken in early winter. From seed, sown in autumn.
POTENTIAL PROBLEMS Slugs, snails.

Mertensia pulmonarioides

M. pulmonarioides *North America*
Virginia bluebells
Foliage: spring. Flowers: mid- to late spring. H:18–24in (45–60cm), S:8–12in (20–30cm). Z:5–9.
The long-tubed flowers, which flare at the mouth, are carried in arching sprays over gray-green leaves. They can be white, but usually the buds are violet-pink, opening to violet-blue. The foliage of this clump-forming plant dies down in mid-summer.

MIMULUS

SCROPHULARIACEAE Monkey flower

Mimulus aurantiacus

A puzzle of horticulture is that in about 1914 the penetrating scent of musk (**M. moschatus**, Z:6–9), once widely grown as a pot plant, disappeared in wild and cultivated populations—and has not returned. Many of the 150 or so species in this widely distributed genus are moisture lovers, and one, the monkey musk or yellow monkey flower (**M. luteus**, Z:6–9) from Chile, is naturalized in ditches and other watery places in many parts of the world. It is a parent of numerous hybrids that are usually treated as annuals. **M. cupreus** (Z:6–9), another Chilean species that has been used in hybridizing, is a low-growing plant, under 12in (30cm) in height, and in the short-lived '**Whitecroft Scarlet**' (Z:6–9) produces flowers of an intense vermilion. Those plants that tolerate drier conditions include the 2 species described and even drier soils suit the shrubby, frost hardy **M. aurantiacus** (Z:7–9), from western North America, an excellent container plant. See also ANNUALS AND BIENNIALS.
CULTIVATION The plants described tolerate full sun or partial shade and require fertile moisture-retentive soil.
PROPAGATION By division, in spring. From seed, sown in autumn or early spring.
POTENTIAL PROBLEMS Slugs, snails; powdery mildew.

M. cardinalis *W. USA to Mexico*
Scarlet monkey flower
Flowers: summer. H:18–36in
(45–90cm), S:9–24in (23–60cm).
Z:7–9.
Erect stems carry snapdragon
flowers over downy foliage. Most
commonly the full lips are red and
the constricted throat yellow, but
there are variations in this color
range as well as pink.

M. lewisii *North America (Alaska
to California)*
Flowers: summer. H:1–2ft (30–
60cm), S:12–18in (30–45cm). Z:5–9.
The leaves of this lax species are
sticky, and the pink or sometimes
white flowers have wispy hairs on
the lip.

MONARDA

LAMIACEAE Bergamot

The common name refers to the
scent of the foliage, which is said
to resemble that of the bergamot
orange. Two perennial plants from
this small North American genus of
about 15 species are involved in
the sun-loving hybrids that provide
color in borders in summer and
early autumn. Although wild
bergamot (***M. fistulosa***, Z:3–9) is
tolerant of drier conditions than
the moisture-loving bee balm (***M.
didyma***, Z:4–9), sometimes known
as Oswego tea, in practice most of
the hybrids do best in soils rich in
organic matter that do not dry out.
CULTIVATION Tolerate full sun or
partial shade and require well-
drained but moist soil.
PROPAGATION By division, in spring.
From basal cuttings, taken in
spring. From seed, sown in autumn
or spring.
POTENTIAL PROBLEMS Slugs;
powdery mildew.

Monarda 'Cambridge Scarlet'

M. hybrids
Flowers: mid-summer to early
autumn. H:2–3ft (60–90cm),
S:14–20in (35–50cm). Z:4–9.
From a base of aromatic pointed
leaves rise square stems carrying
hooded sagelike flowers clustered
in dense whorls. **'Cambridge

Scarlet'**, an old cultivar, remains
one of the most intense of the
reds, the color accentuated by
deep purple-red calyces. The
softest of the pinks is **'Beauty of
Cobham'**, and the darkest in
mauve-purple is **'Prärienacht'**. The
white **'Schneewittchen'** has
smaller flowerheads than the other
hybrids.

MORINA

MORINACEAE

The thistlelike appearance of the
most widely grown of the 4 or 5
species is misleading, but adds to
the fascination of this plant. In the
wild, it is found in stony open land
from eastern Europe to Asia.
CULTIVATION Tolerate partial shade
but best in full sun. Require very
well-drained soil of moderate
fertility.
PROPAGATION From seed, sown as
soon as ripe. From root cuttings,
taken in winter.
POTENTIAL PROBLEMS Slugs.

Morina longifolia

M. longifolia *Himalayas*
Whorlflower
Flowers: mid-summer. H:30–36in
(75–90cm), S:12–18in (30–45cm).
Z:5–8.
The plant has a deep taproot and
forms a rosette of prickly aromatic
leaves. The sturdy reddish-purple
stems carry tiered whorls of
tubular flowers, each whorl
cupped in a thorny bract. The
flowers open white, change to pale
pink and, once fertilized, turn red.
Even when the flowers are over,
the tall stems retain a sketchy
graphic quality.

NEPETA

LAMIACEAE Catnip

The best-known catnips are plants
of well-drained soils, but this is a
large genus with well over 200
species, some of which require
plenty of moisture. They are found
in temperate parts of the Northern
Hemisphere. The shy star among
those for cool moist conditions is
N. govaniana (Z:4–8), more than

3ft (90cm) in height, bearing light
sprays of pale yellow flowers. The
mauve- or purple-blue catnips
described are naturals for romantic
gardens and soften the effect of
bare-stemmed roses and other
bedding over a long season.
CULTIVATION Tolerate partial shade
but best in full sun and those
described require well-drained soil.
PROPAGATION From seed, sown in
autumn. By division, in spring or
autumn. From softwood cuttings,
taken in early summer.
POTENTIAL PROBLEMS Slugs;
powdery mildew.

Nepeta 'Six Hills Giant'

N. × *faassenii*
Flowers: early summer to early
autumn. H and S:18–24in
(45–60cm). Z:4–9.
As an edging plant or skirt to bare-
stemmed shrubs, including roses,
this is hard to beat. The close
stems of gray-green aromatic leaves
are topped by generous sprays of
small mauve-blue flowers. *N.* **'Six
Hills Giant'**, nearly twice the
height, creates an even fuller effect
and makes a long-flowering border
plant. Cutting back after flowering
encourages further flushes.

Nepeta sibirica

N. sibirica *E. Asia, Siberia*
Flowers: mid- to late summer.
H:30–36in (75–90cm), S:18–24in
(45–60cm). Z:3–9.
The roots spread freely, sending up
erect stems that are clothed with
aromatic leaves and terminate in
spikes of mauve-blue flowers.
'Souvenir d'André Chaudron'
(Z:5–9) is dark flowered and
usually under 20in (50cm) tall.

NYMPHAEA

NYMPHAEACEAE Water lily

No other genus provides such a range of floating ornamentals for still water in lakes, ponds, and small pools. There are about 50 species distributed in temperate and tropical regions of the world, only a few of which are cultivated, but there are many hybrids providing a long season of the most elegant flowers. Some are sweetly scented. All have floating leaves that are themselves decorative, give cover to fish, and by casting shade, inhibit the growth of algae. The tender and tropical species, some of which bloom at night, usually hold their flowers well above the surface of the water. Most of the hardy water lilies flower during the day, and their blooms float on or are held close to the water. Water lilies can be planted directly into the silt at the bottom of a pond or lake, but in small pools it is advisable to use lined or micromesh baskets filled with an aquatic media or loam. A mulch of pea gravel helps to keep the soil in place. Very vigorous water lilies, such as the common white water lily (*N. alba*, Z:3–11), can be planted at up to depths of 10ft (3m), but the hardy hybrid water lilies described are suitable for more shallow water. The surface spread of a water lily is about one-and-a-half times its planting depth. However, the area covered by the pads varies considerably according to the growing conditions. A water lily planted in the muddy bottom of a large pool spreads more freely than the same plant container-grown in a small body of water. When first establishing water lilies, it is best to start them in shallow water, the crown of miniatures at a depth of about 3in (7.5cm). They can be put at their final depth as soon as they are making vigorous growth.
CULTIVATION The hardy water lilies described require full sun and, as an alternative to the mud on the floor of a pond, a loam-based or specially formulated aquatic media.
PROPAGATION By division, in spring. From offsets, taken in spring. From seed, sown as soon as ripe submerged under 1in (2.5cm) of water and, for hardy water lilies, at a temperature of 50–55°F (10–13°C).
POTENTIAL PROBLEMS Water lily beetles, water lily aphids, false leaf-mining midges; brown spot, crown rot, water lily leaf spot.

Nymphaea 'Marliacea Chromatella'

N. hybrids
Foliage: late spring to autumn. Flowers: early to late summer. S:1–5ft (30–150cm). Z:3–11.
One of the most striking for large ponds with a depth of up to 6ft (1.8m) is '**Escarboucle**'. It has deep green leaves, 1ft (30cm) across, and fragrant crimson flowers with white-tipped outer petals and bright yellow stamens. The many water lilies of moderate vigor are suitable for water that is 18–30in (45–75cm) deep. Popular examples include '**Gonnère**', with bright green leaves, bronzed at first, and fully double white flowers lit by yellow stamens; '**Froebelii**', its tuliplike deep red flowers opening out among purplish, green leaves; '**Marliacea Chromatella**', with bronze- and purple-marked olive-green leaves and yellow flowers, the sepals and outer petals sometimes tinted pink; '**Odorata Sulphurea Grandiflora**', with heavily mottled dark green leaves setting off large bright yellow star-shaped flowers; and '**Sioux**', with leaves mottled purple and starry flowers that change from yellow to orange and crimson. Toylike water lilies suitable for water 10–18in (25–45cm) deep include '**Aurora**', with cream buds emerging among purple mottled leaves and passing on opening through shades of yellow, orange, and blood red; '**Pygmaea Helvola**', with heavily mottled olive-green leaves and lightly scented yellow flowers; and '**Laydekeri Lilacea**', leaves blotched brown and fragrant pink flowers that deepen to crimson.

Nymphaea 'Sioux'

OENOTHERA

ONAGRACEAE Evening primrose

The common evening primrose, *O. biennis*, naturalized as a charming and common biennial weed of waste ground in many parts of the world, is not in the same league as some of the perennials in this genus of about 125 species from North and South America. These sun-loving plants, many of which thrive in the dry poor soils that suit *O. biennis*, have silky flowers, sometimes fragrant, that individually are fleeting in their beauty but which follow one another in hurried succession for many weeks in summer.
CULTIVATION Require full sun and well-drained soil, most tolerating even poor growing conditions.
PROPAGATION By division, in early spring. From softwood cuttings, taken in late spring to mid-summer. From seed, sown in early spring.
POTENTIAL PROBLEMS Slugs; leaf spot, mildew, root rot.

O. fruticosa E. North America
Sundrops
Flowers: late spring to late summer. H:1–3ft (30–90cm), S:12–18in (30–45cm). Z:4–8.
In yards the species, with yellow flowers up to 2in (5cm) across, is usually represented by **subsp. glauca** with reddish young foliage or by named selections such as '**Fyrverkeri**', with purple-tinted leaves and bright blooms opening from red buds. Another species from the eastern USA, *O. perennis* (Z:4–9), which grows to 18in (45cm), has smaller flowers.

Oenothera macrocarpa

O. macrocarpa S. Central USA
Ozark sundrops
Flowers: late spring to early autumn. H:4–6in (10–15cm), S:18–24in (45–60cm). Z:4–8.
The slouching reddish stems, clothed with silky leaves, suit a rock garden ledge or the front of a bed. The magnificent lemon-yellow flowers are cup shaped and sometimes more than 4in (10cm) across.

O. speciosa *S.W. USA to Mexico*
Flowers: early summer to early
autumn. H and S:12–18in
(30–45cm). Z:5–8.
The cup-shaped flowers of this
low, running plant are usually
white and yellow-centered, but in
'**Rosea**' and '**Siskiyou**' they are
pink, with exquisite veining.

OMPHALODES

BORAGINACEAE Navelwort

The 28 or so species in this genus
are widely distributed in N. Africa,
Asia, and Europe. Some come from
habitats other than the moist
woodland where the most
commonly grown species is found
wild. Its flowers are larger than
those of a forget-me-not but also
blue and borne with an airy grace.
CULTIVATION Require partial shade
and moist organic-rich soil.
PROPAGATION By division, in early
spring. From seed, sown in spring.
POTENTIAL PROBLEMS Slugs, snails.

**Omphalodes cappadocica
'Cherry Ingram'**

O. cappadocica *Turkey*
Flowers: early spring. H:8–10in
(20–25cm), S:16–24in (40–60cm).
Z:5–8.
Small sprays of bright blue flowers
float above a clump of oval leaves.
Named clones include the deep
blue '**Cherry Ingram**' and '**Starry
Eyes**', with a white stripe in the
center of each petal.

OPHIOPOGON

CONVALLARIACEAE Lilyturf

The grasslike leaves are the main
feature of these perennials, most of
which are plants of shade.
Variegated forms of *O. jaburan*
(Z:9–11) and *O. japonicus* (Z:7–9)
are alternatives to the darker plant
described.
CULTIVATION Tolerate full sun but
best in partial shade and require
well-drained but moist slightly acid
soil rich in organic matter (potting
media with added leaf mold).
PROPAGATION By division, in spring.
From seed, sown as soon as ripe.
POTENTIAL PROBLEMS Slugs.

**Ophiopogon planiscapus
'Nigrescens'**

O. planiscapus '**Nigrescens**'
Foliage: year-round. Flowers: mid-
summer. H and S:6–12in
(15–30cm). Z:6–9.
Without the contrast of light-
colored foliage or flowers, the
clumps of near-black leaves are
simply sullen curiosities, but in a
skillfully planted scheme they take
on a sinister charm, especially
when the small mauve flowers are
followed by shiny black berries.

ORIGANUM

LAMIACEAE

Aromatic foliage is a distinctive
feature of this genus from the
Mediterranean, which contains
about 20 species of perennials and
subshrubs, in the wild usually
found on free-draining alkaline
soils. Dittany (*O. dictamnus*,
Z:7–9), for example, a choice plant
for alpine gardeners, with white,
felted leaves and tiny flowers set in
purplish bracts, clings to limestone
cliffs in the gorges and mountains
of Crete. Several are grown as
herbs, the most highly prized
being sweet marjoram (*O.
majorana*, Z:9–10), a frost-hardy
subshrub that is often grown as an
annual or biennial. The slightly
hardier pot marjoram (*O. onites*,
Z:8–10), another subshrubby
perennial, is coarser in flavor. The
slowly spreading low mound of
the golden-leaved common
marjoram (*O. vulgare* '**Aureum**',
Z:6–9) makes a sunny patch beside
a path or in a rock garden. The
leaves become greener late in the
season. The most ornamental of the
species are grown for their small
tubular or funnel-shaped flowers
set among conspicuous bracts.
These bracts are often beautifully
tinted and are long lasting.
CULTIVATION Require full sun and
well-drained, preferably alkaline, soil
(potting media with equal parts
loam, leaf mold, and sharp sand).
PROPAGATION By division, in spring.
From basal cuttings, taken in late
spring. From seed, sown in autumn.
POTENTIAL PROBLEMS Usually none.

O. 'Kent Beauty'
Flowers: summer. H and S:4–8in
(10–20cm). Z:4–8.
This is one of the several hybrids
that have been raised from
O. rotundifolium, a native of
Turkey and neighboring countries
farther east. This lax-stemmed
species has blue-green leaves, and
its soft pink tubular flowers are set
in hoplike bracts of pale apple-
green. The plant is of the same
scale as 'Kent Beauty', but in the
hybrid the tumbling bracts are
flushed pink.

O. laevigatum *Cyprus, Turkey*
Flowers: late spring to autumn.
H:18–24in (45–60cm), S:12–18in
(30–45cm). Z:5–8.
The wiry stems that rise from a
clump of almost scentless gray-
green leaves carry sprays of tiny
purplish-pink flowers. The young
foliage of '**Herrenhausen**' has a
purple tint, and the densely
clustered purplish-pink flowers are
surrounded by darker bracts.

Origanum laevigatum 'Herrenhausen'

OSTEOSPERMUM

ASTERACEAE

The daisy flowers close and sulk in
shade or dull weather but in an
open position and full sun, even
where the skies are a pale
imitation of the radiance of
southern Africa, the home of most
of the 70 or so species, these are
wonderfully bright and free-
flowering plants for beds and
containers, with regular
deadheading prolonging the
flowering season. They are
commonly grown as annuals but
often survive short periods of low
temperatures in winter when
grown on a spartan diet on free-
draining ground.
CULTIVATION Require full sun and
well-drained soil (potting media
with added grit).
PROPAGATION From softwood
cuttings in late spring or semiripe
cuttings, in late summer. From seed,
sown in spring at 64°F (18°C).
POTENTIAL PROBLEMS Aphids;
downy mildew, verticillium wilt.

Osteospermum 'Blue Streak'

O. ecklonis *South Africa (Eastern Cape)*
Flowers: late spring to autumn.
H:18-24in (45-60cm), S:2-3ft (60-90cm). Z:9-10.
The daisies of this subshrubby species provide a striking contrast: the disk is dark blue, the ray flowerets dazzling white but indigo blue on the back. In *O.* **'Blue Streak'** the contrast is between white and slate blue.
The daisies topping the low mat of *O.* **'Prostratum'**, 6-10in (15-25cm) tall, are purplish when closed; when open the white ray flowerets surround a blue-gray disk.

Osteospermum 'Buttermilk'

O. hybrids
Flowers: late spring to autumn.
H:10-24in (25-60cm), S:1-3ft (30-90cm). Z:9-10.
Numerous hybrids have been raised, the contrast between the upper surface and back of the ray flowerets and dark disk flowerets being characteristic of most. The color range includes purple, as in **'Nairobi Purple'**, and yellow in **'Buttermilk'**, in which the back of

Osteospermum 'Whirligig'

the ray flowerets is bronzed. One of the most striking is **'Whirligig'**, in which a white and blue contrast is emphasized by the way the ray flowerets are pinched in the middle, making the tip spoonlike.

Osteospermum jucundum

O. jucundum *E. South Africa*
Flowers: late spring to autumn.
H:12-18in (30-45cm), S:1-2ft (30-60cm). Z:9-10.
Narrow aromatic leaves make sprawling clumps from which the daisies rise in unending succession over several months. The purple disk, which changes to gold as it ages, is surrounded by purplish-pink ray flowerets, usually darker but duller on the underside. A shorter plant, **var. *compactum***, little more than 6in (15cm) tall, is said to be more hardy.

PAEONIA

PAEONIACEAE Peony

From the 30 or so species that are widely distributed in temperate regions of the Northern Hemisphere and the many hybrids derived from them (often listed under *P. lactiflora*), it would be very easy to make a long list of exceptionally beautiful and long-lived garden plants that are suitable for sun or partial shade in well-drained soil. Most have pleasing foliage, in some cases drawing attention to itself in spring or autumn with rich tints, and flowers, often well scented, that are remarkable for their refinement. In the wild these plants have single flowers, usually cup or bowl shaped, with prominent bosses of stamens. The species and the single hybrids derived from them have an entrancingly innocent but short-lived beauty when in bloom. A very long history of selection and hybridizing, beginning centuries ago in China and Japan, has produced numerous double and semidouble peonies as well as a group of anemone form, sometimes called imperial or Japanese peonies, in which the

stamens have been replaced by crowded ribbonlike petals, correctly known as petaloids or staminodes. Miraculously, elaboration has not coarsened these hybrids, which are longer-lasting in their beauty than the single hybrid peonies. See also SHRUBS.
CULTIVATION Tolerate full sun or partial shade and require well-drained soil that contains generous quantities of organic matter.
PROPAGATION From seed, sown in autumn or early winter. By division, in autumn or early spring. From root cuttings, taken in winter.
POTENTIAL PROBLEMS Nematodes; peony gray mold blight, viruses.
WARNING Stomach upsets can occur if any part of the plant is eaten.

Paeonia 'Sarah Bernhardt'

P. hybrids
Flowers: early summer. H and S:2-4ft (60-120cm). Z:3-7.
The key species in the development of the magnificent large-flowered cultivars is *P. lactiflora*, a native of northern and western China and neighboring regions. Its fragrant, bowl-shaped flowers are white or pale pink. The result of centuries of breeding and selection is a group of exceptionally opulent plants in a color range extending from white and pale pink to shades of crimson and maroon. The following small selection is intended to give an idea of the seductive choice presented in specialized catalogs. Single hybrids include **'White Wings'**, with ruffled creamy white petals around the boss of yellow stamens. Among 19th-century double hybrids that can still hold their own are **'Félix Crousse'**, carmine, darker at the center and often with a silvery edge to the ruffled petals; **'Festiva Maxima'**, white with irregular dark crimson flecking; and **'Sarah Bernhardt'**, large and very full, a confection of silvery and darker pinks. **'Bowl of Cream'**, with clustered heads of white flowers

Paeonia 'Bowl of Beauty'

showing yellow stamens in the muddled centers, represents a range of stiff-stemmed American hybrids described by their raisers as "estate" peonies because of their value in landscaping large gardens. Imperial peonies include **'Cheddar Gold'**, white with yellow petaloids; and **'Bowl of Beauty'**, the mass of twisted and tapered petaloids bursting at the center of a pink cup. Some superb American hybrids owe nothing to *P.lactiflora*, and of these *P.* **'Late Windflower'**, with white flowers over finely cut leaves, is a lovely example. The flowers are scented, an inheritance from one of its parents, the Himalayan peony (**P. emodi**).

Paeonia mlokosewitschii

P. mlokosewitschii *Caucasus*
Caucasian peony
Flowers: late spring to early summer. H and S:2–3ft (60–90cm). Z:5–8.
The opening of the single lemon-yellow flowers filled with golden stamens is one of the supreme moments in the gardening calendar, but you must not blink, for the ethereal trembling beauty of the bowls is quickly dashed. Fortunately this peony has other attributes. The emerging foliage makes a cluster of arresting forms in rich copper pink, softening to gray-green divided leaves that accompany the flowers and persist throughout the summer. A surprise in autumn is the combination of scarlet and glossy black when the seedpods split open. Mollie-the-witch, to those defeated by the pronunciation of the specific

name, has a ravishing peer in another Caucasian species, **P. wittmanniana**. This grows to 36in (90cm), has glossy, dark green leaves, tinted pink as they emerge; and the single pale yellow flowers cup yellow anthers and deep pink filaments.

P. officinalis *Europe*
Common peony
Flowers: early to mid-summer. H and S:20–30in (50–75cm). Z:4–8.
The wild plant is a single with deep red or pink cup-shaped flowers over dark green, divided leaves. Much more familiar in cultivation are doubles such as **'Rubra Plena'**, with sheeny full flowers in vivid crimson. Although living in the shadow of opulent plants of eastern origin, this is still an impressive and astonishingly long-lived perennial. Another but slightly smaller European species, *P. peregrina* (Z:6–8), has single flowers with red satiny petals cupping yellow stamens; in **'Otto Froebel'** (Z:6–8) the color is orange-red.

PAPAVER

PAPAVERACEAE Poppy

The Oriental poppies, with crumpled petals opening to large satiny flowers, are the most spectacular of about 70 species, and their magnificent prime makes up for the untidy wreckage of their sprawling leaves and the awkward gap they leave in summer. Representatives of the genus are found in a wide variety of habitats in much of the temperate world. Some of the perennials are short-lived, but in gardens they self-seed freely. The Spanish *P. rupifragum* (Z:6–9), for instance, with fluttering silky, soft orange flowers on stems about 20in (50cm) tall, can be a nuisance if it strays into an inappropriate color scheme. Self-seeding in gritty, free-draining ground is the easiest way of maintaining populations of the small alpine species. The Iceland poppy (**P. nudicaule**, Z:2–7) is best treated as a biennial. Annual species include the field poppy (**P. rhoeas**), a widely naturalized weed of arable land from which the exquisite single to double **Shirley Series** have been developed, and the opium poppy (**P. somniferum**).
CULTIVATION Require full sun and well-drained soil.
PROPAGATION By division, in spring. From root cuttings, taken in early winter. From seed, sown in spring.
POTENTIAL PROBLEMS Aphids; fungal wilts, downy mildew.

P. alpinum *Europe*
Alpine poppy
Flowers: summer. H:6–8in (15–20cm), S:4–10in (10–25cm). Z:4–8.
The name is often used to cover short-growing alpine species with charming tissue-paper flowers in yellow, orange, red, or white. The pale yellow *P. miyabeanum* from Japan is similar in character.

Papaver orientale 'Black and White'

P. orientale *Caucasus, N.E. Turkey, N. Iran*
Oriental poppy
Flowers: late spring to mid-summer. H:18–36in (45–90cm), S:24–36in (60–90cm). Z:3–7.
The species makes clumps of bristly foliage, the leaves 1ft (30cm) or more long with numerous segments cut almost to the central rib. The stems, which often sprawl if not supported, carry orange-red flowers that are up to 6in (15cm) across, with near-black central blotches and stamens around the central knob. A more upright plant, **var. bracteatum** from northern Iran, reaches a height of 4ft (1.2m) and has bracts beneath the large, deep red flowers. The numerous Oriental poppies in a color range from white and pink to red and orange that are usually listed under *P. orientale* are most probably of hybrid origin. All of the following poppies are single and have black or purplish basal blotches: **'Allegro'**, orange-red; **'Beauty of Livermere'**, crimson; **'Black and White'**, white; and **'Mrs. Perry'**, soft pink. **'Türkenlouis'** is pale salmon.

Papaver orientale 'Mrs. Perry'

253

PENSTEMON

SCROPHULARIACEAE

The foxglovelike flowers of the taller penstemons, most of them hybrids, brighten flower beds from mid-summer to autumn. The flowers are tubular and 2-lipped, with 5 lobes at the mouth and hairs (beard) in the throat. Although the border penstemons are generally the most widely grown, this is a large genus of about 250 species distributed in a wide range of habitats, mainly North and Central America. It includes many dwarf species from subalpine and alpine zones, among them some fine subshrubs for rock gardens. Border penstemons are often treated as bedding plants, either raised from seed annually or planted out in spring from cuttings taken in late summer and overwintered under glass. In areas prone to frost, it is sensible to overwinter even the hardiest rooted cuttings under glass. Plants cut back in mid-autumn can be protected with cloches in winter. In the selection below, the alpine penstemons are described before the taller border plants.

CULTIVATION Alpine and border penstemons both require full sun and well-drained soil; alpine penstemons, in fact, require sharply drained soil.

PROPAGATION By division, in spring. From softwood cuttings, in early summer, or semiripe cuttings, in mid-summer. From seed (border penstemons), sown in late winter or spring at 55-64°F (13-18°C).

POTENTIAL PROBLEMS Slugs, snails; powdery mildew.

ALPINE PENSTEMONS

P. davidsonii var. *menziesii*
N.W. USA, W. Canada
Flowers: summer. H:6-10in (15-25cm), S:8-12in (20-30cm). Z:4-9.
Purplish-violet tubular flowers appear above the mat of dark green leathery leaves in summer.

P. fruticosus var. *scouleri*
N.W. USA, W. Canada
Flowers: summer. H and S:12-18in (30-45cm). Z:4-8.
This subspecies of the shrubby penstemon has narrow leathery leaves that are almost lost beneath a profusion of narrow purple flowers. In **f. albus** the creamy-tinged buds open to pure white flowers.

P. newberryi USA
Flowers: early summer. H:6-10in (15-25cm), S:8-12in (20-30cm). Z:6-8.

Similar in form to *P. davidsonii* var. *menziesii*, this plant produces many spikes of vibrant red-pink tubular flowers that hide the mat of green leathery leaves.

Penstemon pinifolius

P. pinifolius Mexico, S. USA
Flowers: summer. H:8-16in (20-40cm), S:8-12in (20-30cm). Z:7-8.
Loose spikes of bright scarlet tubular flowers—bright yellow in 'Mersea Yellow'—rise above the needlelike foliage.

Penstemon pinifolius 'Mersea Yellow'

P. rupicola W. USA
Rock penstemon
Flowers: late spring to early summer. H:3-4in (7.5-10cm), S:12-18in (30-45cm). Z:4-9.
A ground-hugging mat of leathery gray-green leaves produces many clusters of red-pink flowers.

BORDER PENSTEMONS

P. barbatus Mexico, W. USA,
Beardlip penstemon
Flowers: early summer to early autumn. H:3-4ft (90-120cm), S:18-24in (45-60cm). Z:3-8.
The semievergreen clump of basal leaves produces lax, branching stems carrying drooping narrow flowers of bright vermilion. The plant gets its common and specific name from the yellow beards on the lower lips of the flowers.

P. hybrids
Flowers: mid-summer to mid-autumn. H:18-30in (45-75cm), S:1-2ft (30-60cm). Z:6-9.
The hardiness of the tall-growing

Penstemon 'Andenken an Friedrich Hahn'

hybrids, mainly derived from the Mexican species *P. hartwegii* (Z:8-9), varies considerably, but in general, plants with narrow leaves and small flowers, such as those listed below, are the most frost-resistant: '**Andenken an Friedrich Hahn**' (Z:7-9), deep wine-red and almost bell-shaped flowers; '**Apple Blossom**', pale pink with white throat; '**Evelyn**', bright pink with pale striped throat; '**Hidcote Pink**', salmon-pink, veined crimson in the throat; '**Stapleford Gem**', larger in leaf and flower than the others listed here but as hardy; the flowers are a softly opalescent blend of pink and mauve.

Penstemon 'Apple Blossom'

PERSICARIA

POLYGONACEAE Knotweed

Even on a large country estate, the introduction of species such as the Japanese knotweed (*P. cuspidata*) would give cause for great regret: their invasive roots produce thickets of nightmarish density wherever they please. There are better-behaved perennials in this genus of about 75 species, which are widely distributed in both hemispheres. Although they, too, have spreading roots, they are valuable for their ground-covering abilities, especially in moist soil and, in many cases, for their decorative flower spikes, which are produced over a very long period. The main appeal of *P. virginiana* '**Painter's Palette**' (Z:4-8) is quite simply its astonishing foliage: mounds about

2ft (60cm) tall are composed of leaves that combine green, cream, pink, and distinctive V-shaped brown marks.
CULTIVATION Tolerate full sun or partial shade and require moist soil.
PROPAGATION By division, in spring or autumn. From seed, sown in spring.
POTENTIAL PROBLEMS Blackflies (*P. bistorta*), slugs and snails (*P. virginiana* 'Painter's Palette').
WARNING Skin irritations may occur from contact with any part of the plant. Stomach upsets may occur if the sap is swallowed.

P. affinis *Himalayas*
Foliage: autumn. Flowers: mid-summer to mid-autumn. H:8–10in (20–25cm), S:1–2ft (30–60cm). Z:3–8.
Dense mats of lance-shaped leaves are punctuated with spikes of tiny cup-shaped flowers, pink at first, darkening to red before turning brown. The foliage bronzes in autumn and remains russet in the winter months. **'Darjeeling Red'** and **'Donald Lowndes'** are compact, while **'Superba'** is a more luxuriant clone.

Persicaria affinis 'Superba'

P. amplexicaulis *Himalayas*
Bistort
Flowers: mid-summer to early autumn. H and S:3–4ft (90–120cm). Z:5–9.
For many weeks, wiry stems thickened with a slender terminal red spike—crimson in **'Firetail'**—crisscross above dense and expanding clumps of docklike leaves. Another Himalayan species, with a range extending to south-west China, is **P. milletii**, which produces dark red spikes on stems up to 2ft (60cm) tall during summer and autumn.

P. bistorta *Europe, N. and W. Asia*
Bistort
Flowers: early summer to mid-autumn. H:24–30in (60–75cm), S:2–3ft (60–90cm). Z:3–8.
The species, a vigorous colonizer of moist soils, makes dense clumps

of large docklike leaves. In **'Superba'** numerous stiff stems carry soft pink bottlebrushes for many weeks.

Persicaria bistorta 'Superba'

PHLOMIS

LAMIACEAE

In a genus of about 100 widely distributed species, most of that grow in stony, free-draining ground, the best-known perennial is a rough but bold plant that has a substantial base of evergreen leaves.
CULTIVATION Require full sun and well-drained soil.
PROPAGATION By division, in spring or autumn. From seed, sown in spring.
POTENTIAL PROBLEMS None serious.

P. russeliana *Syria, Turkey*
Foliage: year-round. Flowers: late spring to early autumn. H:3–4ft (90–120cm), S:24–30in (60–75cm). Z:6–9.
The heart-shaped leaves, which grow up to 8in (20cm) long, are hairy, like the foliage of many other species in this genus. From the dense clumps rise stiff stems that are ringed at intervals with whorls of hooded, pale yellow flowers. Stems bearing seedheads are attractive left on the plant, or they can be dried for indoor display.

Phlomis russeliana

PHLOX

POLEMONIACEAE

Transformed into showy garden plants, the taller perennial species, which in the wild are found in

river valleys in wooded regions of eastern North America, are commonly known as border phloxes. It is undoubtedly in the border that they shine, as they give a colorful, often bright-eyed display from mid-summer to autumn. As a bonus, they provide fragrant flowers for cutting. This almost exclusively North American genus of 67 species also includes the very popular annual **P. drummondii** and a number of dwarf perennial or subshrubby species that make rock gardens vivid with their generous flowering in spring and early summer. Some of the dwarf species and their hybrids are true alpines, at home in rocky terrain that is fully exposed to sun and wind and where water drains away quickly. Others are low plants of cool moist woodland or its margins. Although they have such diverse habitats and characters, the phloxes are frank about their family connections: the flower in most cases consists of a narrow tube opening to 5 flat petal lobes. In the descriptions below, the dwarf phloxes precede the border phloxes.
CULTIVATION Some dwarf phloxes, among them *P. douglasii* and *P. subulata*, require full sun and well-drained soil, while others, including *P. adsurgens*, *P. divaricata*, and *P. stolonifera*, require partial shade and moist soil containing plenty of organic matter. *P. paniculata* and the many border phloxes tolerate full sun or partial shade and require a well-drained but moist and fertile soil.
PROPAGATION Dwarf phloxes: from basal cuttings, taken in mid-summer; from seed, sown in spring. *P. paniculata* and the numerous border cultivars: from stem cuttings, in early spring; from root cuttings, in late winter or early spring; by division of healthy plants, in autumn or spring; from seed in spring.
POTENTIAL PROBLEMS Nematodes; powdery mildew.

DWARF PHLOXES

P. adsurgens *N.W. USA*
Flowers: late spring to early summer. H and S:10–12in (25–30cm). Z:5–9.
This semievergreen species, with creeping stems that root as they go, is one of several alpine phloxes preferring cool, moist conditions. It is best known for **'Wagon Wheel'**, which has salmon-pink petal lobes that are narrow and spokelike. Another arresting plant requiring

similar conditions and flowering at the same time is *P. divaricata* subsp. *laphamii* 'Chattahoochee' (Z:4–9). Numerous sprays of mauve-blue flowers with a staring purplish red eye arch out on an open, lightly hairy plant about 10in (25cm) tall. The creeping phlox (*P. stolonifera*, Z:3–8) also needs soil rich in organic matter in order to spread. The flowers, held on erect stems up to 6in (15cm) tall, are usually in shades of purple. 'Blue Ridge' (Z:3–8) is mauve-blue.

Phlox douglasii 'Boothman's Variety'

P. douglasii *USA*
(S. Washington to California)
Flowers: late spring to early summer. H:4–8in (10–20cm), S:12–18in (30–45cm). Z:4–9. Even small containers can accommodate the evergreen tufts of needlelike leaves, which are studded for several weeks with short-stemmed, rounded flowers. In the wild, the color is mauve, pink, or white, but there are numerous selections belonging to this species. 'Boothman's Variety' is a cool mauve-blue with an irregular circle of dark purple at the center, while 'Red Admiral' is a rich crimson.

Phlox douglasii 'Red Admiral'

P. subulata *E. to C. USA*
Moss phlox
Flowers: late spring to early summer. H:2–6in (5–15cm), S:18–24in (45–60cm). Z:3–8. When in flower, a tide of color sweeps over the dull evergreen mats of spiky leaves. There is a wonderful choice of cultivars, all

with more or less starry flowers, usually darker at the center and with notched lobes. 'G.F. Wilson' is soft mauve-blue, 'McDaniel's Cushion' deep pink, and 'Temiskaming' dark red.

Phlox subulata 'McDaniel's Cushion'

BORDER PHLOXES

P. paniculata *E. USA*
Perennial phlox
Flowers: late summer to early autumn. H:2–4ft (60–120cm), S:2–3ft (60–90cm). Z:4–8.
The border phloxes derived from this species are the most important perennials of the genus for general garden use. Their fragrant flowers are grouped in dense pyramidal trusses on upright plants, making colorful displays in late summer and even into autumn. The color range goes well beyond that of the plant in the wild, which is restricted to pink, mauve, purple, and white. A contrasting dark eye is an attractive feature of many of the cultivars. Staking is usually not necessary except in exposed gardens. Breeding and selection of border phloxes began in the early 19th century, and there are now many cultivars to choose from. The following is a very small selection: 'Amethyst', violet-blue; 'Bright Eyes', pale pink with red eyes; 'Eventide', mauve-blue; 'Fujiyama', white, and late flowering; 'Norah Leigh', mauve, with white-variegated foliage; 'Prince of Orange', orange-red; 'Starfire', bright red; and the pure white 'White Admiral'. The cluttered density of the flowers and the

Phlox paniculata 'White Admiral'

susceptibility to eelworm attack are drawbacks of the perennial phlox. However, these are not such serious problems with the more slender meadow phlox (*P. maculata*). Growing to 36in (90cm), it carries its fragrant small flowers in cylindrical heads. Plants in the wild are mauve-pink and there is not a wide color range in the few cultivars. 'Omega' is white with a purplish-red eye.

PHORMIUM

AGAVACEAE

Although the flower stems are a curious addition, even without them the 2 evergreen species in this genus are impressive foliage plants, making large clumps of broad straplike leaves, ranging from yellow-green to dark green. The New Zealand flax (*P. tenax*) is found wild in a remarkably wide range of habitats, from coastal sand dunes to mountain gullies. However, in cultivation it is worth giving *P. tenax* and the hybrids between it and the mountain flax (*P. cookianum*), also from New Zealand, the moist conditions in which they do best. A dry mulch will help provide protection from frost between autumn and spring. Limp and discolored leaves should be removed in spring.
CULTIVATION Require full sun and moist well-drained soil.
PROPAGATION By division, in spring. From seed, sown in spring at 55–64°F (13–18°C).
POTENTIAL PROBLEMS Mealybugs.

Phormium cookianum subsp. hookeri 'Tricolor'

P. cookianum *New Zealand*
Mountain flax
Foliage: year-round. Flowers: mid- to late summer. H:4–6ft (1.2–1.8m), S:3–4ft (90–120cm). Z:8–10. Its smaller size and lax arching leaves distinguish the mountain flax from the New Zealand flax. The cream banding of subsp. *hookeri* 'Cream Delight' and the pale yellow and red margins of subsp. *hookeri* 'Tricolor' add to the vivacity of these plants.

Phormium 'Sundowner'

P. hybrids

Flowers: mid- to late summer.
H:30–60in (75–150cm), S:18–36in
(45–90cm). Z:8–10.
Many of the hybrids show the lax
growth of *P. cookianum* and the
small scale of some makes them
adaptable to gardens of moderate
size. The pick of established
hybrids (with an average height for
foliage) includes '**Bronze Baby**',
30in (75cm), purplish-brown
leaves with lax tips; '**Dazzler**', 36in
(90cm), bronze-red with purple,
orange, and pink longitudinal
stripes; '**Sundowner**', 5ft (1.5m),
bronzed-green leaves with deep
pink margins; and '**Yellow Wave**',
36in (90cm), yellow-green leaves
with green striping.

P. tenax *New Zealand*
New Zealand flax
Foliage: year-round. Flowers: mid-
to late summer. H:6–12ft (1.8–
3.7m), S:4–6ft (1.2–1.8m). Z:8–10.
The clump of stiff, swordlike
leaves, which are gray-green and of
leathery texture, has a dramatic
bomb-burst outline. The woody
purple flower stems rise well
above the foliage, and side brackets
carry short rows of erect, dull red
flowers, about 2in (5cm) long.
Flaxes in the **Purpureum Group**
have bronze-purple or coppery
leaves; in '**Variegatum**' the leaves
are striped yellow at the margins.

Phormium tenax Purpureum Group

PHYSOSTEGIA

LAMIACEAE

There are about 12 species of
Physostegia in North America, but
only the surprisingly compliant
P. virginiana, a plant of moist soils,
is in general cultivation. Push an
individual flower in any direction,
and it will hold its position.
CULTIVATION Tolerate full sun or
partial shade and require well-
drained but moist and fertile soil.
PROPAGATION From seed, sown in
autumn. By division, in autumn or
spring.
POTENTIAL PROBLEMS Slugs; fungal
and bacterial rots.

P. virginiana *E. North America*
False dragonhead, obedient plant
Flowers: mid-summer to early
autumn. H:3–4ft (90–120cm),
S:18–24in (45–60cm). Z:3–9.
The running roots make large
clumps of irregularly toothed
leaves. Above the leaves, stems,
which are square in section, carry
spikes of tubular 2-lipped flowers.
In the wild the almost stalkless
flowers are usually mauve-pink or
purple. '**Summer Snow**' is a lovely
white with green bracts; '**Vivid**', a
bright purplish pink. The pale
mauve-pink of **subsp. *speciosa***
'**Bouquet Rose**' is less assertive in
the autumn garden.

Physostegia virginiana

PLATYCODON

CAMPANULACEAE Balloon flower

Once the flowers have opened, it
is very easy to see the connection
with *Campanula* of the single
species within this genus, but it is
the ballooning buds that are more
riveting as they seem to threaten a
sequence of minor explosions. In
the wild it is a plant of high
meadows where there is plenty of
moisture but also the essential
good drainage.
CULTIVATION Requires full sun and
well-drained soil, rich in organic
matter.
PROPAGATION From seed, sown in
spring. By division, in spring.
POTENTIAL PROBLEMS Slugs, snails.

P. grandiflorus *Japan, Korea,*
N. China
Flowers: late summer. H:18–24in
(45–60cm), S:12–18in (30–45cm).
Z:3–9.
The fleshy roots are easily damaged
by careless digging early in the
season because growth is not made
until late spring. The clean-cut
flowers, borne above blue-green
leaves, are a spreading bell shape,
up to 2in (5cm) across. Veining
intensifies their shade of blue or
violet and adds an exquisite
shadow to '**Albus**'. The dwarf
mariesii, which rarely exceeds 1ft
(30cm), flowers early and freely.

Platycodon grandiflorus

PLEIONE

ORCHIDACEAE

A genus of 16 to 20 small orchids
found in an area extending
eastward from North India to
Taiwan are of interest to gardeners
in temperate regions. Where the
climate is mild enough, some can
be grown successfully outdoors. In
the wild they are usually found
perched on tree trunks or mossy
rocks in forested regions where
the rainfall is high, generally at
elevations over 3,000ft (1000m),
but even at much higher altitudes.
They are deciduous, the leaves
usually developing from the short
pseudobulbs after the flowers have
appeared. The conspicuous feature
of the flowers, which are borne
singly or less commonly in pairs on
short stems, is the long trumpet,
fringed at the mouth and often
boldly spotted on the inside. The
plants seem oddly limbless, with
the flowers, often more than 2in
(5cm) across, held just above
ground level.
CULTIVATION Require partial shade
and well-drained fertile soil with
added leaf mold (terrestrial or
epiphytic orchid media).
PROPAGATION By division of
pseudobulbs, in mid- to late spring;
from pseudobulbils, planted in
mid- to late spring.
POTENTIAL PROBLEMS Slugs, aphids.
Under glass: red spider mites,
mealybugs.

P. formosana *E. China, Taiwan*
Flowers: mid- to late spring. H and
S:4-6in (10-15cm). Z:7-9.
Rounded pseudobulbs produce
single or paired mauve-pink
flowers that have a white fringed
trumpet, usually with purplish
spotting on the inside. Among its
cultivars are extremely beautiful
white forms.

Pleione formosana

POLEMONIUM

POLEMONIACEAE

The fanciful common name of
Jacob's ladder (*P. caeruleum*), which
has been grown in Europe since at
least the 16th century, is an allusion
to the foliage and its runglike
arrangement of leaflets. This
perennial, as well as others in a
genus of about 25 species found in
Europe, Asia, and Central and
North America, is a plant of moist
meadows and woodland margins,
but some, including **P. eximium**
(Z:4-8) from western North
America, are alpines. In gardens they
do best in open positions where
the ground drains sharply.
P. caeruleum, like most of the species
in cultivation, deteriorates unless
divided every 2 to 3 years. Cutting
back early-flowering species once
they have bloomed encourages a
second, although smaller, display.
CULTIVATION Tolerate full sun or
partial shade and require well-
drained but moist soil.
PROPAGATION By division, in spring.
From seed, sown in autumn or
spring.
POTENTIAL PROBLEMS Powdery
mildew.

Polemonium caeruleum

P. caeruleum *N. Asia, N. and C.
Europe, W. North America*
Greek valerian, Jacob's ladder
Flowers: early summer. H:18-36in
(45-90cm), S:1-2ft (30-60cm).
Z:3-8.
Rising above the foliage are
numerous arching sprays of bell-
shaped mauve flowers with
orange-yellow stamens. *P.* 'Hopleys'
has dark buds, with bright blue
flowers that fade to near-white, all
stages present at the same time. The
North American species
P. archibaldae is a sturdy version.

P. 'Lambrook Mauve'
Flowers: late spring to early
summer. H and S:16-20in
(40-50cm). Z:3-8.
Many sprays of soft mauve-blue
flowers arch languidly over a
relaxed clump of foliage that has
the characteristic arrangement of
paired leaflets.

POLYGONATUM

CONVALLARIACEAE Solomon's seal

The graceful arching stems and
small bell flowers of the familiar
Solomon's seal are characteristic of
a number of species in a genus of
about 50 woodland perennials,
widely distributed in temperate
regions of the Northern
Hemisphere. They are rhizomatous,
and the taller species are best seen
in bowing colonies making coolly
elegant companions to ferns and
other shade-lovers. A few dwarf
species, including the diminutive
pink-flowered **P. hookeri** (Z:5-8),
are ideal plants for a peat bed.
CULTIVATION Tolerate full or partial
shade and require a well-drained but
moist soil, rich in organic matter.
PROPAGATION By division, in spring.
From seed, sown in autumn.
POTENTIAL PROBLEMS Slugs, sawfly
larvae.
WARNING Stomach upsets may
occur if any parts are swallowed.

P. × hybridum
Common Solomon's seal
Flowers: late spring. H:2-4ft
(60-120cm), S:12-18in (30-45cm).
Z:4-8.
This vigorous hybrid between
P. multiflorum and **P. odoratum**
has outclassed its parents with its
arching stems, alternate leaves, and
ivory, green-tipped bells. The veined
leaves lie horizontally, and the
clusters of 2 to 4 scented flowers
hang from the leaf axils. '**Striatum**'
is a choice variegated plant. The
North American **P. biflorum**
(Z:4-9) is similar to the commonly
grown Solomon's seal, but twice its
size in ideal conditions.

Polygonatum × hybridum

PONTEDERIA

PONTEDERIACEAE

The single widely grown species
from this small New World genus
of 5 species is an impressive
foliage plant of water margins.
CULTIVATION Require full sun. Plant
in loamy soil in water 4-6in
(10-15cm) deep.
PROPAGATION By division, in late
spring. From seed, sown as soon
as ripe.
POTENTIAL PROBLEMS Usually none.

Pontederia cordata

P. cordata *E. North America*
Pickerel weed
Flowers: late summer. H:3-4ft
(90-120cm), S:24-30in (60-75cm).
Z:4-9.
Thick rootstocks ease themselves
out into shallow water, sending up
stiff, crowded stems bearing spear-
shaped glossy leaves with light
shadowing in purplish brown.
During late summer, spikes of
small blue flowers thrust their way
through the magnificent foliage.

POTENTILLA

ROSACEAE Cinquefoil

The sun-loving perennials in this
very large genus of about 500
species, which also contains
numerous shrubs of great garden
value, include many that produce
dazzling flowers in early summer.
The species are found in a wide
variety of habitats in the Northern
Hemisphere—many of them are
plants of open sites and well-
drained ground. The larger species
and their hybrids make bright

accents at the front of beds; the dwarf species, mainly plants of rocky mountainous areas where the drainage is sharp, are good for rock gardens. See also SHRUBS.
CULTIVATION Require full sun and well-drained soil. Rock-garden species require very well-drained, gritty soil.
PROPAGATION From seed, sown in autumn or spring. By division, in spring or autumn.
POTENTIAL PROBLEMS Usually none.

P. hybrids

Flowers: early to late summer. H:1-2ft (30-60cm), S:18-24in (45-60cm). Z:5-8.
One parent of a group of brilliant hybrids is the Himalayan cinquefoil (**P. atrosanguinea**). In itself it is an appealing plant, with flowers the startling red of freshly spilled blood or, in the silver-leaved **var. argyrophylla**, yellow with an orange center. The following hybrids fling out loose sprays of colorful flowers over foliage, which in most cases is green, with strawberrylike leaflets: '**Gibson's Scarlet**', single, dashing scarlet; '**Gloire de Nancy**', double, vermilion; '**William Rollison**', semidouble, orange-red with yellow touches and reverse; and '**Yellow Queen**', semidouble, bright yellow, and silvery foliage.

Potentilla 'Yellow Queen'

P. nepalensis W. Himalayas

Flowers: summer. H:1-3ft (30-90cm), S:18-24in (45-60cm). Z:5-8.
Reddish wiry stems carry hairy palmate leaves and many sprays of saucer-shaped flowers in shades of purplish pink or crimson. '**Miss Willmott**' is 12-18in (30-45cm) tall and has rich pink flowers with a darker center.

P. × tonguei

Flowers: summer. H:4-8in (10-20cm), S:10-14in (25-35cm). Z:5-8.
Although not as compact as many of the cinquefoils suitable for rock gardens, this hybrid flowers generously, and its soft apricot blooms with a dark red eye are instantly appealing.

PRIMULA

PRIMULACEAE

Primula vulgaris

Representatives of this wonderfully varied group of plants have had a long history in cultivation. There are about 400 species, the majority from the Northern Hemisphere with nearly half concentrated in the Himalayas. A very high proportion have flat, primroselike flowers, and some have a mealy powdering (farina) that whitens leaves, stems, and calyces. They are found in a wide range of habitats, from moist woodland, open grassy banks, and alpine meadows to bogs and rugged mountain faces, many on acidic soils but others on lime, among them several choice European species for the alpine house, such as **P. allionii** (Z:6-8). A few primulas—including **P. kewensis** (Z:8-10) and **P. obconica** (Z:8-10)—are grown as short-lived greenhouse or house plants, and the spring-flowering polyanthus hybrids are usually treated as biennials. The groupings used below reflect how they are used in gardens and their history in cultivation. The alpine primulas described represent a tiny proportion of the large number that are appealing to the specialized grower. Many of them are Asiatic, but others are from Europe eastward to the Caucasus and North America. Although the auriculas owe much to the alpine *P. auricula*, these hybrids are a group on their own. They have been much meddled with to give

Primula allionii

rounded, often curiously colored or subtly enameled flowers, with a powerful hold on the affections because of their association with generations of cottage gardeners. The border, bog, and woodland primulas include the European primrose (*P. vulgaris*) as well as representatives of the larger species of Asiatic origin and their hybrids, which demand a reliably moist soil.
CULTIVATION Primulas have varying requirements. Most alpine primulas and auriculas tolerate full sun or partial shade and require a gritty but moist soil, rich in organic matter with leaf mold and grit added. In general, the Asiatic species require more moist conditions than the European alpine species. Some, including *P. frondosa*, require lime-free soil. Other primulas tolerate full sun or partial shade and require a moisture-retentive soil containing generous quantities of organic matter. The candelabra primulas, such as *P. florindae*, require permanently moist conditions and flourish in bogs.
PROPAGATION By division, between autumn and early spring. From basal or offset cuttings, in autumn or early spring. From root cuttings, in winter. From seed, sown in early spring.
POTENTIAL PROBLEMS Aphids, red spider mites, leafhoppers, vine weevils, slugs; gray mold (*Botrytis*), viruses.

Primula farinosa

ALPINE PRIMULAS

P. frondosa C. Bulgaria

Flowers: late spring to early summer. H:4-6in (10-15cm), S:6-10in (15-25cm). Z:5-8.
The underside of the spoon-shaped leaves, the stems, and the buds are powdered white. Up to 30 mauve-pink flowers with prettily notched petal lobes radiate from the top of each stem.
P. farinosa (Z:4-8), which is widely distributed in Europe and northern Asia, is a similar but short-lived plant that is also dusted with farina. The lilac-pink flowers have a yellow eye.

P. marginata *European Alps*
Flowers: early to mid-spring.
H:4–6in (10–15cm), S:6–10in (15–25cm). Z:4–8.
Farina whitens the margins of the leathery leaves and the stems, and the residue in the eye of the mauve-blue flowers gives them a charming bleariness. There are many named clones, some probably of hybrid origin. The combination of dusty whiteness and soft mauve-blue is particularly appealing in '**Linda Pope**'.

P. × pubescens
Flowers: spring. H:4–6in (10–15cm), S:6–10in (15–25cm). Z:4–7.
Many cultivars are listed under this name, which covers hybrids between *P. auricula* and *P. hirsuta*. They are partially evergreen, with strong stems carrying crowded heads of flowers above rosettes of slightly leathery leaves, in some cases powdered with meal. The color range includes white and numerous shades of pink, purple, and red. '**Christine**' is reddish purple, and the old favorite '**Faldonside**' is crimson with a white eye.

AURICULAS

P. auricula *Europe (Alps, Apennines, Carpathians)*
Flowers: spring. H:4–8in (10–20cm), S:4–10in (10–25cm). Z:3–7.
Under the name of a fragrant, yellow-flowered species, which is widely distributed in the mountains of Europe, are listed numerous hybrids that have had a long history in cultivation. They reached their peak of popularity in the 18th and 19th centuries, when they were particularly associated in Britain with the weavers of Lancashire. There are 3 main categories. The show auriculas, which are characterized by a mealy white ring at the center of the flower, have many subdivisions, among the most distinctive being those with flowers edged green or gray. In '**Orb**', for instance, the white ring is surrounded by black and then by a green margin. The selfs, such as the very dark '**Neat and Tidy**', have a single color extending from the white ring to the margins. Easily spoiled by wet and rough weather, the show auriculas are grown under glass. The alpine auriculas have no meal on the flowers or leaves and can be grown outdoors. There is a strong contrast between the yellow or light center and the color of the petal lobes. '**Mark**', for example, is pink with a white

center; '**Bookham Firefly**', red with a gold center. The hearty border auriculas, in some cases with a powdering of meal, are suitable for the open garden. '**Old Red Dusty Miller**' and '**Old Yellow Dusty Miller**' both have meal on the leaves and in the eye of the flowers. Specialized nurseries have many tempting treasures in all 3 categories.

BORDER, BOG, AND WOODLAND
PRIMULAS

Primula denticulata

P. denticulata *Afghanistan to S.E. Tibet, Burma, China*
Drumstick primula
Flowers: mid-spring to summer.
H and S:12–18in (30–45cm). Z:4–7.
The rosette of long leaves, fine-toothed and mealy, reaches its full development after sturdy stems have pushed up a spherical head, as much as 3in (7.5cm) across and packed with flowers. These are yellow eyed and in shades of mauve or purple; in **var. alba** they are white.

P. florindae *S.E. Tibet*
Giant cowslip
Flowers: mid- to late summer.
H:2–4ft (60–120cm), S:2–3ft (60–90cm). Z:5–8.
Where the soil is fertile and unfailingly moist, this is a giant among primroses, making large rosettes of long-stalked leaves and sending up tall stems, with a ring of numerous lemon-yellow flowers dangling from the tip. They are powdered with meal and fragrant. The Himalayan cowslip (**P. sikkimensis**, Z:6–8) is a plant of similar character but usually less than 36in (90cm) in height.

P. japonica *Japan*
Japanese primrose
Flowers: late spring to early summer. H:24–30in (60–75cm), S:9–12in (23–30cm). Z:4–8.
In this plant, the tiered whorls of flowers typical of the candelabra primulas rise above rosettes of pale green leaves. The flowers are

Primula japonica 'Miller's Crimson'

usually a shade of red. '**Miller's Crimson**' is richly colored, and '**Postford White**' is pale pink in bud, opening white with a reddish-pink eye. The Chinese species **P. beesiana** (Z:5–8), which is of similar size and which blooms at the same time, is a piercing magenta. A taller candelabra primula is another Chinese species, **P. pulverulenta** (Z:5–8). It grows to 36in (90cm) in height and has mealy stems and flowers of reddish purple. The **Bartley Hybrids** (Z:5–8) derived from it have pink flowers with red eyes.

Primula japonica 'Postford White'

P. prolifera *Himalayas, E. to mountains of Indonesia*
Flowers: early summer. H:2–3ft (60–90cm), S:9–10in (23–25cm). Z:5–8.
A white-powdered sturdy stem makes a candelabra with up to 7 whorls of fragrant flowers in shades of yellow. The rosette of leaves lasts through the winter. **P. bulleyana** (Z:6–8), of similar size, has orange-tinted flowers. The orange-red **P. aurantiaca** (Z:6–8) is rarely more than 1ft (30cm) tall.

Primula prolifera

P. vialii *China (Sichuan, Yunnan)*
Flowers: summer. H:6–18in
(15–45cm), S:9–12in (23–30cm).
Z:6–7.
Erect stems, rising from a rosette of
upright, hairy leaves, carry single,
rocketlike heads of tightly packed
flowers. At the pointed tips, the
unopened buds are vivid red; the
open flowers below are mauve.

Primula 'Miss Indigo'

P. vulgaris *Europe, W. Turkey*
Primrose
Flowers: early to late spring.
H:6–8in (15–20cm), S:10–14in
(25–35cm). Z:5–8.
The common primrose, one of the
most beautiful of European wild
flowers, was brought into gardens
centuries ago. In spite of their
familiarity, it is hard to improve on
the pale yellow flowers that
emerge in profusion from bright
green corrugated leaves. However,
variations in color and doubling
have long been valued. The
flowers of **subsp. *sibthorpii***, from
the Balkans and farther east, are
usually pale pink. A white double
similar to '**Alba Plena**' was known
in the 16th century. Another
double, *P.* '**Miss Indigo**', has storm-
dark, violet-blue flowers with a
white edge to the petals.

PULMONARIA

BORAGINACEAE Lungwort

As low-growing groundcover in
shade, many of the lungworts,
especially the evergreens with
spotted or silvered leaves, are hard
to beat and their flowers—in a
number of cases making a magical
transition from pink to blue—are
among the first of the year borne
by perennials. The genus, which is
made up of about 14 species,
contains a large number of named
clones from selected seedlings.
The species are found in a wide
range of habitats in Europe and
Asia, usually in partial shade where
the soil is reliably moist but not
waterlogged. Similar conditions
suit these plants in the garden,
either under trees and shrubs or in
the shade of walls.

CULTIVATION Tolerate full or partial
shade and require well-drained but
moist soil, rich in organic matter.
PROPAGATION By division, after
flowering or in autumn. From root
cuttings, in mid-winter. From seed,
sown as soon as ripe.
POTENTIAL PROBLEMS Slugs, snails;
powdery mildew.

P. angustifolia *C., E., and N.E.
Europe*
Blue cowslip
Foliage: spring to autumn. Flowers:
early to late spring. H:9–12in (23–
30cm), S:12–18in (30–45cm). Z:4–8.
This species is deciduous, its
unspotted, lance-shaped, hairy
leaves, up to 16in (40cm) long,
developing as the pink buds open
to blue. The short-growing
'**Munstead Blue**' is very early
flowering. Among named clones
that are deciduous and similar in
character to this species is
P. '**Mawson's Blue**', with flowers
of gentian intensity.

Pulmonaria 'Mawson's Blue'

P. officinalis *Europe*
Jerusalem cowslip, soldiers and
sailors, spotted dog
Foliage: year-round. Flowers: early
to late spring. H:10–12in
(25–30cm), S:12–18in (30–45cm).
Z:4–8.
The bristly, heart-shaped leaves of
this evergreen species are spotted
and its flowers change from pink
through violet to blue. The
selection '**Sissinghurst White**' is
less coarse, with the white flowers
opening from pale pink buds over
thickly spotted leaves.

**Pulmonaria officinalis
'Sissinghurst White'**

P. rubra *S.E. Europe*
Foliage: year-round. Flowers: late
winter to mid-spring. H:12–15in
(30–38cm), S:2–3ft (60–90cm).
Z:4–8.
The unspotted foliage is velvety, and
the red flowers are borne over a
long period from mid-winter. In
'**Bowles' Red**', the leaves are lightly
spotted and the flowers coral.

**Pulmonaria saccharata
'Frühlingshimmel'**

P. saccharata *C. and N. Italy,
S.E. France*
Jerusalem sage
Foliage: year-round. Flowers: late
winter to late spring. H:12–18in
(30–45cm), S:18–24in (45–60cm).
Z:3–7.
The silver or pewter marbling and
splashing of the leaves, which are
up to 1ft (30cm) long, are
outstanding in this evergreen
species. The flowers, which have
purple calyces, open pink but
become blue. In the **Argentea
Group** (Z:4–8), the leaves have an
almost completely metallic finish.
'**Frühlingshimmel**' (Z:4–8) has
sky-blue flowers with a darker
center over lightly spotted leaves.

PULSATILLA

RANUNCULACEAE

The silky hairiness of the pasque
flower (*P. vulgaris*) and many of
its close relatives gives them a
winningly tactile quality. The
genus includes approximately 30
species, widely distributed in the
Northern Hemisphere, usually in
alpine or subalpine zones. They are
often found growing in short turf
where there is plenty of moisture
but also sharp drainage. Alpine
enthusiasts treasure the white-
flowered *P. vernalis* (Z:5–8), the
yellow-flowered *P. alpina* **subsp.
apiifolia** (Z:5–8), and a number of
other species that need protection
from winter wet, as well as gritty,
free-draining soil. Beautiful though
these species undoubtedly are, the
common pasque flower, which has
been grown in gardens since at
least the 16th century, is certainly
their equal.

CULTIVATION Require full sun and very well-drained soil with added grit.
PROPAGATION From seed, sown as soon as ripe.
POTENTIAL PROBLEMS Slugs, snails.
WARNING Skin irritations may occur after sap contact. Stomach upsets may occur if any parts are swallowed.

P. vulgaris *Europe E. to Ukraine*
Pasque flower
Flowers: mid-spring. H and S:8–12in (20–30cm). Z:4–9.
Silken buds push through the ferny tuft of softly hairy leaves, opening to nodding flowers, loaded at the center with rich yellow anthers. In the wild, the color ranges from pale mauve to deep purple; in cultivation it extends to white and shades of pink and red. The tactile fascination of the plant is sustained by feathery seedheads.

Pulsatilla vulgaris

RAMONDA

GESNERIACEAE

Although it shows an astonishing ability to revive after enduring a period of drought, the Pyrenean *R. myconi* and the less familiar plants of this small genus of only 3 species are, in fact, moisture lovers. In the wild, these evergreen perennials lodge tightly in the shady crevices of rock faces. In the garden, excessive moisture around the rosettes during the winter may cause them to rot, a potential problem that can be overcome by setting plants on their sides in a rock wall, such as on the shady side of a raised bed. They look more at home in such a position than on the shelf in an alpine house, where they would need to be given shade from hot sun.
CULTIVATION Require partial shade and well-drained but moist soil, rich in organic matter (equal parts loam, leaf mold, and grit).
PROPAGATION From seed, sown as soon as ripe. From rosette cuttings, in early summer. From leaf cuttings, in early autumn.
POTENTIAL PROBLEMS Slugs, snails.

Ramonda myconi

R. myconi *N.E. Spain, Pyrenees*
Flowers: late spring to early summer. H:4–6in (10–15cm), S:6–8in (15–20cm). Z:6–7.
The dark green, crinkly leaves, which are hairy and have a purplish-red fringe, form a flat rosette. From this, stems emerge usually bearing several, almost flat-faced, purple-blue flowers, each lit at the center by a cluster of yellow anthers. Some seedlings produce white or pink flowers.

RANUNCULUS

RANUNCULACEAE Buttercup

For several centuries the horticultural reputation of this genus, better known for beautiful weeds than garden flowers, was made by the half-hardy tuberous Persian buttercup (*R. asiaticus*), the gorgeous doubles of which are now usually raised commercially under glass. The genus, however, includes about 400 species, some of which are annuals, found in a wide range of habitats, including bogs and watery places, damp meadows, dry grassland, woodland, and mountain slopes. Several species excite alpine specialists, including *R. calandrinioides* (Z:7–8) from the Atlas Mountains, a frail-flowered beauty for the alpine house, and the magnificent but testing giant buttercup (*R. lyallii*, Z:6–7), from the New Zealand Alps. The luster of the flowers is appealing, even in such weedy species as the lesser celandine (*R. ficaria*, Z:4–8) and the creeping buttercup (*R. repens*, Z:4–8).

Ranunculus calandrinioides

R. ficaria has staged a comeback with the darkly glossy '**Brazen Hussy**' (Z:4–8), with chocolate-brown leaves, and such curious doubles as the anemone-flowered '**Collarette**' (Z:4–8).
CULTIVATION The species have varying requirements, but those described tolerate full sun or partial shade and require well-drained moist soil, rich in organic matter.
PROPAGATION By division, in spring or autumn. From seed, sown as soon as ripe.
POTENTIAL PROBLEMS Slugs, snails, aphids; powdery mildew.
WARNING Skin irritation may occur after sap contact.

Ranunculus aconitifolius 'Flore Pleno'

R. aconitifolius 'Flore Pleno'
Fair maids of France, fair maids of Kent, white bachelor's buttons
Flowers: late spring to early summer. H:18–24in (45–60cm), S:12–18in (30–45cm). Z:5–8.
Even the plant with single white buttercups over glossy, jaggedly lobed leaves is attractive in an open woodland garden, but since at least the 16th century it has been outclassed by the double.

R. constantinopolitanus 'Plenus'
Flowers: mid-spring to mid-summer. H:10–12in (25–30cm), S:6–10in (15–25cm). Z:5–8.
Green centers add zest to tidy and sheeny double flowers borne over a handsome clump of leaves with fanned and toothed lobes.

R. montanus 'Molten Gold'
Flowers: early summer. H:4–6in (10–15cm), S:8–12in (20–30cm). Z:4–8.
In a rock garden, this makes a deep green mat of glossy leaves, above which shine cup-shaped yellow flowers.

RAOULIA

ASTERACEAE

Several of the larger plants of this genus of about 20 species, including *R. eximia* (Z:6–7), which can form dense cushions

over 36in (90cm) across and 12in (30cm) or more thick, are known as vegetable sheep: from a distance their gray shapes look like animals grazing on sparse vegetation at the edge of mountain screes. They are difficult plants in cultivation, needing controlled conditions in an alpine house, but in this almost exclusively New Zealand genus, there are other species—some alpines, some plants of gravel river flats—that make attractive evergreen mats in rock gardens, raised beds, or scree beds. The starry flowers are tiny.
CULTIVATION Require full sun and well-drained soil (equal parts loam, leaf mold, and sharp sand with grit topdressing).
PROPAGATION By division of mat-forming species, in spring. From rosette cuttings of cushion-forming species, in early summer and in partial shade.
POTENTIAL PROBLEMS Aphids and red spider mites under glass.

Raoulia australis

R. australis New Zealand
Flowers: summer. H:½in (1cm), S:12-18in (30-45cm). Z:6-9.
Silvery mats of close overlapping leaves, tiny in the **Lutescens Group**, flow among and over rocks, the minute flowers creating a velvety yellow pile.

Raoulia hookeri

R. hookeri New Zealand
Flowers: mid- to late spring. H:½in (1cm), S:8-12in (20-30cm). Z:8-9.
Silky hairs give the packed rosettes of leaves a silvery luster. The small straw-colored or greenish flowers are not long lasting.

RHEUM
POLYGONACEAE Rhubarb

The culinary rhubarb (*R.* × *hybridum*, Z:5-7) gives some idea of the ornamental potential of several large-leaved species with plumelike flower spikes that thrive in moist, fertile soils. The chief interest of a few species, including *R. alexandrae* (Z:6-8) from swampy ground in western China and Tibet, is the conspicuous bracts that hide the flowers. This unusual species, which carries its creamy bracts on stems up to 36in (90cm) tall, has a reputation for being difficult, succeeding only where the soil is permanently wet. There are about 50 species altogether in the genus.
CULTIVATION Tolerate full sun or partial shade and require deep moist soil, rich in organic matter. *R. alexandrae* requires permanently wet soil.
PROPAGATION By division, in early spring. From seed, sown in autumn.
POTENTIAL PROBLEMS Slugs; crown rot, viruses.
WARNING Swallowing the leaves may cause severe stomach upsets.

R. palmatum N.E. Tibet, N.W. China
Chinese rhubarb
Foliage: late spring to mid-summer. Flowers: early summer. H:5-8ft (1.5-2.5m), S:4-6ft (1.2-1.8m). Z:5-9.
The relentless eruption of this plant in spring and early summer is splendid: the jagged leaves, growing up to 36in (90cm) long, reveal their purple-red undersides, and the tall stems shoot up above the leaves, which are plumed cream or red. The tints of **'Atrosanguineum'** are particularly fine, the young leaves purplish-red, the tiny flowers bright crimson; even the seed cases have a rosy flush. The hybrid *R.* **'Ace of Hearts'**, 4ft (1.2m) tall, has heart-shaped leaves that are purplish-red on the back and its thin plumes are pale pink or cream.

Rheum 'Ace of Hearts'

RODGERSIA
SAXIFRAGACEAE

The 6 species in this genus are rhizomatous perennials of forest glades, woodland margins, and streamsides in mountainous country from Burma eastward to Japan. They include several fine foliage plants that, in cultivation, as in the wild, will grow in full sun or light shade, provided there is plenty of moisture in the soil. They are most commonly seen as bog and waterside plants, but also make magnificent stands in damp beds. Although the reputation of the genus is founded on splendid foliage, some species have ornamental plumelike flowers followed by distinctive seedheads.
CULTIVATION Tolerate full sun or partial shade and require moist soil, rich in organic matter, in a sheltered position.
PROPAGATION From seed, sown in spring. By division, in early spring.
POTENTIAL PROBLEMS Slugs.

R. aesculifolia N. China
Foliage: late spring to autumn. Flowers: mid-summer. H:4-6ft (1.2-1.8m), S:2-3ft (60-90cm). Z:5-6.
The impressive stack of foliage, the leaves fingered like those of a giant horse chestnut, with red-brown furring on the stalks and veins, is topped by plumes of tiny, star-shaped white or pink flowers.

Rodgersia pinnata 'Superba'

R. pinnata China (Sichuan, Yunnan)
Foliage: late spring to autumn. Flowers: mid- to late summer. H:3-4ft (90-120cm), S:24-30in (60-75cm). Z:5-7.
The plumes of cream or pink flowers stand well above the dark green foliage base, made up of large overlapping leaves, each composed of 5 to 9 heavily veined and crinkled leaflets up to 8in (20cm) long. In **'Superba'**, which has bright pink flowers and red-brown seedheads, the leaves are bronze tinted when young and usually color richly in autumn.

Rodgersia podophylla

R. podophylla *Japan, Korea*
Foliage: late spring to autumn.
Flowers: mid- to late summer.
H:3–5ft (90–150cm), S:3–6ft
(90–180cm). Z:5–7.
In comparison with the other
widely grown species, this makes
a poor show in flower. However,
the foliage is dramatic, the leaves
usually consisting of 5 wedge-
shaped and jagged leaflets splayed
out like a rosette. They are
bronzed when young, and their
copper tones are particularly rich
later in the year, provided plants
are grown in full sun.

ROMNEYA

PAPAVERACEAE Californian poppy,
matilija poppy, tree poppy

The willfulness of the tree poppy
(there are only 2 species in the
genus) is a fact that has to be
accepted, the wandering roots of
the subshrubs throwing up shoots
in unexpected and not necessarily
convenient places. In the chaparral
of southern California, it is quick to
colonize areas that have been
burned or cleared. In sunny, warm
yards, a colony fluttering with large
white poppies is a glorious sight,
even though disconcertingly ill-
defined in its extent. Plants are
easily battered by winds and need
a sheltered position, in frost-prone
areas at the foot of a warm wall. A
dry mulch, say of straw, will help to
protect plants in winter.
CULTIVATION Require full sun and
well-drained soil.
PROPAGATION From seed, sown in
spring at 55–61°F (13–16°C). From
basal cuttings, in spring. From root
cuttings, in winter.
POTENTIAL PROBLEMS Caterpillars;
verticillium wilt.

R. coulteri *North America
(N. Mexico, S. California)*
Flowers: mid-summer to early
autumn. H and S:4–8ft (1.2–2.5m).
Z:6–9.
Crumpled white petals unfold
around a knob of bright yellow
stamens, and the fragrant flowers,
which can be over 4in (10cm)

across, seem to float randomly in
and above the slashed blue-green
foliage. The fast-spreading '**White
Cloud**' is noted for its very large
flowers and glaucous leaves.

Romneya coulteri

ROSCOEA

ZINGIBERACEAE

At a quick glance, the curious
hooded flowers of these fleshy
rooted perennials seem very
orchidlike. There are nearly 20
species, all of them found in the
Himalayas and China, most of them
growing in cool, moist conditions.
These are the ideal conditions for
them in cultivation as well. Suitable
positions include shady corners of
rock gardens, peat beds, or, in
combination with other choice
woodland plants, in glades among
shrubs or trees. In areas that are
frost-prone, a deep mulch of
leaf mold will help protect plants
in winter.
CULTIVATION Require partial shade
and moist, well-drained soil, rich in
organic matter.
PROPAGATION By division, in spring.
From seed, sown as soon as ripe.
POTENTIAL PROBLEMS Slugs.

R. cautleyoides *China (Sichuan,
Yunnan)*
Flowers: mid-summer. H:16–20in
(40–50cm), S:6–12in (15–30cm).
Z:6–9.
Plants in cultivation usually have
pale yellow flowers with a ghost-
like outline quivering above the
mid-green leaves. However, the
color range also includes purple
and white.

Roscoea cautleyoides

R. humeana *China
(Sichuan, Yunnan)*
Flowers: early summer. H and
S:6–12in (15–30cm). Z:6–9.
This is one of the first of the
species to flower, although the
leaves are usually not fully
developed when it does come into
bloom. In addition to the rich
reddish-purple most commonly
seen in cultivation, the color range
includes white, mauve, and yellow.
R. purpurea (Z:5–9), a taller plant,
usually 1ft (30cm) or more tall and
flowering a few weeks later, has
purple flowers. Occasionally it is bicolored with white and purple
flowers.

RUDBECKIA

ASTERACEAE Coneflower

Rudbeckia 'Goldquelle'

The yellow daisy flowers of the
perennials in this North American
genus of about 20 species have
rather drooping ray flowerets
surrounding the dark-colored or
green central cone. In the wild,
they are plants of open ground,
often near water. They will tolerate
drier conditions in well-cultivated
beds, giving a long display in
summer and early autumn. The
singles have a cleaner look than
the bright yellow **R. 'Goldquelle'**
(Z:4–9) and other doubles. A short-
lived, bristly perennial species,
R. hirta is usually grown as an
annual. The yellow flowerheads
have purplish-brown cones.
CULTIVATION Tolerate full sun or
partial shade and require heavy,
moist, well-drained soil.
PROPAGATION From seed, sown in
early spring. By division, in autumn
or spring.
POTENTIAL PROBLEMS Slugs.

R. fulgida *E. USA*
Black-eyed Susan
Flowers: late summer to mid-
autumn. H:2–3ft (60–90cm), S:18–
24in (45–60cm). Z:3–9.
The pick of these dark-eyed yellow
daisies, widely distributed in
eastern North America, is **var.
sullivantii 'Goldsturm'**. The erect

stems rise above the dark green basal leaves, carrying rich yellow flowers with narrow ray flowerets, up to 5in (12.5cm) across.

Rudbeckia fulgida var. sullivantii 'Goldsturm'

R. 'Herbstsonne'

Flowers: mid-summer to early autumn. H:5–7ft (1.5–2.2m), S:30–36in (75–90cm). Z:3–9.
The stature of **R. nitida** shows in this tall coneflower, of which it is a parent. Above clumps of lobed or toothed glossy leaves, branching stems carry large bright yellow but world-weary flowers, the ray flowerets sagging below the green central knob.

Rudbeckia 'Herbstsonne'

SALVIA

LAMIACEAE

The shrubby culinary sage (**S. officinalis**, Z:7–9) and a few other European representatives of this very large genus—which includes about 900 species of annuals, biennials, perennials, and shrubs—have a long history in cultivation. The species have an enormous spread in temperate and tropical areas of the world. Many plants from a wide range of habitats, especially the tender species, came into cultivation in the 19th century. These tender introductions are, in many instances, true perennials or subshrubs and are grown as such, provided the climate is mild enough. They are also frequently grown as annuals, with new stock raised each year, usually from cuttings taken in autumn or spring.

(Some are treated as such in this book.) Several of the plants described have aromatic foliage, and all have flowers with an upper lip that is hooded and a lower lip that is more spreading. Even when flowers are small, their impact is often enhanced by colorful, long-lasting bracts. The perennial salvias are useful plants for sunny flower beds and they provide some outstanding blues. See also ANNUALS AND BIENNIALS and SHRUBS.
CULTIVATION Salvias have varying requirements but all of those described need full sun and well-drained soil, preferably containing generous quantities of organic matter.
PROPAGATION From seed, especially of *S. patens* and *S. pratensis* Haematodes Group, sown in spring. By division, in spring (not subshrubs).
POTENTIAL PROBLEMS Slugs, snails; aphids, red spider mites, whiteflies (under glass); foot rot, root rot.

Salvia officinalis

S. guaranitica *Argentina, Brazil, Uruguay*

Flowers: late summer to late autumn. H:4–5ft (1.2–1.5m), S:24–30in (60–75cm). Z:7–10.
This lax subshrubby perennial produces stems loaded with deep blue sage flowers in autumn. The flowers of **'Blue Enigma'** (Z:7–9) are fragrant and richly colored, with bright green calyces.

S. nemorosa *Europe to C. Asia*

Flowers: summer. H:2–3ft (60–90cm), S:18–24in (45–60cm). Z:5–9.
The species and several hybrids are bushy plants that branch freely to produce many erect spikes; the effect of the flowers is long lasting because of the bracts that remain even after the flowers have faded. The compact **'Ostfriesland'**, about 18in (45cm) tall, has deep violet-blue flowers and red-purple bracts. Closer to the species in size but with similar coloring to **'Ostfriesland'** is *S. × superba*. Cultivars of the hybrid *S. × sylvestris* range in height from

18–30in (45–75cm). **'Mainacht'** is one of the taller examples, with large, deep blue flowers and purple bracts.

Salvia nemorosa 'Ostfriesland'

S. patens *Mexico*

Flowers: mid-summer to mid-autumn. H:18–24in (45–60cm), S:12–18in (30–45cm). Z:8–10.
Where the climate is mild enough, this makes a superb perennial, for many weeks bearing large paired flowers that gape at the mouth. A contrast between the familiar deep blue species and the pale **'Cambridge Blue'** is very pleasing. The fleshy roots are tuberous and plants can be lifted and stored in a frost-free place over winter. This species is also grown as an annual.

Salvia patens 'Cambridge Blue'

S. pratensis Haematodes Group *Greece*

Flowers: summer. H:2–3ft (60–90cm), S:12–18in (30–45cm). Z:7–9.
The basal rosette consists of large gray-green leaves, crinkled with purple veins. Branched stems carry sprays of mauve-blue flowers. Plants are easily raised from seed.

Salvia pratensis Haematodes Group

265

S. uliginosa *Argentina, Brazil, Uruguay*
Bog sage
Flowers: late summer to mid-autumn. H:5-6ft (1.5-1.8m), S:2-3ft (60-90cm). Z:6-10.
In its carefree grace, this tall species defies the approach of winter, its freely branching stems carrying small spikes of sky-blue flowers well into autumn.

SANGUINARIA

PAPAVERACEAE Bloodroot, red puccoon

The red sap that the plant exudes when damaged has given the one species in this North American genus its generic and common name. A plant of cool, moist woodland, it is well suited to a peat bed or shady area in a rock garden.
CULTIVATION Tolerates deep or partial shade and requires well-drained but moist soil, rich in organic matter.
PROPAGATION By division, immediately after flowering. From seed, sown in autumn.
POTENTIAL PROBLEMS Usually none.

Sanguinaria canadensis 'Plena'

S. canadensis *E. North America*
Flowers: late spring. H:4-6in (10-15cm), S:8-12in (20-30cm). Z:3-8.
The single-flowered form is a pleasing plant, especially in the way the buds are enclosed by the scalloped gray-green leaves, but it is eclipsed by the white purity of the double 'Plena'.

SANGUISORBA

ROSACEAE Burnet

Salad burnet (**S. minor**, Z:4-8), long cultivated as a herb, is a plant of dry grassland. However, the most ornamental of the burnets are moisture lovers, found wild in damp meadows. In late summer or autumn, the pinnate foliage is topped by bottlebrush-like spikes of flowers. There are about 18 species, all from temperate or cool areas of the Northern Hemisphere. Those most commonly grown benefit from light twiggy support.

CULTIVATION Tolerate full sun or partial shade and require moist, well-drained soil.
PROPAGATION By division, in spring or autumn. From seed, sown in spring or autumn.
POTENTIAL PROBLEMS Slugs.

S. canadensis *N.E. North America*
Canadian burnet
Flowers: mid-summer to mid-autumn. H:4-6ft (1.2-1.8m), S:2-3ft (60-90cm). Z:4-8.
The leaves are pale green, and the slender white, occasionally pink-tinted, bottlebrushes are carried on erect stems.

Sanguisorba obtusa

S. obtusa *Japan*
Flowers: mid-summer to early autumn. H:3-4ft (90-120cm), S:2-3ft (60-90cm). Z:5-8.
Lax stems carry soft, arching spikes, their pink a pleasing match for the gray-green foliage.

SAPONARIA

CARYOPHYLLACEAE

Its pretty flowers and easy-going ways made the common soapwort or bouncing bet (**S. officinalis**, Z:5-8) popular as a cottage garden plant, especially in its double pink or white forms; it was also valued for its cleansing properties. An untidy and invasive plant, it is now found naturalized beyond its European homeland. There are about 20 species in the genus. A few compact sun-loving species from mountainous regions in Europe are plants for rock gardens and raised beds. The Pyrenean **S. caespitosa** (Z:4-7), a small congested mat of leaves brightened by pink flowers, is one of these. The plant described becomes loose and untidy unless cut back hard after flowering.
CULTIVATION Require full sun and well-drained soil that is neutral to alkaline.
PROPAGATION From seed, sown in autumn or spring. By division, in spring or autumn. From cuttings, in early summer.
POTENTIAL PROBLEMS Slugs, snails.

Saponaria officinalis

S. ocymoides *Mountains from Spain to former Yugoslavia*
Tumbling Ted
Flowers: all summer. H:3-4in (8-10cm), S:12-18in (30-45cm). Z:4-8.
Tumbling Ted, as this species is sometimes known, rides roughshod over less assertive alpines, but its vigor allows it to plunge recklessly over the edge of retaining walls, trailing dark green drapery that is almost obscured by bright pink flowers. It has its own compact form, '**Rubra Compacta**', and there are several hybrids also of restrained dense growth.
S. 'Bressingham' (Z:5-8) makes a low mat with a spread of about 1ft (30cm), covered by stemless bright pink flowers in mid-summer. The dense cushion of **S. × olivana** (Z:4-7), usually less than half this in size, is covered with pale pink flowers in early summer.

Saponaria ocymoides

SAXIFRAGA

SAXIFRAGACEAE Saxifrage

For the alpine specialist, this is undoubtedly one of the key genera. It contains about 440 species, a large proportion of which are from mountainous habitats in the Northern Hemisphere. Despite their small scale, the species and the large number of hybrids derived from them show a wonderful variety in habit, foliage, and flower. The selection described can only hint at the variety but includes representatives of the most widely grown groups. Among the most spectacular are the silver or encrusted saxifrages, a few of which are mentioned under the entry *S. longifolia*. These are evergreens, forming large rosettes, which are silvered with a liberal encrustation of lime. Plants may take several years before they flower, and after flowering the central rosette usually dies. The mossy saxifrages, which derive this general name from the mosslike growth of their small rounded hummocks or dense mats, are mainly represented in cultivation by hybrids such as *S.* 'Peter Pan'. Two other groups rich in alpine treasures are the Kabschia and Engleria sections. In both, the silver rosettes, encrusted with lime, are densely packed. These saxifrages are often prized plants for an alpine house, but those described can be grown outdoors, ideally in tufa, especially if protected from excessive wet in winter. The purple saxifrage (*S. oppositifolia*) does not fit into any of the above categories, but is one of the most widely distributed of all the alpine species.

Such is the quality and number of the alpine saxifages that the larger species, mainly woodland plants although some of them are well suited to flower beds, are easily overlooked. In the descriptions that follow, border and woodland saxifrages appear after the alpines.

CULTIVATION Saxifrages have varying requirements. Many alpine species are best in light shade and require well-drained soil that is neutral to alkaline (potting media with added limestone chips). *S. longifolia* and the plants described with it thrive in full sun and need very sharp drainage, but *S. cotyledon* and its progeny are best on lime-free soil. The mossy saxifrages such as *S.* 'Peter Pan' require shade and a reasonably moist but well-drained soil that is neutral to slightly acid, with grit added. The border and woodland saxifrages tolerate partial or full shade and require well-drained but moist soil that is rich in organic matter.

PROPAGATION By division, in spring. From rosette cuttings, in late spring or early summer. From seed, sown in autumn.

POTENTIAL PROBLEMS Slugs, aphids, red spider mites.

ALPINE SAXIFRAGES

S. × anglica 'Cranbourne'
Flowers: early summer. H:1in (2.5cm), S:6–8in (15–20cm). Z:4–9.
Even the purists cannot fail to see the winning qualities of this hybrid Kabschia saxifrage. The almost stemless flowers, scattered thickly over huddled gray-green rosettes, are at first a deep and vivid pink, but then turn paler as they age.

S. 'Gregor Mendel'
Flowers: early spring. H:3–4in (8–10cm), S:6–10in (15–25cm). Z:6–7.
Few of the Kabschia saxifrages perform better in the rock garden. In their season, the pale yellow flowers almost obscure the cushion of tight glossy leaves. They also do well planted in walls.

Saxifraga 'Gregor Mendel'

S. 'Jenkinsiae'
Flowers: early spring. H:1–2in (2.5– 5cm), S:8–12in (20–30cm). Z:4–6.
Although the rosettes do not have the exquisite tightness of some Kabschias, the vigor of this hybrid counts when it is grown in the rock garden. Quantities of dark-centered pale pink flowers cover the low gray-green cushion in spring.

Saxifraga 'Jenkinsiae'

S. longifolia *Pyrenees*
Pyrenean saxifrage
Flowers: summer. H:18–24in (45–60cm), S:8–12in (20–30cm). Z:5–7.
In the wild, the species establishes in a cliff-face niche and extends arching sprays that are dense and dazzling with innumerable cup-shaped flowers. *S.* '**Tumbling Waters**', said to be a natural hybrid with *S. longifolia* as one of its parents, is, if it is possible, an even more magnificent plant. Another of the silver or encrusted saxifrages is *S. cotyledon* (Z:5–8), a white-flowered species distributed in mountainous Europe. *S.* '**Southside Seedling**', (Z:5–8), a cultivar or hybrid of it, produces sprays up to 1ft (30cm) tall of white flowers with heavy red markings.

S. oppositifolia *Arctic, mountains of Europe, North America, W. Asia*
Purple saxifrage
Flowers: early summer. H:1in (2.5cm), S:8–12in (20–30cm). Z:2–7.
The astonishingly wide distribution of this alpine species accounts for its varied appearance. As it is usually seen, the cup-shaped, almost stemless, purplish-pink flowers stand shoulder to shoulder above an evergreen mat of hoary leaves.

S. 'Peter Pan'
Flowers: late spring. H:2–3in (5–7.5cm), S:10–12in (25–30cm). Z:4–8.
Like most of the mossy saxifrages in yards, this is a hybrid. In spring, wiry stems make a miniature crimson forest that supports a canopy of pink cups. *S.* '**Triumph**', which has bright red flowers, is one of many on a larger scale, with stems up to 6in (15cm) tall.

Saxifraga 'Peter Pan'

BORDER AND WOODLAND SAXIFRAGES

S. fortunei *Japan*
Foliage: early summer to mid-autumn. Flowers: late summer to early autumn. H:12–18in (30–45cm), S:12–15in (30–38cm). Z:6–8.
The semievergreen foliage is of long-lasting beauty, the scalloped edge echoed in overlapping leaves, which are kidney shaped or rounded and purplish-red on the underside. In some cultivars, such as *S.* '**Rubrifolia**', the upper surface is bronze-red. The showers of small white flowers make a dramatic late appearance, the unequal size of the petals creating the effect of a hovering cloud of insects.

Saxifraga ×urbium

S. × urbium
London pride
Foliage: year-round. Flowers: early summer. H:12–18in (30–45cm), S:18–24in (45–60cm). Z:4–8.
In gardens, London pride has largely displaced **S. umbrosa**, one of its parents. Even on poor soils the interloper makes respectable groundcover. Leathery rosettes of spoon-shaped, toothed leaves spread freely, and in spring tall stems support a haze of tiny white flowers that are pink at the center.

SCABIOSA

DIPSACACEAE Pincushion flower, scabious

The pincushion of the scabious flower, so attractive to bees and butterflies, is formed by a dome of central flowerets with protruding styles, and is surrounded by ray flowerets, which in the showiest species are wavy and overlapping. The 75 or so annual and perennial species are found mostly in the Mediterranean region, but also in the rest of Europe, Africa, Asia, and Japan. They are plants of grassland or rocky slopes, usually on alkaline soils. The star of the perennials is S. caucasica, a long-flowering bedding plant, provided it is deadheaded regularly. It needs to be divided every 3 to 4 years. 'Stäfa' (Z:4–9) is a dark blue clone. A few shorter-growing species, including **S. graminifolia** (Z:5–9), are suitable for rock gardens. Sweet scabious (**S. atropurpurea**), with fragrant flowers in shades of pink to purple or white, is an annual that originates

Scabiosa caucasica 'Stäfa'

from southern Europe.
CULTIVATION Require full sun and well-drained neutral or slightly alkaline soil.
PROPAGATION From seed, sown as soon as ripe or in spring. By division, in spring. From basal cuttings, in spring.
POTENTIAL PROBLEMS Usually none.

Scabiosa 'Butterfly Blue'

S. 'Butterfly Blue'
Flowers: mid- to late summer.
H and S:14–18in (35–45cm). Z:3–9.
The small scabious (**S. columbaria**), which is a plant of alkaline grassland in Europe, is said to be a parent of this hybrid. During the summer, the hybrid provides a long display of mauve-blue flowers over divided gray-green leaves.

Scabiosa caucasica 'Miss Willmott'

S. caucasica *Caucasus, N.E. Turkey, N. Iran*
Flowers: early summer to early autumn. H:18–24in (45–60cm), S:16–20in (40–50cm). Z:4–9.
A basal clump of gray-green leaves produces numerous, almost leafless, stems carrying solitary pale blue or mauve-blue flowers up to 3in (7.5cm) across. Named clones include the soft mauve 'Clive Greaves' and the white 'Miss Willmott'.

SCHIZOSTYLIS

IRIDACEAE Kaffir lily

The single species is found wild in the Drakensberg Mountains of Natal and Lesotho, usually growing near streams. In the garden, it will produce long-lasting spikes of lustrous, cup-shaped flowers in the

autumn, provided it is kept well supplied with moisture through the summer months. The flowers are as good for cutting as they are for garden display.
CULTIVATION Requires full sun and moist, well-drained soil.
PROPAGATION By division, in spring. From seed, sown in spring at 55–61°F (13–16°C).
POTENTIAL PROBLEMS Usually none.

Schizostylis coccinea 'Major'

S. coccinea *Lesotho, South Africa, Swaziland*
Flowers: early autumn. H:24–30in (60–75cm), S:9–12in (23–30cm). Z:6–9.
In moisture-retentive soil, the rhizomatous roots form large, nearly evergreen clumps of narrow, bladelike leaves; in early autumn they are thick with spikes of up to 10 cup-shaped, scarlet flowers that are starry when fully open. Cultivars include the pink and rather small-flowered '**Mrs. Hegarty**' and '**Viscountess Byng**'. Hearty plants with large flowers include '**Major**', which is sheeny red, and '**Sunrise**', with silky salmon-pink flowers.

Schizostylis coccinea 'Sunrise'

SEDUM

CRASSULACEAE Stonecrop

The 400 or so species of succulents in this large genus are of very varied character and widely distributed. The majority are from mountainous regions in the Northern Hemisphere, while some originate in arid parts of South America. The more tender specimens, such as the Mexican

S. striatum *Argentina, Chile*
Flowers: early to mid-summer.
H:12–18in (30–45cm), S:6–12in
(15–30cm). Z:6–9.
The plain-leaved form of this
evergreen is no match ornamentally
for **'Aunt May'**, with its vertical
creamy stripes on irislike leaves.
Stiff stems zigzag above the foliage
from one small cluster of pale
yellow flowers to another.
S. californicum (Z:8–9), about
18in (45cm) tall, has brighter
yellow flowers with dark veining.

Sisyrinchium striatum

SMILACINA

CONVALLARIACEAE False Solomon's
seal

The foliage of the most frequently
grown species shows clearly the
link between this genus and true
Solomon's seals. Most of the 25 or
so rhizomatous perennials in the
genus are woodland plants of
central and eastern Asia as well as
North and Central America.
CULTIVATION Tolerate partial or
deep shade and require moist,
well-drained soil, rich in organic
matter, that is lime-free.
PROPAGATION By division, in spring.
From seed, sown in autumn.
POTENTIAL PROBLEMS Usually none.

S. racemosa *Mexico,
North America*
False spikenard
Foliage: early to late spring.
Flowers: mid- to late spring.
H:30–36in (75–90cm), S:18–24in
(45–60cm). Z:4–9.
The arching stems, clothed with
strongly veined leaves that are

Smilacina racemosa

alternate but closely arranged, are
tipped with fluffy tapering heads
of creamy fragrant flowers.

SOLDANELLA

PRIMULACEAE Snowbell

In lowland gardens, soldanellas do
not take kindly to winter wet, but
where they do succeed, these
European alpines speak modestly
but eloquently of high mountains
being freed from frost and snow.
Panes of glass and cloches may
look unsightly, but can be used
effectively to keep plants dry.
There are about 10 species in all
in the genus.
CULTIVATION Tolerate full sun or
partial shade and require moist,
very well-drained soil, rich in
organic matter (equal parts lime-
free media, leaf mold, and grit).
PROPAGATION By division, in early
spring. From seed, sown as soon as
ripe and subjected to cold.
POTENTIAL PROBLEMS Slugs, snails.

Soldanella carpatica

S. alpina *Mountains of C. and
S. Europe*
Alpine snowbell
Flowers: early spring. H:3–6in
(7.5–15cm), S:6–9in (15–23cm).
Z:5–8.
Blue-purple flowers nod above a
base of thick kidney-shaped
evergreen leaves. The similar
S. carpatica, originating from the
western Carpathians, flowers
more freely.

SOLIDAGO

ASTERACEAE Aaron's rod, goldenrod

The coarse naturalized plants that
cover wasteland in many parts of
the temperate world in late
summer and autumn with their
plumelike heads of fluffy flowers
give an indication of the pushy
character of some of the 100 or so
species in this mainly North
American genus. These are
vigorous colonizers and they self-
seed freely. The best of the taller
kinds of Aaron's rod, such as the
hybrid **'Golden Wings'** (Z:4–9),
which grows to 6ft (1.8m) tall,

have their place in wild gardens
where the soil is poor. More
suitable for flower beds are several
smaller hybrids.
CULTIVATION Require full sun and
light, well-drained soil.
PROPAGATION By division, in autumn
or spring.
POTENTIAL PROBLEMS Powdery
mildew.

Solidago 'Goldenmosa'

S. hybrids
Flowers: late summer to early
autumn. H:24–30in (60–75cm),
S:16–20in (40–50cm). Z:4–9.
'Goldenmosa' is widely used as a
mid-height plant, its yellow froth
reaching a height of 30in (75cm).
'Queenie' is only about 10in
(25cm) tall, and its dense heads
make a bright yellow front-of-bed
plant. **'Luteus'** is often listed under
Solidago, but belongs to a
bigeneric cross (× **Solidaster
luteus**, Z:4–8) between a *Solidago*
and an *Aster.* It has larger daisy
flowers than a true Aaron's rod,
and their lemon-yellow plumes, up
to 30in (75cm) tall, are attractive in
the yard over many weeks and
provide good material for cutting.

STACHYS

LAMIACEAE

Relatively few of the 300 or so
species of this genus find a place
in gardens, but 1, the softly
hairy lambs' ears (*S. byzantina*), is
widely used as a gray foliage plant.
The species are found in a wide
range of habitats, but those in
cultivation are perennials or
subshrubs that need plenty of sun
and good drainage. Rock-garden
species require very well-drained,
gritty soil. Winter wet should be
kept to a minimum by covering
with glass panes or well-ventilated
plastic cloches.
CULTIVATION Require full sun and
well-drained soil (potting media
with added grit).
PROPAGATION By division, in early
spring. From seed, sown in autumn
or spring.
POTENTIAL PROBLEMS Slugs;
powdery mildew.

S. byzantina *Caucasus to Iran*
Lambs' ears, lambs' lugs, lambs' tails, lambs' tongues
Foliage: year-round. Flowers: early summer to early autumn.
H:12–18in (30–45cm), S:1–2ft (30–60cm). Z:4–8.
The thick gray leaves owe their wooly texture and appearance to a dense covering of silvery hairs. '**Silver Carpet**' is nonflowering and particularly effective in making close ground-covering mats. Other cultivars produce wooly square stems with small magenta flowers that are less impressive than the spike itself. '**Cotton Boll**' produces the flower stems, but dispenses with the flowers, contenting itself with a string of curious bobbles.

Stachys byzantina 'Silver Carpet'

S. macrantha *Caucasus, N.E. Turkey, N.W. Iran*
Flowers: early summer to early autumn. H:18–30in (45–75cm), S:12–18in (30–45cm). Z:4–8.
Branching stems that emerge from dark green clumps of wrinkled and scalloped leaves carry whorls of purplish-pink funnel-shaped flowers. '**Robusta**' and '**Superba**' are superior forms.

STOKESIA

ASTERACEAE Stokes' aster

Fringed ray flowerets surround the central disk so that the flowerheads of the single species in this genus from the south-eastern USA have a cornflower-like appearance. Stokes' aster, which is found wild on moist acid soils, is a sprawling plant that is easily stiffened by twiggy supports and best positioned at the front of a moist bed. The rosette of strap-shaped leaves is evergreen. The colorful flowers are particularly good for cutting. A deep, dry mulch should be provided in areas with severe winters.
CULTIVATION Requires full sun and moist, well-drained soil that is acid.
PROPAGATION From seed, sown in autumn. By division, in spring. From root cuttings, in late winter.
POTENTIAL PROBLEMS Usually none.

S. laevis *S.E. USA*
Flowers: mid-summer to early autumn. H:12–18in (30–45cm), S:16–20in (40–50cm). Z:5–9.
Regular deadheading will help to provide a long succession of flowerheads over the evergreen foliage. The long-lasting flowerheads are purplish blue with a creamy center. The white '**Alba**' is equally appealing.

Stokesia laevis

SYMPHYTUM

BORAGINACEAE Comfrey

The watch-spring uncurling of the buds, which open into tubular flowers, is fascinating, but most of the 25 or so species from Europe, North Africa, and western Asia are aggressively colonizing woodland perennials with rhizomatous roots that form large patches of rather coarse foliage. They should be confined to the wildest parts of the garden, where they belong. One of the best for such a position is **S. 'Rubrum'** (Z:4–8), which makes good groundcover about 18in (45cm) tall with red flowers in spring. The pick are those with variegated foliage, all the better if flower stems are cut down.
CULTIVATION Tolerate full sun or partial shade and require moist, fertile soil.
PROPAGATION By division, in spring. From root cuttings, in early winter.
POTENTIAL PROBLEMS Slugs, when establishing.
WARNING Skin irritation may occur from contact with the foliage. Stomach upsets may occur if the root or leaf sections are swallowed.

S. × uplandicum 'Variegatum'
Foliage: mid-spring to autumn.
Flowers: late spring to late summer. H:30–36in (75–90cm), S:24–30in (60–75cm). Z:4–8.
Its tendency to revert, which is more likely if the roots are damaged or the plant is grown in poor soil, is a drawback, but the irregular cream margins of the gray-green leaves make this a very striking plant in shade. Its flowers

Symphytum × uplandicum 'Variegatum'

are mauve-pink. A shorter-growing variegated comfrey is the hybrid **S. 'Goldsmith'**, which makes a mound about 1ft (30cm) tall with yellow and cream markings on dark green. The flowers are blue, pink, or less frequently cream.

Symphytum 'Goldsmith'

TANACETUM

ASTERACEAE

Two herbs belonging to this genus of about 70 species, which are mostly found in dry open sites in the Northern Hemisphere, give a misleading idea of the range the genus encompasses. Feverfew (**T. parthenium**, Z:4–9) is a short-lived but prodigal self-seeder, which in the ornamental garden is best represented by doubles such as '**White Bonnet**' (Z:4–9) or the yellow-leaved '**Aureum**' (Z:4–9). More acridly aromatic is tansy (**T. vulgare**, Z:4–9), fast spreading but with attractively dissected leaves, especially in the curly-leaved **var. crispum** (Z:4–9), and yellow flowerheads. Pyrethrums (**T. coccineum**) are attractive daisies for beds and cutting, and several gray-leaved plants are suitable for rock gardens or edging. They give a second display of flowers if they are cut back after the first flush.
CULTIVATION Require full sun and very well-drained soil.
PROPAGATION By division, in spring or after flowering. From seed, sown in early spring at 50–55°F (10–13°C).
POTENTIAL PROBLEMS Aphids, leaf miners, chrysanthemum nematodes.

WARNING Skin allergies may be aggravated by foliage contact.

T. coccineum *Caucasus, S.W. Asia*

Painted daisy, pyrethrum
Flowers: early summer. H:18–36in (45–90cm), S:16–20in (40–50cm). Z:5–9.
Feathery bright green foliage is topped by yellow-centered daisy flowerheads. These are up to 3in (7.5cm) across in the single and double cultivars which vary in color from white to pink and crimson. The single '**Brenda**' is a vivid cerise-pink.

Tanacetum coccineum 'Brenda'

T. densum subsp. amani
Turkey

Foliage: spring to mid-winter. Flowers: late summer. H:6–8in (15–20cm), S:10–16in (25–40cm). Z:6–8.
Felted, deeply cut leaves make low silvery mounds, which gardeners find more appealing without the clusters of yellow flowers.
T. haradjanii (Z:6–9) is similar but slightly larger in leaf, and the flowerheads have no ray flowerets.

TELLIMA

SAXIFRAGACEAE Fringe cups

The saxifrage family provides in the single species of the genus yet another good plant for groundcover. In the wild, this evergreen is found in moist forest and woodland over a large area of western North America. As a garden plant it is at its best in light shade where the soil is moist. Nevertheless, it is remarkably drought tolerant.
CULTIVATION Tolerates full sun and dry soil, but best in moist soil rich in organic matter, and partial shade.
PROPAGATION By division, in spring. From seed, sown as soon as ripe.
POTENTIAL PROBLEMS Slugs.

T. grandiflora *W. North America (Alaska to California)*

Flowers: late spring to mid-summer. H:18–24in (45–60cm), S:12–18in (30–45cm). Z:4–8.
The hairy leaves, which are round and scalloped, take on crimson

Tellima grandiflora Rubra Group

tints in autumn. The numerous tiny bells, which are carried on erect spikes, open greenish yellow but develop a pink tinge as they age. The leaves of the **Rubra Group** are reddish purple on the underside and color richly in autumn and winter.

THALICTRUM

RANUNCULACEAE Meadow rue

The best of the thalictrums manage to be stately in their general effect, but dainty in their detail, with delicate foliage and fluffy or airy heads of small flowers. There are more than 120 species, most of them plants of the temperate Northern Hemisphere found wild in meadows and woodland, usually in moist soil and often in light shade. The species described are distinguished border plants, but the more fine boned are best among sheltering shrubs that give them some support. Staking is almost fatal to their charm.
CULTIVATION Tolerate full sun or partial shade and a wide range of soils, but best in well-drained but moist soil, preferably neutral to acid, with plenty of organic matter.
PROPAGATION By division, in early spring. From seed, sown as soon as ripe or in early spring.
POTENTIAL PROBLEMS Slugs; powdery mildew.

T. aquilegiifolium *Europe to temperate Asia*

Foliage: late spring to late summer. Flowers: summer. H:2–3ft (60–90cm), S:18–24in (45–60cm). Z:5–8.

Thalictrum aquilegiifolium

The specific name draws attention to the fans of columbine-like foliage, which are carried on purple stems. These are topped by sprays of tiny purplish buds that open to misty clusters of mauve-pink stamens. In '**Thundercloud**' the stamens are dark purple.

T. delavayi *E. Tibet to W. China*

Flowers: mid-summer to early autumn. H:4–5ft (1.2–1.5m), S:18–24in (45–60cm). Z:5–8.
The refined foliage is matched by the swaying grace of large open heads of tiny pendant flowers, their purple sepals opening to show creamy stamens. There is a lovely white, '**Album**', and in '**Hewitt's Double**' an explosion of tiny mauve-blue pompons is magically suspended in midair.

Thalictrum delavayi

T. flavum *Europe to Caucasus and Siberia*

Yellow meadow rue
Flowers: summer. H:4–5ft (1.2–1.5m), S:16–20in (40–50cm). Z:5–9.
This species, with fragrant yellow flowers, is coarser than the others described, but **subsp. glaucum** is impressive in stature and in the combination of blue-gray foliage and pale yellow, fluffy flowers.

TIARELLA

SAXIFRAGACEAE Foam flower

The common name suggests that the flowers are the principal feature of the half dozen or so woodland plants that make up this genus. The airy sprays of small flowers are delightful in spring and early summer, but the foliage is of more enduring appeal and, in this respect, the genus is similar to the closely related *Heuchera*. The best-known species are North American, but the genus is also represented in eastern Asia.
CULTIVATION Tolerate deep or partial shade and require moist, cool soil, rich in organic matter.
PROPAGATION From seed, as soon as ripe or in spring. By division, in spring.
POTENTIAL PROBLEMS Slugs.

T. cordifolia *North America*
Foam flower
Foliage: autumn. Flowers: late spring to early summer. H:6-12in (15-30cm), S:10-14in (25-35cm). Z:3-8. Creeping rhizomes ensure a good, even excessive, cover of greenish-yellow, hairy leaves, which are gently lobed, have a serrated outline, and are deeply veined. Erect stems carry the foaming floral display of tiny, creamy stars.

T. wherryi *USA (Appalachians)*
Foliage: autumn. Flowers: late spring to early summer. H:8-12in (20-30cm), S:8-14in (20-35cm). Z:3-8. This species, which does not have the wandering root system of *T. cordifolia*, slowly builds up a clump of maplelike leaves. Variations of foliage coloring in the wild are reflected in several named clones, **'Bronze Beauty'** showing a mixture of green and purplish-brown. Flower color varies from white to pale pink.

Tiarella wherryi

TOLMIEA

SAXIFRAGACEAE Piggyback plant, youth-on-age

The common names of the single species in this genus refer to the way young plants are produced on the leaves. In the wild it is found spreading freely on the floor of coniferous woodland. Although it is widely grown as a houseplant, it makes effective groundcover under shrubs and trees, when it is protected from strong sun, which will scorch the leaves.
CULTIVATION Tolerates partial or deep shade and requires cool, moist soil, rich in organic matter.
PROPAGATION By division, in spring. By removal of leaf plantlets, mid- to late summer. From seed, sown in autumn.
POTENTIAL PROBLEMS Usually none.

T. menziesii *W. North America*
Piggyback plant, thousand mothers, youth-on-age
Flowers: late spring to early summer. H:12-20in (30-50cm), S:18-24in (45-60cm). Z:6-9.

The hairy leaves, lobed and toothed so that they strongly resemble those of *Tiarella cordifolia*, are more important ornamentally than the spires of small, slightly fragrant, purplish-brown flowers. **'Taff's Gold'** has pale green leaves irregularly speckled with pale yellow.

Tolmiea menziesii 'Taff's Gold'

TRADESCANTIA

COMMELINACEAE Spiderwort

The very varied species in this genus, totaling about 65 and coming from a range of habitats in North, Central, and South America, include several, like the wandering Jew (**T. fluminensis**, Z:10-11), that are best known as conservatory plants. A foliage, mat-forming species, it is most suitable for hanging baskets. The most familiar of the spiderworts seen in temperate gardens are hybrids derived in part from **T. virginiana** (Z:4-9). These all show a preference for moist conditions, although they are prone to making leafy growth at the expense of flowers, if they are grown in a highly fertile soil.
CULTIVATION Tolerate full sun or partial shade and require moist soil.
PROPAGATION By division of hardy species and cultivars, in spring or autumn.
POTENTIAL PROBLEMS Grubs, aphids, vine weevils.
WARNING Skin irritation may occur from contact with the foliage.

T. × andersoniana
Flowers: early summer to early autumn. H and S:18-24in (45-60cm). Z:4-9.
Although individual blooms are short-lived, they come in a long succession, small clusters of 3-petaled flowers, which have a fluff of stamen filaments in the center, spilling from between grooved leaves at the top of the flower stems. The foliage somewhat mars the effect, the amount of coarse untidy leaves being disproportionate to the flowers. The color range includes white, blue-purple, pink, and red-purple.

Tradescantia × andersoniana 'Isis'

'Isis' has large dark blue flowers, while **'J.C. Weguelin'** has large mauve-blue blooms with blue fluff in the center. Cutting back flowered stems prevents seeding and encourages the production of more flowers.

Tradescantia × andersoniana 'J.C. Weguelin'

TRICYRTIS

CONVALLARIACEAE Toad lily

The waxy speckled flowers of the toad lilies hold a unique fascination that makes these perennials worth planting wherever their detail can be enjoyed. The strap-shaped segments open to form a dished star with a sturdy arrangement of stamens and styles in the center. There are about 16 species, all found in Asia, mainly in rugged and wooded habitats where the soil is moist. When they are grown at the margins of their hardiness, they should be protected in winter with a deep mulch.
CULTIVATION Tolerate deep or partial shade and require moist, well-drained soil, rich in organic matter.
PROPAGATION By division, in early spring. From seed, sown as soon as ripe.
POTENTIAL PROBLEMS Slugs, snails.

T. formosana *Taiwan*
Flowers: early autumn. H and S:2-3ft (60-90cm). Z:5-9.
Gently zigzagging stems clothed in glossy oval leaves that are deeply veined carry branched heads of upward-facing pale mauve flowers, heavily spotted with purple.

T. hirta *Japan*
Flowers: late summer to mid-autumn. H and S:24–30in (60–75cm). Z:5–9.
The pale green leaves of this clump-forming species are hairy, and the purple-spotted white flowers are borne in the leaf axils. **'Miyazaki'** has large flowers and an arching growth habit.

Tricyrtis hirta 'Miyazaki'

TRILLIUM

TRILLIACEAE Trinity flower, wood lily

The arrangement of leaves, petals, and calyces in threes is the hallmark of this mainly North American genus of 30 or so woodland species. Their numerical obsession is not the only factor contributing to their homogenous character, for they are all plants preferring cool moist conditions and fertile soil well laced with leaf mold. Most are, at the least, fascinating, and several are plants of sublime radiance and poise, justifying a prime position in a woodland garden. The dwarf species, such as *T. rivale*, with white or pale pink flowers lightly spotted purple, are prize plants for peat beds.
CULTIVATION Tolerate partial or deep shade and require well-drained but moist soil, preferably neutral to acid, that contains plenty of organic matter.
PROPAGATION By rhizome division, in late summer or autumn. From seed, sown as soon as ripe.
POTENTIAL PROBLEMS Slugs, snails.

T. chloropetalum *USA (California)*
Flowers: early spring. H and S:12–18in (30–45cm). Z:4–9.
The fragrant flowers, which are usually greenish white but can also be bright yellow or purplish brown, stand erect above foliage that is mottled with gray-green and maroon. The smaller toad-shade (**T. sessile**, Z:5–9), usually less than 1ft (30cm) tall, which also has marbled and blotched leaves, has maroon flowers with narrow petals standing erect above spread-out sepals. Both sepals and petals are usually a shade of deep maroon.

Trillium chloropetalum

T. grandiflorum *E. North America*
Wake robin
Flowers: late spring to early summer. H and S:12–18in (30–45cm). Z:4–9.
The unrivaled queen of the genus carries its veined but pristine white flowers, backed by green sepals, above a low mound of dark green leaves. When fully open, the flowers are almost triangular in outline, despite the wavy margin of the petals and their recurved tips. The double **Flore Pleno** defies all reservations that purists might have about double flowers.

Trillium grandiflorum

TROLLIUS

RANUNCULACEAE Globeflower

A liking for moisture characterizes the 20 or so species of the buttercup-like, clump-forming globeflower, which are found throughout the temperate regions of the Northern Hemisphere. In gardens, they are generally represented by a range of hybrids, but one of the parents, the common European globeflower (**T. europaeus,** Z:3–7), which is found in northeastern North America as well as Europe, is not to be overlooked. The cool radiance of its exquisite, pale yellow orbs is as telling in the yard as it is in the subalpine meadows where it is most commonly found in the wild. Globeflowers naturalized near water brighten a wild or semiwild garden in late spring and early summer, but their early season also makes them valuable for beds where the soil does not dry out.
CULTIVATION Tolerate full sun or partial shade but best in sun where the soil is permanently moist, as in a bog garden.
PROPAGATION By division, in early spring. From seed, sown as soon as ripe or in spring.
POTENTIAL PROBLEMS Powdery mildew.

Trollius europaeus

T. × cultorum
Flowers: mid-spring to mid-summer. H:2–3ft (60–90cm), S:18–24in (45–60cm). Z:3–7.
The hybrids that go under this name make strong clumps of lobed and jaggedly toothed leaves, the globular flowers held well clear of this attractive glossy green base by erect stems. All have flowers in the yellow to orange range. **'Feuertroll'** and **'Orange Princess'** are in shades of orange, while **'Goldquelle'** is yellow. **'Alabaster'** is a less vigorous hybrid, growing to 2ft (60cm) in height, but the yellowed ivory of its flowers is unique.

Trollius × cultorum 'Alabaster'

UVULARIA

CONVALLARIACEAE Merrybells

The woodland plants in this North American genus of 5 species are shy and easily overlooked if not positioned prominently in a shady flower bed or peat bed.

CULTIVATION Tolerate deep or partial shade and require moist, well-drained soil, rich in organic matter.
PROPAGATION By division, in early spring. From seed, sown as soon as ripe.
POTENTIAL PROBLEMS Slugs, snails.

U. grandiflora *E. North America*
Large merrybells
Flowers: mid- to late spring.
H:24-30in (60-75cm), 9-12in (23-30cm). Z:4-9.
The drooping foliage and the topmost dangling yellow flowers with their curiously twisted bright yellow segments convey the impression that the plant is just pulling itself out of a heavy torpor. The shorter *U. perfoliata*, about 18in (45cm) tall, is slightly later flowering and the flowers are paler in color.

Uvularia grandiflora

VERATRUM

MELANTHIACEAE

The genus contains nearly 50 species, of which only a handful are in general cultivation. Even these are somewhat neglected, perhaps because they are so slow to reach flowering size from seed. Plants of moist ground in woodland or meadows in the Northern Hemisphere, they achieve their full splendor in rich, well-watered soil, preferably lightly shaded, and where a cordon sanitaire keeps drooling slugs and snails at bay.
CULTIVATION Tolerate sun or partial shade and require moist, well-drained soil, rich in organic matter.
PROPAGATION By division, in autumn. From seed, sown as soon as ripe.
POTENTIAL PROBLEMS Slugs, snails.
WARNING Foliage contact may irritate skin. Swallowing any part is very toxic.

V. nigrum *Europe to China, Korea, Siberia*
Foliage: spring to late summer.
Flowers: mid- to late summer.
H:2-5ft (60-150cm), S:18-24in (45-60cm). Z:3-8.
Deeply veined and pleated leaves,

up to 1ft (30cm) long, mound up together to form an impressive base from which rises a tall stem. Its short branches are densely set with small starry flowers of purple-black or maroon. In its almost funereal distinction, this species outclasses the false or white hellebore (*V. album*), with greenish-white flowers.

Veratrum nigrum

VERBASCUM

SCROPHULARIACEAE Mullein

The genus of more than 350 species from Europe, North Africa, and western and central Asia includes many biennials, among them *V. bombyciferum* (Z:6-8), which is silvered with fine hairs. Even most of the perennials, such as the purple mullein (*V. phoeniceum*, Z:6-8), tend to be short-lived. Numerous species survive in very dry, stony landscapes, and most need an open position. They are ideal for growing in gravel or sunny borders. Shorter mulleins, such as *V. 'Letitia'* (Z:6-8), up to 1ft (30cm) with bright yellow flowers, are good for rock gardens or raised flower beds.
CULTIVATION Require full sun and poor, alkaline well-drained soil.
PROPAGATION From seed, sown in late spring or early summer. By division, in spring. From root cuttings, in winter.
POTENTIAL PROBLEMS Weevils, caterpillars; powdery mildew.

V. chaixii *C., E., and S. Europe*
Nettle-leaved mullein
Flowers: mid- to late summer.
H:3-4ft (90-120cm), S:18-24in (45-60cm). Z:5-9.
The plant is anchored by a semi-evergreen rosette of hairy basal leaves, from which rises a felted stem densely set with pale yellow flowers that have bruised purple eyes.

V. 'Helen Johnson'
Flowers: early to late summer.
H:30-36in (75-90cm), S:12-16in (30-40cm). Z:5-8.
Purple-tinted copper and buff, soft-textured flowers combined with gray foliage, felted stems, and wooly buds are a designer success.

Verbascum 'Helen Johnson'

VERBENA

VERBENACEAE

The colorful hybrid verbenas that are popular as bedding and container plants have stolen the limelight from the 250 or so species, most of which come from warm temperate or tropical areas of North, Central, or South America. Although the hybrids are perennials, they are half-hardy and almost invariably grown as annuals. This option is usually followed for the few species that are grown in yards, such as the tuberous *V. rigida* (Z:8-10), with its fragrant, purple flowers. The wiry *V. bonariensis*, at first sight most unlike the hybrid verbenas, makes a tall and airy addition to dry sunny beds and is excellent planted in gravel. It is most attractive when allowed to self-seed and form irregular colonies with individuals nosing their way into other plants. See also ANNUALS AND BIENNIALS.
CULTIVATION Require full sun and well-drained, moist soil.
PROPAGATION From seed, sown in autumn or spring. By division, in spring.
POTENTIAL PROBLEMS Aphids, thrips, slugs; powdery mildew.

Verbena rigida

Verbena bonariensis

V. bonariensis *South America (Brazil to Argentina)*
Flowers: mid-summer to early autumn. H:4-6ft (1.2-1.8m), S:18-24in (45-60cm). Z:7-10.
An angular framework of rigid branching stems rising from a base of rough leaves supports numerous tight clusters of small purplish-pink flowers over a long season. The flowers are fragrant and attractive to butterflies.

VERONICA

SCROPHULARIACEAE Speedwell

Although the color range of the speedwells includes white and pink, it is their blues that stand out in the yard and even make of the irrepressible white-eyed
V. filiformis (Z:4-8) a very beautiful weed. There are about 250 species from a wide range of habitats, most of them in Europe. The low-growing species, including a number of alpines, are usually plants of open sites where the ground drains freely; they are suitable for rock gardens, the front of beds, and for planting among paving or in gravel. The taller species tend to be plants of richer, moister soils. Some species and cultivars require protection from too much winter wet under the shelter of a pane of glass or a very well-ventilated plastic cloche.
CULTIVATION Tolerate full sun or partial shade and require well-drained, loamy, moist soil (equal parts loam, leaf mold, and grit).
PROPAGATION From seed, sown in autumn. By division, in spring or autumn.
POTENTIAL PROBLEMS Powdery mildew, downy mildew.

V. austriaca subsp. **teucrium**
Europe
Flowers: summer. H and S:1-2ft (30-60cm). Z:5-8.
This low-growing plant is usually represented in gardens by named clones that are outstanding for the intensity of their blue spikes. The gentian brilliance of **'Crater Lake Blue'**, 1ft (30cm) tall, is almost

matched by the blue of the slightly taller **'Kapitän'**. The short spikes of a similar species, *V. prostrata* (Z:4-8), are also upright, but the stems lie close to the ground. In **'Trehane'** (Z:4-8), blue flowers are set against yellow-tinged foliage.

Veronica austriaca subsp. teucrium 'Crater Lake Blue'

V. cinerea *E. Mediterranean, Turkey*
Flowers: early summer. H:4-6in (10-15cm), S:9-12in (23-30cm). Z:5-9.
The flowers are tiny, but their blue strikes a piercing note against the dense silvery mat of felted leaves.

V. gentianoides *Caucasus, N. and C. Turkey, Ukraine (Crimea)*
Flowers: early summer. H and S:9-18in (23-45cm). Z:4-8.
Spikes of pale blue flowers rising from mats of fleshy dark green leaves make cool short verticals for the front of flower beds or large rock gardens.

V. peduncularis *Caucasus, Turkey, Ukraine*
Flowers: early spring to early summer. H:4-6in (10-15cm), S:24-30in (60-75cm). Z:6-9.
A low mat or cushion of purple-tinged leaves is swamped in mid-summer by white-eyed blue flowers shaped like saucers. **'Georgia Blue'** is a free-flowering cultivar.

Veronica spicata subsp. incana 'Nana'

V. spicata *Europe to Turkey, C. and E. Asia*
Flowers: summer. H:1-2ft (30-60cm), S:6-12in (15-30cm). Z:4-8.

The cone-shaped flower spikes stand up from a mat of gray-green leaves, pink in **'Heidekind'** and white in **'Icicle'**, variations on the bright blue, star-shaped flowers of the species. The hairy foliage of **subsp. incana**, the silver speedwell, is gray and a good base for the spikes of blue-purple flowers. **'Nana'** has violet-blue flowers.

VIOLA

VIOLACEAE

Generations of gardeners have felt a strong attachment to this genus, so striking in its contrasts of reserve and pertness. There are about 500 species in the genus, annuals and biennials as well as perennials, which are found in a wide variety of habitats in temperate regions of the world. Relatively few of these are seen outside specialized collections; it is the complex hybrids resulting from crosses between a small group of species account for the important role of the genus in gardens. The garden pansies (*V. × wittrockiana*)—and the European heartsease (*V. tricolor*, Z:4-8), which is one of the parents of this large group—are short-lived perennials that are usually grown as biennials. The hybrid violas (and the smaller violettas, which are similar to violas but even more compact, sweetly fragrant, and with no lines radiating from the central eye) are longer-lived. However, their heavy flowering takes its toll, and these plants need to be propagated on a regular basis to maintain their presence. The plants that are described here have many uses but they are particularly effective as a "skirt" to larger perennials and shrubs, at the front of beds, and in the rock garden. Regular deadheading prolongs the flowering season. Straggly plants of *V. cornuta* and hybrid violas that are cut back in mid-summer will make fresh growth and flower again during late summer and autumn. See also ANNUALS AND BIENNIALS.
CULTIVATION Tolerate full sun or partial shade and require well-drained soil that is moist and fertile (potting media with added leaf mold and grit).
PROPAGATION From basal cuttings, in the second half of summer. From seed, sown as soon as ripe or in spring.
POTENTIAL PROBLEMS Slugs, snails, aphids, red spider mites; powdery mildew, leaf spot, rust, mosaic viruses.

Viola cornuta Alba Group

V. cornuta *Spain (Pyrenees)*
Horned violet, viola
Flowers: late spring to late summer. H:6-12in (15-30cm), S:15-24in (38-60cm). Z:6-9.
The horned violet has played an important role in the development of hybrid violas. It is, though, a generous and endearing viola in its own right, filling in the leggy bases of other plants, even climbing among them and showing off over a long season with a prodigious display of mauve-blue flowers. The white of the **Alba Group** is unbeatable in the shade, and all its gradations of blue and purple are worth a place in the garden.

Viola 'Jackanapes'

V. hybrids
Tufted pansy, viola
Flowers: spring to autumn. H:4-8in (10-20cm), S:6-12in (15-30cm). Z:5-7.
Spreading stems clothed in toothed leaves carry masses of flowers over a long season. Some cultivars form sizeable mats, spreading by underground shoots. Most are lightly scented, some are very fragrant, and all have a lively charm. '**Huntercombe Purple**' is deep violet-purple with a tiny white eye; '**Irish Molly**', velvety and an unusual mixture of bronze and lime-green; '**Jackanapes**', small-flowered, with red-brown top petals and rays on the rich yellow lower petals; '**Maggie Mott**', pale mauve with a cream center and well scented; '**Molly Sanderson**', matt black with a tiny yellow eye; '**Vita**', small flowered, pale pink with a yellow eye.

V. odorata *S. and W. Europe*
English violet, garden violet, sweet violet
Flowers: late winter to early spring. H:4-6in (10-15cm), S:12-18in (30-45cm). Z:5-8.
The species, with sweetly scented blue or white flowers, spreads by stolons and self-seeds freely in shady, moist places. Some of the hybrids derived from it, which were once grown commercially on a vast scale, are still available.
V. '**Czar**' is long stemmed, and the large flowers are rich purple.

V. riviniana *Europe, N. Africa*
Common dog violet, wood violet
Flowers: late spring to early summer. H:4-8in (10-20cm), S:10-16in (25-40cm). Z:3-8.
Although its running growth soon makes it a nuisance elsewhere, in the wild garden the blue-purple, scentless flowers of the common dog violet set among heart-shaped leaves are a lovely discovery. The dark purple leaves and light purple flowers of the **Purpurea Group** are seen at their best when contrasted with light colors.

V. sororia *E. North America*
Sister violet, wooly blue violet
Flowers: late spring to summer. H:4-6in (10-15cm), S:6-8in (15-20cm). Z:4-8.
The species is unremarkable, with leaves that are hairy on the underside and flowers that are violet-blue or white with streaking, but '**Freckles**' (Z:4-9), its cultivar, has caught the imagination of gardeners with its spray-gunned spotting of purplish blue.

ZANTEDESCHIA

ARACEAE

All 6 species in this genus of aroids are moisture lovers, and in their home territory of South and East Africa they are found near open water or in swampy ground. The hardiest species is Z. aethiopica but in frost-prone areas the fleshy rhizomes need to be set deep in mud and protected with a mulch in winter. It can also be grown as a marginal aquatic in water no deeper than 1ft (30cm).
CULTIVATION Require full sun and moist soil or potting media rich in organic matter.
PROPAGATION By division, in spring. From seed, sown as soon as ripe at 70-81°F (21-27°C).
POTENTIAL PROBLEMS Aphids; fungal diseases, various viruses.
WARNING Sap contact can irritate skin. Swallowing any parts may cause stomach upsets.

Z. aethiopica *Lesotho, South Africa*
Arum lily
Foliage: spring to autumn. Flowers: late spring to mid-summer. H:3-4ft (90-120cm), S:20-30in (50-75cm). Z:8-10.
Dense clumps of glossy, arrow-shaped leaves make a lovely contrast to the lines of grasses and reeds near water. The flowerlike white spathe swirls with a couturier flourish around the yellow spadix, around which the tiny true flowers are clustered. '**Crowborough**' is said to be a particularly hardy clone. In '**Green Goddess**' the flowers are large and green except for a white throat.

Zantedeschia aethiopica

ZAUSCHNERIA

ONAGRACEAE Californian fuchsia

The 4 species in this genus are from dry stony habitats in western North America. Their tubular, red flowers are profuse from late summer to autumn and are at their best seen showering from a dry stone wall or a stepped rock garden.
CULTIVATION Require full sun and light well-drained soil.
PROPAGATION From basal cuttings, in spring. By division, in spring.
POTENTIAL PROBLEMS Slugs.

Z. californica *USA (California)*
Flowers: late summer to early autumn. H:12-18in (30-45cm), S:18-24in (45-60cm). Z:6-9.
The scarlet-flowered **subsp. cana**, with narrow hairy leaves, is deciduous, like its clone '**Dublin**', with brilliant orange-red flowers.

Zauschneria californica subsp. cana

bulbs, corms, and tubers

Although coming from surprisingly varied habitats, a key group of ornamentals depend on underground storage organs for their survival during seasonally harsh conditions. After their often sensational period in flower, top growth withers away, and new growth is not made until the onset of warmer weather, snow melt, or rain. As bulbs are usually consistent in their spread, few ranges are given in entries. In its strict sense, the term bulb refers to a storage organ consisting of fleshy scales attached to a basal plate. Daffodils are an example where the scales are covered by a papery tunic; in lilies the scales are exposed. In its broader sense, as used here and in plant catalogs, the term covers other types of storage organs as well: that of crocuses and gladioli, for example, is a corm, in fact the swollen base of a stem. Tubers, the storage organs of dahlias, are swollen sections of stem or root. Another kind of storage organ is the rhizome, a stem that develops at ground level or just below the surface. Rhizomatous plants are listed with perennials in this book.

Some of the best-known bulbs provide colorful incident throughout the year in beds, borders, and containers. The species make a less dramatic impact, but they include superb plants for naturalizing in grass.

Top Crocus chrysanthus 'Zwanenburg Bronze'
Center Colchicum agrippinum
Bottom Crocosmia × *crocosmiiflora* 'Emily McKenzie'

ALLIUM

ALLIACEAE Onion

The 500 or so mainly bulbous plants in this large genus include several of inestimable culinary value, among them chives, garlic, leeks, and onions. The onion or garlic smell haunts even the most ornamental species, but is rarely obtrusive except when leaves are bruised. The predominance of purplish mauve in the flower color is a limitation, and in the case of many species, the dying back of foliage before or just as the flowers develop calls for skillful masking of the base. Some species can be bothersome weeds. Even the yellow-flowered *A. moly* (Z:3–9) is best kept in the wild garden. The real strength of the genus lies in the number of summer-flowering bulbs it contains that thrive in hot, dry conditions. Some graceful small species, like the blue-flowered *A. beesianum* (Z:4–8) and *A. cyaneum* (Z:4–8) from China, are suitable for rock gardens. Others, including most of those described here, are impressive in scale and ideal for planting among shrubs and perennials that thrive in Mediterranean conditions. In some species the umbels can be used to make attractive winter decorations when the flowers have dried.
CULTIVATION Require full sun and well-drained soil. Plant in autumn, with bulbs covered to a depth 3 to 4 times the height of the bulb.
PROPAGATION From offsets of bulbous species in autumn. From division of rhizomatous species in spring; from seed as soon as ripe.
POTENTIAL PROBLEMS Fungal diseases, such as white rot.
WARNING Direct contact with bulbs may cause an allergic reaction.

A. atropurpureum *E. Europe*
Flowers: late spring to early summer. H:2–3ft (60–90cm), S:10in (25cm). Z:8–9.
The purplish-black depths of the wine-red flowers make this plant one of the most richly colored in the onion family. The small starry flowers, 2in (5cm) across, are borne in a hemispherical head.

A. caeruleum *N. and C. Asia*
Flowers: early summer. H:1–2ft (30–60cm), S:2in (5cm). Z:2–7.
The linear, mid-green, stem-clasping leaves die back by the time stiff stems carry tight heads, up to 1¾in (4cm) across, of star-shaped, sky-blue flowers. This species sometimes produces bulbils in the flowerhead.

Allium cristophii

A. cristophii *C. Asia, Turkey*
Flowers: early summer. H:10–20in (25–50cm), S:6in (15cm). Z:4–8.
The size of the spherical heads, up to 8in (20cm) across, and the metallic glint of the purple flowers, of which there may be up to 80 in a head, make this an eye-catching plant, and the dried heads are highly ornamental.

A. flavum *S. and E. Europe*
Flowers: mid- to late summer. H:4–12in (10–30cm), S:2–3in (5–7.5cm). Z:4–8.
There are dwarf forms of this variable species that make attractive plants for rock gardens and raised beds. The pale yellow, bell-shaped flowers are usually produced in a loose head. The flowers droop, but the seedheads are erect.

A. giganteum *C. Asia*
Flowers: early summer. H:3–5ft (1–1.5m), S:6in (15cm). Z:4–8.
To be seen to best effect, this impressive species should be planted so that the basal leaves, which die back before flowering, are obscured. The ball-like heads, about 4in (10cm) across, are packed with purplish-pink flowers.

Allium hollandicum 'Purple Sensation'

A. hollandicum *C. Asia*
Flowers: early summer. H:2ft (60cm), S:4in (10cm). Z:4–7.
The spherical heads are as much as 4in (10cm) across and are tightly packed with starry, purplish-pink flowers. The seedheads are also an asset. In **'Purple Sensation'**, the flowers are a richer purple.

A. karataviense *C. Asia*
Flowers: late spring to early summer. H:6–10in (15–25cm), S:4in (10cm). Z:4–8.
Unlike many alliums, the leaves, broad and purplish gray, are attractive in the flowering season. The pale-pink flowers, 50 or more in a head that is up to 4in (10cm) across, dry attractively.

Allium karataviense

A. oreophilum *C. Asia*
Flowers: early to mid-summer. H:4–8in (10–20cm), S:2in (5cm). Z:3–9.
In this dwarf species the rich purplish flowers, which are larger than in most species, are carried in a loose head about 1¼in (3cm) in diameter. When dry, they are pale beige. **'Zwanenburg'** has flowers of exceptionally rich pink.

A. rosenbachianum *C. Asia*
Flowers: late spring to early summer. H:20–36in (50–90cm), S:4in (10cm). Z:4–8.
This is a handsome bulb to plant in drifts. The tall naked stems support spherical heads, 4in (10cm) across, densely packed with small purple flowers, from which protrude violet stamens.

AMARYLLIS

AMARYLLIDACEAE

In warm climates the single species in this genus makes a spectacular appearance in open ground at the onset of the autumn rains. In cooler climates it needs a warm and sheltered position outdoors to get enough heat in the summer. If grown under glass, it will need a position in full light.
CULTIVATION Requires full sun and fertile, well-drained potting media with additional sharp sand. Plant in mid-summer, with the top of the bulb just covered.
PROPAGATION From seed, sown as soon as ripe and kept at a temperature of 61°F (16°C); plants raised this way are likely to take 8 years to flower. By division, as soon as leaves die back in summer.
POTENTIAL PROBLEMS Slugs.

Amaryllis belladonna

A. belladonna *South Africa*
Belladonna lily
Flowers: early to mid-autumn.
H:24–30in (60–75cm), S:4in
(10cm). Z:8–10.
Purplish stems emerge in autumn
and bear a head of 3 or 4 trumpet
flowers, sometimes more, each
4–6in (10–15cm) across and
scented. They are usually bright
pink. The strap-shaped leaves
emerge after the flowers and last
until mid-summer.

ANEMONE

RANUNCULACEAE Windflower

The spring-flowering anemones,
which grow from tubers and
rhizomes, can either be modest
woodlanders that are ideal for
naturalizing under deciduous trees
and among shrubs or bright plants
suitable for growing in sunny rock
gardens. In all of the species, the
petallike segments of the flowers
surround a conspicuous boss of
stamens. See PERENNIALS for
fibrous-rooted anemones.
CULTIVATION A. coronaria and
A. × fulgens require full sun and
well-drained potting medium with
added grit; all the others listed do
well in dappled shade. *A. nemorosa*
needs moist potting media with
added organic matter. Plant in
early to mid-autumn, with
rhizomes or tubers covered by
1½–2in (3–5cm) soil.
PROPAGATION In late summer, from
offsets or by dividing the rhizomes.
POTENTIAL PROBLEMS The hybrids
of *A. coronaria* are susceptible to
viral and fungal diseases.

Anemone blanda

A. blanda *S. to E. Europe, Turkey*
Flowers: early to mid-spring.
H:4–6in (10–15cm), S:6in (15cm).
Z:4–8. One of the loveliest of early
spring flowers, this species, which
grows from a rounded tuber, is
most beguiling when naturalized
in short turf, in the open or under
a light deciduous canopy. It does
particularly well on lime. The
finely divided leaves, consisting of
3 leaflets, emerge before the
yellow-centered flowers, which
have 10 to 20 segments in shades
of blue, pink, and mauve or white.
Cultivars include '**Ingramii**', deep
blue; '**Radar**', purplish pink with a
white center; **var.** *rosea*, pink; and
'**White Splendour**', brilliant white.

Anemone coronaria

A. coronaria *Mediterranean*
Flowers: early to mid-spring.
H:6–18in (15–45cm), S:6in
(15cm). Z:6–9.
The knobbly tubers give no hint of
the charm of the flowers, in the
wild studding open ground with
blooms in red, purple, blue, or
white, 5 to 8 segments around the
central knob. The species has been
displaced in gardens by single- and
double-flowered hybrids between
A. coronaria and closely related
species. By manipulation of the
planting time and forcing, these
can be brought into flower at
almost any season. The **De Caen
Group** is a name covering a race of
giant single anemones producing
many flowers over a long season.
'**Die Braut**' is an outstanding semidouble, a hint of green at the
center setting off the white
segments. The **Saint Brigid Group**
includes giant doubles and semidoubles with good colors, but
which flower less than the singles.

A. × fulgens

Flowers: spring. H:12in (30cm),
S:6in (15cm). Z:7–8.
The Mediterranean peacock
anemone (*A. pavonia*), usually red,
blue, or pink in flower, is a parent
of this hybrid. It can be planted to
create a drift of brilliant scarlet.
The flowers, up to 2in (5cm)
across, have narrow segments.

Anemone × fulgens

A. nemorosa *Europe*
Flowers: early to mid-spring.
H:4–8in (10–20cm), S:8in (20cm).
Z:4–8.
The creeping rhizomes of this
species spread freely in woodland
where the soil is moist, creating
sheets of nodding white flowers,
often suffused with pink or mauve
on the outside, over finely cut
leaves. Few plants so artlessly
establish a feeling of naturalness in
a woodland garden. Most of the
selections available have larger
flowers and stronger coloring
than the type. In '**Allenii**' the
flowers, mauve on the outside,
surround the yellow stamens with
pale blue. '**Robinsoniana**' has
flowers of exquisite soft blue.

Anemone nemorosa 'Robinsoniana'

ARISAEMA

ARACEAE

In addition to the large number of
tropical aroids (see *Arum*), there
are several from temperate zones
that have flowers of fascinating,
even sinister, appeal and attractive
foliage. In the case of aroids, the
term "flower" is used loosely for
the funnellike bract or spathe,
often hooded, that surrounds the
spadix. Here at its base, cluster the
insignificant true flowers. In some
species, including jack-in-the-pulpit
(*A. triphyllum*, Z:4–8), the berries
are a conspicuous feature during
the autumn. There are well over
100 species in this genus of
tuberous and rhizomatous
perennials. Often they do not
make growth above ground before
early summer, so care must be

taken when working around other plantings in spring. Those described below and other reasonably hardy species do well when planted under a light deciduous canopy, in peat beds or in a cool greenhouse.

CULTIVATION Require light shade and neutral to acid soil that is rich in organic matter and moist—leaf mold and grit can be added to improve the soil. Plant the tubers in mid-autumn; cover with 3–6in (7.5–15cm) of soil.

PROPAGATION From offsets in summer, when the leaves have died down.

POTENTIAL PROBLEMS Slugs.

Arisaema candidissimum

A. candidissimum *W. China*
Flowers: early summer. H:10–12in (25–30cm), S:6in (15cm). Z:5–7.
The spathe, which appears before the leaves, is about 4in (10cm) long and consists of a tube opening out into a hood that terminates in a short tail. It is white with vertical stripes, usually of green at the base shading into pale pink, and surrounds a white or greenish-yellow spadix. The large leaves have 3 lobes. This species will grow in boggy ground and in a relatively open position.

Arisaema sikokianum

A. sikokianum *Japan*
Flowers: spring. H:16–20in (40–50cm), S:6in (15cm). Z:5–8.
In flower, this is an eye-catching species. A purplish-brown spathe, with paler striations in the hood, has a white interior around a white club-shaped spadix. The dark leaves have 3 to 5 large leaflets.

ARUM
ARACEAE

In flower, this genus of aroids (see **Arisaema**) is generally more curious than beautiful, but some species have attractive foliage. The plants described are Mediterranean in origin and do best in a reasonably sheltered position in full sun or partial shade.

CULTIVATION Require full sun or partial shade and soil, in organic matter. Plant in autumn or spring with the tubers covered by 4–6in (10–15cm) of soil.

PROPAGATION From offsets, taken during the second half of summer.

POTENTIAL PROBLEMS Slugs, snails.

WARNING Toxic if eaten; the sap may cause an allergic reaction.

Arum italicum 'Marmoratum'

A. italicum *N. Africa, S. Europe, Turkey*
Foliage: autumn to spring. Flowers: spring. Berries: autumn and winter. H:12in (30cm), S:6in (15cm). Z:6–9.
Glossy, white-veined leaves, which resemble a cluster of spearheads, are particularly ornamental in winter, especially in 'Marmoratum'. The green spathe appears in early summer and is soon followed by a spike of red berries, which is usually still vivid when the new leaves are making growth.

BEGONIA
BEGONIACEAE

This large genus has about 900 species, which are found in tropical, subtropical, and warm temperate regions. Among the best known are those with tuberous rootstocks, especially the hybrids, with their often sensationally large and showy flowers. These tender, winter-dormant plants are widely grown in containers and in summer bedding schemes. Male and female flowers are borne on the same plant, but the former are the most eye-catching. See PERENNIALS for rhizomatous and fibrous-rooted begonias.

CULTIVATION Require good light but protection from direct sun, and fertile, neutral to slightly acid soil that is rich in organic matter and drains freely. Start tubers into growth, hollow-side uppermost, in early to mid-spring but in frost-prone areas do not plant outdoors until early summer.

PROPAGATION From basal cuttings in mid-spring. From seed, sown in late winter or early spring.

POTENTIAL PROBLEMS Fungal diseases such as gray mold (*Botrytis*) and powdery mildew.

B. hybrids (Tuberhybrida)
Flowers: summer. H:12–24in (30–60cm), S:12–18in (30–45cm). Z:7–8.
These bushy plants have succulent, brittle stems and glossy, toothed leaves, approximately heart shaped and with a pointed tip.
The attention-seeking double male flowers, which overshadow the few single female flowers, are 6in (15cm) or more in diameter, their color range extending from white, yellow, and pink to orange and red, with subtler intermediate shades and eye-catching picotee bicolors. Breeders have concentrated on perfection of flower form, the flowers of many hybrids resembling a double camellia in the neat layering of segments that open almost flat, others having a rosebud conical center. Examples of upright begonias include '**Anniversary**', yellow and lightly ruffled; '**Bernat Klein**', pure white; '**Fairylight**', ivory flowers touched with pink at the edges; '**Herzog van Sagan**', yellow with notched, red margins; '**Jean Blair**', frilly yellow flowers with scarlet edges; '**Marmorata**', white outlined in red; and '**Roy Hartley**', soft pink. A few hybrids are distinguished from erect begonias by trailing stems, up to 36in (90 cm) long, and the small double flowers, usually 2–3in (5–7.5cm) across. Ideal for hanging baskets, '**Gold Cascade**' is bright yellow; '**Lou Anne**', pale pink; and '**Orange Cascade**', apricot-orange.

Begonia sutherlandii

B. sutherlandii *South Africa, Tanzania*
Flowers: summer. H:10–20in (25–50cm), S:30–40in (75–100cm). Z:8–9.
This offers no competition to the fireworks of the hybrids, but is a fine plant for tall containers and hanging baskets. The generous trailing growth of slightly toothed green leaves gives a display of small apricot-orange flowers.

CALOCHORTUS

LILIACEAE

Although the 60 or so species, natives of open woodland in western North America and Mexico, are rather flimsy plants, with thin stems and linear leaves, the refined beauty of their flowers puts them in the first rank of bulbs. Common names such as cat's ears, fairy lantern, globe lily, and mariposa tulip applied to various species hint at their charm. The flowers have 6 segments, the 3 outer ones usually small, the 3 showier inner petals, sometimes fringed and lined with hairs. They also have a gland at the base, often blotched and surrounded by exquisite markings. The most splendid in this respect is the Californian *C. venustus*. Most species have proved difficult in cultivation outside their native territory, needing dry conditions during their dormancy.
CULTIVATION Require full sun and well-drained potting media with added grit that is dry during dormancy. Plant in autumn, covering the bulbs with 4–6in (10–15cm) of soil.
PROPAGATION From seed, sown as soon as ripe. From offsets, taken in autumn. From bulbils (in the case of species that produce these in the leaf axils), planted in late spring.
POTENTIAL PROBLEMS Usually none.

C. barbatus *Mexico*
Flowers: late summer. H:6–12in (15–30cm), S:3in (7.5cm). Z:6–8.
The nodding, bell-like flowers, which are fringed and hairy, are usually mustard-yellow, but sometimes a purple flush suffuses the outside of the flower.

C. uniflorus *W. USA*
Flowers: late spring to early summer. H:4–8in (10–20cm), S:2in (5cm). Z:6–8.
In the wild this plant thrives in damp, even heavy, soils; in cultivation it will tolerate some moisture during the dormant period. At the end of the stem, several long stalks carry erect mauve flowers, up to 2in (5cm) across, with a purple spot at the center of the inner petals.

Calochortus venustus

C. venustus *USA (California)*
Flowers: late spring to summer. H:8–24in (20–60cm), S:3–4in (7.5–10cm). Z:6–8.
The cup-shaped flowers, up to 3 per stem, vary in color from white or yellow to shades of purplish red. A dark red blotch at the base of each inner petal is ringed with yellow.

CAMASSIA

HYACINTHACEAE Quamash

The 6 species all make basal clumps of strap-shaped leaves above which rise spikes of starry flowers that are pale blue to dark violet or white. In the wild the species are found in damp grassland. They are not so showy as to seem out of place when naturalized in similar conditions. They make useful additions to moist borders, especially those on heavy soils. The bulbs are usually large and weighty.
CULTIVATION Tolerate full sun or partial shade in fertile, moist soil. Plant in autumn, covering the bulbs with about 4in (10cm) of soil.
PROPAGATION From offsets, taken in early autumn. From seed, sown as soon as ripe in summer.
POTENTIAL PROBLEMS Usually none.

Camassia cusickii

C. cusickii *USA (Oregon)*
Flowers: early to mid-summer. H:2–3ft (60–90cm), S:6in (15cm). Z:3–8.
In this species, a stem of blue flowers tops a clump of fleshy leaves that have a wavy margin. The large bulbs mutiply quickly.

C. leichtlinii *W. North America*
Flowers: late spring to early summer. H:30–55in (75–140cm), S:6in (15cm). Z:5–9.
The strong, straight stems of this species carry flowers that vary in color from creamy white through to lovely shades of blue to violet. There are double and semidouble flowers in *subsp. leichtlinii,* and in *subsp. suksdorfii* Caerulea Group, there are also strong blue flowers to choose from.

Camassia quamash

C. quamash *W. Canada and USA*
Camass, quamash
Flowers: early to mid-summer. H:10–36in (25–90cm), S:6in (15cm). Z:4–8.
This is a widespread and variable species, and a number of subspecies have been recognized. It quickly forms large clumps when naturalized in meadowlike conditions. The flowers, up to 2in (5cm) across, are usually bright blue, but they can be darker and also white.

CARDIOCRINUM

LILIACEAE Giant lily

The 3 Asiatic species in this genus are all monocarpic, the bulb dying after flowering while leaving numerous offsets. The bulbs, which have trumpet-shaped flowers, rarely take less than 7 years to reach flowering size from seed and 4 to 5 years from offsets. The species described is hardy and looks spectacular when sited in a dappled glade.
CULTIVATION Require partial shade, shelter, and moist, rich in organic matter, but not stagnant soil, preferably lime-free. Plant in autumn, just covering the bulbs.
PROPAGATION From offsets, taken in autumn. From seed, sown as soon as ripe.
POTENTIAL PROBLEMS Slugs; lily viruses.

Cardiocrinum giganteum

C. giganteum *Himalayas*
Flowers: mid- to late summer.
H:6-10ft (1.8-3m), S:18in (45cm).
Z:6-8.
The stout stem, which is better left
unstaked, develops from a rosette
of large green leaves and bears 10
to 20 downward-facing trumpets,
about 6in (15cm) long and strongly
scented. The flowers are white on
the outside, sometimes tinged
green, while the inside usually has
reddish-purple markings.

CHIONODOXA

HYACINTHACEAE Glory of the snow

In their alpine habitats in the
eastern Mediterranean and in
western Turkey, these are among
the first bulbs to flower. Their star-
shaped flowers appear in the early
spring. Those described are fully
hardy, and their short lax stems of
early, starry flowers, usually blue,
look delightful in rock gardens,
raised beds, and containers. They
also grow vigorously enough in
grass to add to a wild garden.
CULTIVATION Require full sun and
well-drained potting media with
added grit. Plant in early autumn,
covering bulbs with 3in (7.5cm)
of soil or potting mix.
PROPAGATION From offsets, in late
summer. From seed, sown as soon
as ripe.
POTENTIAL PROBLEMS Usually none.

Chionodoxa forbesii 'Pink Giant'

C. forbesii *W. Turkey*
Flowers: late winter to early spring.
H:6-8in (15-20cm), S:1½in (3cm).
Z:4-9.
The lax stem carries 4 to 10
flowers, rich blue with a white eye
and up to ¾in (2cm) across. There
are also white and pink variants.
'Pink Giant' has large flowers
tinted pink around white centers.

Chionodoxa luciliae Gigantea Group

C. luciliae Gigantea Group
W. Turkey
Flowers: late winter to early spring.
H:4-8in (10-20cm), S:1½in (3cm).
Z:4-9.
The stem usually carries 3 blue
starry flowers with white eyes.

C. sardensis *W. Turkey*
Flowers: late winter to early spring.
H:4in (10cm), S:1½in (3cm). Z:4-9.
The stems carry up to 12 slightly
down-turned deep blue flowers.

COLCHICUM

COLCHICACEAE Autumn crocus

Few bulbous plants make such an
impact as the autumn-flowering
colchicums whose irregularly
shaped corms thrust large crocuslike flowers through bare earth.
They teeter elegantly on long
stems before collapsing in autumn
rain and gales. The double-
flowered **'Waterlily'** (Z:5-8)
quickly becomes a mauve-pink
muddle in rough weather. Purplish
pink is the predominant flower
color, and checkered patterns on
the petallike segments are a
distinctive feature of some
colchicums. It is a fault in some
eyes that the leaves of most of
these species do not appear with
the flowers and that when they do
develop in winter or spring they
are large, as much as 3 times the
height of the flowers given below,
and untidy when dying down.
Grass should not be cut until the
leaves have withered, a week or
two before mid-summer. Some
species flower in spring, notably
the yellow *C. luteum* (Z:4-8), but
on the whole these are more
difficult garden plants.

CULTIVATION Tolerate full sun or
partial shade in well-drained
potting media with added grit.
Plant in summer or early autumn;
cover the corms with 4in (10cm)
of soil.
PROPAGATION From offsets, taken
in summer. From seed, sown in
summer as soon as ripe.
POTENTIAL PROBLEMS Slug damage
to corms and leaves.
WARNING All parts toxic if eaten;
skin contact may cause irritation.

C. agrippinum *Origin unknown*
Flowers: late summer to mid-
autumn. H:3-4in (7.5-10cm),
S:3in (7.5cm). Z:5-8.
Each corm produces several starry
flowers with narrow, rather
pointed segments, strongly
patterned with a reddish-purple
checkering. The green-tinted tube
is often rather weak, and the
flowers are easily toppled by rough
weather conditions.

C. autumnale *Europe*
Meadow saffron
Flowers: late summer to mid-
autumn. H:6in (15cm), S:3in
(7.5cm). Z:5-8.
The common name is misleading:
the source of saffron is *Crocus
sativus*. The corms of this robust
species, which is suitable for
naturalizing, produce a jostling
cluster of soft purplish pink, rather
starry, flowers.

C. byzantinum *probably Turkey*
Flowers: late summer to early
autumn. H:6-8in (15-20cm), S:6in
(15cm). Z:6-8.
A corm of this large and free-
flowering species can produce up
to 20 flowers in succession in
soft purplish pink. The broad
leaves appear in spring.

Colchicum 'Lilac Wonder'

C. 'Lilac Wonder'
Flowers: late summer to mid-
autumn. H:6in (15cm), S:6in
(15cm). Z:5-8.
Mauve-pink flowers appear on
short white stems, up to 10 per
corm, have pointed segments, and
are lightly checkered.

Colchicum speciosum

C. speciosum *Caucasus, Iran, N.E. Turkey*

Flowers: early to mid-autumn. H:8–12in (20–30cm), S:6in (15cm). Z:6–8.

The vigor and beauty of goblet-shaped flowers on sturdy stems put this species in the first rank of garden plants. The flowers vary in color from pale to deep purplish pink, often with a white center. '**Album**' has pure-white goblets carried on green stems. In '**Atrorubens**' the flowers, white throated and purplish-crimson, are carried on purple stems.

COSMOS

ASTERACEAE

This tuberous perennial in a genus of 25 species of perennials and annuals originates from Mexico. If mulching is not enough to protect it in winter out of doors, it can be lifted and replanted in spring.
CULTIVATION Require full sun and moist, well-drained soil. Mulch in early autumn or lift and store.
PROPAGATION From basal cuttings in early spring.
POTENTIAL PROBLEMS Aphids, slugs; gray mold (*Botrytis*).

Cosmos atrosanguineus

C. atrosanguineus *Mexico*

Black cosmos, chocolate cosmos
Flowers: mid-summer to autumn. H:30in (75cm), S:18in (45cm). Z:6–9.

From a base of dark-green, divided leaves, purplish stems carry cup-shaped reddish-chocolate flower-heads. Their color is astonishingly matched by a chocolate scent.

CRINUM

AMARYLLIDACEAE

There are more than 100 species in this genus of mainly tropical and subtropical bulbs, the most ornamental carrying clusters (correctly, umbels) of showy, funnel-shaped flowers at the head of stout stems. Among the hardiest are 2 from South Africa, **C. bulbispermum** (Z:7–9) and **C. moorei** (Z:7–9), both plants of soils that are moist in the growing season; in cool temperate gardens, these require warm, sheltered positions and frost protection. They are much less widely grown than the slightly hardier hybrid between them described below.
CULTIVATION Require full sun and fertile, well-drained soil. Plant in mid- to late spring, covering the bulbs with 6–10in (15–25cm) of soil.
PROPAGATION From offsets, removed in early spring. From seed, sown as soon as ripe.
POTENTIAL PROBLEMS Usually none.
WARNING Bulbs likely to cause nausea if eaten; the sap may cause irritation on contact.

Crinum × powellii 'Album'

C. × powellii

Flowers: late summer to early autumn. H:2–3ft (60–90cm), S:1ft (30cm). Z:7–9.

Elegantly curved tubes springing from the head of a stout stem open out to slightly drooping, flared trumpets about 4in (10cm) across at the mouth. There may be as many as 10, and they open in succession. '**Album**', with pure-white flowers, is a cut above the more familiar pink forms. The strap-shaped leaves often look the worse for wear. Congested clumps often flower freely.

CROCOSMIA

IRIDACEAE Montbretia

The montbretias come into their own in the second half of summer, their elegant sprays of funnel-shaped flowers, 6 segments opening at the mouth of a long tube, providing beds with an airy dash of warm colors, from yellow to intense and fiery red. They make fans of grassy leaves. The species, such as **C. masoniorum** (Z:5–9), are from fairly moist grasslands in South Africa, but much more common in cultivation are the slightly hardier hybrids, often covered by the umbrella name *C. × crocosmiiflora*, which are listed here by cultivar name.
CULTIVATION Tolerate full sun or partial shade in fertile, well-drained soil. Plant in early spring, with 3–4in (7.5–10cm) of soil.
PROPAGATION By division in early spring. From seed, sown when ripe.
POTENTIAL PROBLEMS Red spider mites.

Crocosmia × crocosmiiflora 'Solfaterre'

C. × crocosmiiflora

Flowers: late summer to early autumn. H:24in (60cm), S:8in (20cm). Z:5–9.

Among the many hybrids '**Emily McKenzie**' has large flowers, with chocolate splashes on orange, and paler throats. '**Solfaterre**' has soft apricot flowers that are enhanced by the soft bronze tint of the foliage. The taller '**Gerbe d'Or**', which grows to 24–30in (60–75cm), has lemon-yellow flowers. These can be used to cool down red and orange summer schemes.

C. 'Lucifer'

Flowers: mid- to late summer. H:3–4ft (90–120cm), S:8in (20cm). Z:5–9.

The clumps of swordlike leaves have sprays of furnace-red flowers.

Crocosmia 'Lucifer'

CROCUS

IRIDACEAE

Crocuses are best known for their sudden bursts of brilliant or subtle colors (red excluded) in late winter and early spring, but there are also autumn-flowering species and the Dutch crocuses (listed here under *C. vernus*) sometimes flower in mid-spring. In many cases, sweet scent adds to the sheeny perfection of the flowers, made vivid by stamens and styles of contrasting color. The plants grow from corms, distinctively sheathed in a tunic, sometimes with vertical fibers, otherwise arranged in rings or woven tightly. In the case of many species, the linear leaves appear with or just after the flowers, sometimes growing taller than the flowering heights given below. Crocuses that need a dry spell in summer are best grown in an alpine house or frame. Those described generally thrive outdoors in sunny rock gardens and raised beds.

CULTIVATION Most require full sun and well-drained soil; see entries. Plant autumn-flowering crocuses in late summer, winter- and spring-flowering crocuses in early autumn, covering corms with 2–3in (5–7.5cm) of soil.
PROPAGATION From offsets, separated in summer. From seed, sown as soon as ripe in summer.
POTENTIAL PROBLEMS Mice and other rodents (corms), birds; fungal diseases (corms in storage).

C. ancyrensis *Turkey*
Flowers: mid- to late winter.
H:2–3 in (5–7.5cm), S:2in (5cm).
Z:3–9.
The orangey flowers are among the first of the yellow crocuses.

C. angustifolius *Armenia, S. Ukraine*
Cloth of gold
Flowers: late winter to early spring.
H:2–3in (5–7.5cm), S:2in (5cm).
Z:3–9.
The exteriors of the orange-yellow flowers are marked with bronze.

Crocus angustifolius

C. chrysanthus *E. Europe*
Flowers: late winter to early spring.
H:2–3in (5–7.5cm), S:2in (5cm).
Z:4–9.
In wild plants the flowers, globular in outline and honey scented, are usually yellow with darker markings outside. However, the variability of the species and some hybridizing have resulted in numerous free-flowering cultivars in a wide color range that are among the pick of the dwarf crocuses. The opalescent **'Blue Pearl'** is silvery blue, the outside mauve and bronze at the base, and the throat yellow. The very free flowering **'Cream Beauty'** has an orange style and rich yellow throat surrounded by a cream cup. The creamy-yellow flowers of **'E.A. Bowles'** are marked bronze and purple at the base. One of the smallest is **var. *fuscotinctus***, with gold flowers striped with bronzy purple on the outside. **'Ladykiller'** is sheeny white with bold purple over most of the outer segments. More dazzling in its whiteness is **'Snow Bunting'**, with only light purple feathering on the outside and a yellow throat. **'Zwanenburg Bronze'** produces flowers that have a deep red-brown exterior and a vivid orange-yellow interior.

C. goulimyi *S. Greece*
Flowers: early to mid-autumn.
H:4in (10cm), S:2in (5cm). Z:4–8.
The tube of the flower forms a slender stem expanding to a mauve globe surrounding the yellow style and stamens. This sweetly scented species increases rapidly. Leaves appear with the flowers.

C. imperati *S. Italy*
Flowers: mid-winter to early spring.
H:4in (10cm), S:2in (5cm). Z:4–8.
The corms that are most commonly available are of **subsp. *imperati* 'De Jager'** in which the violet inner segments of the flowers contrast exquisitely with the outer ones, which are buff streaked with deep purple. The throat and anthers are yellow, while the style, consisting of numerous threads, is orange. The fully open flowers are up to 3in (7.5cm) across. The leaves are dark green in color and are shiny.

C. kotschyanus *Lebanon, N.W. Syria, Turkey*
Flowers: early to mid-autumn.
H:3in (7.5cm), S:2in (5cm). Z:5–9.
This is the earliest of the autumn-flowering crocuses: the large and curiously irregular corms produce flowers before the leaves appear. The stock usually available is

subsp. *kotschyanus*. The pale tube opens to mauve segments with dark purple veining; bright orange spots ring the yellow throat.

C. × luteus *'Golden Yellow'*
Flowers: late winter to early spring.
H:3–4in (7.5–10cm), S:2in (5cm).
Z:4–9.
This free-flowering crocus, ideal for naturalizing, has clear yellow flowers with a few maroon stripes.

Crocus sieberi 'Hubert Edelsten'

C. sieberi *Greece*
Flowers: late winter to early spring.
H:3in (7.5cm), S:2in (5cm). Z:4–9.
Gold-throated, rather globular flowers have segments in shades of mauve or purple. Its outstanding cultivars include a brilliant white, **'Albus'**, pristine except for the throat and orange style. **'Firefly'** is deep mauve and free-flowering. In **'Hubert Edelsten'** the pale mauve inner segments are cupped by deep purple outer segments, across each of which is an arc of fine white markings. **'Violet Queen'** has numerous beautifully shaped flowers, more purple than violet.

Crocus speciosus

C. speciosus *C. Asia, Caucasus, Iran, S. Ukraine, Turkey*
Flowers: early to mid-autumn.
H:4–6in (10–15cm), S:2in (5cm).
Z:5–9.
The fine-stemmed gobletlike flowers, in shades of mauve or violet-purple, often conspicuously veined, cup an orange-red style. A real asset in the autumn garden, it naturalizes readily in sun or partial shade. Named cultivars include ravishing white-flowered **'Albus'**.

A good crocus to follow it is the shorter **C. medius**, with scarlet style and yellow stamens showing off the rich purple flowers.

Crocus tommasinianus

C. tommasinianus *W. former Yugoslavia*
Flowers: late winter to early spring. H:3–4in (7.5–10cm), S:2in (5cm). Z:4–9.
Although this crocus multiplies profligately in both full sun and partial shade, such a charming plant could hardly be thought a weed. Its shades of mauve and purple are often variable, even within 1 colony. The outer segments are pale, the inner richer in color around an orange style. Cultivars include '**Ruby Giant**', with large reddish-purple flowers (sterile but clumps build up by division), and '**Whitewell Purple**', purple flowers with silver lining. **F. albus** is a lovely white form.

Crocus vernus 'Pickwick'

C. vernus *S. and E. Europe*
Dutch crocus
Flowers: early spring. H:3–4in (7.5–10cm), S:2in (5cm). Z:3–9.
The name covers a number of plants, often regarded as several species, found in mountainous country. It is also under this name that the large-flowered Dutch crocuses are commonly listed. They are vigorous enough to be naturalized in grass in full sun or light shade, and are excellent container plants, but they are too beefy for the rock garden. Taller than the species, their goblet-shaped flowers can be up to 6in (15cm) tall. The following are

widely available: '**Jeanne d'Arc**' has large flowers of white, violet at the base with light feathering, cupping an orange style. In '**Pickwick**', the very pale mauve ground color is dramatically streaked with deep purple to contrast with the yellow stamens and style. The sheeny goblets of '**Purpureus Grandiflorus**' are a deep purple with yellow stamens and style. '**Remembrance**' is striking in the contrast of its violet flowers, streaked with dark purple, and the bright orange style and stamens. '**Vanguard**', the earliest to flower, can produce its slender, mauve flowers in late winter.

CYCLAMEN

PRIMULACEAE Sowbread

The numerous and often subtle variations on a simple theme make the members of this genus delightful plants. The charm of the flowers lies more in their shape and poise than in their limited color range (pink, magenta, and white, but often with attractive dark stains at the mouth). Some are sweetly scented. The petals, sometimes elegantly twisted, are sharply reflexed so that the flowers look like miniature shuttlecocks hovering in midair. In some species they appear before the leaves, in others with them, which are in many cases an outstanding feature on account of the silvering and marbling of their surfaces and variability of size and shape. The more tender species are attractive plants for a cool greenhouse or alpine house.
CULTIVATION Most like partial shade and well-drained, soil rich in organic matter with added leaf mold and grit where they dry out in summer, but see entries. Plant in late summer or early autumn, covering tubers with 1in (2.5cm) of soil.
PROPAGATION From seed, sown as soon as ripe.
POTENTIAL PROBLEMS Mice and other rodents, under glass red spider mites; fungal diseases.

Cyclamen cilicium

C. cilicium *S. Turkey*
Flowers: mid- to late autumn. H:2–4in (5–10cm), S:4–6in (10–15cm). Z:6–8.
Pink or white flowers, which have conspicuous carmine spots at the mouth, appear at the same time as the rounded or heart-shaped leaves, usually marked with silver.

Cyclamen coum

C. coum *Bulgaria, Caucasus, Lebanon, Turkey*
Flowers: early winter to early spring. Foliage: winter and spring. H:2–3in (5–7.5cm), S:4in (10cm). Z:5–8.
The rounded leaves, which are purplish red on the underside and patterned with silver on the upper surface, appear either before or at the same time as the short-petaled flowers. These can be magenta, pink, or white with a carmine flush near the white mouth. White and carmine contrast in **subsp. coum 'Album'**. The cool metallic finish of the leaves is a striking feature of **subsp. coum Pewter Group**.

Cyclamen hederifolium f. *album*

C. hederifolium *Greece, Italy, W. Turkey*
Flowers: late summer to late autumn. Foliage: autumn to spring. H:4in (10cm), S:6–10in (15–25cm). Z:5–8.
This star among dwarf plants tolerates heavy shade, producing many well-proportioned, sometimes fragrant, flowers. Colors include magenta, shades of pink, and white (**f. album**). The ivylike leaves develop while the plant is in flower. They vary in shape and in their silvery markings.

C. purpurascens *C. and E. Europe, N. Italy*

Flowers: mid-summer to autumn. H:4in (10cm). S:4–8in (10–20cm). Z:5–8.

A fragrant species with pink, carmine and, rarely, white flowers. The leaves are more or less evergreen with heart or kidney shapes, faintly patterned with silver or plain green. It is important not to allow it to dry out in the summer.

C. repandum *S. France eastward to Greece*

Flowers: mid- to late spring. H:4–6in (10–15cm), S:4–8in (10–20cm). Z:6–8.

The scented flowers have twisted petals, usually rich pink and darker at the mouth, but carmine and white forms are known. The heart-shaped or triangular leaves are dark green with silvery flecking or patterning above, purple-red on the underside.

DAHLIA

ASTERACEAE

In the 16th century Europeans in Mexico found that the Aztecs were already growing doubles derived from tuberous-rooted species. The thousands of dahlia hybrids that have been produced since, with flowerheads available in an astonishing range of form, color, and size, provide a remarkable demonstration of the mutability of plants as the result of hybridization. One relatively hardy species is included here. However, the remainder are hybrid border dahlias that in frost-prone areas are usually planted out in spring and lifted in autumn, once the leaves have been blackened by the first frosts. Border dahlias, like bedding dahlias, are very often planted out in beds specially prepared for them. They are sometimes simply lined out if they are being grown for cutting or exhibition, for which they remain very popular, but they are also valued for plugging gaps in borders after mid-summer as well as for growing in containers. They are usefully categorized according to the form of their flowerheads, which have the appearance of single flowers but in fact consist of many. For the purposes of exhibition, some categories of dahlia hybrids are subdivided by size of flowerhead into 5 groups: giant, over 10in (25cm); large, 8–10in (20–25cm); medium, 6–8in (15–20cm); small, 4–6in (10–15cm); miniature, less than 4in (10cm). Dahlias with giant, large, and medium flowerheads are

40–60in (100–150cm) in height; small and miniature dahlias are 3–4ft (90–120cm) tall.

CULTIVATION Require full sun and fertile, rich in organic matter, well-drained potting medium with added humus that is well watered throughout the growing season. Plant unsprouted tubers in mid-spring, covering with about 4in (10cm) of soil. Delay planting sprouted tubers until there is minimal risk of frost.

PROPAGATION By division of tubers in early to mid-spring. From basal shoot cuttings in early spring.

POTENTIAL PROBLEMS Aphids, capsid bugs, earwigs, slugs and snails; virus and fungal diseases, including powdery mildew.

SPECIES

D. merckii *Mexico*

Flowers: mid-summer to mid-autumn. H:3–5ft (1–1.5m), S:2–3ft (60–90cm). Z:9–10.

Even in areas that are prone to frost, many gardeners successfully grow this slender species without lifting it every year and value it for the longevity of its flower display. The mauve-pink single flower-heads, with a maroon center showing yellow stamens, are carried on long arching stalks and have a refinement that is lacking in most of the hybrids.

HYBRIDS

Flowers: mid-summer to mid-autumn. H:2–5ft (60–150cm), S:18–48in (45–120cm), but see notes on dimensions below. Z:9–10. In the following descriptions the aim has been to show the character of the main categories (as recognized by The National Dahlia Society of Great Britain) and, where helpful, to give a few representative or outstanding hybrids from a constantly changing selection.

Dahlia 'Yellow Hammer'

Single

These dahlias are up to 2ft (60cm) in height. The flowerheads, up to 4in (10cm) across, have only 1 or 2

rows of ray flowerets, frequently overlapping, surrounding the central cluster of disk flowerets. '**Yellow Hammer**' has rich yellow flowerheads with an orange disk and dark-purple leaves.

Anemone-Flowered

The flattened ray flowerets surround a cluster of tubular, initially erect flowerets, often of contrasting color. Plants are usually less than 4ft (1.2m) in height, and the flowerheads usually 4–6in (10–15cm) in diameter. This category is no longer widely represented in cultivation.

Dahlia 'Clair de Lune'

Collerette

The distinctive feature is a collar of short flowerets surrounding the central disk and set against the single row of ray flowerets. Most hybrids are 30–48in (75–120cm) tall with flowerheads 4–6in (10–15cm) across. '**Clair de Lune**' has a deep yellow center, pale yellow ray flowerets, and a cream collar. In '**Easter Sunday**' the ray flowerets and collar around the yellow center are creamy white. '**La Cierva**' has a banded effect with a white collar surrounded by white-tipped purple ray flowerets.

Dahlia 'John Street'

Waterlily

The flowerheads, much less densely packed than most of the other doubles, have broad ray flowerets that are flat or slightly incurved. There are 5 subdivisions according to size of bloom. The most popular are the small flowered, which include '**Glorie** van Heemstede', noted for its generous display of yellow blooms; **'John Street'**, bright scarlet; and **'Porcelain'**, white with a delicate mauve tinge.

Decorative

The double flowerheads, which have no central disk, consist of layers of broad ray flowerets that are usually blunt tipped. There are 5 subdivisions according to size of flowerhead. **'Arabian Night'** (small) is outstanding for the depth of its dark red. **'David Howard'** (miniature) is pale orange with a darker center and bronzed foliage. **'Duet'** (medium) has startling flowerheads in which the ray flowerets are purplish red with white tips and **'Eveline'** (small) is pearly white tinted with mauve. Giant-flowered examples that are popular for exhibition include **'Hamari Gold'**, bronzed yellow-orange; **'Kidd's Climax'**, pink with yellow shading; and **'Zorro'**, which is deep red.

Dahlia 'Hamari Gold'

Ball

The spherical flowerheads of dahlias in this group have blunt or rounded ray flowerets that are arranged in a spiral. There are 2 sizes of flowerhead, small and miniature, but all hybrids are about 3–4ft (90–120cm) tall. Good miniatures are **'Kathryn's Cupid'** and **'Peach Cupid'**.

Dahlia 'Moor Place'

Pompon

These are in the same mold as the Ball hybrids and of a similar height, but the flowerheads are 2in (5cm)

or less in diameter, and the ray flowerets curve in elegantly over the whole of their length. **'Mi Wong'** is pink with darker touches at the margins of the flowerets; **'Moor Place'** is rich purplish red.

Cactus

The narrow, pointed ray flowerets are quilled for more than half their length, giving the double flowerheads a spiky appearance. There are 5 subdivisions according to size of flowerhead. **'Athalie'** (small) has bronze-tinted pink flowerets; **'Hillcrest Royal'** (medium) is purplish red; and in **'Lady Kerkrade'** (small), the pink flowerheads fade to cream near the center.

Dahlia 'Hillcrest Royal'

Semicactus

There are 5 subdivisions according to size of flowerhead. The ray flowerets are broader than those of cactus dahlias and quilled for less than half their length. Good examples include **'Conway'** (small), purplish-pink flowers with gleams of pale yellow; **'Daleko Jupiter'** (giant), a popular exhibition hybrid in a mixture of red and yellowish pink; **'Dana Iris'** (small), vibrant red; **'Pink Pastelle'** (medium), rich pink; and **'Salmon Keene'** (large), shaggy soft orange with yellow tips and yellow near the flower center.

Miscellaneous

All dahlias not included in the main groups belong here and are classified in informal subgroups, such as Orchid-flowering and Lilliput dahlias. There are considerable differences in size between the groups, the Lilliput dahlias being only 12–18in (30–45 cm) tall with flowerheads up to 1¼in (3cm) across. The peony-flowered **'Bishop of Llandaff'**, however, is 40–48in (100–120cm) in height and has flowerheads that reach up to 2¼in (6cm) across. It is much admired for the combination of its bronze-purple foliage and open, semidouble bright red flowerheads.

Dahlia 'Bishop of Llandaff'

DIERAMA

IRIDACEAE Angel's fishing rod, wandflower

The common names of this South African genus allude to the gracefully arching flower stems, which are weighed down at the tips by the bell-like flowers. A waterside planting meets their requirements while making the most of their languid beauty. In cold areas, annual lifting of the corms will allow the plants to be grown outdoors.

CULTIVATION Require full sun and well-drained soil rich in organic matter with a plentiful supply of moisture during the growing season. Plant in early autumn, covering the corms with 4in (10cm) of soil or, in areas that have cold winters, in mid-spring. Lift the corms in mid-autumn and store them away in conditions that are frost-free.

PROPAGATION From offsets, separated in autumn. From seed, sown in early to mid-spring.

POTENTIAL PROBLEMS Usually none.

D. pulcherrimum S. Africa

Flowers: late summer to mid-autumn. H:4–5ft (1.2–1.5m), S:2ft (60cm). Z:7–9.

Wiry flower stems emerge from a sheaf of narrow leaves and arch over gracefully, loaded toward the tip with violet-purple bells that open from silvered papery bracts. A smaller version of this, **D. pendulum**, grows to about 3ft (90cm) in height.

Dierama pulcherrimum

ERANTHIS

RANUNCULACEAE Winter aconite

The small bulbs, among them the tuberous winter aconites that flourish under the canopy of deciduous trees, are among the chief delights of temperate gardens in late winter and early spring. The genus is small and is mainly represented in gardens by the fully hardy *E. hyemalis*, which naturalizes readily. It can also form extensive colonies, especially when it is planted in alkaline soils.
CULTIVATION Tolerates a wide range of conditions, including full sun or partial shade around trees or deciduous shrubs and well-drained alkaline soils or heavy loams. If possible, plant tubers immediately after flowering in winter or, alternatively, in late summer, covering dry tubers with 1in (2.5cm) of soil.
PROPAGATION By division of tubers in spring, after flowering. From seed, sown as soon as ripe in the late spring.
POTENTIAL PROBLEMS Slugs; smuts, with swellings on stalks bursting to release black spores.
WARNING All parts of the plant are mildly toxic, and the sap can be an irritant.

E. hyemalis *Europe*
Flowers: late winter to early spring. H:2–4in (5–10cm), S:2in (5cm). Z:3–7.
The jaunty flower is a lustrous cup of lemon yellow, about 1in (2.5cm) across, surrounded by a bract that forms a ruff of bright green. The plant forms large colonies dies down by early summer. Other *Eranthis* with distinctive characteristics, but now included with this species, are generally less vigorous plants and are free flowering. The **Cilicica Group**, originating from Turkey, has slightly larger flowers of a richer yellow color. The globular yellow flowers of **'Guinea Gold'**, a selection of the **Tubergenii Group**, are large, and the leaves are an attractive bronze-green.

Eranthis hyemalis

ERYTHRONIUM

LILIACEAE Dog's-tooth violet, trout lily

The poise of their flowers, like scaled-down Turk's-cap lilies, gives these woodland plants a distinctive character. An attractive feature of many, including *E. citrinum* (Z:4–8) and *E. oregonum* (Z:3–8) as well as *E. revolutum*, which is described below, is the purplish-brown mottling of the leaves. Most can be grown with successful results, provided they are given moist conditions under a deciduous canopy, open in spring but cool and shady in summer. The fleshy corms should not be allowed to dry out between lifting and replanting. These plants, representative of those that are easiest in cultivation, are available from specialized nurseries.
CULTIVATION Require dappled or light shade, and moist but not stagnant soil rich in organic matter. Plant in late summer or early autumn, covering the corms with 4–6in (10–15cm) of soil.
PROPAGATION From offsets, taken in summer; from seed, sown when ripe (slow to germinate; plants may take 5 years to reach maturity).
POTENTIAL PROBLEMS Slugs, snails.

Erythronium californicum 'White Beauty'

E. californicum *USA (California)*
Flowers: mid- to late spring. H:6–18in (15–45cm), S:4–6in (10–15 cm). Z:4–8.
Above glossy, dark-green leaves, which are heavily mottled, float cream flowers that have orange-brown markings at the center. In **'White Beauty'** the leaves are marbled and the ring at the throat of the creamy flowers is rust-red.

E. dens-canis *Asia, Europe*
Dog's-tooth violet
Flowers: early to mid-spring. H:4–6in (10–15cm), S:4in (10cm). Z:2–7.
This species is more tolerant than most of dryness in the summer months. In shape the corm is similar to a dog's canine tooth,

hence the common name. The blue-green leaves are strongly mottled. Nodding flowers are variable in color, ranging from purplish pink, through pale pink to white, and the center, usually yellowish, is banded in orange-brown. Named selections include **'Pink Perfection'**, **'Rose Queen'**, and **'Snowflake'**; the many variants are equally delectable.

E. 'Kondo'
Flowers: mid- to late spring. H:8–16in (20–40cm), S:4–6in (10–15cm). Z:4–8.
This vigorous hybrid, of which *E. tuolumnense* is probably a parent, produces several scented flowers per stem. The greenish-yellow flowers are red-brown at the center.

E. 'Pagoda'
Flowers: mid- to late spring. H:10–18in (25–45cm), S:4–6in (10–15cm). Z:4–8.
E. tuolumnense is probably one of the parents of this vigorous hybrid, which has bronze mottling on the leaves and several creamy-yellow flowers per stem.

E. revolutum *Canada and USA (British Columbia to N. California)*
American trout lily
Flowers: mid- to late spring. H:8–14in (20–35cm), S:4–6in (10–15cm). Z:4–8.
Above a brown-mottled clump of leaves, which are wavy at the margins, the upright stems carry several purplish-pink flowers with yellow centers and anthers.

Erythronium tuolumnense

E. tuolumnense *USA (California)*
Flowers: mid- to late spring. H:8–14in (20–35cm), S:4–6in (10–15cm). Z:4–8.
Although it is smaller in flower size than many of the others in the genus, this species does well in cultivation. The very large corms, often over 3in (7.5cm) in length, produce bright-green leaves that have no mottling. The stems of the plant can carry up to 4 yellow flowers, which have attractive green centers.

FREESIA

IRIDACEAE

This South African genus is best known for the numerous hybrids derived from species such as *F. lactea*. Their fragrance, wide color range, and responsiveness to forcing have made them a standby of the florist trade. An appealing feature of species and hybrids is the way the stems, rising above tufts of grassy leaves, angle the flower spike so that the funnel-shaped flowers are more or less erect and open in succession toward the tip. The species and hybrids, which are half-hardy, can be container-grown in a cool greenhouse. Treated corms that flower in summer are sometimes available and can be planted outdoors after the frosts. In areas where the climate is mild enough, untreated corms multiply outdoors.
CULTIVATION Require full sun or well-lit conditions and fertile, well-drained soil, with a plentiful supply of moisture in the growing season. Plant in late summer or early autumn for winter and spring flowering, with corms covered by 2–3in (5–7.5cm) of soil; plant prepared bulbs for summer flowering in mid-spring.
PROPAGATION From offsets, removed in late summer. From seed, sown from early spring to early summer and grown on without check during the summer.
POTENTIAL PROBLEMS Particularly when grown under glass, aphids and red spider mites; fungal diseases, like *Fusarium* wilt, viruses.

Freesia hybrids

F. hybrids
Flowers: under glass, mid-winter to mid-spring; untreated bulbs outdoors, mid- to late spring; treated bulbs outdoors, early to late summer. H:18–24in (45–60cm), S:4–6in (10–15cm). Z:9–10. The funnel-shaped flowers, which are up to 2in (5cm) long, include some doubles, although most are singles, opening out to 6 lobes. In most cases they are fragrant with a color range extending from white and soft pastels to strong oranges, reds, and purples. The throat is usually white or yellow, often streaked with a stronger color.

FRITILLARIA

LILIACEAE Fritillary

The fritillaries have a strong following among specialized growers. Although rarely showy, they are intriguing for their subtle combinations of color, sometimes in checked patterns, and for the secretive way the hanging bells hide the nectaries that glisten at the base of each of the segments. The genus, of about 100 species, is widely distributed in the Northern Hemisphere. It has a core of good plants suitable for borders, woodland, raised beds, or rock gardens. The bulbs should be handled carefully and, if lifted, not allowed to dry out. They consist of 2 or more fleshy scales and some produce large numbers of "rice-grain" bulblets.
CULTIVATION Most of the species described require full sun and well-drained potting media with added grit, but for exceptions see individual entries. Plant in early to mid-autumn, covering the bulbs with a depth of soil equal to at least 4 times the height of the bulb. The large bulbs of *F. imperialis*, for example, should be covered by about 8in (20cm) of soil. In heavy soils, plant on a bed of coarse sand.
PROPAGATION From offsets or bulbils, in late summer. From seed, sown when ripe in mid- to late summer.
POTENTIAL PROBLEMS Attack by lily beetles and slugs.

Fritillaria acmopetala

F. acmopetala *Cyprus, Syria, S. Turkey*
Flowers: late spring. H:12–18in (30–45cm), S:6in (15cm). Z:6–8. This example of the subtle color combinations found in fritillaries does well in a fairly wide range of conditions. From a slender stem, with a few linear leaves, hang 1 to 3 pale green bells, the inner segments with maroon stains and veining and the rim curved back.

Fritillaria camschatcensis

F. camschatcensis *Alaska to N.W. USA, N.E. Asia*
Black sarana
Flowers: late spring to early summer. H:10–16in (25–40cm), S:4–6in (10–15cm). Z:3–8. Stems with glossy, narrow leaves, arranged in whorls, are topped by 1 or, more often, several bell-shaped, near-black purple flowers. This mysterious species, which is unusual in straddling Asia and America, tolerates light shade and thrives in moist soil rich in organic matter, and is ideal for a peat bed.

Fritillaria imperialis

F. imperialis *S.E. Turkey to W. Himalayas*
Crown imperial
Flowers: mid- to late spring. H:2–4ft (60–120cm), S:8–12in (20–30cm). Z:5–8. For many centuries the crown imperial has been admired as a spring bulb of stately grandeur. A stout stem, surrounded by whorls of glossy, twisted leaves to about half its height, is crowned by a tight ring of up to 8 nodding flowers, which can be as much as 2in (5cm) long and as wide at the mouth, topped by a curious green tuft. The color range extends from lemon-yellow to deep brownish red. Recommended cultivars include '**Aurora**', orange-red; '**Maxima Lutea**', deep lemon-yellow; and '**Rubra Maxima**', brick red with darker shading. The crown imperial does well on heavy soils.

291

F. meleagris *C. Europe, W. to Great Britain and N. to Scandinavia*
Snake's head fritillary
Flowers: mid- to late spring.
H:12–18in (30–45cm), S:4–6in (10–15cm). Z:4–8.
Wild and naturalized colonies of this fritillary flourish in damp meadows. However, this checkered species will grow in any reasonably moist soil, producing 1 or 2 square-shouldered bells above grassy, gray-green leaves. The pattern is usually in dark purple on a paler shade. Particularly bewitching when dotted among darker forms are flowers with pale green patterning on white ('**Alba**').

Fritillaria meleagris

F. michailovskyi *N.E. Turkey*
Flowers: early to mid-spring.
H:4–6in (10–15cm), S:2–3in (5–7.5cm). Z:5–8.
The broad yellow rim of the deep-plum, nodding bells is a particularly eye-catching feature. Each stem carries up to 5 flowers, which are about 1in (2.5cm) in length and as much across. The foliage is sparse. In order to prosper, this species requires some dry conditions during the dormant season.

Fritillaria michailovskyi

F. pallidiflora *N.W. China, Siberia*
Flowers: mid-spring. H:12–18in (30–45cm), S:4–6in (10–15cm). Z:5–8.
The stems of this fritillary bear up to 4 square-shouldered cream bells, which are suffused with green and spotted with red on the inside of the flowers.

Fritillaria pyrenaica

F. pyrenaica *Pyrenees*
Flowers: mid-spring. H:10–18in (24–45cm), S:6in (15cm). Z:5–8.
In the wild this species is found in the light shade of open woodland as well as in open rocky terrain, showing a versatility that is useful in the garden. Slender stems carry 1, occasionally 2, bells of very variable coloring. Often it is purple-crimson patterning superimposed on dark purple-brown on the outside, while the interior is tinged greenish yellow.

GALANTHUS

AMARYLLIDACEAE Snowdrop

The snowdrops usually produce foliage and flowers in late winter, the single bloom dangling lightly from a slender stalk beneath the arching tip of the stem or scape. The 3 outer flower segments are typically pure white; the 3 inner ones, which are shorter and notched, are marked with green. The variations of this appealing formula excite passionate enthusiasm. There are doubles as well as singles, differences in vigor as well as in the proportions of the segments and in poise. The distribution of green on the inner segments is another distinguishing feature. There are even a few cases of green on the outer segments and of pale yellow being substituted for green. Also important is the arrangement of the leaves (either 2 pressed flat against each other as they emerge or alternately 1 wrapped around the other), their color, width, and the extent to which the margins are turned back. The first snowdrops appear in autumn with **G. reginae-olgae Winter-flowering Group** (Z:3–8), like an out-of-season common snowdrop (*G. nivalis*). The common snowdrop is one of the most rewarding grown under deciduous trees or shrubs.
CULTIVATION Tolerant of a wide range of conditions (including lime), but most do best in light shade where the soil is moist and heavy. Plant dry bulbs (usually slow to become established) in early autumn, covering with 1–2in (2.5–5cm) of soil; preferably "in the green," that is after, even during, flowering but before leaves die back.
PROPAGATION By division of clumps at or immediately after flowering but while leaves are still green; from seed, sown as soon as ripe.
POTENTIAL PROBLEMS Rodents.

G. 'Atkinsii'
Flowers: mid- to late winter. H:8in (20cm), S:2–3in (5–7.5cm). Z:4–8.
Although setting no seed, this snowdrop increases freely. It shows its *G. nivalis* lineage in its foliage and flower. The outer segments are long, sometimes deformed.

Galanthus 'Atkinsii'

G. caucasicus *Probably Caucasia, Transcaucasia, and Turkey*
Flowers: mid- to late winter.
H:6–8in (15–20cm), S:2–3in (5–7.5cm). Z:4–8.
The broad, gray-green leaves, one wrapped around the other at the base and curving back as they grow, are a distinctive feature. There are green marks at the tips of the inner segments but not the base.

G. elwesii *W. Turkey and adjacent islands*
Flowers: late winter to early spring. H:6–10in (15–25cm), S:2–3in (5–7.5cm). Z:4–8.
The broad, gray-green leaves are wrapped around one another at the base. The inner segments of the large flowers have green markings at the tip and base.

Galanthus elwesii

G. ikariae *Aegean islands*
Flowers: late winter to early spring. H:4–6in (10–15cm), S:2–3in (5–7.5cm). Z:5–8.
The glossy, bright-green leaves, one wrapped around the other at the base, are up to 1in (2.5cm) across and turn back at the tips. Green marks at the tips of the inner segments show between the claw-like outer segments. The very similar **Latifolius Group** from the Caucasus, N.E. Turkey, and N.W. Iran, does well on relatively dry soils.

G. nivalis *Europe, from Spain to the Ukraine*
Common snowdrop
Flowers: mid- to late winter. H:4–6in (10–15cm), S:2–3in (5–7.5cm). Z:3–8.
The strap-shaped leaves, rather narrow and with a light-gray bloom, are flat against each other at the base and the inner segments of the flowers are marked green at the apex. There are numerous selections, some of which are frankly very difficult to tell apart, as well as numerous hybrids, some of which are listed separately. There are also several named doubles, including '**Flore Pleno**', with its irregular dumpy flowers, and the outer segments stretched over green-edged underskirts. This is sterile, but colonies build up quickly from offsets, to form very dense white carpets. The forms in which the green of the flowers is replaced by a pale yellow, such as the single '**Sandersii**', are rather weak-growing curiosities. Other more vigorous variants include the **Scharlockii Group**, in which 2 long spathes stand erect above the flowers, the outer segments of which are touched with green, and '**Viridapicis**', a hearty plant with some green spots at the tips of the outer segments.

Galanthus nivalis 'Flore Pleno'

G. plicatus *Crimea, N. Turkey, Roumania*
Flowers: late winter to early spring. H:6–7.5in (15–20cm), S:2–3in (5–7.5cm). Z:4–8.
The gray-green leaves of this large-flowered snowdrop are pressed flat against each other on emerging and the margins fold back. There is a conspicuous green mark around the notch of the inner flower segments. **Subsp. byzantinus**, from N.W. Turkey, formerly considered a separate species, has green marks at the base of the inner segments as well as at the apex.

Galanthus plicatus

G. 'S. Arnott'
Flowers: mid- to late winter. H:6–8in (15–20cm), S:2–3in (5–7.5cm). Z:4–8.
This hybrid follows the common snowdrop in the arrangement of its leaves and the green markings of the inner flower segments. It is pleasing in its proportions and is one of the best to plant in small groups in prominent positions.

Galanthus 'S. Arnott'

GALTONIA

HYACINTHACEAE

The tall, hyacinth-like stems of pendant bells, which spring from clumps of strap-shaped leaves, are elegant verticals for sunny gardens in late summer and autumn. The 2 species described look best in sheltered beds where the subtle beauty of their white or green-tinted flowers is not overwhelmed by brilliant colors. In areas subject to hard frosts, they are worth growing in pots and keeping under glass during winter.
CULTIVATION Require full sun and well-drained soil with a good supply of moisture in spring and summer. Plant in early to mid-spring, or, where there is little risk of outdoor frost or under glass, in mid-autumn, covering bulbs with about 6in (15cm) of soil.
PROPAGATION From offsets, although these are not abundant, removed in autumn or spring. From seed, sown in early spring.
POTENTIAL PROBLEMS Usually none.

G. candicans *Lesotho, South Africa*
Flowers: late summer to early autumn. H:3–4ft (90–120cm), S:6–8in (15–20cm). Z:7–9.
The most widely grown species has gray-green leaves and up to 30 waxy bells, widely spaced on the stem, that are white, tinted green at the base, and lightly scented.

Galtonia candicans

G. viridiflora *Lesotho, South Africa*
Flowers: late summer to mid-autumn. H:2–3ft (60–90cm), S:6in (15cm). Z:7–9.
The pale green of the wide-spreading bell-shaped flowers has made this a favorite among flower arrangers. The leaves narrow abruptly at their tip from a width of about 4in (10cm).

Galtonia viridiflora

GLADIOLUS

IRIDACEAE

It is by their large-flowered hybrids that gladioli are best known, but there are over 150 species and these, as well as some of the small-flowered hybrids, include some plants of exceptional refinement. There is a concentration of species in southern Africa, but gladioli are also found in other parts of Africa, the Arabian peninsula, western Asia, and Europe, especially the Mediterranean. Their corms produce fans of linear or sword-shaped leaves and spikes of more or less trumpetlike flowers, the tube opening out to 6 lobes that often differ in shape and size. In this selection it is easy to justify the inclusion of the species and the examples of the Nanus Group hybrids. There are only general entries for the other hybrid categories (Grandiflorus Group, Primulinus Group, and Butterfly hybrids) because new hybrids are constantly taking the place of older ones. The hybrids with large spikes are for cutting or exhibiting.

CULTIVATION Require full sun and well-drained potting media with added sharp sand, most needing a plentiful supply of moisture in the growing season. In frost-prone areas, delay planting the summer-flowering gladioli (indicated by A after the flowering season in the entries), including the large-flowered hybrids, until mid- to late spring. Lift the corms once the foliage begins to die down after flowering in order to store them in frost-free conditions. Plant gladioli that flower in late spring or early summer (marked B) in autumn, where the climate is mild enough outdoors, but otherwise cultivate under glass. Cover all the corms with 4-6in (10-15cm) of soil and in heavy soils place them on a bed of coarse sand.

PROPAGATION From cormlets, removed from the soil in the dormant season and planted at the same time as the adult corms. From seed, in late winter or early spring.

POTENTIAL PROBLEMS Aphids and thrips; fungal diseases, including gladiolus corm rot.

Gladiolus 'Amanda Mahy'

G. 'Amanda Mahy'
Flowers: early summer (B). H:20-30in (50-75cm), S:2-4in (5-10cm). Z:6-10.
Upward-tilted flowers, 5 to 7 to a stem and about 2in (5cm) across, are soft pink to apricot, with mauve marks on 3 segments.

G. Butterfly hybrids
Flowers: early to late summer (A). H:2-3ft (60-90cm), S:4-6in (10-15cm). Z:8-10.
The flowers of these hybrids are ruffled or frilled and usually strikingly blotched.

G. callianthus *E. Africa (Ethiopia to Mozambique)*
Flowers: late summer to early autumn (A). H:20-40in (50-100cm), S 4-6in (10-15cm). Z:8-10.
This plant's clump of linear leaves seems unpromising, but is topped by stems carrying 6 to 10 deliciously scented flowers. They arch out on long slender tubes, the pointed segments making an unequal white star 2-3in (5-7.5cm) across, with a deep purple throat. 'Murieliae' is a vigorous selection.

Gladiolus communis subsp. *byzantinus*

G. communis subsp. byzantinus *N. Africa, Sicily, Spain*
Flowers: early summer (B). H:20-30in (50-75cm), S:4in (10cm). Z:7-10.
The intense magenta of the flowers, up to 20 per stem and arranged in 2 alternating ranks, is scarcely relieved by creamy-white stripes on the lower segments.

G. Grandiflorus Group hybrids
Flowers: early to late summer (A). H:3-4ft (90-120cm), S:4-6in (10-15cm). Z:7-10.
The stiff, 1-sided spikes with up to 24 flowers tightly packed one above the other, 8 to 10 often being open at the same time, make these large-flowered hybrids particularly popular in exhibitions. Many have ruffled flowers, some as much as 7in (17cm) across, and the color range, although weak in blue, is exceptional, the lip and throat often contrasting with the main color of the flower. In exhibition, they are divided into 5 categories (Miniature, Small, Medium, Large, and Giant) based on the diameter of the bottom flower, which is the first to open and usually the largest.

G. Nanus Group hybrids
See the separate entries for 'Amanda Mahy', 'Prins Claus', and 'The Bride'.

Gladiolus papilio

G. papilio *South Africa*
Flowers: late summer to early autumn (A). H:2-3ft (60-90cm), S:4in (10cm). Z:7-10.
Although it is not very brightly colored, this is one of the most alluring of the gladioli. Spikes of 5 to 10 flowers are carried above a thin clump of narrow, gray-green leaves. The flowers, very variable in coloring, are almost bell shaped and droop slightly. The foundation color ranges from creamy-yellow to green, usually with bruiselike purple markings on the reverse and with a conspicuous eye on the lower segments. In the **Purpureoauratus Group,** the cream, green-tinted body of the flower is suffused with purple with a purplish-red eye edged with yellow.

G. Primulinus Group hybrids
Flowers: early to late summer (A). H:2-3ft (60-90cm), S:4-6in (10-15cm). Z:8-10.
The alternate arrangement of the flowers makes an obvious zigzag up the stem. The flowers, up to 3in (7.5cm) across, come in an extensive color range; they look like inverted triangles because the central top segments project forward like a hood over the stigma and anthers.

G. 'Prins Claus'
Flowers: early summer (B). H:20-30in (50-75cm), S:2-4in (5-10cm). Z:6-10.
Tonguelike marks of deep pink on the 3 lower segments of this Nanus hybrid stand out against the whiteness of the flowers.

G. 'The Bride'
Flowers: mid-spring to early summer (B). H:18-24in (45-60cm), S:2-4in (5-10cm). Z:6-10.
The starry flowers, which are about 2in (5cm) across and number 3 to

6 per stem, have white, pointed segments around a greenish-yellow throat. This gladiolus is one of the original small-flowered hybrids in the style of, but predating, the Nanus Group.

G. tristis *South Africa (W. Cape)*
Flowers: late winter to late spring (B). H:18–48in (45–120cm), S:3–6in (7.5–15cm). Z:7–10.
The flowers exhale a sweet scent at night. The blooms, usually about 10 per stem but up to 20 in number, are trumpet shaped, flaring to a width of 2in (5cm), and pale yellow or cream, lightly tinged with purplish bronze.

Gladiolus tristis

GLORIOSA

COLCHICACEAE

The botanical name makes extravagant claims, but the single tropical species is not a disappointment. *G. superba* produces vivid, lilylike flowers in summer. The tapering leaves of this slender climber are usually tipped with small hooks that allow the plant to haul itself up into shrubs or artificial supports. In frost-prone areas it is best grown under glass. Whether plants are grown outdoors or under glass, store tubers dry over winter.
CULTIVATION Requires full sun and fertile, well-drained soil with a plentiful supply of moisture in the growing season. Plant in late winter or early spring, covering the tubers with about 4in (10cm) of soil.
PROPAGATION From offsets, detached and planted in late winter. From seed, sown in late winter or early spring and germinated at a temperature of 70–75°F (21–24°C).
POTENTIAL PROBLEMS Aphids.
WARNING Toxic if eaten; the tubers may cause skin irritation.

G. superba *Africa, India*
Flowers: mid- to late summer. H:4–6ft (1.2–1.8m), S:12–18in (30–45cm). Z:9–10.
The long stalks that carry flowers spring from the upper leaf axils at an angle of about 45°. The nodding flowers, like airborne bursts of flame, have wavy-edged, reflexed segments that change as they age from yellow to orange and red. The stamens form a conspicuous circle beneath the segments and the style, instead of protruding vertically, extends abruptly at a right angle. '**Lutea**' has yellow flowers and in '**Rothschildiana**', which can grow to 8ft (2.5m), the red segments are yellow at the base and on the very crimped margins.

Gloriosa superba '**Rothschildiana**'

HERMODACTYLUS

IRIDACEAE

A peculiarity of the ovary puts a single darkly beautiful *Iris* relative in a genus of its own. It needs a warm position, such as the base of a sunny wall where there is room for the creeping tubers to develop.
CULTIVATION Requires full sun and free-draining, preferably alkaline soil with added grit. Plant in autumn, covering tubers with 3–4in (7.5–10cm) of soil.
PROPAGATION By division, as soon as leaves die down.
POTENTIAL PROBLEMS Slugs, snails.

Hermodactylus tuberosus

H. tuberosus *E. Mediterranean, N. Africa, S. Europe*
Flowers: mid- to late spring. H:6–12in (15–30cm), S:2in (5cm). Z:6–9.
The scented flowers, which may seem somber, but are appealing in their subtle color combination and texture, are borne on weak stems. They are about 2in (5cm) across and a shadowed yellowish green color with outer segments (known as the falls) of velvety purplish black. The leaves can grow to 20in (50cm).

HIPPEASTRUM

AMARYLLIDACEAE

The hybridization of Central and South American species of these bulbs, which began in the early 19th century, has produced striking large-flowered plants. These are often incorrectly known as amaryllis, which are popular for winter display under glass. *Hippeastrum* are usually grown in containers.
CULTIVATION Require a well-lit position and well-drained fertile soil with generous supplies of moisture and liquid fertilizer when in active growth. Plant in autumn, only half covering the bulbs with soil.
PROPAGATION From offsets, removed in autumn. From seed, sown as soon as ripe.
POTENTIAL PROBLEMS Bulb scale mite, large narcissus bulb flies; fungal diseases.
WARNING All parts likely to cause stomach upset if eaten.

Hippeastrum '**Apple Blossom**'

H. hybrids
Flowers: H:12–18in (30–45cm), S:4–6in (10–15cm). Z:8–10.
The 4 to 6 funnel-shaped flowers, which are up to 6in (15cm) across, radiate from the top of a stout stem on short stalks. This umbel arrangement, which resembles a cluster of floral megaphones, often looks uncomfortably crowded. The vigor and brilliance of these giant blooms, however, have an understandable appeal during the winter. The color range available includes white, pink, red, and orange. Many of the plants sold are simply identified by their color. Named selections include '**Apple Blossom**', pink-tipped white flowers; '**Picotee**', white with segments outlined in red; '**Red Lion**', brilliant scarlet; '**Star of Holland**', red with a white mark in the throat.

HYACINTHOIDES

HYACINTHACEAE Bluebell

The 2 well-known species of bluebell are superb plants for the wild garden. The blue haze of massed English bluebells in glades among deciduous trees in spring always refreshes the eye. They increase quickly from offsets and seed to make spreading clumps of rather coarse strap-shaped leaves. They can be planted under shrubs, but should be kept out of beds and rock gardens. The 2 species described hybridize freely.
CULTIVATION Tolerate full sun or partial shade and a wide range of soils, preferably moist. Plant in autumn, covering bulbs with about 3in (7.5cm) of soil (the bulbs deteriorate quickly in storage).
PROPAGATION From offsets, removed in summer. From seed, sown as soon as ripe.
POTENTIAL PROBLEMS Usually none.

H. hispanica N. Africa, Portugal, Spain
Spanish bluebell
Flowers: mid-spring to early summer. H:12–16in (30–40cm), S:4–6in (10–15cm). Z:4–9.
An erect stem forms a sturdy campanile carrying up to 15 broad bells. The flowers are unscented and usually pale blue with blue anthers. Yet the color range of cultivars and hybrids includes dark blue, pink, and white.

Hyacinthoides hybrid

H. non-scripta W. Europe
English bluebell
Flowers: mid-spring to early summer. H:10–14in (25–35cm), S:4–6in (10–15cm). Z:4–9.
The bells, 6 to 12 in number, are rather tubelike in shape, but the segments curl back prettily at the mouth. Their rather 1-sided arrangement on the stem bends the slender tip over. Pink and white forms exist, but the lightly scented flowers are usually purplish blue with some cream-colored anthers.

HYACINTHUS

HYACINTHACEAE Hyacinth

The modern hyacinths, sometimes known as florists' or Dutch hyacinths, with columns of densely packed fragrant flowers, are almost the only representatives of the genus in gardens; having displaced the species, *H. orientalis*, from which they are derived, the "improvement" of the species over centuries has produced plants of a rather plastic perfection. However, they are popular because of their heavy scent, the uniform growth of individual cultivars, and their predictable performance when forced and as container and garden plants. Prepared bulbs (heat-treated for forcing) should not be put in a warm room until the flower spike has started to emerge.
CULTIVATION Tolerate full sun or light shade and require well-drained potting media or, for forced bulbs, bulb compost. Plant unprepared bulbs in autumn, covering the bulbs with 3–6in (7.5–15cm) of soil; prepared bulbs in late summer or early autumn with the tops of the bulbs just showing.
PROPAGATION From offsets, removed in summer. By specialist techniques involving scooping or scoring the base of bulbs.
POTENTIAL PROBLEMS Several fungal diseases, including gray bulb rot.
WARNING All parts to some degree toxic if eaten; handling bulbs may cause allergic reactions.

Hyacinthus orientalis 'City of Haarlem'

H. orientalis E. Mediterranean, S. Turkey
Flowers: late winter to late spring; prepared bulbs, mid-winter to early spring. H:8–12in (20–30cm), S:3–4in (7.5–10cm). Z:4–7.
The species, a rather lax-stemmed plant, is barely recognizable in its progeny, except for the powerful fragrance of the bell-like flowers. The modern cultivars, to which the dimensions given above apply, have stout stems carrying 40 or more waxy bells with recurved tips to the lobes and glossy, strap-shaped leaves. The color range extends from white and soft pastel shades of pink, blue, and yellow to vivid hues of red, violet, and orange. Unless stated otherwise, unprepared bulbs of the following cultivars flower from early to mid-spring; those described as late, flower between mid- and late spring: **'Anna Marie'**, single, pale pink, suitable for forcing; **'Blue Jacket'**, single, large deep blue, paler at the edges; **'Carnegie'**, single, white, late; **'City of Haarlem'**, single, soft yellow, late; **'Delft Blue'**, single, soft blue with metallic luster; **'Hollyhock'**, double, carmine-red, late; **'Jan Bos'**, single, dark reddish pink; **'L'Innocence'**, single, less congested than many modern cultivars, pure white; **'Oranje Boven'**, single, salmon pink; **'Ostara'**, single, strong blue with violet band down the center of each segment; and **'Pink Pearl'**, single, glistening deep pink with paler edges, popular for forcing.

Hyacinthus orientalis 'Jan Bos'

IPHEION

ALLIACEAE

The few representatives seen in gardens of this South American genus do not look dramatic, but their clumps of grassy leaves are topped by beautifully formed, scented flowers over many weeks in spring. Their foliage, which smells of onions when bruised, makes growth in late autumn and dies down in summer. It usually recovers well if lightly frost damaged, but in areas prone to prolonged frosts, these are plants for a cold greenhouse.

CULTIVATION Require full sun and well-drained soil. Plant in early autumn, covering bulbs with about 3in (7.5cm) of soil.
PROPAGATION By division of clumps during dormancy in summer. From seed, sown as soon as ripe.
POTENTIAL PROBLEMS Slugs, snails, mice.

I. 'Rolf Fiedler'

Flowers: early to mid-spring.
H:4– 6in (10–15cm), S:4in (10cm).
Z:5–9.
Vivid blue intensified by yellow gives the flowers enameled beauty.

Ipheion uniflorum

I. uniflorum *Argentina, Uruguay*

Flowers: early to mid-spring.
H:6– 8in (15–20cm), S:4in (10cm).
Z:5–9.
The tubular flower opens to an upward-facing star, about 1⅛in (3cm) across, usually silver-blue, but varying in color. In '**Album**', a vigorous grower, brown center lines and green shadows add a somber note to the white flowers. '**Froyle Mill**' is a dark selection with violet flowers. '**Wisley Blue**', with dark central veins, shades from a near-white center, through mauve to violet at the tips.

Ipheion uniflorum '**Froyle Mill**'

IRIS

IRIDACEAE

The horticultural riches of this genus are shared between those that are bulbous and an even larger number that are rhizomatous. The popularity of irises throughout their long history in cultivation owes much to the distinctive makeup of the flower and the numerous variations on the basic formula, usually underlined by rich or subtle coloring. In all irises the flower is made up of 6 segments. The outer 3, the falls, extend on a horizontal or upward-tilted haft with a down-turned, often sharply recurved, blade. The beard that is such a conspicuous feature on the falls of a large group of rhizomatous irises is not present in bulbous irises, but there is sometimes a clearly marked crest. The 3 inner segments, the standards, are more or less erect but can arch outward or even droop and are smaller than the falls. Petallike style branches or arms arch over the falls, each protecting a stamen.

The bulbous irises fall into 3 sections, 2 of which are described. The Juno irises, such as *I. magnifica* and *I. orchioides*, are not represented because of the difficulties they present in cultivation. See PERENNIALS for rhizomatous irises.

RETICULATA IRISES

These late-winter and early-spring flowering dwarf bulbs of jewel-like beauty, astonishingly hardy, are mainly from Turkey, the Caucasus, and farther east. Distinctive features include the netlike (reticulate) tunic of the bulb and the fact that the roots die away during the dormant period. In most species the rather narrow leaves, which have 4 or 8 ribs, are short at flowering but later grow much longer. In the wild, the species experience a long, hot, and dry summer and are often most successful in a bulb frame or alpine house. Most hybrids tolerate moister conditions in free-draining soil.
CULTIVATION Require full sun and well-drained soil, preferably neutral to slightly alkaline (with added grit). Plant in early to mid-autumn, covering bulbs with 3–6in (7.5–15cm) of soil or potting medium.
PROPAGATION From offsets separated in the dormant season. From seed, sown as soon as ripe.
POTENTIAL PROBLEMS Slugs, snails; ink spot fungus.

I. danfordiae *Turkey*

Flowers: mid- to late winter. H:4in (10cm), S:2in (5cm). Z:4–8.
This is one of the first Reticulata irises to flower, and its intense lemon-yellow, with small dark spots on the falls, makes it very conspicuous for its size. The standards are insignificant, so that the flower looks squat and stocky. The honeyed scent is a rarely appreciated feature. The square-sectioned leaves eventually reach a height of about 8in (20cm).

Iris danfordiae

I. histrioides *Turkey*

Flowers: mid- to late winter.
H:4– 6in (10–15cm), S:3–4in (7.5–10cm). Z:5–9.
The royal blue of the clone sold under the name '**Major**' is a dazzling discovery in winter. The flowers, which open before the leaves develop, are up to 3in (7.5cm) across, with falls, extending on nearly horizontal hafts, which have an orange ridge edged by white streaking. The relatively short and broad standards add to the impression of a compact flower. The hybrid *I.* '**Joyce**' has a similar outline. Its broad falls, a deeper blue than the sky-blue of the standards, have a bright yellow ridge with white flecking.

Iris '**Katharine Hodgkin**'

I. 'Katharine Hodgkin'

Flowers: late winter to early spring. H:4–6in (10–15cm), S:3–4in (7.5–10cm). Z:4–8.
In general outline this sturdy hybrid resembles its parents, *I. histrioides* and *I. winogradowii* (Z:5–8), the latter having lemon-yellow flowers with green spots on the falls around a pale orange highlight. The hybrid is white suffused with pale sea green and lightly veined with blue. There are yellow ridges to the falls, which seem to be casually spotted with dark blue.

I. reticulata *E. from C. Turkey to Caucasus, N.E. Iraq, N. Iran*
Flowers: late winter to early spring. H:4–8in (10–20cm), S:2–3in (5–7.5cm). Z:5–9.
The upward-tilted haft of the falls gives a very characteristic shape to the classic Reticulata iris. The solitary scented flower, up to 3in (7.5cm) across, has rather slender segments but proves much less flimsy than its appearance suggests. The stock usually sold under the species name has deep violet-blue flowers with an orange-yellow crest on the falls. The leaves, which have 4 ribs, are normally short at the time of flowering but subsequently extend to about 14in (35cm). There is said to be considerable color variation in the wild, through shades of blue, violet, and purple, which is reflected in the range of cultivars and hybrids, all of them desirable. They include *I.* 'Cantab', pale blue lit on the slightly darker falls by an orange crest edged by white streaking; *I.* 'Clairette', with pale blue and a white blaze on the deep violet falls; and *I.* 'J.S. Dijt', a deep reddish purple in color, the orange ridge, edged by white markings, which extend over a very deep purple blotch.

Iris 'J.S. Dijt'

XIPHIUM IRISES

This section comprises several species from southwest Europe and northwestern Africa, including *I. xiphium* (Z:6–9) itself, and the hybrids, known as English, Dutch, and Spanish irises, derived from them. They are summer flowering; the bulbs have a smooth tunic and there are no fleshy roots that persist throughout the year. The hybrids are popular as cut flowers but they are also useful in beds between spring and full summer.
CULTIVATION Require full sun and well-drained (but moist rather than dry for *I. latifolia* and English hybrids) neutral to slightly alkaline soil. Plant in early to mid-autumn; cover bulbs with 4–6in (10–15cm) of soil.

PROPAGATION From offsets, in late summer or autumn. From seed (species only), sown in spring.
POTENTIAL PROBLEMS Usually none.

I. Dutch hybrids
Dutch iris
Flowers: early summer. H:18–30in (45–75cm), S:3–4in (7.5–10cm). Z:6–9.
The Dutch irises, which are the first of the Xiphium hybrids to flower, are commonly sold as color mixtures, which include white, yellow, bronze, blue, and purple, the flowers often bicolored. Some fine named selections are also available. These include 'Blue Magic', with contrasting pale violet standards and violet falls; 'Golden Harvest', yellow; and 'Wedgwood', pale blue.

I. English hybrids
English iris
Flowers: early to mid-summer. H:16–24in (40–60cm), S:3in (7.5cm). Z:6–9.
The forms and hybrids of *I. latifolia* are more commonly seen than the species itself and are widely sold as mixtures, rarely as named selections. Yellow does not feature in the color range, but there are wonderful shades of blue, purple, and violet as well as pale tints and pure whites. These Xiphium irises follow the species in their general character, having more substantial flowers than the Dutch hybrids, which flower before them.

Spanish (*xiphium*) iris

I. Spanish hybrids
Spanish iris
Flowers: early to mid-summer. H:12–18in (30–45cm), S:3–4in (7.5–10cm). Z:6–9.
Although smaller in all their parts, the Spanish irises resemble the Dutch irises, but flower 2 to 3 weeks later. They are usually sold as mixed colors, including white, cream, yellow, bronze, blue, violet, and purple with a yellow or orange mark. Bicolors have purple standards and bronze falls with an orange blotch.

LEUCOJUM

AMARYLLIDACEAE Snowflake

The snowflakes do not have the ardent following of their relatives the snowdrops, but like them include species of quiet charm that flower in winter, spring, and autumn. The flowers have 6 segments of equal length. The spring and summer snowflakes are hardy bulbs and they perform very well in heavy soils. The slender *L. autumnale* (Z:5–9), which produces small white bells tinged with pink in late summer or early autumn, needs sun and good drainage.
CULTIVATION The species described below tolerate full sun or partial shade and thrive in moisture-retentive soils. Plant *L. autumnale* in mid- to late summer, covering bulbs with 2in (5cm) of soil, and spring-flowering species in autumn, covering bulbs with 3–4in (7.5–10cm) of soil.
PROPAGATION From offsets, separated during dormancy. From seed, sown in autumn.
POTENTIAL PROBLEMS Slugs.

Leucojum aestivum 'Gravetye Giant'

L. aestivum *From British Isles to C. and E. Europe, Caucasus and Turkey*
Summer snowflake
Flowers: mid- to late spring. H:18–24in (45–60cm), S:4–6in (10–15cm). Z:4–9.
This bulb defies its name and flowers in spring. A sturdy leafless stem, above a clump of strap-shaped leaves, terminates in several white bells with green markings just above the tips of the segments. 'Gravetye Giant' is a well-proportioned selection that can grow up to 3ft (90cm).

L. vernum *S. and E. Europe*
Spring snowflake
Flowers: late winter to early spring. H:8–12in (20–30cm), S:2–3in (5–7.5cm). Z:3–9.
The spring snowflake is like an early, shorter-growing summer snowflake but with larger flowers,

usually 1 or 2 per stem, and thrives in the same moist conditions. The robust **var. vagneri** has green markings on the segments, but **var. carpathicum** has yellow tips.

Leucojum vernum

LILIUM

LILIACEAE Lily

No other genus of summer-flowering bulbs can match lilies both as garden and container plants, and there are few genera of any kind that include such a high proportion of outstanding ornamentals. There are about 100 species distributed throughout Europe, Asia, and North America, and the hybrids raised from these are legion. The bulbs of lilies consist of fleshy scales, from which the basal roots develop, and some produce stolons or rhizomes that allow them to spread laterally. Several produce bulbils in the leaf axils or low on the stem as a means of propagation. A large number of lilies, described as stem-rooting (as distinct from the basal-rooting lilies that produce only basal roots), also produce roots on the stem above the bulb. In the descriptions below, stem-rooting lilies are indicated as such after the dimensions. There is a very wide color range, not including blue, and the segments may be spotty and partly covered with warty protuberances known as papillae. The flowers, all arranged in 6 parts, may be upward or outward facing, nodding or down turned, and carried 1 to a stem, in tiered profusion, or in tight clusters. The trumpet, as in *L. regale*, is the classic shape, but equally distinctive is the turk's-cap flower of the martagon lily (*L. martagon*), in which the segments are sharply recurved. Other lilies are said to have flowers of funnel or bowl shape, but many are intermediate in character. Although far from all lilies are scented, some are exceptionally fragrant while a few are rank smelling; its unpleasant scent counts against the easily grown **L. pyrenaicum**, with yellow

turk's-cap flowers. Many of the species are woodland plants from mountainous areas, where there is a plentiful supply of moisture but also good drainage and where the base of plants is often shaded. Some lilies, including the American turk's-cap lily (**L. superbum**, Z:4–9), are plants of marshy ground, and a few species like a warm, sunny position. Most lilies do well in containers, and several that are not fully hardy, including **L. formosanum var. pricei** (Z:5–8) and **L. longiflorum** (Z:7–9), make magnificent plants for cool greenhouses.

A shortcoming of many lilies, including the spectacular Golden-rayed lily (**L. auratum**, Z:4–9) from Japan, is susceptibility to virus diseases. Control of pests such as aphids will help prevent these diseases becoming established.

A classification of lilies into 9 divisions is widely used, all the true species being placed together while the other divisions reflect to some extent the often complex parentage of the hybrids. In the lily selection that follows, the species are given first, followed by the hybrids with the relevant division. *CULTIVATION* Most tolerate partial shade but prefer the flower stem in full sun and the base in shade, and require well-drained soil that is rich in organic matter and neutral to slightly acid with additional leaf mold and grit, but see entries. Plant between mid-autumn and early spring, basal-rooting lilies preferably in autumn. Cover the bulbs of basal-rooting lilies with 3–6in (7.5–15cm) of soil, and stem-rooting lilies with 6–8in (15–20cm). Keep well watered in the growing season. *PROPAGATION* From offsets, scales, bulblets, and bulbils in dormancy (using virus-free stock). From seed, sown in early to mid-autumn. *POTENTIAL PROBLEMS* Pests in and above the soil, including aphids, leatherjackets, lily beetles, and slugs; viruses and fungal diseases, including gray mold (*Botrytis*).

SPECIES

L. canadense *E. North America*
Meadow lily
Flowers: mid-summer. H:3–6ft (1–1.8m), S:10–12in (25–30cm). Z:4–9.
The meadow lily, which requires moist, lime-free soil or potting medium, is exceptionally graceful, the long flower stalks, arched like violin bows, carrying the flowers up and out from the stem before turning over so that the bells hang

vertically. There can be up to 20 lightly scented flowers, but often less than half this number, varying in color from yellow or pale orange to red, marked internally with dark spots. The flowers, which are 2–3in (5–7.5cm) long, have segments that turn at the tips.

L. candidum *E. Mediterranean*
Madonna lily
Flowers: H:3–6ft (1–1.8m), S:8–10in (20–25cm). Z:4–9.
Despite a susceptibility to gray mold, this lily holds its place in the first rank of garden flowers. It does best in full sun and well-drained, slightly alkaline soil, planted with the tips just below the soil surface. The stiff stem carries up to 15 outward-facing, pure white trumpets, 3–4in (7.5–10cm) in length, which flare widely at the mouth. They are heavily scented and lit by the vivid yellow of the anthers. A rosette of overwintering basal leaves appears in early autumn.

L. henryi *C. China*
Flowers: late summer to early autumn. H:3–8ft (1–2.5m), S:12in (30cm). Z:4–8.
The tall stems need staking, but this is a minor shortcoming in a graceful late-flowering lily. The 10 to 20 lightly fragrant turk's-cap flowers, held out from the stem on horizontal stalks, are orange with black spotting among warty protuberances. Neutral to slightly alkaline soils suit this species.

Lilium lancifolium var. splendens

L. lancifolium *China, Japan, Korea*
Tiger lily
Flowers: late summer to early autumn. H:3–6ft (1–1.8m), S:8–10in (20–25cm). Stem rooting. Z:3–9.
Susceptibility to virus is a drawback of this species, which prefers lime-free soil. It does not usually set seed but produces bulblets in the leaf axils. The turk's-cap flowers are orange, spotted on downy stems. There can be as many as 25 to a stem in the vigorous **var. splendens**.

Lilium martagon

L. martagon *Wide spread in Asia and Europe*
Turk's-cap lily
Flowers: early to mid-summer. H:3–5ft (1–1.5m), S:6–10in (15–25cm). Stem rooting. Z:3–8.
In the wild this species, the most widely distributed of the lilies, is found in woodland and open meadows. As a garden plant it does well on alkaline soils and is most appealing when naturalized in dappled shade. The purplish stem can carry up to 50 nodding flowers, usually about 2in (5cm) across, with the segments so tightly rolled back that the tips touch the flower stalk. The flowers, which have a rank scent, are usually purplish pink with darker spotting, but the depth of coloring varies considerably in wild populations. The white **var. album**, with yellow anthers, is exceptionally beautiful. **Var. cattaniae** is tall growing and has unspotted flowers of inky purple.

L. monadelphum *Caucasus, N.E. Turkey*
Flowers: early to mid-summer. H:3–5ft (1–1.5m), S:8–10in (20–25cm). Stem rooting. Z:5–8.
In a well-grown specimen, the stout stem can carry more than 20 nodding scented flowers, up to 4in (10cm) across, of pale or rich yellow. The base and the turned-back tips of the segments are tinged purple, and there is often purple spotting inside the flower.

L. pardalinum *W. USA*
Leopard or panther lily
Flowers: mid-summer. H:5–7ft (1.5 –2.2m), S:10–12in (25–30cm). Z:5–8.
The orange flowers are spotted with purple. Normally 10 per stem, their lively coloring makes this an ideal species to naturalize in dappled shade, bulbs building up in the lime-free soil it requires.

L. pumilum *N. China, N. Korea, Mongolia, Siberia*
Flowers: early summer. H:10–24in (25–60cm), S:6–8in (15–20cm). Stem rooting. Z:3–8.
Unlike some of the short-growing hybrid lilies, this species, which is intolerant of lime, is well proportioned, carrying up to 30 turk's-cap flowers of vivid scarlet. They are scented, and some have black spots at the centers.

Lilium regale

L. regale *W. China*
Regal lily
Flowers: mid-summer. H:3–6ft (1–1.8m), S:6–8in (15–20cm). Stem rooting. Z:3–8.
Popularity cannot spoil the distinction of this lily, which is one of the easiest to grow. A wiry stem carries several richly scented trumpets, often more than 10, that are up to 5in (12.5cm) long. They glisten white, with purple staining on the outside and a yellow throat, from which protrude golden anthers. Flowering plants of this lime-tolerant species can be raised from seed within 2 years. **'Album'** has trumpets of dazzling whiteness warmed by a golden radiance in the throat. **'Royal Gold'** is a surprising variation; the flowers are bright yellow but have a sobering purplish-brown exterior.

Lilium regale 'Album'

L. speciosum *Japan*
Flowers: late summer to early autumn. H:4–6ft (1.2–1.8m), S:10–12in (25–30cm). Stem rooting. Z:4–8.
Although this species and its varieties only do well outdoors in a mild climate, they are well known as greenhouse plants and as cut flowers. They all require lime-free soil. There are usually about 12 strongly scented blooms to a stem, carried on long stalks and outward facing or nodding. They are white or pink, stained pink to crimson at the center. The waxy segments have wavy edges, and the tips turn back revealing a surface warty with dark-colored papillae.
Var. roseum has pink flowers on green stems, but in **var. album**, with white flowers, and the rich carmine-red colored **var. rubrum**, the stems are purplish brown.

Lilium speciosum var. rubrum

L. × testaceum
Nankeen lily
Flowers: mid- to late summer. H:4–6ft (1.2–1.8m), S:8–10in (20–25cm). Z:5–9.
The unique buff color of the flowers is warmed by the orange-red of the anthers and faint spotting in the center. This old garden hybrid has up to 12 flowers per stem, the buds held vertically before opening to nodding turk's-caps about 3in (7.5cm) across.

HYBRIDS

L. African Queen Group
(Trumpet and Aurelian hybrid)
Flowers: mid- to late summer. H:4–6ft (1.2–1.8m), S:10–12in (25–30cm). Stem rooting. FrH.
The richly scented, funnel-shaped flowers in a blend of purplish maroon, tawny peach, and radiant apricot form a compact pyramid at the head of a sturdy stem.

L. 'Bright Star' (Trumpet and Aurelian hybrid)
Flowers: mid-summer. H:30–36in (75–90cm), S:6–8in (15–20cm). Stem rooting. Z:3–8.
The flowers of this lime-tolerant hybrid, usually 5 or more to a stem, hang from nearly horizontal stalks, their ivory-white segments curling back at the tips to reveal a star formed by central, orange-yellow bands, bordered by papillae, on each segment.

Lilium **'Casa Blanca'**

L. 'Casa Blanca' (Oriental hybrid)
Flowers: mid- to late summer.
H:3–4ft (1–1.2m), S:8–10in
(20–25cm). Stem rooting. Z:4–8.
The stiff stem terminates in a
cluster of fragrant bowl-shaped
flowers of splendid whiteness.
Even the papillae are white, but
the anthers are a bold orange-red.

L. 'Côte d'Azur' (Asiatic hybrid)
Flowers: early to mid-summer.
H:16–30in (40–75cm), S:6–8in
(15–20cm). Z:3–8.
Greenish-buff upright buds make
an attractive contrast of color and
form among the bowl-shaped, pink
flowers clustered at the end of a
short stem. **L. 'Red Carpet'**, an
even more compact Asiatic hybrid,
14–16in (35–40cm) tall, with
upward-facing flowers of fiery red,
is good for bedding schemes.

L. 'Fire King' (Asiatic hybrid)
Flowers: mid-summer. H:3–4ft
(1–1.2m), S:8–10in (20–25cm).
Stem rooting. Z:3–8.
The intense orange-red color in a
well-formed head of 5 or more
outward-facing flowers makes this
an arresting lily.

L. 'Journey's End' (Oriental
hybrid)
Flowers: late summer. H:3–5ft
(1–1.5m), S:8–10in (20–25cm).
Stem rooting. Z:4–8.
The erect buds become more
outward facing as they open to
star-shaped, fragrant flowers. These
are up to 8in (20cm) across, with
recurved wavy segments. There is
maroon spotting on the vivid

Lilium **'Journey's End'**

crimson flowers, which pale to
near white at the margins and tips
of the segments. **L. 'Star Gazer'**,
another Oriental hybrid of similar
size with recurved flowers, is
familiar as a cut flower because it
responds well to forcing. The
fragrant blooms have broad, rich
crimson segments, pale at the tip
and margins and liberally spotted
with maroon dots.

L. 'Mont Blanc' (Asiatic hybrid)
Flowers: early to mid-summer.
H:2–3ft (60–90cm), S:6–8in
(15–20cm). Stem rooting. Z:3–8.
Erect pale-pink buds, usually 5 to 8
in number, open to upward-facing
creamy flowers, which are
peppered maroon at the center
and have dark orange anthers.
L. 'Enchantment' is another short
Asiatic hybrid with upward-facing
flowers. They are bowl shaped,
brilliant orange, spotted black in
the center, and there can be as
many as 16 to a stem.

Lilium **'Enchantment'**

L. Pink Perfection Group
(Trumpet and Aurelian hybrid)
Flowers: mid- to late summer.
H:4–6ft (1.2–1.8m), S:10–12in
(25–30cm). Z:4–8.
Stout stems carry several slightly
nodding and strongly scented
trumpet flowers. The pale to
purplish-pink segments curl back
from dark orange anthers.

Lilium **Pink Perfection Group**

L. 'Sterling Star' (Asiatic hybrid)
Flowers: early to mid-summer.
H:3–4ft (1–1.2m), S:8–10in
(20–25cm). Stem rooting. Z:3–8.
Buff-tinted white starry flowers,

usually 6 to 10 per stem, open
nearly flat from pale greenish-pink
buds. The anthers are dark orange,
and dark brown dots speckle the
center. Another Asiatic hybrid of
similar size with upward-facing
flowers is **L. 'Connecticut King'**.
Flowers are star-shaped and a rich
greenish yellow with warmer
shading. **L. 'Montreux'** is slightly
shorter, with greenish buds
opening to nearly flat pink flowers
that have minute brown dots right
at the center.

Lilium **'Montreux'**

MUSCARI

Hyacinthaceae Grape hyacinth

The commonly grown grape
hyacinths represent a relatively
small proportion of the 30 or so
species distributed in Europe and
southwestern Asia. The bulbs are
fleshy and the leaves, basal and
usually grasslike but channeled on
the inside surface, begin to appear
in autumn. A few species are
autumn flowering, but most
produce their spikes of densely
packed bells in spring. The
flowers, in most cases blue and
less than ½in (1cm) in length, are
constricted at the mouth. The
topmost flowers, which are
generally sterile, are often paler
than those lower on the spike.
Some species are sweetly scented.
In general they thrive on well-
drained soil in partial shade as well
as in open positions, but produce
leaves rather than flower spikes
when deprived of sunlight. Some,
especially **M. neglectum** (Z:4–8),
spread so freely that they should
be introduced only with caution.
The less vigorous are attractive in
rock gardens and raised beds. The
strong family resemblance among
Muscari extends to the pick of a
closely related genus, ***Bellevalia
paradoxa*** (***Muscari paradoxum***)
(Z:7–9), although its flowers are
not constricted at the mouth. This
species requires similar conditions
to the *Muscari* described here.
Cultivation Tolerate full sun or
partial shade and require well-
drained soil. Plant in early autumn,

covering bulbs with about 4in (10cm) of soil.

PROPAGATION From offsets, removed in summer. From seed, sown in late summer or early autumn.

POTENTIAL PROBLEMS Viruses.

M. armeniacum *Caucasus to S.E. Europe and Turkey*
Flowers: mid- to late spring. H:8–10in (20–25cm), S:2–3in (5–7.5cm). Z:4–8.
The narrow leaves, which appear in autumn, are rather lax and messy but the spike of tightly packed scented flowers is sturdy. The flowers are bell-like and bright blue, with hints of purple and violet. The constricted mouth has a thin white rim. This is the best grape hyacinth for general planting. '**Blue Spike**' has a heavy head of large, double flowers with strong purple and violet shading. '**Heavenly Blue**' is a misleading name for a selection with single flowers of dark blue.

Muscari aucheri

M. aucheri *N.W. Iran*
Flowers: early to mid-spring. H:6–8in (15–20cm), S:2–3in (5–7.5cm). Z:6–8.
The contrast between the deep blue fertile flowers and the pale blue sterile ones above them is remarkable in this species, sometimes known as the Oxford and Cambridge grape hyacinth.

M. azureum *Caucasus, E. Turkey*
Flowers: early to mid-spring. H:4–6in (10–15cm), S:2in (5cm). Z:7–9.
The short spike, surrounded by broad leaves, is packed with pale blue bells with a darker stripe down the center of each lobe. This species often self-seeds freely but is suitable for a large rock garden.

M. botryoides *C. and S.E. Europe*
Flowers: mid-spring. H:6–8in (15–20cm), S:2in (5cm). Z:2–8.
The spikes have globular blue flowers with a white rim. It and the pearly '**Album**' do not spread so freely as to be a nuisance.

Muscari botryoides 'Album'

M. comosum *Iran, S. Europe, Turkey*
Tassel grape hyacinth
Flowers: late spring to early summer. H:10–20in (25–50cm), S:2–3in (5–7.5cm). Z:4–8.
The species, which is common in the wild in cultivated and rough ground, is easy to grow, but its lax spike of fertile olive-green flowers topped by a tuft of purplish-blue sterile flowers is not of great ornamental value. '**Plumosum**', the feather or grape hyacinth, is, however, an interesting curiosity. All the flowers are sterile, the long-lasting mauve plumes that make it so distinctive consisting of elongated filaments.

NARCISSUS

AMARYLLIDACEAE Daffodil

Daffodils and other narcissi have been enormously popular spring bulbs for hundreds of years. Thousands of cultivars have been developed from the 50 or so species found in Europe, north Africa, and Asia, the strongest concentration being in W. Europe and the Iberian peninsula. In the wild, the species occupy a range of habitats from sea level to the sub-alpine zone, often growing in open meadows or short turf, sometimes on the fringes of woodland. The bulbs produce strap-shaped or rushlike basal leaves and erect leafless stems bearing a solitary flower or umbels with up to 20 flowers breaking out of the sheath at the head of the stem.

What has always fascinated gardeners is that sitting at the center of the 6 petallike segments is a cup or trumpet, a structure known as a corona. Gold, greenish yellow, soft yellow, cream, and white are the predominant colors but among the numerous bicolored cultivars, many have orange and a few have pink coronas. Most of the species and cultivars are fragrant, and some, especially the jonquils (*N. jonquilla* and hybrids of which it is a parent), have sweet scent of

superlative quality. The species and hybrids are a versatile group of garden plants, the more robust being unbeatable for the bold effects they create when naturalized, colonies usually being long-lived, provided the leaves are allowed to die down naturally. The really beefy hybrids are best naturalized in parklike settings, the species and the smaller, well-proportioned hybrids being more suitable for beds and borders and for naturalizing in a wilder setting. There is a wide choice of plants for rock gardens and containers.

All the divisions in the standard categorization of the genus are represented in the following selection (the name of the division is given in the head of the hybrid entries), but it is unapologetically weighted in favor of the species, which are described first, and the more lightly built hybrids. The swept back segments of the cyclamineus hybrids, a trait derived from *N. cyclamineus*, give these well-proportioned daffodils a breezy character. They are among the most versatile of all the narcissi, many naturalizing well and all suitable for beds, borders, rock gardens, and containers.

CULTIVATION Most tolerate full sun or partial shade and require well-drained soil, perhaps with added grit for dwarf species, and a good supply of moisture in spring, but see under headings and individual entries. Plant in early autumn, covering bulbs with 2–6in (5–15cm) of soil, at a depth about 3 times the height of the bulb, deeper in dry soil and in grass.

PROPAGATION From offsets, removed in the dormant season. From seed, sown as soon as ripe.

POTENTIAL PROBLEMS Narcissus bulb flies, narcissus nematodes, slugs; viruses and fungal diseases.

SPECIES

N. bulbocodium *N.W. Africa, Portugal, Spain, S.W. France*
Hoop-petticoat daffodil
Flowers: late winter to early spring. H:4–10in (10–25cm), S:2in (5cm). Z:6–9.
In the wild, this highly distinctive but very variable dwarf species is mainly found in alpine turf. The flowers, produced singly among dark green narrow leaves, are dominated by a funnel-shaped corona 1–2in (2.5–5cm) across, in which can be seen the curved stamens and style. The narrow, short segments, hardly more than vestiges, are the same rich yellow

as the petticoat. The numerous variations on this theme are all remarkable plants, 2 superlative examples being the very free-flowering deep yellow **var. conspicuus** and **var. citrinus**, which has large, lemon-yellow flowers.

Narcissus cyclamineus

N. cyclamineus *Portugal, Spain*
Flowers: late winter to early spring. H:4–8in (10–20cm), S:2in (5cm). Z:6–9.
In damp acid soils that match conditions in its native mountain pasture habitat, this dwarf species, a parent of some of the finest daffodil hybrids, will spread freely to form low drifts even in light shade. The bright yellow flowers have segments swept back from the narrow frilled trumpet.

N. jonquilla *Portugal, Spain*
Wild jonquil
Flowers: mid-spring. H:10–12in (25–30cm), S:2in (5cm). Z:4–9.
The sweet scent is an outstanding feature. The jonquil, which has semicylindrical leaves, produces 3 to 6 deep yellow flowers per stem, the pointed segments radiating from a tiny cup. It does best in full sun on neutral to slightly alkaline soil that is moist in spring.

N. poeticus var. recurvus
Switzerland
Old pheasant's eye
Flowers: late spring. H:14–16in (35–40cm), S:3–4in (7.5–10cm). Z:4–9.
Swept-back segments of glistening white give this variety of the pheasant's eye narcissus a wind-tossed look. The cup is green and yellow rimmed with red. It does best in rather moist soils.

N. pseudonarcissus *Europe*
Wild daffodil, Lent lily
Flowers: early spring. H:6–14in (15–35cm), S:2–4in (5–10cm). Z:4–9.
The fragrant flowers, usually solitary, are carried above a tuft of strap-shaped, gray-green or bluish-green leaves. The trumpet, which

is flared at the mouth, is pale to deep yellow, and the creamy segments are usually slightly twisted. The species, subspecies, and cultivars are among the best daffodils for naturalizing, shaming the heavyweight hybrids by their graceful proportions. **'Lobularis'** is a short-growing bicolored selection, rarely more than 8in (20cm) tall, with slightly drooping flowers. The flowers of **subsp. obvallaris** are a uniform rich yellow, and the trumpet is sometimes more than 2in (5cm) long. The flower stems are about 12in (30cm) tall.

Narcissus pseudonarcissus **subsp. obvallaris**

N. triandrus *Portugal, Spain*
Angel's tears
Flowers: early to mid-spring. H:4–10in (10–25cm), S:2in (5cm). Z:4–8.
The pendulous creamy white flowers are 1 to 6 to a stem with segments swept back. The anthers, protruding from the cup, have a balletic charm that invites close inspection, making this a superb plant for the alpine house. It can be naturalized in short turf, especially on neutral to acid soils.

HYBRIDS

N. 'Actaea' (Poeticus)
Flowers: late spring. H:18–20in (45–50cm), S 4–6in (10–15cm). Z:4–9.
The fragrant flowers can be 3in (7.5cm) across, the crisp white, broad segments around a small yellow cup with a conspicuous red

Narcissus **'Actaea'**

rim. *N.* **'Cantabile'**, a shorter Poeticus daffodil, to 14in (35cm) tall, has brilliant white segments forming a circular outline and a flattened cup, which has bands of green and yellow and an orange-red rim.

Narcissus **'Ice Follies'**

N. 'Carlton' (Large-cupped)
Flowers: early to mid-spring. H:18–20in (45–50cm), S:4in (10cm). Z:4–9.
The flowers are large, but the corona is almost trumpetlike, giving this soft yellow hybrid pleasing proportions. Among daffodils in this division that have pink flowers *N.* **'Satin Pink'** is one of the truest in color and has a long corona. The overlapping segments are pure white.
N. **'Ice Follies'** is a coarser but sturdy hybrid in this division. The overlapping segments are creamy white, and the short gaping cup, frilled at the edge, fades from lemon-yellow to near-white.

Narcissus **'Rip van Winkle'**

N. 'Cheerfulness' (Double)
Flowers: mid-spring. H:16–18in (40–45cm), S:3–4in (7.5–10cm). Z:4–9.
An orange glow emanates from the centers of the creamy double flowers, usually 3 to a stem. The scent is very sweet. *N.* **'Yellow Cheerfulness'** has yellow flowers. The small scale of *N.* **'Rip van Winkle'**, only 6–8in (15–20cm) tall, makes it a more appealing curiosity than larger double daffodils with single flowers. Its green-tinted sunburst is composed of numerous yellow segments.

Narcissus 'February Gold'

N. 'February Gold'
(Cyclamineus)
Flowers: early spring. H:10–12in (25–30cm), S:3in (7.5cm). Z:6–9.
Although rarely as precocious as the name suggests, this stalwart flowers early and is long lasting. The flowers are up to 3in (7.5cm) across with deep yellow trumpets and slightly paler segments.
N. 'February Silver' has a lemon-yellow trumpet, slightly ragged at the mouth, surrounded by creamy-white segments. A slightly taller companion from the same division is N. 'Peeping Tom', with a strikingly long narrow trumpet, flaring at the mouth, and of an almost uniform rich yellow.

N. 'Golden Harvest' (Trumpet)
Flowers: mid-spring. H:16–18in (40–45cm), S:3–4in (7.5–10cm). Z:4–9.
Rich yellow flowers, the trumpet flaring widely and the segments slightly twisted, and its way of increasing freely have made this a favorite among the large trumpet daffodils. Other heavyweights include N. 'Arctic Gold' and N. 'Dutch Master'. Among whites are the glacial N. 'Empress of Ireland' and N. 'Mount Hood'.

N. 'Hawera' (Triandrus)
Flowers: mid-spring. H:8–10in (20–25cm), S:2–3in (5–7.5cm). Z:4–9.
This slender N. triandrus and N. jonquilla hybrid produces several stems per bulb, each with 3 to 5 canary-yellow flowers up to 2in (5cm) across, with swept-back segments. N. 'Petrel' is similar but white, with rounded segments. N. 'Thalia', with several milky flowers to a stem, is 12–14in (30–35cm) tall. The elegant N. 'Rippling Waters' is short cupped, creamy, and taller.

N. 'Jenny' (Cyclamineus)
Flowers: early to mid-spring. H:10–12in (25–30cm), S:2–3in (5–7.5cm). Z:6–9.
The poise and neat proportions of this hybrid are outstanding. The creamy-white pointed segments are swept back from a waisted trumpet that is lemon-yellow on opening but soon fades to palest cream. N. 'Dove Wings' is similar but with more rounded segments. More pronounced bicolored effects in this division are found in N. 'Jack Snipe', with creamy-white segments swept back from a short golden trumpet, and N. 'Itzim', which has strongly reflexed yellow segments and a short orange trumpet, pale at first but intensifying in color. These 2 hybrids are 8–10in (20–25cm) tall.

Narcissus 'Jack Snipe'

N. 'Merlin' (Small-cupped)
Flowers: mid-spring. H:16–18in (40–45cm), S:3–4in (7.5–10cm). Z:4–9.
The overlapping segments make a circular surround of pure white for the yellow corona, with an orange rim. N. 'Birma' has an orange cup with ruffled rim flaring at the center of yellow segments.

Narcissus 'Birma'

N. 'Orangery' (Split corona)
Flowers: mid-spring. H:16–18in (40–45cm), S:3–4in (7.5–10cm). Z:4–9.
The split corona that gives this daffodil its unusual form consists of a ruffled collar with only the margins of the segments showing.

N. 'Rijnveld's Early Sensation' (Trumpet)
Flowers: late winter. H:10–12in (25–30cm), S:2–3in (5–7.5cm). Z:4–9.
This yellow hybrid with lasting blooms is one of the first trumpet daffodils to flower. Short but well proportioned, trumpet hybrids that follow in early spring include N. 'Topolino', 6–8in (15–20cm) tall, with cream segments and a lemon trumpet, and the taller N. 'W.P. Milner' (Z:6–9).

Narcissus 'Rijnveld's Early Sensation'

N. 'Silver Chimes' (Tazetta)
Flowers: mid-spring. H:12–14in (30–35cm), S:3–4in (7.5–10cm). Z:5–9.
Each stem of this vigorous and fragrant hybrid produces a shower of up to 10 nodding white flowers with cups of palest yellow. A taller Tazetta, N. 'Geranium', has a cluttered head of 5 or 6 sweetly scented flowers with orange cups standing out against pure white.

Narcissus 'Sweetness'

N. 'Sweetness' (Jonquilla)
Flowers: mid-spring. H:14–16in (35–40cm), S:3–4in (7.5–10cm). Z:4–9.
This hybrid bears only 1 flower per stem, but it is superbly scented, beautifully proportioned, and a clear yellow throughout.

N. 'Tête-à-Tête' (Miscellaneous)
Flowers: late winter to early spring. H:6–8in (15–20cm), S:2in (5cm). Z:6–9.
This dwarf daffodil shows its Cyclamineus parentage in the yellow segments swept back from a richly colored cup. It deserves its popularity as a container plant, giving an early and long-lasting display. N. 'Jumblie' (Z:4–9) has 2 or 3 short orange-yellow trumpets to a stem.

Narcissus 'Tête-à-Tête'

N. 'Trevithian' (Jonquilla)
Flowers: mid-spring. H:16–20in
(40–50cm), S:3–4in (7.5–10cm).
Z:4–9.
The elegance of the flowers, 2 or 3
to a stem, small cupped and a soft
yellow, make this a distinctive
jonquil, and the purity of the scent
is unimpaired. The shorter *N.* 'Pipit',
about 10in (25cm) tall, has 2 or 3
fragrant lemon flowers to a stem,
their small cups fading to cream.
The dwarf, rich yellow *N.* 'Sundial',
6–8in (15–20cm) tall, has tiny
disklike central cups.

Narcissus 'Trevithian'

NECTAROSCORDUM

ALLIACEAE

Among the most intriguing of the
summer-flowering tall bulbs are
these representatives of the onion
tribe. The basal leaves, linear and
with a sharp keel, smell strongly of
garlic, but the dried seedheads,
which are attractive for indoor
decorations, are scentless. Plants
may self-seed freely.
CULTIVATION Require full sun or
partial shade and well-drained soil.
Plant in autumn, covering the
bulbs with 4–6in (10–15cm) of soil.
PROPAGATION From offsets,
removed in late summer. From
seed, sown as soon as ripe.
POTENTIAL PROBLEMS Usually none.

N. siculum France, Italy
Flowers: late spring to early
summer. H:2–4ft (60–120cm),
S:4–6in (10–15cm). Z:7–9.
The numerous bell-shaped flowers,
spraying out on downward-arching
stalks from the head of a stout

stem, are creamy white with green
tints and reddish-purple markings.
The plant is also attractive when
carrying seeds, the stalks turning
to hold the pods erect. The color
combination of straw, green, and
maroon in **subsp.** *bulgaricum*,
from S.E. Europe, Turkey, and the
Crimea, is even more unusual.

Nectaroscordum siculum **subsp.**
bulgaricum

NERINE

AMARYLLIDACEAE

These bulbs flower in autumn
before the linear leaves appear.
The flowers, which are borne in
umbels, that is, with all the stalks
springing from the end of the
stem, are like small lilies, with 6
strap-shaped segments. These are
often wavy at the margins, curling
back from the thrusting cluster of
stamens and style. Species such as
N. sarniensis and the hybrids do
well in pots, preferring some
crowding to frequent repotting.
The crystalline sparkle of the long-
lasting flowers makes nerines good
for the greenhouse and for cutting.
CULTIVATION Require full sun and
well-drained potting media with
added grit, dry during the dormant
season. Plant in late summer,
either under glass, setting the
bulbs with their tips showing, or
plant outdoors, covering the bulbs
with 3–4in (7.5–10cm) of soil.
PROPAGATION By division of clumps
after flowering. From seed, sown
as soon as ripe.
POTENTIAL PROBLEMS Slug damage.
WARNING All parts may cause
stomach upset if eaten.

Nerine bowdenii

N. bowdenii South Africa
(Eastern Cape, KwaZulu/Natal,
Orange Free State)
Flowers: early to late autumn.
H:18–24in (45–60cm), S:3–4in
(7.5–10cm). Z:7–9.
In cool climates this useful garden
plant needs a favored position,
such as the base of a warm wall,
and it is worth covering the bulbs
with a mulch during winter where
frosts are heavy. The 3 to 9 flowers
at the head of a stiff stem have
glistening pink, rather narrow
segments with crimped edges. In
the vigorous selection, *N.* 'Mark
Fenwick' has a stem that is
purplish green.

ORNITHOGALUM

HYACINTHACEAE Star of Bethlehem

A cool beauty distinguishes a few
among the many species in this
genus. The fleshy bulbs produce
basal leaves that are generally
linear or strap shaped and a stem
carrying numerous starry or cup-
shaped flowers, in many cases
white, with a green stripe on the
reverse of the 6 segments. The
untidy leaves, which sometimes
have a silver stripe, die back just
before or just as plants start
flowering. They will need masking
in beds and borders. The half-
hardy Chincherinchee
(*O. thyrsoides*), familiar as a cut
flower, can be grown in frost-
prone areas, but requires similar
cultivation to hybrid gladioli.
CULTIVATION O. arabicum needs full
sun and well-drained soil; others
tolerate full sun or partial shade
and require well-drained soil. Plant
in mid-autumn (half-hardy species
outdoors in mid-spring), covering
the bulbs with 3–4in (7.5–10cm)
of soil.
PROPAGATION From offsets,
removed in the dormant season.
From seed, sown in autumn or
spring.
POTENTIAL PROBLEMS Usually none.
WARNING All parts may cause
stomach upset if eaten; the sap
may irritate the skin.

O. arabicum Mediterranean
Flowers: late spring to early
summer. H:16–30in (40–75cm),
S:3–4in (7.5–10cm). Z:8–10.
A stout stem carries 6 to 12,
occasionally more, cup-shaped,
scented flowers that are 2in (5cm)
or more across. Their pearly
whiteness is accentuated by the
conspicuous black ovary that is
situated right at the flower's
center. The dark green, semierect
leaves can be up to 24in (60cm)
in length.

Ornithogalum nutans

O. nutans *Europe, S.W Asia*
Flowers: mid- to late spring.
H:12–18in (30–45cm), S:2–3in
(5–7.5cm). Z:5–9.
This true woodlander has widely
distributed naturalized populations
beyond the Balkans, to which it is
thought to be native. The 1-sided
spikes usually carry 10 to 12
flaring bells that are silvery white
on the inside and have a broad,
jade-green stripe on the outside.
The leaves feature a central
gray line.

Ornithogalum umbellatum

O. umbellatum *E. Mediterranean,
Europe, N. Africa, Turkey*
Star of Bethlehem
Flowers: mid- to late spring.
H:6–12in (15–30cm), S:3–4in
(7.5–10cm). Z:4–9.
Although its rapid increase and the
untidiness of its leaves, which have
a central silver stripe, make this
species a nuisance in beds and
borders, in the wild garden it is an
asset. It has sturdy stems that
carry numerous starry white
flowers that are tinted green at
the center and striped green on
the reverse.

OXALIS

OXALIDACEAE

Several of the dwarf species in this
genus have attractive cloverlike
leaves (in some species these fold
at night) and 5-petaled flowers that
are exquisitely furled in bud and
open to wide funnels in sun. These
sun-loving plants are suitable to
grow in rock gardens, raised beds,
and alpine houses.

CULTIVATION Require full sun and
well-drained potting media with
added grit. Plant in early autumn or
early to mid-spring (*O. tetraphylla*),
covering the rootstock with about
2in (5cm) of soil.
PROPAGATION From bulblets pulled
from the roots or division of the
rootstock in the dormant season.
From seed, sown in early spring.
POTENTIAL PROBLEMS Usually none.

Oxalis adenophylla

O. adenophylla *Argentina, Chile*
Flowers: early to mid-summer.
H:3–4in (7.5–10cm), S:4–6in
(10–15cm). Z:5–9.
Once it captures the eye, this
Andean species is beguiling in its
detail. The small bulb, padded
with the fibrous bases of old
leaves, produces a cushion of gray-
green leaves, consisting of
numerous neatly pleated heart-
shaped leaflets. These are studded
with buds that unfurl to reveal
attractive red-purple-throated
flowers with pink veining and
shading on white.

O. enneaphylla *Falkland Islands,
Patagonia*
Flowers: late spring to early
summer. H:3–4in (7.5–10cm),
S:4–6in (10–15cm). Z:6–9.
The blue-green, hairy, fleshy leaves
of this plant are umbrella shaped,
with 9 or more pleated segments.
The numerous solitary flowers that
are borne are white or pink and
darkly veined. 'Rosea' has white-
throated pink flowers that are
tinged with mauve.

O. tetraphylla *Mexico*
Good luck plant, lucky clover
Flowers: early to late summer.
H:6–8in (15–20cm), S:6–10in
(15–25cm). Z:8–9.
The funnel-shaped pink flowers,
4 to 12 to a stem, that are borne
throughout summer are less
interesting than the leaves. These
consist of 4 triangular leaflets that
meet at their apex and fold in as
light fails. In 'Iron Cross' there is a
chocolate band at the center of the
leaf that creates a bold cross when
the leaflets are open.

PUSCHKINIA

HYACINTHACEAE

The single species in this genus is
an early-flowering dwarf bulb that
is closely related to *Scilla* and
glory of the snow (*Chionodoxa*).
In its mountainous native habitat it
is found growing in short turf and
flowers as the snow melts. Its
silvery beauty is seen to good
effect in an alpine house. In the
open garden it looks at home in
front of shrubs or mixed with
other dwarf plants in rock gardens
or raised beds.
CULTIVATION Tolerates full sun or
partial shade and requires well-
drained soil with a plentiful supply
of moisture in the growing season
(add grit if necessary). Plant in
autumn, covering the bulbs with
2–3in (5–7.5cm) of soil.
PROPAGATION From offsets,
removed during the dormant season.
From seed, sown as soon as ripe.
POTENTIAL PROBLEMS Viruses.

**Puschkinia scilloides var.
libanotica**

P. scilloides *Caucasus, Lebanon,
N. Iran, N. Iraq, Turkey*
Flowers: early to mid-spring.
H:6–8in (15–20cm), S:2in (5cm).
Z:5–8.
A pair of strap-shaped leaves flanks
the lax stem, which bears
numerous bell-shaped flowers.
Although the depth of color varies,
they are usually pale blue and each
segment is marked with a darker
blue stripe. In **var. libanotica** the
flowers are smaller and the blue
striping less conspicuous.

RHODOHYPOXIS

HYPOXIDACEAE

The flat flowers of these bright
miniatures are puzzling, the 6
segments being arranged in such a
way that the style and stamens at
the center are obscured. Despite
their diminutive size, the species
and its cultivars or hybrids, here all
listed under *R. baurii*, make a long
and colorful display in tubs and
other containers outside or in the
alpine house as well as in rock

gardens and raised beds. The corm-like rootstocks need protection from excessive wet in winter.
CULTIVATION Require full sun and lime-free, well-drained soil with a plentiful supply of moisture in the growing season (ericaceous medium with added grit). Plant in early autumn, covering the rootstock with about 1in (2.5cm) of soil or medium.
PROPAGATION From offsets, removed in early autumn. From seed, sown in autumn or spring.
POTENTIAL PROBLEMS Usually none.

Rhodohypoxis baurii 'Alba'

R. baurii *South Africa*
Flowers: late spring to early autumn. H:2–4in (5–10cm), S:2–4in (5–10cm). Z:7–10.
A long succession of pale to dark pink flowers, no more than ⅜in (2cm) across, are produced among a tuft of hairy, linear leaves. The cultivars, some of which may be of hybrid origin, similar in general character to the species, include **'Alba'**, white; *R.* **'Appleblossom'**, a soft combination of pink and green; *R.* **'Harlequin'**, small white flowers with a pink suffusion and pink margins; *R.* **'Helen'**, pure white flowers nearly twice as large as those of the species; *R.* **'Tetra Pink'**, large pink flowers; and *R.* **'Tetra Red'**, like a much darker version of *R.* 'Tetra Pink'.

Rhodohypoxis 'Tetra Red'

SCILLA

HYACINTHACEAE

The small species from temperate Europe and S.W. Asia are among the great delights of spring; their

blues include one of the most startlingly vivid of the early garden. The genus is a large one, with representatives in tropical and southern Africa and E. Asia. Naturalized colonies make blue eddies in short grass or among deciduous shrubs, but these species are also suitable for rock gardens and alpine houses.
CULTIVATION S. *peruviana* requires full sun and fertile, well-drained soil; other species tolerate full sun or partial shade and require well-drained soil with added leaf-mold and grit) and a plentiful supply of moisture in spring. Plant in autumn, covering the bulbs of spring-flowering species with 3–4in (7.5–10cm) of soil or compost; set bulbs of *S. peruviana* just below the surface.
PROPAGATION From seed, sown as soon as ripe. From offsets (produced sparingly), removed during the dormant season.
POTENTIAL PROBLEMS Viruses.

S. bifolia *S. Europe to Turkey*
Flowers: late winter to early spring. H:3–6in (7.5–15cm), S:2in (5cm). Z:4–8.
Lax stems seem to teeter among the fleshy leaves, leaning with an arrangement of up to 10 flowers. The flowers face outward or upward and are usually strong blue, although there is considerable variation. **'Rosea'** is pink.

Scilla mischtschenkoana

S. mischtschenkoana *From Georgia to N.W. Iran*
Flowers: late winter to early spring. H:4–6in (10–15cm), S:2in (5cm). Z:4–8.
The precocious blue flowers, with a darker stripe down each segment, seem to emerge from below ground already open. There are several stems to a bulb, each with 2 to 6 flat flowers facing outward.

S. peruviana *Italy, N. Africa, Portugal, Spain*
Flowers: late spring to early summer. H:8–12in (20–30cm), S:6–8in (15–20cm). Z:5–8.
The sturdy stem terminates in a

conelike arrangement of up to 100 starry flowers, which are metallic blue or white. This species does not have a dormant season, with the new linear leaves starting into growth in autumn as the older leaves die off.

Scilla peruviana

S. siberica *Russia and Ukraine to N. Iran and Turkey*
Siberian squill
Flowers: early spring. H:4–8in (10–20cm), S:2in (5cm). Z:2–8.
The piercing blue of the flowers provides one of the most intense color sensations of early spring. There are usually several stems to a bulb, each bearing about 4 down-turned flowers, with some paler forms showing a dark stripe down the center of the segments.
'Spring Beauty' is robust and early flowering with deep coloring.

Scilla siberica

STERNBERGIA

AMARYLLIDACEAE

The best-known species in this small genus of only 8 species produces crocuslike flowers in autumn. Like others in the genus, whether autumn or spring flowering, in the wild it is usually found in stony ground, often on lime, that is baked for several months by an implacable sun. In cooler climates, it does best at the base of a sunny wall.
CULTIVATION Requires full sun and well-drained soil-potting media with added grit, with a dry period in summer. Plant in late summer or early autumn, covering bulbs with 4–6in (10–15cm) of soil.

PROPAGATION From offsets, removed in late summer. From seed, sown as soon as ripe.
POTENTIAL PROBLEMS Narcissus bulb flies and nematodes; narcissus viruses.

Sternbergia lutea

S. lutea *S. Europe to C. Asia*
Flowers: early to mid-autumn. H:4–6in (10–15cm), S:4–6in (10–15cm). Z:6–9.
Linear, deep green leaves show off the sheeny gold of the flowers, which are about 2in (5cm) long. The leaves reach their full length of about 12in (30cm) in spring.

TECOPHILAEA

TECOPHILAEACEAE

There are only 2 species in this South American genus, and the 1 described, a very great beauty, is now extremely rare or extinct in its native habitat in the high Andean meadows of Chile. As a garden plant, it evokes rapturous responses, but success cannot be taken for granted and corms are scarce. In warm gardens, it has been grown successfully outdoors in sunny beds, but because of its rarity, it is usually treated as a treasure for the alpine house.
CULTIVATION Requires full sun and sandy, well-drained soil that dries out in summer (add grit if necessary). Plant in mid-autumn, covering the corms with about 2in (5cm) of soil.
PROPAGATION From offsets, removed in late summer. From seed, sown as soon as ripe.
POTENTIAL PROBLEMS Usually none.

Tecophilaea cyanocrocus 'Leichtlinii'

T. cyanocrocus *South America*
Chilean blue crocus
Flowers: early to mid-spring. H:3–6in (7.5–15cm), S:2in (5cm). Z:6–8.
The stems that rise among the linear basal leaves bear 1 to 3 scented flowers that seem to have been drenched in blue pigment except for a small white center. When the 6 segments open nearly flat, the flowers are about 2in (5cm) across. '**Leichtlinii**' is paler and has more white in the throat.

TIGRIDIA

IRIDACEAE Peacock flower, tiger flower

Of the 20 or so species in this mainly Central American genus, only the gorgeous peacock flower, which is naturalized in many tropical and subtropical countries, is widely known. The exotic blooms only last a day, but each stem bears up to 6 in succession and a fairly long display in late summer can be achieved by planting batches of corms over a period of 5 or 6 weeks.
CULTIVATION Requires full sun and well-drained fertile soil with a plentiful supply of moisture in the growing season (add humus and grit to potting medium). Plant from mid-spring, covering the bulbs with 3–4in (7.5–10cm) of soil.
PROPAGATION From seed, sown in spring.
POTENTIAL PROBLEMS Virus diseases.

Tigridia pavonia

T. pavonia *Guatemala, Mexico*
Peacock flower, tiger flower
Flowers: mid-summer to early autumn. H:16–24in (40–60cm), S:4–6in (10–15cm). Z:8–10.
The vivid flowers, which float above a fan of basal leaves, have 3 large outer segments and when fully open are up to 4in (10cm) across. The color range includes red, orange, yellow, white, and purple. Often their dramatic effect is enhanced by bold spotting or splashing of the central cup and small inner segments, usually in a shade of red on white or yellow.

TULIPA

LILIACEAE Tulip

The tulip is so strongly associated with Holland that the Turkish origins of the flower are often neglected. There are about 100 species, growing mainly in areas with hot, dry summers, many being native to Central Asia. There is much variety in the shape and coloring of the flower, which has 6 segments, and of the foliage. The many hybrids are popular spring bulbs for bedding and containers as well as dry sunny sites.

A standard classification of tulips in 15 divisions is based on flower characteristics, season of flowering, and parentage. The most familiar tulips, with single globular or cup-shaped flowers on stems roughly 12–24in (30–60cm) tall, are found in the Single Early, Triumph, Darwin Hybrid, and Single Late groups. Distinguished from these by their numerous segments are the Double Early and Double Late groups. Another flower shape is provided by the Lily-flowered tulips—their goblet-shaped blooms have long pointed segments that recurve sharply. Other groups with distinctive characteristics include the Fringed tulips, the Viridiflora Group with green suffusions and streaks, and the Parrot Group, flamboyant confections usually with twisted segments that are irregularly striped and cut. Another once greatly prized group, the Rembrandt or "broken" tulips have the main color interrupted by streaks or "feathers" of a darker color. They are not represented as they are no longer readily available, virus being the cause of the color breaking. The Kaufmanniana, Greigii, and Fosteriana Groups each takes its name from a species and includes hybrids in which the character of the species dominates. The waterlily tulip (**T. kaufmanniana**, Z:5–9) is a parent of an important group of showy dwarf hybrids with flowers that open wide to form a 6-pointed star. Some reveal the influence of the taller **T. greigii** (Z:5–9) in the purplish mottling and streaking of gray-green leaves. The brilliance of the scarlet **T. fosteriana** (Z:5–9) has been passed on to other tulips. The Miscellaneous Group contains many characterful species, a counterbalance to the stolid hybrids. In these descriptions, the species precede the hybrids and the division is given with each entry.
CULTIVATION All require full sun and

well-drained soil, the species and hybrids close to them usually require sharper drainage than other hybrids (potting media with additional grit). Plant in mid- to late autumn, covering the bulbs with 4–6in (10–15cm) of soil or compost. Most species as well as Greigii and Kaufmanniana hybrids can be left in the ground from year to year, but lift hybrids when the foliage has died down, ripen under glass, and replant in autumn.

PROPAGATION From offsets, removed when lifting. From seed, sown as soon as ripe.

POTENTIAL PROBLEMS Aphids, stem and bulb nematodes; viruses, tulip fire.

SPECIES

Tulipa clusiana var. chrysantha

T. clusiana *Iran to W. Himalayas*
Lady tulip
Flowers: mid-spring. H:10–12in (25–30cm), S:3–4in (7.5–10cm). Z:5–8.
This slender beauty has white flowers with red bands on the 3 outer segments. As a fully open star, it shows a purple-red blotch at the center. It has gray-green, hairless leaves. **Var.** *chrysantha* is similar, but the flower is yellow with yellow anthers, but with the 3 outer segments flushed red.

Tulipa linifolia

T. linifolia
Afghanistan, N. Iran, Uzbekistan
Flowers: early to mid-spring.
H:6–8in (15–20cm), S:4in (10cm). Z:3–8.
Red flowers with pointed segments

and black at the base stand above gray-green leaves with a wavy red margin. The **Batalinii Group** has yellow flowers. **'Bright Gem'**, with yellow flowers warmed with orange, is one of several cultivars in shades of apricot and bronze.

Tulipa linifolia Batalinii Group

T. marjolletii *S.W. Europe*
Flowers: early to mid-spring.
H:10–20in (25–50cm), S:3–4in (7.5–10cm). Z:4–8.
This lightly built tulip, which may be of garden origin, has yellow cup-shaped flowers with delicate dark pink shading at the segment edges.

T. praestans *C. Asia*
Flowers: mid-spring. H:12–18in (30–45cm), S:4–6in (10–15cm). Z:5–8.
There are up to 5 red flowers to a stem. Vermilion **'Fusilier'** is dramatic and makes a strong statement. **'Unicum'** has variegated foliage with white leaves.

Tulipa saxatilis

T. saxatilis *Crete, W. Turkey*
Flowers: mid- to late spring.
H:12–18in (30–45cm), S:4in (10cm). Z:4–8.
In a sunny position, this tulip spreads to form sizeable clumps. The yellow-centered, purple flowers, 1 to 3 per stem, are up to 3in (7.5cm) across. In the **Bakeri Group**, flowers are deeper colored.

T. sprengeri *Turkey*
Flowers: late spring to early summer. H:18–24in (45–60cm), S:4–6in (10–15cm). Z:5–8.
Few tulips are more satisfactory for naturalizing, and this, one of the

last to flower, does well in the dappled shade of an orchard or open woodland as well as in full sun. The globular flowers are red and have pointed segments.

T. tarda *C. Asia*
Flowers: early spring. H:4–6in (10–15cm), S:3–4in (7.5–10cm). Z:4–8.
When the bunch of starry flowers, 4 to 6 to a stem, are open, they appear yellow with white tips. In fact, the flowers are white, but tinged green or red. It flowers well without annual lifting.

Tulipa tarda

T. urumiensis *N.W. Iran*
Flowers: early spring. H and S:6in (15cm). Z:5–8.
Yellow flowers, tinged lilac on the outside, appear 1 or 2 to a stem above mid-green leaves.

HYBRIDS

***T.* 'Angélique'** (Double late)
Flowers: late spring. H:14–16in (35–40cm), S:4–6in (10–15cm). An.
Pink variations with hints of cream and yellow in the choked center of the cup make this a good double. Slightly taller are the variegated *T.* **'Carnaval de Nice'**, white streaked with dark red, and *T.* **'Mount Tacoma'**, white with some green.

***T.* 'Apeldoorn'** (Darwin hybrid)
Flowers: mid- to late spring. H:24–26in (60–65cm), S:4–6in (10–15cm). An.
The scarlet-orange colors of this sturdy tulip suit a massed display. *T.* **'Golden Apeldoorn'** has yellow goblets shaded greenish bronze.

***T.* 'Artist'** (Viridiflora)
Flowers: late spring. H:12–16in (30–40cm), S:4–6in (10–15cm). An.
A central green stripe runs to the tip of each segment, the margins of which are like wavy flanges of purple and salmon-pink. The inside of the flower has a green flush. **'Groenland'**, a taller Viridiflora tulip, has pale lemon and bright pink edges to green stripes.

Tulipa 'Couleur Cardinal'

T. 'Bellona' (Triumph)
Flowers: mid- to late spring.
H:14–16in (35–40cm), S:4–6in (10–15cm). An.
The yellow flowers are fragrant.
T. 'Couleur Cardinal' is crimson with a gray bloom. '**Prinses Irene**' has orange cups with purple streaks.

T. 'Estella Rijnveld' (Parrot)
Flowers: late spring. H:20–22in (50–55cm), S:4–6in (10–15cm). An.
An extravagant confection of swirling white and red stripes.

Tulipa 'Estella Rijnveld'

T. 'Generaal de Wet'
(Single early)
Flowers: mid-spring. H:14–16in (35–40cm), S:4–6in (10–15cm). An.
Few tulips are better scented, and the cup-shaped flowers are a radiant yellow warmed by rich orange. *T.* '**Keizerskroon**' has scarlet segments with some broad yellow margins.

Tulipa 'Keizerskroon'

T. 'Hamilton' (Fringed)
Flowers: late spring. H:20–22in (50–55cm), S:4–6in (10–15cm). An.
A heavy fringe, thistly, but soft to

the touch, trims a deep yellow, cup-shaped flower in this rather appealing hybrid.

T. 'Heart's Delight'
(Kaufmanniana)
Flowers: early to mid-spring.
H:8–10in (20–25cm), S:6–8in (15–20cm). An.
The flower of this tulip is bright carmine-red with a pale pink edge. This contrasts markedly with the white inside, which has a yellow base. The leaves are streaked with purple-brown. *T.* '**Stresa**', which is another waterlily tulip, has yellow flowers with red markings, including triangular shapes on the 3 outer segments.

Tulipa 'Madame Lefeber'

T. 'Madame Lefeber'
(Fosteriana)
Flowers: mid-spring. H:14–16in (35–40cm), S:4–6in (10–15cm). An.
This vivid scarlet tulip has large, well-shaped flowers with a yellow base. They are touched with a luxurious satin finish.

T. 'New Design' (Triumph)
Flowers: mid- to late spring.
H:18–22in (45–55cm), S:4–6in (10–15cm). An.
On the outside the flowers are pale yellow with reddish-pink margins; inside there is a strong yellow base and apricot flames. The margin of the leaves is silvery with pink staining. *T.* '**Douglas Bader**' is soft pink with darker shading. The flowers of the taller *T.* '**Shirley**', which grows 24in (60cm) tall, are white, edged with a narrow border of purple.

T. 'Purissima' (Fosteriana)
Flowers: mid-spring. H:14–16in (35–40cm), S:4–6in (10–15cm). An.
The milky white flowers of this tulip provide a useful contrast to other more brightly colored spring flowers.

T. 'Queen of Night' (Single late)
Flowers: late spring. H:24–26in (60–65cm), S:4–6in (10–15cm). An.
The velvety maroon of this tulip has great depth. Others in this

division include *T.* '**Bleu Aimable**', mauve-pink darkening to a purple bruise near the stem; *T.* '**Maureen**' has a pure white flower.

Tulipa 'Queen of Night'

T. 'Red Riding Hood' (Greigii)
Flowers: early to mid-spring.
H:8–10in (20–25cm), S:6–8in (15–20cm). Z:5–9.
Compact plants, the foliage strongly mottled, bear waisted flowers of dashing scarlet with black bases.

T. 'Schoonoord' (Double early)
Flowers: mid-spring. H:10–12in (25–30cm), S:4–6in (10–15cm). An.
The pure white flowers are frothy with generous doubling. Another stocky double, *T.* '**Peach Blossom**', has rosy pink flowers that often show greenish white at the base.

T. 'Toronto' (Greigii)
Flowers: early to mid-spring.
H:10–12in (25–30cm), S:6–8in (15–20cm). Z:5–9.
Several flowers to a stem make a reddish pink bouquet above foliage that is only lightly mottled.

T. 'White Triumphator'
(Lily-flowered)
Flowers: late spring. H:24–26in (60–65cm), S:4–6in (10–15cm). An.
The beauty of this tulip depends on its whiteness, the generosity of the cup, and the curve of the pointed segments. In *T.* '**Marilyn**', red flames flicker to the pointed tips of the ivory-white segments. Other shorter lily-flowered tulips include *T.* '**Aladdin**', scarlet with yellow edging; and *T.* '**West Point**', yellow, with narrow pointed tips.

Tulipa 'West Point'

annuals and biennials

Annuals are plants that germinate, grow to maturity, flower, produce seed, and die in a single season. Some biennials are included here, because they can be grown as annuals, although many would grow naturally over 2 years—producing leaves in the first year and flowers and seed in the second. The plants come from both temperate and subtropical climates, and display exceptionally diverse habits of growth.

New cultivars are introduced in large numbers every year, offering fresh color combinations, increased flower production, longer flowering seasons, and disease resistance. One of the best things about annuals is that they can be sown directly in the ground or propagated under glass so that they flower early. Protection is important in climates where they would not normally survive outdoors. The usual temperature range for germination is 59–64°F (15–18°C). If plants require a higher temperature, it is given as part of the propagation information in the introduction to the genus. Marigolds, petunias, and violas are among the many plants that flower exuberantly in containers or hanging baskets (using potting medium). Removal of dead flowerheads encourages the development of more flowers.

Annuals should be planted outdoors only when all risk of frost has passed.

Top Bracteantha bracteata Bright Bikinis Series
Center Eschscholzia californica
Bottom Tagetes Afro-French Group

AGROSTEMMA

CARYOPHYLLACEAE

Corn cockle (*A. githago*), once common on arable land, is the only widely grown species in this genus of 2 to 4 annuals from the Mediterranean and western Asia. The flowers are good for cutting.
CULTIVATION Require full sun and poor, well-drained soil.
PROPAGATION From seed, sown where plants are to flower in autumn or early spring.
POTENTIAL PROBLEMS Usually none.
WARNING Seeds can be toxic.

A. githago *Mediterranean*
Corn cockle
Flowers: summer. H:2–3ft (60–90cm), S:8–12in (20–30cm). An.
Branching downy stems with gray-green leaves carry 5-petaled flowers of purplish-pink with a white eye or, rarely, fully white. Those of **'Milas'** are deep plum-pink and up to 3in (7.5cm) across.

Agrostemma githago

ALCEA

MALVACEAE Hollyhock

The genus comprises about 60 species of biennials and short-lived perennials from temperate parts of Europe and Asia. The long-cultivated hollyhock (*A. rosea*) is troubled by rust and best grown as a usefully tall and striking biennial.
CULTIVATION Require full sun and reasonably fertile, well-drained soil.
PROPAGATION From seed, sown under glass in late winter or where plants are to flower in mid-summer.
POTENTIAL PROBLEMS Cutworms, slugs, mallow flea beetles, aphids, capsid bugs; hollyhock rust.

A. rosea *W. Asia*
Hollyhock
Flowers: summer. H:5–8ft (1.5–2.5m), S:18–24in (45–60cm). Z:6–9.
Tall cultivars may need support and have bare shins, but they make their point by streaking up to carry impressive spikes of single

to fully double flowers. **'Nigra'** is dark maroon with a yellow throat on the funnel-shaped flowers. The color range of **Chater's Double Group** includes red, apricot, white, yellow, and purple. The loss of the well-defined flower shape in the doubles is a shortcoming.

Alcea rosea 'Nigra'

AMARANTHUS

AMARANTHACEAE

Several tropical species in a genus containing about 60 annuals and short-lived perennials have long fascinated gardeners with their catkinlike arrangements of densely clustered flowers and, in the case of Joseph's coat or tampala (cultivars of **A. tricolor**), leaves brightly variegated red, yellow, and green.
CULTIVATION Require full sun in a sheltered site and moist soil, rich in organic matter.
PROPAGATION From seed, sown under glass (at a minimum of 64°F/18°C) from early to mid-spring.
POTENTIAL PROBLEMS Aphids; various virus diseases.

Amaranthus caudatus

A. caudatus *Africa, India, Peru*
Love-lies-bleeding, tassel flower
Flowers: summer to autumn.
H:3–5ft (90–150cm), S:18–30in (45–75cm). An.
Light green leaves on an upright bushy plant make a good background to the tassels of tiny crimson-purple flowers. These can grow up to 18in (45cm) or more long. The tassels of **'Viridis'** are initially vivid green, fading to cream.

ANTIRRHINUM

SCROPHULARIACEAE Snapdragon

The 30 to 40 species of annuals, perennials, and subshrubs, widely distributed in Europe, North Africa, and North America, produce tubular 2-lipped flowers. Most are plants of open rough ground, the widely naturalized snapdragon (*A. majus*), a short-lived perennial, being as much at home on old walls as on rocky outcrops. Named selections of this species were formerly propagated by cuttings; the modern cultivars are, however, grown as annuals from seed. Snapdragons are favorite plants for including in a cottage garden, where they will flower from summer into autumn.
CULTIVATION Require full sun and fertile, well-drained soil.
PROPAGATION From seed, sown thinly under glass from late winter to early spring. Light is necessary for germination.
POTENTIAL PROBLEMS Aphids; antirrhinum rust, powdery mildew.

Antirrhinum majus 'Coronette Cherry'

A. majus *Mediterranean, S.W. Europe*
Flowers: mid-summer to autumn.
H:2–3ft (60–90cm), S:12–18in (30–45cm). An.
The glossy-leaved wild plant produces spikes of flowers that are purplish-pink, but its cultivars cover a wide color range and include bicolors. There are doubles and cultivars selected according to height, weighted in favor of rather congested dwarf kinds with a height of 8–12in (20–30cm). Some cultivars show a degree of resistance to rust, such as the **Monarch Series**, which is intermediate at 1–2ft (30–60cm), and available in a choice of simple colors. The intermediate **Madame Butterfly Series** has variously colored double flowers, described as azalealike. The tall **Coronette Series**, which grows to the same height as the species, comes in various color combinations as well as in single colors.

BELLIS

ASTERACEAE Daisy

The 15 species in the genus, all of them originating from Europe and east to Turkey, are rosette-forming perennials that grow in grass. The British daisy (*B. perennis*) is highly successful as a European lawn weed, but since the Middle Ages numerous variants have been grown, usually as biennials, for the attraction of their charming spring flowers.
CULTIVATION Require full sun or partial shade and well-drained, reasonably fertile soil.
PROPAGATION From seed, sown thinly in a seedbed in early summer. By division, in spring after flowering (*B. perennis* 'Dresden China' and 'Rob Roy').
POTENTIAL PROBLEMS Usually none.

Bellis perennis Pomponette Series

B. perennis *Europe*
Common British daisy
Flowers: late winter to summer.
H and S:2-8in (5-20cm). Z:4-8.
The short-stemmed flowerheads standing above fresh green leaf rosettes have yellow centers surrounded by white ray flowerets that are often tinged pink or red. Cultivars available as seed, such as the **Carpet Series**, have fully double flowerheads in white, pink, or red. The tight flowerheads of the **Pomponette Series** have quilled ray flowerets. Cultivars not available from seed include **'Dresden China'**, with very neat pink flowerheads, and **'Rob Roy'**, a rich red.

BIDENS

ASTERACEAE

A few perennials from this diverse genus of about 200 very widely distributed species are grown as annuals, usually in containers.
CULTIVATION Require full sun and fertile, moist but well-drained soil.
PROPAGATION From seed, sown under glass in early to mid-spring. From stem cuttings, taken in spring or late summer.
POTENTIAL PROBLEMS Usually none.

Bidens ferulifolia

B. ferulifolia *Mexico, S. USA*
Flowers: summer to autumn.
H:9-12in (23-30cm), S:indefinite.
An.
The plant flings out slender stems with finely dissected leaves, bearing sprays of starry rich yellow flowerheads over a long season.

BRACHYSCOME

ASTERACEAE

Of the 60 to 70 species, from New Guinea or Australasia, the best known is the Swan river daisy (*B. iberidifolia*), a free-flowering dwarf annual. There are dwarf perennials such as the frost-hardy **B. rigidula** (Z:7-9).
CULTIVATION Require full sun in a sheltered site and fertile, well-drained soil.
PROPAGATION From seed, sown under glass (at a minimum of 64°F/18°C) in early spring.
POTENTIAL PROBLEMS Slugs, snails.

B. iberidifolia *Australia*
Swan river daisy
Flowers: summer. H:8-16in (20-40cm), S:10-18in (25-45cm). An.
Small bushes with divided leaves bear fragrant, yellow-centered daisies, in shades of blue, purple, or pink, and white. The **Splendour Series** gives a representative range.

Brachyscome iberidifolia
Splendour Series

BRACTEANTHA

ASTERACEAE

There are about 7 species of annuals and perennials in this Australian genus, and all are plants of open scrubland or grassland. The flowerheads are daisylike, with papery bracts around a central corolla (whorl of petals).
CULTIVATION Require full sun and a poor, light soil (for good flower color) or a more moist, fertile soil for more numerous flowers.
PROPAGATION From seed, sown under glass (at a minimum of 64°F/18°C) from late winter to early spring.
POTENTIAL PROBLEMS Downy mildew.

B. bracteata *Australia*
Golden everlasting, strawflower
Flowers: spring to autumn.
H:12-48in (30-120cm), S:8-12in (20-30cm). Z:9-10.
This is unreliably perennial but as an annual is one of the most widely grown of the "everlasting" flowers with bright daisylike flowerheads. The color range covers yellow, orange, pink, red, and white. In the dwarf **Bright Bikinis Series**, 12-18in (30-45cm) tall, the double flowerheads are as much as 3in (7.5cm) across. The frost-hardy **'Dargan Hill Monarch'** is a vivid yellow single.

Bracteantha bracteata
Bright Bikinis Series

BRASSICA

BRASSICACEAE

The genus contains 30 species, mainly annuals and biennials found on rocky slopes and wasteland from the Mediterranean to Asia. Its value lies in the number of vegetables developed from a few species, especially *B. oleracea*. A vegetable patch with broccoli, cabbages, cauliflowers, and brussels sprouts is beautiful, but ornamental kales and cabbages are more striking.
CULTIVATION Require full sun and fertile, well-drained soil, preferably rich in lime.
PROPAGATION From seed, sown under glass in early spring or where plants are to grow from mid- to late spring.
POTENTIAL PROBLEMS Aphids, whiteflies, root flies, flea beetles, caterpillars; blackleg, downy mildew, clubroot.

B. oleracea *W. Europe*
Ornamental cabbage and kale
Foliage: autumn to winter. H and
S:10–18in (25–45cm). An.
Ornamental kinds are inedible but
are strikingly colored, mostly in
shades of red, pink, green, and
white. Ornamental cabbages
(**B. oleracea var. capitata**), such
as the ruffled **Osaka Series** and
the smooth-edged '**Tokyo**', tend
to form rounded, compact heads
of foliage, while ornamental kale
(**B. oleracea var. acephala**) such
as '**Nagoya**' have a more open
habit and deeply cut leaves. Plants
prefer cool conditions, and colors
intensify as night temperatures fall
below 50°F (10°C).

Brassica oleracea var. *capitata*
'Osaka Red'

CALENDULA

ASTERACEAE Marigold

The genus includes 20 to 30 species
of annuals and biennials that are
found in rough open ground or as
weeds of cultivated ground in the
Mediterranean region and North
Africa. The pot marigold
(*C. officinalis*), one of the easiest
and most satisfying ornamentals to
grow and long cultivated as a
medicinal herb, as a flavoring, a
food colorant, and an ornamental,
is widely naturalized.
CULTIVATION Tolerate full sun or
partial shade and poor soil, provided
it is well drained.
PROPAGATION From seed, sown
where plants are to flower in early
autumn or spring. In cold areas
autumn-sown seedlings need
cloche protection.
POTENTIAL PROBLEMS Aphids;
powdery mildew, cucumber
mosaic virus.

C. officinalis *N. Africa to*
S. Europe
Pot marigold
Flowers: summer to autumn.
H:12–28in (30–70cm), S:12–18in
(30–45cm). An.
Fast-growing bushy plants with
aromatic spoon-shaped leaves
produce many daisylike single to
double flowerheads, up to 4in

(10cm) across, in shades of yellow
and orange. The semidouble **Art**
Shades Mixed, up to 2ft (60cm)
tall, include subtle tones of apricot
and cream, and the dwarf **Fiesta**
Gitana Mixed, up to 1ft (30cm)
tall, produce mostly double
flowerheads in pastel shades of
orange and yellow.

Calendula officinalis **Art**
Shades Mixed

CALLISTEPHUS

ASTERACEAE China aster

The single species in this genus
is a Chinese annual of rough open
ground and cultivated fields. The
modern cultivars produce single
to double chrysanthemum-like
flowerheads that are excellent
for cutting.
CULTIVATION Requires full sun and
a fertile, moist but well-drained
soil, preferably alkaline to neutral.
PROPAGATION From seed, sown
under glass in early spring or
where plants are to flower from
late spring to early summer.
POTENTIAL PROBLEMS Aphids,
cutworms; aster wilt, cucumber
wilt, tomato spotted wilt.

C. chinensis cultivars
Flowers: summer to autumn.
H:8–24in (20–60cm), S:4–8in
(10–20cm). An.
These fast-growing bushy plants
with coarsely toothed leaves bear
showy flowerheads. The petallike
ray flowerets are predominantly
violet-blue and purple in color but
also include white and shades of
pink, crimson, and yellow. Tall

Callistephus chinensis
Duchesse Series

cultivars, about 2ft (60cm) tall,
include the **Duchesse Series**, with
double incurved flowerheads, the
Ostrich Plume Series, also double,
with wide-spreading narrow ray-
flowerets, and the **Princess Series**,
semidouble, with incurved quill-
like ray flowerets. The compact
Milady Series, which grows to
about 1ft (30cm) tall, has double
flowerheads.

CENTAUREA

ASTERACEAE

Modern farming methods have
almost eliminated bachelor's
buttons (*C. cyanus*) from arable
land so that this, the best-known
annual of a genus of 450 species,
mainly from Europe, now takes
refuge in the yard. The more
variously colored and scented
sweet sultan (**Amberboa**
moschata), which resembles a large
version, was formerly included in
this genus. See also PERENNIALS.
CULTIVATION Require full sun and
well-drained soil.
PROPAGATION From seed, sown
where plants are to flower in early
autumn or early spring.
POTENTIAL PROBLEMS Usually none.

Centaurea cyanus

C. cyanus *Northern temperate*
regions
Bachelor's buttons, blue-bottle,
cornflower
Flowers: summer. H:10–36in (25–
90cm), S:12–18in (30–45cm). An.
The flowers of the species are
intense violet-blue. Cultivars with
pink, purple, red, or white flowers
are available, but they miss the
point. '**Blue Diadem**' is a piercing
blue tall double. Short-growing
mixtures include the **Florence**
Series, up to 14in (35cm) tall.

CLARKIA

ONAGRACEAE

The genus includes about 36
species of annuals, which are
widely distributed in dry, open
habitats, sometimes in
mountainous country, in North
America and South America.

CULTIVATION Require full sun and moderately fertile, moist but well-drained soil, preferably slightly acid.
PROPAGATION From seed, sown where plants are to flower in early autumn or early spring. In cold areas autumn-sown seedlings need cloche protection.
POTENTIAL PROBLEMS Foot rot, root rot, stem rot.

C. amoena *USA (California)*
Farewell-to-spring
Flowers: summer. H:20–30in (50–75cm), S:8–12in (20–30cm). An.
The sheeny flowers, borne at the tips of stems, are spreading and funnel shaped, each with 4 petals. Many cultivars, sometimes described as "azalea-flowered," have semidouble or double flowers, the petals often prettily frilled. Shades of pink and red predominate, often with contrasting colors in the same flower, as in plants in the **Grace Series** and the dwarf **Satin Series**, up to 8–12in (20–30cm) tall. Both of these have single flowers.

Clarkia amoena Satin Series

C. unguiculata *USA (California)*
Flowers: summer. H:1–3ft (30–90cm), S:6–8in (15–20cm). An.
Slender reddish stems carry single spidery flowers in the upper leaf axils. Many of the cultivars have more dense double flowers. Their color range covers shades of pink, red, and purple and, less commonly, white. **Royal Bouquet Series** has double frilly flowers.

CLEOME

CAPPARARIDAEAE

This tropical and subtropical genus contains about 150 species, most of them annuals. The only one widely grown is described here and is a useful filler in a border.
CULTIVATION Require full sun and fertile, free-draining soil.
PROPAGATION From seed, sown under glass (at a minimum of 64°F/18°C) in spring, or self-seeds.
POTENTIAL PROBLEMS Aphids.

C. hassleriana *South America*
Spider flower
Flowers: summer. H:4–5ft (1.2–1.5m), S:16–20in (40–50cm). An.
The plant is erect and bushy, with palmate leaves, the long leafstalks having spines at the base. The fragrant white and pink flowers, which form rounded clusters at the ends of stems, have prominent stamens that justify the common name. The flowers of the **Queen Series** are carmine and violet-pink.

Cleome hassleriana 'Pink Queen'

CONSOLIDA

RANUNCULACEAE

The genus, closely related to *Delphinium*, comprises about 40 species of annuals. These are erect, slender-stemmed plants usually found on rough open ground, including fields and steppes, from southern Europe and the Mediterranean and eastward to central Asia. The species described here is a showy plant producing dense spikes of spurred flowers that are excellent for cutting and drying.
CULTIVATION Require full sun and light, fertile, well-drained soil. Tall cultivars benefit from support.
PROPAGATION From seed, sown where plants are to flower in early autumn or from spring to early summer. In cold areas, autumn-sown seedlings need cloche protection.
POTENTIAL PROBLEMS Slugs, snails; powdery mildew, crown rot.
WARNING The seeds are toxic.

C. ajacis *Mediterranean*
Rocket larkspur
Flowers: summer. H:2–3ft (60–90cm), S:9–12in (23–30cm). An.
Upright well-branched plants bear finely dissected leaves and densely packed spikes of single or double flowers in shades of pink, blue, and purple or in white. There are dumpy short-growing cultivars, such as the **Dwarf Rocket Series**, which grow to 12–20in (30–50cm) tall, but they are poor alternatives to the tall kinds, such as the **Giant Imperial Series**.

Consolida ajacis Dwarf Rocket Series

COSMOS

ASTERACEAE

There are annuals and perennials, some bulbous, in this genus of about 25 species, most of them growing in grass or scrubland in southern USA or Central America. The species described is renowned for its airy grace. While it produces its long-stemmed flowers in pinks and reds, as well as white, the equally elegant *C. sulphureus* provides blooms in rich shades of orange and yellow. See also BULBS, CORMS, AND TUBERS.
CULTIVATION Require full sun and moderately fertile, moist but well-drained soil.
PROPAGATION From seed, sown under glass from early to mid-spring or where plants are to flower in late spring.
POTENTIAL PROBLEMS Aphids, slugs; gray mold (*Botrytis*).

Cosmos bipinnatus Sensation Series

C. bipinnatus *Mexico*
Flowers: summer. H:2–4ft (60–120cm), S:10–18in (25–45cm). An.
Saucer-shaped yellow-centered flowerheads that are white, pink, or crimson are carried freely above feathery foliage on a slender but wiry and erect plant. Cultivars in the **Sensation Series** grow to about 36in (90cm) tall, and the flowers are 3in (7.5cm) across. **'Sea Shells'**, also tall, has flowers with tubular ray flowerets. The **Sonata Series** is compact, with a spread of 12–18in (30–45cm), but at the expense of gracefulness.

DIGITALIS

SCROPHULARIACEAE Foxglove

The 22 or so species are biennials and short-lived perennials, most from woodland in Europe and east to central Asia. The genus is noted for its spires of tubular to bell-shaped flowers, making vertical accents among freer shapes.

D. × **mertonensis** (Z:4–8), which is reasonably perennial, has spires up to 36in (90 cm) tall with large flowers of an unusual bruised pink. The biennial rusty foxglove (**D. ferruginea**) has small flowers, but their tawny gold spikes, up to 4ft (1.2m), are very arresting.

CULTIVATION Tolerate full sun or shade and any soil except those that are very wet or dry.

PROPAGATION From seed, sown where plants are to flower from late spring to early summer.

POTENTIAL PROBLEMS Powdery mildew, leaf spot.

WARNING All parts can be toxic if ingested.

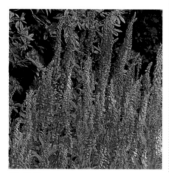

Digitalis purpurea

D. purpurea *Europe*
Common foxglove
Flowers: summer. H:3–6ft (90–180cm), S:18–24in (45–60cm). Z:4–8.
Tall one-sided spikes carry steeply angled, purple, pink, or white flowers, spotted maroon or purple inside. This variable biennial or short-lived perennial seeds itself too freely for ordered gardens. The white **f. albiflora** gives woodland a spectral beauty. The **Excelsior Group** are hefty, the flowers, in shades of creamy yellow, white, purple, or pink, evenly spaced around the stem and held horizontally.

DOROTHEANTHUS

AIZOACEAE

This South African genus contains 10 species of succulent annuals of open ground and stony or sandy soils. They have glistening leaves and numerous daisylike flowerheads that are sensitive to light, closing on gray days.

CULTIVATION Require full sun and well-drained, preferably poor, sandy soil.

PROPAGATION From seed, sown under glass from late winter to early spring.

POTENTIAL PROBLEMS Slugs, snails, greenflies; foot rot.

**Dorotheanthus bellidiformis
Magic Carpet Series**

D. bellidiformis *South Africa (W. Cape)*
Livingstone daisy
Flowers: summer. H:4–6in (10–15cm), S:10–12in (25–30cm). An. Dazzling flowerheads in shades of pink, red, orange, and yellow, usually with a paler zone around the dark central disk, beam up from a mat of fleshy leaves. Livingstone daisies are usually available only as mixtures such as **'Magic Carpet'**. **'Lunette'**, which has red-centered yellow flowers, is a happy exception.

ERYSIMUM

BRASSICACEAE Wallflower

Among the 80 species in this genus, there are annuals, biennials, and a number of woody-based evergreen perennials, although these are sometimes not long lived. Wherever they are found— in Europe, North Africa, North America, and western Asia—they are usually plants that prefer sunny positions where the ground is free-draining and often calcareous. The flowers, consisting of 4 petals arranged in a cross, are usually carried in dense spikes. Those described below are grown as biennials but the fully hardy **'Bowles' Mauve'** (Z:5–8) is a bushy, short-lived perennial, which gives a long but unscented display of dark mauve flowers.

CULTIVATION Require full sun and poor to moderately fertile, well-drained soil, preferably neutral to alkaline. Pinch out the growing tips when plants are 6in (15cm) tall to encourage branching.

PROPAGATION From seed, sown in a seedbed from late spring to early summer.

POTENTIAL PROBLEMS Slugs, snails, flea beetles; various fungal and bacterial diseases, including clubroot and mildew.

E. × **allionii**
Siberian wallflower
Flowers: spring. H:20–24in (50–60cm), S:10–12in (25–30cm). Z:4–7.
The mound of deep green, often toothed leaves is topped by erect spikes of scented orange flowers.

E. cheiri *S. Europe*
Wallflower
Flowers: spring. H:10–30in (25–75cm), S:12–16in (30–40cm). Z:6–7.
Wallflowers that seed themselves in old walls often prove perennial, but as bedding plants they are grown as biennials. The velvety, sweetly scented flowers are predominantly orange and yellow, but the color range includes pink and cream as well as deep reds and bronze. Cultivars include the **Bedder Series**, compact plants producing flowers in orange, scarlet, primrose, and yellow, and **'Fire King'**, bearing orange flowers.

Erysimum cheiri 'Golden Bedder'

ESCHSCHOLZIA

PAPAVERACEAE California poppy

The 8 to 10 species, from western North America, are annuals and perennials of dry, sunny places. The poppylike flowers, carried above finely cut leaves, tend to close in bad weather.

CULTIVATION Require full sun and poor, well-drained soil.

PROPAGATION From seed, sown where plants are to flower in early autumn or mid-spring.

POTENTIAL PROBLEMS Usually none.

E. californica *USA (western coastal regions)*
California poppy
Flowers: summer. H:8–12in (20–30cm), S:6–8in (15–20cm). An. Silky saucer-shaped flowers up to 3in (7.5cm) across, produced prolifically over ferny blue-green leaves, are predominantly orange,

but the color range includes cream, yellow, and scarlet. Long cylindrical seedpods follow. Several selections, including 'Ballerina' and the frilly 'Monarch Art Shades', have semidouble or double flowers.

Eschscholzia californica

IBERIS

BRASSICACEAE Candytuft

There are about 40 species of annuals, perennials, and evergreen sub-shrubs in this genus, most of them found in open and rocky habitats, predominantly on lime-rich soils. The flowers, typically white, with 2 long and 2 short petals, are borne in dense clusters. The evergreen *I. sempervirens* (Z:3-8) is a spreading bushy plant that is grown in rock gardens for its dazzling, fragrant, white flowers from spring to early summer.
CULTIVATION Require full sun and fertile, moist but well-drained soil, preferably neutral to alkaline.
PROPAGATION From seed, sown where plants are to flower in early autumn or from early to mid-spring.
POTENTIAL PROBLEMS Slugs, snails, caterpillars; clubroot.

Iberis umbellata Fairy Series

I. umbellata S. Europe
Common candytuft
Flowers: spring to summer.
H:6-12in (15-30cm), S:8-10in (20-25cm). An.
The leaves of the common candytuft are almost hidden by dense clusters, up to 4in (10cm) across, of small scented flowers in a color range that includes mauve,

purple, crimson, white, and some bicolors, the full range being available in the **Fairy Series**. Another annual species, the summer-flowering *I. amara*, is a taller plant with stems growing to a height of 12-18in (30-45cm) and supporting cones of predominantly white flowers.

IMPATIENS

BALSAMINACEAE

The plants in this genus of about 850 annuals, evergreen perennials, and subshrubs have brittle, fleshy stems and lush foliage. The 5-petaled flowers are borne singly or in clusters. Most species and cultivars are excellent for summer bedding and as houseplants. *Impatiens* thrive even in shady conditions, making them particularly useful plants for brightening up out-of-the-way corners that receive little sun.
CULTIVATION Require partial shade with shelter from wind and fertile, moist but well-drained soil. Under glass, require good light and moderate to high humidity.
PROPAGATION From seed, sown under glass in early spring; freely self-seeds.
POTENTIAL PROBLEMS Aphids; gray mold (*Botrytis*).

I. balsamina China, India
Balsam
Flowers: summer to autumn.
H:24-30in (60-75cm), S:14-18in (35-45cm). An.
This sparsely branched annual produces cup-shaped, hooded flowers, 1-2in (2.5-5cm) across, in shades of pink, red, purple, or white. Cultivars include **Camellia-flowered Series** with large, double, pink or red flowers that are mottled with white.

I. **New Guinea Group hybrids**
Flowers: summer to autumn.
H and S:12-20in (30-50cm). An.
These hybrid perennials, derived from *I. hawkeri* and other species, are usually grown as annuals. They are excellent in mixed container plantings and as individual pot plants. The foliage is ornamental, often attractively bronzed or dark, glossy green. The striking flowers are mostly available in vibrant shades of red, pink, and purple.

I. walleriana E. Africa
Busy Lizzie
Flowers: summer. H and S:18-24in (45-60cm). An.
This subshrublike perennial is usually represented in gardens by dwarf hybrids that are grown as

annuals. They grow just 6-12in (15-30cm) tall and bear flattened, spurred flowers in a wealth of colors. The **Accent Series**, the **Impulse Series**, the **Super Elfin Series**, and the **Tempo Series** are among those offering blooms in a range of bright and sometimes pastel colors, some bicolored or with a conspicuous eye.

Impatiens walleriana Accent Series

LAVATERA

MALVACEAE Mallow

The 25 species in this widely distributed genus are annuals, biennials, perennials, and shrubs. The leaves of mallows are rather coarse, but the flowers are nicely formed, especially in the commonly grown annual, *L. trimestris*. See also SHRUBS.
CULTIVATION Require full sun in a sheltered site and well-drained soil.
PROPAGATION From seed, sown where plants are to flower in early autumn or from mid- to late spring.
POTENTIAL PROBLEMS Stem rot, rust, soilborne fungal diseases.

Lavatera trimestris 'Mont Blanc'

L. trimestris Mediterranean
Bush mallow
Flowers: summer. H:2-3ft (60-90cm), S:14-18in (35-45cm). An.
Upright bushy plants with lobed mid-green leaves bear open, funnel-shaped flowers, 3-4in (7.5-10cm) across, in shades of pink, reddish pink, or white. Cultivars include **'Mont Blanc'**, with dark green foliage and white flowers, and **'Silver Cup'**, which has pink flowers, with darker veining. Both grow to 20in (50cm).

LIMNANTHES

LIMNANTHACEAE

This genus comprises about 17 species of annuals from western North America. Most are plants of moist soils, but the poached-egg plant (*L. douglasii*), the only species commonly grown, self-seeds successfully wherever it can get a cool root run, doing well in chinks between paving stones.
CULTIVATION Requires full sun and fertile, moist but well-drained soil.
PROPAGATION From seed, sown where plants are to flower in early autumn or early spring.
POTENTIAL PROBLEMS Usually none.

L. douglasii USA (California, Oregon)
Poached-egg plant
Flowers: summer to autumn.
H and S:6–8in (15–20cm). An.
Sprawling plants with slightly fleshy, light green leaves bear a profusion of broadly funnel-shaped flowers, which are white with a yellow "yolk." They are lightly scented and a nectar-rich enticement to bees.

Limnanthes douglasii

LIMONIUM

PLUMBAGINACEAE Sea lavender, statice

About 150 species of annuals, biennials, and perennials are distributed worldwide, many of them adapted to extreme desert and salt-marsh conditions. The small flowers are papery and long lasting, making statice one of the most popular flowers for drying. The annual *Psylliostachys suworowii*, which grows to 18in (45cm) and produces narrow branching spikes packed with small, deep pink flowers, was formerly placed in this genus.
CULTIVATION Require full sun and well-drained, preferably sandy soil.
PROPAGATION From seed, sown under glass from late winter to early spring or where plants are to flower from mid- to late spring.
POTENTIAL PROBLEMS Powdery mildew.

L. sinuatum Mediterranean
Statice
Flowers: summer to autumn.
H:16–24in (40–60cm), S:10–12in (25–30cm). An.
A perennial grown as an annual, statice has stiff, winged stems that branch to carry clusters of tiny flowers surrounded by long-lasting papery calyces. In the cultivars the white and mauve-blue color range has been extended; the **California Series** includes 9 different strong colors, among them blue, purplish-pink, and yellow. The **Fortress Series** has both strong and pastel shades.

Limonium sinuatum Fortress Series

LINARIA

SCROPHULARIACEAE Toadflax

The genus includes about 100 species of annuals, biennials, and perennials. These sun-loving plants are found in open habitats on free-draining soils in the temperate Northern Hemisphere. The small flowers are spurred and have 2 lips. Many species are lightweight, and only 1 annual is widely grown. See also PERENNIALS.
CULTIVATION Require full sun and light, well-drained, preferably sandy soil.
PROPAGATION From seed, sown in a seedbed from early to mid-spring.
POTENTIAL PROBLEMS Aphids; powdery mildew.

Linaria maroccana 'Fairy Bouquet'

L. maroccana N. Africa (Morocco)
Flowers: summer. H:9–18in (23–45cm), S:4–6in (10–15cm). An.
Erect bushy plants with linear

leaves produce slender stems carrying numerous miniature snapdragons with a white or yellow blotch on the lower lip. **'Fairy Bouquet'** and the longer-flowering **'Northern Lights'** both have flowers in white, yellow, orange, mauve, and carmine and in shades of pink.

LOBULARIA

BRASSICACEAE

There are 5 species in this genus, but only 1 is commonly grown. In the past, sweet alyssum (*L. maritima*) has been used to excess in conventional planting, but it is an adaptable plant for containers and the open garden and is tolerant of coastal conditions.
CULTIVATION Requires full sun and light, well-drained soil.
PROPAGATION From seed, sown where plants are to flower from early to mid-spring .
POTENTIAL PROBLEMS Slugs, flea beetles; downy mildew, clubroot, white blister.

Lobularia maritima 'Carpet of Snow'

L. maritima Mediterranean
Sweet alyssum
Flowers: summer to autumn.
H:3–6in (7.5–15cm), S:8–12in (20–30cm). An.
Freely branching, bushy plants bear tiny fragrant flowers clustered densely at the ends of stems. The flowers have 4 petals arranged in a cross shape, and the color range in the cultivars includes white, pink, and purple. **'Carpet of Snow'** is a low-spreading plant with white flowers. The **Easter Bonnet Series**, compact and early flowering, covers the whole color range.

LUNARIA

BRASSICACEAE Honesty

The 3 species in this genus are adaptable plants, readily colonizing disturbed or open ground in a range of habitats in Europe and western Asia. The familiar annual money plant (*L. annua*) self-seeds with great success in shrubberies and wild gardens. Both it and the

hardy perennial **L. rediviva** (Z:4–8), from Europe and western Siberia, flower in spring and bear translucent seedpods, those of *L. rediviva* being more elliptical.
CULTIVATION Tolerate full sun or partial shade and require fertile, moist but well-drained soil.
PROPAGATION From seed, sown in a seedbed from late spring to early summer.
POTENTIAL PROBLEMS Clubroot, white blister, viruses.

Lunaria annua var. albiflora

L. annua *Europe*
Money plants, honesty, satin flower
Flowers: spring and summer.
H:30–36in (75–90cm), S:10–12in (25–30cm). An.
Upright stems, well clothed with heart-shaped to triangular, coarsely toothed leaves, bear numerous 4-petaled flowers that are purple or white. The shimmering round disks that follow are highly ornamental both in the garden and in dried flower arrangements.
'**Alba Variegata**' has white flowers, and the leaves are frosted white.

MALOPE

MALVACEAE

The 4 species of annuals and perennials are found in scrubland and fields on lime-rich soils in the Mediterranean region and western Asia. The species described is grown for its dramatic, papery, trumpet-shaped flowers, which are ideal at the front of a bed as well as for cutting.
CULTIVATION Require full sun and moist but well-drained soil.
PROPAGATION From seed, sown where plants are to flower from early to mid-spring.
POTENTIAL PROBLEMS Aphids; rust.

M. trifida *W. Mediterranean*
Mallowwort
Flowers: summer to autumn.
H:30–36in (75–90cm), S:8–10in (20–25cm). An.
Upright plants carry the purplish-pink mallow flowers singly in the leaf axils. The flowers are as much as 3in (7.5cm) across, and dark

purple veining adds to their glamour. The flowers of '**Vulcan**' are large and magenta, those of '**White Queen**' pure white.

Malope trifida

MATTHIOLA

BRASSICACEAE Gillyflower, stock

Only a few of the 50 or so species are grown, but these have long been valued for their rich fragrance. Night-scented stock (*M. longipetala* **subsp.** *bicornis*), a hardy annual from Greece and eastward into Asia, seems inconsequential, but a scattering among other plants exhales a seductive perfume as dusk falls.
CULTIVATION Require full sun in a sheltered site and fertile, moist but well-drained soil, preferably neutral to slightly alkaline.
PROPAGATION From seed, sown under glass from late winter to early spring or where plants are to flower from mid- to late spring.
POTENTIAL PROBLEMS Aphids, flea beetles, cabbage root flies; fungal diseases, including clubroot, downy mildew, and gray mold (*Botrytis*).

Matthiola incana **East Lothian Mixed**

M. incana *Europe (S. and W. coastal regions)*
Gillyflower, stock
Flowers: spring to summer.
H:12–30in (30–75cm), S:10–12in (25–30cm). An.
In the wild, this woody-based perennial bears fragrant cross-shaped single flowers that are purple, pink, or white. Doubles and a more varied color range,

including mauve-blue violet, crimson, and yellow, have been in cultivation for centuries, the stiff plants usually being grown as annuals or biennials. The cultivars, often a mixture of single and double flowers, fall into a number of categories. **Brompton** stocks, bushy upright plants about 18in (45cm) tall, are grown as biennials. The similar but more compact and smaller-flowered **East Lothian** stocks, about 1ft (30cm) tall, can be grown as biennials or spring sown. **Ten Week** stocks, with dwarf and tall cultivars, and the even faster-maturing **Trisomic Seven Week** stocks, about 18in (45cm) tall, are grown as annuals.

MIMULUS:

SCROPHULARIACEAE Monkey flower

Several of the monkey flowers are plants of dry habitats, but of some 150 species most are annuals, perennials, and evergreen shrubs of moist, often boggy conditions. The yellow-flowered Chilean *M. luteus* (Z:6–9) and the North American *M. guttatus* (Z:6–9), also yellow but often heavily spotted, have played an important role in hybridizing.
CULTIVATION Require full sun or light shade and very moist soil that is rich in organic matter.
PROPAGATION From seed, sown under glass late winter.
POTENTIAL PROBLEMS Slugs, snails; powdery mildew.

Mimulus × hybridus **Calypso Mixed**

M. × hybridus
Flowers: summer. H:5–12in (12.5–30cm), S:10–14in (25–35cm). An.
These bushy perennials are usually grown as annuals. The solitary flowers, borne in the leaf axils, are tubular and then flare open, with lobed lips. The flowers are usually spotted in a contrasting color, the color range in cultivars such as **Calypso Mixed** and the low and spreading **Malibu Series** including yellow, orange, and red. The early-flowering **Magic Series** has small blooms and includes pastel shades and bicolors.

319

MYOSOTIS

BORAGINACEAE Forget-me-not

Despite having small flowers, many forget-me-nots make a strong impression with their sprays of dainty, mainly blue flowers. There are about 50 species, including annuals, biennials, and perennials, which are widely distributed throughout the world in habitats ranging from woodland and meadows to swampy ground and the water's edge.
CULTIVATION Tolerate full sun or partial shade and a range of soils but do best in moist, well-drained conditions that are not too rich.
PROPAGATION From seed, sown in a seedbed from late spring to early summer.
POTENTIAL PROBLEMS Powdery mildew, downy mildew.

Myosotis sylvatica 'Blue Ball'

M. sylvatica *Europe*
Flowers: spring to summer. H:6–14in (15–35cm), S:6–8in (15–20cm). Bi.
The familiar forget-me-not is a pleasing biennial self-seeder in woodland, among shrubs, and in the wild garden, but it is also often used in a more disciplined way in bedding schemes, its flowering coinciding with that of tulips. Colors other than blue seem a curious lapse, but there are white and pink cultivars. The emphasis in seed catalogs is on compact cultivars such as the **Ball Series**, about 6–8in (15–20cm) tall, but fortunately there are taller cultivars, such as '**Royal Blue**'.

NEMESIA

SCROPHULARIACEAE

This South African genus includes about 50 species of annuals, perennials, and subshrubs, many of them plants of scrubland or more open ground where the soil is free-draining but seasonally moist. The flowers are 2-lipped—the upper lip with 4 lobes, the lower lip with 2—and are borne singly in the leaf axils or in short racemes at the stem tips. A perennial, sometimes woody-based species, **N. caerulea** is less showy than the well-known annual species, but gives a long display from mid-spring to autumn, its flowers sometimes white but usually ranging from pale mauve or pink to violet-purple with a yellow mark in the center. It is frost hardy and cultivars like deep violet '**Joan Wilder**' are best treated as short-lived and annually propagated from cuttings in late summer.
CULTIVATION Require full sun and moderately fertile, moist but well-drained soil, preferably slightly acid.
PROPAGATION From seed, sown under glass from early to mid-spring.
POTENTIAL PROBLEMS Foot rot, root rot.

Nemesia caerulea 'Joan Wilder'

N. strumosa *South Africa*
Flowers: summer. H:6–12in (15–30cm), S:4–6in (10–15cm). An.
The small but distinctive flowers, with a broad lower lip and a fanned upper lip, are carried in profusion on erect bushy plants. The color range in the cultivars is very wide, some being bicolored and almost all having yellow throats. '**Blue Gem**' has bright blue flowers, the **Carnival Series** is compact with a mixture of jolly colors, and '**Mello Red and White**' is boldly bicolored. '**Mello White**' has a deep yellow center.

Nemesia strumosa 'Mello White'

NEMOPHILA

HYDROPHYLLACEAE

Saucer- or bell-shaped blue or white flowers are borne by the 11 species of annuals in this genus. They are all natives of western North America, but they are found in a wide range of habitats.
CULTIVATION Require full sun or partial shade and fertile, moist but well-drained soil.
PROPAGATION From seed, sown where plants are to flower in early autumn or early spring.
POTENTIAL PROBLEMS Aphids.

Nemophila maculata

N. maculata *USA (California)*
Five-spot
Flowers: summer. H and S:6–12in (15–30cm). An.
Low plants carry profuse long-stalked, saucer-shaped flowers, each with 5 white petals, sometimes veined or tinted mauve, and tipped with violet-blue. Baby blue-eyes (**N. menziesii**), a slightly larger species, has bright blue flowers with lighter centers.

NICOTIANA

SOLANACEAE Tobacco plant

Hybrids derived from the South American **N. alata** are the most commonly grown of the tobacco plants, but a few of the 67 species are unusual short-lived garden plants. **N. langsdorffii**, a scentless Brazilian annual up to 5ft (1.5m) tall, has green tubular flowers that open to a 5-lobed mouth. The equally tall **N. sylvestris** from Argentina, usually grown as a biennial, bears long-tubed slender white trumpets that are sweetly fragrant. These half-hardy species do well in moist dappled shade.
CULTIVATION Tolerate full sun or partial shade and fertile, moist but well-drained soil.
PROPAGATION From seed, surface-sown under glass (at a minimum of 64°/18°C) from late winter to early spring.
POTENTIAL PROBLEMS Aphids.
WARNING Contact with the foliage may irritate the skin.

Nicotiana sylvestris

N. hybrids

Flowers: summer. H:10-24in (25-60cm), S:9-12in (23-30cm). An. *N. alata* is a short-lived perennial that is sticky to the touch. It has white flowers that are usually closed during the day but are strongly scented when open at night. The hybrids of which it is a parent are grown as annuals and come in a color range that includes white, pink, red, and lime-green; their flowers are open during the day, but except for some whites, are almost unscented. The **Domino Series**, about 18in (45cm) tall, has upward-facing flowers in a wide color range. The **Havana Series** is more compact, and the dwarf **Merlin Series** is usually under 1ft (30cm) in height. '**Lime Green**', about 2ft (60cm) tall, has yellow-green flowers.

Nicotiana 'Lime Green'

NIGELLA

RANUNCULACEAE

There are about 20 species in the genus, all annuals of open stony ground, including fields and wasteland, in the Mediterranean region, North Africa, and eastward into Asia. A few other species are sometimes seen, but love-in-a-mist (*N. damascena*) is by far the most commonly grown, ensuring its place by self-seeding freely.

CULTIVATION Require full sun and well-drained soil.
PROPAGATION From seed, sown where plants are to flower in early autumn or early spring.
POTENTIAL PROBLEMS Usually none.

N. damascena *N. Africa, S. Europe*

Devil-in-a-bush, love-in-a-mist
Flowers: summer. H:16-24in (40-60cm), S:8-10in (20-25cm). An. This upright bushy annual has feathery foliage and sky-blue flowers that sit within a rufflike outline of wispy leaves. These are followed by inflated seed capsules that dry well. The blooms also make good cut flowers. There are dwarf cultivars under 16in (40cm) in height, but the tall '**Miss Jekyll**', with semidouble bright blue flowers, and the intermediate **Persian Jewel Series**, which is semidouble and available in shades of blue, pink, or in white, are better poised.

Nigella damascena 'Miss Jekyll'

PETUNIA

SOLANACEAE

It is hard to believe that the fashion for petunias ever waned. The long-flowering plants that are so popular now in bedding and container gardening, like the petunias that were all the rage in the 19th century, are perennial hybrids that are grown as annuals. The genus originates from South America and contains about 40 species, which are found in a range of habitats, but mostly on open and stony ground.
CULTIVATION Require full sun in a sheltered site and light, well-drained soil.
PROPAGATION From seed, sown under glass in early spring.
POTENTIAL PROBLEMS Aphids, slugs; virus diseases.

P. hybrids

Flowers: spring to autumn.
H:8-16in (20-40cm), S:10-36in (25-90cm). An.
These are bushy or trailing plants bearing single or double trumpet-shaped flowers with a broad 5-lobed mouth. The color range in the numerous seed strains includes blue and yellow as well as white, pink, purple, and red. Deep veining and contrasting colors in the mouth, at the edges, or in the form of a superimposed star add to the variety in the mixtures, but the range of single colors is limited. Compact cultivars have a spread of 10-16in (25-40cm), trailing kinds of 18-36in (45-90cm). There are 2 main groups, although some hybrids are of intermediate character. The **Grandiflora** petunias have large flowers up to 4in (10cm) across, often rather floppy and vulnerable to weather damage. They include the early-flowering **Daddy Series**, with heavily veined and ruffled single flowers; the **Picotee Series**, with single ruffled flowers outlined in white; and the **Surfinia Series**, freely branching and trailing, with many flowers that stand up well to rough weather. The **Multiflora** petunias bear many weatherproof flowers that are about 2in (5cm) across. They include compact hybrids such as the **Carpet Series**, usually less than 10in (25cm) tall; the **Duo Series**, with double flowers; and the **Primetime Series**, with a wide color range.

Petunia 'Daddy Blue'

RESEDA

RESEDACEAE

About 55 to 60 species of annuals and perennials in this genus are found in the wild in the Mediterranean region, Africa, and Asia, mainly on stony hillsides, in scrubland, and at the edges of cultivated fields. Few are grown other than mignonette (*R. odorata*), which has long been valued for its scented flowers.
CULTIVATION Require full sun or partial shade and moderately fertile, well-drained soil, preferably alkaline.
PROPAGATION From seed, sown where plants are to flower in early autumn or from early to mid-spring.
POTENTIAL PROBLEMS Usually none.

R. odorata *N. Africa*
Mignonette
Flowers: summer to autumn.
H:1-2ft (30-60cm), S:8-10in
(20-25cm). An.
Upright branching plants bear
loose, conical heads of starry
flowers. These are tiny and usually
buff or greenish white, the central
tuft of orange stamens being the
most conspicuous feature. They
are grown for their scent, which
lingers strongly even in dried plants.

Reseda odorata

SALPIGLOSSIS

SOLANACEAE

The 2 species from the southern
Andes are annuals or short-lived
perennials of rough, open, and
often dry terrain. Cultivars of the
single species in general cultivation
have long-lasting, richly colored
flowers.
CULTIVATION Require full sun in a
sheltered site and moist, well-
drained soil, rich in organic matter.
PROPAGATION From seed, sown
under glass (at a minimum of
64°F/ 18°C) from late winter
to mid-spring.
POTENTIAL PROBLEMS Aphids; gray
mold (*Botrytis*), foot rot, root rot.

Salpiglossis sinuata Casino Series

S. sinuata *Argentina, Peru*
Flowers: summer to autumn.
Painted tongue
H:18-24in (45-60cm), S:10-12in
(25-30cm). An.
Lightly branched, erect, and sticky
plants bear funnel-shaped flowers,
about 2in (5cm) across, each with
5 notched lobes. The flowers,
often burnished with gold, come

in shades of yellow, orange, red,
purple, or blue with darker or
contrasting veining. The cultivars in
the **Casino** and **Festival Series** are
compact, about 18in (45cm) tall.

SALVIA

LAMIACEAE

This large genus of 900 species is
represented in several categories.
In frost-prone areas, tender
perennials and subshrubs are
usually grown as annuals. See also
PERENNIALS and SHRUBS.
CULTIVATION Require full sun and
well-drained soil.
PROPAGATION From seed, sown
under glass from late winter to
early spring (frost-tender plants) or
where plants are to flower from
early to mid-spring or in summer
(full hardy plants).
POTENTIAL PROBLEMS Slugs, snails.

Salvia farinacea 'Victoria'

S. farinacea *Mexico, USA (Texas)*
Mealycup sage
Flowers: summer to autumn.
H:20-24in (50-60cm), S:10-12in
(25-30cm). Z:9-10.
In mild climates this is perennial,
but it is commonly grown as an
annual. Mealy white stems carry
slender spikes of purplish-blue
flowers clear of the glossy foliage.
'**Alba**' bears white flowers, while
'**Victoria**' has intense purple-blue
flowers and stems.

S. sclarea var. turkestanica
C. Asia, Europe
Flowers: spring to summer.
H:30-36in (75-90cm), S:12-16in
(30-40cm). Bi.
The leaves of this biennial clary are
large, hairy, and coarsely aromatic
and the branching flower spikes
create a long-lasting haze of pink
and mauve, the purplish bracts
persisting when the flowers have
finished. The plant seeds itself
freely in dry gardens.

S. splendens *Brazil*
Scarlet sage
Flowers: summer to autumn.
H:10-16in (25-40cm), S:10-14in
(25-35cm). An.
This upright, bushy perennial,
usually grown as an annual, looks
shocking with its dense spikes of
long-tubed, bright red flowers,
which are surrounded by scarlet
bracts. There are some less
strident colors in the **Cleopatra
Series**, including red, salmon-pink,
purple, and white.

S. viridis *Mediterranean*
Annual clary
Flowers: summer. H:18-20in (45-
50cm), S:8-10in (20-25cm). An.
The flowers are insignificant, but
they are surrounded by bracts up
to 1½in (3cm) long that are pink,
purple, or white with darker veins.
There is a comprehensive color
range in the **Claryssa Series**,
plants that are well branched and
grow to a height of about 16in
(40cm).

SCHIZANTHUS

SOLANACEAE Butterfly flower

This South American genus
comprises about 12 to 15 species
of annuals and biennials, which are
mainly found in dry rocky habitats.
S. pinnatus has superficially orchidlike flowers; its showy cultivars,
which can be grown under glass or
as bedding plants, are the most
commonly seen representatives of
the genus.
CULTIVATION Require full sun and
fertile, moist but well-drained soil.
PROPAGATION From seed, sown
under glass from early to mid-
spring.
POTENTIAL PROBLEMS Aphids.

S. pinnatus *Chile*
Butterfly flower, poor man's orchid
Flowers: spring to autumn.
H:10-24in (25-60cm), S:8-12in
(20-30cm). An.
The ferny, light green leaves are
overlooked when the plants are in
bloom because the effect of their
dense clusters of flared bright

Schizanthus pinnatus 'Hit Parade'

flowers is dazzling. The main colors are pink, red, purple, yellow, or white, and usually there is a striking yellow flash in the throat that is splashed with dark markings. Contrasting colors add zest to the compact **'Hit Parade'**, with plants about 1ft (30cm) tall.

SOLENOPSIS

CAMPANULACEAE

In this genus of about 25 annuals and perennials, 1 species, *L. axillaris*, is a long-flowering and pretty edging and container plant. In the wild, this Australian species, like others in the genus from Central and South America, is a plant of dry open habitats.
CULTIVATION Require full sun and moderately fertile, well-drained soil.
PROPAGATION From seed, sown under glass from late winter to early spring.
POTENTIAL PROBLEMS Aphids.

S. axillaris *Australia*
Flowers: spring to autumn. H and S:10-12in (25-30cm). An.
Long tubular buds that burst open into starry flowers with 5 narrow lobes stand tall above a dome of feathery green leaves. The flowers, lightly scented in the evening, are mainly blue, and sometimes white or pink. This is perennial but usually raised annually from seed.

Solenopsis axillaris

TAGETES

ASTERACEAE Marigold

There are in all about 50 species of annuals and perennials in the genus, most of them occupying hot and often dry habitats from southern USA to Argentina. The well-known bedding and container marigolds of gardens are hybrids of 3 Mexican species, *T. erecta*, *T. patula*, and *T. tenuifolia*. They have vividly colored flowerheads, mostly in shades of yellow and orange, and are borne on neat, upright plants above divided green leaves that emit a pungent smell when bruised. They fall into 4 main groups, and it is under these

that the cultivars and hybrids are described below.
CULTIVATION Require full sun and moderately fertile, well-drained soil.
PROPAGATION From seed, sown under glass (at a minimum of 64°F/18°C) from early to mid-spring or where plants are to flower in late spring.
POTENTIAL PROBLEMS Red spider mites, whiteflies, slugs, snails; foot rot, gray mold (*Botrytis*).

T. African Group cultivars and hybrids
African marigold
Flowers: spring to autumn. H:8-18in (20-45cm), S:12-18in (30-45cm). An.
Derived from *T. erecta*, these are compact bushy plants topped by large, densely double, pomponlike flowerheads, up to 5in (12.5cm) across. Plants in the **Antigua Series** and the **Excel Series** grow to about 1ft (30cm) and are in a range of yellow and orange shades.

T. Afro-French Group cultivars and hybrids
Afro-French marigold
Flowers: spring to autumn. H:8-18in (20-45cm), S:12-16in (30-40cm). An.
These bushy annuals, derived from *T. erecta* and *T. patula* crosses, bear many small, single or double flowerheads, 1-2¼in (2.5-6cm) across, usually orange or yellow and sometimes marked with red-brown. The **Beaux Series** has double flowerheads in shades of rich yellow, orange splashed with red, or copper-red. In the **Zenith Series** the flowerheads are red, orange, and shades of yellow. In both of these series, plants grow to about 1ft (30cm).

T. French Group cultivars and hybrids
French marigold
Flowers: spring to autumn. H:8-18in (20-45cm), S:6-12in (15-30cm). An.
The plants, derived from *T. patula*, are usually compact with single or double flowerheads about 2in (5cm) across, their color range including yellow and orange, often with red-brown markings. Plants in the robust **Boy Series**, about 6in (15cm) tall, have dense crested flowerheads in a range of orange, yellow, and reddish-brown shades, the crest sometimes contrasting with the rest of the flowerhead. The **Disco Series**, 8-10in (20-25cm) tall, is a selection with single flowerheads in yellow, orange, and orange-red, some of them with reddish-brown

markings. The pert **'Naughty Marietta'** produces single yellow flowerheads with mahogany markings at the center.

Tagetes 'Disco Golden Yellow'

T. Signet Group cultivars and hybrids
Signet marigold
Flowers: spring to autumn. H:8-18in (20-45cm), S:10-16in (25-40cm). An.
These plants derived from *T. tenuifolia* are upright and they branch freely to carry numerous single flowerheads, about 1in (2.5cm) across, in shades of yellow and orange. Plants in the **Gem Series** grow to a height of approximately 10in (25cm). The starry, clear lemon-yellow flowers of **'Lemon Gem'**, above the bright green ferny foliage, correct the rather common impression that marigold flowers are simply blobs of crude color.

VERBENA

VERBENACEAE

Out of a total of about 250 species, most of them from the Americas, only a small number of tropical and subtropical perennials, including the scarlet-flowered *V. peruviana*, have been involved in the crosses that have produced the long-flowering hybrid verbenas. At the height of their popularity as bedding plants in the 19th century, enormous numbers were propagated annually from cuttings, but most of the modern hybrids are raised from seed. The small, sometimes scented flowers, clustered in a domed or flattish head at the end of stems, have 5 lobes, 2 upper and 3 lower ones. See also PERENNIALS.
CULTIVATION Require full sun and moderately fertile, moist but well-drained soil.
PROPAGATION From seed, sown under glass (at a minimum of 64°F/18°C) from mid-winter to early spring.
POTENTIAL PROBLEMS Aphids, thrips, leafhoppers, slugs; powdery mildew.

Verbena × hybrida
'Peaches and Cream'

V. hybrids

Flowers: summer to autumn.
H:6–18in (15–45cm), S:10–36in
(25–90cm). An.
The many colorful hybrids raised
from seed include bushy upright
plants, with a spread of 10–14in
(25–35cm), and others that are
low and sprawling, with a spread
of 18–36in (45–90cm). The bushy
plants in the **Novalis Series** cover
a broad range of colors, some
plants having a conspicuous white
eye. **'Imagination'**, with small
flowers of intense violet-blue,
makes a spreading mound about
1ft (30cm) tall. **'Peaches and
Cream'**, also spreading but with
stiffer stems and larger flowers,
combines shades of cream, yellow,
orange, and salmon pink. The
Romance Series is bushy but
compact with bright-eyed flowers
of single colors. Cultivars that do
not come true from seed and are
raised from cuttings include **'Silver
Anne'** (Z:7–10), a sprawling plant
with lightly scented flowers that
are bright pink when first open
but fade to near white, and the
mat-forming **'Sissinghurst'**, with
bright pink flowers.

VIOLA

VIOLACEAE

About 500 species, mainly annuals,
biennials, and perennials, are
found in the temperate regions of
the world, in a variety of habitats.
Heartsease (*V. tricolor*, Z:3–8), a
small-flowered short-lived species
widely distributed in Europe and
Asia, has played a major role in the
complex breeding that has
produced the garden pansy (*V. ×
wittrockiana*). The hybrids, too,
can be short-lived perennials, but
they are most commonly grown as
annuals and biennials. In the
heartsease flower, the 5 petals are
clearly defined: the spurred lower
petal is flanked by 2 laterals and
topped by another 2. In breeding
the garden pansy, trouble was
taken to defy this distinctive shape
and create a rounded flower to

satisfy a notion of floral perfection.
Heartsease retains the affection of
gardeners, with self-seeding
colonies giving a spring or summer
display of flowers in purple, blue,
yellow, and white. There are many
equally pretty hybrids or cultivars,
such as **'Bowles' Black'**, yellow-
eyed but of the deepest black-
purple, and **'Prince Henry'**, with
dark purple flowers. See also
PERENNIALS.
CULTIVATION Tolerate full sun or
partial shade and require fertile,
moist but well-drained soil.
PROPAGATION From seed, sown
under glass from late winter to early
spring (for summer flowering) or in
a seedbed from mid- to late summer
(for winter flowering).
POTENTIAL PROBLEMS Slugs, snails,
aphids, red spider mites, violet leaf
midge; leaf spot, mosaic viruses,
rust, powdery mildew.

Viola × wittrockiana Universal
Series **'True Blue'**

V. × wittrockiana

Pansy
Flowers: spring to summer.
H:6–9in (15–23cm), S:9–12in
(23–30cm). An.
The garden pansies are usually
spreading plants producing a
profusion of flowers, in some
cases as much as 4in (10cm)
across, and continuing in flower
over a long season provided they
are regularly deadheaded and fed
generously. Some are grown
exclusively for their summer
display, but there are in addition
winter-flowering pansies that in
mild weather bloom from autumn
to spring. The color range is
exceptional; there are single colors
and bold bicolors, some with
central masks and numerous
combinations of colors. Summer-
flowering pansies include the
following: **'Bambini'**, which has
small flowers in many colors,
usually with a white or yellow face
and whiskered; the **Clear Crystal
Series**, with medium-sized flowers
in a wide range of clear, single
colors; the **Joker Series**, having
medium-sized bicolored flowers
with strongly marked faces; the

Princess Series, with small
flowers, mainly in shades of
yellow and blue; and the **Super
Chalon Giants**, with large, ruffled,
bicolored flowers. The best-known
winter-flowering pansies are those
of the **Universal Series**, with
medium-sized flowers in single
colors or bicolors, many with a
dark central blotch. The **Ultima
Series** also has medium-sized
flowers in a wide color range,
from early winter to spring.

ZINNIA

ASTERACEAE

Most of the annuals, perennials,
and subshrubs in this genus are
plants of dry scrubland or more
open habitats. Many of the 20
species are from Mexico but
representatives are found from
southern USA to South America.
Those in cultivation are among the
most successful annuals in areas
that have dry hot summers.
CULTIVATION Require full sun and
fertile, well-drained soil that is rich
in organic matter.
PROPAGATION From seed, sown
under glass in early spring or where
plants are to flower in late spring.
POTENTIAL PROBLEMS Usually none.

Z. elegans *North America*

Flowers: summer. H:18–30in (45–
75cm), S:6–12in (15–30cm). An.
The flowerheads of the wild
species are purplish-red, but those
topping the stiffly upright cultivars
come in a wide variety of bright
colors and are single to fully
double. Tall zinnias include the
Cactus-flowered Group, with
semidouble flowerheads up to
5in (12.5cm) across, composed
of quilled flowerets; **'State Fair'**,
a mixture with fully double flowerheads; and **'Envy'**, a semidouble of
unusual lime-green coloring. There
are also numerous short-growing
and dwarf cultivars, among them
the **Peter Pan Series** and the
Thumbelina Series. These
cultivars grow to a height of
4–12in (10–30cm).

Zinnia elegans Peter Pan Series
'Peter Pan Orange'

bamboos, grasses, grasslike plants, and ferns

Recognition that grasses have ornamental value in the garden other than as constituents of a lawn is recent. The exceptions to this generalization are the bamboos, which are shrubby grasses with woody, usually hollow, canes (known technically as culms). The bamboos are included here with other true grasses, annuals as well as perennials, and the sedges, rushes, and cat's tails, three groups of plants with an appearance superficially like that of grasses. The chief ornamental feature of many of these plants is their foliage, with a wide color range, variegation in some cases producing very bold effects. The flowers are less showy, but their plumes, spikes, and spraylike arrangements are in many cases graceful. The scale, deportment, and texture of tufts and clumps vary so enormously that an exciting garden can be made entirely of grasses and grasslike plants.

Ferns have no rival for providing soft, feathery foliage and fine lacy patterns in the garden with their gently arching fronds. These ancient and primitive plants have no flowers or seeds, but reproduce by means of spores, which are found in clusters called sori on the undersides of their leaves.

The best time for planting is in autumn or late spring. Dead flower stalks and foliage should be cut back in spring.

Top Pleioblastus variegatus
Center Imperata cylindrica 'Rubra'
Bottom Matteuccia struthiopteris

BAMBOOS, GRASSES, AND GRASSLIKE PLANTS

ALOPECURUS

POACEAE Foxtail grass

The foxtail grasses owe their generic and common names to their bushy cylindrical flower spikes. There are about 35 annual and perennial species found in a wide range of habitats in the Northern Hemisphere, including subarctic tundra, moist fertile meadows, and dry screes. The wooly foxtail grass (*A. lanatus*, Z:4-8), with blue-green leaves covered in soft hairs, demands a very free draining gritty soil and protection from excessive wet.
CULTIVATION Tolerate full sun or partial shade and require fertile moist but well-drained soil.
PROPAGATION By division in late spring or early summer.
POTENTIAL PROBLEMS Usually none.

A. pratensis 'Aureovariegatus'
Foliage: spring and summer.
Flowers: mid-spring to mid-summer. H:8-12in (20-30cm),
S:10-14in (25-35cm). Z:4-8.
Rich yellow variegation makes this a bright plant for a frontal position. The clumps are topped by green or purplish flower spikes, but these are sacrificed if the plants are clipped to achieve a dense, radiant foliage effect. The leaves of '**Aureus**' are almost rich yellow.

Alopecurus pratensis 'Aureus'

ARUNDO

POACEAE

The 2 or 3 species are evergreen rhizomatous perennials that are native to warm temperate regions of the Northern Hemisphere. In the wild the best known, the giant reed (*A. donax*), often forms large stands at the edge of rivers and in other watery places, but in cultivation, it also adapts to drier conditions.
CULTIVATION Full sun and preferably moist conditions. Cut stems back annually for the best foliage effect.

PROPAGATION From stem cuttings taken in summer; by division of the rootstock in late spring; from seed, sown in spring.
POTENTIAL PROBLEMS Usually none.

A. donax S. Europe
Giant reed
Foliage: year-round. H:12-15ft (3.7-4m), S:4-6ft (1.2-1.8m).
Z:7-10.
This is one of the most impressive grasses of the temperate world. Clumps of stout stems carry broad, drooping, blue-gray leaves, about 2ft (60cm) long. Feathery plumes, purple at first but later nearly white, are produced on second-year stems where the climate is mild enough.

Arundo donax

BRIZA

POACEAE Quaking grass

Several annual and perennial species have sprays of pretty spikelets that tremble in the lightest breeze and rattle when shaken hard. These are widely distributed grasses of temperate regions; the annuals, which naturalize in dry open ground beyond their original homeland, often self-seed freely.
CULTIVATION Annual species require full sun. Perennial species tolerate full sun or partial shade. All need well-drained soil.
PROPAGATION From seed, in spring or autumn. *B. media* by division, in late spring or early summer.
POTENTIAL PROBLEMS Usually none.

Briza maxima

B. maxima Mediterranean
Greater quaking grass, puffed wheat
Flowers: late spring to mid-summer. H:16-24in (40-60cm),
S:6-10in (15-25cm). Z:4-8.
The elongated, heart-shaped spikelets of this annual are pale green tinged with red-brown or purple. They dangle on fine stalks above loose tufts of narrow leaves and, like the foliage, become straw colored in late summer.

B. media Europe, W. Asia
Common quaking grass, trembling grass
Flowers: late spring to late summer. H:1-2ft (30-60cm),
S:8-12in (20-30cm). Z:4-8.
This perennial species, which spreads slowly by creeping rhizomes, has blue-green leaves and sprays of heart-shaped shiny spikelets. These are purplish green at first, later fading to beige.

CALAMAGROSTIS

POACEAE

The most commonly grown reed grass is a hybrid between
C. arundinacea (Z:5-9) and
C. epigejos (Z:5-9), 2 of some 250 species of rhizomatous perennials found on moist soils in woodland and open heathland in temperate regions. Its cultivars remain attractive in autumn and winter when the clumps turn shades of soft brown and off-white.
CULTIVATION Tolerate full sun or partial shade and a wide range of soils provided they are fairly moist.
PROPAGATION By division, in mid-to late spring.
POTENTIAL PROBLEMS Usually none.

Calamagrostis × acutiflora 'Overdam'

C. × acutiflora 'Karl Foerster'
Feather reed grass
Foliage: year-round. Flowers: mid-to late summer. H:5-6ft (1.5- 1.8m),
S:18-24in (45-60cm). Z:5-9.
The narrow column of gray-green leaves is topped by soft pink-

bronze plumes, which fade to buff. **'Overdam'**, up to 4ft (1.2m) tall, has purplish plumes that age to silvery pink and makes a loose clump of arching leaves with yellow margins.

CAREX

CYPERACEAE Sedge

Although sedges are common to boggy and peaty areas in temperate and arctic regions, members of this large genus, with more than 1,500 perennial species, are found in a range of moist, rather than dry, habitats, extending to high elevations in the tropics. The main feature of the few grown in gardens is the grasslike foliage.
CULTIVATION Tolerate full sun or partial shade and require moist soil (but see also individual entries).
PROPAGATION By division, in late spring or early summer; from seed, sown in spring. (The seed of Northern Hemisphere species generally needs a period of winter cold to germinate.)
POTENTIAL PROBLEMS Usually none.

C. buchananii New Zealand
Leatherleaf sedge
Foliage: year-round. Flowers: mid- to late summer. H:20–30in (50–75cm), S:2–3ft (60–90cm). Z:6–8.
The very narrow, cylindrical-looking leaves are in fact 3-angled, and taper to a fine curled point, forming an orange-brown tussock. The flower spikes are brown.

C. conica **'Snowline'**
Foliage: year-round. Flowers: early summer. H:6–12in (15–30cm), S:10–14in (25–35cm). Z:6–8.
The silver tufts of arching leaves have white margins. The flower spikes are purplish brown.

C. elata **'Aurea'**
Bowles' golden sedge
Foliage: spring to summer. Flowers: late spring to early summer. H:20–28in (50–70cm), S:16–20in (40–50cm). Z:5–9.
In early summer this variant of the tufted sedge, a European fenland

Carex elata **'Aurea'**

plant that will grow in shallow water, has arching bright yellow leaves with narrow green margins. As summer advances, the overall effect becomes greener. The brown male flower spikes are borne above the stalkless green female spikes.

C. **'Frosted Curls'**
Foliage: year-round. H and S:12–18in (30–45cm). Z:5–9.
The silvery green tuft is dense, but softened by the curling tips of the arching leaves.

C. hachioensis **'Evergold'**
Foliage: year-round. Flowers: mid- to late spring. H:10–18in (25–45cm), S:12–18in (30–45cm). Z:4–9.
This outstanding variegated form of an evergreen Japanese species is best grown in light shade. The dark green in the leaves brightens the central yellow stripe, which ages to a creamy yellow. The flower spikes are brown. The variegated *C. morrowii* **'Fisher's Form'** (Z:5–9) makes a larger clump, 18–20in (45–50cm) high, with leaves edged and striped with yellow that fades to creamy white.

C. pendula Europe, N. Africa
Drooping sedge, pendulous sedge, weeping sedge
Foliage: year-round. Flowers: late spring to early summer. H and S:4–5ft (1.2–1.5m). Z:5–9.
Arching stems rising through dense evergreen clumps of shiny leaves bear green-brown flower spikes, which are erect at first but then hang like catkins. This shade-tolerant woodland sedge also looks graceful by the water's edge.

CORTADERIA

POACEAE

The 20 or so species, mainly from South America and New Zealand, include several distinctive grasses that make large mounds of narrow leaves topped by magnificent plumes. The South American pampas grass (*C. selloana*) is the best known, but the New Zealand toe toe (*C. richardii*, Z:7–9) is useful in a large planting of grasses since it flowers in early to mid-summer. Although plants of long-lasting beauty, they can be difficult to place in small yards, reflecting, perhaps unfairly, the suburban landscape at its most dispiriting.
CULTIVATION Require full sun and well-drained soil. Wearing gloves, remove dead leaves in spring.
PROPAGATION By division, in spring; from seed, sown in spring.
POTENTIAL PROBLEMS Usually none.

Cortaderia richardii

C. selloana Temperate South America
Pampas grass
Foliage: year-round. Flowers: late summer to mid-autumn. H:7–10ft (2.2–3m), S:4–5ft (1.2–1.5m). Z:7–9.
The gray-green tussock of narrow, arching leaves is impressive, but the plant is transformed by the tall glistening plumes, usually creamy white or silver, sometimes tinged purple or red. The gold variegated **'Aureolineata'** is shorter, and the free-flowering **'Pumila'** only reaches 4–6ft (1.2–1.8m). The long-lasting plumes of **'Sunningdale Silver'** are silvery white.

Cortaderia selloana **'Sunningdale Silver'**

DESCHAMPSIA

POACEAE

Among the 40 to 50 species in this genus of mainly perennial grasses, widely distributed in temperate regions, are several highly ornamental species. Those described are plants of moist acid soils, often found in poorly drained boggy and peaty areas.
CULTIVATION Tolerate full sun or light shade and require moist neutral to acid soil.
PROPAGATION By division, in late spring; from seed, sown in autumn or spring.
POTENTIAL PROBLEMS Usually none.

Deschampsia caespitosa 'Goldschleier'

D. caespitosa *Temperate and arctic Eurasia, mountains of Africa*
Tufted hair grass, tussock grass
Foliage: year-round. Flowers: all summer. H:4-6ft (1.2-1.8m), S:4-5ft (1.2-1.5m). Z:4-7.
Narrow dark green leaves form a dense evergreen tussock, but this base, attractive enough in winter and spring, is overwhelmed by airy plumes from early summer. Their color, usually starting green or purplish, changes as the season advances. In **'Bronzeschleier'** the plumes progress from silvery green to bronzy yellow, in **'Goldschleier'** to pale sheeny gold.

D. flexuosa *Europe, N. Asia, N.E. USA, temperate South America*
Crinkled hair grass
Foliage: year-round. Flowers: early to mid-summer. H and S:20-30in (50-75cm). Z:3-9.
The evergreen clump of threadlike leaves is topped by light flower plumes that are silvery, brown, or purple. The leaves of **'Tatra Gold'** are bright yellow-green throughout most of the year, and stiff stems carry bronzed flowerheads.

FARGESIA

POACEAE

Fargesia murieliae

Two outstanding bamboos that have endured several changes of name now rest in this small genus. In the wild they are clump-forming plants of moist forest margins. In the yard the clumps expand slowly but never get out of hand. Their fountainlike shape makes them effective when they are grown as isolated clumps, but they are also appealing planted as a small grove. *F. murieliae*, more wind tolerant than *F. nitida*, provides an elegant hedge; both make impressive container plants.
CULTIVATION Require moisture-retentive soil (potting soil with added organic matter). *F. murieliae* tolerates sun or shade, and *F. nitida* requires partial shade and shelter from cold winds.
PROPAGATION By division, in mid- to late spring.
POTENTIAL PROBLEMS Usually none.

F. murieliae *China*
Umbrella bamboo
Foliage: year-round. H:10-12ft (3-3.7m), S:4-6ft (1.2-1.8m). Z:4-9.
Slender yellow-green canes, with a white bloom when young, surge up as a column before arching out under the cumulative weight of numerous narrow leaves.

F. nitida *China*
Fountain bamboo
Foliage: year-round. H:12-15ft (3.7-4.5m), S:4-6ft (1.2-1.8m). Z:4-9.
This thin-leaved bamboo needs shade and shelter from cold winds in order to make a column of arching purplish-gray canes with an elegant burden of narrow leaves.

FESTUCA

POACEAE Fescue

The fescues, a large genus of more than 300 species, are among the most important pasture grasses in the temperate world (they are also found in mountains of the tropics). Some, such as *F. rubra* (Z:4-8), look good in ornamental turf. Several evergreen perennial fescues, mainly plants of dry rough terrain, have a more sophisticated ornamental value, their short bluish tufts providing contrasts of color and texture and making stubby edgings.
CULTIVATION Require full sun and well-drained soil.
PROPAGATION By division, in autumn or spring; from seed, sown in mid-spring.
POTENTIAL PROBLEMS Usually none.

F. glauca
Blue or gray fescue
Foliage: year-round. Flowers: early to mid-summer. H:6-12in (15-30cm), S:8-10in (20-25cm). Z:4-8.
Dense tufts bristling with narrow blue-green leaves send up stiff stems with blue-green flower plumes tinged violet. The steel-blue foliage is particularly striking in the compact **'Blaufuchs'** and in the taller **'Elijah Blue'**. The compact *F. valesiaca* **'Silbersee'** has pale silvery-blue foliage. The large blue fescue (*F. amethystina*), which grows to 18in (45cm), has a hint of mauve in its blue-gray foliage.

Festuca glauca

HAKONECHLOA

POACEAE

The genus includes a single deciduous perennial, **H. macra** (Z:5-8), a woodland grass of Japan, found mainly in mountainous areas. The plain-leaved plant, which has yellow-green foliage, is outshone by its variegated forms.
CULTIVATION Tolerate full sun or partial shade and require moist, organic-rich soil (potting soil with added organic matter.)
PROPAGATION By division, in mid- to late spring.
POTENTIAL PROBLEMS Usually none.

Hakonechloa macra 'Aureola'

H. macra 'Aureola'
Foliage: spring to autumn. Flowers: late summer to early autumn. H:8-14in (20-35cm), S:14-18in (35-45cm). Z:5-8.
Tapering ribbonlike leaves, piled one on top of another to form a soft mound, are bright yellow with fine green stripes. In late summer and autumn, when sprays of pale green flowers are produced, the foliage often takes on a pink or red tint. The leaves of **'Alboaurea'** are slightly broader, and the narrow white, yellow, and green stripes are often flushed bronze.

HELICTOTRICHON

POACEAE

The grass described, one of about 50 deciduous and evergreen species found in the temperate Northern Hemisphere, is a plant of stony ground on calcareous soils. It is suitable for sunny beds and for planting in gravel.
CULTIVATION Requires full sun and well-drained soil, preferably alkaline.
PROPAGATION By division, in spring; from seed sown in spring.
POTENTIAL PROBLEMS Usually none.

Helictotrichon sempervirens

H. sempervirens
Blue oat grass
Foliage: year-round. Flowers: early to mid-summer. H:3–4ft (90–120cm), S:18–24in (45–60cm). Z:5–8.
Narrow blue-green leaves, which are erect in the center but surrounded by others arching out, form a spiky clump. Slender stems carry small sheeny plumes well clear of the foliage.

HORDEUM

POACEAE

Barley (**H. vulgare**), one of the first cultivated cereal crops, is among the 20 or so annual and perennial grasses in this genus, most of which are found on rather dry soils in temperate regions, often where the ground has been disturbed. The flowers of the annual species described are remarkable for their long awns (bristles).
CULTIVATION Require full sun and well-drained soil.

Hordeum jubatum

PROPAGATION From seed, sown where plants are to grow in autumn or spring.
POTENTIAL PROBLEMS Usually none.

H. jubatum N.E. Asia, North America
Squirrel tail grass
Flowers: early to mid-summer. H:20–24in (50–60cm), S:10–12in (25–30cm). Z:5–8.
Erect stems rising from short tufts of green leaves arch over to form a silky head with long soft hairs. The spikelets are pale green at first, but often have a red or purple flush before the color bleaches.

IMPERATA

POACEAE

This small genus of rhizomatous perennials from tropical or warm temperate regions contains a species, *I. cylindrica*, grown for the red staining of its foliage. In a warm climate it can spread with weedlike abandon, but in cool temperate regions, it is suitable for the open yard or a container.
CULTIVATION Tolerate full sun or dappled shade and require moist, soil rich in organic matter (potting soil with added organic matter.)
PROPAGATION By division, in late spring.
POTENTIAL PROBLEMS Usually none.

Imperata cylindrica 'Rubra'

I. cylindrica S. Europe to Japan and Australia
Foliage: spring to autumn. Flowers: late summer to early autumn. H:16–24in (40–60cm), S:10–12in (25–30cm). Z:5–10.
The plant usually seen is '**Rubra**' from Japan, remarkable for the strong red staining of the flat upright leaves, which becomes more bloodied as summer advances. The flowers are silvery.

JUNCUS

JUNCACEAE Rush

The rushes, a large genus of about 300 grasslike evergreen or deciduous plants, are found in many parts of the world in marshy conditions, particularly on acid soils. Rushes are a common feature of boggy ground in cool temperate regions. The relatively few species that are cultivated are useful marginals for ponds.
CULTIVATION Requires full sun and wet soil, tolerating water to a depth of about 4in (10cm).
PROPAGATION By division, in mid- to late spring.
POTENTIAL PROBLEMS Usually none.

Juncus effusus 'Spiralis'

J. effusus 'Spiralis'
Corkscrew rush
Foliage: spring to autumn. Flowers: early to late summer. H:16–20in (40–50cm), S:12–18in (30–45cm). Z:4–9.
The corkscrew variant of the soft rush is a curiosity for the margin of a small pool. The glossy, dark green stems spiral randomly, some lying coiled on the ground in the tangle. The cluster of brownish flowers emerges well below the stem tip.

LAGURUS

POACEAE Hare's tail

The bobbing flowerheads of the annual hare's tail (*L. ovatus*), the single species in this genus, are a familiar sight in sandy coastal areas of the Mediterranean region. It is an easily grown garden plant and can be dried.
CULTIVATION Requires full sun and well-drained soil.
PROPAGATION From seed, sown where plants are to grow in spring or autumn, or in autumn under glass in containers.
POTENTIAL PROBLEMS Usually none.

Lagurus ovatus

L. ovatus *Mediterranean*
Hare's tail
Flowers: early to late summer.
H:12–18in (30–45cm), S:6–10in
(15–25cm). An.
The slender erect stems rising from
tufts of downy gray-green leaves
carry fluffy, silky, egg-shaped heads
that are greenish white at first,
usually with a purplish tinge, and
eventually turn beige.

LUZULA

JUNCACEAE Woodrush

The woodrushes are mainly plants
of moist woodlands, with about 80
species, the majority perennials,
widely distributed in temperate
regions of the world. These grasslike plants, which are closely
related to the true rushes (*Juncus*),
have rather broad leaves and
produce clusters of very small
flowers. They make unspectacular
but useful groundcover in shade.
CULTIVATION Tolerate full sun or
partial shade and require moist
soil, rich in organic matter, that
does not dry out. *L. nivea* needs
full sun.
PROPAGATION By division, in late
spring or early summer; from seed,
sown in containers in autumn
or spring.
POTENTIAL PROBLEMS Usually none.

L. nivea *S. and C. Europe*
Snowy woodrush
Foliage: year-round. Flowers: early
to late summer. H:18–24in (45–
60cm), S:14–18in (35–45cm).
Z:5–9.
This evergreen perennial forms
tufts of deep green leaves topped
by clustered heads of lustrous, pale
buff flowers, which dry well.

Luzula sylvatica 'Aurea'

L. sylvatica *S., W., and C. Europe,*
S.W. Asia
Greater woodrush
Foliage: year-round. Flowers: mid-
spring to early summer. H:28–32in
(70–80cm), S:18–20in (45–50cm).
Z:5–9.
Dense evergreen tussocks provide
groundcover under trees and
shrubs. Airy heads of tiny brown

flowers appear above glossy dark
green leaves. 'Aurea' has yellow-
green leaves that turn bright
yellow in winter, and the leaves
of 'Marginata' have a cream edge.

MILIUM

POACEAE

This small genus of annual and
perennial woodland grasses
includes the semievergreen wood
millet (*M. effusum*, Z:5–8), which is
widely distributed in Europe and
North America. The plain-leaved
plant is rarely grown, although the
light green of its foliage shows up
well in semishade.
CULTIVATION Require partial shade
and moist soil, rich in organic
matter.
PROPAGATION By division in spring;
from seed, sown in spring.
POTENTIAL PROBLEMS Usually none.

Milium effusum 'Aureum'

M. effusum 'Aureum'
Bowles' golden grass, golden wood
millet
Foliage: spring to late summer.
Flowers: late spring to mid-
summer. H:16–24in (40–60cm),
S:10–12in (25–30in). Z:5–8.
Even on a cloudy day in spring, the
rich yellow, ribbonlike leaves of
this perennial catch the light. Tiny
golden flowers shimmer on slender
stems. The limp foliage becomes
greener as the season advances.

MISCANTHUS

POACEAE

There are about 20 species of
these elegant perennial grasses,
and although widely distributed, a
high proportion come from Japan
and China, where they are usually
found in moist, even marshy soils
with other grasses and herbaceous
plants. Those plants described,
which increase steadily without
being invasive, remain beautiful
when reduced to bleached
parchment in winter, but should
be cut down before new growth is
made in spring.
CULTIVATION Require full sun and
fertile, moist, but well-drained soil.

PROPAGATION By division in mid-
to late spring; from seed, sown in
spring.
POTENTIAL PROBLEMS Usually none.

Miscanthus sacchariflorus

M. sacchariflorus *S.E. Asia*
Silver banner grass
Foliage: year-round. Flowers: late
summer to early autumn. H:6–10ft
(1.8–3m), S:3–5ft (90–150cm).
Z:8–10.
In a large-scale waterside planting,
this is a match for giants such as
Gunnera manicata. The purple-
brown flowerheads rarely appear
in cool temperate regions, but the
bamboolike clumps, with their long
rustling leaves, arch gracefully.

M. sinensis *S.E. Asia*
Flowers: mid-autumn. Foliage:
year-round. H:4–10ft (1.2–3m),
S:3–5ft (90–150cm). Z:5–9.
The wild form has been displaced
in gardens by a range of beautiful
cultivars, the leaves making an
arching counterpoint to the
vigorous upward thrust of the
stems. The silky buff-pink sprays of
M. 'Silberfeder', up to 8ft (2.5m)
tall, and less dependent than most
on a warm summer to flower, are
in a class of their own. Other fine
cultivars include 'Gracillimus'
(Z:4–9), up to 5ft (1.5m) tall and
gracefully slender; 'Grosse
Fontäne', a vigorous grower up to
6½ft (2m) with purple stems and
cascading leaves, with distinctive
white mid-ribs, and red-tinted
plumes; 'Malepartus', up to 8ft
(2.5m) tall, with silver-veined
leaves that turn purplish in autumn
and large mahogany plumes aging

Miscanthus sinensis 'Zebrinus'

to silver; and '**Zebrinus**', the zebra grass, which grows to 6ft (1.8m), with irregular horizontal banding in shades of cream or yellow.

MOLINIA

POACEAE

The genus contains only 2 species, both of them perennial grasses of moist acidic boggy and peaty areas. In cultivation, however, the purple moor grass (*M. caerulea*) and its variegated cultivars succeed in a fairly wide range of conditions. They are suitable for beds and woodland yards, while the smaller dwarf kinds are ideal for outcrops in rock gardens.
CULTIVATION Tolerate full sun or partial shade and require moist soil, preferably neutral to acid.
PROPAGATION By division, in late spring; from seed, sown in spring.
POTENTIAL PROBLEMS Usually none.

Molinia caerulea subsp. caerulea 'Moorhexe'

M. caerulea *Europe, N. and S.W. Asia*
Purple moor grass
Flowers: mid-summer to early autumn. Foliage: spring to autumn. H:2–4ft (60–120cm), S:18–24in (45–60cm). Z:5–8.
The dense tussocks from which stiff stems rise bear purplish flowers. The tall flower stems of **subsp. arundinacea**, about 4ft (1.2m) high, even up to 7ft (2.2m) in '**Windspiel**', turn amber yellow in autumn. The narrow upright growth of **subsp. caerulea 'Moorhexe'**, only 18in (45cm) tall and topped by dark flowers, contrasts well with rambling plants. The pick of these grasses is **subsp. caerulea 'Variegata'**, which has arching leaves, with cream stripes, and feathery purplish buff plumes. It reaches 18–24in (45–60cm) tall.

PENNISETUM

POACEAE

Over 100 species are distributed from warm temperate to tropical regions of the world. The Kikuyu

grass (*P. clandestinum*, Z:8–10), grown for pasture, is of economic importance. The appealing flowerheads of those grown ornamentally resemble hairy caterpillars. The species described are plants of open grassland and tolerant of dry conditions.
CULTIVATION Require full sun and well-drained soil.
PROPAGATION By division, in late spring; from seed, sown in spring.
POTENTIAL PROBLEMS Usually none.

P. alopecuroides *E. Asia to W. Australia*
Fountain grass
Flowers: Early to mid-autumn. Foliage: year-round. H and S:2–4ft (60–120cm). Z:5–9.
This evergreen species makes a dark green mound of narrow leaves, its arching growth emphasized in autumn when fuzzy purplish flowerheads weigh down the stem tips. '**Hameln**' is compact and flowers in late summer.

P. orientale *C. and S.W. Asia, N. India*
Flowers: mid-summer to early autumn. Foliage: spring to autumn. H and S:18–24in (45–60cm). Z:7–9.
In cool temperate regions this deciduous perennial can be grown as an annual, started under glass in early spring. Large caterpillarlike flowerheads, at first mauve pink, later buff to near white, sway above clumps of narrow leaves.

Pennisetum villosum

P. villosum *Mountains of N.E. tropical Africa*
Feathertop
Flowers: late summer to early autumn. Foliage: spring to autumn. H and S:20–24in (50–60cm). Z:7–9.
Where the climate suits it, as in parts of Australia, this deciduous perennial grass is a weed. Like *P. orientale*, it can be grown as an annual. Beige flowerheads, their long hairs tactile and feathery, bob in the breeze above a clump of arching gray-green leaves.

PHALARIS

POACEAE

The genus includes annual and perennial grasses from a wide variety of habitats, but the representatives usually seen in yards are variegated forms of a moisture-loving evergreen perennial, reed canary grass (*P. arundinacea*).
CULTIVATION Tolerate full sun or partial shade and wet to moderately moist soil.
PROPAGATION By division, from mid-spring to early summer.
POTENTIAL PROBLEMS Usually none.

Phalaris arundinacea var. picta 'Feesey'

P. arundinacea var. picta 'Feesey'
Gardeners' garters
Foliage: year-round. Flowers: early to mid-summer. H and S:2–3ft (60–90cm). Z:4–9.
This is a sport of the vigorous **var. picta**, one of the first variegated grasses for yards. Half-and-half longitudinal green and white striping on ribbonlike leaves make it tempting, although it is invasive. '**Feesey**' is whiter and paler green and spreads slowly to form dense clumps. The pale green to buff spikelets stand clear of the leaves.

PHYLLOSTACHYS

POACEAE

Several graceful bamboos belong to this genus of about 80 species, most of them woodland plants from the Himalayas and farther east. In addition to an elegant form and beautiful foliage, several have distinctive canes, including the fishpole or golden bamboo (*P. aurea*, Z:5–10). The young shoots of many, including *P. edulis* (Z:7–10), are edible. The giant timber bamboo (*P. bambusoides*, Z:7–10) has commercial value.
CULTIVATION Tolerate full sun or partial shade and require moist well-drained soil (potting soil).
PROPAGATION By division, in mid- to late spring.
POTENTIAL PROBLEMS Slugs.

Phyllostachys nigra

P. nigra *E. and C. China*
Black bamboo
Foliage and canes: year-round.
H:5-10ft (1.5-3m), S: 6-10ft
(1.8-3m). Z:7-10.
The rich foliage is a feature of this
clump-forming bamboo, as are the
arching canes that turn from green
in the first year to mottled brown
and then nearly black in
the second or third year. **'Boryana'**
produces yellowish green canes
with purple-brown marks. The
canes of **var. henonis** are bright
green at first, turning yellow-
brown as they mature. The leaves
are dark green.

PLEIOBLASTUS

POACEAE

This Asiatic genus of about 20
bamboos includes several
characterful low-growing species.
In the wild these bamboos, most
of which have running roots, form
thickets on woodland margins and
in glades. The low-growing species,
P. humilis (Z:5-10) and
P. pygmaeus (Z:6-10), make
attractive container plants.
CULTIVATION Tolerate full sun or
partial shade (variegation is best in
full sun), moist soil (potting soil),
and shelter from cold winds.
PROPAGATION By division, in mid-
to late spring.
POTENTIAL PROBLEMS Usually none.

Pleioblastus auricomus

P. auricomus *Japan*
Foliage: year-round. H and S:2-5ft
(60-150cm). Z:5-10.
In shade the leaves of this bamboo
look sickly green but make a bright
yellow splash in full sun, which
brings out the rich yellow striping.

P. variegatus *Japan*
Foliage: year-round. H and S:2-4ft
(60-120cm). Z:7-10.
The pale green canes carry spiky
tufts of narrow downy leaves with
bold dark green and white stripes.
The roots run but this charmingly
bright bamboo is easily controlled.

SEMIARUNDINARIA

POACEAE

The 10 or so tall bamboos that
make up this genus are from China
and Japan. In the wild they usually
form large thickets in or at the
margins of woodland in rough
mountainous country. In a cool
temperate climate, the species
described forms a dense clump
from which rhizomes establish
neighboring clumps.
CULTIVATION Requires full sun or
light shade and moist, well-drained
soil, rich in organic matter.
PROPAGATION By division of young
rhizomes, in spring.
POTENTIAL PROBLEMS Slugs.

Semiarundinaria fastuosa

S. fastuosa *Japan*
Narihira bamboo
Foliage and canes: year-round.
H:15-25ft (4.5-7.5m), S:5-8ft
(1.5-2.5m). Z:7-10.
The shiny green leaves are carried
high up on tall stiff canes, which
eventually turn yellow-brown, but
when young are glossy green with
purple stains at the nodes. It
makes a good hedge or screen.

STIPA

POACEAE Feather grass

Many of the species in this large
genus of several hundred
temperate and tropical grasses,
most of them perennial, are highly
ornamental as well as remarkably
tolerant of dry conditions. The

leaves are usually quill-like with
rolled-in margins.
CULTIVATION Require full sun
and well-drained soil. Tolerate
dry conditions except for
S. arundinacea.
PROPAGATION By division in
mid- to late spring; from seed,
sown in spring.
POTENTIAL PROBLEMS Usually none.

S. arundinacea *New Zealand*
Pheasant's tail grass
Flowers: mid-summer to early
autumn. H:18-24in (45-60cm),
S:3-4ft (90-120cm). Z:5-8.
The orange and russet tones that
develop in the arching clumps
throughout summer make a
striking feature during the winter.
The flower stems are light and
weighed down by a haze of soft
brown flowers.

S. calamagrostis *S. Europe*
Flowers: summer to early autumn.
H and S:3-4ft (90-120cm). Z:7-9.
This free-flowering deciduous
grass makes a lax clump that is
improved by light support. The
feathery green plumes eventually
turn warm buff and last through
the winter.

S. gigantea *Spain, Portugal*
Giant feather grass, golden oats
Flowers: early to mid-summer.
H:6-8ft (1.8-2.5m), S:3-4ft
(90-120cm). Z:7-9.
The lax evergreen or semievergreen clump of narrow leaves
is undistinguished, but the tall
flowering stems that spring from it
carry heads of oatlike, pinkish
purple flowers. These turn to gold
and spangle beautifully in the
lightest breeze.

Stipa tenuissima

S. tenuissima *USA (Texas, New
Mexico), Mexico, Argentina*
Flowers: mid-summer to autumn.
H:18-24in (45-60cm), S:10-12in
(25-30cm). Z:6-9.
The fine, bright green leaves make
a soft-textured vaselike clump with
a billowing silky head of silver-
green flowers that turn
buff as they age.

FERNS

ADIANTUM

ADIANTACEAE Maidenhair fern

This genus consists of over 200 species of evergreen, semi-evergreen, and deciduous ferns. Many occur in tropical and sub-tropical forest in North and South America, while others are found in temperate woodland or woodland margins in Europe, Asia, Australasia, and North America. The variable fronds are divided, with oval or rounded segments carried on long, thin, shiny, purple-black leafstalks. True maidenhair fern (*A. capillus-veneris*, Z:7-10), often grown as a pot plant, is notable for its light green triangular fronds.
CULTIVATION Prefer full or partial shade and moist, well-drained soil. Do not let the soil dry out or become waterlogged.
PROPAGATION By division, in spring. From spores, sown ripe.
POTENTIAL PROBLEMS Usually none.

A. pedatum *North America*
H:6-8in (15-20cm), S:12-24in (30-60cm). Z:3-8.
Light green, lance-shaped, deciduous fronds with toothed margins are borne on thin, glossy, purple stalks. The Aleutian maidenhair fern (**A. pedatum var. subpumilum**, Z:2-8), which is also fully hardy, is considerably larger than the species, with a height and spread of 30in (75cm). Blackish-purple stems support finely divided, fingered fronds that are tinged pink when young, later turning pale to mid-green.

Adiantum pedatum

A. venustum *China, Tibet*
Himalayan maidenhair fern
Foliage: year-round. H and S:6-9in (15-23cm). Z:4-8.
Vivid bronze-pink fronds emerge in late winter and early spring. As the fronds develop, they turn mid-green and open out into a triangular shape, with narrowly fan-shaped segments.

ASPLENIUM

ASPLENIACEAE Spleenwort

The plants in this large genus of over 700 semievergreen and evergreen ferns are found in most parts of the world in a wide range of habitats. The fronds grow in tufts on short, erect, or creeping rhizomes, and are deeply divided or entire. The bird's nest fern (**A. nidus**, Z:10-11), which is a tropical epiphyte, has green glossy fronds, rather like long tongues, arranged in a rosette. This fern is, however, susceptible to attacks from scale. In contrast, the terrestrial rusty-backed fern (**A. ceterach**, Z:5-8) has fronds made up of small, round green leaflets, with feltlike brown scales beneath.
CULTIVATION Prefer partial shade. Require a sheltered site and well-drained soil rich in organic matter.
PROPAGATION From spores, sown as soon as ripe. By division, in spring.
POTENTIAL PROBLEMS Usually none.

Asplenium scolopendrium **Crispum Group**

A. scolopendrium *Asia, Europe, North America*
Hart's tongue fern
Foliage: year-round. H:12-24in (30-60cm), S:10-20in (25-50cm). Z:3-8.
The clusters of tufty fronds are light green with a leathery texture and resemble shuttlecocks. Its variations include the **Crispum Group**, with fronds that have a pronounced wavy margin; the **Cristatum Group**, with crested and ruffled fronds; and the **Undulatum Group**, with fronds that have irregular wavy margins.

A. trichomanes *Most temperate regions*
Maidenhair spleenwort
Foliage: year-round. H and S:3-9in (7.5-23cm). Z:3-8.
Attractive fronds of dark green leaflets with rounded tips are produced on thin, glossy, dark brown to black stems. The fronds grow in dense tufts on short, erect, occasionally creeping rhizomes.

ATHYRIUM

ATHYRIACEAE Lady fern

Over 180 species of deciduous lady ferns occur throughout the world in moist temperate and tropical woodland, yet very few have been cultivated for garden use. The common lady fern (*A. filix-femina*), much loved by Victorian gardeners, is highly variable, with numerous cultivars.
CULTIVATION Require partial or full shade and fertile, moist, neutral to slightly acid soil.
PROPAGATION By division, in spring. From spores, sown as soon as ripe.
POTENTIAL PROBLEMS Usually none.

Athyrium filix-femina 'Frizelliae'

A. filix-femina *Temperate Northern Hemisphere*
Lady fern
H and S:18-36in (45-90cm). Z:4-8.
The arching outline of this fern is one of its chief assets. The fronds, rising from erect rhizomes, are finely divided into long, pointed leaflets. **'Frizelliae'** (Mrs. Frizell's lady fern, tatting fern) has small, rounded segments on the fronds, 8in (20cm) long, which resemble "tatting" (intricate lace).

A. niponicum var. **pictum**
Japanese painted fern
H and S:12-18in (30-45cm). Z:3-8.
This slow-spreading Japanese fern, with individual fronds produced from a creeping rhizome, will cover small areas with a carpet of silver-green fronds. The midribs are flushed maroon-purple.

Athyrium niponicum var. **pictum**

333

BLECHNUM

BLECHNACEAE Hard fern

Between 150 and 200 species of hard ferns, the majority of which are evergreen, occur mostly in moist, acid, sheltered sites in temperate and tropical regions. The hardiest and most garden-worthy of these ferns make useful evergreen groundcover plants for moist, acid soils. The drooping or nearly prostrate infertile fronds and the erect, spore-bearing fronds, developed in the center of the foliage rosettes, provide a striking contrast in form.
CULTIVATION Require partial or full shade and moist, acid soil rich in organic matter.
PROPAGATION By division, in spring. From spores, sown in late summer.
POTENTIAL PROBLEMS Usually none.

Blechnum penna-marina

B. penna-marina *Australasia, South America*
Foliage: year-round. H:4-8in (10-20cm), S:indefinite. Z:6-9.
Creeping rhizomes produce dense tufts of evergreen fronds. The fertile fronds have more widely spaced segments than those of the sterile fronds.

B. spicant *Europe, N. Asia, W. North America*
Hard fern
Foliage: year-round. H:12-18in (30- 45cm), S:18-24in (45-60cm). Z:4-8.
Fertile fronds, standing bolt upright, are produced in the center of large rosettes of sterile fronds. Variations in shape include crested and serrated segments.

CYSTOPTERIS

ATHYRIACEAE Bladder fern

The 10 to 20 deciduous ferns in this genus occur in temperate and subtropical regions, where they grow on rocky mountainsides, in woodland, and in damp valleys, usually in alkaline soil. The sori of their delicately bowed, soft, very finely divided fronds have a bladderlike covering that gives the group its common name. Some species, such as *C. bulbifera*, produce small bulbils on the frond stalk; the bulbils drop when ripe and sprout new ferns.
CULTIVATION Require partial shade, shelter from cold, drying winds, and fertile, moist but well-drained soil with stone chips added.
PROPAGATION From bulbils, in late summer (*C. bulbifera*). By division, in spring. From spores, sown in late summer.
POTENTIAL PROBLEMS Usually none.

C. bulbifera *E. North America*
H:12-18in (30-45cm), S:8-12in (20-30cm). Z:3-7.
This lime-tolerant fern has graceful, swirling rosettes of light green, slender, divided fronds with curving tips. Bulbils develop beneath the midribs, which are lightly tinged with red.

C. fragilis *E. North America*
Brittle bladder fern
H and S:8-10in (20-25cm). Z:2-9.
Widely distributed in northern temperate regions and also found in Chile, this clump-forming fern produces lacy tufts of gray-green, divided fronds.

Cystopteris fragilis

DICKSONIA

DICKSONIACEAE

There are about 25 species of evergreen and semievergreen ferns in this genus, occurring in sheltered forests in temperate and tropical regions of Australasia, S.E. Asia, and South America. The rhizomes are often thick, trunklike, and upright, but occasionally creeping. Dark glossy green, leathery, divided fronds form terminal clusters. Man fern (*D. antarctica*) grows successfully in coastal regions.
CULTIVATION Prefer full or partial shade, but tolerate full sun. Prefer moist, acid soil rich in organic matter.
PROPAGATION From spores, sown as soon as ripe.
POTENTIAL PROBLEMS Usually none.

Dicksonia antarctica

D. antarctica *E. Australia (including Tasmania)*
Man fern, soft tree fern, wooly tree fern
Foliage: year-round. H and S:6-12ft (1.8-3.7m). Z:9-11.
This statuesque, slow-growing fern gradually develops into a single furry trunk made up of the fibrous remains of old leafstalks. The large, finely divided fronds, up to 6ft (1.8m) long, are glossy mid-green on the upper side and matt green on the underside.

DRYOPTERIS

ASPIDIACEAE Buckler fern

There are about 200 species of ferns in this genus. They are found in the temperate Northern Hemisphere, often in woodland or on mountainsides and near water. Most are deciduous, but a few stay green in winter if grown in favorable conditions.
CULTIVATION Require partial or full shade, a sheltered site, and moist soil rich in organic matter. Golden male fern (*D. affinis*) tolerates a less sheltered site.
PROPAGATION By division, in spring or autumn. From spores, sown as soon as ripe.
POTENTIAL PROBLEMS Usually none.

Dryopteris affinis

D. affinis *Mediterranean to Himalayas, W. Europe*
Golden male fern
Foliage: year-round in mild winters. H and S:2-4ft (60- 120cm). Z:4-9.
Golden brown scales on each frond midrib show to best effect as

the young growth unfurls in spring. The leathery fronds are dark green. Among cultivars, **'Cristata The King'** (Z:4–8) has the brightest golden scales and is notable for the heavily crested tip to each frond.

D. dilatata *C. and N.W. Europe*
Broad buckler fern
H and S:2–4ft (60–120cm). Z:4–8. Arching, triangular, divided fronds rise from erect rhizomes to create an elegant shuttlecock form. The fronds are pale green in spring, maturing to dark green. The midribs are covered with brown scales with buff-brown margins.

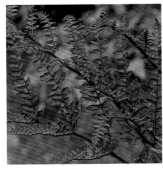

Dryopteris erythrosora

D. erythrosora *China, Japan*
Japanese shield fern, autumn fern Foliage: year-round in mild winters. H and S:18–24in (45–60cm). Z:5–8. Slowly creeping rhizomes make loose tufts of spreading, triangular, divided fronds, showy copper-red while young, fading to dark green. Bright red young sori often show well against the summer foliage.

D. filix-mas *Europe, North America*
Male fern
H and S:2–4ft (60–120cm). Z:4–8. Spear-shaped, deep glossy green, finely divided fronds arch so that the tips almost touch the ground. This fern spores prolifically. Slower-growing **'Crispa Cristata'** has crested fronds and crested, wavy-edged leaflets. Less vigorous **'Cristata'** (crested buckler fern) is more spreading; the fronds are yellow-green with finely divided, crinkled edges. **'Linearis'** has delicate-looking fronds.

D. wallichiana *Himalayas to S.E. Asia*
Wallich's wood fern
Foliage: spring to autumn. H:3–5ft (1–1.5m), S:30–36in (75–90cm). Z:4–8.
A massive shuttlecock of lance-shaped, divided, dark green fronds form a bold feature. The brownish-black midrib scales contrast with the yellow-green spring foliage.

MATTEUCCIA

ASPIDIACEAE

This genus comprises 3 or 4 species of deciduous ferns, widely distributed in deciduous woodland in the Northern Hemisphere. The large, finely divided fronds appear in spring, and are followed by fertile, spore-bearing fronds in mid-summer, which persist into winter.
CULTIVATION Prefer partial or dappled shade, but tolerate sun. Require moist, well-drained soil rich in organic matter.
PROPAGATION From spores, sown as soon as ripe. By division, in early spring.
POTENTIAL PROBLEMS Usually none.

M. struthiopteris *Asia, Europe, North America*
Shuttlecock fern
H:3–5ft (1–1.5m), S:2–3ft (60–90cm). Z:2–9.
This deciduous fern has an outer rim of gently arching, yellow-green sterile fronds, up to 3ft (90cm) long. The shorter greenish-brown inner fronds are fertile. Both inner and outer fronds are spear shaped, very thin, and deeply cut, with blackish-brown midribs.

Matteuccia struthiopteris

ONOCLEA

ASPIDIACEAE

Genus of a single species of deciduous fern occurring in damp sites. It is ideal for a damp shady border or beside water.
CULTIVATION Prefers partial shade (the fronds may burn in full sun) and moist, preferably acid, soil.
PROPAGATION By division, in autumn or early spring. From spores, sown as soon as ripe.
POTENTIAL PROBLEMS Usually none.

O. sensibilis *E. Asia, E. USA*
Foliage: autumn. H:12–24in (30–60cm), S:indefinite. Z:3–8. Bright green sterile fronds, often bronze-pink in spring, turn butter-yellow in autumn. Shorter spore-bearing fronds, which are stiffly upright, turn dark brown.

Onoclea sensibilis

OSMUNDA

OSMUNDACEAE

These deciduous, moisture-loving ferns, approximately 12 species in total, are found in damp places and watersides in all continents except Australia. The mid-green, broadly spear-shaped, very finely divided fronds arch gently from the base. The undersides of the inner fronds are covered with spore capsules, which turn brown when ripe, usually in mid-summer.
CULTIVATION Prefer partial shade. Tolerate full sun in a damp site.
PROPAGATION From spores, sown as soon as ripe. By division, in late spring.
POTENTIAL PROBLEMS Usually none.

O. regalis *Temperate and subtropical regions*
Flowering fern, royal fern
H and S:4–5ft (1.2–1.5m). Z:4–9. The broadly triangular, bright green sterile fronds are followed by fertile fronds with long, tassel-like tips. This fern gradually builds up a mass of crowns and matted black roots 2–3ft (60–90cm) above the ground.

Osmunda regalis

POLYPODIUM

POLYPODIACEAE

Most of the 75 or more species are evergreen, epiphytic ferns from tropical regions in the Americas. Some species tolerate drought more than most other ferns.
CULTIVATION Require dappled or full shade and moderately fertile, acid, gritty, well-drained soil.

PROPAGATION By division, in spring or early summer. From spores, sown when ripe.
POTENTIAL PROBLEMS Usually none.

P. vulgare *Europe, Africa, E. Asia*
Common polypody
Foliage: year-round. H:6–15in (15–38cm), S:indefinite. Z:5–8.
This fern is grown for its lance-shaped, leathery, dark green fronds, which rise from tough, creeping rhizomes. Growing either epiphytically or terrestrially, it grows in dry-stone walls, on mossy boulders, and tree stumps, or on banks or dunes. 'Cornubiense Grandiceps' has finely divided fronds, crested or branched in quite a pronounced manner at each frond tip.

Polypodium vulgare

POLYSTICHUM

ASPIDIACEAE Shield fern

There are nearly 200 species of these ferns, most of which are evergreen. They occur in a wide range of habitats, from alpine cliffs to tropical forests worldwide, and are resilient and tolerant of dry conditions. Many have intricately divided dark green fronds, which spiral in shuttlecocks around erect central rhizomes. Characteristic of many species are the toothed segments, terminating in a sharp point or bristle and giving the fronds sharp definition.
CULTIVATION Require full sun or dappled to deep shade and moderately fertile, gritty soil.
PROPAGATION By division, in spring. From spores, sown when ripe. From bulbils (cultivars of *P. setiferum*), in autumn.
POTENTIAL PROBLEMS Usually none.

P. aculeatum *C. and N.W. Europe*
Hard shield fern, prickly shield fern
Foliage: year-round. H:2–3ft (60–90cm), S:12–30in (30–75cm). Z:4–8.
A handsome fern with a broad, arching, vase-shaped shuttlecock formed by the leathery, narrow, divided fronds.

Polystichum aculeatum

P. munitum *N.W. North America*
Sword fern
Foliage: year-round. H:2–4ft (60–120cm), S:3–4ft (90–120cm). Z:5–8.
The leathery, lance-shaped fronds are matt dark green, hairy on the underside, and form shuttlecocks. The leaflets are spiny toothed.

P. setiferum *Europe*
Soft shield fern
Foliage: year-round in mild winters. H:2–4ft (60–120cm), S:30–36in (75–90cm). Z:5–8.
The divided, soft-textured, dark green fronds make a drooping and ornamental, vase-shaped shuttlecock. Each frond stem is covered in soft brown scales. Ferns in the Acutilobum Group have pronounced long, pointed fronds, spiraling elegantly around the crown. They are drought tolerant—even thriving in full sun on fertile, moist soils—and produce bulbils on frond midribs. Divisilobum Group contains ferns with intricately divided fronds and long, narrow, leathery leaflets earning them the name 'Filigree Fern'. Bulbils often form along the frond midribs. 'Herrenhausen' has broad fronds, spreading to flattened shuttlecocks as much as 20in (50cm) across.

THELYPTERIS

THELYPTERIDACEAE

The 2 ferns in this genus are deciduous, from bogs and swamps in temperate regions throughout the world. They are often mat-forming, producing a roving mass of rhizomatous roots from which emerge lance-shaped fronds with deeply divided leaflets. They are ideal plants for a moist border or beside a pond.
CULTIVATION Tolerate full sun or partial shade and require perpetually moist, moderately fertile soil.
PROPAGATION By division, in spring or summer. From spores, sown as soon as ripe.
POTENTIAL PROBLEMS Usually none.

T. palustris *Europe, Asia*
Marsh fern
H and S:2–3ft (60–90cm). Z:4–8.
This fern spreads into a dainty gray-green, soft-fronded edge and thrives in bogs or by water. The long-stalked, lance-shaped, divided fronds rise from amid the creeping rhizomes.

Thelypteris palustris

WOODWARDIA

BLECHNACEAE Chain fern

Of the 10 species of evergreen and deciduous ferns in this genus, only 2 are commonly cultivated in temperate gardens. Their natural habitats are moist, shady banks near water or acid bogs, in warm temperate and tropical zones. Where winters are mild, they are among the largest and grandest of ferns, with broad, arching fronds. The sori are arranged in chains, hence the common name.
CULTIVATION Require partial shade and a sheltered position, and moderately fertile, moist soil.
PROPAGATION By division, in spring. From spores, sown in late summer or early autumn. From bulbils, in autumn.
POTENTIAL PROBLEMS Usually none.

W. radicans *Atlantic Islands, S.W. Europe*
European chain fern
Foliage: year-round. H:3–4ft (90–120cm), S:4–8ft (1.2–2.5m). Z:9–10.
Broad, lance-shaped fronds, with finely toothed leaflets, form bold, spreading arches. A single bulbil is produced at the tip of each frond.

Woodwardia radicans

Special Plant Lists

In the following lists, selections of plants are grouped according to the conditions in which they grow best. Unless there are differences within a genus, only the genus name is given. Some genera will tolerate a wide range of conditions and these appear under several headings. More detailed information on cultivation can be found in the entries, on pp. 106–336.

Plants for Major Growing Conditions

Full Sun

The following lists do not cover the plants that thrive in reasonably moisture-retentive but well-drained soils, the aim being to draw attention to those that are better suited to conditions that are drier or moister than the average. Some of the plants here will tolerate light or dappled shade, especially when grown in warm climates, but in cool temperate regions lose their character or do not thrive unless grown in open in full sun.

Dry Soils

The plants in this list vary in their tolerance of drought but all require well-drained conditions and as mature plants are to some degree capable of withstanding dry periods. However, as young plants they all are dependent on regular supplies of water and even when established need moisture during their peak period of growth.

TREES
Acer negundo
Betula
Carpinus betulus
Cercis siliquastrum
Fagus sylvatica
Gleditsia
Ilex
Populus alba
P. tremula
Prunus
  laurocerasus
P. lusitanica
Robinia

SHRUBS
Ballota
Berberis
Calluna
Cistus
Convolvulus
Cotoneaster
Elaeagnus
Erica
Genista
Helianthemum

Hypericum (some)
Lavandula
Ruta
Salvia
Santolina
Tamarix
Thymus
Yucca

CONIFERS
Ginkgo
Juniperus
  communis
J. × pfitzeriana
Pinus
Taxus

CLIMBERS
Lathyrus latifolius
Solanum crispum
  'Glasnevin'

PERENNIALS
Acaena
Acanthus
Achillea

Anaphalis
  margaritacea
Anthemis
Armeria
Artemisia
Asphodeline
Aubrieta
Aurinia
Centaurea
Centranthus
Crambe
Cynara
Dianthus
Diascia
Dictamnus
Echinops
Eryngium
Euphorbia
  characias
E. myrsinites
Gypsophila
Iris, bearded
Iris unguicularis
Linum
Lychnis
Oenothera

Origanum
Penstemon
Phlomis
Phlox douglasii
Salvia
Saponaria
Sedum
Sempervivum
Stachys
Verbascum
Zauschneria

BULBS, CORMS, AND TUBERS
Allium
Anemone
  coronaria
Crocus
Gladiolus
Nectaroscordum

ANNUALS AND BIENNIALS
Calendula
  officinalis
Centaurea cyanus

Erysimum
Eschscholzia
  californica
Limnanthes
  douglasii
Limonium
  sinuatum
Salvia viridis

GRASSES
Festuca
Helictotrichon
Imperata
Pennisetum
Stipa

Moist Soils

The plants in the following lists will often survive short periods of drought but only achieve their full potential when growing in soils that are reliably moist.

TREES
Alnus
Amelanchier
Betula pendula
Crataegus
  laevigata
Populus
Quercus palustris
Salix
Sorbus aucuparia

SHRUBS
Amelanchier
Ceratostigma
Cornus alba
C. stolonifera
Salix
Sambucus
Viburnum opulus

CONIFERS
Metasequoia
Taxodium

PERENNIALS
Ajuga
Alchemilla
Aruncus
Astilbe
Astrantia
Canna
Inula
Iris ensata
I. sibirica
Ligularia
Lobelia
Lysimachia
Lythrum
Macleaya

Monarda
Ranunculus
Rheum

BULBS, CORMS, AND TUBERS
Camassia
Dahlia
Fritillaria
  meleagris
Narcissus
  cyclamineus

BAMBOOS
Fargesia

GRASSES
Calamagrostis
Carex pendula
Miscanthus

Light and Partial Shade

The following lists cover some of the plants that will grow in shaded areas for at least part of the day during the growing season. This is a common situation in nature where many plants grow on the fringes of woodland or under deciduous trees. Many of the plants listed here (see next page) will produce a flush of early spring growth before the trees come into full leaf and cast shade over the ground below.

Dry Soils

The plants in the following list vary in the amount of shade they prefer but they must have a well-drained soil in which to grow and thrive. Once they are established, they can withstand dry conditions for considerable periods of time. Some of these plants may require watering soon after transplanting to speed up their establishment.

TREES
Carpinus
Parrotia
Sorbus
Stewartia
Trachycarpus

SHRUBS
Chaenomeles
Cornus kousa
Corylus
Cotinus
Euonymus
Garrya
Hypericum (some)
Osmanthus

Pachysandra
Philadelphus
Pyracantha
Rubus 'Benenden'
Symphoricarpos
Weigela

CONIFERS
Chamaecyparis
Cryptomeria
× Cupressocyparis
Juniperus
Taxus

CLIMBERS
Celastrus
Hedera
Lapageria rosea
Lonicera
Parthenocissus
Tropaeolum

PERENNIALS
Bergenia
Helleborus

BULBS, CORMS, AND TUBERS
Anemone blanda
Colchicum
  autumnale
Cyclamen coum
C. hederifolium
Eranthis
Hyacinthus
Lilium lancifolium
L. regale
L. speciosum
Muscari
Narcissus

ANNUALS AND BIENNIALS
Bellis
Digitalis

GRASSES
Briza media
Luzula nivea

FERNS
Asplenium
Polystichum

Moist Soils

The plants in the following list vary in the amount of shade they prefer but they must have at least a moist soil in which to grow. Some will grow well in wet soils and mature plants can often withstand damp soil conditions for considerable periods of time.

TREES
Acer griseum
A. palmatum
Aesculus
Crataegus
Davidia
Ilex
Liriodendron
Nyssa
Populus
Prunus
Styrax
Tilia

SHRUBS
Acer palmatum
A. japonicum
Amelanchier
Buxus
  sempervirens
Camellia
Cassiope
Corylopsis
Daphne
Enkianthus
Fatsia
Forsythia
Fuchsia
Gaultheria
Hamamelis
Hebe
Hydrangea
Leucothoe
Lonicera
Magnolia
Mahonia
Pachysandra
Pieris
Rhododendron
Sarcococca
Skimmia
Viburnum

CONIFERS
Abies
Chamaecyparis

Cryptomeria
× Cupressocyparis
Juniperus
Metasequoia
Taxodium
Tsuga

CLIMBERS
Aconitum
Akebia
Ampelopsis
Berberidopsis
Clematis
Codonopsis
  convolulacaea
Fallopia
Hedera
Humulus
Hydrangea
  anomala
Lonicera
Passiflora
Schisandra
Schizophragma
Trachelospermum
Tropaeolum

PERENNIALS
Aconitum
Actaea
Ajuga
Alchemilla
Alstroemeria
Anaphalis
Anemone
  hupehensis
Aquilegia
Aruncus
Astilbe
Astilboides
Astrantia
Bletilla
Brunnera
Chelone
Chiastophyllum
Cimicifuga

Convallaria
Cynoglossum
Darmera
Dicentra
Dodecathion
Doronicum
Epimedium
Eupatorium
Euphorbia
  amygdaloides
E. griffithii
E. polychroma
E. schillingii
Filipendula
Gaura
Gentiana
Geranium
Geum
Gunnera
Hepatica
Heuchera
Hosta
Houttuynia
Incarvillea
Inula hookeri
Kirengeshoma
Lamium
Ligularia
Lobelia
Lychnis
Lysichiton
Lysimachia
Meconopsis
Mertensia
Monarda
Omphalodes
Ophiopogon
Penstemon (some)
Persicaria
Physostegia
Pleione
Polemonium
Polygonatum
Primula
Pulmonaria
Ramonda

Ranunculus
Rheum
Rodgersia
Roscoea
Rudbeckia
Sanguinaria
Saxifraga (some)
Silene (some)
Soldanella
Symphytum
Tellima
Thalictrum
Tiarella
Tolmiea
Tricyrtis
Trollius
Uvularia
Veratrum
Veronica
Viola

BULBS, CORMS, AND TUBERS
Anemone
  nemorosa
Arisaema
Camassia
Cardiocrinum
Erythronium
Galanthus
Hyacinthoides
Leucojum
Lilium canadense
L. henryi
L. martagon
L. pardalinum

ANNUALS AND BIENNIALS
Impatiens
Mimulus
Myosotis
Nemophila
Nicotiana
Viola

GRASSES
Alopecurus
Calamagrostis
Carex
Deschampsia
Hakonechloa
Imperata
Luzula sylvatica
Milium
Molinia
Phalaris

BAMBOOS
Fargesia
Phyllostachys
Pleioblastus
Semiarundinaria

FERNS
Adiantum
Athyrium
Blechnum
Cystopteris
Dicksonia
Dryopteris
Matteuccia
Onoclea
Osmunda
Thelypteris
Woodwardia

PLANT FOR PARTICULAR GROWING CONDITIONS

PLANTS FOR COASTAL AREAS

Plants that grow close to the sea have a number of problems peculiar to their localized environment. High concentrations of salt are found in both the air and the soil. To cope with this, many plants have developed adaptations for conserving any fresh water they receive for use during their growing processes. Most coastal areas are subject to high winds for at least part of the year and, often, this high wind carries yet more salt. Some plants have extra thick coatings or hairs on their leaves to protect them from this salt. Others have leaves that are modified to reduce the amount of moisture lost during windy and dry periods.

TREES
Arbutus
Eucalyptus
Laburnum
Populus
Quercus ilex
Sorbus aucuparia
Trachycarpus

SHRUBS
Berberis
Brachyglottis
Buddleja
Calluna
Camellia
Ceanothus
Cistus
Cordyline
Cytisus
Daphne
Elaeagnus
Escallonia
Euonymus

Fatsia
Fuchsia
Genista
Hebe
Helianthemum
Magnolia
Myrtus
Rhododendron
Santolina
Tamarix
Thymus

CONIFERS
Cupressus
Juniperus
Picea
Pinus

ROSES
Rosa nitida
R. rugosa
R. 'Mermaid'
R. 'Zépherine
  Drouhin'

CLIMBERS
Berberidopsis
Eccremocarpus
Lapageria rosea
Solanum
Tropaeolum

PERENNIALS
Agapanthus
Agave
Astilbe
Bergenia
Catananche
Dianthus
Echinops
Eryngium
Geum
Hemerocallis
Heuchera
Osteospermum
Phormium

**BULBS, CORMS,
AND TUBERS**
Colchicum
Crocosmia
Crocus
Galanthus
Narcissus
Nerine
Tigridia
Tulipa

**ANNUALS AND
BIENNIALS**
Agrostemma
Brachyscome
Bracteantha
Calendula
Consolida
Dorotheanthus
Eschscholtzia
Limonium
Lobularia
Malope

Salvia
Tagetes

GRASSES
Cortaderia
Festuca
Lagurus
Stipa

BAMBOOS
Fargesia nitida

PLANTS FOR BOG AND WATERSIDE

All plants need water and are unable to function without it, and while some drought-tolerant plants need very little, others love as much as possible. Many of the plants in this list need moist soil at the very least, while others are happy to spend long periods of time with their "feet" in several inches of water. While they are not true aquatic plants, many of these subjects will only thrive well when their roots are able to grow in a cool, moist soil.

TREES
Betula
Populus
Salix
Tilia

SHRUBS
Cornus alba
Daphne
Pachysandra
Salix

Sambucus
Symphoricarpos

CONIFERS
Metasequoia
Taxodium

PERENNIALS
Acorus
Alchemilla
Astilbe

Astilboides
Caltha
Chelone
Darmera
Filipendula
Houttuynia
Iris laevigata
I. pseudocorus
Ligularia
Lobelia cardinalis
Lysichiton

Lythrum
Mimulus luteus
Pontederia
Primula vialii
Rheum
Rodgersia
Trollius
Veratrum
Zantedeschia

GRASSES
Carex elata
C. pendula
Juncus
Luzula (some)
Phalaris

FERNS
Osmunda
Thelypteris
Woodwardia

PLANTS FOR DEEP SHADE

Most gardens have an area that is shaded for at least part of the day and some have areas in permanent shade, where no direct sunlight ever penetrates. Some plants grow quite well in these conditions and they often have large, glossy leaves and green stems that have developed to catch as much of the available light as possible. Those listed below are a selection of plants that are capable of growing in the deepest shade in the garden.

SHRUBS
Aucuba
Buxus
Gaultheria
Lonicera
Mahonia
Pachysandra
Prunus
  laurocerasus
Sarcococca
Skimmia
Symphoricarpos
Viburnum tinus

CONIFERS
Chamaecyparis
Cryptomeria
× Cupressocyparis
Juniperus (some)
Taxus

CLIMBERS
Aconitum
Akebia
Ampelopsis
Berberidopsis
Fallopia
  baldschuanica
Hedera
Hydrangea
  anomala
Lonicera
Passiflora

Schizophragma
Tropaeolum

PERENNIALS
Aconitum
Ajuga
Aruncus
Astilbe
Bergenia
Brunnera
Convallaria
Darmera
Epimedium
Filipendula
Geranium
Gunnera
Hepatica
Houttynia
Lamium

Liriope
Persicaria
Primula (some)
Pulmonaria
Rodgersia
Sanguinaria
Symphytum
Tellima
Tolmiea
Tricyrtis
Uvularia
Veratrum
Viola

**BULBS, CORMS
AND TUBERS**
Anemone (some)
Arisaema
Cardiocrinum

Erythronium
Galanthus
Hyacinthoides
Leucojum

FERNS
Athyrium
Blechnum
Cystopteris
Dryopteris
Matteuccia
Onoclea
Osmunda
Thelypteris
Woodwardia

SMALL PLANTS FOR RAISED BEDS AND ROCK GARDENS

The term "alpine" is often used to describe dwarf or slow-growing plants that originate from higher altitudes and mountainous regions. These plants have certain shared characteristics, such as a preference for thin, free-draining soil with low fertility; a capacity to tolerate extremely low temperatures; and a dislike of very wet and polluted atmospheres. Many of the plants in this list are capable of growing perfectly well in hot, dry conditions.

SHRUBS	CONIFERS	*Incarvillea*	*Veronica* (some)	ANNUALS AND
Berberis ×	*Cryptomeria*	*Lewisia*	*Zauschneria*	BIENNIALS
stenophylla	*japonica*	*Linaria*		*Agrostemma*
'Corallina	'Vilmoriniana'	*Mertensia*	BULBS, CORMS	*Bellis*
Compacta'	*Juniperus conferta*	*Penstemon* (some)	AND TUBERS	*Dorotheanthus*
Calluna	*J. horizontalis*	*Phlox* (some)	*Allium flavum*	*Iberis*
Cassiope	*Pinus mugo* 'Mops'	*Pleione*	*Anemone* × *fulgens*	*Limnanthes*
Cistus		*Primula allionii*	*Calochortus*	*Lobularia*
Convolvulus	PERENNIALS	*Pulsatilla alpina*	*uniflorus*	
Coronilla	*Anacyclus*	*Ramonda*	*Chionodoxa*	GRASSES
Daphne (some)	*Androsace*	*Raoulia*	*Ipheion*	*Lagurus*
Erica	*Arenaria*	*Sanguinaria*	*Iris histrioides*	
Euonymus (some)	*Aurinia*	*Saponaria*	*Ornithogalum*	FERNS
Hebe (some)	*Chiastophyllum*	*Saxifraga*	*arabicum*	*Polypodium*
Helianthemum	*Dianthus* (some)	*Sedum* (some)	*Oxalis*	
Hypericum (some)	*Dodecatheon*	*Sempervivum*	*Puschkinia*	
Lithodora	*Draba*	*Silene*	*Rhodohypoxis*	
Salix hastata	*Erodium*	*Sisyrinchium*	*Sternbergia*	
Santolina	*Gentiana*	*Soldanella*		
	Geranium (some)	*Thalictrum*		

PLANTS WITH SPECIFIC NEEDS

PLANTS REQUIRING LIME-FREE SOILS

The acidity or alkalinity of a soil is measured on a pH scale. This ranges from 0 (very acid) to 14 (very alkaline). Most plants prefer a pH of 6.5–7.5, but some are unable to obtain minerals from the soil if the pH is too high. These plants prefer to grow in acid soil conditions and are often called 'ericaceous' plants when they should, more accurately, be called calcifuges. Members of the Ericaceae family enjoy acid conditions, but so do members of other plant families such as *Camellia, Cardiocrinum,* and *Hamamelis.* Although these are not related to heaths (*Erica*), they will only grow successfully in soils with a low pH.

TREES	*Daphne*	*Picea*	*Kirengeshoma*	*Lilium lancifolium*
Arbutus	*Enkianthus*	*Pinus parviflora*	*Lewisia*	*L. pumilum*
Betula	*Erica*	*Pseudolarix*	*Liriope*	*Rhodohypoxis*
Eucalyptus	*Fothergilla*	*Taxodium*	*Lupinus*	
Eucryphia	*Gaultheria*	*Thuja*	*Meconopsis*	ANNUALS AND
Nyssa	*Hamamelis*		*Ophiopogon*	BIENNIALS
Quercus coccinea	*Kalmia*	CLIMBERS	*Sidalcea*	*Clarkia*
Q. rubra	*Leucothoë*	*Berberidopsis*	*Smilacina*	*Nemesia*
Stewartia	*Magnolia*	*Lapageria*	*Soldanella*	
	Pieris	*Schisandra*	*Stokesia*	GRASSES
SHRUBS	*Rhododendron*	*Schizophragma*	*Thalictrum*	*Deschampsia*
Calluna	*Skimmia*		*Trillium*	*Molinia*
Camellia		PERENNIALS		
Cassiope	CONIFERS	*Anemonopsis*	BULBS, CORMS,	FERNS
Cornus canadensis	*Abies*	*Corydalis*	AND TUBERS	*Athyrium*
C. kousa	*Chamaecyparis*	*cashmeriana*	*Arisaema*	*Blechnum*
Corylopsis	*Cryptomeria*	*Gentiana*	*Begonia*	*Onoclea*
Daboecia	*Metasequoia*	*sino-ornata*	*Cardiocrinum*	*Woodwardia*

PLANTS THRIVING IN ALKALINE SOILS

Many gardeners are faced with the prospect of growing plants in alkaline soils or in areas where the water supply is alkaline. This does not present a problem if a few basic rules are followed. The soil should be cultivated so that adequate quantities of water and plant food are available to the plants and, most importantly, plants should be chosen that will grow well in these conditions. The list of plants below, while not extensive, does give an indication of the range of plants that can be grown in alkaline soils.

TREES	*Lithodora*	*Erodium*	*Silene*	ANNUALS AND
Fagus	*Sarcococca*	*Gypsophila*	*Sisyrinchium*	BIENNIALS
Fraxinus	*Syringa*	*Helianthus*	*Verbascum*	*Antirrhinum*
Genista		*Helleborus*		*Brassica*
Laburnum	CLIMBERS	*Hepatica*	BULBS, CORMS,	*Callistephus*
	Clematis	*Inula*	AND TUBERS	*Erysimum*
SHRUBS	*Wisteria*	*Iris unguicularis*	*Eranthis*	*Iberis*
Cytisus		*Knautia*	*Galanthus*	*Lobularia*
Escallonia	PERENNIALS	*Origanum*	*Hermodactylus*	*Malope*
Euonymus	*Aubrieta*	*Primula*	*Iris reticulata*	*Matthiola*
Fremontodendron	*Aurinia*	*marginata*	*I. xiphium*	
Genista	*Centaurea*	*Saponaria*	*Lilium candidum*	GRASSES
Hebe	*Centranthus*	*Saxifraga* (some)	*L. henryi*	*Helictotrichon*
Helianthemum	*Dianthus*	*Scabiosa*	*L. martagon*	
Hibiscus	*Dictamnus*	*Sedum*	*Sternbergia*	

GENERAL INDEX

PLANT INDEX

Page numbers in *italics* refer to illustrations. Plants in **bold** represent David Joyce's top 250 plants. There are cross-references for genus and species synonyms as well as for common names. Those cultivars with a specific common name or names are cross-referenced to the relevant species in the index and are given with the species in the Directory.

345

Picture Credits

KEY a = above b = bottom c = center l = left
m = middle r = right t = top

All photographs taken by Jerry Harpur unless stated otherwise.

PRELIMINARY PAGES AND INTRODUCTION
Photographer's credits: 1 RHS Wisely; Surrey; 2 RHS Rosemoor; Great Torrington, Devon; 3 Park Farm, Great Waltham; 4-5 designers: Oehme & van Sweden Associates, Washington DC; 6 Beth Chatto, Elmstead Market, Essex; 8 t Beth Chatto as before; 8 b RHS Wisely; 9 Rita & Samuel Robert, Nantucket Island, Mass. Architect Edward Knowles; 10 The Garden House, Buckland Monachorum, Devon; 11 t Bellevue Botanic Garden, Seattle; 11 b Savill Garden, Englefield Green, Surrey; 12 t Tresco Abbey Gardens, Isles of Scilly; 12 b Beth Chatto as before; 13 t Tresco Abbey Gardens, Isles of Scilly; 13 b Beth Chatto; 14-15 "Les Quatres Vents", La Malbaie, Quebec, Canada.

PLANT COMMUNITIES IN NATURE
Bruce Coleman Ltd
Stephen Bond 20-21 b; Fred Bruemmer 46 tr; Bob and Clara Calhoun 18 rm; Mr P Clement 36 abr; Alain Compost 28 abr; Derek Croucher 43 tr; Gerald Cubitt 30-31c; 33 rm; Adrian Davies 47 t; Geoff Dore 34 bl; 41 t 42 tr; MPL Fogden 16 rm, 17 rm, 28-29 b; Jeff Foott Productions 19 b, 44-45 b; Christer Frederiksson 28 l; Sir Jeremy Grayson 36 tr, 37 tr; 39 tl; Peter A Hinchliffe 46 tl; Janos Jurka 22-23b; CC Lockwood 45 c, 46 bl; Luiz Claudio Marigo 28 btr & br; George McCarthy 42 tl; Dr Eckart Pott 38 br; Marie Read 22 bl; Hans Reinhard 18 tr 19 t; 35 tr, 40 t; Dr Frieder Sauer 34-35 t; Dr Sabine M Schmidt 34 ml; John Shaw 23 ar, 30-31 b, 34 tl, 40 rm; 45 br; Kim Taylor 44 bl, 45 tr; G Ziesler 24 t, 38 t, 43 tl.

Robert Harding Picture Library
36 btr; Norma Joseph 32 t; John Miller 47 br; James Strachan 26 b.

Images Colour Library
16 t, 17 t, btl, br, 18 tl, 21 c, 22-23 c, 23 br, 30 tl, 40-41 b, 42-43 b, 44 cb, 44-45 t, 45 cr.

Impact Photos
Colin Jones 21 br; David Palmer 27 c.

NHPA
L Campbell 39 tr; Paal Hermansen 36-37 b; Helio and Van Ingen 35 br; Alberto Nardi 46-47 b; Rod Planck 33 tl; Christophe Ratier 32 c; David Woodfall 39 bl.

Jerry Pavia
20 t; 24-25 c; 41 ml.

Wildlight
Mark Lang 24-25 b; 26 c; Milton Wordley 31 tr.

PLANT ASSOCIATIONS IN THE GARDEN
Photographers credits: 48-49 Dr J R Smart "Marwood Hill", Nr Barnstaple, Devon; 50 t Beth Chatto's woodland; 50-51 b RHS Wisely, Surrey; 51 t Garden in the Woods, Framingham, Mass.; 51 m Great Dixter, Northiam, Sussex; 51 b The Old Rectory, Kirby Bedon, Norfolk; 52 t House of Pitmuies, Guthrie-by-Forfar, Tayside; 52 b Carl Niels, Dallas, Texas; 53 l Xa Tollemache's design for The Evening Standard at RHS Chelsea 1997; 53 tr Beth Chatto as before; 53 br Manor House, Heslington, York; 54 t Springfields Garden, Spalding, Lincs.; 54 bl Peter Wooster, Roxbury, Connecticut; 54 br Linda Teague, Del Mar, Ca.; 55 t Manor House, Heslington, York; 55 b Rita & Sam Robert, Nantucket, Mass.; 56 t The Garden House as before; 56 bl Beth Chatto as before; 56-57 Beth Chatto; 57 t The Garden House; 58 t Rita & Sam Robert as before; 58-59 Eastgrove Cottage Garden, Sankyns Green, Nr Worcs.; 59 tc Designers: Charles Price & Glen Whitty, Seattle, Wa.; 59tr Eastgrove Cottage as before; 59 b RHS Rosemoor as before; 60 tl Tessa King-Farlow, Edgbaston, Birmingham; 60 m Savill Garden as before; 60 b RHS Wisely; 61 tl Stone House Cottage, Stone, Worcs.; 61 tr Designer: Tessa Hobbs, The Red House, Kirby Cane, Suffolk; 61 b Saling Hall, Great Saling, Essex; 62 l The Manor House, Bledlow, Bucks; 62 tr Great Dixter as before; 62-63 "The Dingle", Welshpool, Powys; 64-65 t Writtle Horticultural College, Essex; 64 m Designer: Sylvia Oxenford, Patagonia; 64-65 b Great Dixter as before; 65 m Great Dixter; 66 t "Dolwen", Llanrhaeadr-ym-Mochnant, Powys; 66 b Westonbirt

Arboretum, Glos.; 67 t House of Pitmuies as before; 67 m Blandy Gardens, Madeira; 67 b Highdown, Goring-by-Sea, West Sussex; 68 tl Burford House, Tenbury Wells, Worcs.; 68-69 Helmingham Hall, Stowmarket, Suffolk; 68 br Designer: Tessa Hobbs as before; 69 tr Tessa King-Farlow as before; 69 bl Shelia McQueen, Leverstock Green, Herts.; 70 tl Barnsley House, Barnsley, Glos.; 70 bl Valley Garden, Englefield, Surrey; 70-71 Exbury Gardens, Nr Southampton, Hants; 71 tmr Designer: Margaret Locket, Seattle; 71 br Beth Chatto as before; 72 l Designer: Dan Hinkley, "Heronswood", Seattle, Wa.; 72 tr Mr & Mrs Lucas, Castle Hedingham, Ex.; 72-73 Exbury Gardens as before; 73 Winterhur, Wilmington, Delaware; 74 Foxgrove Plants, Enborne, Berks.; 74 ml Eastgrove Cottage as before; 74 mr Mr & Mrs Lucas as before; 74-75 b Dr. Chris Grey Wilson, Suffolk; 75 r Savill Garden, Englefield Green, Surrey; 76t Dr & Mrs Stalbow, Stanmore; 76 b "Inverewe", Poolewe, Ross & Cromarty; 77 t Joe Eck & Wayne Winterrowd, Readsboro, Vermont; 77 mr RHS Wisely as before; 77 b Beth Chatto gravel garden as before; 78 tl Park Farm, Chelmsford, Essex; 78b Ebrington Village, Glos.; 78-79 t Highdown, Goring-by-Sea, Sussex; 79 tr Valley Garden, Englefield Green; 79 b Stone House Cottage as before; 80 t,m,b all Valley Garden; 81 lb & rb Savill Garden as before; 82-83 t "Dolwen" as before; 82-83 m Wollerton Old Hall, Wollerton, Shropshire; 83 t Peter Wooster as before; 83 b Beth Chatto; 84 tl "Dolwen" as before; 84-85 Beth Chatto; 84 br Burnby Hall Gardens, Pocklington, Yorks.; 85 b Designer: Ken Ruzicka, Patchogue, NY; 86 m Beth Chatto; 86 b Wave Hill, The Bronx, New York; 86-87 "Marwood Hill" as before; 87 t Beth Chatto as before; 87 b Burnby Gardens as before; 88 t Beth Chatto; 88 m Sun House, Long Melford, Suffolk; 88-89 b Moat House, Cockfield, Suffolk; 89 t Beth Chatto's gravel garden as before; 89 b Beth Chatto; 90 t Tresco Abbey Gardens as before; 90 r Domaine Rayol, Rayol, South of France , designer: Gilles Clement; 91 t Gardenworld, Keysborough, Victoria, Australia; 91 m&b Huntington Botanic Garden, Ca.; 92 l Eastgrove Cottage Garden; 92 tr & 92-93 m The Garden House as before; 92-93 b Dr & Mrs Rivers, Balscote, Oxon.; 93 t Foxgrove Plants, Enborne, Berks.; 94 l Sylvia Oxenford, Patagonia; 94 r Highdown as before; 95 t Shepherd House, Inveresk, Midlothian; 95 m Burnby Hall as before; 95 b Shepherd House as before; 96 tl Domaine Rayol as before; 96 bl Tresco as before; 97 t Mme Ferrari, Hyères, South of France; 97 b Inverewe, Poolewe, Ross & Cromarty; 98 t Orchid Garden, Singapore Botanic; 98 bl Mrs Ileana de Teran, Costa Rica; 98-99 Orchid Garden, Singapore as before; 99 tr Fern Valley, The Domain, Auckland, New Zealand; 99 mr Fairchild Tropical Garden, Miami, Fla; 99 br on a house wall in Funchal, Madeira; 100 tl Wally Berg's Garden, Miami; 100 bl Bok Tower Gardens, Lake Wales, Fla.; 100 br Longwood Gardens, Kennett Square, Pennsylvania; 101 t Mrs McLemare, Miami; 101 tr &101 b Orchid Garden, Singapore Botanic.

DIRECTORY
Andrew Lawson:
104; Trees: 106 c; 107 r; 108 lb; 109 cb & r; 110 rb; 111 lt & rt; 113 lt; 115 l; 116 l; 118 r; Shrubs: 125 c; 130 lb; 132 l & cb; 135 r; 137 c; 146 l; 150 l & cb; 157 l & r; 158 lb; 161 c & r; 162 rt & rb Conifers: 166 c; 169 c; 171 l; 173 c; 174 lt & c; Roses: 192 l & lb; Perennials: 199 cb; 200 c; 201 cb; 203 c; 205 l; 214 rb; 217 lt; 221 l & c; 245 r; 247 lt; 251 r; 257 r; 272 c & r; 276 c; Bulbs, Corms, and Tubers:298 c; Annuals and Biennials: 312 ct; 313 cb; 314 r; 324 l; Bamboos, Grasses, and Grasslike Plants: 326 cb; 328 l; 329 rb.

Photos Horticultural:
Trees: 107 ct; 114 r; 117 c & rt; Shrubs: 124 c; 129 cb & rt; 144 c; Conifers: 167 rt; 168 cb; 171 rb; 173 lt; Climbers: 176 l; 177 c; 178 l; 181 l; 186 l & r; 188 c; Perennials: 202 r; 210 l; 216 l; 219 ct; 223 rb; 228 lb; 232 r; 236 cb; 243 l; 245 ct; 262 ct & r; 268 ct; 270 ct & cb; 271 c; 273 l; 275 cb; 276 l; Bulbs, Corms, and Tubers: 291 l; 294 l; 295 cb; 306 c; 308 c; Annuals and Biennials: 313 l; 314 l & ct & cb; 315 t; 316 c; 317 rb; 318 cb & r; 319 cb & r; 320 cb; 321 c & r; 322 lb & rb; 323 r; Bamboos, Grasses, and Grasslike Plants: 328 lb; 329 lb & rt; 332 c; Ferns: 334 c; 336 l.

Clive Nichols:
Perennials: 250 ct.

John Glover Photography:
Perennials: 216 rb; 217 r; 220 r; 224 cb; 247 ct; 263 r.

Bruce Coleman:
Perennials: 207 lt: Sir Jeremy Grayson.

The Garden Picture Library:
Ferns: 336 rb.

AUTHOR'S ACKNOWLEDGMENTS

I regret the lack of space to record the influence of individual gardeners and their gardens in this book, not to mention countless landscapes where plants grow in the wild. But it is a pleasure to acknowledge here the enormous debt I owe to others for information and to recognize humbly the many influences that have helped to form my opinions.

Many people have played a role in the making of this book, some of whom I cannot adequately thank. First among these is Caroline Davison, the project editor, who has shown extraordinary commitment, great ability as

an organizer, and keen judgement during a testing production schedule. I also gratefully acknowledge the enormous amount of work put in by the editors Jane Chapman and Stella Vayne, and by the art editor, Paul Tilby. The work of Jerry and Marcus Harpur and the other photographers speaks for itself.

I join the publishers in thanking the following individuals for their help in compiling this book: Steven Bradley, Cathy Buchanan, Liz Dobbs, Sue Fisher, Jenny Hendy, and John Swithinbank.

PHOTOGRAPHER'S ACKNOWLEDGMENTS

Jerry Harpur would like to thank Susan Rowley for her conscientious help in the editing of his transparencies, liaising with the publisher and keeping delivery to schedule. Without her, and his son Marcus, who photographed many of the plants and some of the gardens in Great Britain, this book would not have been possible.

He would also like to thank the following garden owners, nurseries, and designers for their generous cooperation:

Jacques Amand Ltd., Stanmore, Middlx; Ruth Bancroft Garden, Walnut Creek, Ca.; D. Barker, NCCPG Epimediums Collection, Danbury, Essex; Bellevue Botanical Garden, Seattle; Blandy Gardens, Madeira; Botanic Gardens, Funchal, Madeira; Rupert Bowlby, Reigate, Surrey; Broadleigh Gardens, Bishops Hull, Somerset; Burnby Hall, Pocklington, Yorks.; Sheila Chapman, Chelmsford, Essex; Molly Chappellet, Napa Valley, Ca.; Beth Chatto, Elmstead Market, Essex; Bradenham Hall, Norfolk; Simone de Chazal, Funchal, Madeira; "Chiffchaffs", Bourton, Dorset; Mr & Mrs N Coote, Oxford, Oxon.; Copford Bulbs, Colchester, Essex; The Dingle Nursery, Welshpool, Wales; "Dolwen", Llanrhaeadr-ym-Mochnant, Powys; The Domain, Auckland, New Zealand; Domaine Rayol, Rayol, France; Eastgrove Cottage Garden, nr. Worcester; Joe Eck and Wayne Winterrowd, Readsboro, Vt.; Exbury Gardens, Hants; Foxgrove Plants, Enborne, Berks.; Sonny Garcia, San Francisco, Ca.; Gardenworld, Keysborough, Vic., Australia; Garden House, Buckland Monachorum, Devon; "Glen Chantry", Wickambishops, Essex; Great Dixter, Northiam, Sussex, "Heronswood",

Kingston, Seattle; "Heronswood", Dromona, Vic., Australia; Hillier Arboretum, Hants; "Highdown", Goring-by-Sea, Sussex; Hoecroft Plants, nr Dereham, Norfolk; V. H. Humphrey, Dorking, Surrey; Huntington Botanic, LA, Ca.; W.E Th. Ingwersen, East Grinstead, Sussex; La Casella, Opio, South of France; Langthorns Plantery, Dunmow, Essex; Rod & Jane Leeds, nr Lavenham, Norfolk; Philippe Levrat, Hyères, France; Lincluden Nursery, Bisley, Surrey; Margaret Locket, Seattle, Wa.; Longwood Gardens, Kennett Square, Pa.; Manor House, Heslington, York; "Marwood Hill", nr Barnstaple, Devon; New York Botanical Garden; Paradise Centre, Bures, Suffolk; Parc Bagatelle, Paris, France; Park Farm, Chelmsford, Essex; Plantsman Nursery, Okehampton, Devon; Potterton & Martin, Nr Caistor, Lincs.; RHS Hyde Hall, Rettendon, Essex; RHS Rosemoor, Great Torrington, Devon; Rougham Hall Nurseries, Bury St. Edmunds, Suffolk; Royal Botanic Garden, Kirstenbosch, RSA; Royal Botanic Garden, Melbourne, Australia; Royal Botanic Garden, Kew, Surrey; Royal National Rose Society, St Albans, Herts.; Susan Ryley, Victoria, BC, Canada; Saling Hall, Essex; Savill Garden, Englefield Green, Surrey; Scott Arboretum, Swarthmore, Pa.; Secrett's Nursery, Milford, Surrey; Shepherd House, Inveresk, Midlothian; Singapore Botanic Garden; Springfields Gardens, Spalding, Lincs.; Stone House Cottage, Stone, Worcs.; Sun House, Long Melford, Suffolk; Linda Teague, Del Mar, Ca.; Ileana de Teran, Costa Rica; Tresco Abbey Gardens, Isles of Scilly; Villa Roquebrune, Cannes; J. Walkers Bulbs, nr. Spalding, Lincs.; Wave Hill, The Bronx, New York; Westonbirt Arboretum, Glos.; Wildflower Research Centre, Austin, Texas; Winterthur; RHS Wisely, Surrey; Wollerton Old Hall, Shropshire; Peter Wooster, Roxbury, Connecticut; Writtle Horticultural College, Essex.